PENGUIN REFERENCE

The New Penguin Dictionary of Abbreviations

Rosalind Fergusson was born in Liverpool in 1953 and obtained her degree in French from Exeter University. From here she took a teaching certificate and became an assistant teacher at a school in West Sussex. From 1978 to 1984 she worked for Market House Books where she trained as an assistant editor and rose to the position of Senior Editor. During this time she worked on a range of reference books. Since leaving Market House Books she has worked as a freelance editor.

Her other publications include *The Penguin Dictionary of Proverbs* (1983), *The Penguin Rhyming Dictionary* (1985), *Choose your Baby's Name* (1987), *The Hamlyn Dictionary of Quotations* (1989), *The Penguin Dictionary of English Synonyms and Antonyms* (1992), *Chambers Dictionary of Foreign Words and Phrases* (1995) and *Cassell Dictionary of English Idioms* (1999). Rosalind Fergusson has also edited and co-edited a number of dictionaries and reference books, and has contributed to *The Bloomsbury Good Word Guide* (1988) and *Brewer's Dictionary of 20th-Century Phrase and Fable* (1991), among others.

Rosalind Fergusson is married and lives in Kent. Her leisure interests include walking, sailing and music.

The New Penguin Dictionary of

Abbreviations

From A to zz

Rosalind Fergusson

PENGUIN BOOKS

PENGUIN BOOKS

Published by the Penguin Group
Penguin Books Ltd, 80 Strand, London WC2 0RL, England
Penguin Putnam Inc., 375 Hudson Street, New York, New York 10014, USA
Penguin Books Australia Ltd, Ringwood, Victoria, Australia
Penguin Books Canada Ltd, 10 Alcorn Avenue, Toronto, Ontario, Canada M4V 3B2
Penguin Books India (P) Ltd, 11, Community Centre, Panscheel Park, New Delhi – 110 017, India
Penguin Books (NZ) Ltd, Cnr Rosedale and Airborne Roads, Albany, Auckland, New Zealand
Penguin Books (South Africa) (Pty) Ltd, 24 Sturdee Avenue, Rosebank 2196, South Africa

Penguin Books Ltd, Registered Offices: 80 Strand, London WC2 0RL, England

www.penguin.com

First published 2000
8

Set in ITC Stone
Typeset by Rowland Phototypesetting Ltd, Bury St Edmunds, Suffolk
Printed in England by Clays Ltd, St Ives plc

Contents

Introduction

The New Penguin Dictionary of Abbreviations contains over 40,000 entries, listed under more than 20,000 headwords. Abbreviations abound in all walks of modern life, and no dictionary of abbreviations can hope to be fully comprehensive, but users of this book should find in its pages most of the abbreviations they are likely to encounter, whether they are reading a magazine, listening to the news, browsing on the Internet, buying a house, or applying for a job.

Abbreviations fall into five main categories. There are *shortenings*, in which a word is simply truncated, as in **Co.** and **technol.**; *contractions*, which contain the first and last letters of the full word, as in **Ltd** and **Dr**; *initialisms*, made up of the first letters of a series of words, as in **BBC** and **e.g.**; *acronyms*, in which the first letters or syllables of a name or phrase are pronounced as a word, as in **NATO** and **Ofsted**; and *symbols*, which often belong to the fields of science and technology and may or may not be related to the words they represent, such as **km** and **Pb** (meaning 'lead'). The scope of *The New Penguin Dictionary of Abbreviations* has been broadened to include some items that are not classified as abbreviations in many standard dictionaries because they are – or have become – part of the English language as words in their own right, such as the acronyms **radar** and **laser** and informal short forms such as **fridge** and **pub**.

Abbreviations are perhaps most frequently used to save time and space in writing and printing, and the form that they take may vary from person to person, or from publication to publication. Some acronyms can appear in print either as a lower-case word with a capital initial or as a string of capitals, as in **Unesco** or **UNESCO**. Initialisms may often be capital or lower-case, with or without full stops or other punctuation, as in **ASAP** or **a.s.a.p.** (In *The New Penguin Dictionary of Abbreviations* we have tended to prefer the all-capital form of acronyms, unless an alternative form is known to be more frequent or favoured by the organization concerned; for lower-case initialisms we have usually retained the full stops.) Many users of British English signal the difference between shortenings and contractions by putting a full stop at the end of the former but not the latter, a convention that has been followed in this dictionary.

Order of entries

The abbreviations are listed in alphabetical order. Where two or more abbreviations differ only in capitalization and/or punctuation, all the forms containing capitals precede those in lower case, and unpunctuated forms precede those with slashes, full stops, spaces, etc. Abbreviations containing numbers follow those made up of the letter or letters before (or after) the number: **3M** comes between **M**, **m.**, etc. and **MA**, and **Y2K** comes between **Y**, **y.**, etc. and **YA**. The ampersand symbol has been alphabetized as 'and', so **R&A** follows **RANCOM**.

Within each entry, the full forms are listed in character-by-character alphabetical order, ignoring any letters or words in brackets.

Some Useful Groups of Abbreviations

Abbreviations used in advertisements

personal

ALA	all letters answered
ALAWP	all letters answered with photograph
ARA	all replies answered
GL	good-looking
GSOH	good sense of humour
n/m	not married
NS	nonsmoker
n/s	nonsmoker
NSP	nonsmoker preferred
NTW	no time wasters
OHAC	own house and car
PA	photograph appreciated
SOH	sense of humour
TDH	tall, dark and handsome
TLEH	true love and everlasting happiness
VGL	very good-looking
VGSOH	very good sense of humour
VYAH	very young at heart
WLTM	would like to meet
YAH	young at heart

for cars

a/b	airbag(s)
a/con.	air conditioning
AT	automatic transmission
AW	alloy wheels
b/bar	bull-bar
b/kit	body kit
C/C	cruise control
CDL	central door locking
ch.	chassis
CL	central locking
c/lock.	central locking
COL	centrally operated locking
EDS	electrically adjusted driver's seat
EFW	electric front windows
EPS	electrically positioned seats
ESC	electric seat control; etched security code
ESR	electric sunroof
EW	electric windows
FAR	front arm rests
FSH	full service history
g/box	gearbox
h'back	hatchback
HFS	heated front seats
HLW	headlamp wipers
HLWW	headlamp wash and wipe
HRW	heated rear window
HWW	headlamp wash and wipe
IRL	infrared (remote) locking
IS	independent suspension
l.h.d.	left-hand drive
LSW	lights spray and wipe
LUD	leather-upholstered dashboard
LW&S	lights wipe and spray
MDS	memory-adjusted driver's seat
mlg.	mileage
MSR	manual sunroof
OBC	on-board computer

OTG	outside temperature gauge	**s/hist.**	service history
p.a.s.	power-assisted steering	**spd**	speed
PS	power steering	**s/r**	sunroof
PW	power windows	**s/roof**	sunroof
r/belt	rear seat belt	**s/susp.**	sports suspension
r.h.d.	right-hand drive	**T&T**	taxed and tested
RHR	rear head restraints	**WW**	walnut wood (trim)

for houses, flats, etc.

balc.	balcony	**lhld**	leasehold
bath.	bathroom	**lnge**	lounge
bed.	bedroom	**LU**	lock-up
bedrm	bedroom	**magnif.**	magnificent
beds	bedrooms	**mais.**	maisonette
bung.	bungalow	**mod.**	modernized
c&c	carpets and curtains	**OCH**	oil central heating
CH	central heating	**o'lkng**	overlooking
c.h.	central heating	**o.p.**	open-plan
clkrm	cloakroom	**ORP**	off-road parking
conserv.	conservatory	**OSCH**	off-peak (or overnight) storage central heating
CW	cavity wall		
det.	detached	**OSP**	off-street parking
d-f	double-fronted	**p/b**	purpose-built
DG	double glazed (or glazing)	**p.p.**	planning permission
DR	dining room	**ptr**	porter
ens.	en suite	**rec.**	reception room
EOT	end of terrace	**recpt.**	reception room
e/s	en suite	**rest.**	restored
FCH	full central heating	**rm**	room
FF	fixtures and fittings; fully fitted	**SD**	semi-detached
		sh.	shower
FGCH	full gas central heating	**shwr**	shower
F/H	freehold	**sit.**	sitting room
fhld	freehold	**sitt.**	sitting room
FTB	first-time buyer	**SOF**	share of freehold
fttgs	fittings	**spac.**	spacious
GCH	gas central heating	**s/pool**	swimming pool
g/f	ground floor	**SSTC**	sold subject to contract
GFCH	gas-fired central heating	**STC**	subject to contract
gge	garage	**t&s**	toilet and shower
K	kitchen	**terrd**	terraced
k&b	kitchen and bathroom	**unmod.**	unmodernized
kit.	kitchen	**util.**	utility room
lge	lounge	**W/W**	wall-to-wall
L/H	leasehold		

for rented accommodation, hotels, etc.

B	bathroom	**BBEM**	bed, breakfast and evening meal
b.	bedroom		
BB	bed and breakfast	**DBB**	dinner, bed and breakfast
BBB	bed, breakfast and bath	**ED**	evening dinner

EM	evening meal	**SD**	spin dryer
ens.	en suite	**sh.**	shower
e/s	en suite	**shwr**	shower
f.	furnished	**SWF**	single white female
FB	full board	**SWM**	single white male
f.b.	full board	**SWPF**	single white professional female
FF	fully furnished		
f/furn	fully furnished	**SWPM**	single white professional male
furn.	furnished		
p.a.x.	per annum, exclusive	**t&s**	toilet and shower
penthse	penthouse	**u/f**	unfurnished
SC	self-contained	**unfurn.**	unfurnished
s/c	self-catering; self-contained	**WM**	washing machine

general

a/nw	as new	**o.v.n.o.**	or very near offer
g.c.	good condition	**P/E**	part exchange
immac.	immaculate	**POA**	price on application
neg.	negotiable	**pt ex.**	part exchange
o.b.o.	or best offer	**PX**	part exchange
OIEO	offers in excess of	**v.g.c.**	very good condition
OIRO	offers in the region of	**WM**	well maintained
o.n.o.	or near(est) offer	**WTP**	willing to pay
o/o	offers over		

Abbreviations used on the Internet

.ac.uk	UK academic institution (in Internet address)
AFK	away from the keyboard (in Internet chat)
ANSI	American National Standards Institute
ARPANET	Advanced Research Projects Agency Network
ASCII	American Standard Code for Information Interchange
.at	Austria (in Internet address)
ATK	at the keyboard (in Internet chat)
ATM	asynchronous transfer mode; at the moment (in Internet chat and e-mail)
.au	Australia (in Internet address)
BBL	be back later (in Internet chat)
BBS	be back soon (in Internet chat); bulletin board system
BCNU	be seein' you (in Internet chat)
.be	Belgium (in Internet address)
BITNET	Because It's Time Network
BRB	be right back (in Internet chat)
BTDT	been there, done that (in Internet chat)
BTW	by the way (in Internet chat and e-mail)
.ca	Canada (in Internet address)
.com	(US) commercial organization (in Internet address)
.co.uk	UK commercial organization (in Internet address)
.de	Germany (in Internet address)
.dk	Denmark (in Internet address)
DL	download

DNS	domain name system
EBCDIC	extended binary-coded decimal-interchange code
EOF	end of file
EOM	end of message
.es	Spain (in Internet address)
FAQ	frequently asked question
FOAF	friend of a friend
FOHCL	falls off her/his chair laughing (in Internet chat)
.fr	France (in Internet address)
FTP	file-transfer protocol
FWIW	for what it's worth (in Internet chat and e-mail)
GIF	graphics interchange format
GMTA	great minds think alike (in Internet chat)
.gov	government (in Internet address)
.gov.uk	UK government (in Internet address)
.gr	Greece (in Internet address)
.hk	Hong Kong (in Internet address)
HTML	hypertext markup language
HTTP	hypertext transfer protocol
IAB	Internet architecture board
IAP	Internet access provider
.ie	Ireland (in Internet address)
IETF	Internet Engineering Task Force
IMHO	in my humble opinion (in Internet chat and e-mail)
IMO	in my opinion (in Internet chat and e-mail)
IOW	in other words (in Internet chat and e-mail)
IP	Internet protocol
IRC	Internet relay chat
IRL	in real life (in Internet chat)
ISDN	Integrated Services Digital Network
ISP	Internet service provider
.it	Italy (in Internet address)
IVL	in virtual life (in Internet chat)
.jp	Japan (in Internet address)
LOL	laughs out loud (in Internet chat)
.lu	Luxembourg (in Internet address)
.mil	US military (in Internet address)
MIME	multipurpose Internet mail extension
.mod.uk	Ministry of Defence (in Internet address)
MUD	multi-user dungeon (or dimension) (in game)
.mx	Mexico (in Internet address)
.net	network (in Internet address)
.nl	Netherlands (in Internet address)
NNTP	net(work) news transfer protocol
.nz	New Zealand (in Internet address)
.org	noncommercial organization (in Internet address)
OTOH	on the other hand (in Internet chat and e-mail)
PC	personal computer
POP	point of presence; post office protocol
PPP	point-to-point protocol
.pt	Portugal (in Internet address)
ROTFL	rolls on the floor laughing (in Internet chat)

.ru	Russia (in Internet address)
.sg	Singapore (in Internet address)
SGML	standard generalized markup language
SLIP	serial line Internet protocol
SMTP	simple mail transfer protocol
TCP	transmission control protocol
TCP/IP	transmission control protocol/Internet protocol
.uk	United Kingdom (in Internet address)
UL	upload
URL	Uniform Resource Locator (address of Internet location)
.us	United States of America (in Internet address)
WAIS	wide-area information service
WAN	wide-area network
WLAN	wireless local area network
WWW	World Wide Web
wysiwyg	what you see is what you get
XML	extensible markup language

Foreign business abbreviations

a.	*accepté* (French: accepted); *akzeptiert* (German: accepted)
A/B	*Aktiebolaget* (Swedish: joint-stock company)
a.B	*auf Bestellung* (German: on order)
abb.	*abbuono* (Italian: allowance, discount)
abl	*abril* (Spanish: April)
a.b.s.	*aux bons soins (de)* (French: care of, c/o) (in postal addresses)
a/c	*ai cuidado (de)* (Portuguese: care of, c/o) (in postal addresses)
a.c.	*à compte* (French: on account); *année courante* (French: this year)
a cta	*a cuenta* (Spanish: on account)
AG	*Aktiengesellschaft* (German: public limited company, plc)
ago.	*agosto* (Italian or Spanish: August)
Akt	*Aktiebolaget* (Swedish: joint-stock company)
Aktb	*Aktiebolaget* (Swedish: joint-stock company)
a.l.	*après livraison* (French: after delivery)
AM	*assurance mutuelle* (French: mutual insurance)
anme	*anonyme* (French: limited liability; of company)
AP	*à protester* (French: to be protested; on bill of exchange)
Apr.	*April* (German: April)
apr.	*aprile* (Italian: April)
A/S	*Aksjeselskap* (Norwegian: limited company, Ltd); *Aktieselskab* (Danish: joint-stock company)
a/s de	*aux soins (de)* (French: care of, c/o) (in postal addresses)
ASP	*accepté sous protêt* (French: accepted under protest)
ASPC	*accepté sous protêt pour compte* (French: accepted under protest for account)
Aug.	*August* (German: August)
av.	*avril* (French: April)
b. à p.	*billets à payer* (French: bills payable)
b. à r.	*billets à recevoir* (French: bills receivable)
Best.	*Bestellung* (German: order)
b.p.f.	*bon pour francs* (French: value in francs)

BV	*Besloten Vennootschap* (Dutch: limited company, Ltd)
Ca	*compagnia* (Italian: company, Co.); *companhia* (Portuguese: company, Co.); *compañia* (Spanish: company, Co.)
CAF	*coût, assurance, fret* (French: cost, insurance, freight, CIF)
c/c	*compte courant* (French: current account); *conto corrente* (Italian: current account)
ccc	*cwmni cyfyngedig cyhoeddus* (Welsh: public limited company, plc)
cedex	*courrier d'entreprise à distribution exceptionnelle* (French: special business postal code)
Cia	*compagnia* (Italian: company, Co.); *companhia* (Portuguese: company, Co.); *compañia* (Spanish: company, Co.)
Cie	*compagnie* (French: company, Co.)
CO	*compte ouvert* (French: open account)
cour.	*courant* (French: current, this month, inst.) (in correspondence)
ct	*courant* (French: current, this month, inst.) (in correspondence)
dbre	*diciembre* (Spanish: December)
déc.	*décembre* (French: December)
Dez.	*Dezember* (German: December)
dic.	*dicembre* (Italian: December)
dim.	*dimanche* (French: Sunday)
d.M	*dieses Monats* (German: this month, inst.)
Do.	*Donnerstag* (German: Thursday)
dom.	*domenica* (Italian: Sunday); *domingo* (Spanish: Sunday)
Dtg	*Dienstag* (German: Tuesday)
EGmbH	*Eingetragene Gesellschaft mit beschränkter Haftung* (German: registered limited company)
eno	*enero* (Spanish: January)
e.o.o.e.	*erreur ou omission exceptée* (French: errors and omissions excepted)
Fa	*Firma* (German: firm, business)
fa	*factura* (Spanish: invoice)
f. à b.	*franco à bord* (French: free on board)
facta	*factura* (Spanish: invoice)
fbro	*febrero* (Spanish: February)
febb.	*febbraio* (Italian: February)
Febr.	*Februar* (German: February)
fév.	*février* (French: February)
Fr.	*Frau* (German: Mrs)
Fre.	*Freitag* (German: Friday)
fre	*facture* (French: invoice)
Frk.	*Fröken* (Swedish: Miss); *Frøken* (Danish or Norwegian: Miss)
Frl.	*Fräulein* (German: Miss)
genn.	*gennaio* (Italian: January)
Ges.	*Gesellschaft* (German: company, society)
gio.	*giovedì* (Italian: Thursday)
giu.	*giugno* (Italian: June)
GmbH	*Gesellschaft mit beschränkter Haftung* (German: limited company, Ltd)
H/F	*Hlutafjelagid* (Icelandic: limited company, Ltd)
Hr	*Herr* (German: Mr, Sir)
Jan.	*Januar* (German: January)
janv.	*janvier* (French: January)
jeu.	*jeudi* (French: Thursday)
juev.	*jueves* (Spanish: Thursday)

juil.	*juillet* (French: July)
jul.	*julio* (Spanish: July)
jun.	*junio* (Spanish: June)
KG	*Kommanditgesellschaft* (German: limited partnership)
KK	*Kabushiki Kaisha* (Japanese: joint-stock company)
Komp.	*Kompanie* (German: company)
Kto	*Konto* (German: account)
Lda	*Sociedade de responsabilidade limitada* (Portuguese: limited company, Ltd)
liv.	*livraison* (French: delivery)
L/L	*Lutlang* (Norwegian: limited company, Ltd)
l/o	*leur ordre* (French: their order)
l.R	*laufen der Rechnung* (German: current account)
lu.	*luglio* (Italian: July)
lun.	*lundi* (French: Monday); *lunedì* (Italian: Monday); *lunes* (Spanish: Monday)
M	*Monsieur* (French: Mr, Sir)
magg.	*maggio* (Italian: May)
mar.	*mardi* (French: Tuesday); *martedì* (Italian: Tuesday); *martes* (Spanish: Tuesday); *marzo* (Italian or Spanish: March)
mbH	*mit beschränkter Haftung* (German: with limited liability) (of company)
m.c.	*mois courant* (French: current month)
mer.	*mercoledì* (Italian: Wednesday); *mercredi* (French: Wednesday)
miér.	*miércoles* (Spanish: Wednesday)
Mit.	*Mittwoch* (German: Wednesday)
Mlle	*Mademoiselle* (French: Miss)
Mme	*Madame* (French: Mrs)
Mmes	*Mesdames* (French: plural of Mme)
moms	*mervaerdiomsaetningsskat* (Danish: value-added tax); *mervardesomsattningsskatt* (Swedish: value-added tax)
Mon.	*Montag* (German: Monday)
Mpy	*Maatschappij* (Dutch: company, Co.)
nbre	*noviembre* (Spanish: November)
Nov.	*November* (German: November)
nov.	*novembre* (French or Italian: November)
NV	*Naamloze Vennootschap* (Dutch: public limited company, plc)
obre	*octobre* (French: October)
oct.	*octubre* (Spanish: October)
OHG	*Offene Handelsgesellschaft* (German: partnership)
Okt.	*Oktober* (German: October)
ott.	*ottobre* (Italian: October)
p.A	*per Adresse* (German: care of, c/o) (in postal addresses)
p. Adr.	*per Adresse* (German: care of, c/o) (in postal addresses)
SA	*sociedad anónima* (Spanish: (public) limited company, plc or Ltd); *sociedade anónima* (Portuguese: (public) limited company, plc or Ltd); *società anonima* (Italian: (public) limited company, plc or Ltd); *société anonyme* (French: (public) limited company, plc or Ltd)
sab.	*sabato* (Italian: Saturday)
sáb.	*sábado* (Spanish: Saturday)
Sam.	*Samstag* (German: Saturday)
sam.	*samedi* (French: Saturday)
Sarl	*société à responsabilité limitée* (French: limited company, Ltd)
Sas	*società in accomandita semplice* (Italian: limited partnership)

sbre	*septiembre* (Spanish: September)
S en C	*sociedad en comandita* (Spanish: limited partnership); *société en commandite* (French: limited partnership)
S en NC	*société en nom collectif* (French: partnership)
Sept.	*September* (German: September)
sept.	*septembre* (French: September)
sett.	*settembre* (Italian: September)
s.f.	*sans frais* (French: no expenses)
So.	*Sonntag* (German: Sunday)
Soc.	*società* (Italian: company)
SpA	*società per azioni* (Italian: public limited company, plc)
sprl	*société de personnes à responsabilité limitée* (French: limited company, Ltd)
SRC	*sociedad regular colectiva* (Spanish: partnership)
Srl.	*società a responsabilità limitata* (Italian: limited company, Ltd)
Sté	*société* (French: company, Co.)
t.p.	*tout payé* (French: all (expenses) paid)
TVA	*taxe à la valeur ajoutée* (French: value-added tax, VAT)
ven.	*vendredi* (French: Friday); *venerdì* (Italian: Friday)
Ver.	*Verein* (German: association, company)
vier.	*viernes* (Spanish: Friday)
z.H	*zu Händen* (German: for the attention of, f.a.o., care of, c/o) (in postal addresses)

Symbols for chemical elements

Ac	actinium	**Dy**	dysprosium
Ag	silver (from Latin *argentum*)	**Er**	erbium
Al	aluminium	**Es**	einsteinium
Am	americium	**Eu**	europium
Ar	argon	**F**	fluorine
As	arsenic	**Fe**	iron (from Latin *ferrum*)
At	astatine	**Fm**	fermium
Au	gold (from Latin *aurum*)	**Fr**	francium
B	boron	**Ga**	gallium
Ba	barium	**Gd**	gadolinium
Be	beryllium	**Ge**	germanium
Bh	bohrium	**H**	hydrogen
Bi	bismuth	**Ha**	hahnium
Bk	berkelium	**He**	helium
Br	bromine	**Hf**	hafnium
C	carbon	**Hg**	mercury (from Latin *hydrargyrum*)
Ca	calcium		
Cd	cadmium	**Ho**	holmium
Ce	cerium	**Hs**	hassium
Cf	californium	**I**	iodine
Cl	chlorine	**In**	indium
Cm	curium	**Ir**	iridium
Co	cobalt	**K**	potassium (from Latin *kalium*)
Cr	chromium		
Cs	caesium	**Kr**	krypton
Cu	copper (from Latin *cuprum*)		

Ku	kurchatovium (alternative name for rutherfordium)	**Re**	rhenium
		Rf	rutherfordium
La	lanthanum	**Rh**	rhodium
Li	lithium	**Rn**	radon
Lr	lawrencium	**Ru**	ruthenium
Lu	lutetium	**S**	sulphur
Md	mendelevium	**Sb**	antimony (from Latin *stibium*)
Mg	magnesium		
Mn	manganese	**Sc**	scandium
Mo	molybdenum	**Se**	selenium
Mt	meitnerium	**Sg**	seaborgium
N	nitrogen	**Si**	silicon
Na	sodium (from Latin *natrium*)	**Sm**	samarium
		Sn	tin (from Latin *stannum*)
Nb	niobium	**Sr**	strontium
Nd	neodymium	**Ta**	tantalum
Ne	neon	**Tb**	terbium
Ni	nickel	**Tc**	technetium
No	nobelium	**Te**	tellurium
Np	neptunium	**Th**	thorium
O	oxygen	**Ti**	titanium
Os	osmium	**Tl**	thallium
P	phosphorus	**Tm**	thulium
Pa	protactinium	**U**	uranium
Pb	lead (from Latin *plumbum*)	**V**	vanadium
Pd	palladium	**W**	tungsten (from former name wolfram)
Pm	promethium		
Po	polonium	**Xe**	xenon
Pr	praseodymium	**Y**	yttrium
Pt	platinum	**Yb**	ytterbium
Pu	plutonium	**Zn**	zinc
Ra	radium	**Zr**	zirconium
Rb	rubidium		

UK vehicle registration letters

AA	Bournemouth	**AP**	Brighton
AB	Worcester	**AR**	Chelmsford
AC	Coventry	**AS**	Inverness
AD	Gloucester	**AT**	Hull
AE	Bristol	**AU**	Nottingham
AF	Truro	**AV**	Peterborough
AG	Hull	**AW**	Shrewsbury
AH	Norwich	**AX**	Cardiff
AJ	Middlesbrough	**AY**	Leicester
AK	Sheffield	**AZ**	Belfast
AL	Nottingham	**BA**	Manchester
AM	Swindon	**BB**	Newcastle upon Tyne
AN	Reading	**BC**	Leicester
AO	Carlisle	**BD**	Northampton

BE	Lincoln	**DJ**	Liverpool
BF	Stoke-on-Trent	**DK**	Manchester
BG	Liverpool	**DL**	Portsmouth
BH	Luton	**DM**	Chester
BJ	Ipswich	**DN**	Leeds
BK	Portsmouth	**DO**	Lincoln
BL	Reading	**DP**	Reading
BM	Luton	**DR**	Exeter
BN	Manchester	**DS**	Glasgow
BO	Cardiff	**DT**	Sheffield
BP	Portsmouth	**DU**	Coventry
BR	Newcastle upon Tyne	**DV**	Exeter
BS	Aberdeen	**DW**	Cardiff
BT	Leeds	**DX**	Ipswich
BU	Manchester	**DY**	Brighton
BV	Preston	**DZ**	Antrim
BW	Oxford	**EA**	Dudley
BX	Haverfordwest	**EB**	Peterborough
BY	northwest London	**EC**	Preston
BZ	Down	**ED**	Liverpool
CA	Chester	**EE**	Lincoln
CB	Manchester	**EF**	Middlesbrough
CC	Bangor	**EG**	Peterborough
CD	Brighton	**EH**	Stoke-on-Trent
CE	Peterborough	**EJ**	Haverfordwest
CF	Reading	**EK**	Liverpool
CG	Bournemouth	**EL**	Bournemouth
CH	Nottingham	**EM**	Liverpool
CJ	Gloucester	**EN**	Manchester
CK	Preston	**EO**	Preston
CL	Norwich	**EP**	Swansea
CM	Liverpool	**ER**	Peterborough
CN	Newcastle upon Tyne	**ES**	Dundee
CO	Exeter	**ET**	Sheffield
CP	Huddersfield	**EU**	Bristol
CR	Portsmouth	**EV**	Chelmsford
CS	Glasgow	**EW**	Peterborough
CT	Lincoln	**EX**	Norwich
CU	Newcastle upon Tyne	**EY**	Bangor
CV	Truro	**EZ**	Belfast
CW	Preston	**FA**	Stoke-on-Trent
CX	Huddersfield	**FB**	Bristol
CY	Swansea	**FC**	Oxford
CZ	Belfast	**FD**	Dudley
DA	Birmingham	**FE**	Lincoln
DB	Manchester	**FF**	Bangor
DC	Middlesbrough	**FG**	Brighton
DD	Gloucester	**FH**	Gloucester
DE	Haverfordwest	**FJ**	Exeter
DF	Gloucester	**FK**	Dudley
DG	Gloucester	**FL**	Peterborough
DH	Dudley	**FM**	Chester

FN	Maidstone	**HS**	Glasgow
FO	Gloucester	**HT**	Bristol
FP	Leicester	**HU**	Bristol
FR	Preston	**HV**	central London
FS	Edinburgh	**HW**	Bristol
FT	Newcastle upon Tyne	**HX**	central London
FU	Lincoln	**HY**	Bristol
FV	Preston	**HZ**	Tyrone
FW	Lincoln	**IA**	Antrim
FX	Bournemouth	**IB**	Armagh
FY	Liverpool	**IJ**	Down
FZ	Belfast	**IL**	Fermanagh
GA	Glasgow	**IW**	Londonderry
GB	Glasgow	**J**	Durham
GC	southwest London	**JA**	Manchester
GD	Glasgow	**JB**	Reading
GE	Glasgow	**JC**	Bangor
GF	southwest London	**JD**	central London
GG	Glasgow	**JE**	Peterborough
GH	southwest London	**JF**	Leicester
GJ	southwest London	**JG**	Maidstone
GK	southwest London	**JH**	Reading
GL	Truro	**JI**	Tyrone
GM	Reading	**JJ**	Maidstone
GN	southwest London	**JK**	Brighton
GO	southwest London	**JL**	Lincoln
GP	southwest London	**JM**	Reading
GR	Newcastle upon Tyne	**JN**	Chelmsford
GS	Luton	**JO**	Oxford
GT	southwest London	**JP**	Liverpool
GU	southeast London	**JR**	Newcastle upon Tyne
GV	Ipswich	**JS**	Inverness
GW	southeast London	**JT**	Bournemouth
GX	southeast London	**JU**	Leicester
GY	southeast London	**JV**	Lincoln
GZ	Belfast	**JW**	Birmingham
HA	Dudley	**JX**	Huddersfield
HB	Cardiff	**JY**	Exeter
HC	Brighton	**JZ**	Down
HD	Huddersfield	**K**	Liverpool
HE	Sheffield	**KA**	Liverpool
HF	Liverpool	**KB**	Liverpool
HG	Preston	**KC**	Liverpool
HH	Carlisle	**KD**	Liverpool
HJ	Chelmsford	**KE**	Maidstone
HK	Chelmsford	**KF**	Liverpool
HL	Sheffield	**KG**	Cardiff
HM	central London	**KH**	Hull
HN	Middlesbrough	**KJ**	Maidstone
HO	Bournemouth	**KK**	Maidstone
HP	Coventry	**KL**	Maidstone
HR	Swindon	**KM**	Maidstone

KN	Maidstone	**MT**	northeast London
KO	Maidstone	**MU**	northeast London
KP	Maidstone	**MV**	southeast London
KR	Maidstone	**MW**	Swindon
KS	Edinburgh	**MX**	southeast London
KT	Maidstone	**MY**	southeast London
KU	Sheffield	**MZ**	Belfast
KV	Coventry	**NA**	Manchester
KW	Sheffield	**NB**	Manchester
KX	Luton	**NC**	Manchester
KY	Sheffield	**ND**	Manchester
KZ	Antrim	**NE**	Manchester
LA	northwest London	**NF**	Manchester
LB	northwest London	**NG**	Norwich
LC	northwest London	**NH**	Northampton
LD	northwest London	**NJ**	Brighton
LE	northwest London	**NK**	Luton
LF	northwest London	**NL**	Newcastle upon Tyne
LG	Chester	**NM**	Luton
LH	northwest London	**NN**	Nottingham
LJ	Bournemouth	**NO**	Chelmsford
LK	northwest London	**NP**	Worcester
LL	northwest London	**NR**	Leicester
LM	northwest London	**NS**	Glasgow
LN	northwest London	**NT**	Shrewsbury
LO	northwest London	**NU**	Nottingham
LP	northwest London	**NV**	Northampton
LR	northwest London	**NW**	Leeds
LS	Edinburgh	**NX**	Dudley
LT	northwest London	**NY**	Cardiff
LU	northwest London	**NZ**	Londonderry
LV	Liverpool	**OA**	Birmingham
LW	northwest London	**OB**	Birmingham
LX	northwest London	**OC**	Birmingham
LY	northwest London	**OD**	Exeter
LZ	Armagh	**OE**	Birmingham
MA	Chester	**OF**	Birmingham
MB	Chester	**OG**	Birmingham
MC	northeast London	**OH**	Birmingham
MD	northeast London	**OI**	Belfast
ME	northeast London	**OJ**	Birmingham
MF	northeast London	**OK**	Birmingham
MG	northeast London	**OL**	Birmingham
MH	northeast London	**OM**	Birmingham
MJ	Luton	**ON**	Birmingham
MK	northeast London	**OO**	Chelmsford
ML	northeast London	**OP**	Birmingham
MM	northeast London	**OR**	Portsmouth
MO	Reading	**OS**	Glasgow
MP	northeast London	**OT**	Portsmouth
MR	Swindon	**OU**	Bristol
MS	Edinburgh	**OV**	Birmingham

OW	Portsmouth	**SA**	Aberdeen
OX	Birmingham	**SB**	Glasgow
OY	northwest London	**SC**	Edinburgh
OZ	Belfast	**SCY**	Truro (Isles of Scilly)
PA	Guildford	**SD**	Glasgow
PB	Guildford	**SE**	Aberdeen
PC	Guildford	**SF**	Edinburgh
PD	Guildford	**SG**	Edinburgh
PE	Guildford	**SH**	Edinburgh
PF	Guildford	**SJ**	Glasgow
PG	Guildford	**SK**	Inverness
PH	Guildford	**SL**	Dundee
PJ	Guildford	**SM**	Carlisle
PK	Guildford	**SN**	Dundee
PL	Guildford	**SO**	Aberdeen
PM	Guildford	**SP**	Dundee
PN	Brighton	**SR**	Dundee
PO	Portsmouth	**SS**	Aberdeen
PP	Luton	**ST**	Inverness
PR	Bournemouth	**SU**	Glasgow
PS	Aberdeen	**SV**	Carlisle
PT	Newcastle upon Tyne	**SW**	Glasgow
PU	Chelmsford	**SX**	Edinburgh
PV	Ipswich	**SZ**	Down
PW	Norwich	**TA**	Exeter
PX	Portsmouth	**TB**	Liverpool
PY	Middlesbrough	**TC**	Bristol
PZ	Belfast	**TD**	Manchester
RA	Nottingham	**TE**	Manchester
RB	Nottingham	**TF**	Reading
RC	Nottingham	**TG**	Cardiff
RD	Reading	**TH**	Swansea
RE	Stoke-on-Trent	**TJ**	Liverpool
RF	Stoke-on-Trent	**TK**	Exeter
RG	Newcastle upon Tyne	**TL**	Lincoln
RH	Hull	**TM**	Luton
RJ	Manchester	**TN**	Newcastle upon Tyne
RK	northwest London	**TO**	Nottingham
RL	Truro	**TP**	Portsmouth
RM	Carlisle	**TR**	Portsmouth
RN	Preston	**TS**	Dundee
RO	Luton	**TT**	Exeter
RP	Northampton	**TU**	Chester
RR	Nottingham	**TV**	Nottingham
RS	Aberdeen	**TW**	Chelmsford
RT	Ipswich	**TX**	Cardiff
RU	Bournemouth	**TY**	Newcastle upon Tyne
RV	Portsmouth	**TZ**	Belfast
RW	Coventry	**UA**	Leeds
RX	Reading	**UB**	Leeds
RY	Leicester	**UC**	central London
RZ	Antrim	**UD**	Oxford

UE	Dudley	**WD**	Dudley
UF	Brighton	**WE**	Sheffield
UG	Leeds	**WF**	Sheffield
UH	Cardiff	**WG**	Sheffield
UI	Londonderry	**WH**	Manchester
UJ	Shrewsbury	**WJ**	Sheffield
UK	Birmingham	**WK**	Coventry
UL	central London	**WL**	Oxford
UM	Leeds	**WM**	Liverpool
UN	Exeter	**WN**	Swansea
UO	Exeter	**WO**	Cardiff
UP	Newcastle upon Tyne	**WP**	Worcester
UR	Luton	**WR**	Leeds
US	Glasgow	**WS**	Bristol
UT	Leicester	**WT**	Leeds
UU	central London	**WU**	Leeds
UV	central London	**WV**	Brighton
UW	central London	**WW**	Leeds
UX	Shrewsbury	**WX**	Leeds
UY	Worcester	**WY**	Leeds
UZ	Belfast	**WZ**	Belfast
VA	Peterborough	**XI**	Belfast
VB	Maidstone	**XZ**	Armagh
VC	Coventry	**YA**	Taunton
VE	Peterborough	**YB**	Taunton
VF	Norwich	**YC**	Taunton
VG	Norwich	**YD**	Taunton
VH	Huddersfield	**YE**	central London
VJ	Gloucester	**YF**	central London
VK	Newcastle upon Tyne	**YG**	Leeds
VL	Lincoln	**YH**	central London
VM	Manchester	**YJ**	Brighton
VN	Middlesbrough	**YK**	central London
VO	Nottingham	**YL**	central London
VP	Birmingham	**YM**	central London
VR	Manchester	**YN**	central London
VS	Luton	**YO**	central London
VT	Stoke-on-Trent	**YP**	central London
VU	Manchester	**YR**	central London
VV	Northampton	**YS**	Glasgow
VW	Chelmsford	**YT**	central London
VX	Chelmsford	**YU**	central London
VY	Leeds	**YV**	central London
VZ	Tyrone	**YW**	central London
WA	Sheffield	**YX**	central London
WB	Sheffield	**YY**	central London
WC	Chelmsford	**YZ**	Londonderry

International vehicle registration marks

A	Austria
AFG	Afghanistan
AL	Albania
AND	Andorra
AUS	Australia
AZ	Azerbaijan
B	Belgium
BD	Bangladesh
BDS	Barbados
BF	Burkina Faso
BG	Bulgaria
BIH	Bosnia-Herzegovina
BOL	Bolivia
BR	Brazil
BRN	Bahrain
BRU	Brunei
BS	Bahamas
BUR	Myanmar (from former name Burma)
BVI	British Virgin Islands
BY	Belarus (from alternative name Byelorussia)
BZ	Belize
C	Cuba
CAM	Cameroon
CDN	Canada
CH	Switzerland (from French *Confédération Helvétique* or Latin *Confederatio Helvetica*)
CI	Côte d'Ivoire (Ivory Coast)
CL	Sri Lanka (from former name Ceylon)
CO	Colombia
CR	Costa Rica
CY	Cyprus
CZ	Czech Republic
D	Germany (from German *Deutschland*)
DK	Denmark and Greenland
DOM	Dominican Republic
DY	Benin (from former name Dahomey)
DZ	Algeria (from Arabic *Djazïr*)
E	Spain (from Spanish *España*)
EAK	(East Africa) Kenya
EAT	(East Africa) Tanzania
EAU	(East Africa) Uganda
EAZ	(East Africa) Tanzania (formerly Zanzibar)
EC	Ecuador
ES	El Salvador
EST	Estonia
ET	(Arab Republic of) Egypt
ETH	Ethiopia
F	France
FIN	Finland
FJI	Fiji
FL	Liechtenstein (from German *Fürstentum Liechtenstein*)
FR	Faeroe Islands
G	Gabon
GB	Great Britain
GBA	Alderney
GBG	Guernsey
GBJ	Jersey
GBM	Isle of Man
GBZ	Gibraltar
GCA	Guatemala (Central America)
GE	Georgia
GH	Ghana
GR	Greece
GUY	Guyana
H	Hungary
HK	Hong Kong
HKJ	(Hashemite Kingdom of) Jordan
HR	Croatia (from Croatian *Hrvatska*)
I	Italy
IL	Israel
IND	India
IR	Iran
IRL	Ireland
IRQ	Iraq
IS	Iceland (from Icelandic *Ísland*)
J	Japan
JA	Jamaica
K	Cambodia (from former name Kampuchea)
KS	Kyrgyzstan
KWT	Kuwait

KZ	Kazakhstan
L	Luxembourg
LAO	Laos
LAR	Libya (Arab Republic)
LB	Liberia
LS	Lesotho
LT	Lithuania
LV	Latvia
M	Malta
MA	Morocco
MAL	Malaysia
MC	Monaco
MD	Moldova
MEX	Mexico
MK	Macedonia
MOC	Mozambique (from Portuguese *Moçambique*)
MS	Mauritius
MW	Malawi
N	Norway
NA	Netherlands Antilles
NAM	Namibia
NAU	Nauru
NEP	Nepal
NGR	Nigeria
NIC	Nicaragua
NL	Netherlands
NZ	New Zealand
P	Portugal
PA	Panama
PE	Peru
PK	Pakistan
PL	Poland
PNG	Papua New Guinea
PY	Paraguay
Q	Qatar
RA	(Republic of) Argentina
RB	(Republic of) Botswana
RC	Taiwan (Republic of China)
RCA	Central African Republic (from French *République Centrafricaine*)
RCB	(Republic of) Congo (from former name Congo-Brazzaville)
RCH	(Republic of) Chile
RG	(Republic of) Guinea
RH	(Republic of) Haiti
RI	(Republic of) Indonesia
RIM	(Islamic Republic of) Mauritania (from French *République Islamique de Mauritanie*)
RL	(Republic of) Lebanon
RM	(Republic of) Madagascar
RMM	(Republic of) Mali
RN	(Republic of) Niger
RO	Romania
ROK	(Republic of) Korea
ROU	(Republic of) Uruguay
RP	(Republic of the) Philippines
RSM	(Republic of) San Marino
RU	(Republic of) Burundi (from former name Urundi)
RUS	Russia
RWA	Rwanda
S	Sweden
SA	Saudi Arabia
SD	Swaziland
SGP	Singapore
SK	Slovakia
SLO	Slovenia
SME	Suriname
SN	Senegal
SO	Somalia
SUD	Sudan
SY	Seychelles
SYR	Syria
T	Thailand
TCH	Chad (from French *Tchad*)
TG	Togo
TJ	Tajikistan
TM	Turkmenistan
TN	Tunisia
TR	Turkey
TT	Trinidad and Tobago
UA	Ukraine
USA	United States of America
V	Vatican City State
VN	Vietnam
WAG	(West Africa) Gambia
WAL	(West Africa) Sierra Leone
WD	(Windward Islands) Dominica
WG	(Windward Islands) Grenada
WL	(Windward Islands) St Lucia
WS	(Western) Samoa

WV	(Windward Islands) St Vincent	**Z**	Zambia
YAR	Yemen (Arab Republic)	**ZA**	South Africa (from Afrikaans *Zuid Afrika*)
YU	Yugoslavia	**ZW**	Zimbabwe
YV	Venezuela		

UK postcodes

AB	Aberdeen	**HA**	Harrow
AL	St Albans	**HD**	Huddersfield
B	Birmingham	**HG**	Harrogate
BA	Bath	**HP**	Hemel Hempstead
BB	Blackburn	**HR**	Hereford
BD	Bradford	**HU**	Hull
BH	Bournemouth	**HX**	Halifax
BL	Bolton	**IG**	Ilford
BN	Brighton	**IM**	Isle of Man
BR	Bromley	**IP**	Ipswich
BS	Bristol	**IV**	Inverness
BT	Belfast	**JE**	Jersey
CA	Carlisle	**KA**	Kilmarnock
CB	Cambridge	**KT**	Kingston-upon-Thames
CF	Cardiff	**KW**	Kirkwall (Orkney)
CH	Chester	**KY**	Kirkcaldy
CM	Chelmsford	**L**	Liverpool
CO	Colchester	**LA**	Lancaster
CR	Croydon	**LD**	Llandrindod Wells
CT	Canterbury	**LE**	Leicester
CV	Coventry	**LL**	Llandudno
CW	Crewe	**LN**	Lincoln
DA	Dartford	**LS**	Leeds
DD	Dundee	**LU**	Luton
DE	Derby	**M**	Manchester
DG	Dumfries	**ME**	Medway
DH	Durham	**MK**	Milton Keynes
DL	Darlington	**ML**	Motherwell
DN	Doncaster	**N**	north London
DT	Dorchester	**NE**	Newcastle upon Tyne
DY	Dudley	**NG**	Nottingham
E	east London	**NN**	Northampton
EC	east central London	**NP**	Newport
EH	Edinburgh	**NR**	Norwich
EN	Enfield	**NW**	northwest London
EX	Exeter	**OL**	Oldham
FK	Falkirk	**OX**	Oxford
FY	Blackpool	**PA**	Paisley
G	Glasgow	**PE**	Peterborough
GL	Gloucester	**PH**	Perth
GU	Guildford	**PL**	Plymouth
GY	Guernsey	**PO**	Portsmouth

PR	Preston	**TD**	Galashiels
RG	Reading	**TF**	Telford
RH	Redhill	**TN**	Tonbridge
RM	Romford	**TQ**	Torquay
S	Sheffield	**TR**	Truro
SA	Swansea	**TS**	Cleveland
SE	southeast London	**TW**	Twickenham
SG	Stevenage	**UB**	Uxbridge
SK	Stockport	**W**	west London
SL	Slough	**WA**	Warrington
SM	Sutton (Surrey)	**WC**	west central London
SN	Swindon	**WD**	Watford
SO	Southampton	**WF**	Wakefield
SP	Salisbury	**WN**	Wigan
SR	Sunderland	**WR**	Worcester
SS	Southend-on-Sea	**WS**	Walsall
ST	Stoke-on-Trent	**WV**	Wolverhampton
SW	southwest London	**YO**	York
SY	Shrewsbury	**ZE**	Lerwick
TA	Taunton		

US postcodes (zip codes)

AK	Alaska	**MT**	Montana
AL	Alabama	**NC**	North Carolina
AR	Arkansas	**ND**	North Dakota
AZ	Arizona	**NE**	Nebraska
CA	California	**NH**	New Hampshire
CO	Colorado	**NJ**	New Jersey
CT	Connecticut	**NM**	New Mexico
DC	District of Columbia	**NV**	Nevada
DE	Delaware	**NY**	New York
FL	Florida	**OH**	Ohio
GA	Georgia	**OK**	Oklahoma
HI	Hawaii	**OR**	Oregon
IA	Iowa	**PA**	Pennsylvania
ID	Idaho	**RI**	Rhode Island
IL	Illinois	**SC**	South Carolina
IN	Indiana	**SD**	South Dakota
KS	Kansas	**TN**	Tennessee
KY	Kentucky	**TX**	Texas
LA	Louisiana	**UT**	Utah
MA	Massachusetts	**VA**	Virginia
MD	Maryland	**VT**	Vermont
ME	Maine	**WA**	Washington
MI	Michigan	**WI**	Wisconsin
MN	Minnesota	**WV**	West Virginia
MO	Missouri	**WY**	Wyoming
MS	Mississippi		

A

A [fishing port] Aberdeen; [physics] absolute (temperature); academician; academy; [card games] ace; acre; acreage; adjutant; admiral; [cinema] adult (former film classification); [education] advanced (as in **A level**); air; *Altesse* (French: Highness); [music] alto; amateur; America; American; ammeter (in circuit diagrams); [Bible] Amos; ampere; ampere-turn; analog; [botany] androecium (in floral formula); angstrom; [horticulture] annual; anode; answer; anterior; April; area; armoured; art; arterial road (as in **A27**); article; artillery; assault (as in **A-day**); assistant; associate; athletic; atom(ic) (as in **A-bomb**); atomic weight; August; Australia; Australian; [international vehicle registration] Austria; *avancer* (French: go faster) (on clock or watch regulator); [medicine] blood group; [education] highest grade or mark; managerial or professional (occupational group); [physics] mass number; [music] note of scale; ten (in hexadecimal notation)

A [physics] absorbance; [chemistry] activity; [chemistry] affinity; [mathematics] area

a *année* (French: year); *annus* (Latin: year); are (unit of area); atto- (indicates 10^{-18}, as in **am** = attometre)

a [physics] acceleration; [physics] amplitude

a. about; absent; accepted; [finance] *accepté* (French: accepted) (on bill of exchange); acre; acreage; acting; [grammar] active; actual; address; adjective; advance; advanced; afternoon; age; [finance] *akzeptiert* (German: accepted) (on bill of exchange); [music] alto; amateur; *anno* (Latin: in the year); anonymous; answer; *ante* (Latin: before); anterior; *aqua* (Latin: water); arrive; arriving; [baseball] assist

A0 [paper size] 841 × 1189 mm

A1 [paper size] 594 × 841 mm; in first-class condition

A2 [paper size] 420 × 594 mm; [civil aircraft marking] Botswana

a2 [music] *a due* (Italian: for two (instruments or voices))

A3 [paper size] 297 × 420 mm; [civil aircraft marking] Tonga

A4 [paper size] 210 × 297 mm

A5 [paper size] 148 × 210 mm; [civil aircraft marking] Bhutan

A6 [paper size] 105 × 148 mm; [civil aircraft marking] United Arab Emirates

A7 [paper size] 74 × 105 mm; [civil aircraft marking] Qatar

A8 [paper size] 52 × 74 mm

A9 [paper size] 37 × 52 mm

A9C [civil aircraft marking] Bahrain

A10 [paper size] 26 × 37 mm

A40 [civil aircraft marking] Oman

3A [civil aircraft marking] Monaco

5A [civil aircraft marking] Libya

9A [civil aircraft marking] Croatia

AA [cinema] accompanied by adult (former film classification); achievement age; administrative assistant; advertising agency; Advertising Association; [taxation] age allowance; air attaché; Alcoholics Anonymous; [fishing port] Alloa; American Aviation; [biochemistry] amino acid; Anglers' Association; [military] anti-aircraft; Architectural Association; Army Act; [biochemistry] ascorbic acid; Associate in Accounting; Associate in Agriculture; Associate in Arts; Association of Agriculture; *Astronautica Acta* (journal of IAF); [physics] atomic absorption; [physics] atomic adsorption; Augustinians of the Assumption; Australian Army; author's alteration; Automobile Association; [vehicle registration] Bournemouth

a.a. absolute alcohol; acting appointment; after arrival; [shipping] always afloat; approximate absolute; area administrator; arithmetic average; attendance allowance; author's alteration

AAA [medicine] abdominal aortic aneurysm; [USA] Agricultural Adjustment Act; [USA] Agricultural Adjustment Administration; Allied Artists of America; Amateur Athletic Association; American Accounting Association; American Automobile Association; [biochemistry] amino acid analogue; [military] anti-aircraft artillery; [USA] Army Audit Agency; Association of Average Adjusters; Australian Association of Accountants; Australian Automobile Association; Automobile Association of America

AAAA Amateur Athletic Association of America; American Association of Advertising Agencies; Associated Actors and Artistes of America; Australian Association of Advertising Agencies

AAAC all-aluminium alloy conductor

AAAI American Association for Artificial Intelligence

AAAL American Academy of Arts and Letters

AAAM American Association of Aircraft Manufacturers

AA&QMG Assistant Adjutant and Quartermaster-General

AAAS American Academy of Arts and Sciences; American Academy of Asian Studies; American Association for the Advancement of Science; Associate of the American Antiquarian Society

AAB Aircraft Accident Board; Association of Applied Biologists

AABC American Amateur Baseball Congress

AABL Associated Australian Banks in London

AABM Australian Association of British Manufacturers

AABT American Association of Behavior Therapists

AABW Antarctic Bottom Water

AAC Aeronautical Advisory Council; Agricultural Advisory Council; [US air force] Alaskan Air Command; amateur athletic club; *anno ante Christum* (Latin: in the year before Christ); Army Air Corps; [electronics] automatic amplitude control

AACB [USA] Aeronautics and Astronautics Coordinating Board; Association of African Central Banks

AACC American Association of Clinical Chemists; [aeronautics] area-approach control centre

AACP American Association for Child Psychiatry; Anglo-American Council on Productivity

AACR [bibliography] Anglo-American Cataloguing Rules

AACS Aberdeen-Angus Cattle Society; [USA] Airways and Air Communications Service; [computing] automated-access control system

AAD [medicine] atlantoaxial dislocation

AADC air aide-de-camp; [USA] Army–Air Defense Command

AADFI Association of African Development Finance Institutions

AADS [USA] Army–Air Defense System

AAE American Association of Engineers

AAEC Australian Atomic Energy Commission

AAEE Aircraft and Armament Experimental Establishment

AAeE Associate in Aeronautical Engineering

AAES Association of Agricultural Education Staffs; Australian Army Education Service

AAEW [military] Atlantic airborne early warning

AAF Allied Air Forces; [USA] Army Air Forces

AAFC [military] anti-aircraft fire control

AAFCE Allied Air Forces in Central Europe

AAFIS Army and Air Force Intelligence Staff

AAFNE Allied Air Forces in Northern Europe

AAFSE Allied Air Forces in Southern Europe

AAG Air Adjutant-General; Assistant Adjutant-General; Association of American Geographers
AAgr Associate in Agriculture
AAGS Association of African Geological Surveys
AAHPER American Association for Health, Physical Education, and Recreation
AAIA Associate of the Association of International Accountants; Associate of the Australian Institute of Advertising; Association of American Indian Affairs
AAIB Air Accidents Investigation Branch
AAII Associate of the Australian Insurance Institute
AAIL American Academy and Institute of Arts and Letters
AAL [meteorology] above aerodrome level; Academy of Art and Literature; [USA] Arctic Aeromedical Laboratory; Association of Assistant Librarians
AALA American Association for Laboratory Accreditation
AALD Australian Army Legal Department
AALL American Association of Law Libraries
AAM air-to-air missile; American Association of Microbiology; American Association of Museums; Anti-Apartheid Movement; Association of Assistant Mistresses in Secondary Schools; Australian Air Mission
AAMI [medicine] age-associated memory impairment
AAMW [USA] Association of Advertising Men and Women
AAMWS Australian Army Medical Women's Service
AANA Australian Association of National Advertisers
A&A additions and amendments
A&AEE Aeroplane and Armament Experimental Establishment
a&b assault and battery
A&C addenda and corrigenda
A&E [medicine] accident and emergency (hospital department)
a&h [insurance] accident and health
A&I [USA] Agricultural and Industrial (college)
a&i [insurance] accident and indemnity
A&M [USA] Agricultural and Mechanical (college); Ancient and Modern (hymn book)
A&N Army and Navy (stores or club)
A&NI Andaman and Nicobar Islands
A&P [commerce] advertising and promotion; [New Zealand] Agricultural and Pastoral (show or association)
A&R artists and recording; artists and repertoire (as in **A&R man**)
a&r assault and robbery
a&s [insurance] accident and sickness
A&SH [military] Argyll and Sutherland Highlanders
A&W alive and well
AANS Australian Army Nursing Service
AAO American Association of Orthodontists; Anglo-Australian Observatory
aaO *am angeführten Orte* (German: at the place quoted)
AAOC Australian Army Ordnance Corps
AAOM American Academy of Occupational Medicine
AAP affirmative action programme; [US astronautics] Apollo Applications Program; Association of American Publishers; Australian Associated Press (news agency)
AAPA Advertising Agency Production Association; American Association of Port Authorities
AAPB American Association of Pathologists and Bacteriologists
AAPC All African People's Conference
AAPE American Academy of Physical Education
AAPG American Association of Petroleum Geologists
AAPHI Associate of the Association of Public Health Inspectors
AAPM American Association of Physicists in Medicine
AAPS American Association for the Promotion of Science
AAPSO Afro-Asian People's Solidarity Organization
AAPSS American Academy of Political and Social Science
AAPSW Associate of the Association of Psychiatric Social Workers
AAPT American Association of Physics Teachers
AAR Association of American Railroads
a.a.r. after action report; [insurance]

against all risks; aircraft accident record; aircraft accident report; average annual rainfall

AARP American Association of Retired Persons

AAS *Academiae Americanae Socius* (Latin: Fellow of the American Academy (of Arts and Sciences)); *Acta Apostolicae Sedis* (Latin: Acts of the Apostolic See) (publication of Roman Catholic Church); American Academy of Sciences; American Antiquarian Society; American Astronautical Society; American Astronomical Society; Andersen air sampler; Army Air Service; Associate in Applied Science; Association of Architects and Surveyors; Association of Asian Studies; atomic absorption spectrometry; Australian Academy of Science; Auxiliary Ambulance Service

AASA Associate of the Australian Society of Accountants

AASB [aeronautics] aerodynamically air-staged burner; American Association of Small Businesses

AASC Allied Air Support Command; Australian Army Service Corps

AASF Advanced Air Striking Force

AASG Association of American State Geologists

A'asia Australasia

AASM Associated African States and Madagascar (treaty)

AASR Airport and Airways Surveillance Radar

AASS *Americanae Antiquarianae Societatis Socius* (Latin: Associate of the American Antiquarian Society)

AAT [psychology] achievement anxiety test; Anglo-Australian Telescope (Siding Spring, Australia); Association of Accounting Technicians; [medicine] asymptomatic autoimmune thyroiditis; Australian Antarctic Territory

AATA Anglo-American Tourist Association

AATNU *Administration de l'assistance technique des Nations Unies* (French: United Nations Technical Assistance Administration)

AATT American Association of Textile Technology

AATTA Arab Association of Tourism and Travel Agents

AATUF All-African Trade Union Federation (replaced by OATUU)

AAU [USA] Amateur Athletic Union; Association of American Universities

AAUN American Association for United Nations; Australian Association for United Nations

AAUP American Association of University Presses; American Association of University Professors

AAUW American Association of University Women

AAV [medicine] adeno-associated virus; assault amphibious vehicle

AAVC Australian Army Veterinary Corps

AAVS American Anti-Vivisection Society

AAWC Australian Advisory War Council

AAZPA American Association of Zoological Parks and Aquariums

AB [UK postcode] Aberdeen; [fishing port] Aberystwyth; able-bodied seaman; advisory board; air board; airborne; [US air force] Airman Basic; Alberta; *Alliance balkanique* (French: Balkan Alliance); ammonia for bees (used to treat stings); antiballistic (missile); [medicine] asthmatic bronchitis; [baseball] at bat; [USA] Bachelor of Arts (from Latin *Artium Baccalaureus*); [medicine] blood group; [vehicle registration] Worcester

A/B [commerce] *Aktiebolaget* (Swedish: joint-stock company)

Ab antibody

a.B [commerce] *auf Bestellung* (German: on order)

a/b airbag(s) (in car advertisement); airborne

ab. about; abridgment

a.b. anchor bolt; [baseball] at bat

ABA Amateur Boxing Association; American Badminton Association; American Bankers' Association; American Bar Association; American Basketball Association (became part of NBA); American Book Award; American Booksellers Association; Antiquarian Booksellers Association; Associate in Business Administration; Association of British Archaeologists; Australian Bankers' Association

ABAA Antiquarian Booksellers Association of America
ABAC Association of British Aero Clubs and Centres
ABB [accounting] activity-based budgeting
Abb. Abbess; Abbey; Abbot
abb. abbey; [commerce] *abbuono* (Italian: allowance, discount)
ABBA Amateur Basketball Association; American Board of Bio-Analysis
abbr. abbreviated; abbreviation
abbrev. abbreviated; abbreviation
ABC [accounting] activity-based costing (as in **ABC method**); Advance Booking Charter (airline ticket); advanced biomedical capsule; Aerated Bread Company; air bridge to Canada; [medicine] airway, breathing, circulation (in first aid); America–Britain–Canada; American book-prices current; American Broadcasting Companies; analysis of benefits and costs; animal birth control; Arab Banking Corporation; Argentina–Brazil–Chile; Aruba, Bonaire, Curaçao (group of islands); Associated British Cinemas; [computing] Atanasoff–Berry computer; atomic, biological, and chemical (weapons or warfare); Audit Bureau of Circulation; Australian Broadcasting Corporation; [computing] automatic binary computer; automatic brake control
ABCA American Business Communication Association; Army Bureau of Current Affairs
ABCB Association of Birmingham Clearing Banks
ABCC Association of British Chambers of Commerce; Association of British Correspondence Colleges
ABCD [military] American, British, Chinese, Dutch (in World War II); atomic, biological and chemical protection and damage control
ABCFM American Board of Commissioners for Foreign Missions
ABCM Associate of the Bandsmen's College of Music
ABD [US military] advanced base depot; all but dissertation (of higher degree candidate); average body dose (of radiation)
abd abdicated; abridged
abd. abdicate; abdomen; abdominal
ABDA [military] American, British, Dutch, Australian (in World War II)
abdom. abdomen; abdominal
ABDP Association of British Directory Publishers
ABE acetone–butanol–ethanol (solvent)
ABEd [USA] Bachelor of Arts in Education
Aber. Aberdeen; Aberdonian
ABERCOR Associated Banks of Europe Corporation
ABF [informal] absolute bloody final (drink); Actors' Benevolent Fund; Associated British Foods
Abf. *Abfahrt* (German: departure)
ABFD Association of British Factors and Discounters
ABFM American Board of Foreign Missions
ABGB [Austria] *Allgemeines Bürgerliches Gesetzbuch* (German: General Civil Code)
abgk. *abgekürzt* (German: abbreviated)
ABGWIU [USA] Aluminum Brick and Glass Workers International Union
ABH actual bodily harm
Abh. *Abhandlungen* (German: transactions, treatises)
ABI [computing] application binary interface; Associate of the Institute of Book-keepers; Association of British Insurers
ABIA Association of British Introduction Agencies
ab init. *ab initio* (Latin: from the beginning)
ABINZ Associate of the Bankers' Institute of New Zealand
ABL atmospheric boundary layer
abl *abril* (Spanish: April)
abl. [grammar] ablative
ABLA American Business Law Association
ablat. [grammar] ablative
ABLJ adjustable buoyancy lifejacket
ABLS Association of British Library Schools; [USA] Bachelor of Arts in Library Science
ABM antiballistic missile; Associate in Business Management; Australian Board of Missions; automatic batch mix
ABMA Army Ballistic Missile Agency

ABMAC Association of British Manufacturers of Agricultural Chemicals
ABMEWS antiballistic missile early warning system
ABMPM Association of British Manufacturers of Printers' Machinery
ABMT [medicine] autologous bone marrow transplant(ation)
ABN [chemistry] acid–base–neutral; Anti-Bolshevik Bloc of Nations
Abn Aberdeen
abn airborne
ABNE Association for the Benefit of Non-contract Employees
ABO American Board of Ophthalmology; American Board of Orthodontics; American Board of Otolaryngology; [medicine] blood group system
ABOF Association of British Organic Fertilizers
ABOG American Board of Obstetrics and Gynecology
A-bomb atomic bomb
ABOS American Board of Oral Surgery; American Board of Orthopedic Surgery
ABP American Board of Pathology; American Board of Pediatrics; American Board of Peridontology; American Board of Prosthodontics; [biochemistry] androgen-binding protein; [medicine] arterial blood pressure; Associated Book Publishers; Associated British Ports
Abp Archbishop
ABPA Australian Book Publishers' Association
ABPC American Book Publishers' Council; Associated British Picture Corporation
ABPI Association of the British Pharmaceutical Industry
ABPN American Board of Psychiatry and Neurology; Association of British Paediatric Nurses
ABPO Advanced Base Personnel Officer
ABPS American Board of Plastic Surgery
ABPVM Association of British Plywood and Veneer Manufacturers
ABR American Board of Radiology; [medicine] auditory brainstem recording
abr. abridge; abridged; abridgment
ABRACADABRA Abbreviations and Related Acronyms Associated with Defense, Astronautics, Business and Radio-electronics (US publication)
ABRC Advisory Board for the Research Councils
ABRES advanced ballistic re-entry system
ABRO Animal Breeding Research Organization; Army in Burma Reserve of Officers
ABRS Association of British Riding Schools
ABRSM Associated Board of the Royal Schools of Music
ABRV [military] advanced ballistic re-entry vehicle
ABS acrylonitrile–butadiene–styrene (type of plastic); [chemistry] alkyl benzene sulphonate; American Bible Society; American Board of Surgery; American Bureau of Shipping; *Antiblockiersystem* (German: antilocking system (for brakes)); antilock braking system; Architects' Benevolent Society; Association of Broadcasting Staff; Australian Bureau of Statistics
abs. absence; absent; absolute; absolutely; absorbent; abstract
a.b.s. *aux bons soins* (*de*) (French: care of, c/o) (in postal addresses)
ABSA Association of Business Sponsorship of the Arts
abse. re. [law] *absente reo* (Latin: the defendant being absent)
abs. feb. [medicine] *absente febre* (Latin: when there is no fever)
ABSIE American Broadcasting Station in Europe (in World War II)
ABSM Associate of the Birmingham School of Music
ABSM(TTD) Associate of the Birmingham School of Music (Teacher's Training Diploma)
absol. absolute; absolutely
abs. re. [law] *absente reo* (Latin: the defendant being absent)
abstr. abstract; abstracted
abs. visc. absolute viscosity
ABSW Association of British Science Writers
ABT advanced backplane technology; [computing] advanced bi-CMOS technology; Association of Building Technicians
Abt. *Abteilung* (German: division, part)
abt about

ABTA Allied Brewery Traders' Association; Association of British Travel Agents Limited; Australian British Trade Association

ABTAC Australian Book Trade Advisory Committee

ABTUC All-Burma Trade Union Congress

ABU Asian Broadcasting Union; Assembly of the Baptist Union

A-BU Anglo-Belgian Union

abv. above

ABWR [nuclear technology] advanced boiling-water reactor

AC [chemistry] activated carbon; [chemistry] activated charcoal; [medicine] acute cholecystitis; adult contemporary (music); [computing] advanced CMOS; aero club; Air Command; Air Commodore; air conditioning; air control; Air Corps; Air Council; aircraftman; Alcohol Concern; Alpine Club; [physics] alternating current; Ambulance Corps; analogue computer; analytical chemist; angular correlation; annual conference; *ante Christum* (Latin: before Christ, BC); [law] Appeal Case; appeal court; *appellation contrôlée* (French: name controlled) (wine classification); Army Corps; Army Council; artillery college; Arts Council; Assistant Commissioner; athletic club; Atlantic Charter; *Auditor Camerae* (Latin: Auditor of the Papal Treasury); *Azione Cattolica* (Italian: Catholic Action) (social organization); Companion of the Order of Australia; [vehicle registration] Coventry

A/C account; account current; air conditioning; aircraft; aircraftman

Ac [chemistry] acetyl; [chemical element] actinium

Ac [meteorology] altocumulus

aC *antes de Cristo* (Portuguese: before Christ, BC); *avanti Cristo* (Italian: before Christ, BC)

a/c account; account current; *ai cuidado* (*de*) (Portuguese: care of, c/o) (in postal addresses)

ac. acre; activity

a.c. *a capo* (Italian: new line); *à compte* (French: on account); advisory committee; [physics] alternating current; *année courante* (French: this year); *anno corrente* (Latin: this year); [medicine] *ante cibum* (Latin: before meals) (in prescriptions); [finance] *assegno circolare* (Italian: banker's draft); author's correction

ACA [telecommunications] adjacent-channel attenuation; advanced combat aircraft; Agricultural Cooperative Association; American Camping Association; American Canoe Association; Anglers' Cooperative Association; Arts Council of America; Associate of the Institute of Chartered Accountants; Association of Consulting Actuaries; Australian Consumers' Association; Australian Council for Aeronautics

ACAA Agricultural Conservation and Adjustment Administration; American Coal Ash Association

ACAB [USA] Army Contract Adjustment Board

Acad. Academy

acad. academic; academy

Acad. fran. *Académie française* (French: French academy)

ACADI *Association des cadres dirigeants de l'industrie* (French: Association of Industrial Executives)

ACAE Advisory Council for Adult and Continuing Education

ACAL Advanced Computer Architecture Laboratory

AC&U [USA] Association of Colleges and Universities

ACAO Assistant County Advisory Officer

Acap. Acapulco

ACARD Advisory Council for Applied Research and Development

ACAS Advisory, Conciliation, and Arbitration Service; Assistant Chief of Air Staff

ACB *Association canadienne des bibliothèques* (French: Canadian Library Association)

ACBG [medicine] aorto-coronary bypass graft

ACBS Accrediting Commission for Business Schools

ACBSI Associate of the Chartered Building Societies Institute

ACBWS automatic chemical–biological warning system

ACC [New Zealand] Accident Compensation Corporation; [computing] accumulator; [medicine] acute cardiovascular collapse; Administrative Coordination Committee; advanced communication course; Agricultural Credit Corporation Limited; Anglican Consultative Council; annual capital charge; army cadet college; Army Catering Corps; Assistant County Commissioner (in Scouting); Associated Chemical Companies; Association of County Councils

acc. accelerate; acceleration; accent; [commerce] acceptance; [commerce] accepted; [music] accompanied (by); [music] accompaniment; according (to); account; accountant; [grammar] accusative

ACCA Aeronautical Chamber of Commerce of America; Agricultural Central Cooperative Association; Associate of the Chartered Association of Certified Accountants; Association of Certified and Corporate Accountants

ACCC Association of Canadian Community Colleges

ACCD American Coalition of Citizens with Disabilities

acce [commerce] acceptance

accel. [music] *accelerando* (Italian: with increasing speed)

access. accessory

ACCHAN Allied Command Channel (in NATO)

ACCM Advisory Council for the Church's Ministry

ACCO Association of Child Care Officers

accom. accommodation

accomp. accompanied; accompaniment; accompany

ACCP American College of Chest Physicians

accred. accredited

ACCS Associate of the Corporation of Secretaries (formerly Associate of the Corporation of Certified Secretaries)

ACCT Association of Cinematograph, Television and Allied Technicians

acct account; accountant

acct. accounting

acctd accented

accum. accumulative

accus. [grammar] accusative

accy accountancy; accuracy

ACD [medicine] acid citrate dextrose (as in **ACD solution**); [medicine] acquired cystic disease of the kidney

acd accord

ACDA Advisory Committee on Distinction Awards; [USA] Arms Control and Disarmament Agency; Aviation Combat Development Agency

ACDAS automatic control and data acquisition system

AC/DC [physics] alternating current/direct current; [informal] bisexual

ACDCM Archbishop of Canterbury's Diploma in Church Music

ACdre Air Commodore

ACDS Assistant Chief of Defence Staff

acdt accident

ACE [astronomy] Advanced Composition Explorer; advanced computing environment; [engineering] advanced cooled engine; Advisory Centre for Education; [medicine] alcohol–chloroform–ether (anaesthetic); Allied Command Europe; American Council on Education; [medicine] angiotensin-converting enzyme (as in **ACE inhibitor**); [USA] Army Corps of Engineers; Association for the Conservation of Energy; Association of Conference Executives; Association of Consulting Engineers; Association of Cultural Exchange; Australian College of Education; [computing] Automatic Computing Engine

ACEA Action Committee for European Aerospace

ACEd. Associate in Commercial Education

ACEEE American Council for an Energy-Efficient Economy

ACEF Australian Council of Employers' Federations

ACER Australian Council for Educational Research

ACERT Advisory Council for the Education of Romanies and other Travellers

ACET Advisory Committee on Electronics and Telecommunications; [medicine] Aids care, education and treatment

acet. acetate; acetone

ACEWEX Allied Command Europe Weather Exchange

ACF *Académie Canadienne Française* (French: French Canadian Academy); [South Africa] Active Citizen Force; Army

Cadet Force; *Automobile Club de France* (French: Automobile Club of France)
ACFA Army Cadet Force Association
ACFAS *Association canadienne-française pour l'avancement des sciences* (French: French-Canadian Association for the Advancement of Science)
ACFHE Association of Colleges of Further and Higher Education
ACFI Associate of the Clothing and Footwear Institute
acft aircraft
ACG *An Comunn Gaidhealach* (Gaelic: The Gaelic Society); Assistant Chaplain-General; automatic control gear
ACGB Arts Council of Great Britain
ACGBI Automobile Club of Great Britain and Ireland
ACGI Associate of the City and Guilds (of London) Institute
ACGME Accreditation Council for Graduate Medical Education
ACGS Assistant Chief of the General Staff
ACH [banking] automated clearing house
ach [building] air changes per hour
ACHR American Convention on Human Rights
AChS Associate of the Society of Chiropodists
ACI *Alliance coopérative internationale* (French: International Cooperative Alliance); Alloy Castings Institute; American Concrete Institute; army council instruction; Associate of the Institute of Commerce; *Automobile Club d'Italia* (Italian: Automobile Club of Italy)
ACIA Associate of the Corporation of Insurance Agents; [computing] asynchronous communications interface adapter
ACIAA Australian Commercial and Industrial Artists' Association
ACIArb Associate of the Chartered Institute of Arbitrators
ACIB Associate of the Chartered Institute of Bankers; Associate of the Corporation of Insurance Brokers
ACIC [USA] Aeronautical Charting and Information Center
ACIGS Assistant Chief of the Imperial General Staff
ACII Associate of the Chartered Insurance Institute
ACILA Associate of the Chartered Institute of Loss Adjusters
ACINF [USA] Advisory Committee on Irradiated and Novel Foods
ACIOPJF *Association catholique internationale des œuvres de protection de la jeune fille* (French: International Catholic Girls' Society)
ACIS American Committee for Irish Studies; Associate of the Institute of Chartered Secretaries and Administrators (formerly Associate of the Chartered Institute of Secretaries)
ACIT Associate of the Chartered Institute of Transport
ACJP airways corporations joint pensions
ACK [telecommunications] acknowledgment
ack. acknowledge; acknowledgment
ack-ack anti-aircraft (from former phonetic alphabet for AA)
ackgt acknowledgment
ackt acknowledgment
ACL [computing] access control list; action-centred leadership; Analytical Chemistry Laboratory; Atlas Computer Laboratory
ACLA Anti-Communist League of America
ACLANT Allied Command Atlantic
ACLC Air Cadet League of Canada
ACLP Association of Contact Lens Practitioners
ACLS American Council of Learned Societies
ACLS automatic carrier landing system
ACLU American Civil Liberties Union; American College of Life Underwriters
ACM Air Chief Marshal; air combat manœuvring; American Campaign Medal; asbestos-containing material; [USA] Assistant Chief of Mission; Association for Computing Machinery; authorized controlled material
ACMA Agricultural Cooperative Managers' Association; Associate of the Chartered Institute of Management Accountants
ACMC Association of Canadian Medical Colleges
ACME [USA] Advisory Council on Medical Education; [USA] Association of Consulting Management Engineers

ACMET Advisory Council on Middle East Trade
ACMF [USA] Air Corps Medical Forces; Allied Central Mediterranean Forces; Australian Commonwealth Military Forces
ACMM Associate of the Conservatorium of Music, Melbourne
ACMP Advisory Committee on Marine Pollution; Assistant Commissioner of the Metropolitan Police
acmp. accompany
ACMRR Advisory Committee on Marine Resources Research
ACMT American College of Medical Technologies
ACN [chemistry] alkane carbon number; American College of Neuropsychiatrists; *ante Christum natum* (Latin: before the birth of Christ)
a.c.n. all concerned notified
ACNA [USA] Advisory Council on Naval Affairs; Arctic Institute of North America
ACNS Assistant Chief of Naval Staff; Associated Correspondents News Service
ACNY Advertising Club of New York
ACO Admiralty Compass Observatory; Association of Children's Officers
AC of S Assistant Chief of Staff
ac.o.g. aircraft on ground
ACom Associate in Commerce
AComm Associate in Commerce
a/con. air conditioning (in car advertisement)
ACOPS Advisory Commission on Pollution of the Sea
ACOR American Center for Oriental Research
ACORD Advisory Council on Research and Development
ACORN *A Classification of Residential Neighbourhoods* (directory); [computing] associative content retrieval network; [computing] automatic checkout and recording network
ACOS Advisory Committee on Safety; American College of Osteopathic Surgeons; Assistant Chief of Staff
ACOST Advisory Council on Science and Technology
ACP advanced computer program; advanced computer project; African, Caribbean and Pacific (countries); American College of Pharmacists; American College of Physicians; Associate of the College of Preceptors; Association of Circus Proprietors of Great Britain; Association of Clinical Pathologists; *Automóvel Clube de Portugal* (Portuguese: Automobile Club of Portugal)
ACPM American Congress of Physical Medicine and Rehabilitation
ACPO Association of Chief Police Officers
acpt. [commerce] acceptance
ACPU auxiliary computer power unit
acq. acquire; acquisition; acquittal
ACR Admiral Commanding Reserves; advanced capabilities radar; aircraft control room; American College in Rome; [aeronautics] approach control radar; Association of College Registrars; audio cassette recorder
ACRB *Aero-Club royal de Belgique* (French: Royal Belgian Aero Club)
acrd accrued
ACRE Action with Communities in Rural England; Advisory Committee on Releases to the Environment; automatic climatological recording equipment
ACRF Advanced Computing Research Facility
acrg. acreage
ACRI [USA] Air-Conditioning and Refrigeration Institute
ACRL [USA] Association of College and Research Libraries
acron. acronym
ACRR American Council on Race Relations
ACRS [taxation] accelerated cost recovery system; Advisory Committee on Reactor Safeguards
ACS [aeronautics] active control system; Admiral Commanding Submarines; Admiralty computing service; advanced communications system; air-conditioning system; airport catering services; [aeronautics] altitude control system; American Cancer Society; American Ceramic Society; American Chemical Society; American College of Surgeons; assembly control system; Associate in Commercial Science; Association of Caribbean States; Association of Commonwealth Students; Australian

Computer Society; [finance] automated confirmation service; [computing] automated control system

ACSA Allied Communications Security Agency; Associate of the Institute of Chartered Secretaries and Administrators

ACSE [Australia] Association of Consulting Structural Engineers

ACSEA Allied Command South East Asia

ACSL [computing] advanced continuous simulation language; assistant Cub Scout leader

ACSM American Congress on Surveying and Mapping

ACSN Association of Collegiate Schools of Nursing

ACSPA Australian Council of Salaried and Professional Associations

a/cs pay. accounts payable

a/cs rec. accounts receivable

ACSS [printing] automated colour separation system

ACSTT Advisory Committee on the Supply and Training of Teachers

ACT activated-complex theory; [aeronautics] active control technology; advance corporation tax; [computing] advanced CMOS with TTL inputs; advanced coal technology; Advisory Council on Technology; Agricultural Central Trading Limited; Air Council for Training; American College Test; [computing] analogical circuit technique; Associate of the College of Technology; Associated Container Transportation; Association of Corporate Treasurers; Australian Capital Territory; Australian College of Theology

act. acting; [grammar] active; activities; actor; actual; actuary

a cta *a cuenta* (Spanish: on account)

ACTC Art Class Teacher's Certificate

actg acting

ACTH [biochemistry] adrenocorticotrophic hormone

ACTO Advisory Council on the Treatment of Offenders

ACTP American College Testing Program

ACTS [USA] Acoustic Control and Telemetry System; Action of Churches Together in Scotland; Australian Catholic Truth Society

ACTT Association of Cinematograph, Television and Allied Technicians (became part of BECTU)

ACTU Australian Council of Trade Unions

ACTWU [USA] Amalgamated Clothing and Textile Workers Union

ACU Actors' Church Union; American Congregational Union; Asian Clearing Union; Association of Commonwealth Universities; Auto-Cycle Union; [computing] automatic calling unit

ACUA Association of Cambridge University Assistants

ACUE American Committee of United Europe

.ac.uk UK academic institution (in Internet address)

ACUS Atlantic Council of the United States

ACV actual cash value; air-cushion vehicle; Associate of the College of Violinists; Associated Commercial Vehicles

ACW agricultural crop waste; Air Command and Warning; Air Control and Warning; aircraftwoman; [physics] alternating continuous wave; automatic car wash

ACWS aircraft control and warning system

ACWW Associated Country Women of the World

ACY average crop yield

AD [insurance] accidental damage; *Acción Democrática* (Spanish: Democratic Action Party) (in Venezuela); accumulated dose (of radiation); [military] active duty; administrative department; [military] air defence; air dried; [currency] Algerian dinar; [medicine] Alzheimer's disease; *anno Domini* (Latin: in the year of the Lord, AD) (in dates); [fishing port] Ardrossan; armament depot; art director; assembly district; assistant director; Australian Democrat (or Democrats); autograph document; average deviation; Dame of the Order of Australia; [vehicle registration] Gloucester

A-D Albrecht Dürer (German artist)

A/D aerodrome; after date; [computing] analog–digital (conversion or converter)

a.D *ausser Dienst* (German: retired, on half pay)

ad [US short form] advantage (in tennis); [short form] advertisement
ad. adapt; adaptation; adapted; adapter; [medicine] *addantur* (Latin: let there be added) (in prescriptions); [medicine] *adde* (Latin: add) (in prescriptions); [grammar] adverb; advertisement
.ad Andorra (in Internet address)
a.d. after date; *ante diem* (Latin: before the day); autograph document
ADA [medicine] adenosine deaminase (as in **ADA deficiency**); Agricultural Development Association; [USA] Air Defense Agency; Aluminium Development Association; American Dental Association; American Diabetes Association; Americans for Democratic Action; Association of Drainage Authorities; Atomic Development Authority; Australian Dental Association
ADAA Art Dealers Association of America
ADAD [USA] automatic telephone dialing–announcing device
adag. [music] *adagio* (Italian: slowly)
adap. adapted
Adapt Access for Disabled People to Arts Today
ADAPTS [USA] Air-Deliverable Antipollution Transfer System (in Coast Guard)
ADAS Agricultural Development and Advisory Service; [computing] automatic data acquisition system; [computing] auxiliary data annotation set
ADAWS [military] action data automation and weapons systems; Assistant Director of Army Welfare Services
A-day assault day
ADB accidental death benefit; African Development Bank; Asian Development Bank; Associate of the Drama Board; [USA] Bachelor of Domestic Arts
ADC advanced developing country (or countries); [telecommunications] advice of duration and charge; aerodrome control; [Jamaica] Agricultural Development Corporation; aide-de-camp; [medicine] Aids dementia complex; Aid to Dependent Children; [USA] Air Defense Command; amateur dramatic club; [computing] analog–digital converter; apparent diffusion coefficient; Art Directors' Club; Assistant District Commissioner (in Scouting); Association of District Councils; [computing] automated distribution control; automatic digital calculator
ADCC [USA] Air Defense Control Center
ADCCP [computing] advanced data communication control procedure
ADCI American Die Casting Institute
ADCM Archbishop of Canterbury's Diploma in Church Music
ADCONSEN [USA] advice and consent of the Senate
ADCP personal aide-de-camp (to the monarch)
ADCT Art Directors' Club, Toronto
ADD [aeronautics] airstream direction detector; [medicine] attention deficit disorder
add. [medicine] *addantur* (Latin: let there be added) (in prescriptions); [medicine] *adde* (Latin: add) (in prescriptions); addenda; addendum; addition; additional; address; addressed
ADDC [USA] Air Defense Direction Center
ADDF Abu Dhabi Defence Force
addl additional
addn addition
addnl additional
addsd addressed
ADEF *Agence d'évaluation financière* (French: financial rating agency)
ad effect. [medicine] *ad effectum* (Latin: until effective) (in prescriptions)
ADEME Assistant Director, Electrical and Mechanical Engineering
ad eund. *ad eundem gradum* (Latin: to the same degree)
ADF [Australia] approved deposit fund; Asian Development Fund; Australian Defence Force; [navigation] automatic direction finder
a.d.f. after deducting freight
ad fin. *ad finem* (Latin: at the end, near the end)
ADFManc Art and Design Fellow, Manchester
ADFW Assistant Director of Fortifications and Works
ADG Assistant Director-General
ADGB Air Defence of Great Britain
ADGMS Assistant Director-General of Medical Services

ad gr. acid. [medicine] *ad gratam aciditatem* (Latin: to an agreeable acidity) (in prescriptions)
ad gr. gust. [medicine] *ad gratam gustum* (Latin: to an agreeable taste) (in prescriptions)
ADH [biochemistry] antidiuretic hormone; Assistant Director of Hygiene; Association of Dental Hospitals
ADHD [medicine] attention deficit hyperactivity disorder
ad h.l. *ad hunc locum* (Latin: at this place, on this passage)
ADI [medicine] acceptable daily intake (of toxic substance); approved driving instructor
ad inf. *ad infinitum* (Latin: to infinity)
ad init. *ad initium* (Latin: at the beginning)
ad int. *ad interim* (Latin: in the meantime)
ADIZ [USA] air defense identification zone
ADJ [meteorology] adjacent
adj. adjacent; [grammar] adjective; adjoining; [mathematics] adjoint; adjourned; adjudged; adjunct; [insurance, banking] adjustment; adjutant
AdjA [USA] Adjunct in Arts
ADJAG Assistant Deputy Judge Advocate-General
Adj-Gen Adjutant-General
adjt adjutant
Adjt-Gen Adjutant-General
ADL [electronics] acoustic delay line; [medicine] activities of daily living (or life); [computing] ADA design language; [USA] Anti-Defamation League (of B'nai B'rith); Assistant Director of Labour
ad lib. *ad libitum* (Latin: according to pleasure, freely)
ad loc. *ad locum* (Latin: at the place, on this passage)
ADLP Australian Democratic Labor Party
ADM Advanced Diploma in Midwifery; annual delegate meeting; Association of Domestic Management; atomic demolition munitions; average daily membership
Adm. Admiral; Admiralty
adm. administration; administrative; administrator; admission; admitted
ADMA American Drug Manufacturers' Association; [USA] Aviation Distributors' and Manufacturers' Association
admin [short form] administration
admin. administration; administrative; administrator
Adml Admiral
ADMO(CA) Assistant Director of the Meteorological Office (Civil Aviation)
ADMOS [computing] automatic device for mechanical order selection
admov. [medicine] *admoveatur* (Latin: let it be applied) (in prescriptions)
Adm. Rev. *Admodum Reverendus* (Latin: Very Reverend)
ADMS Assistant Director of Medical Services
ADMT Association of Dental Manufacturers and Traders of the United Kingdom
admx administratrix
ADN *Allgemeiner deutscher Nachrichtendienst* (German news agency)
ADNA Assistant Director of Naval Accounts
ADNC Assistant Director of Naval Construction
ad neut. [medicine] *ad neutralizandum* (Latin: until neutral)
ADNI Assistant Director of Naval Intelligence
ADNOC Abu Dhabi National Oil Company
ADNS Assistant Director of Nursing Services
ADO [USA] advanced development objective; air defence officer; assistant district officer; Association of Dispensing Opticians; automotive diesel oil
ADOF Assistant Director of Ordnance Factories
ADOS Assistant Director of Ordnance Services
ADP [biochemistry] adenosine diphosphate; air defence position; [physics] area density of particles; Association of Dental Prosthesis; [computing] automatic data processing
ADPA Associate Diploma of Public Administration
ADPCM [computing] adaptive differential pulse code modulation
ADPLAN advanced planning

ADPR Assistant Director of Public Relations
ADPSO Association of Data Processing Service Organizations
ADR accident data recorder; [law] alternative dispute resolution; [stock exchange] American Depository Receipt
ADRA Animal Diseases Research Association (Edinburgh)
ADS [computing] accurately defined systems; advanced dressing station; [USA] air defense sector; American Dialect Society; [engineering] articulated drill string; Astrophysics Data System; [engineering] automatic depressurization system
A.d.S. *Académie des sciences* (French: Academy of Sciences)
a.d.s. autograph document signed
ad s. [law] *ad sectam* (Latin: at the suit of)
ad saec. *ad saeculum* (Latin: to the century)
ADS&T Assistant Director of Supplies and Transport
ad sat. [medicine] *ad saturandum* (Latin: to saturation)
ADSOC [USA] Administrative Support Operations Center
ADSS Association of Directors of Social Services; Australian Defence Scientific Service
ADST [finance] approved deferred share trust
adst. feb. [medicine] *adstante febre* (Latin: when fever is present)
ADT American District Telegraph; Assistant Director of Transport; Atlantic Daylight Time; [electronics] automatic double tracking; average daily traffic
ADTECH advanced decoy technology
ADTS Automated Data and Telecommunications Service
ad us. *ad usum* (Latin: according to the custom)
ad us. ext. [medicine] *ad usum externum* (Latin: for external use) (in prescriptions)
Adv. Advent; Advocate
adv. advance; [grammar] adverb; [grammar] adverbial; *adversus* (Latin: against); advertisement; advertising; advice; advise; adviser; advisory; advocate
ad val. *ad valorem* (Latin: according to value)
advb [grammar] adverb
adven. adventure
adv. pmt advance payment
ADVS Advanced Diploma in Voice Studies; Assistant Director of Veterinary Services
advt advertisement
advv. [grammar] adverbs
ADW air defence warning; Assistant Director of Works
ADWE&M Assistant Director of Works, Electrical and Mechanical
ADX [computing] automatic data exchange; [telecommunications] automatic digital exchange
AE account executive; [physics] acoustic emission; adult education; aeronautical engineer; aeronautical engineering; [taxation] age exemption; *Agence Europe* (news agency); agricultural engineer; agricultural engineering; Air Efficiency Award; *Aktiebolaget Atomenergi* (Swedish: Atomic Energy Corporation); All England; American English; army education; Associate in Education; Associate in Engineering; atomic energy; [photography] autoexposure; [vehicle registration] Bristol; pen-name of George Russell (Irish poet)
ae. [numismatics] *aeneus* (Latin: made of copper); *aetatis* (Latin: at the age of, aged)
.ae United Arab Emirates (in Internet address)
AEA [physics] acoustic emission analysis; [USA] Actors' Equity Association; [engineering] air entraining agent; American Economic Association; [USA] Atomic Energy Act; Atomic Energy Authority
AEAA *Asociación de Escritores y Artistas Americanos* (Spanish: Association of Spanish-American Writers and Artists)
AEAF Allied Expeditionary Air Force
AE&MP Ambassador Extraordinary and Minister Plenipotentiary
AE&P Ambassador Extraordinary and Plenipotentiary
AEAUSA Adult Education Association of the United States of America
AEB Area Electricity Board; Associated Examining Board

AEBP atmospheric equivalent boiling point
AEC [insurance] additional extended cover(age); Agricultural Executive Council; American Express Company; Army Electronics Command; Associated Equipment Company; Association of Education Committees; [USA] Atomic Energy Commission; [South Africa] Atomic Energy Corporation; [USA] Atomic Energy Council; [photography] automatic exposure control
a.e.c. at earliest convenience
AECB [USA] Atomic Energy Control Board
AECCG African Elephant Conservation Coordinating Group
AECI African Explosives and Chemical Industries; Associate of the Institute of Employment Consultants
AECL Atomic Energy of Canada Limited
AED advanced electronics design; Algol Extended for Design (computer programming language); Association of Engineering Distributors; automated engineering design; Doctor of Fine Arts (from Latin *Artium Elegantium Doctor*)
AEd Associate in Education
AEDE *Association européenne des enseignants* (French: European Teachers' Association)
AEDOT Advanced Energy Design and Operation Technologies
AEDP [USA] Alternative Energy Development Program
AEDS [USA] Association for Educational Data Systems; Atomic Energy Detection Systems
AEDU Admiralty Experimental Diving Unit
AEE airborne evaluation equipment; Atomic Energy Establishment
AeE aeronautical engineer
AEEC [USA] Airlines Electronic Engineering Committee
AEEE [Canada] Army Equipment Engineering Establishment
AEEN *Agence européenne pour l'energie nucléaire* (French: European Agency for Atomic Energy)
AEEU Amalgamated Engineering and Electrical Union
AEF Allied Expeditionary Force; American Expeditionary Force(s); Australian Expeditionary Force
A-effect [theatre] alienation effect
AEFM *Association européenne des festivals de musique* (French: European Association of Music Festivals)
AEG *Allgemeine Elektrizitäts-Gesellschaft* (German manufacturer of electrical goods)
a.e.g. *ad eundem gradum* (Latin: to the same degree); [bookbinding] all edges gilt
AEGIS Aid for the Elderly in Government Institutions; [computing] an existing general information system
AEGM Anglican Evangelical Group Movement
AEH A(lfred) E(dward) Housman (British poet)
AEI [USA] Alternative Energy Institute; American Express International; Associated Electrical Industries; *Association des écoles internationales* (French: International Schools Association)
AEIOU *Austriae Est Imperare Orbi Universi* (Latin: it is given to Austria to rule the whole world); *Austria Erit In Orbe Ultima* (Latin: Austria will be the world's last survivor)
AEJ Association for Education in Journalism
AEL Admiralty Engineering Laboratory; aeronautical engine laboratory; aircraft engine laboratory; Associated Engineering Limited; automation engineering laboratory
AELE *Association européenne de libre-échange* (French: European Free Trade Association, EFTA)
AELTC All England Lawn Tennis Club
AEM Air Efficiency Medal; analytical electron microscope (or microscopy)
AEMT Association of Electrical Machinery Trades
AEMU [astronautics] Advanced Extra-vehicular Mobility Unit
AEn Associate in English
Aen. *The Aeneid* (epic poem by Virgil)
aen. [numismatics] *aeneus* (Latin: made of copper)
AENA All England Netball Association
AEng Associate in Engineering
AEO Assistant Education Officer; Assistant

Experimental Officer; Association of Exhibition Organizers
AEP *Agence européenne de productivité* (French: European Production Agency); American Electric Power
AEPI American Educational Publishers Institute
aeq. *aequalis* (Latin: equal)
AER Army Emergency Reserve
aer. aeronautics; aeroplane
AERA American Educational Research Association; Associate Engraver, Royal Academy
aera. aeration
AERE Atomic Energy Research Establishment (Harwell)
AerE aeronautical engineer
AERI Agricultural Economics Research Institute (Oxford University)
AERNO aeronautical equipment reference number
AERO Air Education and Recreation Organization
aero. aeronautic(al)
Aeroflot Aero Flotilla (Russian airline company)
aeron. aeronautic(al); aeronautics
aerosp. aerospace
AES advanced energy system; [USA] Aerospace Electrical Society; Agricultural Economics Society (Reading University); [USA] Airways Engineering Society; [physics] atomic emission spectrum; Audio Engineering Society
Aes. Aesop (ancient Greek writer of fables)
AESE [USA] Association of Earth Science Editors
AESL [USA] Aerospace Energy Systems Laboratory
aesth. aesthetics
AET Associate in Electrical (or Electronic) Technology
aet. *aetatis* (Latin: at the age of, aged)
a.e.t. after extra time
aetat. *aetatis* (Latin: at the age of, aged)
AEU Amalgamated Engineering Union (became part of AEEU); American Ethical Union
AEV aerothermodynamic elastic vehicle; air evacuation; [microbiology] avian erythroblastosis virus
AEW Admiralty Experimental Works; airborne early warning (aircraft)
AEW&C airborne early warning and control
AEWHA All England Women's Hockey Association
AEWLA All England Women's Lacrosse Association
AEWS advanced earth satellite weapons system; aircraft early warning system
AF *Académie française* (French: French Academy); Admiral of the Fleet; air force; [USA] Air Foundation; Anglo-French; *Armée française* (French: French Army); Associated Fisheries; Associate Fellow; audiofrequency; [photography] autofocus; automatic (smoke) filter; [vehicle registration] Truro
A/F antiflooding; as found (in auction catalogue)
Af [currency] afgháni (used in Afghanistan)
Af. Africa; African; Afrikaans; [currency] Aruban florin
a/f [commerce] *a favor* (Spanish: in favour); as found (in auction catalogue)
.af Afghanistan (in Internet address)
a.f. advanced freight; [commerce] *a favor* (Spanish: in favour); *anno futuro* (Latin: next year); audiofrequency
AFA [nuclear technology] advanced fuel assembly; African Football Association; Air Force Act; [USA] Air Force Association; Amateur Fencing Association; Amateur Football Alliance; American Foundrymen's Association; Associate in Fine Arts; Associate of the Faculty of Actuaries
AFAC American Fisheries Advisory Committee
AFAEP Association of Fashion Advertising and Editorial Photographers
AFAFC [USA] Air Force Accounting and Finance Center
AFAIAA Associate Fellow of the American Institute of Aeronautics and Astronautics
AFAIM Associate Fellow of the Australian Institute of Management
AFAITC [USA] Armed Forces Air Intelligence Training Center
AFAL [USA] Air Force Astronautical Laboratory
AFAM Ancient Free and Accepted Masons

AF&AM Ancient Free and Accepted Masons

AFAS *Association française pour l'avancement des sciences* (French: French Association for the Advancement of the Sciences)

AFASIC Association for all Speech-Impaired Children

AFB [USA] Air Force Base; American Federation for the Blind

AFBD Association of Futures Brokers and Dealers

AFBF American Farm Bureau Federation

AFBMD [USA] Air Force Ballistic Missile Division

AFBPsS Associate Fellow of the British Psychological Society

AFBS American and Foreign Bible Society

AFC Air Force Cross; amateur football club; American Football Conference; [immunology] antibody-forming cell; association football club; Australian Flying Corps; automatic flight control; automatic frequency control; average fixed costs

a.f.c. automatic flight control; automatic frequency control

AFCAI Associate Fellow of the Canadian Aeronautical Institute

AFCE Associate in Fuel Technology and Chemical Engineering; automatic flight control equipment

AFCEA [USA] Armed Forces Communications and Electronics Association

AFCent Allied Forces in Central Europe

AFCO Admiralty Fleet Confidential Order

afco [engineering] automatic fuel cut-off

AFCRL [USA] Air Force Cambridge Research Laboratories

AFCS Air Force Communications Service; automatic flight control system

AFCU American and Foreign Christian Union

AFCW Association of Family Case Workers

AFD accelerated freeze dried; accelerated freeze drying; air force depot; [USA] Doctor of Fine Arts

AFDC [USA] Aid to Families with Dependent Children

AFDCS Association of First Division Civil Servants (formerly FDA)

AFDM [engineering] advanced fluid-dynamics model

AFDS Air Fighting Development Squadron

AFEA American Farm Economics Association; American Film Export Association

AFEE Airborne Forces Experimental Establishment

AFEIS Advanced Further Education Information Service

AFERO Asia and the Far East Regional Office

AFES Admiralty Fuel Experimental Station

AFESC [USA] Air Force Engineering and Services Center

AFESD Arab Fund for Economic and Social Development

AFEX [USA] Air Forces Europe Exchange; [USA] Armed Forces Exchange

AFF [photography] aberration-free focus

aff. affairs; affectionate; affectionately; affiliate; affiliated; affirmative; affix

affil. affiliate; affiliated

Aff.IP Affiliate of the Institute of Plumbing

AFFL Agricultural Finance Federation Limited

afft affidavit

AFFTC [USA] Air Force Flight Test Center

AFG [international vehicle registration] Afghanistan

Afg. Afghan; Afghanistan

AFGE American Federation of Government Employees

Afgh. Afghan; Afghanistan

Afghan. Afghanistan

AFGL [USA] Air Force Geophysics Laboratory

AFGM American Federation of Grain Millers

AFH American Foundation for Homeopathy

AFHC Air Force Headquarters Command

AFHQ Allied Forces Headquarters; Armed Forces Headquarters

AFI American Film Institute

AFIA American Foreign Insurance Association; Apparel and Fashion Industry

AFIAP *Artiste de la Fédération internationale de l'art photographique* (French: Artist of the International Federation of Photographic Art)

AFICD Associate Fellow of the Institute of Civil Defence
AFII American Federation of International Institutes
AFIIM Associate Fellow of the Institution of Industrial Managers
AFIMA Associate Fellow of the Institute of Mathematics and its Applications
AFIPS American Federation of Information Processing Societies (Incorporated)
AFK away from the keyboard (in Internet chat)
AFL [computing] abstract family of languages; Air Force List; American Federation of Labor; American Football League; *Associação de Futebol de Lisboa* (Portuguese: Lisbon Football Association)
AFLA Amateur Fencers' League of America; Asian Federation of Library Associations
AFLC [USA] Air Force Logistics Command
AFL-CIO American Federation of Labor and Congress of Industrial Organizations
aflt afloat
AFM [engineering] abrasive flow machining; Air Force Medal; American Federation of Musicians of the United States and Canada; assistant field manager; Associated Feed Manufacturers; [physics] atomic force microscope (or microscopy); [telecommunications] audiofrequency modulation
AFMA Armed Forces Management Association; Artificial Flower Manufacturers' Association of Great Britain
AFMDC [USA] Air Force Missile Development Center
AFMEC African Methodist Episcopal Church
AFMed Allied Forces in Mediterranean
afmo *afectísimo* (Spanish: very affectionately) (in correspondence)
AFMTC [USA] Air Force Missile Test Center
AFN American Forces Network; Armed Forces Network; Association of Free Newspapers
AFNIL *Agence francophone pour la numérotation internationale du livre* (French: French Agency for International Book Numbering, ISBN)
AFNOR *Association française de normalisation* (French: French Standardization Association)
AFNorth Allied Forces in Northern Europe
AFO Admiralty Fleet Order; army forwarding officer
AFOAR [USA] Air Force Office of Aerospace Research
AFOAS [USA] Air Force Office of Aerospace Sciences
AF of M American Federation of Musicians of the United States and Canada
AFOM Associate of the Faculty of Occupational Medicine
AFOSR [USA] Air Force Office of Scientific Research
AFP *Agence France Presse* (French news agency); [medicine] alpha-fetoprotein
AFPRB Armed Forces Pay Review Board
AFR accident frequency rate; air-fuel ratio; automatic fingerprint recognition
AFr. Anglo-French
Afr. Africa; African; Afrikaans
AFRA American Farm Research Association
AFRAeS Associate Fellow of the Royal Aeronautical Society
AFRC Agricultural and Food Research Council (formerly ARC)
Afrik. Afrikaans
AFRO African Regional Office
AFRTS [USA] Armed Forces Radio and Television Service
AFS Advanced Flying School; air force station; Alaska Ferry Service; American Field Service; Army Fire Service; Atlantic Ferry Service; auxiliary fire service
AFSA American Foreign Service Association; [USA] Armed Forces Security Agency
AFSBO American Federation of Small Business Organizations
AFSC Air Force Systems Command; American Friends Service Committee; Armed Forces Staff College
AFSCME American Federation of State, County and Municipal Employees
afsd aforesaid
AFSIL Accommodation for Students in London
AFSLAET Associate Fellow of the Society

of Licensed Aircraft Engineers and Technologists
AFSouth Allied Forces in Southern Europe
AFT American Federation of Teachers; axial-flow turbine
aft. after; afternoon
AFTA ASEAN Free Trade Area
AFTE American Federation of Technical Engineers
AFTM American Foundation of Tropical Medicine; [computing] anonymous file transfer protocol
AFTN Aeronautical Fixed Telecommunications Network
aftn afternoon
AFTR American Federal Tax Reports
AFTRA American Federation of Television and Radio Artists
AFU advanced flying unit
AFULE Australian Federated Union of Locomotive Enginemen
AFV armoured fighting vehicle; armoured force vehicle
AFVG [aeronautics] Anglo-French variable geometry
AFVPA Advertising Film and Videotape Producers' Association
AFW army field workshop
AFWAL [USA] Air Force Wright Aeronautical Laboratories
AG Accountant-General; Action Group Party (in Nigeria); Adjutant-General; Agent-General (of colonies); air gunner; [commerce] *Aktiengesellschaft* (German: public limited company, plc); *Alberghi per la Gioventù* (Italian: Youth Hostels); art gallery; Attorney-General; [vehicle registration] Hull
Ag antigen; [chemical element] silver (from Latin *argentum*)
Ag. August
ag. against; agent; agreement; agricultural; agriculture
.ag Antigua and Barbuda (in Internet address)
a.g. anti-gas
AGA air-to-ground-to-air; *Aktiebolaget Gasaccumulator* (Swedish gas company, original manufacturer of stoves); Amateur Gymnastics Association; American Gas Association; American Genetic Association; [obstetrics] appropriate for gestational age; Australian Garrison Artillery
AGAC American Guild of Authors and Composers
AGACS automatic ground-to-air communications system
AGARD Advisory Group for Aerospace Research and Development (in NATO)
a.g.b. a good brand; any good brand
AGBI Artists' General Benevolent Institution
AGC [USA] advanced graduate certificate; American Grassland Council; [electronics] automatic gain control
AGCA [aeronautics] automatic ground-controlled approach
AGCAS Association of Graduate Careers Advisory Service
AGCC Arab Gulf Cooperation Council
AGCL [aeronautics] automatic ground-controlled landing
AGCM [meteorology] atmospheric general circulation model
agcy agency
agd agreed
a.g.d. [engineering] axial gear differential
AGDC [Freemasonry] Assistant Grand Director of Ceremonies
AGDL Attorney-General of the Duchy of Lancaster
AGE Admiralty Gunnery Establishment; aerospace ground equipment; Associate in General Education; automatic guidance electronics
AgE agricultural engineer
AGES Association of Agricultural Education Staffs
AGF Adjutant-General to the Forces; army ground forces
Agfa *Aktiengesellschaft für Anilinfabrikation* (German chemical company)
ag. feb. [medicine] *aggrediente febre* (Latin: when the fever increases)
agg. aggregate
aggr. aggregate
AGH Australian General Hospital
AGI [USA] adjusted gross income (in tax returns); American Geographical Institute; American Geological Institute; annual general inspection; *Artistes graphiques internationaux* (French: International Graphic Artists); Associate of the Institute of Certificated Grocers

AGIP *Agenzia Generale Italiana Petroli* (Italian oil company)
agit. [medicine] *agitatum* (Latin: shaken)
agit. ante sum. [medicine] *agita ante sumendum* (Latin: shake before taking) (in prescriptions)
Agitprop *Agitpropbyuro* (Russian: Agitation and Propaganda Bureau) (former bureau of Soviet Communist Party)
AGK *Astronomische Gesellschaft Katalog* (German: Astronomical Society Catalogue)
AGL above ground level
aglm. agglomerate
AGM advisory group meeting; [medicine] African green monkey; air-to-ground missile; annual general meeting; Award of Garden Merit (Royal Horticultural Society award)
AGMA American Guild of Musical Artists; Athletic Goods Manufacturers' Association
AGN [astronomy] active galactic nucleus
agn again; agnomen
agnos. agnostic
ago. *agosto* (Italian or Spanish: August)
AGOR Auxiliary-General Oceanographic Research
AGP Academy of General Practice; [computing] accelerated graphics port; [computing] advanced graphics port; aviation general policy
AGPA American Group Psychotherapy Association
AGPL *Administração-Geral do Pôrto de Lisboa* (Portuguese: Port of Lisbon Authority)
AGR [nuclear technology] advanced gas-cooled reactor; Association of Graduate Recruiters
agr. agreed; agreement; agricultural; agriculture; agriculturist
AGRA Army Group Royal Artillery; Association of Genealogists and Record Agents
AGREE Advisory Group on Reliability of Electronic Equipment
AGRF American Geriatric Research Foundation
agric. agricultural; agriculture; agriculturist
AGRM Adjutant-General, Royal Marines
agron. agronomy
AGS [astronautics] abort guidance system; aircraft general standard; Air Gunnery School; Alpine Garden Society; American Geographical Society; Associate in General Studies
AGSM Associate of the Guildhall School of Music (and Drama); Australian Graduate of the School of Management
AGSRO Association of Government Supervisors and Radio Officers
AGSS American Geographical and Statistical Society
agst against
AGT advanced gas turbine; Art Gallery of Toronto; [USA] Association of Geology Teachers
agt agent; agreement
AGU American Geophysical Union
AGV [pharmacology] aniline gentian violet; automated guided vehicle; [electronics] autonomous guided vehicle
AGVA American Guild of Variety Artists
AGW actual gross weight
AGWAC Australian Guided Weapons and Analogue Computer
AGWY [insurance] Atlantic, Gulf, West Indies
agy agency
AH *anno Hebraico* (Latin: in the Jewish year); *anno Hegirae* (Latin: in the year of the Hegira) (in Muslim calendar); [insurance] Antwerp–Hamburg coastal ports; [fishing port] Arbroath; [chemistry] aromatic hydrocarbon; [medicine] artificial hyperglycaemia; [vehicle registration] Norwich
a.h. [shipping] after hatch; [shipping] aft hatch; ampere-hour; armed helicopter
AHA American Heart Association; American Historical Association; American Hospitals Association; area health authority; Australian Hotels Association
AHAM [USA] Association of Home Appliance Manufacturers
AH&FITB Agricultural, Horticultural and Forestry Industry Training Board
AHAUS Amateur Hockey Association of the United States
AHC Accepting Houses Committee; American Horticultural Council; Army Hospital Corps
AHD *American Heritage Dictionary*

ahd ahead
AHDL [medicine] alveolar hydatid disease of the liver
AHE [USA] Associate in Home Economics; [USA] Association for Higher Education
AHEM Association of Hydraulic Equipment Manufacturers
AHF [medicine] antihaemophilic factor
AHG [medicine] antihaemophilic globulin
AHGMR Ad Hoc Group on Missile Reliability
AHI American Health Institute; American Hospital Institute
AHIL [USA] Association of Hospital and Institutional Libraries
AHL American Hockey League
a.h.l. *ad hunc locum* (Latin: at this place, on this passage)
AHMC Association of Hospital Management Committees
AHMPS Association of Headmistresses of Preparatory Schools
AHMS American Home Mission Society
AHNCV Area of High Nature Conservation Value
AHP [engineering] absorption heat pump; assistant house physician
ahp air horsepower
AHPR Association of Health and Pleasure Resorts
AHQ Air Headquarters; Allied Headquarters; Army Headquarters
a.h.r. acceptable hazard rate (in risk analysis)
AHRC Australian Humanities Research Council
AHRHS Associate of Honour of the Royal Horticultural Society
AHRIH [New Zealand] Associate of Honour of the Royal Institute of Horticulture
AHS adult health study; American Helicopter Society; *anno humanae salutis* (Latin: in the year of human salvation); annual housing survey; assistant house surgeon
AHSA American Horse Shows Association
AHSB Authority, Health and Safety Branch (of Atomic Energy Authority)
AHSM Associate of the Institute of Health Services Management
AHT absorption heat transformer; acoustic homing torpedo; Animal Health Trust; Association of Highway Technicians
a.h.v. *ad hanc vocem* (Latin: at this word) (in reference book)
AHWA Association of Hospital and Welfare Administrators
AI Admiralty instruction; Admiralty Islands; [computing] Adobe Illustrator; air interception; air interdiction; *Altesse Impériale* (French: Imperial Highness); American Institute; Amnesty International; *anno inventionis* (Latin: in the year of the discovery); Anthropological Institute; Army Intelligence; artificial insemination; artificial intelligence
a.i. *ad interim* (Latin: for the meantime)
AIA Abrasive Industries Association; [USA] Aerospace Industries Association; American Institute of Aeronautics; American Institute of Architects; American Insurance Association; Anglo-Indian Association; Archeological Institute of America; Associate of the Institute of Actuaries; Association of International Accountants; Association of International Artists; automated image analysis; [New Zealand] Aviation Industry Association
AIAA Aircraft Industries Association of America; American Institute of Aeronautics and Astronautics; Association of International Advertising Agencies
AIAB Associate of the International Association of Book-keepers
AIAC Air Industries Association of Canada; *Association internationale d'archéologie classique* (French: International Association for Classical Archaeology)
AIAE Associate of the Institution of Automobile Engineers
AIAgrE Associate of the Institution of Agricultural Engineers
AIAL Associate Member of the International Institute of Arts and Letters
AIAS Australian Institute of Agricultural Science
AIB [insurance] accidents investigation branch (of insurance company); American Institute of Banking; Association of Independent Businesses; *Associazione Italiana Biblioteche* (Italian: Italian Library Association)
AIBA *Association internationale de boxe*

amateur (French: International Amateur Boxing Association)

AIBC Architectural Institute of British Columbia

AIBD Associate of the Institute of British Decorators; Association of International Bond Dealers

AIBM *Association internationale des bibliothèques musicales* (French: International Association of Music Libraries)

AIBP Associate of the Institute of British Photographers

AIBS American Institute of Biological Sciences

AIBScot Associate of the Institute of Bankers in Scotland

AIC Agricultural Improvement Council; Agricultural Institute of Canada; American Institute of Chemists; artificial insemination centre; Art Institute of Chicago

AICA Associate Member of the Commonwealth Institute of Accountants; *Association internationale des critiques d'art* (French: International Association of Art Critics)

AICB *Association internationale contre le bruit* (French: International Association Against Noise)

AICBM anti-intercontinental ballistic missile

AICC All India Congress Committee

AICE American Institute of Chemical Engineers; American Institute of Consulting Engineers; Associate of the Institution of Civil Engineers

AIChE American Institute of Chemical Engineers

AICMA *Association internationale des constructeurs de matériel aérospatial* (French: International Association of Aerospace Equipment Manufacturers)

AICRO Association of Independent Contract Research Organizations

AICS Associate of the Institute of Chartered Shipbrokers; *Association internationale du cinéma scientifique* (French: International Scientific Film Association)

AICTA Associate of the Imperial College of Tropical Agriculture

AICV armoured infantry combat vehicle

AID [medicine] acute infectious disease; Aeronautical Inspection Directorate; [USA] Agency for International Development; agricultural industrial development; Aircraft Intelligence Department; American Institute of Decorators; American Institute of Interior Designers; Army Intelligence Department; [medicine] artificial insemination by donor; *Association internationale pour le développement* (French: International Development Association)

AIDA *Association internationale de droit africain* (French: International African Law Association); *Association internationale de la distribution alimentaire* (French: International Association of Food Distribution); [marketing] attention, interest, desire, action (of customer)

AIDAS Agricultural Industry Development Advisory Service

AIDD American Institute for Design and Drafting

AIDF African Industrial Development Fund

AIDL [New Zealand] Auckland Industrial Development Laboratory

AIDP Associate of the Institute of Data Processing; *Association internationale de droit pénal* (French: International Association of Penal Law)

AIDS accident information display system; [medicine] acquired immune deficiency syndrome; aircraft integrated data system; air force intelligence data-handling system

Aids [medicine] acquired immune deficiency syndrome

AIEA *Agence internationale de l'énergie atomique* (French: International Atomic Energy Agency)

AIED *Association internationale des étudiants dentaires* (French: International Association of Dental Students)

AIEE Associate of the Institution of Electrical Engineers; *Association des instituts d'études européennes* (French: Association of Institutes for European Studies)

AIEP [USA] Association of Independent Electricity Producers

AIF *Alliance internationale des femmes* (French: International Alliance of Women); [USA] Atomic Industrial Forum; Australian Imperial Forces

AIFA Associate of the International Faculty of Arts
AIFF Associate of the Institute of Freight Forwarders
AIFireE Associate of the Institution of Fire Engineers
AIFM *Association internationale des femmes médecins* (French: International Association of Women Doctors)
AIG Adjutant Inspector-General; Assistant Inspector-General; Assistant Instructor of Gunnery
AIGA American Institute of Graphic Arts
AIGCM Associate of the Incorporated Guild of Church Musicians
AIGS Agricultural Investment Grant Schemes
AIH all in hand; [medicine] artificial insemination by husband; *Association internationale de l'hôtellerie* (French: International Hotel Association)
AIHA American Industrial Hygiene Association
AIIA Australian Institute of International Affairs
AIIE American Institute of Industrial Engineers
AIIExE Associate of the Institution of Incorporated Executive Engineers
AIInfSc Associate of the Institute of Information Scientists
AIITech Associate Member of the Institute of Industrial Technicians
AIJD *Association internationale des juristes démocrates* (French: International Association of Democratic Lawyers)
AIJPF *Association internationale des journalistes de la presse féminine et familiale* (French: International Association of Women's Press Journalists)
AIL air intelligence liaison; Associate of the Institute of Linguists
AILAS [aeronautics] automatic instrument-landing approach system
AILO air intelligence liaison officer
AILocoE Associate of the Institution of Locomotive Engineers
AIM Africa Inland Mission; Alternative Investment Market; American Indian Movement (civil-rights organization); American Institute of Management; Amsterdam International Market; analytical ion microscopy; Australian Inland Mission (in Presbyterianism); Australian Institute of Management
a.i.m.a. as interest may appear
AIMarE Associate of the Institute of Marine Engineers
AIMCO [USA] Association of Internal Management Consultants
AIME American Institute of Mechanical Engineers; American Institute of Mining Engineers
AIMechE Associate of the Institution of Mechanical Engineers
AIMI Associate of the Institute of the Motor Industry
AIMM Australasian Institute of Mining and Metallurgy
AIMO Association of Industrial Medical Officers
AIMPA *Association internationale de météorologie et de physique de l'atmosphère* (French: International Association of Meteorology and Atmospheric Physics)
AIMS Association for Improvement in Maternity Services
AIMU American Institute of Marine Underwriters
AIN American Institute of Nutrition
AINEC All-India Newspaper Editors' Conference
AInstP Associate of the Institute of Physics
AInstPI Associate of the Institute of Patentees and Inventors
AINucE Associate of the Institution of Nuclear Engineers
AIP American Institute of Physics; Associate of the Institute of Plumbing; Association of Independent Producers
AIPA Associate of the Institute of Practitioners in Advertising; *Association internationale de psychologie appliquée* (French: International Association of Applied Psychology)
AIPO American Institute of Public Opinion
AIPR Associate of the Institute of Public Relations
AIPS *Association internationale de la presse sportive* (French: International Sports Press Association); astronomical image-processing system
AIQS Associate of the Institute of Quantity Surveyors

AIR All India Radio; American Institute of Refrigeration
a-i-r artist-in-residence
AIRA [USA] air attaché
AIRC Association of Independent Radio Companies
AIRCENT Allied Air Forces, Central Europe
AIRCOM airways communications system
air con. air conditioning
AIRG Agency for Intellectual Relief in Germany
AIRH *Association internationale de recherches hydrauliques* (French: International Association of Hydraulic Research)
AIRPASS aircraft interception radar and pilots attack sight system
AIRS [physics, electronics] acoustic-imaging recognition system
AIRTE Associate of the Institute of Road Transport Engineers
AIRTO Association of Independent Research and Technology Organizations
AIS [commerce] agreed industry standard; androgen insensitivity syndrome; Anglo-Italian Society; *Association internationale de sociologie* (French: International Sociological Association); Australian Illawarra Shorthorn (breed of cattle)
AISA Associate of the Incorporated Secretaries Association
AISE *Association internationale des sciences économiques* (French: International Economics Association)
AISI American Iron and Steel Institute
AISJ *Association internationale des sciences juridiques* (French: International Association of Legal Science)
AISS *Association internationale de la sécurité sociale* (French: International Social Security Association)
AIST [USA] Agency of Industrial Science and Technology
AIStructE Associate of the Institution of Structural Engineers
AIT *Alliance internationale de tourisme* (French: International Tourism Alliance); [meteorology] artificial ionospheric turbulence; Asian Institute of Technology; Association of HM Inspectors of Taxes; Association of Investment Trusts
AITA *Association internationale du théâtre d'amateurs* (French: International Amateur Theatre Association)
AITC *Association internationale des traducteurs de conférence* (French: International Association of Conference Translators); Association of Investment Trust Companies
AITO Association of Independent Tour Operators
AIU *Association internationale des universités* (French: International Association of Universities)
AIV *Association internationale de volcanologie* (French: International Association of Volcanology)
AIW (International Union of) Allied Industrial Workers of America; Atlantic-Intercoastal Waterway (from Cape Cod to Florida Bay)
AIWC All-India Women's Conference
AIWEM Associate of the Institution of Water and Environmental Management
AIWM American Institute of Weights and Measures
AIX [computing] advanced interactive executive
AJ ankle jerk; [telecommunications] anti-jam; *Archaeological Journal*; Associate in Journalism; [vehicle registration] Middlesbrough
AJA American of Japanese ancestry; Anglo-Jewish Association; Australian Journalists' Association
AJAG Assistant Judge Advocate-General
AJC Australian Jockey Club
AJCC American Joint Committee on Cancer
AJE [accounting] adjusting journal entry
AJEX Association of Jewish Ex-Service Men and Women
AJPM *ad Jesum per Mariam* (Latin: to Jesus through Mary)
AJR Association of Jewish Refugees; Australian Jurist Reports
AJY Association for Jewish Youth
AK above knee; [US postcode] Alaska; automatic Kalashnikov (type of rifle, as in **AK-47**); Knight of the Order of Australia; [vehicle registration] Sheffield
a.k.a. also known as

Akad. *Akademie* (German: academy)
AKC American Kennel Club; Associate of King's College (London)
AKEL *Anorthotikon Komma Ergazomanou Laou* (Greek: Progressive Party of the Working People) (in Cyprus)
AKOE Anti-Killer Organization of Expatriates (in Cyprus)
AKR auroral kilometric radiation (from the earth)
Akt [commerce] *Aktiebolaget* (Swedish: joint-stock company)
Aktb [commerce] *Aktiebolaget* (Swedish: joint-stock company)
Aktieb [commerce] *Aktiebolaget* (Swedish: joint-stock company)
AL Abraham Lincoln (US president); [medicine] activity of living; Admiralty letter; [US postcode] Alabama; [international vehicle registration] Albania; *América Latina* (Spanish: Latin America); [baseball] American League; American Legion; Anglo-Latin; *anno lucis* (Latin: in the year of light); army list; [vehicle registration] Nottingham; [UK postcode] St Albans
Al [chemical element] aluminium
al. alcohol; alcoholic; *alia* (Latin: other things); *alii* (Latin: others)
.al Albania (in Internet address)
a.l. [finance] allotment letter; [commerce] *après livraison* (French: after delivery); autograph letter
ALA Air Licensing Authority; all letters answered (in personal advertisement); American Library Association; Associate in Liberal Arts; Associate of the Library Association; Association of London Authorities; Authors' League of America
Ala. Alabama
ALAA Associate of the Library Association of Australia
ALAC Artificial Limb and Appliance Centre
ALACP American League to Abolish Capital Punishment
ALADI *Asociación Latino-Americana de Integración* (Spanish: Latin-American Integration Association)
ALAI *Association littéraire et artistique internationale* (French: International Literary and Artistic Association)
ALA-ISAD American Library Association–Information Science and Automation Division
ALAM Associate of the London Academy of Music (and Dramatic Art)
ALAP as low as practicable (referring to radiation level or dose)
ALARA as low as reasonably achievable (referring to radiation level or dose)
Alas. Alaska
ALAWP all letters answered with photograph (in personal advertisement)
Alb. Albania; Albanian; Alberta; Albion
alb. [medicine] albumin
Alba Alberta
Alban. *Albanensis* (Latin: (Bishop) of St Albans)
ALBM air-launched ballistic missile
Albq. Albuquerque
ALBSU Adult Literacy and Basic Skills Unit
ALC Agricultural Land Commission
alc. alcohol
a.l.c. à la carte
ALCAN Aluminium Company of Canada
ALCD Associate of the London College of Divinity
alch. alchemy
ALCM air-launched cruise missile; Associate of London College of Music
ALCS Authors' Lending and Copyright Society
ALD [medicine] adrenoleukodystrophy; [computing] automatic line drawing
Ald. Alderman
ALDEV African Land Development
Aldm. Alderman
ALE [insurance] additional living expense; Association for Liberal Education
A level [education] Advanced level
ALF Animal Liberation Front; Arab Liberation Front (in Iraq); automatic letter facer (machine for sorting mail)
ALFSEA Allied Land Forces South-East Asia
ALG [medicine] antilymphocyte globulin
Alg. Algeria; Algerian; Algiers
alg. algebra; algebraic
a.l.g. advanced landing ground
ALGES Association of Local Government Engineers and Surveyors
ALGFO Association of Local Government Financial Officers
Algol [computing] algorithmic language

ALH Australian Light Horse
ALI American Library Institute; Argyll Light Infantry; Associate of the Landscape Institute
ALICE Autistic and Language-Impaired Children's Education
align. alignment
ALJ Administration Law Judge; Australian Law Journal
ALJR Australian Law Journal Reports
alk. alkali; alkaline
ALL [medicine] acute lymphatic leukaemia
ALLC Association for Literary and Linguistic Computing
alleg. allegation; allegorical; allegory
All H. All Hallows
all'ingr. *all'ingrosso* (Italian: wholesale)
allo [music] *allegro* (Italian: quickly)
all'ott. [music] *all'ottava* (Italian: an octave higher)
All S. All Souls
All SS All Saints
ALM [medicine] alveolar lining material; Association of Lloyd's Members; audio-lingual method (in foreign-language teaching); Master of the Liberal Arts (from Latin *Artium Liberalium Magister*)
ALN [medicine] axillary lymph nodes
ALNA *Armée de libération nationale d'Angola* (French: Angolan National Liberation Army)
ALO air liaison officer; allied liaison officer
ALOE A Lady of England (pen-name of Charlotte M. Tucker, British novelist)
ALP American Labor Party; Australian Labor Party; automated language processing; automated learning process; [USA] automated library program
alp. alpine
ALPA Air Line Pilots' Association
ALPAL [computing] A Livermore Physics Applications Language
alph. alphabetic(al)
alphanum. alphanumeric
ALPO Association of Land and Property Owners; Association of Lunar and Planetary Observers
ALPSP Association of Learned and Professional Society Publishers
ALPURCOMS all-purpose communications system
ALR American Law Reports
alr *aliter* (Latin: otherwise)
ALRC Anti-Locust Research Centre
ALRI airborne long-range input
ALS accident localization system; Agricultural Land Service; [medicine] amyotrophic lateral sclerosis; [immunology] antilymphocytic serum; [aeronautics] approach lighting system(s); Associate of the Linnean Society; autograph letter signed; automated library system
a.l.s. autograph letter signed
Alsat. Alsatian
al seg. [music] *al segno* (Italian: to the sign, at the sign)
ALSEP Apollo Lunar Surface Experiment Package
ALT Agricultural Land Tribunal
Alt [computing] alternate (key)
Alt. *Altesse* (French: Highness)
alt. alteration; altered; alternate; alternative; alternator; altimeter; altitude; [music] alto
Alta Alberta
alt. dieb. [medicine] *nis diebus* (Latin: every other day)
alter. alteration
alt. hor. [medicine] *alternis horis* (Latin: every other hour)
alt. noct. [medicine] *alternis noctibus* (Latin: every other night)
ALTPR Association of London Theatre Press Representatives
ALTU Association of Liberal Trade Unionists
ALU [computing] arithmetic and logic unit
alum. aluminium; alumna(e); alumnus (or alumni)
ALV [microbiology] avian leucosis virus
ALWR [nuclear technology] advanced light-water reactor
AM Academy of Management; administrative memorandum; [astronautics] airlock module; air mail; Air Marshal; Air Ministry; Albert Medal; Alpes-Maritimes (French department); [radio] amplitude modulation; [physics] angular momentum; *anno mundi* (Latin: in the year of the world); *annus mirabilis* (Latin: year of wonders, 1666); *ante meridiem* (Latin: before noon); area manager;

army manual; assistant manager; Associate Member; [insurance] *assurance mutuelle* (French: mutual insurance); *Ave Maria* (Latin: Hail Mary); Award of Merit; [USA] Master of Arts (from Latin *Artium Magister*); Member of the Order of Australia; [vehicle registration] Swindon
Am [chemical element] americium
Am. America; American; [Bible] Amos
aM *am Main* (German: on the River Main) (in place-names)
am attometre
a/m above-mentioned
am. amateur; ammeter; ammunition
.am Armenia (in Internet address)
a.m. [radio] amplitude modulation; *ante meridiem* (Latin: before noon)
AMA against medical advice; American Management Association; American Marketing Association; American Medical Association; American Missionary Association; American Motorcycle Association; Assistant Masters Association; Associate of the Museums Association; Association of Metropolitan Authorities; Australian Medical Association
AMAB Army Medical Advisory Board
AMAE American Museum of Atomic Energy
amal. amalgamated
amalg. amalgamated
AMAmIEE Associate Member of the American Institute of Electrical Engineers
AMARC Associated Marine and Related Charities
AMASCE Associate Member of the American Society of Civil Engineers
amat. amateur
AMAusIMM Associate Member of the Australasian Institute of Mining and Metallurgy
AMB Air Ministry bulletin; [USA] Airways Modernization Board
Amb. Ambassador; ambulance
AMBAC Associate Member of the British Association of Chemists
Ambas. Ambassador
ambig. ambiguity; ambiguous
AMBIM Associate Member of the British Institute of Management
AMC [USA] Aerospace Manufacturers' Council; Agricultural Mortgage Corporation Limited; American Motors Corporation; [USA] Army Missile Command; [USA] Army Mobile Command; [USA] Army Munitions Command; Art Master's Certificate; Association of Management Consultants; Association of Municipal Corporations
AMCA Architectural Metal Craftsmen's Association
AMCIB Associate Member of the Corporation of Insurance Brokers
AMCIOB Associate Member of the Chartered Institute of Building
AMCL Association of Metropolitan Chief Librarians
AMCS airborne missile control system
AMCT Associate of the Manchester College of Technology
am. cur. [law] *amicus curiae* (Latin: friend of the court)
AMD acid-mine drainage; Admiralty machinery depot; aerospace medical division; [meteorology] air movement data; Army Medical Department
amd amend
AMDB Agricultural Machinery Development Board
AMDEA Association of Manufacturers of Domestic Electrical Appliances
AMDEC Agricultural Marketing Development Executive Committee
AMDG *ad majorem Dei gloriam* (Latin: to the greater glory of God) (motto of Jesuits)
amdt amendment
AME [USA] Advanced Master of Education; African Methodist Episcopal; Association of Municipal Engineers
AMEC Australian Minerals and Energy Council
AMEDS [USA] Army Medical Service
AMEE Admiralty Marine Engineering Establishment; Association of Managerial Electrical Executives
AMEIC Associate Member of the Engineering Institute of Canada
AMEM African Methodist Episcopal Mission
Am. Emb. American Embassy
AMEME Association of Mining Electrical and Mechanical Engineers

amend. amendment
amendt amendment
Amer. America; American
Amer. Ind. American Indian
Amer. Std American Standard
AMES Air Ministry Experimental Station; Association of Marine Engineering Schools
AMet Associate of Metallurgy
AMETS Association for Management Education and Training in Scotland
AMEWA Associated Manufacturers of Electric Wiring Accessories
Amex American Express; American Stock Exchange
AMEZC African Methodist Episcopal Zion Church
AMF Allied Mobile Force (of NATO); Australian Marine Force; Australian Military Forces
AMG Allied Military Government
amg among
a.m.g. [aeronautics] automatic magnetic guidance
AMGO Assistant Master-General of Ordnance
AMGOT Allied Military Government of Occupied Territory (in World War II)
AMI [medicine] acute myocardial infarction; American Meat Institute; American Military Institute; Ancient Monuments Inspectorate; *Association Montessori internationale* (French: International Montessori Association)
a.m.i. [military] advanced manned interceptor; [aeronautics] air mileage indicator
AMIAE Associate Member of the Institution of Automobile Engineers
AMIAP Associate Member of the Institution of Analysts and Programmers
AMIBF Associate Member of the Institute of British Foundrymen
AMICE Associate Member of the Institution of Civil Engineers
AMICEI Associate Member of the Institution of Civil Engineers of Ireland
AMIChemE Associate Member of the Institution of Chemical Engineers
AMICW Associate Member of the Institute of Clerks of Works of Great Britain
AMIED Associate Member of the Institution of Engineering Designers
AmIEE American Institute of Electrical Engineers
AMIEI Associate Member of the Institution of Engineering Inspection
AMIEx Associate Member of the Institute of Export
AMIFireE Associate Member of the Institution of Fire Engineers
AMIGasE Associate Member of the Institution of Gas Engineers
AMIHT Associate Member of the Institution of Highways and Transportation
AMII Association of Musical Instrument Industries
AMIIE Associate Member of the Institution of Incorporated Engineers
AMIIM Associate Member of the Institution of Industrial Managers
AMILocoE Associate Member of the Institution of Locomotive Engineers
AMIMarE Associate Member of the Institute of Marine Engineers
AMIMechE Associate Member of the Institution of Mechanical Engineers
AMIMGTechE Associate Member of the Institution of Mechanical and General Technician Engineers
AMIMI Associate Member of the Institute of the Motor Industry
AMIMM Associate Member of the Institution of Mining and Metallurgy
Am. Ind. American Indian
AMinlsTech Associate in Minerals Technology
AMInstBE Associate Member of the Institution of British Engineers
AMInstR Associate Member of the Institute of Refrigeration
AMINucE Associate Member of the Institution of Nuclear Engineers
AMIOP Associate Member of the Institute of Printing
AMIPA Associate Member of the Institute of Practitioners in Advertising
AMIPRE Associate Member of the Incorporated Practitioners in Radio and Electronics
AMIQA Associate Member of the Institute of Quality Assurance
AMIRA Australian Mineral Industries Research Association
AMIRSE Associate Member of the Institute of Railway Signalling Engineers

AMIStructE Associate Member of the Institution of Structural Engineers
AMITA Associate Member of the Industrial Transport Association
AMIWEM Associate Member of the Institution of Water and Environmental Management
AMJ *Assemblée mondiale de la jeunesse* (French: World Assembly of Youth)
AML abandoned mine land; [medicine] acute myeloid leukaemia; Admiralty materials laboratory; [New Zealand] applied mathematics laboratory
AMLS [USA] Master of Arts in Library Science
AMM antimissile missile; assistant marketing manager; *Association médicale mondiale* (French: World Medical Association)
amm. ammunition
AMMA Assistant Masters' and Mistresses' Association
AMMI American Merchant Marine Institute
amn ammunition
AMNECInst Associate Member of the North East Coast Institution of Engineers and Shipbuilders
AMNILP Associate Member of the National Institute of Licensing Practitioners
AMO Air Ministry order; area medical officer; assistant medical officer; Association of Managerial Officers
AMOB automatic meteorological oceanographic buoy
AMORC Ancient Mystical Order Rosae Crucis (= Rosicrucians)
amort. amortization
AMOS automatic meteorological observing station
AMP [biochemistry] adenosine monophosphate; Air Member for Personnel (in RAF); Associated Master Plumbers and Domestic Engineers; Australian Mutual Provident Society
amp [short form] ampere; [short form] amplifier
amp. amperage; ampere; amplification; amplified; amplifier; amplitude
AMPAS [USA] Academy of Motion Picture Arts and Sciences
AMPC [USA] automatic message processing center; auxiliary military pioneer corps
amph. amphibian; amphibious
AMPHIBEX amphibious exercise
ampl. amplifier
AMPS [finance] auction market preferred stock; automatic message processing system
AMPSS advanced manned precision strike system
AMQ American medical qualification
AMR Atlantic missile range; automated meter reading; automatic message routing
AMRAAM advanced medium-range air-to-air missile
AMRINA Associate Member of the Royal Institution of Naval Architects
Amrit. Amritsar
AMRO Association of Medical Record Officers
AMRS Air Ministry radio station
AMS accident-monitoring system; [USA] Agricultural Marketing Service; American Mathematical Society; American Meteorological Society; American Microscopical Society; American Musicological Society; Ancient Monuments Society; [astronautics] Apollo mission simulator; army map service; army medical services; army medical staff; assistant military secretary; Australian medical services; automatic music search
AMSA advanced manned strategic aircraft
AMSAM antimissile surface-to-air missile
Am. Sam. American Samoa
AMSE Associate Member of the Society of Engineers
AMSEF anti-minesweeping explosive float
AMSERT Associate Member of the Society of Electronic and Radio Technicians
AMSGA Association of Manufacturers and Suppliers for the Graphic Arts
AMSL above mean sea level
AMSO Air Member for Supply and Organization (in RAF); Association of Market Survey Organizations
AMSST Associate Member of the Society of Surveying Technicians
Amst. Amsterdam
Amstrad Alan Michael Sugar Trading (computer manufacturer)

AMSW [USA] Master of Arts in Social Work
AMT Academy of Medicine, Toronto; airmail transfer; Air Member for Training (in RAF); [USA] alternative minimum tax; area management team; Associate in Mechanical Technology; Associate in Medical Technology; Association of Marine Traders; [USA] Master of Arts in Teaching
amt amount
AMTA Association of Multiple Travel Agents
AMTC Art Master's Teaching Certificate
AMTDA Agricultural Machinery Tractor Dealers' Association
AMTE Admiralty Marine Technology Establishment
AMTI airborne moving target indicator
AMTRI Advanced Manufacturing Technology Research Institute
AMTS Associate Member of the Television Society
AMU Associated Metalworkers' Union; [USA] Associated Midwestern Universities; Association of Master Upholsterers
amu [physics] atomic mass unit
AMUA Associate of Music, University of Adelaide
AMus Associate in Music
AMusD Doctor of Musical Arts
AMusLCM Associate in Music, London College of Music
AMusTCL Associate in Music, Trinity College of Music, London
AMV *Association mondiale vétérinaire* (French: World Veterinary Association); [microbiology] avian myeloblastosis virus
AMVAP Associated Manufacturers of Veterinary and Agricultural Products
AMVERS automated merchant vessel report system
AMVETS American Veterans (of World War II etc.)
AMW average molecular weight
AN [chemistry] acid number; [chemistry] ammonium nitrate; Anglo-Norman; [medicine] antenatal; Associate in Nursing; [physics] audible noise; [medicine] avascular necrosis; [civil aircraft marking] Nicaragua; [vehicle registration] Reading
A/N advice note; alphanumeric
An [chemistry] actinon
An. Annam
an. *anno* (Latin: in the year); anonymous; answer
.an Netherlands Antilles (in Internet address)
a.n. above named
ANA All Nippon Airways; American Nature Association; American Neurological Association; American Newspaper Association; American Numismatic Association; American Nurses' Association; [commerce] Article Number Association; [USA] Associate National Academician; Association of Nurse Administrators; Australian Natives' Association
anaes. anaesthesia; anaesthetic
anag. anagram
anal. analogous; analogy; analyse; analysis; analytic(al)
ANAPO *Allianza Nacional Popular* (Spanish: National Popular Alliance) (in Colombia)
ANARE Australian National Antarctic Research Expedition
anat. anatomic(al); anatomy
ANC advanced nuclear computer; African National Congress; Army Nurse Corps; Australian Newspapers Council
anc. ancient
anch. anchored
ANCUN Australian National Committee for the United Nations
AND [international vehicle registration] Andorra
And [astronomy] Andromeda
and. [music] *andante* (Italian: at moderate speed)
ANDB [USA] Air Navigation Development Board
ANDI [medicine] abnormal development and involution
ANEC American Nuclear Energy Council
ANECInst Associate of the North East Coast Institution of Engineers and Shipbuilders
ANERI [USA] Advanced Nuclear Equipment Research Institute
ANF [USA] Advanced Nuclear Fuels (Corporation); antinuclear factor; Atlantic Nuclear Force; [medicine] atrial natriur-

etic factor; Australian National Flag Association
ANG [USA] Air National Guard; Australian Newspaper Guild
Ang. Anglesey; *Anglice* (Latin: in English)
ang. angle; angular
ANGB [USA] Air National Guard Base
Angl. *Angleterre* (French: England); Anglican; Anglicized
Anglo-Fr. Anglo-French
Anglo-Ind. Anglo-Indian
Anglo-Ir. Anglo-Irish
Anglo-L Anglo-Latin
Anglo-Sax. Anglo-Saxon
ANGUS Air National Guard of the United States
Anh. *Anhang* (German: appendix) (of book etc.)
anhyd. [chemistry] anhydrous
anhydr. [chemistry] anhydrous
ANI *Agência Nacional de Informações* (Portuguese: National Information Agency); American Nuclear Insurers
anim. [music] *animato* (Italian: in a lively manner)
Ank. *Ankunft* (German: arrival)
ANL Anti-Nazi League; *Archaeological News Letter*; [USA] Argonne National Laboratory; [engineering] automatic noise limiting; National Library of Australia
ANM Admiralty Notices to Mariners
Anm. *Anmerkung* (German: note) (in book etc.)
anme [commerce] *anonyme* (French: limited liability) (of company)
ANN [telecommunications] all-figure numbers now; [computing] artificial neural network
ann. annals; *anni* (Latin: years); *anno* (Latin: in the year); annual; annuity
ANNA [USA] Army–Navy–NASA–Air Force satellite
anniv. anniversary
annot. annotate; annotation; annotator
annuit. annuitant
annul. annulled; annulment
Annunc. Annunciation
ANO [USA] Association of Nuclear Operators
anon. anonymous; anonymously
ANOVA [mathematics] analysis of variance
ANP advanced nursing practice; aircraft nuclear propulsion; *Algemeen Nederlands Persbureau* (Dutch news agency); ammonium nitrate–phosphate (fertilizer); Australian National Party
ANPA American Newspaper Publishers' Association; Australian National Publicity Association
anr another
anrac aids navigation radio control
ANRC American National Red Cross; Australian National Research Council
ANRE advanced nuclear rocket engine
ANRPC Association of Natural Rubber Producing Countries
ANS [physics] advanced neutron source; American Nuclear Society; Army News Service; Army Nursing Service; [computing] artificial neural system; Astronomical Netherlands Satellite; [anatomy] autonomic nervous system
ans. answer
a.n.s. autograph note signed
ANSA *Agenzia Nazionale Stampa Associata* (Italian news agency); Independent Union for Abbey National Staff (formerly Abbey National Staff Association)
ANSI American National Standards Institute
ANSI–SPARC American National Standards Institute/Systems Planning and Requirements Committee
ANSL Australian National Standards Laboratory
ANSP Academy of Natural Sciences of Philadelphia; Australian National Socialist Party
ANSR [nuclear technology] advanced neutron-source reactor
ANSTI African Network of Scientific and Technological Institutions
ANSTO Australian Nuclear Science and Technology Organization
Ant [astronomy] Antlia
Ant. Antarctica; Antigua; Antrim
ant. antenna; anterior; anticipated; antilogarithm; antiquarian; antique; antiquity; antonym
ANTA American National Theater and Academy; Australian National Travel Association
Antarc. Antarctic
anthol. anthology

anthrop. anthropological; anthropology
anthropol. anthropological; anthropology
Antig. Antigua
antilog [short form] antilogarithm
antiq. antiquarian; antiquities
antiq. antiquity
Ant. Lat. antique Latin
ant. ld antique laid (paper)
anton. antonym
ANTOR Association of National Tourist Office Representatives
Antr. Antrim
ant. wo. antique wove (paper)
ANU Australian National University
a/nw as new (in advertisement)
ANWR Arctic National Wildlife Refuge
anx annex
ANZ Australia and New Zealand
ANZAAS Australia and New Zealand Association for the Advancement of Science
Anzac Australia and New Zealand Army Corps (in World War I)
ANZAM Australia, New Zealand and Malaysia (defence strategy)
ANZAMRS Australia and New Zealand Association for Medieval and Renaissance Studies
ANZCAN Australia, New Zealand and Canada
ANZIA Associate of the New Zealand Institute of Architects
ANZUK Australia, New Zealand and United Kingdom (defence force)
ANZUS Australia, New Zealand and the United States (defence alliance)
AO accountant officer; Air Officer; air ordnance; *anno ordinis* (Latin: in the year of the order); [chemistry] anthracene oil; area office; army order; Australian Opera; [vehicle registration] Carlisle; Officer of the Order of Australia
A/O [accounting] account of; and others
aO *an der Oder* (German: on the River Oder) (in place-names)
a/o [accounting] account of
.ao Angola (in Internet address)
AOA activity-on-arrow; [USA] Administration on Aging; Aerodrome Owners' Association; Air Officer in charge of Administration; American Ordnance Association; American Orthopedic Association; American Osteopathic Association; American Overseas Association
AOB advanced operational base; Antediluvian Order of Buffaloes; any other business
a.o.b. any other business; at or below
AOC Air Officer Commanding; *anno orbis Conditi* (Latin: in the year of the Creation); any other colour; *appellation d'origine contrôlée* (French: name of origin controlled) (wine classification); Army Ordnance Corps; Artists of Chelsea
AOCB any other competent business
AOC-in-C Air Officer Commanding-in-Chief
AOCM [US air force] aircraft out of commission for maintenance
AOD acousto-optic device; advanced ordnance depot; Ancient Order of Druids; Army Ordnance Department
AOER Army Officers' Emergency Reserve
AOF *Afrique Occidentale Française* (French: French West Africa); Ancient Order of Foresters; Australian Olympic Federation
A of F Admiral of the Fleet
AOFP absolute open-flow potential
A of S Academy of Science
AOG aircraft on ground
AOH Ancient Order of Hibernians
AoI aims of industry
aoi angle of incidence
a.o.i.v. [engineering] automatically operated inlet valve
A-OK [USA] all OK
AOL [USA] absent over leave; Admiralty Oil Laboratory; America Online (Internet service provider); [USA] Atlantic Oceanographic Laboratories; [Canada] Atlantic Oceanographic Laboratory
AOM amorphous organic matter
AON activity-on-node
AONB area of outstanding natural beauty
AOP Association of Optical Practitioners
AOPU Asian Oceanic Postal Union
AOQ average outgoing quality
AOQL average outgoing quality limit
AOR [music] adult-oriented rock; [US law] advice of rights; [USA] album-oriented radio; [music] album-oriented rock
aor angle of reflection

a/or and/or
aor. aorist
AOS [astronautics] acquisition of signal; American Opera Society; American Ophthalmological Society; Ancient Order of Shepherds; automated office system
AOSIS Association of Small Island States
AOSO advanced orbiting solar observatory
AOSS *Americanae Orientalis Societatis Socius* (Latin: Fellow of the American Oriental Society)
AOSTRA Alberta Oil Sands Technology and Research Authority
AOSW Association of Official Shorthand Writers
AOT [engineering] allowed outage time; [engineering] allowed out-of-service time
AOTA American Occupational Therapy Association
AOU American Ornithologists' Union
AOV any other variety
AP [insurance] additional premium; [grammar] adjective phrase; aerosol particle; [USA] airplane; [USA] Air Police; air pollution; air publication (of Ministry of Defence); *Alianza Popular* (Spanish: Popular Alliance) (political party); [USA] American plan (for payment of hotel bills); [surveying] *Amsterdamsch Peil* (German: Amsterdam level) (mean level used in parts of northern Europe); Andhra Pradesh; [medicine] angina pectoris; [medicine] anterior pituitary; [medicine] anteroposterior; antipersonnel; [commerce] *à protester* (French: to be protested) (on bill of exchange); armour-piercing; [computing] array processor; [medicine] arterial (blood) pressure; Associated Presbyterian; Associated Press (news agency); atomic power; authority to pay; authority to purchase; automotive products; [insurance] average payable; [vehicle registration] Brighton; [civil aircraft marking] Pakistan
Ap. apostle; Apostolic; April
ap. apostle; apothecaries' (weight or measure); apothecary; apparent; apparently; *apud* (Latin: in the works of, according to)
a.p. above proof; [insurance] additional premium; advanced post; [medicine] *ante prandium* (Latin: before meals) (in prescriptions); [mathematics] arithmetical progression; author's proof
APA [taxation] additional personal allowance; Alaska Power Authority; [Australia] All Parties Administration; [computing] all points addressable (as in **APA mode**); American Philological Association; American Physicists Association; American Pilots Association; American Press Association; American Protestant Association; American Psychiatric Association; American Psychological Association; [telecommunications] annular phased array; Associate in Public Administration; Association for the Prevention of Addiction; Association of Public Analysts; Australian Physiotherapy Association; *Austria Presse Agentur* (Austrian news agency)
APACL Asian People's Anti-Communist League
APACS Association for Payment Clearing Services
APAE Association of Public Address Engineers
apart. apartment
APB Accounting Principles Board; [USA] all-points bulletin (police alert); Auditing Practices Board
APBA American Power Boat Association
APBF Accredited Poultry Breeders' Federation
APC [engineering] advanced process control; air-pollution control; All People's Congress (in Sierra Leone); American Philatelic Congress; [immunology] antigen-presenting cell; Appalachian Power Company; armoured personnel carrier; aspirin, phenacetin and caffeine; Assistant Principal Chaplain; Associated Portland Cement; Auditing Practices Committee; automatic phase control; [electronics] automatic power control; automatic public convenience
a.p.c. average propensity to consume
APCA [USA] Air Pollution Control Association; Anglo-Polish Catholic Association
APCIMS Association of Private Client Investment Managers and Stockbrokers
APCK Association for Promoting Christian Knowledge (in Church of Ireland)
APCN *anno post Christum natum* (Latin: in the year after the birth of Christ)

APCO Association of Pleasure Craft Operators
APCOL All-Pakistan Confederation of Labour
APD Administrative Planning Division; [USA] Air Pollution Division; Army Pay Department
apd approved
APDC Apple and Pear Development Council
Ap. Deleg. Apostolic Delegate
AP/DOS [computing] advanced pick/disk operating system
APE Amalgamated Power Engineering; automatic photomapping equipment; [physics] available potential energy
APEC Asia-Pacific Economic Cooperation Conference
APEX advance-purchase excursion (reduced fare on train or aeroplane); Association of Professional, Executive, Clerical and Computer Staff (became part of GMB)
APF Association for the Propagation of the Faith
APFC Asia-Pacific Forestry Commission
APG [US air force] air proving ground
APGA American Public Gas Association
APH A(lan) P(atrick) Herbert (British writer and politician); [medicine] antepartum haemorrhage; [biochemistry] anterior pituitary hormone
aph. aphorism
APHA American Public Health Association
APHC Association of Plumbing and Heating Contractors
aphet. aphetic
APHI Association of Public Health Inspectors
APHIS [USA] Animal and Plant Health Inspection Service
API air-pollution index; air-position indicator; American Petroleum Institute (as in **API scale** for measuring specific gravity of petroleum products); [computing] application program(mer) interface; *Association phonétique internationale* (French: International Phonetic Association); atmospheric pressure ionization
APIS Army Photographic Intelligence Service
ap. J-C *après Jésus-Christ* (French: after Jesus Christ, AD)
APL Alberta Power Limited; alternating polarization laser; [USA] Applied Physics Laboratory (Johns Hopkins University); [computing] A Programming Language
Apl April
APLA Azanian People's Liberation Army
APLE Association of Public Lighting Engineers
APM [USA] Academy of Physical Medicine; airborne particulate matter; Assistant Paymaster; Assistant Provost-Marshal; [astronomy] automatic plate-measuring machine
APMC Allied Political and Military Commission
APMG Assistant Postmaster-General
APMI Associate of the Pensions Management Institute
apmt appointment
APNEC All-Pakistan Newspaper Employees' Confederation
APO Acting Pilot Officer; African People's Organization; Armed Forces Post Office; Army Post Office; Asian Productivity Organization
apo. apogee
Apoc. Apocalypse; Apocrypha; Apocryphal
Apocr. Apocrypha; Apocryphal
apog. apogee
Apos. Apostolic
apos. apostrophe
APOTA automatic positioning telemetering antenna
apoth. apothecary
APP African People's Party (became part of KANU); [computing] application portability profile
App. Apostles
app. apparatus; apparent; apparently; appeal; appended; appendix (of book); applied; appointed; appointment; appreciated; apprentice; approval; approved; approximate; approximately
APPA African Petroleum Producers Association
appar. apparatus; apparent; apparently
app. crit. *apparatus criticus* (Latin: critical apparatus) (list of variant readings)
appd approved

APPITA Australian Pulp and Paper Industries Technical Association
appl appeal
appl. appellant; applicable; applied
appos. appositive
APPR [USA] Army Package Power Reactor
appr. apprentice; approved
appro [short form] approval
approx. approximate; approximately; approximation
apps appendices
appt appoint; appointment
apptd appointed
APPU Australian Primary Producers' Union
appurts appurtenances
appx appendix (of book)
APR Accredited Public Relations Practitioner; annual percentage rate (of interest); annual progress report; annual purchase rate (on hire purchase)
Apr. April; *April* (German: April)
apr. *aprile* (Italian: April)
APRA Air Public Relations Association
APRC *anno post Romam conditam* (Latin: in the year from the foundation of Rome)
A/Prin. Assistant Principal
apr. J-C *après Jésus-Christ* (French: after Jesus Christ, AD)
APRS [navigation] acoustic position reference system; Association for the Protection of Rural Scotland; Association of Professional Recording Studios
APS [Australia] Aborigines' Protection Society; Advanced Photo System; Algeria Press Service (news agency); American Peace Society; American Philatelic Society; American Philosophical Society; American Physics Society; American Physiological Society; American Protestant Society; Arizona Public Service (Company); army postal service; assistant private secretary; Associate of the Pharmaceutical Society; Associate of the Philosophical Society
Aps [astronomy] Apus
a.p.s. autograph poem signed; average propensity to save
APSA American Political Science Association; Associate of the Photographic Society of America; Australian Political Studies Association
APSE [computing] Ada programming support environment
APSL Acting Paymaster Sublieutenant
APST Association of Professional Scientists and Technologists
APSW Association of Psychiatric Social Workers
APT advanced passenger train; advanced process technology; [nautical] after peak tank; [medicine] alum-precipitated (diphtheria) toxoid; Association of Polytechnic Teachers; Association of Printing Technologists; Association of Private Traders; automatic picture transmission (from satellite)
apt apartment
APTC Army Physical Training Corps
APTI Association of Principals of Technical Institutions
APTIS all-purpose ticket-issuing systems
APTS [astronautics] Automatic Picture Transmission Subsystem
APTU African Postal and Telecommunications Union
APU acute psychiatric unit; Arab Postal Union; [education] Assessment of Performance Unit; [aeronautics] auxiliary power unit
APUC Association for Promoting Unity of Christendom
APUD amine-precursor uptake and decarboxylation (as in **APUD cell**)
a.p.v. adjusted present value
APWA All Pakistan Women's Association; American Public Welfare Association; American Public Works Association
APWR [nuclear technology] advanced pressurized-water reactor
APWU American Postal Workers Union
apx. approximately
AQ [psychology] accomplishment quotient; [psychology] achievement quotient; [military] Administration and Quartering
Aq. [horticulture] aquatic
aq. *aqua* (Latin: water); aqueous
.aq Antarctica (in Internet address)
aq. bull. [pharmacology] *aqua bulliens* (Latin: boiling water)
AQC Associate of Queen's College (London)

aq. cal. [pharmacology] *aqua calida* (Latin: warm water)
aq. com. [pharmacology] *aqua communis* (Latin: tap water)
aq. dest. [pharmacology] *aqua destillata* (Latin: distilled water)
aq. ferv. [pharmacology] *aqua fervens* (Latin: hot water)
aq. frig. [pharmacology] *aqua frigida* (Latin: cold water)
AQI air-quality index
AQL acceptable quality level
Aql [astronomy] Aquila
AQMG Assistant Quartermaster-General
aq. m. pip. [pharmacology] *aqua menthae piperitae* (Latin: peppermint water)
AQPS *autre que pur sang* (French: other than pure blood) (in horse-breeding)
aq. pur. [pharmacology] *aqua pura* (Latin: pure water)
Aqr [astronomy] Aquarius
aq. tep. [pharmacology] *aqua tepida* (Latin: tepid water)
aque. aqueduct
AR [psychology] accomplishment ratio; account receivable; [psychology] achievement ratio; acid resisting; acrylic rubber; [medicine] acute rejection; [physiology] adrenergic receptor; advice of receipt; *Agencja Robotnicza* (Polish workers' news agency); [USA] airman recruit; *Altesse Royale* (French: Royal Highness); [physiology] androgen receptor; *Anna Regina* (Latin: Queen Anne); *anno regni* (Latin: in the year of the reign); annual register; *Annual Register of World Events*; annual report; [taxation] annual return; [medicine] aortic regurgitation; [numismatics] *argentum* (Latin: silver); [US postcode] Arkansas; Army Regulation(s); artificial respiration; [image technology] aspect ratio; Assistant Resident; Associated Rediffusion; Autonomous Region; Autonomous Republic; [fishing port] Ayr; [vehicle registration] Chelmsford
Ar [chemical element] argon
Ar. Arab; Arabia; Arabian; Arabic; Aramaic
aR *am Rhein* (German: on the River Rhine) (in place-names)
a/r [insurance] all risks
ar. arrival; arrive(s); arrived
.ar Argentina (in Internet address)
a.r. [insurance] all risks; *anno regni* (Latin: in the year of the reign)
ARA Aircraft Research Association; all replies answered (in personal advertisement); Amateur Rowing Association; American Railway Association; Army Rifle Association; Associate of the Royal Academy; Association of the River Authorities; [New Zealand] Auckland Regional Authority
Arab. Arabia; Arabian; Arabic
ARAC Associate of the Royal Agricultural College
arach. arachnology
ARACI Associate of the Royal Australian Chemical Institute
ARAD Associate of the Royal Academy of Dancing
ARAeS Associate of the Royal Aeronautical Society
ARAIA Associate of the Royal Australian Institute of Architects
ARAM Associate of the Royal Academy of Music
Aram. Aramaic
ARAMCO Arabian-American Oil Company
ARAS Associate of the Royal Astronomical Society
ARB Air Registration Board (in civil aviation); Air Research Bureau
arb. arbiter; arbitrageur; arbitrary; arbitration; arbitrator
ARBA Associate of the Royal Society of British Artists
ARBE *Académie royale des beaux-arts, école supérieure des arts décoratifs et école supérieure d'architecture de Bruxelles* (French: Brussels Royal Academy of Fine Arts)
arbor. arboriculture
ARBS Associate of the Royal Society of British Sculptors
ARC Aeronautical Research Council; Agricultural Research Council (former name of AFRC); [medicine] Aids-related complex; American Red Cross; [USA] Ames Research Center; Archaeological Resource Centre (York); Architects' Registration Council; Arthritis and Rheumatism Council; Astrophysical Research Consortium; Atlantic Research Corporation
arc. [music] *arcato* (Italian: bowed);

[music] *coll'arco* (Italian: with the bow)
ARCA Associate of the Royal Cambrian Academy; Associate of the Royal Canadian Academy of Arts; Associate of the Royal College of Art
ARCamA Associate of the Royal Cambrian Academy
arccos [mathematics] arc cosine
arccosec [mathematics] arc cosecant
arccot [mathematics] arc cotangent
Arch. Archbishop; Archdeacon; Archduke
arch. archaic; archaism; archery; archipelago; architect; architectural; architecture
archaeol. archaeology
Archbp Archbishop
Archd. Archdeacon; Archduke
archit. architect; architectural; architecture
archt architect
ARCIC Anglican/Roman Catholic International Commission
ARCM Associate of the Royal College of Music
Arcnet attached resource computing network
ARCO Associate of the Royal College of Organists
ARCO(CHM) Associate of the Royal College of Organists with Diploma in Choir Training
ARCOS Anglo-Russian Cooperative Society
ARCPsych Associate of the Royal College of Psychiatrists
ARCS Associate of the Royal College of Science; Associate of the Royal College of Surgeons (of England); Australian Red Cross Society
arcsec [mathematics] arc secant; arc second
arcsin [mathematics] arc sine
ARCST Associate of the Royal College of Science and Technology (Glasgow)
arctan [mathematics] arc tangent
ARCUK Architects' Registration Council of the United Kingdom
ARCVS Associate of the Royal College of Veterinary Surgeons
ARD [medicine] acute radiation disease; [medicine] acute respiratory disease
ARDC [USA] Air Research and Development Command
ARDEC [USA] Army Research Development and Engineering Center
ARDMS automated route design and management system
ARDS [medicine] adult respiratory distress syndrome
ARE activated reactive evaporation; Admiralty Research Establishment; Arab Republic of Egypt; Associate of the Royal Society of Painter-Printmakers (formerly Associate of the Royal Society of Painter-Etchers and Engravers)
ARELS Association of Recognized English Language Schools
ARENA *Aliança Renovadora Nacional* (Spanish: National Renewal Alliance) (in Brazil)
ARF [medicine] acute renal failure; [medicine] acute respiratory failure; Advertising Research Foundation
Arg. [heraldry] argent; Argentina; Argentine; Argentinian; Argyll(shire)
aRh. *am Rhein* (German: on the River Rhine) (in place-names)
ARHA Associate of the Royal Hibernian Academy
ARHS Associate of the Royal Horticultural Society
ARI [medicine] acute respiratory infection
Ari [astronomy] Aries
ARIA automated radioimmunoassay
ARIAS Associate of the Royal Incorporation of Architects in Scotland
ARIBA Associate of the Royal Institute of British Architects
ARICS Professional Associate of the Royal Institution of Chartered Surveyors
ARIEL Automated Real-time Investments Exchange Limited (former share-dealing system)
ARIMA [computing] autoregressive integrated moving average
ARINA Associate of the Royal Institution of Naval Architects
ARIPHH Associate of the Royal Institute of Public Health and Hygiene
ARIS advanced range instrumentation ship
Arist. Aristotle (ancient Greek philosopher)
Aristoph. Aristophanes (ancient Greek dramatist)
arith. arithmetic; arithmetical; arithmetician

Ariz. Arizona
Ark. Arkansas
ARL Admiralty Research Laboratory; Aeronautical Research Laboratory; Arctic Research Laboratory; [USA] Association of Research Libraries; Australian Rugby League
ARLA Association of Residential Letting Agents
ARLL [computing] advanced run length limited
ARM [USA] adjustable-rate mortgage; *Alliance réformée mondiale* (French: Worldwide Presbyterian Alliance); antiradar missile; antiradiation missile; [medicine] artificial rupture of membranes; atomic resolution microscope; Australian Republican Movement
ArM Master of Architecture (from Latin *Architecturae Magister*)
Arm. Armagh; Armenia; Armenian; Armorica; Armorican
ARMA Association of Residential Managing Agents; [computing] autoregressive moving average
ARMCM Associate of the Royal Manchester College of Music
armd armoured
ARMIT Associate of the Royal Melbourne Institute of Technology
ARMS Action for Research into Multiple Sclerosis; Associate of the Royal Society of Miniature Painters
ARNA Arab Revolution News Agency
ARO army routine order; Asian Regional Organization; Associate Member of the Register of Osteopaths
AROD airborne remote operated device
AROS African Regional Organization for Standardization
ARP [US finance] adjustable rate preferred (stock); air-raid precautions; Associated Reformed Presbyterian
arp. [music] *arpeggiato* (Italian: played as arpeggio); [music] arpeggio
ARPA Advanced Research Projects Agency (former name of DARPA)
ARPANET [computing] Advanced Research Projects Agency Network
ARPO Association of Resort Publicity Officers
ARPS Associate of the Royal Photographic Society; Association of Railway Preservation Societies
ARR accounting rate of return; *anno regni Reginae* (Latin: in the year of the Queen's reign); *anno regni Regis* (Latin: in the year of the King's reign); Association of Radiation Research
arr. [music] arranged (by); [music] arrangement; [music] arranger; arrival; arrive(s); arrived
ARRC Associate of the Royal Red Cross
arrd arrived
arron. *arrondissement* (French: administrative district)
ARRS American Roentgen Ray Society
ARS [medicine] acute radiation syndrome; [USA] Agricultural Research Service; American Records Society; American Recreation Society; American Rocket Society; *anno reparatae salutis* (Latin: in the year of our redemption); [medicine] aortic regurgitation and stenosis; Army Radio School
ARSA Associate of the Royal Scottish Academy; Associate of the Royal Society of Arts
ARSAP [USA] Advanced Reactor Severe Accident Program
ARSCM Associate of the Royal School of Church Music
ARSH Associate of the Royal Society of Health
ARSL Associate of the Royal Society of Literature
ARSM Associate of the Royal School of Mines
ARSR air route surveillance radar
ARSW Associate of the Royal Scottish Water Colour Society
ART [computing] algebraic reconstruction technique; [computing] automated reasoning tool
Art. Artemis (ancient Greek goddess)
art. article; artificer; artificial; artillery; artist
ARTC air route traffic control
artic [short form] articulated truck
artic. articulated
artif. artificer
art. pf artist's proof
arty artillery
ARU American Railway Union; [computing] audio response unit

ARV [medicine] Aids-associated retrovirus; [Bible] American (Standard) Revised Version
ARVA Associate of the Rating and Valuation Association
ARWA Associate of the Royal West of England Academy
ARWS Associate of the Royal Watercolour Society
AS Academy of Science; Admiral Superintendent; [education] Advanced Supplementary (as in **AS level**); air speed; air staff; [insurance] all sections; [music] *al segno* (Italian: to the sign, at the sign); [geology] aluminium silicate; American Samoa; [computing] analogue states; Anglo-Saxon; *anno salutis* (Latin: in the year of salvation); *anno Salvatoris* (Latin: in the year of the Saviour); antisubmarine; assistant secretary; assistant surgeon; Associate in Science; [vehicle registration] Inverness; [taxation] personal allowance
A/S account sales; [education] Advanced Supplementary (as in **A/S level**); [banking] after sight; [commerce] *Aksjeselskap* (Norwegian: limited company, Ltd); [commerce] *Aktieselskab* (Danish: joint-stock company); alongside
As [chemical element] arsenic
As [meteorology] altostratus
As. Asia; Asian; Asiatic
a.s. account sales; aggregate supply
ASA Acoustical Society of America; [USA] Addiction Services Agency; Advertising Standards Authority; Amateur Swimming Association; American Sociological Association; American Standards Association; American Statistical Association; Army Sailing Association; [USA] Associate of the Society of Actuaries; Australian Society of Accountants
ASAA Associate of the Society of Incorporated Accountants and Auditors
ASAB Association for the Study of Animal Behaviour
ASAI Associate of the Society of Architectural Illustrators
ASAM Associate of the Society of Art Masters
AS&TS of SA Associated Scientific and Technical Societies of South Africa
ASAP as soon as possible; automated shipboard aerological programme
a.s.a.p. as soon as possible
ASAT [military] antisatellite (interceptor)
ASB Accounting Standards Board; [South Africa] *Afrikaanse Studentebond* (Afrikaans: South African students' union); Alternative Service Book (in Church of England); American Society of Bacteriologists; [medicine] anencephaly and spina bifida
asb. asbestos
a.s.b. aircraft safety beacon
ASBAH Association for Spina Bifida and Hydrocephalus
ASBM air-to-surface ballistic missile
ASBSBSW Amalgamated Society of Boilermakers, Shipwrights, Blacksmiths and Structural Workers
ASC Accounting Standards Committee; Administrative Staff College (Henley); [USA] Air Service Command; altered state of consciousness; American Society of Cinematographers; Anglo-Soviet Committee; Asian Socialist Conference
ASc Associate in Science
Asc. [astrology] Ascendant
asc. ascend; ascent
ASCA Associate of the Society of Company and Commercial Accountants
ASCAB Armed Services Consultant Approval Board
ASCAP American Society of Composers, Authors, and Publishers
ASCC Accounting Standards Steering Committee; Association of Scottish Climbing Clubs; [computing] Automatic Sequence Controlled Calculator
ASCE American Society of Civil Engineers
ASCII [computing] American Standard Code for Information Interchange
ASCM Australian Student Christian Movement
ASCS [engineering] advanced Stirling conversion system
ASCU [USA] Association of State Colleges and Universities
ASD [engineering] adjustable speed drive; Admiralty Salvage Department; [engineering] antislip drive; Armament Supply Department; [medicine] atrial septal defect
Asda Associated Dairies

ASDAR aircraft-to-satellite data relay
ASDC Associate of the Society of Dyers and Colourists
ASDE Airport Surface Detection Equipment
a/s de *aux soins de* (French: care of, c/o) (in postal addresses)
ASDIC Allied Submarine Detection Investigation Committee (early form of sonar); [USA] Armed Services Documents Intelligence Center
ASE Admiralty Signal Establishment; American Stock Exchange; [physics] amplified spontaneous emission; Army School of Education; Associate of the Society of Engineers; Association for Science Education; automotive Stirling engine
ASEA Association of South East Asia
ASEAN Association of South East Asian Nations
ASEC [USA] Applied Solar Energy Corporation
ASEE American Society for Engineering Education; Association of Supervisory and Executive Engineers (became part of IIExE)
ASF [computing] aspect source flag; Associate of the Institute of Shipping and Forwarding Agents
ASG Acting Secretary-General; Assistant Secretary-General
ASGB Aeronautical Society of Great Britain; Anthroposophical Society of Great Britain
ASGBI Anatomical Society of Great Britain and Ireland
asgd assigned
asgmt assignment
ASH Action on Smoking and Health
ashp airship
ASHRAE American Society of Heating, Refrigeration and Air-Conditioning Engineers
ASI airspeed indicator; *Association soroptimiste internationale* (French: Soroptimist International Association)
ASIA Airlines Staff International Association
ASIC [electronics] application-specific integrated circuit
ASIF Amateur Swimming International Federation
ASIO Australian Security Intelligence Organization
ASIP [astronomy] all-sky imaging photometer
ASIRC [USA] Aquatic Sciences Information Retrieval Center (Rhode Island)
ASIS [astronautics] abort sensing and implementation system; American Society for Information Science
ASL above sea level; Acting Sublieutenant; Advanced Student in Law; American Sign Language; American Soccer League; assistant Scout leader
ASLA American Society of Landscape Architects
ASLB [USA] Atomic Safety and Licensing Board
ASLE American Society of Lubrication Engineers
ASLEF Associated Society of Locomotive Engineers and Firemen
ASLEP [astronautics] Apollo surface lunar experiments package
AS level [education] Advanced Supplementary level
A/S level [education] Advanced Supplementary level
ASLIB Association for Information Management (formerly Association of Special Libraries and Information Bureaux)
ASLO American Society of Limnology and Oceanography; Australian Scientific Liaison Office
ASLP Amalgamated Society of Lithographic Printers
ASLW Amalgamated Society of Leather Workers
ASM Acting Sergeant-Major; air-to-surface missile; [computing] algorithmic state machine; American Society for Metals; assistant sales manager; assistant Scoutmaster; assistant stage manager; assistant station master; Association of Senior Members
ASME American Society of Mechanical Engineers; Association for the Study of Medical Education
As. Mem. Associate Member
ASMO Arab Organization for Standardization and Metrology
ASMP American Society of Magazine Photographers

ASN army service number; average sample number
ASNE American Society of Newspaper Editors
ASO Air Staff Officer; American Symphony Orchestra; area supplies officer
ASOS automatic storm observation service
ASP [commerce] *accepté sous protêt* (French: accepted under protest); [US air force] aerospace plane; African Special Project (of IUCN); Afro-Shirazi Party (in Tanzania); American selling price; [USA] Anglo-Saxon Protestant; Astronomical Society of the Pacific
ASPA Australian Sugar Producers' Association
ASPAC Asian and Pacific Council
ASPC [commerce] *accepté sous protêt pour compte* (French: accepted under protest for account); Association of Swimming Pool Contractors
ASPCA American Society for the Prevention of Cruelty to Animals
ASPEP Association of Scientists and Professional Engineering Personnel
ASPF Association of Superannuation and Pension Funds
ASPI [computing] advanced SCSI programming interface
ASR airport surveillance radar; air-sea rescue; [meteorology] altimeter setting region; answer, send and receive; [computing] automatic send and receive
ASRE Admiralty Signal and Radar Establishment
A/SRS air-sea rescue service
ASS automatic space station
Ass. Associate; Associated; Association
ass. assembly; assistance; assistant; association; assurance
ASSC Accounting Standards Steering Committee
Ass-Com-Gen Assistant-Commissary-General
ASSET [US air force] aerothermodynamic-elastic structural systems environmental tests
ASSGB Association of Ski Schools in Great Britain
assigt assignment
assim. assimilate; assimilated
assmt assessment
assn association
assoc. associate; associated; association
AssocEng Associate of Engineering
AssocMCT Associateship of Manchester College of Technology
assocn association
AssocSc Associate in Science
ASSR Autonomous Soviet Socialist Republic
asst assistant
asstd assorted
ASSU American Sunday School Union
assy assembly
Assyr. Assyrian
AST above-ground storage tank; advanced supersonic transport; air service training; assured shorthold tenancy; Atlantic Standard Time; automated screen trading; automatic station tuning
ASTA American Society of Travel Agents; [New Zealand] Auckland Science Teachers' Association
ASTC Administrative Service Training Course; Associate of the Sydney Technical College
ASTIA [USA] Armed Services Technical Information Agency
ASTM American Society for Testing and Materials
ASTMS Association of Scientific, Technical and Managerial Staffs
ASTOR antisubmarine torpedo ordnance rocket
ASTP Apollo–Soyuz test project
astr. astronomer; astronomical; astronomy
ASTRO [USA] Air Space Travel Research Organization
astro. astronautics; astronomer; astronomy
astrol. astrologer; astrological; astrology
astron. astronomer; astronomical; astronomy
astrophys. astrophysical
Ast. T astronomical time
ASU American Students Union; Arab Socialist Union
ASUA Amateur Swimming Union of the Americas
ASV aircraft-to-surface vessel; [Bible] American Standard Version; [microbiology] avian sarcoma virus

ASVA Associate of the Incorporated Society of Valuers and Auctioneers
ASVU Army Security Vetting Unit
ASW Amalgamated Society of Wood Workers; antisubmarine warfare; antisubmarine work; Association of Scientific Workers; Association of Social Workers
ASWDU Air Sea Warfare Development Unit
ASWE Admiralty Surface Weapons Establishment
AT achievement test; administrative trainee; Advanced Technologies; [immunology] agglutination test; alternative technology; *Angling Times*; antitank; apparent time; [USA] appropriate technology; arrival time; [medicine] ataxia telangiectasia; Atlantic Time; [education] attainment target; Australia Telescope; automatic transmission (in car advertisement); [vehicle registration] Hull
A/T American terms
At ampere-turn; [chemical element] astatine; [informal] (member of the) Auxiliary Territorial Service
at. atmosphere; atomic; [navigation] attitude; attorney
.at Austria (in Internet address)
ATA [computing] Advanced Technologies attachment; [nuclear technology] advanced test accelerator; Air Transport Association; Air Transport Auxiliary; American Translators' Association; Amusement Trades Association; Animal Technicians' Association; Associate Technical Aide; Atlantic Treaty Association
ATAC Air Transport Advisory Council
ATAE Association of Tutors in Adult Education
ATAF Allied Tactical Air Force
ATAM Association for Teaching Aids in Mathematics
AT&T American Telephone and Telegraph Company
Atapi [computing] Advanced Technologies attachment packet interface
ATAS Air Transport Auxiliary Service
ATB advanced technology bomber; all-terrain bike; at the time of the bomb(ing)
ATBM antitactical ballistic missile
ATC acid-treated coal; air traffic control; Air Training Command; Air Training Corps; Air Transport Command; [law] Annotated Tax Cases; Art Teacher's Certificate; [computing] authorization to copy (software); automatic temperature control; automatic train control
a.t.c. average total costs
ATCC air traffic control centre
ATCE [astronautics] ablative thrust chamber engine
atchd attached
ATCL Associate of Trinity College of Music, London
ATCO Air Traffic Control Officer
ATCRBS air traffic control radar beacon system
ATCSP Association of Teachers of the Chartered Society of Physiotherapy
ATD actual time of departure; advanced technology development; Art Teacher's Diploma; Australian Tax Decisions
ATDS Association of Teachers of Domestic Science
ATE Amusement Trades Exhibition; Automatic Telephone and Electric (Company); [electronics] automatic test equipment
ATEC Air Transport Electronics Council
a tem. [music] *a tempo* (Italian: in time)
ATF [nuclear technology] accelerator test facility; [nuclear technology] advanced toroidal facility
ATFS Association of Track and Field Statisticians
ATG [medicine] antithymocyte globulin
ath. athlete; athletic
ATHE Association of Teachers in Higher Education
Athen. Athenian
athl. athlete; athletic
ATI Associate of the Textile Institute; Association of Technical Institutions
ATII Associate of the Taxation Institute, Incorporated (member of Chartered Institute of Taxation)
ATK at the keyboard (in Internet chat)
ATL [insurance] actual total loss; [medicine] adult T-cell leukaemia; Association of Teachers and Lecturers; [computing] automated (or automatic) tape library
Atl. Atlantic
ATLAS [astronomy] airborne tunable laser absorption spectrometer; [USA] Argonne tandem-linac accelerator system; auto-

matic tabulating, listing and sorting package; automatic telephone line address system
ATLB Air Transport Licensing Board
ATLV [medicine] adult T-cell leukaemia virus
ATM [computing] Adobe Type Manager; air training memorandum; antitank missile; approved testing material; Association of Teachers of Management; Association of Teachers of Mathematics; [computing] asynchronous transfer mode; at the moment (in Internet chat and e-mail); [banking] automated teller machine
atm atmosphere (unit of pressure)
atm. atmospheric
ATMS assumption-based truth maintenance system
ATN [medicine] acute tubular necrosis; [mathematics] arc tangent; [telecommunications] augmented transition network
ATNA Australasian Trained Nurses' Association
ATNF Australia Telescope National Facility
at. no. atomic number
ATO Ammunition Technical Officer (bomb-disposal officer); [aeronautics] assisted take-off
A to A air-to-air
A to J [New Zealand] Appendices to Journals (of parliament)
ATOL Air Travel Organizers' Licence
ATP [biochemistry] adenosine triphosphate; [aeronautics] advanced turboprop; [commerce] aid trade provision; Air Technical Publications; Associated Theatre Properties; Association of Tennis Professionals; [railways] automatic train protection
ATPAS Association of Teachers of Printing and Allied Subjects
ATPC Association of Tin Producing Countries
ATPG automatic test-pattern generation
ATPL(A) Airline Transport Pilot's Licence (Aeroplanes)
ATPL(H) Airline Transport Pilot's Licence (Helicopters)
ATR [nuclear technology] advanced test reactor; [nuclear technology] advanced thermal reactor; [aeronautics] air turbo-ram (jet engine); [radar] anti-transmit-receive (as in **ATR tube**); Association of Teachers of Russian; [military] automatic target recognition
ATRAN automatic terrain recognition and navigation
a.t.r.i.m.a. [law] as their respective interests may appear
ATS [Australia] Amalgamated Television Services; American Temperance Society; American Tract Society; American Transport Service; [medicine] antitetanus serum; [USA] Army Transport Service; Associate of Theological Study; automated trade system; Auxiliary Territorial Service (in World War II)
a.t.s. [law] at the suit of
ATSC Associate of the Tonic Sol-Fa College
ATSDR [USA] Agency for Toxic Substances and Disease Registry
ATSIS [computing] automated technical-specification information system
ATSS Association for the Teaching of Social Sciences
ATT antitetanus toxoid
att. attached; attention; attorney
Att-Gen Attorney-General
attn attention; for the attention of
attrac. attractive
attrib. attribute; attributed (to); attribution; [grammar] attributive; attributively
atty attorney
Atty-Gen Attorney-General
ATU [USA] Amalgamated Transit Union
ATUC African Trade Union Confederation
ATV all-terrain vehicle; Associated Television
at. wt atomic weight
AU [USA] Actors' Union; [printing] all up (i.e. all set in type); angstrom unit; arithmetic(al) unit; astronomical unit; [vehicle registration] Nottingham
Au [chemical element] gold (from Latin *aurum*)
.au Australia (in Internet address)
AUA [finance] agricultural unit of account (in EU); American Unitarian Association; American Urological Association
AUBC Association of Universities of the British Commonwealth

AUBTW Amalgamated Union of Building Trade Workers

AUC *ab urbe condita* (Latin: (in the year) from the founding of the city (of Rome)); *anno urbis conditae* (Latin: in the year from the founding of the city (of Rome)); [mathematics] area under the curve (on graph); Association of Underwater Contractors; Australian Universities Commission

AUCAS Association of University Clinical Academic Staff

aud. audit; audited; auditor

Aud-Gen Auditor-General

AUEW Amalgamated Union of Engineering Workers (became part of AEEU)

Aufl. *Auflage* (German: edition)

AUFW Amalgamated Union of Foundry Workers

Aug. August; *August* (German: August)

aug. augment; [grammar] augmentative; augmented

augm. augment; [grammar] augmentative; *augmenté* (French: enlarged)

AUI [computing] attachment unit interface

AULLA Australasian Universities Language and Literature Association

AUM air-to-underwater missile

AUMLA Australian Universities Modern Language Association

a.u.n. *absque ulla nota* (Latin: with no identifying mark)

AUO African Unity Organization

AUP Aberdeen University Press; acceptable use policy; Australian United Press (news agency)

Aur [astronomy] Auriga

AUS Army of the United States; assistant undersecretary; [international vehicle registration] Australia

Aus. Australia; Australian; Austria; Austrian

AUSA Association of the United States Army

Ausg. *Ausgabe* (German: edition)

Aust. Australia; Australian; Austria; Austrian

Austral. Australasia; Australasian; Australia; Australian

AUT Association of University Teachers

Aut. *Autriche* (French: Austria)

aut. autograph; autumn

AUTA Association of University Teachers of Accounting

AUTEC [US navy] Atlantic Underwater Test Evaluation Center

auth. authentic; author; authority; authorize; authorized

Auth. Ver. [Bible] Authorized Version

AUTIF Association of Unit Trusts and Investment Funds

auto. automatic; automobile; automotive

autobiog. autobiographical; autobiography

autog. autograph

AUT(S) Association of University Teachers (Scotland)

a.u.w. all-up-weight

AUWE Admiralty Underwater Weapons Establishment

AUX [linguistics] auxiliary verb

aux. auxiliary

AV [chemistry] acid value; [finance] *ad valorem* (Latin: according to value); [photography] aperture value; Artillery Volunteers; [medicine] atrioventricular (as in **AV node**); audiovisual; [numismatics] *aurum* (Latin: gold); [Bible] Authorized Version; average value; [vehicle registration] Peterborough

Av. Avenue; *Avocat* (French: lawyer)

a/v [finance] *ad valorem* (Latin: according to value)

av. avenue; average; avoirdupois; *avril* (French: April)

a.v. *annos vixit* (Latin: (he/she) lived . . . years); [finance] asset value

AVA Alberta Veterinary Association; Amateur Volleyball Association (of Great Britain); audiovisual aids; Audiovisual Association; Australian Veterinary Association

avail. available

AVB [medicine] atrioventricular block

AVC additional voluntary contribution (to pension scheme); American Veterans' Committee; [electronics] automatic volume control

av. C *avanti Cristo* (Italian: before Christ, BC)

a.v.c. [electronics] automatic volume control; average variable costs

Av. Cert. Aviator's Certificate

AVCM Associate of Victoria College of Music
AVCO [accounting] average cost
AVD Army Veterinary Department
avdp. avoirdupois
Ave. Avenue
ave. average
AVF [US military] all-volunteer force
avg. average
AVGAS aviation gasoline
avge [cricket] average
AVI Association of Veterinary Inspectors; audio-video interleaved; automatic vehicle identification
avia. aviation
av. J-C *avant Jésus-Christ* (French: before Jesus Christ, BC)
AVL [computing] Adel'son-Vel'skii-Landis (as in **AVL tree**); automatic vehicle location
AVLA Audio Visual Language Association
AVLIS atomic vapour laser isotope separation
AVM Air Vice-Marshal; [medicine] arteriovenous malformation; automatic vending machine
AVMA Action for the Victims of Medical Accidents; Automatic Vending Machine Association
AVN [medicine] atrioventricular node
avn aviation
AVO administrative veterinary officer; average vehicle occupancy
avoir. avoirdupois
AVR Army Volunteer Reserve
AVRI Animal Virus Research Institute
AVRO A. V. Roe and Company Limited (aircraft manufacturer)
AVRP audiovisual recording and presentation
AVS Anti-Vivisection Society
AVSL assistant Venture Scout leader
AVTRW Association of Veterinary Teachers and Research Workers
AW added water (in food); Alfred Wainwright (British walker and writer); alloy wheels (in car advertisement); Armstrong Whitworth (aircraft manufacturer); Articles of War; atomic warfare; [vehicle registration] Shrewsbury
a/w actual weight; airworthy; artwork
.aw Aruba (in Internet address)
a.w. actual weight; [shipping] all water; atomic weight
AWACS airborne warning and control system
AWAM Association of West African Merchants
AWAS Australian Women's Army Service
AWB [South Africa] *Afrikaner Weerstandsbeweging* (Afrikaans: Afrikaner Resistance Movement) (right-wing political party); Agricultural Wages Board; [USA] air waybill; Australian Wages Board
AWC Allied Works Council; [USA] Army War College; Australian Wool Corporation
AWE Atomic Weapons Establishment
AWEA American Wind Energy Association
AWeldI Associate of the Welding Institute
AWG American Wire Gauge; Art Workers' Guild
AWHA Australian Women's Home Army
AWJ [engineering] abrasive water jet
AWL absent with leave
AWMC Association of Workers for Maladjusted Children
AWNL Australian Women's National League
AWO American Waterways Operators (Incorporated)
AWOL absent without (official) leave
AWP amusements with prizes (in British Gaming Acts); annual wood production
AWPR Association of Women in Public Relations
AWR Association for the Study of the World Refugee Problem
AWRA Australian Wood Realization Agency
AWRE Atomic Weapons Research Establishment
AWS [geology] acoustic well sounding; Agricultural Wholesale Society; American Welding Society; automatic warning system
AWSA American Water Ski Association
AWU Australian Workers' Union
AX [vehicle registration] Cardiff
ax. axiom
AXAF Advanced X-ray Astrophysical Facility (at NASA)

AY [vehicle registration] Leicester
AYH American Youth Hostels
AYM [Freemasonry] Ancient York Mason
Ayr. Ayrshire
AZ [US postcode] Arizona; [international vehicle registration] Azerbaijan; [vehicle registration] Belfast
az. azimuth; azure
.az Azerbaijan (in Internet address)
Azapo [South Africa] Azanian People's Organization
az. ld [printing] azure laid (paper)
Azo. Azores
AZT [medicine] azidothymidine (used to treat Aids)
az. wo. [printing] azure wove (paper)

B

B administrative or professional (occupational group); Bachelor; [currency] baht (used in Thailand); [currency] balboa (used in Panama); [fishing port] Ballina; Baptist; Baron; [physics] baryon number; [chemistry] base-catalysed reaction; [music] bass; [music] basso; bathroom (in accommodation advertisement); battle; Baumé (temperature scale); bay (on map); *Beatus* (Latin: Blessed); [fishing port] Belfast; [international vehicle registration] Belgium; Benediction; best (wrought iron); Bey; Bible; billion; [UK postcode] Birmingham; Bishop; [chess] bishop; black (soft pencil lead); Blessed; [medicine] blood group; blue; board; boatswain; [currency] bolívar (used in Venezuela); bomber (aircraft) (as in **B-52**); [immunology] bone marrow (as in **B-cell**); book; [chemical element] boron; breadth; Britain; British; brotherhood; [photography] B-setting (shutter setting); building; [civil aircraft marking] China; eleven (in hexadecimal notation); [music] note of scale; of secondary importance (as in **B-side**); secondary road (as in **B5053**); [education] second highest grade or mark; [civil aircraft marking] Taiwan
b [physics] barn (unit of nuclear cross-section); [meteorology] blue sky; [physics] bottom (quark flavour)
b. bag; bale; ball; barrel; base; [music] bass; [music] basso; bath; batsman; bay; beam; bedroom (in accommodation advertisement); before; billion; *bis* (Latin: twice); bitch; bloody; book; born; bound; [medicine] bowels; [cricket] bowled (by); breadth; brother; [informal] bugger; bust; by; [cricket] bye
B0 [paper size] 1000 × 1414 mm
B1 [paper size] 707 × 1000 mm
B2 [paper size] 500 × 707 mm
B3 [paper size] 353 × 500 mm
B4 [paper size] 250 × 353 mm
B5 [paper size] 176 × 250 mm
B6 [paper size] 125 × 176 mm
B7 [paper size] 88 × 125 mm
B8 [paper size] 62 × 88 mm
B9 [paper size] 44 × 62 mm
B10 [paper size] 31 × 44 mm
2B double black (very soft pencil lead)
3B [civil aircraft marking] Mauritius; treble black (very soft pencil lead)
5B [civil aircraft marking] Cyprus
BA able-bodied seaman; Bachelor of Arts; [fishing port] Ballantrae; [finance] bank acceptance; [finance] banker's acceptance; [UK postcode] Bath; [medicine] biliary atresia; [USA] *Biological Abstracts*; Board of Agriculture; Booksellers' Association (of Great Britain and Ireland); [chemistry] boric acid; British Academy; British Airways; British America; British Association (for the Advancement of Science); [medicine] bronchial asthma; Buenos Aires; [computing] bus automaton; [vehicle registration] Manchester
Ba [chemical element] barium
.ba Bosnia-Herzegovina (in Internet address)
b.a. [taxation] balancing allowance; blind approach
BAA Bachelor of Applied Arts; Booking Agents' Association of Great Britain; British Accounting Association; British

Airports Authority; British Archaeological Association; British Astronomical Association
BAA&A British Association of Accountants and Auditors
BAAB British Amateur Athletic Board
BA(Admin) Bachelor of Arts in Administration
BAAF British Agencies for Adoption and Fostering
BAAL British Association for Applied Linguistics
BA(Art) Bachelor of Arts in Art
BAAS British Association for the Advancement of Science
Bab. Babylonia; Babylonian
BABIE British Association for Betterment of Infertility and Education
BABS [aeronautics] beam approach beacon system; [aeronautics] blind approach beacon system
BAC biologically active compound(s); blood-alcohol concentration; blood-alcohol content; British Aircraft Corporation; British Association of Chemists; [medicine] bronchoalveolar cell(s); Business Archives Council
BAc Bachelor of Acupuncture
Bac. Baccalauréat (French school-leaving examination); *Baccalaureus* (Latin: Bachelor)
BACAH British Association of Consultants in Agriculture and Horticulture
BACAN British Association for the Control of Aircraft Noise
BACAT barge aboard catamaran; barge canal traffic
BAcc Bachelor of Accountancy
bach. bachelor
BACIE British Association for Commercial and Industrial Education
BACM British Association of Colliery Management
BACO British Aluminium Company (Limited)
BACS Bankers Automated Clearing System
bact. bacteria; bacterial; bacteriological; bacteriology; bacterium
bacteriol. bacteriological; bacteriology
BAD base air depot; British Association of Dermatology
BADA British Antique Dealers' Association
BADGE base air defence ground environment
BAdmin Bachelor of Administration
BAE Bachelor of Aeronautical Engineering; Bachelor of Arts in Education; Badminton Association of England; Belfast Association of Engineers; [USA] Bureau of Agricultural Economics
BAe British Aerospace
BAEA British Actors' Equity Association
BAEC Bangladesh Atomic Energy Commission; British Agricultural Export Council
BA(Econ) Bachelor of Arts in Economics
BA(ED) Bachelor of Arts in Environmental Design
BA(Ed) Bachelor of Arts in Education
BAEF Belgian-American Educational Foundation
BAF biological aerated filter; British Athletics Federation
BAFM British Association of Forensic Medicine; British Association of the Friends of Museums
BAFMA British and Foreign Maritime Agencies
BAFO British Air Forces of Occupation; British Army Forces Overseas
BAFRA British Antique Furniture Restorers' Association
BAFSC British Association of Field and Sports Contractors
BAFSV British Armed Forces Special Vouchers
BAFTA British Academy of Film and Television Arts
BAG Bank Action Group
BAGA British Amateur Gymnastics Association
BAGB Bicycle Association of Great Britain
BAgEc Bachelor of Agricultural Economics
BAgr Bachelor of Agriculture
BAgrSc Bachelor of Agricultural Science
Bah. Bahamas
BAHA British Association of Hotel Accountants
BAHOH British Association for the Hard of Hearing
BAHS British Agricultural History Society

BAI Bachelor of Engineering (from Latin *Baccalaureus Artis Ingeniariae*); [military] battlefield air interdiction; Book Association of Ireland; [medicine] bronchial arterial infusion
BAIE British Association of Industrial Editors
BAIR British Airports Information Retrieval
BAJ Bachelor of Arts in Journalism
BAL blood alcohol level; British anti-lewisite (antidote to gas and metal poisoning); [medicine] bronchoalveolar lavage
Bal. Ballarat
bal. [accounting] balance
balc. balcony (in property advertisement)
BALH British Association for Local History
ball. ballast; ballistics
BALPA British Air Line Pilots' Association
bals. balsam
Balt. Baltic; Baltimore
balun [telecommunications] balanced unbalanced (transformer)
BAM Bachelor of Applied Mathematics; Bachelor of Arts in Music
BaM [medicine] barium meal
BAMA British Aerosol Manufacturers' Association; British Amsterdam Maritime Agencies; British Army Motoring Association
BAMBI ballistic missile boost intercept
BAMTM British Association of Machine Tool Merchants
BA(Mus) Bachelor of Arts in Music
BAMW British Association of Meat Wholesalers
BAN British Association of Neurologists
Ban. Bangor; Bantu
BANC British Association of National Coaches; British Association of Nature Conservationists
Banc. Sup. [law] *Bancus Superior* (Latin: higher bench, Queen's Bench, King's Bench)
B&B bed and breakfast
B&C [insurance] building and contents
B&D bondage and discipline; bondage and domination
b&e beginning and ending
B&FBS British and Foreign Bible Society
B&Q (Richard) Block and (David) Quayle (British founders of chain of DIY stores)
B&S brandy and soda; Browne and Sharpe (wire gauge)
B&W black and white
B&WE Bristol and West of England
BANS British Association of Numismatic Societies
BANZARE British, Australian, New Zealand Antarctic Research Expedition
BAO Bachelor of Arts in Obstetrics; Bankruptcy Annulment Order; British American Oil
BAOD British Airways Overseas Division
BA of E Badminton Association of England
BAOMS British Association of Oral and Maxillofacial Surgeons
BAOR British Army of the Rhine
Bap. Baptist
bap. baptize; baptized
b. à p. *billets à payer* (French: bills payable)
BAPA British Amateur Press Association
BAPC British Aircraft Preservation Council
BAPCO Bahrain Petroleum Company
BA(PE) Bachelor of Arts in Physical Education
BAPL Bettis Atomic Power Laboratory
BAPLA British Association of Picture Libraries and Agencies
BAPM British Association of Physical Medicine
BAppArts Bachelor of Applied Arts
BAppSc Bachelor of Applied Science
BAppSc(MT) Bachelor of Applied Science (Medical Technology)
BAPS beacon automated processing system (for lighthouses); British Association of Paediatric Surgeons; British Association of Plastic Surgeons
BAPT British Association for Physical Training
Bapt. Baptist
bapt. baptism; baptized
BAR [computing] base address register; *Book Auction Records*; British Association of Removers; Browning Automatic Rifle; [computing] buffer address register
Bar. Baritone; Barrister; [Bible] Baruch (book of Apocrypha)
bar. baritone; barleycorn (former unit of

length); barometer; barometric; barrel; barrister
b. à r. *billets à recevoir* (French: bills receivable)
BARB British Association of Rose Breeders; British Audience Research Bureau; Broadcasters' Audience Research Board
Barb. Barbados
barbie [Australian short form] barbecue
BARC British Automobile Racing Club
BArch Bachelor of Architecture
BArchE Bachelor of Architectural Engineering
barg. bargain
barit. baritone
BARLA British Amateur Rugby League Association
BARP British Association of Retired Persons
BARR British Association of Rheumatology and Rehabilitation
Barr. Barrister
BARS [commerce] behaviourally anchored rating scales; British Association of Residential Settlements
Bart Baronet
Bart's St Bartholomew's Hospital (London)
BAS Bachelor of Agricultural Science; Bachelor of Applied Science; British Antarctic Survey
BASA British Architectural Students' Association; British Australian Studies Association
BASAF British and South Africa Forum
BASC British Association for Shooting and Conservation
BASc Bachelor of Agricultural Science; Bachelor of Applied Science
BASCA British Academy of Songwriters, Composers and Authors
BASF *Badische Anilin- und Soda-Fabrik* (German chemical and electronics company)
BASI British Association of Ski Instructors
Basic beginners' all-purpose symbolic instruction code (computer programming language); British-American scientific international commercial (as in **Basic English**)
BASMA Boot and Shoe Manufacturers' Association and Leather Trades Protection Society
bass. con. [music] *basso continuo* (Italian: continuous bass)
BASW British Association of Social Workers
BAT best available technology; British Aerial Transport; British-American Tobacco Company; [medicine] brown adipose tissue
Bat. Batavia
bat. battalion; battery; battle
BATF [USA] Bureau of Alcohol, Tobacco and Firearms
bath. bathroom (in property advertisement)
BA(Theol) Bachelor of Arts in Theology
bathrm bathroom (in property advertisement)
BATO [aeronautics] balloon-assisted take-off
BA(TP) Bachelor of Arts in Town and Country Planning
BATS [ecology] biosphere–atmosphere transfer scheme
batt. battalion; [military] battery
battn battalion
BAU British Association Unit; business as usual
BAUA Business Aircraft Users' Association
BAUS British Association of Urological Surgeons
Bav. Bavaria; Bavarian
b. à v. [finance] *bon à vue* (French: good at sight)
BAWA British Amateur Wrestling Association
BAWLA British Amateur Weightlifters' Association
BAYS British Association of Young Scientists
BB bail bond; balloon barrage; bank book; bed and breakfast (in accommodation advertisement); best best (wrought iron); [UK postcode] Blackburn; Blue Book; B'nai B'rith (Jewish society); Boys' Brigade; Brigitte Bardot (French actress); double black (very soft pencil lead); [vehicle registration] Newcastle upon Tyne
Bb. bishops
bb. books
.bb Barbados (in Internet address)
b.b. ball bearing; bearer bonds; [nautical] below bridges

BBA Bachelor of Business Administration; [obstetrics] born before arrival; British Backgammon Association; British Bankers' Association; British Beekeepers' Association; British Bloodstock Association; British Board of Agrément; British Bobsleigh Association
BBAC British Balloon and Airship Club
b/bar bull-bar (in car advertisement)
BBB bed, breakfast and bath (in accommodation advertisement); [USA] Better Business Bureau; [physiology] blood–brain barrier; treble black (very soft pencil lead)
BBBC British Boxing Board of Control
BBC British Broadcasting Corporation
BBCC British Bottle Collectors' Club
BBCCS British Beer Can Collectors Society
BBCM Bandmaster of the Bandsmen's College of Music
BBCMA British Baby Carriage Manufacturers' Association
BBCS British Beer Mat Collectors Society; British Butterfly Conservation Society
BBEM bed, breakfast and evening meal (in accommodation advertisement)
BBF British Baseball Federation
BBFC British Board of Film Classification (formerly British Board of Film Censors)
BBI British Bottlers' Institute
BBIP *British Books in Print*
BBIRA British Baking Industries' Research Association
B Bisc. Bay of Biscay
BBL be back later (in Internet chat); British Bridge League
bbl barrel
BBMA British Brush Manufacturers' Association; British Button Manufacturers' Association
BBMC British Board of Marbles Control
BBQ barbecue
BBQC British Board of Quality Control
BBS Bachelor of Business Science; Bachelor of Business Studies; be back soon (in Internet chat); [computing] bulletin board system
BBSR Bermuda Biological Station for Research
BBSRC Biotechnology and Biological Sciences Research Council
BBT [medicine] basal body temperature
BC Bachelor of Chemistry; Bachelor of Commerce; Bachelor of Surgery (from Latin *Baccalaureus Chirurgiae*); badminton club; [taxation] balancing charge; bank clearing; bankruptcy court; basketball club; [music] *basso continuo* (Italian: continuous bass); Battery Commander; battle cruiser; bayonet cap (on light bulb); before Christ (in dates); bicycle club; billiards club; bills for collection; birth control; bishop and confessor; [medicine] blood consumption; board of control; boat club; boating club; [biochemistry] body composition; [astronomy] bolometric correction; Bomber Command; borough council; bowling club; bowls club; boxing club; boys' club; Bristol Channel; British Coal; British Columbia; British Commonwealth; British Council; [medicine] bronchial carcinoma; budgeted cost; [education] Burnham Committee; [vehicle registration] Leicester
B/C bills for collection
b.c. [music] *basso continuo* (Italian: continuous bass); blind copy; bulk carrier
BCA [New Zealand] Bachelor of Commerce and Administration; Book Club Associates; Boys' Clubs of America; British-Caribbean Association; [angling] British Casting Association; British Chicken Association; British Chiropractic Association
BCAB Birth Control Advisory Bureau; British Computer Association for the Blind
BCAC British Conference on Automation and Computation
BC&T [USA] Bakery, Confectionery and Tobacco Workers International Union
BCAP British Code of Advertising Practice
BCAR British Civil Airworthiness Requirements; British Council for Aid to Refugees
BCAS British Compressed Air Society
BCAT Birmingham Centre for Art Therapies
BCBC British Cattle Breeders' Club; British Citizens Band Council
BCC [medicine] basal-cell carcinoma; British Caravanners Club; British Coal Corporation (replacement for NCB); British Colour Council; British Copy-

right Council; British Council of Churches; British Crown Colony; Bus and Coach Council

b.c.c. blind carbon copy

BCCA British Cyclo-Cross Association

BCCG British Cooperative Clinical Group

BCCI Bank of Credit and Commerce International

BCD [USA] bad conduct discharge; [computing] binary coded decimal; [astronomy] blue compact dwarf

BCDP [medicine] balloon catheter dilation of the prostate

BCDTA British Chemical and Dyestuffs Traders' Association

BCE Bachelor of Chemical Engineering; Bachelor of Civil Engineering; before Christian Era (in dates); before Common Era (in dates); Board of Customs and Excise

BCEAO *Banque centrale des états de l'Afrique de l'Ouest* (French: Central Bank of West African States)

BCECC British and Central European Chamber of Commerce

BCF battle cruiser force; billion cubic feet; British Chess Federation; British Cycling Federation; [chemistry] bromochlorodifluoromethane (used in fire extinguishers); [textiles] bulked continuous filament; [USA] Bureau of Commercial Fisheries

BCFA British–China Friendship Association

BCG [medicine] bacille Calmette–Guérin (vaccine against tuberculosis); [medicine] ballistocardiography; [astronomy] blue compact galaxy

BCGA British Commercial Gas Association; British Cotton Growing Association

BCH [computing] Bose–Chaudhuri–Hocquenghem (code)

BCh Bachelor of Surgery (from Latin *Baccalaureus Chirurgiae*)

bch branch; bunch

BChD Bachelor of Dental Surgery (from Latin *Baccalaureus Chirurgiae Dentalis*)

BChE Bachelor of Chemical Engineering

BChemEng Bachelor of Chemical Engineering

BChir Bachelor of Surgery (from Latin *Baccalaureus Chirurgiae*)

BCINA British Commonwealth International Newsfilm Agency

BCIRA British Cast-Iron Research Association

BCIS Building Cost Information Service; *Bureau central international de séismologie* (French: International Central Bureau of Seismology)

BCK [fishing port] Buckie

BCL Bachelor of Canon Law; Bachelor of Civil Law

BCM [USA] Boston Conservatory of Music; British Commercial Monomark; British Consular Mail

BCMA British Colour Makers' Association; British Columbia Medical Association; British Complementary Medicine Association; British Country Music Association

BCMD biological and chemical munitions disposal

BCMF British Ceramic Manufacturers' Federation

BCMG Birmingham Contemporary Music Group

BCMS Bible Churchmen's Missionary Society

BCN British Commonwealth of Nations

bcn beacon

BCNU be seein' you (in Internet chat)

BCNZ Broadcasting Corporation of New Zealand

BCO [medicine] bilateral carotid (artery) occlusion; British College of Optometrists (or Ophthalmic Opticians)

BCOG British College of Obstetricians and Gynaecologists

BCom Bachelor of Commerce

BComm Bachelor of Commerce

BComSc Bachelor of Commercial Science

BCP Book of Common Prayer; Bulgarian Communist Party (former name of BSP)

BCPC British Crop Protection Council

BCPIT British Council for the Promotion of International Trade

BCPL [computing] Basic Combined Programming Language; [computing] Basic Computer Programming Language

BCPMA British Chemical Plant Manufacturers' Association

BCR battlefield casualty replacement

BCRA British Carbonization Research Association; British Ceramic Research Association

BCRC British Cave Rescue Council; British Columbia Research Council
BCRD British Council for the Rehabilitation of the Disabled
BCRU British Committee on Radiological Units
BCRUM British Committee on Radiation Units and Measurements
BCS Bachelor of Chemical Science; Bachelor of Commercial Science; [physics] Bardeen–Cooper–Schrieffer (theory of superconductivity); battle cruiser squadron; Bengal Civil Service; British Calibration Service; British Cardiac Society; British Computer Society; British Crossbow Society; [USA] Bureau of Criminal Statistics
BCSA British Constructional Steelwork Association
bcst broadcast
BCT Belfast Chamber of Trade; [medicine] body computer tomograph; Building Conservation Trust
BCTA British Canadian Trade Association; British Children's Theatre Association
BCTGA British Christmas Tree Growers Association
BCTV [microbiology] beet curly top virus
BCU [cinema] big close-up; British Canoe Union; British Commonwealth Union
BCURA British Coal Utilization Research Association
BCVA British Columbia Veterinary Association
BCWMA British Clock and Watch Manufacturers' Association
BCYC British Corinthian Yacht Club
BD Bachelor of Divinity; [currency] Bahraini dinar; [international vehicle registration] Bangladesh; battle dress; [physics] beam deflection; [fishing port] Bideford; [medicine] bile duct; [commerce] bill(s) discounted; bomb disposal; [medicine] bone density; [astronomy] Bonner Durchmusterung (star catalogue); boom defence; [UK postcode] Bradford; *Bundesrepublik Deutschland* (German: Federal Republic of Germany); [vehicle registration] Northampton
B/D bank draft; banker's draft; [commerce] bill(s) discounted; [book-keeping] brought down
Bd *Band* (German: volume); [computing] baud; Board; Boulevard
bd board; [printing] bold; [finance] bond; [bookbinding] bound; broad
b/d barrels per day; [book-keeping] brought down
bd. bundle
.bd Bangladesh (in Internet address)
b.d. [commerce] bill(s) discounted; [medicine] *bis (in) die* (Latin: twice a day) (in prescriptions)
BDA Bachelor of Domestic Arts; Bachelor of Dramatic Art; bomb damage assessment; British Deaf Association; British Decorators Association; British Dental Association; British Diabetic Association; British Dyslexia Association
BDBJ Board of Deputies of British Jews
BDC Book Development Council
b.d.c. [engineering] bottom dead centre
BDCC British Defence Coordinating Committee
Bde *Bände* (German: volumes); Brigade
BDentSc Bachelor of Dental Science
BDes Bachelor of Design
BDF [computing] backward differentiation formulae (as in **BDF methods**); Ballroom Dancers Federation; Botswana Defence Force
BDFA British Dairy Farmers' Association
bd ft board foot (unit of timber length)
BDG [bookbinding] binding
BDG/ND [bookbinding] binding, no date (given)
BDH British Drug Houses
BDI British Dyslexia Institute; *Bundesverband der deutschen Industrie* (German: Federal Association of German Industry)
b.d.i. bearing deviation indicator; both dates (or days) included
BDL below detectable limits; British Drama League
bdl. bundle
bdle bundle
BDM births, deaths, marriages; bomber defence missile; branch delegates' meeting
BDMA British Direct Marketing Association; British Disinfectant Manufacturers' Association
BDMAA British Direct Mail Advertising Association
Bdmr Bandmaster

BDNF [medicine] brain-derived neurotrophic factor
BDO Boom Defence Officer; British Darts Organization
BDP breakdown pressure
Bdr Bombardier; Brigadier
BDRA British Drag Racing Association
bdrm bedroom (in property or accommodation advertisement)
BDS Bachelor of Dental Surgery; [international vehicle registration] Barbados; bomb disposal squad; British Deer Society; British Dragonfly Society; British Driving Society
bds [bookbinding] boards; bundles
b.d.s. [medicine] *bis (in) die sumendus* (Latin: to be taken twice a day) (in prescriptions)
BDSA [USA] Business and Defense Services Administration
BDSc Bachelor of Dental Science
BDST British Double Summer Time
BDU [astronomy] baryon-dominated universe; bomb disposal unit
BDV breakdown voltage; [accounting] budget day value
Bdx Bordeaux
BE Bachelor of Economics; Bachelor of Education; Bachelor of Engineering; Bank of England; [fishing port] Barnstaple; best estimate; bill of exchange; [computing] binary encounter; [physics] binding energy; [USA] Board of Education; borough engineer; [physics] Bose–Einstein; British Element; British Embassy; British Empire; [vehicle registration] Lincoln
B/E bill of entry; bill of exchange
Be [chemical element] beryllium
Bé Baumé (temperature scale)
be. *bezüglich* (German: with reference to)
.be Belgium (in Internet address)
b.e. bill of entry; bill of exchange; binding edge
BEA British East Africa; British Epilepsy Association; British Esperanto Association; British European Airways (former airline company)
BEAB British Electrical Approvals Board
BEAC *Banque des états de l'Afrique centrale* (French: Bank of Central African States)
BEAIRE British Electrical and Allied Industries' Research Association
BEAM [medicine] brain electrical activity mapping
BEAMA (Federation of) British Electrotechnical and Allied Manufacturers' Associations
bearb. *bearbeitet* (German: compiled, edited)
BEAS British Educational Administration Society
BEC Building Employers' Confederation; *Bureau européen du café* (French: European Coffee Bureau); [USA] Bureau of Employees' Compensation
BEc Bachelor of Economics
bec. because
BECA British Exhibition Contractors' Association
Bech. Bechuanaland (former name of Botswana)
BE(Chem) Bachelor of Chemical Engineering
BECO booster-engine cut-off
BEcon Bachelor of Economics
BEcon(IA) Bachelor of Economics in Industrial Administration
BEcon(PA) Bachelor of Economics in Public Administration
BECTU Broadcasting, Entertainment, Cinematograph and Theatre Union
BEd Bachelor of Education
bed. bedroom (in property advertisement)
BEDA British Electrical Development Association; Bureau of European Designers' Associations
BEd(Com) Bachelor of Education in Commerce
BEd(HEc) Bachelor of Education in Home Economics
BEd(N) Bachelor of Education in Nursing
BEd(PE) Bachelor of Education in Physical Education
bedrm bedroom (in property advertisement)
Beds Bedfordshire
beds bedrooms (in property advertisement)
BEd(Sc) Bachelor of Education in Science
BEE Bachelor of Electrical Engineering
Beeb [short form] British Broadcasting Corporation

BEEL biological equivalent exposure limit (of radiation)
BEF British Equestrian Federation; British Expeditionary Force
bef. before
b.e.f. blunt end first
BEFA British Emigrant Families Association
BEG [USA] Bureau of Economic Geology
beg. beginning
BEHA British Export Houses Association
BEI Bachelor of Engineering (Dublin); *Banque européenne d'investissement* (French: European Investment Bank, EIB)
Beibl. *Beiblatt* (German: supplement)
BEIC British Egg Industry Council
beigeb. *beigebunden* (German: bound, in with something else)
beil. *beiliegend* (German: enclosed)
BEIR biological effects of ionizing radiation
BEL British Electrotechnical Committee
Bel. Belgian; Belgium
bel ex. *bel exemplaire* (French: fine copy) (of book or engraving)
Belf. Belfast
Belfox Belgian Futures and Options Exchange
Belg. Belgian; Belgic; Belgium
BEM British Empire Medal; bug-eyed monster
BEMA British Essence Manufacturers' Association
BEMAC British Exports Marketing Advisory Committee
BEMAS British Education Management and Administration Society
BEMB British Egg Marketing Board
BEME Brigade Electrical and Mechanical Engineer
BEMSA British Eastern Merchant Shippers' Association
BEN [electronics] broadband electrostatic noise
ben. *benedictio* (Latin: blessing); benediction
Bend. Bendigo (Australia)
BenDr *Bachelier en droit* (French: Bachelor of Law)
benef. benefice
Benelux Belgium, Netherlands, Luxembourg
BEng Bachelor of Engineering
Beng. Bengal; Bengali
BEngr Bachelor of Engraving
BenH *Bachelier en humanité* (French: Bachelor of Humanities)
BEO Base Engineer Officer
BEPC British Electrical Power Convention
beq. bequeath
beqt bequest
Ber. Berlin
BERCO British Electric Resistance Company
Berks Berkshire
Berl. Berlin
Berm. Bermuda
BERSA British Elastic Rope Sports Association
Berw. Berwick(shire)
BES Bachelor of Engineering Science; Bachelor of Environmental Studies; Biological Engineering Society; British Ecological Society; Business Expansion Scheme (replaced by EIS)
bes. *besonders* (German: especially)
BESA British Esperanto Scientific Association
BèsA *Bachelier ès arts* (French: Bachelor of Arts)
BESI bus electronic scanning indicator
BèsL *Bachelier ès lettres* (French: Bachelor of Letters)
BESO British Executive Service Overseas
BESS Bank of England Statistical Summary; bottom environmental sensing system (in oceanography)
BèsS *Bachelier ès sciences* (French: Bachelor of Science)
BEST British Expertise in Science and Technology (database)
Best. [commerce] *Bestellung* (German: order)
BET British Electric Traction Company; buildings energy technology
bet. between
BETA Broadcasting and Entertainment Trades Alliance (became part of BECTU); Business Equipment Trades' Association
BETAA British Export Trade Advertising Association
BETRO British Export Trade Research Organization
betw. between

BEU [engineering] batch extraction unit; Benelux Economic Union
BEUC *Bureau européen des unions de consommateurs* (French: European Bureau of Consumers' Unions)
BEV Black English Vernacular
BeV [USA] billion electronvolts
bev. bevel; beverage
BEVA British Exhibition Venues' Association
BEXA British Exporters Association
bez. *bezahlt* (German: paid); *bezüglich* (German: with reference to)
bezw. *beziehungsweise* (German: respectively)
BF Bachelor of Forestry; [fishing port] Banff; *Banque de France* (French: Bank of France); [currency] Belgian franc; black face (sheep); blast furnace; [informal] bloody fool; body fat; breathing frequency; British Funds; [international vehicle registration] Burkina Faso; [vehicle registration] Stoke-on-Trent
B/F bring forward; [book-keeping] brought forward
bf brief
b/f bring forward; [book-keeping] brought forward
.bf Burkina Faso (in Internet address)
b.f. bankruptcy fee; base frequency; beer firkin; [informal] bloody fool; [printing] bold face; bona fide
BFA Bachelor of Fine Arts; British Film Academy
BFAP British Forces Arabian Peninsula
BFASS [nuclear technology] BWR fuel assembly sealing system
b'fast breakfast
BFAWU Bakers', Food and Allied Workers' Union
BFBB British Federation of Brass Bands
BFBPW British Federation of Business and Professional Women
BFBS British and Foreign Bible Society; British Forces Broadcasting Service
BFCA British Federation of Commodity Associations
BFCS British Friesian Cattle Society
BFEBS British Far Eastern Broadcasting Service
BFET [electronics] ballistic field-effect transistor
BFFA British Film Fund Agency
BFFC British Federation of Folk Clubs
BFFS British Federation of Film Societies
BFG Big Friendly Giant (in children's book by Roald Dahl)
BFI British Film Institute
BFIA British Flower Industry Association
BFMA British Farm Mechanization Association
BFMF British Federation of Music Festivals; British Footwear Manufacturers' Federation
BFMIRA British Food Manufacturing Industries' Research Association
BFMP British Federation of Master Printers
BFN [informal] bye for now
Bfn Bloemfontein; British Forces Network
BFO beat-frequency oscillator
BFor Bachelor of Forestry
BForSc Bachelor of Forestry Science
BFP Bureau of Freelance Photographers
BFPA British Film Producers' Association
BFPC British Farm Produce Council
BFPO British Forces Post Office
BFr [currency] Belgian franc
BFS [mining] blast-furnace slag; British Fuchsia Society
BFSA British Fire Services' Association
BFSS British and Foreign Sailors' Society; British Field Sports Society
BFT biofeedback training
BFTA British Fur Trade Alliance
BFUW British Federation of University Women
BFV [military] Bradley fighting vehicle
BG Birmingham (Wire) Gauge; blood group; Brigadier-General; British Guiana (former name of Guyana); [international vehicle registration] Bulgaria; [vehicle registration] Liverpool
bg [commerce] bag
b/g bonded goods
.bg Bulgaria (in Internet address)
b.g. [horseracing] bay gelding
BGA [USA] Better Government Association; British Gliding Association; British Graduates Association
BGB *Bürgerliches Gesetzbuch* (German: code of civil law)
BGC bank giro credit
BGCS Botanic Gardens Conservation Secretariat

BGEA Billy Graham Evangelistic Association
BGenEd Bachelor of General Education
BGF [Australia] Banana Growers' Federation
BGH [biochemistry] bovine growth hormone
BGIRA British Glass Industry Research Association
BGL Bachelor of General Laws
b.g.l. below ground level
bglr bugler
BGM Bethnal Green Museum
BGMA British Gear Manufacturers' Association
BGMV [microbiology] bean golden mosaic virus
BGRB British Greyhound Racing Board
BGS Brigadier General Staff; British Geological Survey; British Geriatrics Society; British Goat Society; Brothers of the Good Shepherd
bgt bought
BGV below-ground vault
BH base hospital; [astronomy] black hole; [fishing port] Blyth; [UK postcode] Bournemouth; [metallurgy] Brinell hardness; British Honduras (former name of Belize); British Hovercraft; Burlington House (London) (home of Royal Academy); [vehicle registration] Luton
B/H bill of health
Bh [chemical element] bohrium
b/h barrels per hour
.bh Bahrain (in Internet address)
b.h. [informal] bloody hell
BHA [mining] bottom-hole assembly; British Handball Association; British Homeopathic Association; British Humanist Association
B'ham Birmingham
BHB British Hockey Board
BHC [medicine] benign hereditary chorea; benzene hexachloride (insecticide); British High Commissioner
bhd beachhead; billhead; bulkhead
BHDF British Hospital Doctors' Federation
BHE Bachelor of Home Economics
B'head Birkenhead
BHF British Hardware Federation; British Heart Foundation
Bhf *Bahnhof* (German: railway station)
BHGA British Hang Gliding Association
BHI British Horological Institute; *Bureau hydrographique international* (French: International Hydrographic Bureau)
BHL biological half-life
Bhm Birmingham
BHMRA British Hydromechanics' Research Association
BHN [metallurgy] Brinell hardness number
BHort Bachelor of Horticulture
BHortSc Bachelor of Horticultural Science
BHP [Australia] Broken Hill Proprietary
bhp brake horsepower
bhpric bishopric
BHQ Brigade Headquarters
BHRA British Hydromechanics' Research Association
BHRCA British Hotels, Restaurants and Caterers' Association
BHS boys' high school; British Home Stores; British Horse Society
BHT [electronics] bipolar heterojunction transistor; [mining] bottom-hole temperature
BHTA British Herring Trade Association
Bhu. Bhutan
BHy Bachelor of Hygiene
BI background information; Bahama Islands; Balearic Islands; base ignition; Befrienders International; Bermuda Islands; [medicine] bone injury; bulk issue
Bi [chemical element] bismuth
.bi Burundi (in Internet address)
BIA British Institute of Acupuncture; British Insurance Association; British Ironfounders' Association; [USA] Bureau of Indian Affairs
BIAA British Industrial Advertising Association
BIAC Business and Industry Advisory Committee
BIAE British Institute of Adult Education
BIAS Bristol Industrial Archaeological Society
BIAT British Institute of Architectural Technologists
BIATA British Independent Air Transport Association
BIB [military] baby incendiary bomb
Bib. Bible; Biblical

bib. [medicine] *bibe* (Latin: drink); biblical; *bibliothèque* (French: library)
BIBA British Insurance Brokers' Association (former name of BIIBA)
BIBC British Isles Bowling Council
BIBF British and Irish Basketball Federation
bibl. biblical; bibliographer; bibliographical; bibliography
biblio. bibliography
bibliog. bibliographer; bibliographical; bibliography
BIBRA British Industrial Biological Research Association
BIC Bahá'i International Community; [electronics] biased ion collector; *Bureau international du cinéma* (French: International Cinema Bureau); Butter Information Council
bicarb [short form] bicarbonate of soda
BICC Berne International Copyright Convention; British Insulated Callender's Cables Limited
BICE *Bureau international catholique de l'enfance* (French: International Catholic Child Bureau)
BICEMA British Internal Combustion Engine Manufacturers' Association
BICEP British Industrial Collaborative Exponential Programme
BICERI British Internal Combustion Engine Research Institute
BICFET [electronics] bipolar inversion-channel field-effect transistor
bi-CMOS [electronics] (merged) bipolar/complementary metal oxide semiconductor
BICS British Institution of Cleaning Science
BID Bachelor of Industrial Design; Bachelor of Interior Design; [medicine] brought in dead
b.i.d. [medicine] *bis in die* (Latin: twice a day) (in prescriptions)
BIDS British Institute of Dealers in Securities
BIE Bachelor of Industrial Engineering; [mathematics] boundary integral equation; *Bureau international d'éducation* (French: International Bureau of Education); *Bureau international des expositions* (French: International Exhibition Bureau)
BIEE British Institute of Energy Economics
bien. biennial
bienn. biennial
BIET British Institute of Engineering Technology
BIF [geology] banded iron formation; British Industries Fair
BIFFEX Baltic International Freight Futures Market (formerly Baltic International Freight Futures Exchange)
BIFU Banking, Insurance and Finance Union
BIH [medicine] benign intracranial hypertension; [international vehicle registration] Bosnia-Herzegovina; *Bureau international de l'heure* (French: International Time Bureau)
BIHA British Ice Hockey Association
BIIBA British Insurance and Investment Brokers' Association (formerly BIBA)
bike [short form] bicycle
BIM [mathematics] boundary integral method; British Institute of Management; British Insulin Manufacturers
bim. *bimestrale* (Italian: bimonthly); *bimestre* (Italian: two-month period)
BIMA [astronomy] Berkeley–Illinois–Maryland Association (array)
BIMBO buy-in management buyout
BIMCAM British Industrial Measuring and Control Apparatus Manufacturers' Association
BIN *Bulletin of International News*
bin. [mathematics] binary
BINC Building Industries' National Council
bind. binding
BIO [Canada] Bedford Institute of Oceanography
biochem. biochemical; biochemistry
biodeg. biodegradable
biog. biographer; biographical; biography
biogeog. biogeography
biol. biological; biologist; biology
BIOS [computing] basic input–output system; Biological Investigation of Space; [astronautics] biological satellite; British Intelligence Objectives Subcommittee
BIOT British Indian Ocean Territory
BIP Botswana Independence Party; British

Industrial Plastics; British Institute in Paris

BIPCA *Bureau international permanent de chimie analytique pour les matières destinées à l'alimentation de l'homme et des animaux* (French: Permanent International Bureau of Analytical Chemistry of Human and Animal Food)

BIPL Burmah Industrial Products Limited

BIPM *Bureau international des poids et mésures* (French: International Bureau of Weights and Measures)

BIPP [medicine] bismuth iodoform paraffin paste (formerly applied to wounds); British Institute of Practical Psychology

BIR Board of Inland Revenue; British Institute of Radiology

BIRD *Banque internationale pour la reconstruction et le développement* (French: International Bank for Reconstruction and Development, IBRD)

BIRF Brewing Industry Research Foundation

Birm. Birmingham

BIRMO British Infra-Red Manufacturers' Organization

BIRS British Institute of Recorded Sound

BIS Bank for International Settlements; British Information Services; British Interplanetary Society; *Bureau international du scoutisme* (French: Boy Scouts International Bureau); business information system

bis. bissextile

BISA British International Studies Association

Bisc. Biscayan

BISF British Iron and Steel Federation

BISFA British Industrial and Scientific Film Association

bish. bishop

bis in 7d. [medicine] *bis in septem diebus* (Latin: twice a week) (in prescriptions)

BISPA British Independent Steel Producers' Association

BISRA British Iron and Steel Research Association

BISYNC [computing] binary synchronous communications

BIT *Bureau international du travail* (French: International Labour Office)

bit [computing] binary digit

bit. bitumen; bituminous

BITA British Industrial Truck Association

bitm. bituminous

BITNET [computing] Because It's Time Network

BITO British Institution of Training Officers

BITOA British Incoming Tour Operators' Association

bitum. bituminous

BIU Bermuda Industrial Union; *Bureau international des universités* (French: International University Bureau)

biv. bivouac

BIWF British–Israel World Federation

BIWS Bureau of International Whaling Statistics

BIZ *Bank für internationalen Zahlungsausgleich* (German: Bank for International Settlements)

BJ Bachelor of Journalism; [vehicle registration] Ipswich

.bj Benin (in Internet address)

BJA British Judo Association

BJCEB British Joint Communications Electronics Board

BJJ [electronics] boundary Josephson junction

BJJA British Ju Jitsu Association

BJOS *British Journal of Occupational Safety*

BJP [India] Bharatiya Janata Party

BJSM British Joint Services Mission

BJT [electronics] bipolar junction transistor

BJTRA British Jute Trade Research Association

BJur Bachelor of Jurisprudence

BJuris Bachelor of Jurisprudence

BK [fishing port] Berwick-on-Tweed; [trademark] Burger King; [vehicle registration] Portsmouth

Bk [chemical element] berkelium

bk backwardation; bank; bark; barrack; black; block; book; break

BKA British Karate Association; *Bundeskriminalamt* (German: criminal investigations office)

bkble bookable

bkcy bankruptcy

BKD [medicine] bacterial kidney disease

bkd blackboard; booked

bkfst breakfast

bkg banking; booking; book-keeping

bkgd background
b/kit body kit (in car advertisement)
bkkg book-keeping
bklr [printing] black letter
bklt booklet
Bklyn [USA] Brooklyn
bkm buckram
bkpg book-keeping
bkpt bankrupt
bkrpt bankrupt
bks barracks; books
BKSTS British Kinematograph, Sound and Television Society
bkt basket; bracket; bucket
BL Bachelor of Law; Bachelor of Letters; Bachelor of Literature; Barrister-at-Law; base line; bill lodged; bill of lading; [printing] black letter; [medicine] blood lead; Boatswain Lieutenant; Bodleian Library (Oxford); [UK postcode] Bolton; [fishing port] Bristol; British Legion; British Leyland (former vehicle manufacturer); British Library; [medicine] Burkitt's lymphoma; [vehicle registration] Reading
B/L bill of lading
Bl. *Blatt* (German: newspaper); Blessed
bl barrel
bl. bale; black; blue
b.l. bill of lading; breech-loading (rifle)
BLA Bachelor of Landscape Architecture; Bachelor of Liberal Arts; British Legal Association; British Liberation Army
BLACC British and Latin American Chamber of Commerce
BLAISE British Library Automated Information Service
BLAVA British Laboratory Animals Veterinary Association
BLB [horticulture] bacterial leaf blight; [medicine] Boothby, Lovelace and Bulbulian (nasal oxygen mask)
BLBSD British Library, Bibliographic Services Division
BLC British Lighting Council
bld [printing] bold (face)
bldg building
BLDSC British Library, Document Supply Centre
BLE [USA] Brotherhood of Locomotive Engineers
bleaters [informal] born losers expending all their energy rubbishing success
BLESMA British Limbless Ex-Servicemen's Association
BLEU Belgo-Luxembourg Economic Union; [aeronautics] Blind Landing Experimental Unit
BLG *Burke's Landed Gentry*
BLH British Legion Headquarters
BLHSS British Library, Humanities and Social Sciences
BLI British Lighting Industries
BLib Bachelor of Library Science
BLibSc Bachelor of Library Science
BLIC *Bureau de liaison des industries du caoutchouc de la CE* (French: Rubber Industries Liaison Bureau of the EU)
BLIS [USA] Bibliographic Literature Information System
Bliss baby life support systems; [military] bend, low silhouette, irregular shape, small, secluded (pilots' escape technique)
BLit Bachelor of Literature
BLitt Bachelor of Letters (from Latin *Baccalaureus Litterarum*)
blk black; blank; block; bulk
BLL Bachelor of Laws
BLLD British Library, Lending Division
BLM blind landing machine; [USA] Bureau of Land Management
BLMA British Lead Manufacturers' Association
BLMAS Bible Lands Missions' Aid Society
BLMRA British Leather Manufacturers' Research Association
BLNL British Library Newspaper Library
BLOF British Lace Operatives' Federation
BLOX [finance] block order exposure system
BLP Barbados Labour Party
b.l.r. breech-loading rifle
BLRA British Launderers' Research Association
BLRD British Library, Reference Division
BLRG [astronomy] broad-line radio galaxy
BLS Bachelor of Library Science; basic life support; *benevolenti lectori salutem* (Latin: greeting to the well-wishing reader); Branch Line Society; [USA] Bureau of Labor Statistics
BLSN [meteorology] blowing snow
BLT bacon, lettuce and tomato (sandwich)
blt built

BLV [microbiology] bovine leukaemia virus; British Legion Village
Blvd Boulevard
BLWA British Laboratory Ware Association
BLWN [electronics] band-limited white noise
BM Bachelor of Medicine; Bachelor of Music; bandmaster; [medicine] basal metabolism; base metal; *beatae memoriae* (Latin: of blessed memory); *Beata Maria* (Latin: Blessed Mary); [surveying] bench-mark; Bishop and Martyr; *bonae memoriae* (Latin: of happy memory); [medicine] bone marrow; [computing] Boyer–Moore (algorithm); brigade major; British Monomark; British Museum; [fishing port] Brixham; bronze medal; bronze medallist; [USA] Bureau of Mines; [vehicle registration] Luton
b.m. *bene merenti* (Latin: to the well-deserving); [horseracing] black mare; board measure (of wood); [medicine] bowel movement; breech mechanism (of firearm)
BMA Bahrain Monetary Agency; British Manufacturers' Association; British Medical Association; British Midland Airways
BMath Bachelor of Mathematics
BMATT British Military Advisory and Training Team
BMBF British Mountain Bike Federation
BMC [medicine] bone marrow cell(s); [medicine] bone mineral content (or concentration); Book Marketing Council; British Match Corporation; British Medical Council; British Metal Corporation; British Motor Corporation (vehicle manufacturer); British Mountaineering Council; British Museum Catalogue (of 15th-century books)
BMCIS Building Maintenance Cost Information Service
BMD ballistic missile defence; births, marriages and deaths; [medicine] bone mineral density
BMDM [medicine] bone-marrow-derived macrophage(s); British Museum Department of Manuscripts
BMDO [USA] Ballistic Missile Defense Organization
Bmdr Bombardier
BME Bachelor of Mechanical Engineering; Bachelor of Mining Engineering; Bachelor of Music Education; [medicine] benign myalgic encephalomyelitis
BMEC British Marine Equipment Council
BMed Bachelor of Medicine
BMedSci Bachelor of Medical Science
BMEF British Mechanical Engineering Federation
BMEG Building Materials Export Group
BMEO British Middle East Office
BMEP [engineering] brake mean effective pressure
BMet Bachelor of Metallurgy
BMetE Bachelor of Metallurgical Engineering
BMEWS ballistic missile early warning system
BMF Builders Merchants Federation
BMFA Boston Museum of Fine Arts
BMH British Military Hospital
BMI ballistic missile interceptor; Birmingham and Midland Institute; body-mass index; Broadcast Music Incorporated
BMJ *British Medical Journal*
BML Bachelor of Modern Languages; British Museum Library
BMM British Military Mission
BMMA Bacon and Meat Marketing Association
b.m.o. business machine operator
B'mouth Bournemouth
BMP biochemical methane potential; biochemical methane production; [computing] bitmap (format)
bmp brake mean power
BMPA British Metalworking Plantmakers' Association
BMPS British Musicians' Pension Society
BMR [physiology] basal metabolic rate
BMRA Brigade Major Royal Artillery
BMRB British Market Research Bureau
BMRMC British Motor Racing Marshals' Club
BMRR [USA] Brookhaven Medical Research Reactor
BMS Bachelor of Marine Science; Baptist Missionary Society; British Mycological Society; building management system; business modelling system
BMSE Baltic Mercantile and Shipping Exchange

BMT basic motion time-study; bone-marrow transplant; borehole-mining tool; British Mean Time
BMTA British Motor Trade Association
BMus Bachelor of Music
BMusEd Bachelor of Music Education
BMV Blessed Mary the Virgin; [microbiology] brome mosaic virus
BMW *Bayerische Motorenwerke* (German vehicle manufacturer)
BMWE [USA] Brotherhood of Maintenance of Way Employees
BMWS ballistic missile weapon system
BMX bicycle motocross
BN Bachelor of Nursing; bank note; [astronomy] Becklin–Neugebauer (object); [fishing port] Boston; [UK postcode] Brighton; Britten–Norman (aircraft); [vehicle registration] Manchester
Bn Baron; Battalion
bn bassoon; battalion; beacon; been; billion; born
.bn Brunei (in Internet address)
BNA British Naturalists' Association; British North America; [insurance] British North Atlantic; British Nursing Association
BNAF British North Africa Force
BNB [physiology] blood–nerve barrier; *British National Bibliography*
BNBC British National Book Centre
BNC [computing] bayonet nut couplers; [linguistics] British National Corpus
BNCAR British National Committee for Antarctic Research
BNCC British National Committee for Chemistry
BNCI *Banque nationale pour le commerce et l'industrie* (French: National Bank for Commerce and Industry) (in Madagascar)
BNCM *Bibliothèque nationale du conservatoire de musique* (French: National Library of Music) (in Paris)
BNCS British National Carnation Society
BNCSAA British National Committee on Surface-Active Agents
BNCSR British National Committee on Space Research
BND *Bundesnachrichtendienst* (German: national intelligence service)
B/ND [bookbinding] binding, no date (given)
BNDD [USA] Bureau of Narcotics and Dangerous Drugs
Bndr Bandmaster
BNEC British National Export Council; British Nuclear Energy Conference
BNES British Nuclear Energy Society
BNF [computing] Backus–Naur form; [computing] Backus normal form; [pharmacology] British National Formulary; British Nuclear Fuels; British Nutrition Foundation
BnF *Bibliothèque nationale de France* (French: National Library of France)
BNFC British National Film Catalogue
BNFL British Nuclear Fuels Limited
BNFMF British Non-Ferrous Metals Federation
BNGA British Nursery Goods Association
BNGM British Naval Gunnery Mission
BNHQ battalion headquarters
bnkg banking
BNL *Banca Nazionale del Lavoro* (Italian: National Bank of Labour); Brookhaven National Laboratory
BNM *Bureau national de métrologie* (French: National Bureau of Metrology)
BNO [medicine] bowels not opened
BNOC British National Oil Corporation; British National Opera Company
BNP *Banque nationale de Paris* (French: National Bank of Paris); Barbados National Party; British National Party
BNS Bachelor of Natural Science; Bathymetric Navigation System; British Numismatic Society; buyer no seller
BNSC British National Space Centre
BNSc Bachelor of Nursing Science
BNTA British Numismatic Trade Association
BNurs Bachelor of Nursing
BNX British Nuclear Export Executive
bnzn [chemistry] benzoin
BO Bachelor of Oratory; biological oceanography; [informal] body odour; [fishing port] Borrowstounness (Bo'ness); [medicine] bowels opened; box office; branch office; [vehicle registration] Cardiff
B/O [book-keeping] brought over; buyer's option
b/o [book-keeping] brought over
.bo Bolivia (in Internet address)
b.o. back order; blackout; broker's order; buyer's option

BOA British Olympic Association; British Optical Association; British Orthopaedic Association; broad ocean area
BOAC British Overseas Airways Corporation (former airline company)
BOAD *Banque ouest-africaine de développement* (French: West African Development Bank)
BOA(Disp) British Optical Association, Dispensing Certificate
BOAI [medicine] balloon occluded arterial infusion
BOAT byroad open to all traffic
BOBA British Overseas Banks' Association
BOBMA British Oil Burner Manufacturers' Association
BOBS Board of Banking Supervision
BOC [computing] beginning of cycle; [computing] bimodal optical computer; British Oxygen Corporation; Burmah Oil Company
BOCE Board of Customs and Excise
BOCM British Oil and Cake Mills Limited
BOD biochemical oxygen demand
Bod. Bodleian Library (Oxford)
Bodl. Bodleian Library (Oxford)
BODMAS brackets, of, division, multiplication, addition, subtraction (mnemonic for order of arithmetical operations)
Body British Organ Donor Society
BOE Bank of England; Board of Education; [building] brick on edge (as in **BOE sill**)
BOF basic oxygen furnace; [computing] beginning of file; British Orienteering Federation; British Overseas Fairs
B of E Bank of England
B of H Band of Hope Union
BOGMC Bangladesh Oil, Gas and Minerals Corporation
Boh. Bohemia; Bohemian
BOHA [medicine] balloon occlusion hepatic angiography
BOJ Bank of Japan
BOL beginning of life; [international vehicle registration] Bolivia
Bol. (Simon) Bolívar (South American statesman); Bolivia; Bolivian
bol. [medicine] bolus (large pill)
BOLTON better on lips than on notepaper (on envelope of love letter)
BOM bill of materials; [USA] Bureau of Mines
Bom. Bombay
b.o.m. bill of materials
Bomb. Bombardier; Bombay
BomCS Bombay Civil Service
BomSC Bombay Staff Corps
BON British Organization of Non-Parents
bon *bataillon* (French: battalion)
BONUS [finance] Borrower's Option for Notes and Underwritten Standby
Boo [astronomy] Bootes
BOP [chemistry] basic oxygen process; [mining] blowout preventer; *Boy's Own Paper*
BOptom Bachelor of Optometry
BOQ [US military] bachelor officers' quarters; base officers' quarters
BOr Bachelor of Orientation
bor. borough
BORAD British Oxygen Research and Development Association
boro. borough
BOS basic oxygen steelmaking; [computing] business operating system
bos'n boatswain
Bos Pops [USA] Boston Pops Orchestra
BOSS Bioastronautic Orbiting Space Station; [South Africa] Bureau of State Security
Boswash [USA] Boston–Washington, DC (urban area)
BOT [computing] beginning of tape (marker); Board of Trade (became part of DTI)
bot bought
bot. botanic(al); botanist; botany; bottle; bottom
BOTB British Overseas Trade Board
BOU British Ornithologists' Union
Boul. Boulevard
BOV brown oil of vitriol (commercial sulphuric acid)
BOWO Brigade Ordnance Warrant Officer
BP Bachelor of Pharmacy; Bachelor of Philosophy; back projection; (Robert) Baden Powell (founder of Scout movement); barometric pressure; [finance] basis point; [military] beach party; before present (in dates); be prepared (motto of Scout movement); [shipping] between perpendiculars; [medicine] blood pressure; *Blue Peter* (television programme);

Boerenpartij (Dutch: Farmers' Party); boiling point; British Patent; British Petroleum; British Pharmacopoeia; British Public; [vehicle registration] Portsmouth

B/P bills payable

Bp Bishop

b/p bills payable; blueprint

bp. baptized; birthplace

b.p. below proof (of alcohol); bills payable; [medicine] blood pressure; boiling point; *bonum publicum* (Latin: the public good)

BPA Bachelor of Professional Arts; *Bahnpostamt* (German: railway post office); [USA] Biological Photographic Association; Bookmakers' Protection Association; British Paediatric Association; British Parachute Association; British Philatelic Association; [USA] Brookhaven (National Laboratory) Plant Analyzer; [USA] Business Publications Audit of Circulation

BPAA British Poster Advertising Association

BPAGB Bicycle Polo Association of Great Britain

BPAS British Pregnancy Advisory Service

b.p.b. bank post bills

BPBF British Paper Box Federation

BPBIRA British Paper and Board Industry Research Association

BPBMA British Paper and Board Makers' Association

BPC Book Prices Current; British Pharmaceutical Codex; British Pharmacopoeia Commission; British Printing Corporation; British Productivity Council; [USA] Business and Professional Code

BPCA British Pest Control Association

BPCC British Printing and Communication Corporation

bpcd barrels per calendar day

BPCF British Precast Concrete Federation

BPCR Brakes on Pedal Cycle Regulations

BPCRA British Professional Cycle Racing Association

BPd Bachelor of Pedagogy

bpd barrels per day

BPDB Bangladesh Power Development Board

BPDMS [military] basic point defence missile system

BPE Bachelor of Physical Education

BPEd Bachelor of Physical Education

BPF bottom pressure fluctuation; British Plastics Federation; British Polio Fellowship

b.p.f. [commerce] *bon pour francs* (French: value in francs)

BPG Broadcasting Press Guild

BPH Bachelor of Public Health; [medicine] benign prostatic hypertrophy (or hyperplasia)

BPh Bachelor of Philosophy

bph barrels per hour

BPharm Bachelor of Pharmacy

BPhil Bachelor of Philosophy

BPI Booksellers' Provident Institution; British Pacific Islands

bpi [computing] bits per inch; [computing] bytes per inch

BPICA *Bureau permanent international des constructeurs d'automobiles* (French: International Permanent Bureau of Motor Manufacturers)

BPIF British Printing Industries' Federation

Bpl. Barnstaple

bpl. birthplace

bpm barrels per minute; [music] beats per minute

BPMA British Premium Merchandise Association; British Pump Manufacturers' Association

BPMF British Postgraduate Medical Federation; British Pottery Manufacturers' Federation

BPO base post office; Berlin Philharmonic Orchestra

BPOE Benevolent and Protective Order of Elks

BPP Botswana People's Party

BPPMA British Power-Press Manufacturers' Association

BPR business process re-engineering

BPRA Book Publishers' Representatives' Association

BPRO Blind Persons Resettlement Officer

BPS [medicine] blood-pool scintigraphy; border patrol sector; border patrol station; British Pharmacological Society; British Psychological Society; [USA] Bureau of Professional Standards (Internal Affairs)

BPs Bachelor of Psychology

bps [computing] bits per second; [computing] bytes per second
BPsS British Psychological Society
Bp Suff. Bishop Suffragan
BPsych Bachelor of Psychology
BPT Bachelor of Physiotherapy; battle practice target; British Petroleum Tanker
bpt [computing] bits per track
BPV [microbiology] bovine papilloma virus
BQ *bene quiescat* (Latin: may he/she rest well)
Bq becquerel (unit of radioactivity)
bq. barque
BQA British Quality Association
BQMS Battery Quartermaster-Sergeant
bque barque
BR [law] *Bancus Reginae* (Latin: Queen's Bench); [law] *Bancus Regis* (Latin: King's Bench); bioaccumulation ratio; [medicine] blink reflex; [education] block release; book of reference; [international vehicle registration] Brazil; [nuclear technology] breeder reactor; breeding ratio; [physics] bremsstrahlung radiation; [fishing port] Bridgwater; British Rail; [UK postcode] Bromley; (poly)butadiene rubber; butyl rubber; [vehicle registration] Newcastle upon Tyne
B/R bills receivable; Bordeaux or Rouen (in grain trade); [insurance] builders' risks
Br [currency] birr (used in Ethiopia); Bombardier; [chemical element] bromine; [Roman Catholic Church] Brother; [military] Bugler
Br. Branch; Brazil; Breton; Britain; British
br. bearing; branch; bridge; brief; brig; bronze; brother; brown
.br Brazil (in Internet address)
b.r. bank rate; bills receivable
BRA Bee Research Association; Brigadier Royal Artillery; British Records Association; British Rheumatism and Arthritis Association
bra [short form] brassière
BRAD *British Rates and Data* (directory of publications)
Brad. Bradford
Br. Am. British America
BRAS ballistic rocket air suppression
Braz. Brazil; Brazilian
Brazza. Brazzaville
BRB be right back (in Internet chat); [medicine] blood retinal barrier
BRC [USA] base residence course; Biological Records Centre (Nature Conservancy Council); British Radio Corporation; business reply card
Br. C British Columbia
brch branch
BRCS British Red Cross Society
BRD [fishing port] Broadford; [USA] Building Research Division (National Bureau of Standards)
brd board
BRDC British Racing Drivers' Club
brdcst broadcast
BRE Bachelor of Religious Education; British Rail Engineering; Building Research Establishment
Brec. Brecon
b. rec. bills receivable
BREL British Rail Engineering Limited
BREMA British Radio Equipment Manufacturers' Association
Bren Brno and Enfield (places of manufacture of Bren gun)
Br'er Brother
Bret. Breton
brev. brevet; *breveté* (French: patent); *brevetto* (Italian: patent)
brew. brewer; brewery; brewing
BRF Bible Reading Fellowship; British Road Federation
brf [law] brief
BRFC [angling] British Record Fish Committee
brg bearing
br. g. [horseracing] brown gelding
BRI *Banque des règlements internationaux* (French: Bank for International Settlements, BIS); [computing] basic-rate ISDN; [USA] Biological Research Institute; [USA] Brain Research Institute
Br. I British India; British Isles
Brig. Brigade; Brigadier
Brig-Gen Brigadier-General
brill [short form] brilliant
brill. [music] *brillante* (Italian: brilliant)
BRIMEC British Mechanical Engineering Confederation
BRINCO British Newfoundland Corporation Limited
Brisb. Brisbane

Brist. Bristol
Brit. Britain; Britannia; British; Briton
Brit. Mus. British Museum
Brit. Pat. British Patent
brk brick
brkf. breakfast
brklyr bricklayer
brkt bracket
brkwtr breakwater
BRL Ballistic Research Laboratory; [USA] Bible Research Library
brl barrel
BRM [computing] binary-rate multiplier; [medicine] biological response modifier; British Racing Motors
BRMA Board of Registration of Medical Auxiliaries; British Rubber Manufacturers' Association
BRMCA British Ready-Mixed Concrete Association
BRMF British Rainwear Manufacturers' Federation
BRN [international vehicle registration] Bahrain
brn brown
BRNC Britannia Royal Naval College
brng [navigation] bearing; burning
BRO brigade routine order
Bro. Brotherhood
bro. brother
brom. [chemistry] bromide
Bros. Brothers
bros. brothers
BRP biological reclamation process
BRS British Record Society; British Road Services; Building Research Station
BRSA British Rail Staff Association
BRSCC British Racing and Sports Car Club
BRT *Belgische Radio en Televisie* (Belgian broadcasting company); [shipping] *Brutto-Registertonnen* (German: gross register tons)
brt bright
BRTA British Racing Toboggan Association; British Regional Television Association; British Road Tar Association
BRU [international vehicle registration] Brunei
Brum Brummagem (informal name for Birmingham)
Brunsw. Brunswick
BRurSc Bachelor of Rural Science
Brux. *Bruxelles* (French: Brussels)
BRW British Relay Wireless
bry. bryology
bryol. bryology
brz. bronze
BS [vehicle registration] Aberdeen; [USA] Bachelor of Science; Bachelor of Surgery; [international vehicle registration] Bahamas; battleship; battle squadron; [fishing port] Beaumaris; below specification; Bibliographical Society; bill of sale; [computing] binary state; Biochemical Society; Blackfriars Settlement; Blessed Sacrament; [medicine] blood sugar; Boy Scouts; [angling] breaking strain (of line); [medicine] breath sounds; [UK postcode] Bristol; [aeronautics] Bristol Siddeley; British Standard; British Steel (plc); Budgerigar Society; building society; [slang] bullshit; [computing] bus switch
B/S bill of sale; [commerce] bill of store
Bs [currency] bolívar (used in Venezuela)
bs bags; bales
.bs Bahamas (in Internet address)
b.s. backstage; balance sheet; bill of sale; [slang] bullshit
BSA Bachelor of Science in Agriculture; Bachelor of Scientific Agriculture; Bibliographical Society of America; Birmingham Small Arms Company; [medicine] body surface area; [medicine] bovine serum albumin; Boy Scouts' Association; Boy Scouts of America; British School at Athens; British Speleological Association; Building Societies' Association
BSAA Bachelor of Science in Applied Arts; British School of Archaeology at Athens
BSAC British Sub-Aqua Club
BSAdv Bachelor of Science in Advertising
BSAE Bachelor of Science in Aeronautical Engineering; Bachelor of Science in Agricultural Engineering
BSAeEng Bachelor of Science in Aeronautical Engineering
BSAgE Bachelor of Science in Agricultural Engineering
BSAgr Bachelor of Science in Agriculture
BS&W basic (or bottom) sediment and water
BSAP British Society of Animal Production

BSArch Bachelor of Science in Architecture
BSAS British Ship Adoption Society
BSAVA British Small Animals Veterinary Association
BSB British Satellite Broadcasting (became part of BSkyB); British Standard brass (screw thread)
Bsb. Brisbane
BSBA Bachelor of Science in Business Administration
BSBC British Social Biology Council
BSBI Botanical Society of the British Isles
BSBus Bachelor of Science in Business
BSC Bachelor of Science in Commerce; Bengal Staff Corps; Bibliographical Society of Canada; [computing] binary symmetric channel; [computing] binary synchronous communications; Biomedical Sciences Corporation; British Safety Council; British Shoe Corporation; British Society of Cinematographers; British Standard Channel; British Stationery Council; British Steel Corporation; British Sugar Corporation; British Supply Council; Broadcasting Standards Council; Building Societies Commission
BSc Bachelor of Science
bsc basic
BSCA British Swimming Coaches' Association; [USA] Bureau of Security and Consular Affairs
BSc(A) Bachelor of Science in Agriculture
BSc(Acc) Bachelor of Science in Accounting
BSc(Ag) Bachelor of Science in Agriculture
BScApp Bachelor of Applied Science
BSc(Arch) Bachelor of Science in Architecture
BSCC British Society of Clinical Cytology; British Synchronous Clock Conference
BSc(ChemE) Bachelor of Science in Chemical Engineering
BScD Bachelor of Dental Science
BSc(Dent) Bachelor of Science in Dentistry
BSCE Bachelor of Science in Civil Engineering
BSc(Econ) Bachelor of Science in Economics
BSc(Ed) Bachelor of Science in Education
BSc(Eng) Bachelor of Science in Engineering
BSChE Bachelor of Science in Chemical Engineering
BSc(Hort) Bachelor of Science in Horticulture
BScMed Bachelor of Medical Science
BSc(Nutr) Bachelor of Science in Nutrition
BSCP British Standard Code of Practice
BSCRA British Steel Castings Research Association
BScSoc Bachelor of Social Science
BScTech Bachelor of Technical Science
BSD Bachelor of Science in Design; ballistic system division; [computing] Berkeley Systems Distribution; British Society of Dowsers; British Space Development
BSDes Bachelor of Science in Design
b.s.d.l. boresight datum line
BSE Bachelor of Science in Education; Bachelor of Science in Engineering; [veterinary science] bovine spongiform encephalopathy; [medicine] breast self-examination
b.s.e. base support equipment
BSEc Bachelor of Science in Economics
BSECP Black Sea Economic Cooperation Project
BSEd Bachelor of Science in Education
BSEE Bachelor of Science in Electrical Engineering; Bachelor of Science in Elementary Education
BSEEng Bachelor of Science in Electrical Engineering
BSEIE Bachelor of Science in Electronic Engineering
BSEM Bachelor of Science in Engineering of Mines
BSEng Bachelor of Science in Engineering
BSES Bachelor of Science in Engineering Sciences; British Schools Exploring Society
BSF Bachelor of Science in Forestry; British Salonica Force; British Shipping Federation (Limited); British Slag Federation; British Standard fine (screw thread); British Stone Federation
BSFA British Science Fiction Association; British Steel Founders' Association
b.s.f.c. brake specific fuel consumption
BSFL British Shipping Federation Limited

BSFM Bachelor of Science in Forestry Management
BSFor Bachelor of Science in Forestry
BSFS Bachelor of Science in Foreign Service; British Soviet Friendship Society
BSFT Bachelor of Science in Fuel Technology
BSG British Standard Gauge
b.s.g.d.g. *breveté sans garantie du gouvernement* (French: patented without government guarantee)
BSGE Bachelor of Science in General Engineering
BSH British Society of Hypnotherapists; British Standard Hardness
bsh. bushel
BSHA Bachelor of Science in Hospital Administration
BSHE Bachelor of Science in Home Economics
BSHEc Bachelor of Science in Home Economics
BSHS British Society for the History of Science
BSHyg Bachelor of Science in Hygiene
BSI British Sailors' Institute; British Standards Institution; Building Societies' Institute
BSIA British Security Industry Association
BSIB Boy Scouts International Bureau
BSIC British Ski Instruction Council
BSIE Bachelor of Science in Industrial Engineering
BSIP British Solomon Islands Protectorate
BSIRA British Scientific Instrument Research Association
BSIS Business Sponsorship Incentive Scheme
BSIU British Society for International Understanding
BSJ Bachelor of Science in Journalism
BSJA British Show Jumping Association
bsk. basket
bskt basket
BSkyB British Sky Broadcasting
BSL Bachelor of Sacred Literature; Bachelor of Science in Linguistics; [medicine] bacterial skin lesion; Boatswain Sublieutenant; British Sign Language
Bs/L bills of lading
BSLS Bachelor of Science in Library Science
BSM Bachelor of Sacred Music; Bachelor of Science in Medicine; Battery Sergeant-Major; branch sales manager; British School of Motoring; [USA] bronze star medal
BSMA British Skate Makers' Association
BSME Bachelor of Science in Mechanical Engineering; Bachelor of Science in Mining Engineering
BSMedTech Bachelor of Science in Medical Technology
BSMet Bachelor of Science in Metallurgy
BSMetE Bachelor of Science in Metallurgical Engineering
BSMGP British Society of Master Glass-Painters
BSMT Bachelor of Science in Medical Technology
bsmt basement
BSMV [microbiology] barley stripe mosaic virus
BSN Bachelor of Science in Nursing
BSNE Bachelor of Science in Nuclear Engineering
BSNS Bachelor of Naval Science
BSO base supply officer; Boston Symphony Orchestra; Bournemouth Symphony Orchestra; Business Statistics Office
BSocSc Bachelor of Social Science
BSOT Bachelor of Science in Occupational Therapy
BSP Bachelor of Science in Pharmacy; Bering Sea Patrol; [computing] binary space-partitioning (as in **BSP tree**); Birmingham School of Printing; [printing] bleached sulphite pulp; British Standard pipe (screw thread); Bulgarian Socialist Party (formerly BCP); business systems planning
BSPA Bachelor of Science in Public Administration
BSPE Bachelor of Science in Physical Education
BSPH Bachelor of Science in Public Health
BSPhar Bachelor of Science in Pharmacy
BSPharm Bachelor of Science in Pharmacy
BSPhTh Bachelor of Science in Physical Therapy
BSPT Bachelor of Science in Physical Therapy
BSR Birmingham Sound Reproducers;

[medicine] blood sedimentation rate; Board for Social Responsibility (in Church of England); British School at Rome
BSRA British Ship Research Association; British Society for Research on Ageing; British Sound Recording Association
BSRAE British Society for Research in Agricultural Engineering
BSRC [USA] Biological Serial Record Center
BSRT Bachelor of Science in Radiological Technology
BSS Bachelor of Secretarial Science; Bachelor of Social Science; [medicine] balanced salt solution; basic safety standards; Bibliothèque Saint-Sulpice (Montreal library); [geology] borehole seismic system; British Sailors' Society; British Standard size; British Standards Specification
BSSA Bachelor of Science in Secretarial Administration
BSSc Bachelor of Social Science
BSSE Bachelor of Science in Secondary Education
BSSG [USA] Biomedical Sciences Support Grant
BSSO British Society for the Study of Orthodontics
BSSS Bachelor of Science in Secretarial Studies; Bachelor of Science in Social Science; British Society of Soil Science
BST Bachelor of Sacred Theology; bovine somatotrophin; British Standard Time; British Summer Time; bulk supply tariff
B/St bill of sight
BSTA British Surgical Trades' Association
BSTC British Student Travel Centre
bstd bastard
bstr booster
bstr rkt booster rocket
BSU [engineering] bench scale unit
BSurv Bachelor of Surveying
BSW Bachelor of Social Work; British Standard Whitworth (screw thread)
b.s.w. barrels of salt water
BSWB Boy Scouts World Bureau
BSWE British Scouts in Western Europe
BSWIA British Steel Wire Industries' Association
BT Bachelor of Teaching; Bachelor of Theology; basic trainer; basic training; [psychology] behaviour therapy; [UK postcode] Belfast; [medicine] benign tumour; bishop's transcript; British Telecommunications (plc) (formerly British Telecom); [vehicle registration] Leeds
Bt [currency] baht (used in Thailand); Baronet; [military] brevet
bt beat; benefit; bent; bought
.bt Bhutan (in Internet address)
BTA Billiards Trade Association; [USA] Blood Transfusion Association; British Theatre Association; British Tourist Authority (formerly British Travel Association); British Tuberculosis Association
BTAC [computing] binary tree algebraic computation
BTASA Book Trade Association of South Africa
BTB [medicine] blood–tumour barrier; [medicine] breakthrough bleeding
BTBA British Tenpin Bowling Association
BTBS Book Trade Benevolent Society
BTC [USA] Bankers' Trust Company; [USA] basic training center; British Textile Confederation; British Transport Commission
btca *biblioteca* (Spanish: library)
BTCC Board of Transportation Commissioners of Canada
BTCh Bachelor of Textile Chemistry
BTCP Bachelor of Town and Country Planning
BTCV British Trust for Conservation Volunteers
b.t.d. bomb testing device
BTDB Bermuda Trade Development Board
b.t.d.c. [engineering] before top dead centre
BTDT been there, done that (in Internet chat)
BTE Bachelor of Textile Engineering
bté *breveté* (French: patent)
BTEC Business and Technology Education Council
BTech Bachelor of Technology
BTechEd Bachelor of Technical Education
BTechFood Bachelor of Food Technology
BTEF Book Trade Employers' Federation
BTEMA British Tanning Extract Manufacturers' Association

BTEX benzene, toluene, ethylbenzene and xylene (solvents)
BTF British Trawlers Federation; British Turkey Federation
b.t.f. balance to follow; barrels of total fuel; bomb tail fuse
BTG British Technology Group
BTH British Thomson-Houston Company
BTh Bachelor of Theology
bth bath; berth
bth. bathroom (in property or accommodation advertisement)
BTHMA British Toy and Hobby Manufacturers' Association
BthU British thermal unit
BTI *British Technology Index*
BTIA British Tar Industries' Association
btk buttock
btl. bottle
BTM bromotrifluoromethane (used in firefighting)
btm bottom
BTMA British Typewriter Manufacturers' Association
BTN Brussels Tariff Nomenclature
btn baton; button
BTO big-time operator; British Trust for Ornithology; Brussels Treaty Organization (replaced by WEU)
BTP Bachelor of Town Planning
BTR [physics] bimetric theory of relativity; *British Tax Review*; British Telecommunications Research
BTRA Bombay Textile Industry's Research Association
BTRP Bachelor of Town and Regional Planning
btry [military] battery
BTS Blood Transfusion Service; British Telecommunications Systems
Btss Baronetess
BTTA British Thoracic and Tuberculosis Association
BTU Board of Trade unit; [USA] British thermal unit
Btu British thermal unit
BTUC Bahamas Trade Union Congress
BTW by the way (in Internet chat and e-mail)
btw. between
btwn between
BTX benzene, toluene and xylene (solvents)
bty [military] battery
BU Bakers, Food and Allied Workers Union; Baptist Union (of Great Britain and Ireland); Brown University (Rhode Island); [fishing port] Burntisland; [vehicle registration] Manchester
Bu. Bureau
bu. bureau; bushel
b.u. base unit; [finance] break-up
BuAer [USA] Bureau of Aeronautics
BUAF British United Air Ferries
BUA of E Badminton Umpires' Association of England
BUAV British Union for the Abolition of Vivisection
BUC Bangor University College
buck. buckram
Bucks Buckinghamshire
BUCOP *British Union Catalogue of Periodicals*
Bud. Buddhism; Buddhist
bud. budget
Budd. Buddhism; Buddhist
BuDocks [US navy] Bureau of Yards and Docks
Budpst Budapest
BUF British Union of Fascists
BUIC back-up interceptor control
BUJ Bachelor of Canon and Civil Law (from Latin *Baccalaureus Utriusque Juris*)
bul. bulletin
Bulg. Bulgaria; Bulgarian
bull. bulla (seal on papal bull); bulletin; [medicine] *bulliat* (Latin: let it boil)
buloga business logistics game
BULVA Belfast and Ulster Licensed Vintners' Association
BuMed [US navy] Bureau of Medicine and Surgery
BUN [medicine] blood urea nitrogen
Buna [trademark] butadiene and natrium (synthetic rubber)
BUNAC British Universities North America Club
BUNCH Burroughs, Univac, NCR, Control Data, Honeywell (computer manufacturers)
bung. bungalow (in property advertisement)
BuOrd [US navy] Bureau of Ordnance
BUP British United Press
BUPA British United Provident Association (company providing health insurance)

BuPers [US navy] Bureau of Naval Personnel
BuPubAff [USA] Bureau of Public Affairs
BUR [international vehicle registration] Myanmar (from former name Burma)
Bur. Burma; Burmese
bur. bureau; buried
BuRec [USA] Bureau of Reclamation
burg. burgess; burgomaster
burl. burlesque
Burm. Burma; Burmese
BURMA be undressed ready, my angel (on envelope of love letter)
burp [informal] bankrupt unemployed rejected person
Burs. Bursar
bus [short form] omnibus
bus. bushel; business
BuS&A [US navy] Bureau of Supply and Accounts
BUSF British Universities' Sports Federation
bush. bushel
BuShips [US navy] Bureau of Ships
bus. mgr business manager
BUSWE British Union of Social Work Employees
but. butter; button
buy. buyer; buying
BV *Beata Virgo* (Latin: Blessed Virgin); *Beatitudo Vestra* (Latin: Your Holiness); *bene vale* (Latin: farewell); [commerce] *Besloten Vennootschap* (Dutch: limited company, Ltd); Bible Version (of Psalms); Blessed Virgin; [medicine] blood vessel; [medicine] blood volume; [shipping] *Bureau Veritas* (French shipping classification society); [vehicle registration] Preston
b.v. balanced voltage; [accounting] book value
BVA British Veterinary Association
BVD [veterinary science] bovine virus diarrhoea
BVetMed Bachelor of Veterinary Medicine
BVetSc Bachelor of Veterinary Science
BVI [international vehicle registration] British Virgin Islands
BVJ *British Veterinary Journal*
BVK *Bundesverdienstkreuz* (German: Federal Cross of Merit)
BVM Bachelor of Veterinary Medicine; *Beata Virgo Maria* (Latin: Blessed Virgin Mary); Blessed Virgin Mary
BVMA British Valve Manufacturers' Association
BVMS Bachelor of Veterinary Medicine and Surgery
BVO *Bundesverdienstorden* (German: Federal Order of Merit)
BVP British Visitors' Passport; British Volunteer Programme
BVRLA British Vehicle Rental and Leasing Association Limited
BVS Bachelor of Veterinary Surgery
BVSc Bachelor of Veterinary Science
BVSc&AH Bachelor of Veterinary Science and Animal Husbandry
bvt brevet
BW bacteriological warfare; [fishing port] Barrow; Bath and Wells (bishop's see); biological warfare; black and white; Black Watch; Board of Works; body water; [medicine] body weight; bonded warehouse; British Waterways; business week; [vehicle registration] Oxford
B/W black and white
b/w black and white
.bw Botswana (in Internet address)
b.w. *bitte wenden* (German: please turn over, PTO); bridleway(s)
BWA backward wave amplifier; Baptist World Alliance; British Waterworks Association; British West Africa
B-way [USA] Broadway
BWB British Waterways Board
BWC [USA] Board of War Communications; British War Cabinet
BWCC British Weed Control Conference
BWD [veterinary science] bacillary white diarrhoea
bwd backward
BWF British Whiting Federation; British Wool Federation
BWG Birmingham Wire Gauge
BWI British West Indies
BWIA British West Indian Airways
BWIR British West India Regiment
BWISA British West Indies Sugar Association
bwk brickwork; bulwark
BWM British War Medal
BWMA British Woodwork Manufacturers' Association
BWMB British Wool Marketing Board

BWO backward wave oscillator
BWP basic war plan
BWPA backward wave power amplifier; British Waste Paper Association; British Word Preserving Association
bwpd barrels of water per day
bwph barrels of water per hour
BWPUC British Wastepaper Utilization Council
BWR [nuclear technology] boiling-water reactor
BWS [medicine] battered wife (or woman) syndrome; British Watercolour Society
BWSF British Water Ski Federation
BWTA British Women's Temperance Association
BWU Barbados Workers' Union
BWV [music] *Bach Werke-Verzeichnis* (German: Catalogue of (J. S.) Bach's Works)
b.w.v. back water valve
BWVA British War Veterans of America
BWWA British Waterworks Association
BX [US air force] Base Exchange; British Xylonite; [vehicle registration] Haverfordwest
bx box
BY [international vehicle registration] Belarus (from alternative name Byelorussia); [vehicle registration] northwest London
By Barony
.by Belarus (in Internet address)
b.y. billion years
BYDV [microbiology] barley yellow dwarf virus
BYO bring your own
Byo Bulawayo
BYOB bring your own beer; bring your own booze; bring your own bottle
BYOG bring your own girl
byr billion years
BYT [informal] bright young things
BYU [USA] Brigham Young University
Byz. Byzantine; Byzantium
BZ [international vehicle registration] Belize; B'nai Zion; Brazil; British Zone; [vehicle registration] Down
Bz [chemistry] benzene (used in formulae)
.bz Belize (in Internet address)
BZH Brittany (from Breton *Breizh*)
bzw. *beziehungsweise* (German: respectively)

C

C *Caballeros* (Spanish: gentlemen); Caesar; *caldo* (Italian: hot); *caliente* (Spanish: hot); *calle* (Spanish: street); [geology] Cambrian; [civil aircraft marking] Canada; [informal] cancer; candle; canon; canto; Cape; Captain; [chemical element] carbon; [geology] Carboniferous; Cardinal; [USA] cargo transport (aircraft); [chess] castle; catechism; Catholic; Celsius; Celtic; centigrade; [theatre] centre (of stage); century; Chancellor; Chancery; *chaud* (French: hot); chief; Christ; Christian; circuit; *ciudad* (Spanish: town); [card games] clubs; [slang] cocaine; cold (water); Commander; Command Paper (1870–99) (in parliamentary procedure); commended; Commodore; Companion; [immunology] complement; Confessor; [pharmacology] *congius* (Latin: gallon); Congregation; Congregational; Congress; Conservative; contract; copyright; [fishing port] Cork; [botany] corolla (in floral formula); Corps; coulomb; council; Count; [music] countertenor; county; coupon; cross; [paper size] crown; cruiser; [international vehicle registration] Cuba; curacy; curate; current (electricity); [Roman numeral] hundred; [music] note of scale
C [physics] capacitance; [physics] charm quantum number; [physics] compliance; [physics] heat capacity; [chemistry] molecular concentration
© copyright
c centi- (indicates one-hundredth, as in **cl** = centilitre); [physics] charm (quark flavour); [chemistry] concentration; [mathematics] constant; cubic; [Roman numeral] hundred

c [physics] specific heat capacity; [physics] speed of light in vacuum

c. canine (tooth); capacity; *caput* (Latin: chapter); carat; carbon (paper); carton; case; [baseball] catcher; cathode; cattle; [cricket] caught (by); [currency] cent (hundredth of dollar etc.); [currency] centavo (hundredth of peso etc.); [currency] centime (hundredth of franc etc.); central; centre; century; chairman; chairwoman; chapter; charge; chest; child; church; [medicine] *cibus* (Latin: meal); *circiter* (Latin: approximately); *circum* (Latin: around); city; class; cloudy; cold; collected; college; colt; compound; conductor; constable; consul; *contra* (Latin: against); contralto; contrast; convection; copy; copyright; court; cousin; crowned; [medicine] *cum* (Latin: with) (in prescriptions); cup; currency; current (electricity); cycle(s)

c. *circa* (Latin: about) (in dates)

c/- [Australia, New Zealand] care of (in postal addresses); case; coupon; currency

C1 supervisory or clerical (occupational group)

C2 [civil aircraft marking] Nauru; skilled manual (occupational group)

C3 [civil aircraft marking] Andorra

C³I [military] command, control, communications and intelligence

C4 Channel Four (television company); [paper size] crown quarto (7.5 × 10 in)

C5 Channel Five (television company); [civil aircraft marking] Gambia

C6 [civil aircraft marking] Bahamas

C8 [paper size] crown octavo (5 × 7.5 in)

C9 [civil aircraft marking] Mozambique

C16 [paper size] crown 16mo (3.75 × 5 in)

C32 [paper size] crown 32mo (2.5 × 3.75 in)

3C [civil aircraft marking] Equatorial Guinea

CA [US postcode] California; Canadian army; capital account; [taxation] capital allowances; cardiac arrest; [fishing port] Cardigan; [UK postcode] Carlisle; Caterers' Association; Catholic Association; [chemistry] cellulose acetate; Central America; certificate of airworthiness; chargé d'affaires; [Scotland] Chartered Accountant; *Chemical Abstracts*; [vehicle registration] Chester; chief accountant; [genetics] chromosomal aberration; chronological age; Church Army; Church Assembly; citric acid; city architect; city attorney; civil affairs; civil aviation; Classical Association; clean air; coast artillery; College of Arms; commercial agent; community association; Companies Act; [USA] Confederate Army; constituent assembly; consular agent; Consumers' Association; [medicine] contrast angiography; Contributions Agency; controlled atmosphere; controller of accounts; cooperative agreement; *Corps d'armée* (French: Army Corps); county alderman; county architect; Court of Appeal; Croquet Association; Crown Agent; Cruising Association; [commerce] current assets

C/A capital account; credit account; current account

Ca [chemical element] calcium; [commerce] *compagnia* (Italian: company, Co.); [commerce] *companhia* (Portuguese: company, Co.); [commerce] *compañia* (Spanish: company, Co.)

Ca. California; Canada; Canadian

ca centiare (unit of area)

c/a cash account

ca. [medicine] carcinoma; [law] case(s)

ca. *circa* (Latin: about) (in dates)

.ca Canada (in Internet address)

c.a. [commerce] capital asset; [engineering] close annealed; [music] *coll'arco* (Italian: with the bow); [physics] *corriente alterna* (Spanish: alternating current); [physics] *courant alternatif* (French: alternating current)

CAA Campaign for the Abolition of Angling; Canadian Authors' Association; [commerce] Capital Allowances Act; Central African Airways Corporation; [USA] Civil Aeronautics Administration; [USA] Civil Aeronautics Administrator; Civil Aviation Authority; Clean Air Act; Commonwealth Association of Architects; [USA] Community Action Agency; Concert Artists' Association; [medicine] coronary artery aneurysm; Cost Accountants' Association; County Agricultural Adviser

CAAA Canadian Association of Advertising Agencies

CAADRP civil aircraft airworthiness data recording program
CAAE Canadian Association of Adult Education
CAAIS computer-aided (or -assisted) action information system(s)
CAAR compressed-air accumulator rocket
CAARC Commonwealth Advisory Aeronautical Research Council
CAAT Campaign Against Arms Trade; [Canada] College of Applied Arts and Technology; [accounting] computer-aided (or -assisted) audit technique
CAAtt Civil Air Attaché
CAAV Central Association of Agricultural Valuers
CAB Canadian Association of Broadcasters; [chemistry] cellulose acetate butyrate; Citizens' Advice Bureau; [USA] Civil Aeronautics Board; Commonwealth Agricultural Bureaux (former name of CABI)
cab. cabalistic; cabin; cabinet; cable
CABAS City and Borough Architects' Society
CABEI Central American Bank for Economic Integration
CABG [medicine] coronary artery bypass graft
CABI CAB International (formerly Commonwealth Agricultural Bureaux)
CABM Commonwealth of Australia Bureau of Meteorology
CABMA Canadian Association of British Manufacturers and Agencies
CABS [medicine] coronary artery bypass surgery
cabtmkr cabinetmaker
CAC Campaign Against Censorship; Canadian Armoured Corps; Central Advisory Committee; Central Arbitration Committee; [USA] Climate Analysis Center; Colonial Advisory Council; *Compagnie des agents de change* (French: stockbrokers' association); [USA] Consumer Advisory Council; County Agricultural Committee
CACA Canadian Agricultural Chemicals Association
CAC&W continental aircraft control and warning
CACC Civil Aviation Communications Centre; Council for the Accreditation of Correspondence Colleges (former name of ODLQC)
CACD computer-aided (or -assisted) circuit design
CACDS Centre for Advanced Computing and Decision Support
CACE Central Advisory Council for Education
CACGP Commission on Atmospheric Chemistry and Global Pollution
CACLB Churches' Advisory Committee on Local Broadcasting
CACM Central Advisory Council for the Ministry; Central American Common Market
CACSD computer-aided (or -assisted) control system design
CACUL Canadian Association of College and University Libraries
CAD cash against documents; [USA] civil air defense; *comité d'aide au développement* (French: development assistance committee); compact audio disc; computer-aided (or -assisted) design; computer-aided (or -assisted) drawing; contract award date; [medicine] coronary artery disease; Crown Agent's Department
Cád. Cádiz
cad. *cadauno* (Italian: each); [medicine] cadaver; [music] cadenza; cadet
c.a.d. cash against disbursements; cash against documents
c-à-d *c'est-à-dire* (French: that is to say)
cadav. [medicine] cadaver
CADC central air-data computer; colour analysis display computer
CADCAM computer-aided (or -assisted) design and manufacture
CADD computer-aided (or -assisted) drafting and design
CADF Commutated Antenna Direction Finder
CADIN [USA] continental air defense integration north
CADIS computer-aided (or -assisted) design information system
CADMAT computer-aided (or -assisted) design, manufacture and testing
CADO [USA] central air documents office
CADPO communications and data-processing operation

CADPOS communications and data-processing operations system
CADS computer-aided (or -assisted) design system
CAE Canadian Aviation Electronics; Chartered Automobile Engineer; *cóbrese al entregar* (Spanish: cash on delivery, COD); [Australia] College of Advanced Education; computer-aided (or -assisted) education; computer-aided (or -assisted) engineering
Cae [astronomy] Caelum
CAEC Central American Economic Community; County Agricultural Executive Committee
CAEM *Conseil d'assistance économique mutuelle* (French: Council for Mutual Economic Aid, COMECON)
CAER Conservative Action for Electoral Reform
Caern. Caernarvon(shire)
Caerns Caernarvonshire
CAES compressed-air energy storage
Caes. Caesar
CAEU Council of Arab Economic Unity
CAF [medicine] cardiac assessment factor; Central African Federation; charities aid foundation; charities aid fund; clerical, administrative and fiscal; [commerce] cost and freight; [commerce] *coût, assurance, fret* (French: cost, insurance, freight, CIF)
caf. cafeteria
c.a.f. [commerce] cost and freight; [commerce] *coût, assurance, fret* (French: cost, insurance, freight, c.i.f.)
CAFE [USA] Corporate Average Fuel Economy (fuel consumption standard for cars)
CAFEA-ICC Commission on Asian and Far Eastern Affairs of the International Chamber of Commerce
CAFIC Combined Allied Forces Information Centre
c.a.f.m. commercial air freight movement
Cafod Catholic Fund for Overseas Development
CAFR [accounting] comprehensive annual financial report
CAFS [computing] content-addressable file system
CAFU civil aviation flying unit
CAG Canadian Association of Geographers; [US navy] carrier air group; [USA] civil air guard; commercial arbitration group; Commercial Artists' Guild; Concert Artists' Guild
CAGI [USA] Compressed Air and Gas Institute
CAGR [nuclear technology] civil advanced gas-cooled reactor; [nuclear technology] commercial advanced gas-cooled reactor
CAGS [USA] Certificate of Advanced Graduate Study
CAH [medicine] chronic active hepatitis; [medicine] congenital adrenal hyperplasia; [chemistry] cyanacetic hydrazide
CAI Canadian Aeronautical Institute; *Club Alpino Italiano* (Italian: Italian Alpine Club); colour alteration indices; computer-aided (or -assisted) instruction; Confederation of Aerial Industries Limited; [chemical engineering] controlled air incineration (or incinerator); [forestry] current annual increment
Cai. Caithness
CAIRC [USA] Caribbean Air Command
CAISM Central Association of Irish Schoolmistresses
CAISSE computer-aided (or -assisted) information system on solar energy
Caith. Caithness
CAL computer-aided (or -assisted) learning; Continental Airlines; [computing] conversational algebraic language; [USA] Cornell (University) Aeronautical Laboratory
Cal kilocalorie (from alternative name Calorie)
Cal. Calcutta; Caledonia; Calends; California
cal calorie
cal. [music] *calando* (Italian: lowering, falling away); calendar; calibre
CALA Civil Aviation Licensing Act
CALANS Caribbean and Latin American News Service
Calc. Calcutta
Calç. *Calçada* (Portuguese: street)
calc. calculate; calculated; calculation; calculator; calculus
cald calculated
CALE Canadian Army Liaison Executive
Calg. Calgary
calg calculating
calibr. calibrate; calibration

Calif. California
Cal. Mac. Caledonian MacBrayne (Scottish ferry company)
caln calculation
CALPA Canadian Air Line Pilots' Association
Caltech California Institute of Technology
Caltex California Texas Petroleum Corporation
Calv. (John) Calvin (French theologian); Calvinism; Calvinistic
Calz. *Calzada* (Spanish: boulevard)
CAM [international vehicle registration] Cameroon; [computing] cellular automata machine; commercial air movement; Commonwealth Association of Museums; communication, advertising and marketing (as in **CAM Foundation**); computer-aided (or -assisted) manufacture; [computing] content-addressable memory; continuous air monitor
Cam [astronomy] Camelopardalis
Cam. Cambodia; Cambodian; Cambrian; Cambridge; Cameroon
cam. camber; camouflage
CAMA Civil Aerospace Medical Association
CAMAL continuous airborne missile-launched and low-level system
Camb. Cambrian; Cambridge(shire)
Cambs Cambridgeshire
CAMC Canadian Army Medical Corps
CAMD [chemistry] computer-aided (or -assisted) molecular design
CAMDA Car and Motorcycle Drivers' Association
CAMDS chemical agent munitions disposal system
CAMM computer-aided (or -assisted) maintenance management
CAMRA Campaign for Real Ale
CAMRIC Campaign for Real Ice Cream
CAMS Certificate of Advanced Musical Study; [engineering] computer-aided (or -assisted) manipulation system
CaMV [microbiology] cauliflower mosaic virus
CAMW Central Association for Mental Welfare
CAN Committee on Aircraft Noise; customs-assigned number
Can. Canada; Canadian; Canal; Canberra; Canon; Canonry; *Cantoris* (Latin: of the precentor) (side of church choir)
can. canal; cancel; cannon; canon; canto; canton
CANA Caribbean News Agency; Clergy Against Nuclear Arms
Canad. Canada; Canadian
Canc. *Cancellarius* (Latin: Chancellor)
canc. cancellation; cancelled
CANCIRCO Cancer International Research Cooperative
CAND Campaign Against Nuclear Dumping
cand. candidate
C&A Clemens and Auguste (Breeninkmeyer) (Dutch founders of chain store)
c&b [cricket] caught and bowled (by)
c&c carpets and curtains (in property advertisement); command and control
c&d collection and delivery
C&E Customs and Excise
c&e consultation and education
c&f cost and freight
C&G Cheltenham and Gloucester (Building Society); City and Guilds
C&I commerce and industry; commercial and industrial
c&i cost and insurance
C&J clean and jerk (in weightlifting)
c&m care and maintenance
c&p carriage and packing; [bookbinding] collated and perfect
c&r convalescence and rehabilitation
CANDU [nuclear technology] Canadian Deuterium Uranium Reactor
C&W country and western (music)
C&W Ck caution and warning (system) check
CANEL [USA] Connecticut Advanced Nuclear Engineering Laboratory
Can. Fr. Canadian French
Can. I Canary Islands
CANO chief area nursing officer
Can. Pac. Canadian Pacific
CANSG Civil Aviation Navigational Services Group
Cant. Canterbury; [Bible] Canticles; Cantonese
cant. cantilever
Cantab. *Cantabrigiensis* (Latin: of Cambridge (University))
canton. [military] cantonment

CANTRAN cancel in transmission
Cantuar. *Cantuariensis* (Latin: (Archbishop) of Canterbury)
CANUS [military] Canada–United States
canv. canvas
CAO chief accountant officer; chief administrative officer; county advisory officer; county agricultural officer; Crimean Astrophysical Laboratory
CAORB Civil Aviation Operational Research Branch
CAORG Canadian Army Operational Research Group
CAOT Canadian Association of Occupational Therapy
CAP Canadian Association of Physicists; [genetics] catabolite activator protein; Church Action on Poverty; [USA] civil air patrol; Code of Advertising Practice; College of American Pathologists; [USA] combat air patrol; Common Agricultural Policy (in EU); [USA] Community Action Program; computer-aided (or -assisted) planning; computer-aided (or -assisted) production
Cap [astronomy] Capricornus
Cap. Captain
cap. capacity; [medicine] *capiat* (Latin: let him/her take) (in prescriptions); capital; capitalize; capital letter; *capitulum* (Latin: chapter, heading); *caput* (Latin: chapter, heading); foolscap
c.a.p. *codice di avviamento postale* (Italian: postcode number)
CAPA Canadian Association of Purchasing Agents
CAPAC Composers', Authors' and Publishers' Association of Canada
CAPCOM capsule communicator (in NASA)
CAPD [medicine] continuous ambulatory peritoneal dialysis
CAPE Clifton Assessment Procedures for the Elderly
CAPM [accounting] capital asset pricing model; computer-aided (or -assisted) production management
Capn Captain
CAPO Canadian Army Post Office; Chief Administrative Pharmaceutical Officer
CAPP computer-aided (or -assisted) process planning
Capric. Capricorn
CAPS Captive Animals' Protection Society; [USA] Center for Analysis of Particle Scattering
caps. capital letters; capsule
Capt. Captain
capt. caption
CAR Canadian Association of Radiologists; Central African Republic; Civil Air Regulations; [aeronautics] cloudtop altitude radiometer; [nuclear technology] collisionally activated reaction; [Australia] *Commonwealth Arbitration Reports*; [finance] compound annual return; compounded annual rate (of interest); computer-aided (or -assisted) retrieval; [computing] contents of address register
Car [astronomy] Carina
Car. Carlow; *Carolus* (Latin: Charles)
car. carat
CARA combat air rescue aircraft
CARAC Civil Aviation Radio Advisory Committee
CARAF Christians Against Racism and Fascism
CARB California Air Resources Board
carb [short form] carburettor
carb. carbon; [chemistry] carbonate
CARD Campaign Against Racial Discrimination; compact automatic retrieval device; computer-augmented road design
Card. Cardinal
card. cardinal
CARDE Canadian Armament Research and Development Establishment
Cards Cardiganshire (former name of Ceredigion)
CARE Christian Action for Research and Education; [psychology] communicated authenticity, regard, empathy; computer-aided (or -assisted) risk evaluation; continuous aircraft reliability evaluation; Cooperative for American Relief Everywhere; Cottage and Rural Enterprises
CAREC Caribbean Epidemiology Centre
Carib. Caribbean
CARIBANK Caribbean Investment Bank
CARICAD Caribbean Centre for Administration Development
CARICOM Caribbean Community and Common Market
CARIFTA Caribbean Free Trade Area

Carliol. *Carlioliensis* (Latin: (Bishop) of Carlisle)
Carms Carmarthenshire
carn. carnival
Carns Caernarvonshire
Carp. Carpathian (Mountains); Carpentaria
carp. carpenter; carpentry
carr. fwd [commerce] carriage forward
CARS Canadian Arthritis and Rheumatism Society
CART collision avoidance radar trainer
cart. cartage; carton
Carth. Carthage
cartog. cartographer; cartographic; cartography
CAS Cambridge Antiquarian Society; Carib Advertising Services (in Guyana); Centre for Administrative Studies; CERN Accelerator School; [USA] Certificate of Advanced Studies; Chemical Abstracts Service; Chief of Air Staff; Children's Aid Society; close air support; [aeronautics] collision avoidance system; *Connecticutensis Academiae Socius* (Latin: Fellow of the Connecticut Academy of Arts and Sciences); controlled airspace; [medicine] coronary arterial stenosis
Cas [astronomy] Cassiopeia
cas. castle; casual; casualty
CASA [USA] Coal Advisory Service Association; Contemporary Art Society of Australia
CA(SA) Chartered Accountant (South Africa)
ca. sa. [law] *capias ad satisfaciendum* (Latin: writ of execution)
CASAC [USA] Clean Air Scientific Advisory Committee
CASE Campaign for State Education; Centre for Advanced Studies in Environment; [USA] Committee on Academic Science and Engineering; computer-aided (or -assisted) software engineering; computer-aided (or -assisted) system engineering; Confederation for the Advancement of State Education; Cooperative Awards in Science and Engineering
casevac [military] casualty evacuation
cash. cashier
CASI Canadian Aeronautics and Space Institute
CASIG Careers Advisory Service in Industry for Girls
CASLE Commonwealth Association of Surveying and Land Economy
Caspar [physics] Cambridge analog simulator for predicting atomic reactions
cass. cassette
CAST Consolidated African Selection Trust
Cast. Castile; Castilian
CASTE Civil Aviation Signals Training Establishment
CASU Cooperative Association of Suez Canal Users
CASW [USA] Council for the Advancement of Scientific Writing
CAT Centre for Alternative Technology; [psychology] Children's Apperception Test; Civil Air Transport; cleanup and treatment; [aeronautics] clear-air turbulence; College of Advanced Technology; compressed-air tunnel; [medicine] compute(rize)d axial tomography (as in **CAT scanner**); computer-aided (or -assisted) teaching; computer-aided (or -assisted) testing; [medicine] computer-aided (or -assisted) tomography; computer-aided (or -assisted) trading; computer-aided (or -assisted) training; computer-aided (or -assisted) translation; computer-aided (or -assisted) typesetting; low charges, easy access, fair terms (as in **CAT standard** for ISAs)
Cat. Catalan; Catholic; Catullus (Roman poet)
cat [short form] catalytic converter; [short form] catamaran
cat. catalogue; catamaran; [medicine] cataplasm (poultice); catapult; catechism; category; cattle
CATA Commonwealth Association of Tax Administration
catachr. catachresis; catachrestic
Catal. Catalan; Catalonian
CATC Commonwealth Air Transport Commission
CATCC Canadian Association of Textile Colorists and Chemists
CATE Committee for the Accreditation of Teacher Education
Cath. Cathedral; Catholic
cath. cathedral; cathode

CATI computer-aided (or -assisted) telephone interviewing
CATOR Combined Air Transport Operations Room
CATRA Cutlery and Allied Trades Research Association
CATS [education] credit accumulation transfer scheme
CATU Ceramic and Allied Trade Union
CATV community antenna television (= cable television)
caus. causation; causative
CAV constant air-volume (control system); [computing] constant angular velocity; [law] *curia advisari vult* (Latin: the court wishes to consider it) (used in reports when judgment follows hearing); [medicine] cyclophosphamide, adriamycin and vincristine (used in chemotherapy)
Cav. *Cavaliere* (Italian: Knight); Cavalry; Cavan
cav. cavalier; cavalry; [law] caveat
CAVD Completion, Arithmetic Problems, Vocabulary, Following Directions (intelligence test)
CAVI *Centre audio-visuel international* (French: International Audio-Visual Centre)
Caviar Cinema and Video Industry Audience Research
CAWU Clerical and Administrative Workers' Union (became part of GMB)
Cay. Cayenne; Cayman Islands
CAYA Catholic Association of Young Adults
CB [civil aircraft marking] Bolivia; [UK postcode] Cambridge; Cape Breton (Canada); carbon black; carte blanche; cash book; cavalry brigade; [USA] Census Bureau; [theatre] centre back (of stage); centre of buoyancy; chemical and biological (weapons or warfare); Chief Baron; chlorobromomethane (used in firefighting); Citizens' Band (radio); Coal Board; [law] Common Bench; Companion of the Order of the Bath; [physics] conduction band; confidential book (in Royal Navy); confined to barracks; construction battalion; *contrabasso* (Italian: double bass); cost-benefit; county borough; [chemistry] covalent bonding; currency bond; [vehicle registration] Manchester
Cb [chemical element] columbium (former name of niobium)
Cb [meteorology] cumulonimbus
c/b [cricket] caught and bowled; cost-benefit
c.b. cash book; cast brass; centre of buoyancy; circuit breaker; compass bearing; continuous breakdown
CBA [physics] colliding-beam accelerator; Commercial Bank of Australia; Commonwealth Broadcasting Association; [USA] Community Broadcasters' Association; cost-benefit analysis; Council for British Archaeology
CBAA Canadian Business Aircraft Association
CB&PGNCS circuit breaker and primary guidance navigation control system
CBAT [USA] College Board Achievement Test
CBB Campaign for Better Broadcasting
CBBC Children's BBC
CBC Canadian Broadcasting Corporation; Caribbean Broadcasting Company; [USA] Children's Book Council; [Australia] Christian Brothers' College; [computing] cipher block chaining; [medicine] complete blood count; county borough council
CBCRL Cape Breton Coal Research Laboratory
CBCS [Australia] Commonwealth Bureau of Census and Statistics
CBD cash before delivery; central business district; [anatomy] common bile duct
c.b.d. cash before delivery
CBDC Cape Breton Development Corporation
CBE chemical, biological and environmental (weapons or warfare); Commander of the Order of the British Empire; Council for Basic Education
CBEL *Cambridge Bibliography of English Literature*
CBEVE Central Bureau for Educational Visits and Exchanges
CBF Central Board of Finance; [medicine] cerebral blood flow
CBI Cape Breton Island; computer-based information; computer-based instruction; Confederation of British Industry; [USA] *Cumulative Book Index*
c.b.i. complete background investigation

CBIM Companion of the British Institute of Management
CBiol Chartered Biologist
CBIS computer-based information system
CBIV computer-based interactive videodisc
CBJO Coordinating Board of Jewish Organizations
cbk chequebook
CBL commercial bill of lading; computer-based learning; [meteorology] convective boundary layer
cbl. cable
CBM Californian Business Machines; confidence building measure; conveyor belt monitor(ing)
CBMIS computer-based management information system
CBMM Council of Building Materials Manufacturers
CBMPE Council of British Manufacturers of Petroleum Equipment
CBMS [USA] Conference Board of Mathematical Sciences
CBNM [USA] Central Bureau for Nuclear Measurements
CBNS Commander British Navy Staff
CBO Conference of Baltic Oceanographers; [USA] Congressional Budget Office; Counter-Battery Officer
Cbo Colombo (Sri Lanka)
CBOE Chicago Board of Options Exchange
C-bomb cobalt bomb
CBOT Chicago Board of Trade
CBPC Canadian Book Publishers' Council
CBQ civilian bachelor quarters
CBR [USA] Center for Brain Research; chemical, bacteriological and radiation (weapons or warfare); [aeronautics] cloud base recorder; [immunology] complement-binding reaction; [medicine] complete bed rest; [computing] constant bit rate; [astronomy] cosmic background radiation; crude birth rate
CBRI [India] Central Building Research Institute
CBS Canadian Biochemical Society; *Centraal Bureau voor de Statistiek* (Dutch: Central Statistical Bureau); Church Building Society; [medicine] citrate-buffered saline; [computing] close binary system; [USA] Columbia Broadcasting System; [medicine] computerized bone scanning; [Roman Catholic Church] Confraternity of the Blessed Sacrament
CBSA Clay Bird Shooting Association
CBSI Chartered Building Societies Institute
CBSM conveyor-belt service machine
CBSO City of Birmingham Symphony Orchestra
CBT Chicago Board of Trade; computer-based teaching; computer-based training
CBU Clearing Banks Union; [commerce] completely built-up (goods for immediate use)
c.b.u. cluster(ed) bomb unit; [commerce] completely built-up (goods for immediate use)
CBV [medicine] cerebral blood volume
CBW chemical and biological warfare
CBX [telecommunications] company branch exchange
CBZ coastal boundary zone
CC [vehicle registration] Bangor; Cape Colony; Caribbean Commission; central committee; Chamber of Commerce; Charity Commission; chess club; chief clerk; [civil aircraft marking] Chile; circuit court; city council; city councillor; [insurance] civil commotion; civil court; [physics] close coupling; closed circuit (transmission); collision course; colour centre; [photography] colour conversion; [photography] colour correction; community council; [genetics] compact chromosome; Companion of the Order of Canada; company commander; [electronics] compensating current; computer code; concave; [military] confined to camp; consular clerk; [commerce] continuation clause; control computer; [medicine] corpus callosum; [medicine] corpus cardiacum; [physics] correction coil; [physics] *corriente continua* (Spanish: direct current); Countryside Commission; county clerk; county commissioner; county council; county councillor; county court; [electronics] coupled channel; credit card; cricket club; croquet club; Crown Clerk; cruise control (in car advertisement); cruising club; Curate in Charge; cushion craft; cycling club
C/C cruise control (in car advertisement)

Cc [meteorology] cirrocumulus
cc carbon copy (or copies); cruise control (in car advertisement); cubic centimetre
c/c *compte courant* (French: current account); *conto corrente* (Italian: current account)
cc. centuries; chapters
c.c. carbon copy (or copies); cash credit; change course; chronometer correction; close control; colour code; *compte courant* (French: current account); *conto corrente* (Italian: current account); contra credit; [physics] *courant continu* (French: direct current); cubic centimetre
CCA Canadian Construction Association; [US navy] carrier-controlled approach; Chief Clerk of the Admiralty; [USA] Circuit Court of Appeals; [medicine] common carotid artery; Commonwealth Correspondents' Association; [USA] Consumers' Cooperative Association; continental control area; [USA] Council for Colored Affairs; County Councils' Association; [USA] County Court of Appeals; current-cost accounting
CCAB Canadian Circulations Audit Board; Consultative Committee of Accountancy Bodies
CCAFS [USA] Cape Canaveral Air Force Station
CCAHC Central Council for Agricultural and Horticultural Cooperation
CCAM Canadian Congress of Applied Mechanics
CCAMLR Commission for the Conservation of Antarctic Marine Living Resources
CCAT Central Council for the Amateur Theatre
CCB [South Africa] Civil Cooperation Bureau
c.c.b. cubic capacity of bunkers
CCBI Council of Churches for Great Britain and Ireland
CCBN Central Council for British Naturism
CCBW Committee on Chemical and Biological Warfare
CCC Camping and Caravanning Club (of Great Britain and Ireland); Canadian Chamber of Commerce; Central Control Commission; Central Criminal Court; [USA] Chemical Control Corporation; [USA] Civilian Conservation Corps; Club Cricket Conference; Commodity Credit Corporation; *Conseil de coopération culturelle* (French: European Council for Cultural Cooperation); Council for the Care of Churches; county cricket club; cross-country club; Customs Cooperation Council
ccc [commerce] *cwmni cyfyngedig cyhoeddus* (Welsh: public limited company, plc)
CCCA Cocoa, Chocolate and Confectionery Alliance; Corps Commander, Coast Artillery
CCCBR Central Council of Church Bell Ringers
CCCC Charity Christmas Card Council
CCCI [military] command, control, communications and intelligence
CCCM Central Committee for Community Medicine
CCCO Committee on Climatic Changes and the Ocean
CCCP *Soyuz Sovietskikh Sotsialisticheskikh Respublik* (Russian: Union of Soviet Socialist Republics, USSR) (transcription of Cyrillic characters, transliterated as SSSR)
CCCR [medicine] closed-chest cardiac resuscitation; Coordinating Committee for Cancer Research
CCCS Commonwealth and Continental Church Society
CCD Central Council for the Disabled; [electronics] charge-coupled device; *Conseil de coopération douanière* (French: Customs Cooperation Council)
CCDA [USA] Commercial Chemical Development Association
CCE [chemistry] carbon-chloroform extract; Chartered Civil Engineer; compound-cycle engine; *Conseil des communes d'Europe* (French: Council of European Municipalities); [USA] Council of Construction Employers; [accounting] current cash equivalent; [electronics] current-carrying element
c.c.e.i. composite cost-effectiveness index
CCETSW Central Council for Education and Training in Social Work
CCETT *Centre commun d'études de télédiffusion et télécommunications* (French:

Television and Telecommunications Research Centre)
CCF central computing facility; central control function; Combined Cadet Force; common-cause failure; Common Cold Foundation; concentrated complete fertilizer; [medicine] congestive cardiac failure; [Canada] Cooperative Commonwealth Federation; [statistics] cross-correlation function
CCFA Combined Cadet Force Association
CCFD [statistics] complementary cumulative frequency distribution
CCFL [electronics] counter-current flow limit
CCFM Combined Cadet Forces Medal
CCFP Certificate of the College of Family Physicians
CCG Control Commission for Germany
CCGB Cycling Council of Great Britain
c.c.h. commercial clearing house; cubic capacity of holds
CCHE Central Council for Health Education
CChem Chartered Chemist
CCHF Children's Country Holidays Fund
CCHMS Central Committee for Hospital Medical Services
CCI Calculated Cetane Index; *Chambre de commerce internationale* (French: International Chamber of Commerce)
CCIA Commission of the Churches on International Affairs; [USA] Consumer Credit Insurance Association
CCIC *Comité consultatif international du coton* (French: International Cotton Advisory Committee)
CCIE [computing] Cisco Certified Internetworking Expert
CCIR Catholic Council for International Relations; *Comité consultatif international des radiocommunications* (French: International Radio Consultative Committee)
CCIS command control information system
CCITT *Comité consultatif international télégraphique et téléphonique* (French: International Telegraph and Telephone Consultative Committee)
CCITU Coordinating Committee of Independent Trade Unions
CCIVS Coordinating Committee for International Voluntary Service
CCJ circuit court judge; Council of Christians and Jews; county court judge; [medicine] cranio-cervical junction
CCJO Consultative Council of Jewish Organizations
CCK [biochemistry] cholecystokinin
CCL Canadian Congress of Labour; [USA] commodity control list
CCLGF Consultative Committee on Local Government Finance
CCLRC Council for the Central Laboratory of the Research Councils
CCM [medicine] caffeine clearance measurement; [physics] constant current modulation; [physics] controlled carrier modulation; Cornish Chamber of Mines
CCMA Call Centre Management Association; Commander, Corps Medium Artillery; Contract Cleaning and Maintenance Association
CCMD [USA] Carnegie Committee for Music and Drama; [physics] continuous-current monitoring device
CCMS Committee on the Challenge of Modern Society (in NATO)
CCN [meteorology] cloud condensation nuclei; command control number; contract change notice; contract change notification
CCNDT Canadian Council for Non-Destructive Technology
CCNR Consultative Committee for Nuclear Research (in Council of Europe)
CCNSC [USA] Cancer Chemotherapy National Service Center
CCNY Carnegie Corporation of New York; City College of the City University of New York
CCO Central Coding Office; current-controlled oscillator
CCOA County Court Officers' Association
CCOFI California Cooperative Oceanic Fisheries Investigations
CCP Chinese Communist Party; Code of Civil Procedure; Committee on Commodity Problems; Court of Common Pleas; [nuclear technology] critical compression pressure
c.c.p. credit-card purchase
CCPE Canadian Council of Professional Engineers
CCPF *Comité central de la propriété forestière*

de la CE (French: Central Committee on Forest Property for the EU)

CCPI Cyanamid Canada Pipeline Incorporated

CCPIT China Committee for the Promotion of International Trade

CCPL [USA] Computer Center Program Library

CCPO *Comité central permanent de l'opium* (French: Permanent Central Opium Board)

CCPR Central Council of Physical Recreation

CCPS Consultative Committee for Postal Studies

CCR cassette camera recorder; [USA] Commission of Civil Rights; Common Centre of Research; [law] contract change request; [medicine] cranial cavity ratio; critical compression ratio

CCRA Commander Corps of Royal Artillery

CCRE Commander Corps of Royal Engineers

CCREME Commander Corps of Royal Electrical and Mechanical Engineers

CCRSigs Commander Corps of Royal Signals

CCRU [USA] Common Cold Research Unit

CCS [computing] calculus of communicating systems; Canadian Cancer Society; Canadian Ceramic Society; casualty clearing station; child-care service; collective call sign; [USA] Combined Chiefs of Staff; controlled combustion system

CCSA Canadian Committee on Sugar Analysis

CCSATU Coordinating Council of South African Trade Unions

CCSC Central Consultants and Specialists Committee (in BMA)

CCSD [computing] coupled-cluster single and double

CCSEM computer-controlled scanning electron microscope (or microscopy)

CCSS centrifugally cast stainless steel

CCST [USA] Center for Computer Sciences and Technology

CCSU Council of Civil Service Unions

CCT [medicine] cerebral circulation time; [USA] clean coal technology; common customs tariff (in EU); compulsory competitive tendering; [electronics] contact charge-transfer; correct corps time; [medicine] cranial compute(rize)d tomography

CCTA Central Computer and Telecommunications Agency; *Commission de coopération technique pour l'Afrique* (French: Commission for Technical Cooperation in Africa); Coordinating Committee of Technical Assistance

CCTG constant concentration tracer gas (system)

CCTR [nuclear technology] cassette compact toroid reactor

CCTS [USA] Canaveral Council of Technical Societies; Combat Crew Training Squadron

CCTV closed-circuit television

CCU [medicine] coronary care unit

CCUS Chamber of Commerce of the United States

CCV [aeronautics] control-configured vehicle

CCW [nuclear technology] component cooling water; Curriculum Council for Wales

ccw. counterclockwise

CCWS [nuclear technology] component cooling water system

CD [vehicle registration] Brighton; Canadian Forces Decoration; [electronics] carrier density; certificate of deposit; [law] Chancery Division; Civil Defence; civil disobedience; closing date; [immunology] cluster of differentiation; coal dust; College Diploma; [Jamaica] Commander of the Order of Distinction; commercial dock; compact disc; Conference on Disarmament (of UN); confidential document; [USA] Congressional District; [medicine] contagious disease; [image technology] contrast detail; [astronomy] Córdoba Durchmusterung (star catalogue); [nuclear technology] core damage; *Corps diplomatique* (French: Diplomatic Corps); countdown; [Freemasonry] Court of Deliberation; cross-dresser (= transvestite); [electronics] current density

C/D consular declaration; customs declaration

Cd [chemical element] cadmium; [military]

Command; Command Paper (1900–18) (in parliamentary procedure); [military] Commissioned
cd candela (unit of luminous intensity); *ciudad* (Spanish: city); command; cord; could
c/d [book-keeping] carried down
c.d. [book-keeping] carried down; cash discount; [finance] cum dividend (i.e. with dividend)
CDA Canadian Dental Association; *Centre de données astronomiques* (French: Centre for Astronomical Data); [South Africa] Christian Democratic Alliance; Civil Defence Act; College Diploma in Agriculture; [computing] compound document architecture; [Canada] Conference of Defence Associations; Copper Development Association
CDAA Churches Drought Action in Africa
CDAAA Committee to Defend America by Aiding the Allies
CD&G compact disc and graphics
Cd Armn Commissioned Airman
CDAS Civil Defence Ambulance Service
CDB [computing] comprehensive database
Cd B Commissioned Boatswain
cdbd cardboard
Cd Bndr Commissioned Bandmaster
CDC Canada Development Corporation; canister decontamination cell (or chamber); [chemistry] carbon derived from coal; Caribbean Defence Command; [USA] Center for Disease Control; [USA] Combat Development Command; [computing] command and data-handling console; Commissioners of the District of Columbia; [computing] common development cycle; Commonwealth Development Corporation; Control Data Corporation (computer manufacturer); cost determination committee; [electronics] critical density of current
Cd CO Commissioned Communication Officer
Cd Con. Commissioned Constructor
CDD [USA] certificate of disability for discharge; [electronics] charge-density distribution
CDDI [computing] copper distributed data interface
CDE chemical defence ensemble; compact disc erasable
CD-E compact disc erasable
CDEE Chemical Defence Experimental Establishment
C de G *Croix de Guerre* (French: War Cross) (military decoration)
CDEM crop disease environment monitor
Cd Eng. Commissioned Engineer
CDEU Christian Democratic European Union
CDF [computing] central database facility; Collider Detector at Fermilab; [nuclear technology] core-damage frequency
c.d.f. [statistics] cumulative distribution function
CDFC Commonwealth Development Finance Company
Cdg. Cardigan
Cd Gr Commissioned Gunner
CDH College Diploma in Horticulture; [medicine] congenital disease of the heart; [medicine] congenital dislocation of the hip
CDHS California Department of Health Services
CDI compact disc interactive
CD-I compact disc interactive
CDIC [USA] Carbon Dioxide Information Center
CDIF [computing] CASE data interchange format
Cd In. O Commissioned Instructor Officer
CDipAF Certified Diploma in Accounting and Finance
c. div. [finance] cum dividend (i.e. with dividend)
CDL Central Dockyard Laboratory (in Ministry of Defence); central door locking (in car advertisement); [chemistry] coal-derived liquid; Council of the Duchy of Lancaster; [Australia] County and Democratic League
Cdl Cardinal
CDLD [medicine] chronic diffuse liver disease
CDM [astronomy] cold dark matter (as in **CDM theory**)
Cd MAA Commissioned Master-at-Arms
CDN [international vehicle registration] Canada; *Chicago Daily News*
Cdn Canadian
cDNA [biochemistry] complementary DNA
Cd O Commissioned Officer

Cdo Commando
Cd Obs. Commissioned Observer
Cd OE Commissioned Ordnance Engineer
CDOI Colorado Department of Institutions
Cd OO Commissioned Ordnance Officer
CDOS [computing] concurrent disk operating system
CDP Committee of Directors of Polytechnics
CDPE continental daily parcels express
CDPS [computing] compound document protocol specification
CDR carbon dioxide research; Committees for the Defence of the Revolution (in Cuba); compact disc recordable; [computing] contents of decrement register; critical design review; crude death rate
CD-R [computing] compact disc recordable
Cdr Commander; Conductor
CDRA Committee of Directors of Research Associations
Cd Rad. O Commissioned Radio Officer
CDRB Canadian Defence Research Board
CDRC Civil Defence Regional Commissioner
CDRD [USA] Carbon Dioxide Research Division
Cdre Commodore
CDRF Canadian Dental Research Foundation
CDRH [USA] Center for Devices and Radiological Health
CDRI [India] Central Drug Research Institute
CD-ROM [computing] compact disc read-only memory
CD-ROM XA [computing] CD-ROM extended architecture
CDRS Civil Defence Rescue Service
CD-RW [computing] compact disc rewritable
CDS Chief of the Defence Staff; Civil Defence Services
CDSC Communicable Disease Surveillance Centre
CDSE computer-driven simulation environment
Cd Sh. Commissioned Shipwright
CDSO Companion of the Distinguished Service Order
Cd SO Commissioned Stores Officer; Commissioned Supply Officer
CDT Carnegie Dunfermline Trust; [USA, Canada] Central Daylight Time; craft, design and technology (school subject)
Cdt Cadet; Commandant
Cdt Mid. Cadet Midshipman
CDTV [computing] Commodore Dynamic Total Vision; compact-disc television
CDU *Christlich-Demokratische Union* (German: Christian Democratic Union) (political party)
CDUCE Christian Democratic Union of Central Europe
CDV [microbiology] canine distemper virus; Civil Defence Volunteers; compact-disc video; current domestic value
c.d.v. *carte-de-visite* (French: visiting card)
CDW [USA] collision damage waiver (in car insurance)
c.d.w. chilled drinking water; cold drinking water
Cd Wdr Commissioned Wardmaster
CD-WO [computing] compact disc write once
CDWR California Department of Water Resources
CDWS Civil Defence Wardens' Service
Cdz Cádiz
CE Canada East; carbon equivalent; centre of effort; [medicine] cerebral embolism; Chancellor of the Exchequer; chemical engineer; chief engineer; Christian Endeavour; Christian Era (in dates); Church of England; [computing] circular error; civil engineer; [medicine] clinical evaluation; [fishing port] Coleraine; Combustion Engineering (Incorporated); [education] Common Entrance; Common Era (in dates); *Communauté européenne* (French: European Community); community education; compass error; compression engine; [computing] computing efficiency; contrast-enhanced (of picture image); Corps of Engineers; Council of Europe; counter-espionage; [electronics] current efficiency; [vehicle registration] Peterborough
Ce [chemical element] cerium
c.e. [law] *caveat emptor* (Latin: let the buyer beware); centre of effort; [computing] circular error; compass error; critical examination

CEA Canadian Electrical Association; [medicine] carcino-embryonic antigen; Central Electricity Authority; Cinematograph Exhibitors Association; Combustion Engineering Association; *Comité européen des assurances* (French: European Insurance Committee); [commerce] commodity exchange authority; *Confédération européenne de l'agriculture* (French: European Confederation of Agriculture); Conference of Educational Associations; control electronics assembly; [USA] Council of Economic Advisors; Council of Educational Advance

CEAA [USA] Center for Editions of American Authors; Council of European-American Associations

CEAC [USA] Citizens Energy Advisory Committee; *Commission européenne de l'aviation civile* (French: European Civil Aviation Commission)

CEB Central Electricity Board

CEBAR chemical, biological and radiological warfare

CEC California Energy Commission; Canadian Electrical Code (of standardization); Catholic Education Council; Central Ethical Committee (in BMA); Centre for Economic Cooperation (in UN); Church Education Corporation; Civil Engineering Corps; Clothing Export Council; Commission of the European Communities; Commonwealth Economic Committee; Commonwealth Education Conference; Commonwealth Engineering Conference; Community Education Centre; Council for Exceptional Children

CECA *Communauté européenne du charbon et de l'acier* (French: European Coal and Steel Community)

CECD *Confédération européenne du commerce de détail* (French: European Confederation of Retail Trades)

CECE Committee for European Construction Equipment

CECG Consumers in the European Community Group

CECLES *Conseil européen pour la construction de lanceurs d'engins spatiaux* (French: European Space Launching Development Organization)

CECS Church of England Children's Society; civil engineering computing system; Communications Electronics Coordination Section

CED Committee for Economic Development; computer entry device; [USA] Council for Economic Development

CEDA Committee for Economic Development of Australia

CEDAR coupling, energetics and dynamics of atmospheric regions

CEDC Committee on Economic Cooperation among Developing Countries

CEDEL *Centrale de livraison de valeurs mobilières* (French: eurobond settlement service)

cedex *courrier d'entreprise à distribution exceptionnelle* (French: special business postal code)

CEDI *Centre européen de documentation et d'information* (French: European Documentation and Information Centre)

CEDIC Church Estates Development and Improvement Company

CEDO Centre for Educational Development Overseas

CEDR Centre for Dispute Resolution

CEE Central Engineering Establishment; Certificate of Extended Education; *Commission économique pour l'Europe* (French: Economic Commission for Europe); *Commission internationale de réglementation en vue de l'approbation de l'équipement électrique* (French: International Commission on Rules for the Approval of Electrical Equipment); Common Entrance Examination; *Communauté économique européenne* (French: European Economic Community); Council for Environmental Education

CEEA *Communauté européenne de l'énergie atomique* (French: European Atomic Energy Community)

CEEB [USA] College Entrance Examination Board

CEEC Council for European Economic Cooperation

CEED Centre for Economic and Environmental Development

CEEP *Centre européen d'études de population* (French: European Centre for Population Studies)

CEF Canadian Expeditionary Force; Chinese Expeditionary Force; [chemistry] crystalline electric field

CEFTA Central European Free Trade Area

CEFTRI [India] Central Food Technological Research Institute

CEG *collège d'enseignement général* (French: college of general education); Computer Education Group

CEGB Central Electricity Generating Board

CEGGS Church of England Girls' Grammar School

CEGS Church of England Grammar School

CEI [Switzerland] *Centre d'études industrielles* (French: Centre for Industrial Studies); *Commission électrotechnique internationale* (French: International Electrotechnical Commission); Committee for Environmental Information; communications-electronics instructions; cost-effectiveness index; Council of Engineering Institutions

CEIF Council of European Industrial Federations

CEIR Corporation for Economic and Industrial Research

CEL [USA] Constitutional Educational League

Cel. Celsius

cel. celebrate; celebrated; celebration; celery; [music] celesta; celibate

CELA Council for Exports to Latin America

CELC Commonwealth Education Liaison Committee

celeb [short form] celebrity

celest. celestial

CELEX *Communitatis Europeae Lex* (Latin: European Community Law) (computerized documentation system)

CELJ Conference of Editors of Learned Journals

cello [short form] violoncello

Cels. Celsius

CELSS controlled ecological life-support system

Celt. Celtic

CEM *Companhia Electricidade de Macáu* (Macao electricity company); [physics] continuous emission monitoring; cost and effectiveness method; [astronautics] crew-escape module

cem. cement; cemetery

CEMA Canadian Electrical Manufacturers' Association; Catering Equipment Manufacturers' Association; Conveyor Equipment Manufacturers' Association; Council for Economic Mutual Assistance; Council for the Encouragement of Music and the Arts

CEMAC Committee of European Associations of Manufacturers of Active Electronic Components; *Communauté économique et monétaire de l'Afrique central* (French: Central African Economic and Monetary Community)

CEMAP *Commission européenne des méthodes d'analyse des pesticides* (French: Collaborative Pesticides Analytical Committee)

CEMF [electronics] counter-electromotive force

CEMLA *Centro de Estudios Monetarios Latino-Americanos* (Spanish: Latin-American Centre for Monetary Studies)

CEMR Council of European Municipalities and Regions

CEMS Church of England Men's Society

CEN *Comité européen de normalisation* (French: European Standardization Committee)

Cen [astronomy] Centaurus

cen. central; centre; century

CEND Civil Engineers for Nuclear Disarmament

CENELEC *Comité européen de normalisation électrotechnique* (French: European Electrotechnical Standardization Committee)

CEng Chartered Engineer

cens. censor; censored; censorship

cent. [currency] centavo (hundredth of peso etc.); [currency] centesimo (hundredth of peso etc.); centigrade; [currency] centime (hundredth of franc etc.); central; centrifugal; *centum* (Latin: hundred); century

CENTA Combined Edible Nut Trade Association

CENTAG Central (European) Army Group (in NATO)

centenn. centennial

centig. centigrade

Cento Central Treaty Organization

CEO chief education officer; chief execu-

tive officer; Confederation of Employee Organizations
CEOA Central European Operating Agency (in NATO)
CEP [computing] circular error probability
Cep [astronomy] Cepheus
CEPCEO *Comité d'études des producteurs de charbon d'Europe occidentale* (French: Western European Coal Producers' Association)
CEPES *Comité européen pour le progrès économique et social* (French: European Committee for Economic and Social Progress)
CEPIS Council of European Professional Informatics Societies
CEPO Central European Pipeline Office
CEPR Centre for Economic Policy Research
CEPS Central European Pipeline System; Centre for European Policy Studies; Cornish Engine Preservation Society
CEPT *Conférence européenne des administrations des postes et des télécommunications* (French: European Conference of Postal and Telecommunications Administrations)
CEQ [USA] Council on Environmental Quality
CEQA [USA] California Environmental Quality Act
CER carbon dioxide evolution rate; carbon dioxide exchange rate; [Australia, New Zealand] closer economic relations; Community of European Railways
cer. ceramic
ceram. ceramic
CERC [USA] Center for Energy Research Computation; Civil Engineering Research Council
CERCA Commonwealth and Empire Radio for Civil Aviation
CERCLA [USA] Comprehensive Environmental Response, Compensation and Liability Act
Cerdip [computing] ceramic dual in-line package
CERES [USA] Coalition for Environmentally Responsible Economies; Consumers for Ethics in Research Group
CERG Conservative European Reform Group
CERI Centre for Educational Research and Innovation (of OECD)
CERL Central Electricity Research Laboratories
CERN *Conseil européen pour la recherche nucléaire* (French: European Organization for Nuclear Research)
CERP *Centre européen des relations publiques* (French: European Centre of Public Relations)
CERT Charities Effectiveness Review Trust; computer emergency response team
cert [short form] certainty
cert. certain; certificate; certificated; certification; certified; certify
CertCAM Certificate in Communication, Advertising and Marketing
CertEd Certificate in Education
CertHE Certificate in Higher Education
certif. certificate; certificated; certified
cert. inv. certified invoice
cerv. [medicine] cervical
CES [USA] Center for Energy Studies; Centre for Environmental Studies; Christian Evidence Society; *collège d'enseignement secondaire* (French: college of secondary education); community energy system; cost-estimating system
CESAR [USA] Center for Engineering Systems Advanced Research
CESC Conference on European Security and Cooperation
CESE [USA] Center for Earth Science and Engineering
CESP Confederation of European Socialist Parties
CESR [USA] Cornell electron storage ring
CESSAC Church of England Soldiers', Sailors' and Airmen's Clubs
CESSI Church of England Sunday School Institution
CEST Centre for Exploitation of Science and Technology
Cestr. *Cestrensis* (Latin: (Bishop) of Chester)
CET Central European Time; *collège d'enseignement technique* (French: college of technical education); Common External Tariff; Council for Educational Technology
Cet [astronomy] Cetus
CETA [USA] Comprehensive Employment and Training Act
CETEX Committee on Extra-Terrestrial Exploration

CETHV Council for the Education and Training of Health Visitors
CETI communications with extraterrestrial intelligence
CETO Centre for Educational Television Overseas
cet. par. *ceteris paribus* (Latin: other things being equal)
CETS chemical energy transmission systems; Church of England Temperance Society
CEU Christian Endeavour Union
CEUS Central and Eastern United States
CEUSA Committee for Exports to the United States of America
CEVS [USA] controlled environment vitrification system
CEWC Council for Education in World Citizenship
CEWMS Church of England Working Men's Society
Cey. Ceylon
CEYC Church of England Youth Council
Ceyl. Ceylon
CEZMS Church of England Zenana Missionary Society
CF calibration factor; [civil aircraft marking] Canada; Canadian Forces; capacity factor; [fishing port] Cardiff; [UK postcode] Cardiff; [commerce] carried forward; centre of flotation; Chaplain to the Forces; charcoal-filtered; *Comédie Française* (French national theatre); Commonwealth Fund; [currency] Comorian franc; compensation fee; [medicine] conventional fractionation radiotherapy; Corresponding Fellow; cost and freight; [chemistry] crystal field (as in **CF theory**); [medicine] cystic fibrosis; [vehicle registration] Reading
Cf [chemical element] californium
Cf. [Roman Catholic Church] Confessions
c/f [book-keeping] carried forward; cost and freight
cf. [bookbinding] calfskin; *confer* (Latin: compare)
.cf Central African Republic (in Internet address)
c.f. [music] *cantus firmus* (Latin: fixed song); [book-keeping] carried forward; [sports] centre field; [baseball] centre fielder; [sports] centre forward; centre of flotation; *chemin de fer* (French: railway); communication factor; context free; cost and freight; cubic feet
CFA Canadian Federation of Agriculture; Canadian Field Artillery; Canadian Forestry Association; cash-flow accounting; [USA] Chartered Financial Analyst; Commission of Fine Arts; Commonwealth Forestry Association; *Communauté financière africaine* (French: African Financial Community, as in **CFA franc**); [medicine] complete Freund's adjuvant; Consumer Federation of America; Contract Flooring Association Limited; Cookery and Food Association; Council for Acupuncture; Council of Foreign Affairs; [electrical engineering] cross-field amplifier; [medicine] cryptogenic fibrosing alveolitis
CFAF [currency] CFA franc (used in some countries of Africa)
CFAL current food additives legislation
CFAM cogeneration feasibility analysis model
CFAP Canadian Foundation for the Advancement of Pharmacy
CFAR constant false alarm rate
CFAT Carnegie Foundation for the Advancement of Teaching
CFB [computing] cipher feedback; [USA] Consumer Fraud Bureau; Council of Foreign Bondholders
CFBAC Central Fire Brigade Advisory Council (of England and Wales)
CFBS Canadian Federation of Biological Sciences
CFC carbon-fibre composite; chlorofluorocarbon (chemical harmful to ozone layer); [microbiology] colony-forming cell; Common Fund for Commodities (in UN); *Congregatio Fratrum Christianorum* (Latin: Congregation of Christian Brothers); consolidation freight classification
CFCE *Conseil des fédérations commerciales d'Europe* (French: Council of European Commercial Federations)
CFD [computing] compact floppy disk; [engineering] computational fluid dynamics
cfd cubic feet per day
CFDC Canadian Film Development Corporation
CFDT *Confederation française démocratique*

du travail (French: Democratic Federation of Labour)
CFE Central Fighter Establishment; College of Further Education; [microbiology] colony-forming efficiency; [physics] control fuel element; Conventional (Armed) Forces in Europe (as in **CFE treaty**)
CFF *Chemins de fer fédéraux suisses* (French: Swiss federal railways); [computing] critical flicker frequency; [physics] critical fusion frequency
CFFLS [USA] Consortium for Fossil Fuel Liquefaction Science
c.f.g. cubic feet of gas
cfh cubic feet per hour
CFHT Canada–France–Hawaii Telescope (Mauna Kea, Hawaii)
CFI Campaign for Freedom of Information; chief flying instructor; cost, freight and insurance; Court of First Instance (in EU)
c.f.i. cost, freight and insurance
CFL Canadian Football League; ceasefire line; Central Film Library
CFLP Central Fire Liaison Panel
CFM Cadet Forces Medal; [chemistry] chlorofluoromethane; Council of Foreign Ministers
cfm confirm; cubic feet per minute
cfm. confirmation
CfN Council for Nature
CFO [meteorology] Central Forecasting Office; chief financial officer; chief fire officer
c.f.o. calling for orders; channel for orders
CFOA Chief Fire Officers' Association
CFOD Catholic Fund for Overseas Development
CFP Common Fisheries Policy (of EU); *Communauté financière du Pacifique* (French: Pacific Financial Community, as in **CFP franc**); *Compagnie française des pétroles* (French petroleum company)
CFPF [currency] CFP franc (used in some countries of Pacific)
CFPP coal-fired power plant
CFR [USA] Code of Federal Regulations; Commander of the Order of the Federal Republic of Nigeria; [nuclear technology] commercial fast reactor; [engineering] Cooperative Fuel Research (Committee) (as in **CFR engine**); [medicine] coronary flow reserve; [metallurgy] corrosion-fatigue resistance; Council on Foreign Relations
cfr chauffeur
cfr. *confronta* (Italian: compare)
CFRI [USA] Central Fuel Research Institute
CFRP carbon-fibre reinforced plastic
CFS central flying school; [medicine] chronic fatigue syndrome; Clergy Friendly Society; [telecommunications] combination frequency signal; [computing] common file system
cfs cubic feet per second
CFSAN [USA] Center for Food Safety and Applied Nutrition
CFSL Central Forensic Science Laboratory
CFSP Common Foreign and Security Policy (in EU)
CFSTI [USA] Clearinghouse for Federal Scientific and Technical Information
CFT *Compagnie française de télévision* (French television company); [medicine] complement fixation test; [engineering] cross-flow turbine; Cystic Fibrosis Trust
cft craft
CFTB Commonwealth Forestry and Timber Bureau
CFTC [USA] Commodity Futures Trading Commission; Commonwealth Fund for Technical Cooperation
cftmn craftsman
CFU [microbiology] colony-forming unit
CFV continuous-flow ventilation
CFWI County Federation of Women's Institutes
CFX [Roman Catholic Church] *Congregatio Fratrum Xaverianorum* (Latin: Congregation of Xaverian Brothers)
CG [vehicle registration] Bournemouth; Captain-General; Captain of the Guard; centre of gravity; Chaplain-General; [aeronautics] cloud-to-ground; coastguard; Coldstream Guards; [US army] Commanding General; Commissary-General; computer graphics; concentration guide; conjugate gradient; Consul-General; Covent Garden (opera house); *Croix de Guerre* (French: War Cross) (military decoration)
C-G Chaplain-General
cg centigram
.cg (Republic of) Congo (in Internet address)

c.g. centre of gravity
CGA [commerce] cargo's proportion of general average; Certified General Accountant; [USA] Coast Guard Academy; [USA] Coast Guard Auxiliary; [computing] colour graphics adapter; Community of the Glorious Ascension; Country Gentlemen's Association
CGAT City Gallery Arts Trust
CGB Commonwealth Geographical Bureau
CGBR central government borrowing requirement
CGC [USA] Coast Guard cutter; Commonwealth Games Council; *Confédération générale des cadres* (French: General Confederation of Executive Staff); Conspicuous Gallantry Cross
CGD [medicine] chronic granulomatous disease
CGDK Coalition Government of Democratic Kampuchea
CGE Conservative Group for Europe
cge carriage; charge
cge fwd carriage forward
cge pd carriage paid
CGF Commonwealth Games Federation
CGH Cape of Good Hope; computer-generated hologram
CGI Catholic Guides of Ireland; chief ground instructor; chief gunnery instructor; City and Guilds Institute; commercial grade item; [computing] common gateway interface; computer graphics interface
c.g.i. corrugated galvanized iron
CGIA City and Guilds (of London) Insignia Award
CGIAR Consultative Group in International Agricultural Research
CGIL *Confederazione Generale Italiana del Lavoro* (Italian: General Italian Confederation of Labour)
CGLI City and Guilds of London Institute
CGM computer graphics metafile; Conspicuous Gallantry Medal
cgm centigram
CGMW Commission for the Geological Map of the World
cgo cargo; [finance] contango
CGOU [USA] Coast Guard Oceanographic Unit
CGP College of General Practitioners
CGPM *Conférence générale des poids et mesures* (French: General Conference of Weights and Measures); *Conseil général des pêches pour la Méditerranée* (French: General Fisheries Council for the Mediterranean)
CGPS Canadian Government Purchasing System
CGRI [India] Central Glass and Ceramic Research Institute
CGRM Commandant-General, Royal Marines
CGRO Compton Gamma Ray Observatory
CGS central gunnery school; Chief of the General Staff; Coast and Geodetic Survey; [US army] Commissary General of Subsistence; Cottage Gardens Society
cgs centimetre-gram-second (as in **cgs units**)
CGSB Canadian Government Specifications Board
CGSC [USA] Command and General Staff College
CGSS [USA] Command and General Staff School
CGSUS Council of Graduate Schools in the United States
CGT capital gains tax; ceramic gas turbine; closed gas turbine; *Compagnie générale transatlantique* (French shipping company); compressed-gas turbometer; *Confederación general del trabajo* (Spanish: General Confederation of Labour) (in Argentina); *Confédération générale du travail* (French: General Confederation of Labour)
CGTB Canadian Government Travel Bureau
CGT-FO *Confédération générale du travail–force ouvrière* (French: General Confederation of Labour/Workers' Force)
c.g.u. ceramic glazed units
CH [military] Captain of the Horse; [Freemasonry] Captain of the Host; Carnegie Hall; central heating (in property advertisement); [medicine] cerebral haemorrhage; chapter house; [fishing port] Chester; [UK postcode] Chester; Christ's Hospital; clearing house; Companion of Honour; [medicine] contact hypersensitivity; [astronomy] coronal hole; corporate hospitality; custom(s) house; [vehicle registration] Nottingham; [inter-

national vehicle registration] Switzerland (from French *Confédération Helvétique* or Latin *Confederatio Helvetica*)
C/H central heating (in property advertisement)
Ch. chairman; chairwoman; Chaldean; Chaldee; Chamber; Champion; Chancellor; Chancery; Chapter; Chile; Chilean; China; Chinese; *Chirurgiae* (Latin: of Surgery) (in academic degrees); Christ; [Bible] Chronicles; Church
ch [mathematics] hyperbolic cosine
.ch Switzerland (in Internet address)
ch. chain (crochet stitch); chain (unit of length); chaldron (unit of capacity); *chambre(s)* (French: room(s)); champion; chaplain; chapter; charge(s); chart; [horseracing] chase; chassis (in car advertisement); [chess] check; cheese; chemical; chemistry; cheque; [horseracing] chestnut; *cheval-vapeur* (French: horsepower); chief; child; children; choir; choke; church
c.h. candle hour; central heating (in property advertisement); [sports] centre half; clearing house; club house; compass heading; court house; custom(s) house
CHA Catholic Hospital Association; Chest and Heart Association; Community Health Association; Countrywide Holidays Association
Cha [astronomy] Chamaeleon
chacom chain of command
Chal. Chaldaic; Chaldean; Chaldee
chal. chaldron (unit of capacity); *chaleur* (French: heat); challenge
Chald. Chaldaic; Chaldean; Chaldee
Chamb. Chamberlain; Chambers
Chan. Chancellor; Chancery
chan. chancel; channel
Chanc. Chancellor; Chancery
CHANCOM Channel Committee (in NATO)
chap. chapel; chaplain; chaplaincy; chapter
CHAPS Clearing House Automated Payment System
chapt. chapter
CHAR Campaign for Homeless People (formerly Campaign for the Homeless and Rootless)
char. character; characteristic; characterize; charity; charter
charc. charcoal
CHAS Catholic Housing Aid Society
Chas. Charles
Chauc. (Geoffrey) Chaucer (English poet)
CHB Companion of Honour of Barbados; [medicine] complete heart block
ChB Bachelor of Surgery (from Latin *Chirurgiae Baccalaureus*); [USA] Chief of the Bureau
Chb. Cherbourg
CHC child health clinic; choke coil; Clerk to the House of Commons; Community Health Council; [USA] Confederate High Command; [chemistry] cyclohexylamine carbonate
ch. cent. *chauffage central* (French: central heating)
Ch. Clk Chief Clerk
CHD [medicine] congenital heart disease; [medicine] coronary heart disease
ChD Doctor of Chemistry; Doctor of Surgery (from Latin *Chirurgiae Doctor*)
Ch. Div. [law] Chancery Division
CHDL computer hardware description language
CHE Campaign for Homosexual Equality
ChE chemical engineer; chief engineer
CHEAR Council on Higher Education in the American Republics
CHEC Commonwealth Human Ecology Council
Cheka *Chrezvychainaya Comissiya* (Russian: Special Commission (for fighting counter-revolution and sabotage)) (former Soviet security organization)
CHEL *Cambridge History of English Literature*
Chelm Cheltenham
CHEM chemical health effects (assessment) methodology
chem. chemical; chemically; chemist; chemistry
ChemE chemical engineer
Ches. Cheshire
CHESS [USA] Cornell high-energy synchrotron source
Chev. Chevalier
chev. chevron
CHF Carnegie Hero Fund; [medicine] congestive heart failure
ChF Chaplain of the Fleet
chf chief
ch. fwd charges forward

chg. change; charge
chgd charged
chge charge
chgph. choreographer; choreographic; choreography
Chi. Chicago; Chichester; China; Chinese
Chic. Chicago
Chich. Chichester
Chicom Chinese communist
childn children
CHILL [computing] CCITT high-level language
Chin. China; Chinese
CHIPS Clearing House Inter-Bank Payments System
CHIRP Confidential Human Incidence Reporting Programme (civil aviation safety scheme)
Chi. Trib. *Chicago Tribune*
chiv. chivalry
Ch. J Chief Justice
Ch. K Christ the King
chk check
chkd checked
chkpt checkpoint
chkr checker
Chl [botany] chlorophyll
chl. chloride; chloroform
Ch. Lbr chief librarian
ChLJ Chaplain of the Order of St Lazarus of Jerusalem
chlo. chloride; chloroform
CHLW [nuclear technology] commercial high-level waste
ChM Master of Surgery (from Latin *Chirurgiae Magister*)
chm. chairman; [chess] checkmate; choirmaster
CHMC [USA] Children's Hospital Medical Center
chmn chairman
CHMR [USA] Center for Hazardous Materials Research
CHNT Community Health Nurse Tutor
CHO Confederation of Healing Organizations; Crop Husbandry Officer
cho. choral; chorister; chorus
choc. chocolate
Ch. of S Chamber of Shipping
Ch. of the F Chaplain of the Fleet
CHOGM Commonwealth Heads of Government Meeting
choirm. choirmaster
chor. choral; chorister; chorus
CHP chemical heat pump; combined heat and power; *Cumhuriyet Halk Partisi* (Turkish: Republican People's Party)
ch. pd charges paid
ch. ppd charges prepaid
CHQ Commonwealth Headquarters (of Girl Guides Association); [military] Corps Headquarters
chq. cheque
Chr. Christ; Christian; Christianity; Christmas; [Bible] Chronicles
CHRI Commonwealth Human Rights Initiative
chrm. chairman
Chron. [Bible] Chronicles
chron. chronicle; chronological; chronologically; chronology; chronometry
chronol. chronological; chronologically; chronology
Chrs Chambers
CHS Canadian Hydrographic Service; Church Historical Society; [computing] cylinders, heads and sectors
chs chapters
CHSA Chest, Heart and Stroke Association
CHSC Central Health Services Council
ch'ship championship
Ch. Skr chief skipper
ChStJ Chaplain of the Order of St John of Jerusalem
c.h.t. cylinder-head temperature
chtg charting
ch. v. check valve
c.h.w. constant hot water
chwdn churchwarden
chyd churchyard
Chy Div. [law] Chancery Division
CI [medicine] cardiac index; [medicine] cerebral infarction; Channel Islands; [Freemasonry] Chapter of Instruction; chemical inspectorate; chemical ionization; Chief Inspector; chief instructor; [astronomy] Colour Index; [medicine] combined injury; [chemistry] combustion index; Commonwealth Institute; Communist International; compression-ignition (as in **CI engine**); [statistics] confidence interval; [chemistry] configuration interaction; consular invoice; [commerce] continuous improvement; [photography] contrast index;

[astronomy] coronal index (of solar activity); [engineering] corrosion inhibitor; [international vehicle registration] Côte d'Ivoire (Ivory Coast); counter-intelligence; (Imperial Order of the) Crown of India

Ci curie (unit of radioactivity)

Ci [meteorology] cirrus

.ci Côte d'Ivoire (Ivory Coast, in Internet address)

c.i. cast iron

CIA Cancer Information Association; cash in advance; [USA] Central Intelligence Agency; Chemical Industries' Association; Chief Inspector of Armaments; *Conseil international des archives* (French: International Council on Archives); Corporation of Insurance Agents; Culinary Institute of America

Cia [commerce] *compagnia* (Italian: company, Co.); [commerce] *companhia* (Portuguese: company, Co.); [commerce] *compañia* (Spanish: company, Co.)

CIAA *Centre international d'aviation agricole* (French: International Agricultural Aviation Centre); Coordinator of Inter-American Affairs

CIAB [USA] Coal Industry Advisory Board; *Conseil international des agences bénévoles* (French: International Council of Voluntary Agencies)

CIAC Construction Industry Advisory Council

CIAgrE Companion of the Institution of Agricultural Engineers

CIAI Commerce and Industry Association Institute

CIAL Corresponding Member of the International Institute of Arts and Letters

CIAPG *Confédération internationale des anciens prisonniers de guerre* (French: International Confederation of Former Prisoners of War)

CIArb Chartered Institute of Arbitrators

CIAS Conference of Independent African States

CIB Campaign for an Independent Britain; Central Intelligence Board; Chartered Institute of Bankers (formerly IOB); Corporation of Insurance Brokers; [New Zealand] Criminal Investigation Branch

CIBS Chartered Institute of Building Services (former name of CIBSE); Chartered Institution of Building Societies

CIBSE Chartered Institution of Building Services Engineers (formerly CIBS)

CIC Capital Issues Committee; Chemical Institute of Canada; Cinema International Corporation; [immunology] circulating immune complexes; [USA] Combat Information Center; Commander-in-Chief; [USA] Command Information Center; Commonwealth Information Centre; [USA] Counterintelligence Corps; [USA] Critical Issues Council

Cic. (Marcus Tullius) Cicero (Roman orator)

CICA Canadian Institute of Chartered Accountants

CICADA central instrumentation control and data acquisition

CICAR Cooperative Investigations of the Caribbean and Adjacent Regions

CICB Criminal Injuries Compensation Board

CICC [electronics] cable-in-conduit conductor; *Conférénce internationale des charités catholiques* (French: International Conference of Catholic Charities)

Cicestr. *Cicestrensis* (Latin: (Bishop) of Chichester)

CICG *Centre international du commerce de gros* (French: International Centre for Wholesale Trade)

CICHE Committee for International Cooperation in Higher Education

CICI Confederation of Information Communication Industries

CICP [USA] Committee to Investigate Copyright Problems

CICR *Comité international de la Croix-Rouge* (French: International Committee of the Red Cross)

CICRC *Commission internationale contre le régime concentrationnaire* (French: International Commission Against Concentration Camp Practices)

CICRIS Cooperative Industrial and Commercial Reference and Information Service

CICS [computing] customer information control system

CICT *Conseil international du cinéma et de*

la télévision (French: International Film and Television Council)

CID [electronics] charge injection device; Committee for Imperial Defence; Council of Industrial Design; Criminal Investigation Department

CIDA Canadian International Development Agency; *Comisión interamericano de desarrollo agricola* (Spanish: Inter-American Committee for Agricultural Development); *Comité intergouvernemental du droit d'auteur* (French: Intergovernmental Copyright Committee)

CIDADEC *Confédération internationale des associations d'experts et de conseils* (French: International Confederation of Associations of Experts and Consultants)

CIDE *Comisión de inversion y desarrollo económico* (Spanish: Commission for Investment and Economic Development) (in Uruguay)

CIDESA *Centre international de documentation économique et sociale africaine* (French: International Centre for African Social and Economic Documentation)

CIDNP chemically induced dynamic nuclear polarization

CIDOC [Mexico] Centre for Intercultural Documentation

CIE captain's imperfect entry; *Centre international de l'enfance* (French: International Children's Centre); *Commission internationale de l'éclairage* (French: International Commission on Illumination, ICI); Companion of the Order of the Indian Empire; *Confédération internationale des étudiants* (French: International Confederation of Students); [Ireland] *Córas Iompair Éireann* (Gaelic: Transport Organization of Ireland)

Cie [commerce] *compagnie* (French: company, Co.)

CIEC *Centre international d'études criminologiques* (French: International Centre of Criminological Studies); *Commission internationale de l'état civil* (French: International Commission on Civil Status)

CIEE Companion of the Institution of Electrical Engineers

CIEO Catholic International Education Office

CIEPS *Conseil international de l'éducation physique et sportive* (French: International Council of Sport and Physical Education)

CIF Canadian Institute of Forestry; *Clube internacional de futebol* (Portuguese: International Football Club); *Conseil international des femmes* (French: International Council of Women); [commerce] cost, insurance and freight

c.i.f. [commerce] cost, insurance and freight

CIFA Corporation of Insurance and Financial Advisers

c.i.f.c. [commerce] cost, insurance, freight and commission

c.i.f.c.i. [commerce] cost, insurance, freight, commission and interest

CIFE Colleges and Institutes for Further Education; *Conseil des fédérations industrielles d'Europe* (French: Council of European Industrial Federations); *Conseil international du film d'enseignement* (French: International Council for Educational Films)

c.i.f.e. [commerce] cost, insurance, freight and exchange

c.i.f.i. [commerce] cost, insurance, freight and interest

CIFJ *Centre international du film pour la jeunesse* (French: International Centre of Films for Children)

c.i.f.L.t. [commerce] cost, insurance and freight, London terms

CIG *Comité international de géophysique* (French: International Geophysical Committee)

cig [short form] cigarette

CIGA *Compagnia Italiana dei Grandi Alberghi* (Italian hotel company)

CIGAR [nuclear technology] channel inspection and gauging apparatus of reactors

CIGAS Cambridge Intercollegiate Graduate Application Scheme

CIGasE Companion of the Institution of Gas Engineers

CIGR *Commission internationale du génie rural* (French: International Commission of Agricultural Engineering)

CIGS Chief of the Imperial General Staff

CIH Certificate in Industrial Health; Chartered Institute of Housing; [medicine] chronic inactive hepatitis

CIHA *Comité international d'histoire de l'art* (French: International Committee on the History of Art)
CIHE Council for Industry and Higher Education
CII Centre for Industrial Innovation (of University of Strathclyde); Chartered Insurance Institute; *Conseil international des infirmières* (French: International Council of Nurses)
CIIA Canadian Institute of International Affairs; *Commission internationale des industries agricoles* (French: International Commission for Agricultural Industries)
CIIR Catholic Institute for International Relations
CIJ Chartered Institute of Journalists; *Commission internationale de juristes* (French: International Commission of Jurists)
CIL Confederation of Irish Labour
CILB *Commission internationale de lutte biologique contre les ennemis des plantes* (French: International Commission for Biological Control)
CILECT *Centre international de liaison des écoles de cinéma et de télévision* (French: International Association of National Film Schools)
CILG Construction Industry Information Liaison Group
CIM Canadian Institute of Mining; Chartered Institute of Marketing; China Inland Mission; Commission for Industry and Manpower; computer input on microfilm; computer-integrated manufacturing; *Conférence islamique mondial* (French: World Muslim Conference); *Conseil international de la musique* (French: International Music Council); Cooperative Investment Management
CIMA Chartered Institute of Management Accountants; [USA] Construction Industry Manufacturers' Association
CIMarE Companion of the Institute of Marine Engineers
CIMAS continuous iron-making and steel-making
CIMB Construction Industry Manpower Board
CIME *Comité intergouvernemental pour les migrations européennes* (French: Intergovernmental Committee for European Migration); Council of Industry for Management Education
CIMechE Companion of the Institution of Mechanical Engineers
CIMGTechE Companion of the Institution of Mechanical and General Technician Engineers
CIMM Canadian Institute of Mining and Metallurgy
CIMPM *Comité international de médecine et de pharmacie militaires* (French: International Committee of Military Medicine and Pharmacy)
CIMS [USA] chemical information management systems
CIMTP *Congrès international de médecine tropicale et de paludisme* (French: International Congress of Tropical Medicine and Malaria)
CIN [medicine] cervical intraepithelial neoplasia (in cervical smear); *Commission internationale de numismatique* (French: International Numismatic Commission)
C-in-C Commander-in-Chief
CINCENT Commander-in-Chief Allied Forces Central Europe
CINCLANT Commander-in-Chief Atlantic
CINCNORTH Commander-in-Chief Allied Forces Northern Europe
CINCPAC Commander-in-Chief Pacific
CINCSOUTH Commander-in-Chief Allied Forces Southern Europe
CINFO Chief of Information
Cinn. Cincinnati
CINO Chief Inspector of Naval Ordnance
CINR [USA] Central Institute for Nuclear Research
CINS [USA] child(ren) in need of supervision
CInstR Companion of the Institute of Refrigeration
CIO Church Information Office; *Comité international olympique* (French: International Olympic Committee); *Commission internationale d'optique* (French: International Commission for Optics); [USA] Congress of Industrial Organizations
CIOB Chartered Institute of Building (formerly IOB)
CIOMS Council for International Organizations of Medical Sciences
CIOS Combined Intelligence Objectives

Subcommittee; *Conseil international pour l'organisation scientifique* (French: International Committee of Scientific Management)

CIOT Chartered Institute of Taxation

CIP [mining] carbon-in-pulp; Cataloguing in Publication; *Centre d'information de la presse* (Belgian news agency); [engineering] cold isostatic pressing; Common Industrial Policy (of EU); [engineering] constant-injection pressure

CIPA Canadian Industrial Preparedness Association; Chartered Institute of Patent Agents

CIPFA Chartered Institute of Public Finance and Accountancy

CIPL *Comité international permanent des linguistes* (French: International Standing Committee of Linguists)

CIPM *Commission internationale des poids et mesures* (French: International Committee on Weights and Measures); [USA] Council for International Progress in Management

CIPO *Comité international pour la préservation des oiseaux* (French: International Committee for Bird Preservation)

CIPP *Conseil indo-pacifique des pêches* (French: Indo-Pacific Fisheries Council)

CIPR *Commission internationale de protection contre les radiations* (French: International Commission on Radiological Protection)

CIPS Central Illinois Public Service (Company); Chartered Institute of Purchasing and Supply; Choice in Personal Safety

CIPSH *Conseil international de la philosophie et des sciences humaines* (French: International Council for Philosophy and the Humanities)

CIR Canada India reactor; Commission (or Council) on Industrial Relations; Commissioners of Inland Revenue; cost information report; [computing] current instruction register

Cir [astronomy] Circinus

cir. circle; circuit; circular; circulation; circumference; circus

cir. *circa* (Latin: about) (in dates)

CIRA Conference of Industrial Research Associations

circ. circle; circuit; circular; circulation; circumcision; circumference; circus

circ. *circa* (Latin: about) (in dates)

CIRCCE *Confédération internationale de la représentation commerciale de la communauté européenne* (French: International Confederation of Commercial Representation in the European Community)

circs [short form] circumstances

circum. circumference

CIRF *Centre international d'information et de recherche sur la formation professionelle* (French: International Vocational Training Information and Research Centre); Corn Industries Research Foundation

CIRIA Construction Industry Research and Information Association

CIRIEC *Centre international de recherches et d'information sur l'économie collective* (French: International Centre of Research and Information on Collective Economy)

CIRP *Collège international pour recherche et production* (French: International Institution for Production Engineering Research)

CIRRPC [USA] Committee on Interagency Radiation Research and Policy Coordination

CIRS [computing] cross-interleaved Reed-Solomon (as in **CIRS scheme**)

CIRT Community Initiative Research Trust

CIS [medicine] carcinoma in situ; cataloguing in source; [USA] Catholic Information Society; [USA] Center for International Studies; Central Information Service on Occupational Health and Safety (of RoSPA); Chartered Institute of Secretaries (former name of ICSA); Coal Industry Society; [medicine] combined-injury syndrome; Commonwealth of Independent States (former Soviet republics); Cooperative Insurance Society

CISA Canadian Industrial Safety Association

CISAC Centre for International Security and Arms Control; *Confédération internationale des sociétés d'auteurs et compositeurs* (French: International Confederation of Societies of Authors and Composers)

CISBH *Comité international de standardis-*

ation en biologie humaine (French: International Committee for Standardization in Human Biology)
CISC complex instruction-set chip; complex instruction-set computer
CISCO City Group for Smaller Companies; Civil Service Catering Organization
CIS-COBOL [computing] compact interactive standard Cobol
CISF *Confédération internationale des sages-femmes* (French: International Confederation of Midwives)
CISL *Confédération internationale des syndicats libres* (French: International Confederation of Free Trade Unions); *Confederazione Italiana Sindacati Lavoratori* (Italian: Italian Confederation of Workers' Trade Unions)
CISM *Conseil international du sport militaire* (French: International Military Sports Council)
CISPR *Comité international spécial des perturbations radioélectriques* (French: International Special Committee on Radio Interference)
CISS Centre for International Sports Studies; *Conseil international des sciences sociales* (French: International Social Science Council)
Cist. Cistercian
CISTI Canadian Institute for Scientific and Technological Information
CISV Children's International Summer Village Association
CIT [USA] California Institute of Technology; [USA] Carnegie Institute of Technology; [New Zealand] Central Institute of Technology; Chartered Institute of Transport; [astronomy] circumstellar imaging telescope; *Comité international des transports par chemin de fer* (French: International Railway Transport Committee); [nuclear technology] compact ignition tokamak; *Compagnia Italiana Turismo* (Italian tourism company)
cit. citadel; citation; cited; citizen; citrate
c.i.t. compression in transit
CITB Construction Industry Training Board
CITC Canadian Institute of Timber Construction; Construction Industry Training Centre
CITEL Committee for Inter-American Telecommunications
CITES Convention on International Trade in Endangered Species
CITI *Confédération internationale des travailleurs intellectuels* (French: International Confederation of Professional and Intellectual Workers)
cito disp. [medicine] *cito dispensatur* (Latin: let it be dispensed quickly) (in prescriptions)
CITV Children's Independent Television
CIU Club and Institute Union
CIUS *Conseil international des unions scientifiques* (French: International Council of Scientific Unions)
CIUSS Catholic International Union for Social Service
CIV City Imperial Volunteers; *Commission internationale du verre* (French: International Glass Commission)
civ. civil; civilian; civilization; civilize
CivE civil engineer
civvies [short form] civilian clothes
civvy [short form] civilian (as in **civvy street**)
CIW [USA] Carnegie Institute of Washington
CIWF Compassion in World Farming
CIX commercial Internet exchange
CJ Chief Justice; [vehicle registration] Gloucester
cj. conjectural
CJA Commonwealth Journalists' Association; Criminal Justice Act
CJCC Commonwealth Joint Communications Committee
CJD [medicine] Creutzfeld–Jakob disease
CJEC Court of Justice of the European Communities
CJM *Code de justice militaire* (French: Code of Military Justice); [Roman Catholic Church] Congregation of Jesus and Mary; *Congrès juif mondial* (French: World Jewish Congress)
CK [trademark] Calvin Klein; certified kosher; [fishing port] Colchester; [vehicle registration] Preston
ck cask; check; cook
CKD [computing] centre for key distribution; [commerce] completely knocked down (of goods sold in parts)
ckout checkout

ckpt cockpit
ckw. clockwise
CL calendar line; [fishing port] Carlisle; cathode luminescence; central locking (in car advertisement); civil law; Civil Lord; [Belgium] Commander of the Order of Leopold; common law; Communication Lieutenant; confidence limits; craft loss; critical list; [medicine] cruciate ligament; [vehicle registration] Norwich; [international vehicle registration] Sri Lanka (from former name Ceylon)
Cl [chemical element] chlorine
cl centilitre; council
c/l cash letter; craft loss
cl. claim; clarinet; class; classical; classics; classification; clause; clearance; clergy; clergyman; clerk; climb; close; closet; closure; cloth; clove
.cl Chile (in Internet address)
c.l. carload; central locking (in car advertisement); centre line; *cum laude* (Latin: with praise); cut lengths
CLA Canadian Library Association; Canadian Lumbermen's Association; Copyright Licensing Agency; Country Landowners' Association
Cla. Clackmannan(shire)
Clack. Clackmannan(shire)
CL(ADO) Contact Lens Diploma of the Association of Dispensing Opticians
CLAM chemical ramjet low-altitude missile
CLAN [computing] cordless local-area network
CLAP [USA] Citizens Lobbying Against Prostitution
CLAPA Cleft Lip and Palate Association
Clar. [heraldry] Clarenceux (King of Arms)
clar. [printing] clarendon (typeface); clarinet
Clarnico Clark, Nichols and Coombes (Limited) (confectionery manufacturers)
CLASS Computer-based Laboratory for Automated School Systems
class. classic; classical; classification; classified; classify
clav. [music] clavier
CLAW Consortium of Local Authorities in Wales
CLB [USA] Cape Lookout Bight (North Carolina); Church Lads' Brigade
CLC Canadian Labour Congress; Chartered Life Underwriter of Canada; Commonwealth Liaison Committee
CLCB Committee of London Clearing Banks
CLCr Communication Lieutenant-Commander
CLD [medicine] chronic liver disease; Doctor of Civil Law
cld [stock exchange] called; cancelled; cleared; coloured; cooled; could
CLE Council of Legal Education
CLEA Council of Local Education Authorities
CLEAPSE Consortium of Local Education Authorities for the Provision of Science Equipment
cler. clerical
cl. gt [bookbinding] cloth gilt
CLH *Croix de la Légion d'Honneur* (French: Cross of the Legion of Honour)
CLI [computing] command-line interface; cost-of-living index
CLIC Cancer and Leukaemia in Children
clim. climate; climatic
CLIMAP Climate: Long-range Interpretation, Mapping and Prediction (international project)
clin. clinic; clinical
CLit Companion of Literature
CLitt Companion of Literature
CLJ *Cambridge Law Journal*; Commander of the Order of St Lazarus of Jerusalem
clk clerk; clock
clkrm cloakroom (in property advertisement)
clks cloaks (= cloakroom)
clkw. clockwise
CLL [medicine] chronic lymphatic leukaemia
cl. L classical Latin
CLLR International Symposium on Computing in Literary and Linguistic Research
Cllr Councillor
CLM coal–liquid mixture; conservation and load management
clm column
CLML *Current List of Medical Literature*
CLNS [computing] connectionless network service
CLO chief liaison officer; cod liver oil

Clo. Close (in road name)
clo. closet; clothing
cloakrm cloakroom (in property advertisement)
c/lock. central locking (in car advertisement)
CLP China Light and Power (Company Limited); [computing] concurrent logic programming; Constituency Labour Party; [computing] constraint logic programming
CLPA Common Law Procedure Acts
CLR Central London Railway; City of London Rifles; computer-language recorder; [USA] Council on Library Resources
clr clear; colour; cooler
CLRAE Conference of Local and Regional Authorities of Europe
clrm classroom
CLRU Cambridge Language Research Unit
CLS Certificate in Library Science; Christian Literature Society; [statistics] classical least-squares; [statistics] constrained least-squares; Courts of London Sessions
cls. close
CLSB Committee of London and Scottish Bankers
CLT *Canadian Law Times*; *Compagnie Luxembourgeoise de Télédiffusion* (European media company); computer-language translator
CLU Chartered Life Underwriter
CLV [microbiology] carnation latent virus; [microbiology] cassava latent virus; [computing] constant linear velocity
clvd clavichord
CM Canadian Militia; Catholic Mission; [USA] Central Maine; central meridian; [physics] centre of mass; Certificated Master; Certificate of Merit; Certified Master; [UK postcode] Chelmsford; church mission; church missionary; circulation manager; [USA] Cleveland Museum (of Art); combustion modification; [astronautics] command module; Common Market; [music] common metre; complex mixture; composite material; condition monitoring; [computing] configuration management; [Roman Catholic Church] Congregation of the Mission; contrast medium (in radiology); [nuclear technology] core meltdown; corporate membership; Corresponding Member; court martial; [microbiology] culture medium; [vehicle registration] Liverpool; Master of Surgery (from Latin *Chirurgiae Magister*); Member of the Order of Canada
Cm Command Paper (1987–); [chemical element] curium
cM [genetics] centimorgan
cm centimetre
.cm Cameroon (in Internet address)
c.m. *carat métrique* (French: metric carat); *causa mortis* (Latin: by reason of death); [physics] centre of mass; [music] common metre; [medicine] *cras mane* (Latin: tomorrow morning)
CMA Cable Makers' Association; [chemistry] calcium magnesium acetate; Canadian Medical Association; Catering Managers' Association; [USA] Certificate of Management Accounting; Chartered Management Accountant; Church Music Association; civil–military affairs; coal–mineral analysis; [USA] Colorado Mining Association; Commonwealth Medical Association; Communication Managers' Association; cost and management accountant; Country Music Association; Court of Military Appeals
CMa [astronomy] Canis Major
CMAC Catholic Marriage Advisory Council
CMACP *Conseil mondial pour l'assemblée constituante des peuples* (French: World Council for the People's World Convention)
CMAS Clergy Mutual Assurance Society; *Confédération mondiale des activités subaquatiques* (French: World Underwater Federation)
CMB Central Medical Board; Central Midwives Board; Chase Manhattan Bank; [chemistry] chemical mass balance; coastal motor boat; [astronomy] cosmic microwave background
CMBHI Craft Member of the British Horological Institute
CMBI Caribbean Marine Biological Institute
cmbt combat
CMC Canadian Marconi Company; Canadian Meteorological Centre; Canadian

Music Council; [chemistry] carboxymethyl cellulose; Catholic Media Council; Central Manpower Committee; ceramic-matrix composite; [USA] certified management consultant; Collective Measures Committee (of UN); Commandant of the Marine Corps; Conservation Monitoring Centre

CMCW Calvinistic Methodist Church of Wales

CMD [astronomy] colour-magnitude diagram; [music] common metre double; conventional munitions disposal; [physics] cryogenic magnetic detector

Cmd Command Paper (1919–56) (in parliamentary procedure)

cmdg commanding

Cmdr Commander

Cmdre Commodore

Cmdt Commandant

CME Chicago Mercantile Exchange; *Conférence mondiale de l'énergie* (French: World Power Conference); [astronomy] coronal mass ejection; [USA] cost and manufacturability expert

CMEA Council for Mutual Economic Assistance

CMF Cement Makers' Federation; Central Mediterranean Force; [Australia] Citizen Military Forces; Coal Merchants' Federation; [physics] coherent memory filter; Commonwealth Military Forces; [physics] compressed magnetic field; [Roman Catholic Church] *Cordis Mariae Filii* (Latin: Missionary Sons of the Immaculate Heart of Mary)

CMG Commission on Marine Geology; Companion of the Order of St Michael and St George; Computer Management Group

CMH Campaign for the Mentally Handicapped; combined military hospital; [USA] Congressional Medal of Honor

CMHA Canadian Mental Health Association

CMHC [Canada] Central Mortgage and Housing Corporation

CMHR combustion modified highly resilient

CMI [medicine] cell-mediated immunity; *Comité maritime international* (French: International Maritime Committee); *Commission mixte internationale pour la protection des lignes de télécommunication et des canalisations* (French: Joint International Committee for the Protection of Telecommunication Lines and Ducts); Commonwealth Mycological Institute; computer-managed instruction

CMi [astronomy] Canis Minor

CMIA Coal Mining Institute of America

CMIPS [computing] common management information protocol/service

CMIR [USA] Center for Medical Imaging Research

CMJ Church's Ministry among the Jews

CML Central Music Library; [medicine] chronic myeloid leukaemia; computer-managed learning; Council of Mortgage Lenders; [computing] current mode logic

cml commercial

CMLA Chief Martial Law Administrator

CMLJ Commander of Merit of the Order of St Lazarus of Jerusalem

CMM [computing] capability and maturity model; [Canada] Commander of the Order of Military Merit

CMMA [USA] Coal Mining Management College; Concrete Mixer Manufacturers' Association

cmn commission

Cmnd Command Paper (1957–86) (in parliamentary procedure)

cmnr commissioner

CMO Central Merchandising Office (in Zambia); chief medical officer; [USA] collateralized mortgage-backed obligation; [astronomy] compact massive object

CMOPE *Confédération mondiale des organisations de la profession enseignante* (French: World Confederation of Organizations of the Teaching Profession)

CMOS [electronics] complementary metal oxide semiconductor; [electronics] complementary metal oxide silicon

CMP [USA] Central Maine Power Company; Christian Movement for Peace; [astronautics] command module pilot; Commissioner of the Metropolitan Police; cost of maintaining project

cmp. compromise

cmpd compound

CMPDI [USA] Central Mine Planning and Design Institute

cm. pf. cumulative preference (shares); cumulative preferred (shares)

Cmpn Companion
CMR Cape Mounted Rifles; central meter reading; cerebral metabolic rate; [electronics] common mode rejection
CMRA Chemical Marketing Research Association
CMRC [USA] Coal Mining Research Company
CMRO County Milk Regulations Officer
CMRR [electronics] common mode rejection ratio
CMRS [USA] Central Mining Research Station
CMS Catholic Missionary Society; [USA] Center for Measurement of Science; central materials supply; Certificate in Management Studies; Church Missionary Society; [computing] conversational monitor system
c.m.s. [medicine] *cras mane sumendus* (Latin: to be taken tomorrow morning) (in prescriptions)
CMSER [USA] Commission on Marine Science, Engineering and Resources
CM/SM [astronautics] command module service module
cmt cement
CMV [medicine] cerebral major vessel; [medicine] conventional mechanical ventilation; [microbiology] cucumber mosaic virus; [medicine] cytomegalovirus
CMY [computing] cyan, magenta, yellow
CMYK [computing] cyan, magenta, yellow, black
CMZS Corresponding Member of the Zoological Society
CN [fishing port] Campbeltown; Canadian National (Railway); [chemistry] cellulose nitrate; Chinese Nationalists; [chemistry] chloracetophenone; *Code Napoléon* (French: Napoleonic Code); common network; [physics] compound nucleus; [physics] condensation nucleus; Confederate Navy; [commerce] credit note; [civil aircraft marking] Morocco; [vehicle registration] Newcastle upon Tyne
C/N [ecology] carbon–nitrogen (as in **C/N ratio**); circular note; consignment note; contract note; [insurance] cover note; [commerce] credit note
Cn [ecclesiastical] Canon
.cn China (in Internet address)
c.n. [medicine] *cras nocte* (Latin: tomorrow night)
CNA Canadian Nuclear Association; [US navy] Center for Naval Analyses; Central News Agency (in Taiwan); [USA] Chemical Notation Association; [astronomy] cosmic noise absorption; Cyprus News Agency
CNAA Council for National Academic Awards
CNADS Conference of National Armaments Directors (in NATO)
CNAR Chief of Naval Air Services; [finance] compound net annual rate
CNC computerized numerical control
Cnc [astronomy] Cancer
CNCIEC China National Coal Import and Export Corporation
Cncl Council
Cnclr Councillor
CNCMH Canadian National Committee for Mental Hygiene
cncr. concurrent
CND Campaign for Nuclear Disarmament
CNDC Cherished Numbers Dealers Association; China Nuclear Data Centre
CNE *Comisión nacional de energía* (Spanish: National Energy Commission)
CNEAF coal, nuclear, electric and alternate fuels
CN(Eng)O Chief Naval Engineering Officer
CNES *Centre national d'études spatiales* (French: National Space Centre)
CNF Challis National Forest; Commonwealth Nurses' Federation
CNFD [USA] Commercial Nuclear Fuel Division
CNG compressed natural gas; consolidated natural gas
CNI Chief of Naval Information; Companion of the Nautical Institute
CNIP Ciskei National Independence Party
CNIPA Committee of National Institutes of Patent Agents
CNL Canadian National Library; [Australia] Commonwealth National Library; [USA] Crocker Nuclear Laboratory
cnl cancel
CNLA [USA] Council of National Library Associations
CNLS [statistics] complex nonlinear least-square

CNM [USA] Certified Nurse-Midwife
CNN Cable News Network; Certified Nursery Nurse
CNO chief nursing officer; Chief of Naval Operations
CNP Chief of Naval Personnel; Council for National Parks
CNR Canadian National Railway; Civil Nursing Reserve; *Conseil national de la révolution* (French: National Revolutionary Council) (in Burkina Faso); Council of National Representatives
cnr corner
CNRE [USA] cooperative networks on rural energy
CNRS *Centre national de la recherche scientifique* (French: National Centre for Scientific Research)
CNS [anatomy] central nervous system; [USA] Cherokee Nuclear Station; Chief of Naval Staff; China News Service (news agency); Community Nursing Services; Congress of Neurological Surgeons
c.n.s. [medicine] *cras nocte sumendus* (Latin: to be taken tomorrow night) (in prescriptions)
CNSI [USA] Chem-Nuclear Systems Incorporated
CNSLD chronic nonspecific lung disease
CNSSO Chief Naval Supply and Secretariat Officer
CNT Canadian National Telegraphs; celestial navigation trainer; [USA] Center for Neighborhood Technology; Commission for the New Towns; *Confederación nacional del trabajo* (Spanish: National Confederation of Labour)
cntn contain
cntr container
cntr. contribute; contribution
cnvt convict
CO Cabinet Office; [fishing port] Caernarvon; [medicine] cardiac output; careers officer; central office; chief officer; clerical officer; [UK postcode] Colchester; [international vehicle registration] Colombia; [US postcode] Colorado; [military] combined operations; commanding officer; command order; Commissioner of Oaths; Commonwealth Office (became part of FCO); [finance] *compte ouvert* (French: open account); conscientious objector; criminal offence; Crown Office; [electronics] current oscillations; [vehicle registration] Exeter
C/O case oil; cash order; certificate of origin
Co [chemical element] cobalt
Co. Coalition; Colorado; Company; County
c/o care of (in postal addresses); [bookkeeping] carried over; change over
.co Colombia (in Internet address)
co. [navigation] course
c.o. [medicine] complains of; [bookkeeping] carried over
CO_2 carbon dioxide
COA change of address; College of Aeronautics; [medicine] condition on admission
coad. coadjutor
Coal. Coalition
COAS Council of the Organization of American States
coax [short form] coaxial cable
c.o.b. close of business
COBE [astronomy] Cosmic Background Explorer
Cobol [computing] common business-oriented language
c.o.b.q. *cum omnibus bonis quiescat* (Latin: may he/she rest with all good souls)
Cobra Cabinet Office Briefing Room
COC Chamber of Commerce; Clerk of the Chapel; [USA] combat operations center; [medicine] combined oral contraceptive; Corps of Commissionaires
coc. cocaine
COCA [USA] consent order and compliance agreement
COCAST Council for Overseas Colleges of Arts, Science and Technology
COCEMA *Comité des constructeurs européens de matériel alimentaire* (French: Committee of European Machinery Manufacturers for the Food Industries)
coch. [medicine] *cochleare* (Latin: spoonful)
coch. amp. [medicine] *cochleare amplum* (Latin: heaped spoonful)
cochl. [medicine] *cochleare* (Latin: spoonful)
coch. mag. [medicine] *cochleare magnum* (Latin: tablespoonful)

coch. med. [medicine] *cochleare medium* (Latin: dessertspoonful)
coch. parv. [medicine] *cochleare parvum* (Latin: teaspoonful)
COCI Consortium on Chemical Information
COCOM Coordinating Committee for Multinational Export Controls
COCOMO [computing] constructive cost model
COD cash on delivery; cause of death; Chamber of Deputies; chemical oxygen demand; [USA] collect on delivery; *Concise Oxford Dictionary*
Cod. Codex
cod. codex; codicil; codification
c.o.d. cargo on deck; cash on delivery; [USA] collect on delivery
CODAG [engineering] combined diesel and gas turbine
CODAN [telecommunications] carrier-operated device anti-noise
CODASYL [computing] Conference on Data Systems Languages
CODATA Confederation of Design and Technology Associations
codd. codices
codec [computing] coder-decoder
Codesh Convention for a Democratic South Africa
CODIPHASE [computing] coherent digital phased array system
CODOG [engineering] combined diesel or gas turbine
CODOT *Classification of Occupations and Directory of Occupational Titles*
COE Chamber Orchestra of Europe; *Conseil oecuménique des églises* (French: World Council of Churches); [USA] Corps of Engineers; cost of electricity; cost of energy
COED computer-operated electronic display; *Concise Oxford English Dictionary*
co-ed [short form] coeducational
coeff. coefficient
CoEnCo Committee for Environmental Conservation
COESA [USA] Committee on Extension to the Standard Atmosphere
COF *Comité olympique française* (French: French Olympic Committee)
C of A Certificate of Airworthiness; College of Arms
COFACE [commerce] *Compagnie française pour l'assurance du commerce extérieur* (French: French export credit guarantee company)
C of B confirmation of balance
C of C Chamber of Commerce
C of E Church of England; Council of Europe
C of ECS Church of England Children's Society
C of F Chaplain of the Fleet; chief of finance; [engineering] coefficient of friction
C of G centre of gravity
C of GH Cape of Good Hope
COFI Committee on Fisheries
C of I Church of Ireland
C of L City of London
C of M [aeronautics] Certificate of Maintenance
C of S Chief of Staff; Church of Scotland; conditions of service
COG Cleansing Officers' Guild
CoG centre of gravity
cog. cognate; cognizant; cognomen
c.o.g. centre of gravity
COGAG [engineering] combined gas and gas turbine
COGB certified official government business
COGECA *Comité général de la coopération agricole des pays de la CE* (French: General Committee for Agricultural Cooperation in the EU Countries)
Cogene Committee on Genetic Experimentation
COGLA Canada Oil and Gas Lands Administration
COGMA Concrete Garage Manufacturers' Association
COGS [astronautics] continual orbital guidance system; [accounting] cost of goods sold
coh. coheir
c.o.h. cash on hand
COHSE Confederation of Health Service Employees (became part of Unison)
COI Central Office of Information; certificate of origin and interest; *Commission océanographique intergouvernementale* (French: Intergovernmental Oceanographic Commission); [USA] cost of illness
COIC Canadian Oceanographic Identifica-

tion Centre; Careers and Occupational Information Centre
COID Council on International Development
CoID Council of Industrial Design (former name of Design Council)
COIE Committee on Invisible Exports
COIF Control of Intensive Farming
COIL chemical oxygen–iodine laser
COIN [USA] counter-insurgency
COINS [USA] Committee on Improvement of National Statistics
COJO Conference of Jewish Organizations
COL centrally operated locking (in car advertisement); computer-oriented language; cost of living
Col [astronomy] Columba
Col. Colombia; Colombian; Colonel; Colorado; [Bible] Colossians
col. collect; collected; collection; collector; college; collegiate; colon; colonial; colony; colour; coloured; column
COLA Camping and Outdoor Leisure Association; [USA] cost-of-living adjustment (in employment contract)
Col. Comdt Colonel Commandant
COLD [medicine] chronic obstructive lung disease
Coling International Conference on Computational Linguistics
Coll. College
coll. collateral; colleague; collect; collected; collection; collective; collector; college; collegiate; colloquial; colloquialism; [medicine] collyrium (eyewash)
collab. collaborate; (in) collaboration (with); collaborator
collat. collateral; collaterally
collect. collective; collectively
colloq. colloquial; colloquialism; colloquially
coll'ott. [music] *coll'ottava* (Italian: in octaves)
collr collector
colly colliery
Colo. Colorado
colog. cologarithm
Coloss. [Bible] Colossians
Col. P [advertising] colour page
COLS [computing] communications for online systems
cols columns
Col-Sgt Colour-Sergeant
COM coal–oil mixture; [US navy] Commander; [chemistry] complex organic mixture; computerized operations management; computer output on microfiche (or microfilm)
Com [astronomy] Coma Berenices
Com. Commander; Commissary; Commissioner; Committee; Commodore; Commonwealth; Communist
com. comedy; comic; comma; commentary; commerce; commercial; commission; commissioner; committee; common; commoner; commonly; commune; communicate; communicated; communication(s); community
.com (US) commercial organization (in Internet address)
COMA Committee on Medical Aspects of Food Policy
COMAF *Comité des constructeurs de matériel frigorifique de la CE* (French: Committee of Refrigerating Plant Manufacturers of the EU)
COMAL [computing] common algorithmic language
COMAR [USA] Code of Maryland Air Regulations
COMARE [USA] Committee on Medical Aspects of Radiation in the Environment
COMART Commander, Marine Air Reserve Training
comb. combination; combine; combined; combining; combustible; combustion
Comd. Commander
comd command
comd. commanding
COMDEV Commonwealth Development Finance Company
Comdg [military] Commanding
Comdr Commander
Comdt Commandant
COME Chief Ordnance Mechanical Engineer
COMECON Council for Mutual Economic Assistance
Comet Committee for Middle East Trade; computer-operated management evaluation technique
COMEX [USA] Commodity Exchange (New York)
COMEXO Committee for Exploitation of the Oceans
comfy [short form] comfortable

Com-Gen Commissary-General
COMIBOL *Corporación Minera de Bolivia* (Bolivian state mining company)
Cominform Communist Information Bureau
COMINT communications intelligence
Comintern Communist International
coml commercial
COMLOGNET [US air force] combat logistics network
Comm. Commander; Commodore
comm. commentary; commerce; commercial; commercially; committee; commonwealth; communal; communication
Commd [military] Commissioned
commem. commemoration; commemorative
Commiss. Commissary
Commissr Commissioner
Commn Commission
commn commission
Commnd [military] Commissioned
Commr Commissioner
comms communications
commun. communication; community
Commy Commissary
COMO Committee of Marketing Organizations
Comp. Companion (of institute or institution)
comp. companion; comparative; compare; comparison; compass; compensation; compete; competition; competitive; competitor; compilation; compiled; compiler; complete; compose; composer; composite; composition; compositor; compound; compounded; comprehensive; compression; comprising
COMPAC Commonwealth Trans-Pacific Telephone Cable
compar. comparative; comparison
compd compound
Comp-Gen Comptroller-General
compl. complement; complete; compliment; complimentary
complt complainant; complaint
compo. composition
compr. compressive
Compsac International Computer Software and Applications Conference
compt compartment
Compt. Comptroller
Comptr Comptroller
Comr Commissioner
Com. Rom. Common Romance (language)
comsat communications satellite
ComSec Commonwealth Secretariat
COMSER Commission on Marine Science and Engineering Research (in UN)
Com. Teut. Common Teutonic (language)
Com. Ver. [Bible] Common Version
Com. W Ger. Common West Germanic (language)
Comy-Gen Commissary-General
Con. Conformist; Conservative; [finance] Consols; Constable; [military] Constructor; Consul; [music] contralto
con. concentration; concerning; concerto; conclusion; conditioning; confidence; conics; *conjunx* (Latin: wife); connection; conservation; consolidate; consolidated; [finance] consols; continue; continued; *contra* (Latin: against); convenience; conversation
CONAC [USA] Continental Air Command
CONAD [USA] Continental Air Defense Command
CONARC [USA] Continental Army Command
CONBA Council of National Beekeeping Associations of the United Kingdom
conbd contributed
Con. C Constructor Captain
conc. concentrate; concentrated; concentration; concerning; concerto; concise
concd concentrated
concg concentrating
conch. conchology
conchie [short form] conscientious objector
concn concentration
Con. Cr Constructor Commander
concr. concrete
con. cr. [book-keeping] contra credit
cond. condense; condensed; condenser; condition; conditional; conduct; conducted; conductivity; conductor
condr conductor
con esp. [music] *con espressione* (Italian: with expression)
con espr. [music] *con espressione* (Italian: with expression)
conf. confection; confectionery; *confer* (Latin: compare); conference; confession; confessor; confidential

confab [short form] confabulation
Confed. Confederacy; Confederate; Confederation
confed. confederate; confederated; confederation
Cong. Congregational; Congregationalist; Congress; Congressional
cong. [pharmacology] *congius* (Latin: gallon); congregation; congregational
Cong. R [USA] Congressional Records
Cong. Rec. [USA] Congressional Records
CONGU Council of National Golf Unions
CONI *Comitato Olimpico Nazionale Italiano* (Italian: Italian National Olympic Committee)
con. inv. consular invoice
conj. conjecture; [grammar] conjugation; [grammar] conjunction; conjunctive
Con. L Constructor Lieutenant
CONLAN [computing] consensus language
Con. LCr Constructor Lieutenant-Commander
Conn. Connecticut
conn. connect; connected; connection; connotation
conq. conquer; conquered; conqueror; conquest
CONS [computing] connection-oriented network service
Cons. Conservative; Conservatoire; Conservatorium; Conservatory; Constable; Constitution; Consul
cons. consecrate; consecrated; consecration; consecutive; consequence; conservation; conservative; conserve; consider; consigned; consignment; consolidated; consonant; constable; constitution; constitutional; construction; consul; consult; consulting
con. sec. conic section
Conserv. Conservatoire; Conservatorium; Conservatory
conserv. conservatory (in property advertisement)
cons. et prud. *consilio et prudentia* (Latin: by counsel and prudence)
consgt consignment
consid. consideration
Con. SL Constructor Sub-Lieutenant
consol. consolidated
consols [short form] consolidated annuities (or stock)
Const. Constable; Constitution
const. constable; constant; constituency; constitution; constitutional; construction
constit. constituent
constl constitutional
constr. construct; construction; construe
cont. container; containing; contents; continent; continental; continue; continued; [music] continuo; continuum; *contra* (Latin: against); contract; contraction; control; controller
contag. contagious
contbd contraband
contbg contributing
cont. bon. mor. *contra bonos mores* (Latin: contrary to good manners)
contd contained; continued
contemp. contemporary
contg containing
contn continuation
contr. contract(s); contracted; contraction; contralto; contrary; contrast; contrasted; control; controller
contr. bon. mor. *contra bonos mores* (Latin: contrary to good manners)
cont. rem. [medicine] *continuantur remedia* (Latin: let the medication be continued) (in prescriptions)
contrib. contributed; contributing; contribution; contributor
CONUS continental United States
Conv. Convocation
conv. convenience; convenient; convent; convention; conventional; conversation; conversion; converter; convertible
convce conveyance
COOC [insurance] contact with oil or other cargo
co-op [short form] cooperative (society or store)
COP [New Zealand] Certificate of Proficiency (university pass); coefficient of performance (in thermodynamics); [USA] community-oriented policing; custom of port
Cop. Copernican; Coptic
cop. copper; copulative; copyright; copyrighted
COPA *Comité des organisations professionnelles agricoles de la CE* (French: Committee of Agricultural Organizations in the EU)

COPAL Cocoa Producers' Alliance
COPD [medicine] chronic obstructive pulmonary disease
Copec Conference on Christian Politics, Economics and Citizenship
COPPSO Conference of Professional and Public Service Organizations
copr. copyright
COPS Council of Polytechnic Secretaries
Copt. Coptic
coptr copartner
COPUOS Committee on the Peaceful Uses of Outer Space
COPUS Committee on the Public Understanding of Science
COR Committee of the Regions (in EU)
Cor. [Bible] Corinthians; Coroner
cor. corner; cornet; [music] *corno* (Italian: horn); coroner; *corpus* (Latin: the body); correct; corrected; correction; correlative; correspondence; correspondent; corresponding; corrupt
Coral [computing] common real-time application language
Corat Christian Organizations Research and Advisory Trust
CORBA [computing] common object request broker architecture
CORD [medicine] chronic obstructive respiratory disease
Corda Coronary Artery Disease Research Association
CORE [USA] Congress of Racial Equality
CORES computer-aided (or -assisted) order routing and execution system (in Tokyo Stock Exchange)
CORGI Council for Registered Gas Installers
Cor. Mem. Corresponding Member
Corn. Cornish; Cornwall
Cornh. *Cornhill Magazine*
corol. corollary
coroll. corollary
Corp. Corporal; Corporation
Corpl Corporal
Corpn Corporation
corr. correct; corrected; correction; corrective; correlative; *corrente* (Italian: current); correspond; correspondence; correspondent; corresponding; corrigenda; corrugated; corrupt; corrupted; corruption
CORRA Combined Overseas Rehabilitation Relief Appeal
correl. correlative
corresp. correspondence; corresponding
Corresp. Mem. Corresponding Member
corrupt. corruption
CORS Chief of the Regulating Staff
Cors. Corsica; Corsican
Cor. Sec. corresponding secretary
CORSO [New Zealand] Council of Organizations for Relief Services Overseas
CORT Council of Regional Theatres; Council of Repertory Theatres
cort. cortex
COS [commerce] cash on shipment; Chamber of Shipping; Charity Organization Society; Chief of Staff; Cinema Organ Society
CoS Chief of Staff
Cos. Companies; Counties
cos [mathematics] cosine
c.o.s. [commerce] cash on shipment
COSA Colliery Officials and Staffs Association; [accounting] cost of sales adjustment
co. sa *come sopra* (Italian: as above)
COSAG [shipping] combined steam turbine and gas turbine
COSAR compression scanning array radar
COSATI Committee on Scientific and Technical Information
COSATU Congress of South African Trade Unions
COSBA Computer Services and Bureaux Association
COSE [computing] common open software environment
COSEC Coordinating Secretariat of the National Union of Students
cosec [mathematics] cosecant
cosech [mathematics] hyperbolic cosecant
COSFPS Commons, Open Spaces and Footpaths Preservation Society
cosh [mathematics] hyperbolic cosine
COSHEP Committee of Scottish Higher Education Principals
COSHH Control of Substances Hazardous to Health
CoSIRA Council for Small Industries in Rural Areas
COSLA Convention of Scottish Local Authorities
COSMD Combined Operations Signals Maintenance Division

cosmog. cosmogony; cosmographical; cosmography
COSMOS Coast Survey Marine Observation System
co. so. *come sopra* (Italian: as above)
COSPAR Committee on Space Research
Coss. *Consules* (Latin: Consuls)
COSSAC Chief of Staff to Supreme Allied Commander
COSSEC Cambridge, Oxford and Southern School Examinations Council
COST Committee for Overseas Science and Technology
COT [physics] change of temperature
CoT College of Technology
cot [mathematics] cotangent
cotan [mathematics] cotangent
COTC Canadian Officers' Training Corps
coth [mathematics] hyperbolic cotangent
COTR [USA] contracting officers' technical representative
Cots Childlessness Overcome Through Surrogacy
COTT [South Africa] Central Organization for Technical Training
couch. [heraldry] couchant
.co.uk UK commercial organization (in Internet address)
Coun. Council; Councillor; Counsellor
cour. *courant* (French: current, this month, inst.) (in correspondence)
COV [statistics] coefficient of variation; [chemistry] concentrated oil of vitriol; [electronics] corona onset voltage; [statistics] covariance; [genetics] crossover value
Cov. Coventry
cov. [statistics] covariance; covenant
covers [mathematics] coversed sine
cov. pt [cricket] cover point
COW character-oriented windows
COWAR Committee on Water Research
COWPS [USA] Council on Wages and Price Stability
Coy [military] company
COZI communications zone indicator
CP [civil aircraft marking] Bolivia; [medicine] Campylobacter pylori (bacterium causing gastric illness); Canadian Pacific (Railway); Canadian Press (news agency); Cape Province (former South African province); Captain of the Parish (in Isle of Man); [navigation] cardinal point; *casella postale* (Italian: post office box); [computing] central processor; [aeronautics] centre of pressure; centrifugal pump; [medicine] cerebral palsy; [surveying] change point; [physics] charge parity; charter party; chemically pure; Chief of Police; Chief Patriarch; [medicine] chronic pancreatitis; [medicine] cisplatin (used to treat cancer); civil power; civil procedure; Clarendon Press; Clerk of the Peace; code of procedure; *Codice Penale* (Italian: Penal Code); College of Preceptors; colour printing (as in **CP filter**); [military] Command Post; commercial paper; Common Pleas; Common Prayer; Communist Party; community physician; community programme; *Companhia dos Caminhos de Ferro Portugueses* (Portuguese railway company); [stock exchange] concert party; condensation product; conference paper; conference proceedings; [Roman Catholic Church] *Congregatio Passionis* (Latin: Congregation of the Passion); [India] Congress Party; [South Africa] Conservative Party; convict prison; corporal punishment; [Australia] Country Party (former name of National Party); county primary (school); Court of Probate; [biochemistry] creatine phosphate; [physics] cross polarization; current paper; [vehicle registration] Huddersfield
C/P charter party
Cp. [Roman Catholic Church] compline
cp. compare
c.p. candlepower; carriage paid; [aeronautics] centre of pressure; chemically pure; constant pressure
CPA Canadian Pharmaceutical Association; Canadian Psychological Association; central planning area; [USA] Certified Public Accountant; Chartered Patent Agent; Chick Producers' Association; [insurance] claims payable abroad; Clyde Port Authority; Commonwealth Parliamentary Association; Communist Party of Australia; Construction Plant Association; Contractors' Plant Association; contract price adjustment; cost planning and appraisal; Council of Provincial Associations; [computing] critical path analysis

CPAC Collaborative Pesticides Analytical Committee; Consumer Protection Advisory Committee
CPAG Child Poverty Action Group; [USA] Collision Prevention Advisory Group
CPAI Canvas Products Association International
C Pal. Crystal Palace
CPAM Committee of Purchasers of Aircraft Material
CPAS Catholic Prisoners' Aid Society; Church Pastoral Aid Society
CPB [medicine] cardiopulmonary bypass; [book-keeping] casual payments book; Central Planning Bureau; Communist Party of Britain
CPBF Campaign for Press and Broadcasting Freedom
CPC [USA] City Planning Commission; city police commissioner; Clerk of the Privy Council; [medicine] clinicopathological conference; Communist Party of China; Conservative Political Centre
CPCIZ *Comité permanent des congrès internationaux de zoologie* (French: Standing Committee of International Zoological Congresses)
CPCU [USA] Chartered Property and Casualty Underwriter
CPD [astronomy] Cape Photographic Durchmusterung (star catalogue); [medicine] chronic pulmonary disease; [electronics] contact potential difference; continuing professional development
cpd compound
c.p.d. [commerce] charterers pay dues
CPDL Canadian Patents and Developments Limited
CPDM Centre for Physical Distribution Management
CPE Certificate of Physical Education; [USA] Certified Property Exchanger; [medicine] chronic pulmonary emphysema; College of Physical Education; [law] Common Professional Examination; *Congrès du peuple européen* (French: Congress of European People); contractor performance evaluation; [microbiology] cytopathic effect
CPEA Catholic Parents' and Electors' Association; [USA] Cooperative Program for Educational Administration
c. pén. *code pénal* (French: penal code)
CPEQ Corporation of Professional Engineers of Quebec
CPF contributory pension fund
CPFF cost plus fixed fee
CPFS Council for the Promotion of Field Studies
CPG Coronary Prevention Group
CPGB Communist Party of Great Britain
CPH Certificate in Public Health
cph cycles per hour
CPHA Canadian Public Health Association
CPhys Chartered Physicist
CPI chief pilot instructor; Communist Party of India; consumer price index
cpi [printing] characters per inch
CPJI *Cour permanente de justice internationale* (French: Permanent Court of International Justice)
CPL Cats' Protection League; central public library; Colonial Products Laboratory; [computing] combined programming language; commercial pilot's licence
Cpl Corporal
cpl [printing] characters per line
CPM [USA] Certified Property Manager; Colonial Police Medal; [music] common particular metre; Communist Party of Malaya; computer program module; [computing] critical path method
CP/M [trademark] Control Program for Microcomputers
cpm [computing] characters per minute; cycles per minute
CPMEE&W Council for Postgraduate Medical Education in England and Wales
CPN *Communistische Partij van Nederland* (Dutch: Netherlands Communist Party); community psychiatric nurse
Cpn Copenhagen
cpn coupon
CPNA Council of Photographic News Agencies
Cpnhgn Copenhagen
CPNZ Communist Party of New Zealand
CPO cancel previous order; [chemistry] catalytic partial oxidation; Chief Petty Officer; command pay office; Commonwealth Producers' Organization; compulsory purchase order; county planning officer; crime prevention officer

CPP chemical processing plant; Convention People's Party (in Ghana); [computing] critical path plan(ning); current purchasing power (as in **CPP accounting**)
c.p.p. controllable pitch propeller
CPPA Canadian Pulp and Paper Association
CPPCC Chinese People's Political Consultative Conference
CPPS [computing] critical path planning and scheduling
CPR Canadian Pacific Railway; [medicine] cardiopulmonary resuscitation
CPRC Central Price Regulation Committee
CPRE Council for the Protection of Rural England
CPRS Central Policy Review Staff
CPRW Council for the Protection of Rural Wales
CPS Centre for Policy Studies; cents per share; [USA] Certified Professional Secretary; Church Patronage Society; Clerk of Petty Sessions; Commonwealth Public Service; Communist Party of Syria; Congregational Publishing Society; Crown Prosecution Service; *Custos Privati Sigilli* (Latin: Keeper of the Privy Seal)
cps [computing] characters per second; cycles per second
CPSA Civil and Public Services Association; Clay Pigeon Shooting Association
CPSC [USA] Consumer Product Safety Commission
CPSS Certificate in Public Service Studies
CPSU Communist Party of the Soviet Union
CPsychol Chartered Psychologist
CPT Canadian Pacific Telegraphs; [physics] charge parity–time; cost per thousand; [computing] critical path technique
Cpt. Captain
cpt cockpit; counterpoint
CPTB Clay Products Technical Bureau
CPU central packaging unit; [computing] central processing unit; collective protection unit; Commonwealth Press Union
CPUSA Communist Party of the United States of America
CPVE Certificate of Pre-vocational Education
CQ [military] charge of quarters; conditionally qualified
CQM Chief Quartermaster; Company Quartermaster
CQMS Company Quartermaster-Sergeant
CQR *Church Quarterly Review*
CQS Court of Quarter Sessions
CQSW Certificate of Qualification in Social Work
CR *Carolina Regina* (Latin: Queen Caroline); *Carolus Rex* (Latin: King Charles); carriage return; carrier's risk; cash receipts; central railway; central registry; Chief Ranger; [medicine] chronic rejection; *Civis Romanus* (Latin: Roman citizen); [USA] Commendation Ribbon; Community of the Resurrection (Anglican monastic order); company's risk; [medicine] complete regression; [medicine] complete remission; [engineering] compression ratio; [medicine] computed radiography; [chemistry] concentration ratio; [psychology] conditioned reflex; [psychology] conditioned response; conference report; Congo red (dye); consciousness raising; control relay; cosmic rays; [international vehicle registration] Costa Rica; crease-resistant; credit; credit rating; credit report; [statistics] critical ratio; [UK postcode] Croydon; current rate; *Custos Rotulorum* (Latin: Keeper of the Rolls); [vehicle registration] Portsmouth; [civil aircraft marking] Portugal
Cr [chemical element] chromium; Commander; Councillor; cruiser
c/r company's risk
cr. created; creation; credit; creditor; creek; [music] *crescendo* (Italian: with increasing loudness); crew; crimson; crown; cruise; *crux* (Latin: cross)
.cr Costa Rica (in Internet address)
c.r. *con riserva* (Italian: with reservations); [finance] cum rights (i.e. with rights)
CRA California Redwood Association; Canadian Rheumatism Association; [Northern Ireland] Civil Rights Association; Coal Research Association of New Zealand; Commander of the Royal Artillery; Commercial Rabbit Association; composite research aircraft; corrosion-resistant alloy
CrA [astronomy] Corona Australis
CrAA Commander-at-Arms

CRAC Careers Research and Advisory Centre; Central Religious Advisory Committee; Construction Research Advisory Council

CRAD Committee for Research into Apparatus for the Disabled

CRAE Committee for the Reform of Animal Experimentation

CRAeS Companion of the Royal Aeronautical Society

CRAF [USA] Civil Reserve Air Fleet

CRAMRA Convention on the Regulation of Antarctic Mineral Resource Activities

cran. craniology

craniol. craniology

craniom. craniometry

CRASC Commander of the Royal Army Service Corps

CRB Central Radio Bureau

CrB [astronomy] Corona Borealis

CRC [printing] camera-ready copy; Cancer Research Campaign; child-resistant closure; Civil Rights Commission; coal rank code; Community Relations Council; [printing] composing room chapel; [USA] Coordinating Research Council; cycle racing club; [computing] cyclic redundancy check

CRCC Canadian Red Cross Committee

CRCH central register and clearing house

CRCP Certificant of the Royal College of Physicians

CRCS Certificant of the Royal College of Surgeons (of England)

CRD [medicine] chronic respiratory disease; Crop Research Division

CRDEC [USA] Chemical Research, Development and Engineering Center

CRDF cathode-ray direction-finding

CRE [USA] Coal Research Establishment; Commander of the Royal Engineers; Commercial Relations and Exports; Commission for Racial Equality; cumulative radiation effect

CREFAL *Centro Regional de Educación Fundamental para la América Latina* (Spanish: Regional Centre of Fundamental Education for Latin America)

Cres. Crescent (in road name)

cres. [music] *crescendo* (Italian: with increasing loudness)

cresc. [music] *crescendo* (Italian: with increasing loudness)

CRF [finance] capital recovery factor; [medicine] chronic renal failure; [medicine] coagulase reacting factor; [biochemistry] corticotrophin-releasing factor

crg. carriage

CRH [biochemistry] corticotrophin-releasing hormone

CRI Caribbean Research Institute; Children's Relief International; [medicine] chronic renal insufficiency; [photography] colour reversal intermediate; [USA] Cray Research Incorporated; *Croce Rossa Italiana* (Italian: Italian Red Cross)

CRIB Current Research in Britain

CRIC [Roman Catholic Church] Canons Regular of the Immaculate Conception; Commercial Radio International Committee

crim. criminal

crim. con. [law] criminal conversation (i.e. adultery)

criminol. criminology

CRIS [medicine] clinical radiology imaging system; [computing] command retrieval information system; current research information system

crit. criterion; critic; critical; critically; criticism

Crk Cork (Ireland)

CRL [Roman Catholic Church] Canons Regular of the Lateran; Certified Record Librarian; Certified Reference Librarian; Chemical Research Laboratory

CRM [USA] Central Rocky Mountains; certified reference material; counter-radar missile; count-rate meter; cruise missile

CRMA Cotton and Rayon Merchants' Association

CRMF Cancer Relief Macmillan Fund

CRMP Corps of Royal Military Police

crn crown

crn. crane

CRNA Campaign for the Restoration of the National Anthem and Flag; Clinical Research Nurses' Association

CRNCM Companion of the Royal Northern College of Music

CRNSS Chief of the Royal Naval Scientific Service

CRO cathode-ray oscilloscope (or oscillograph); Cave Rescue Organization of Great Britain; chief recruiting officer; Commonwealth Relations Office (became part of FCO); community relations officer; Companies Registration Office; compulsory rights order; Criminal Records Office

Croat. Croatia; Croatian

CRP *Calendarium Rotulorum Patentium* (Latin: Calendar of the Patent Rolls); [Roman Catholic Church] Canons Regular of Prémontré; capacity requirement plan; [India] Central Reserve Police; coordinated research programme

CRPL [USA] Central Radio Propagation Laboratory

CRPPH [USA] Committee on Radiation Protection and Public Health

CRR constant ratio rule; Curia Regis Roll

CRS Catholic Record Society; Cereals Research Station; cold-rolled steel; Cooperative Retail Society; cosmic radio source

CRSI [USA] Concrete Reinforcing Steel Institute

CRT cathode-ray tube; [mathematics] Chinese remainder theorem; combat readiness training; composite rate tax

Crt Court; [astronomy] Crater

CRTC Canadian Radio-Television Commission

crtkr caretaker

CRTS Commonwealth Reconstruction Training Scheme

CRU civil resettlement unit; [computing] control register user

Cru [astronomy] Crux

Crv [astronomy] Corvus

crypto. cryptographic; cryptography

cryst. crystal; crystalline; crystallography

crystallog. crystallography

crystd crystallized

crystn crystallization

CRZZ *Centralna Rada Związków Zawadowych* (Polish: Central Council of Trade Unions)

CS [medicine] Caesarean section; [chemistry] calcium silicate; capital stock; carbon steel; (Ben) Carson and (Roger) Stoughton (as in **CS gas**); [biochemistry] casein; cast steel; Certificate in Statistics; Chartered Surveyor; Chemical Society; Chief of Staff; chief secretary; [computing] chip select; Christian Science; Christian Scientist; city surveyor; civil servant; Civil Service; Clerk of Session; Clerk to the Signet; [medicine] clinical stage; close shot; close support; College of Science; [mining] colliery screened; [psychology] conditioned stimulus; [USA] Confederate States; [Roman Catholic Church] Congregation of Salesians; [physics] coolant system; Cooperative Society; cotton seed; county surveyor; Court of Session; [fishing port] Cowes; credit sales; cruiser squadron; *Custos Sigilli* (Latin: Keeper of the Seal); [vehicle registration] Glasgow; [civil aircraft marking] Portugal

C/S channel shank (buttons); cycles per second

Cs [chemical element] caesium

Cs [meteorology] cirrostratus

c/s cases; cycles per second

cs. case; census; consul

c.s. capital stock; *come sopra* (Italian: as above)

CSA Canadian Standards Association; Casualty Surgeons' Association; Channel Swimming Association; Child Support Agency; Common Services Agency; [USA] Community Services Administration; [Canada] Computer Science Association; Confederate States Army; Confederate States of America

CSAA Child Study Association of America

CSAB Civil Service Appeal Board

CSAE Canadian Society of Agricultural Engineering

CSAP Canadian Society of Animal Production

CSAR Communication Satellite Advanced Research

CSB Bachelor of Christian Science; [engineering] calcium silicate brick; Central Statistical Board; [medicine] chemical stimulation of the brain

CSBF Civil Service Benevolent Fund

CSBGM Committee of Scottish Bank General Managers

CSBM [military] confidence- and security-building measures

CSC Civil Service Commission; Commonwealth Science Council; Comprehensive Schools Committee; [Belgium] *Confédération des syndicats chrétiens* (French: Federation of Christian Trade Unions); Conspicuous Service Cross (replaced by DSC)

csc [mathematics] cosecant
CSCB Committee of Scottish Clearing Bankers
CSCBS Commodore Superintendent, Contract-Built Ships
CSCC Civil Service Commission of Canada; Council of Scottish Chambers of Commerce
CSCE Conference on Security and Cooperation in Europe (former name of OSCE)
CSCFE Civil Service Council for Further Education
CSCW computer-supported cooperative working
CSD Chartered Society of Designers (formerly SIAD); Civil Service Department; Commonwealth Society for the Deaf; [engineering] constant speed drive; Cooperative Secretaries Diploma; Doctor of Christian Science
CSDE Central Servicing Development Establishment (in RAF)
CSE Campaign for State Education; Central Signals Establishment; Certificate of Secondary Education (replaced by GCSE); [computing] cognitive systems engineering; Council of the Stock Exchange
cse course
CSEA [USA] Civil Service Employees Association
C-section [medicine] Caesarean section
CSED [US navy] coordinated ship electronics design
CSEU Confederation of Shipbuilding and Engineering Unions
CSF [medicine] cerebrospinal fluid; Coil Spring Federation; [medicine] colony-stimulating factor
CSFA Canadian Scientific Film Association
CSFE Canadian Society of Forest Engineers
CSG Catholic Social Guild; Companion of the Order of the Star of Ghana; [computing] constructive solid geometry
CSGA Canadian Seed Growers' Association
CS gas tear gas invented by (Ben) Carson and (Roger) Stoughton
CSH [chemistry] calcium silicate hydrate
csh cash
CSI Chartered Surveyors' Institution; Church of South India; *Commission sportive internationale* (French: International Sporting Commission); [image technology] compact source iodide (as in **CSI lamp**); Companion of the Order of the Star of India; [USA] Construction Specifications Institute
CSICC Canadian Steel Industries Construction Council
CSIP Committee for the Scientific Investigation of the Paranormal
CSIR Council for Scientific and Industrial Research
CSIRA Council for Small Industries in Rural Areas
CSIRO Commonwealth Scientific and Industrial Research Organization (Australia)
CSJ *Christian Science Journal*
csk cask; countersink
CSL [Australia] Commonwealth Serum Laboratories; Communication Sub-Lieutenant; computer simulation language; [computing] control and simulation language; Cub Scout leader
CSLATP Canadian Society of Landscape Architects and Town Planners
CSLO Canadian Scientific Liaison Office; Combined Services Liaison Officer
CSLT Canadian Society of Laboratory Technologists
CSM [medicine] cerebrospinal meningitis; *Christian Science Monitor*; Christian Socialist Movement; [astronautics] command service module; Commission for Synoptic Meteorology; Committee on Safety of Medicines; Company Sergeant-Major; [USA] corn, soya, milk (food supplement)
CSMA [computing] carrier sense multiple access; Chemical Specialities Manufacturers' Association; Civil Service Motoring Association
CSMA/CD [computing] carrier sense multiple access, collision detection (network protocol)
CSMMG Chartered Society of Massage and Medical Gymnastics
CSMTS Card Setting Machine Tenters' Society
CSN Confederate States Navy
CSNI [USA] Committee on the Safety of Nuclear Installations

CSO Caltech Submillimeter Observatory; Central Selling Organization; Central Statistical Office; chief scientific officer; Chief Signal Officer; Chief Staff Officer; Colonial Secretary's Office; [image technology] colour separation overlay; Command Signals Officer; Commonwealth Scientific Office; community service order

CSP Chartered Society of Physiotherapy; Civil Service of Pakistan; [computing] communicating sequential processes; Congregation of Saint Paul; Council for Scientific Policy

CSPAA *Conférence de solidarité des pays afro-asiatiques* (French: Afro-Asian People's Solidarity Conference)

CSPCA Canadian Society for the Prevention of Cruelty to Animals

CSPR [chemistry] chlorosulphonated polyethylene rubber

CSR [Australia] Colonial Sugar Refining Company; combat-stress reaction; Czechoslovak Socialist Republic

CSS [computing] centralized structure store; Certificate in Social Service; computer systems simulator; (member of the) Congregation of the Holy Ghost (from Latin *Sanctus Spiritus*); Council for Science and Society

CSSA Civil Service Supply Association

CSSB Civil Service Selection Board

CSSDA [USA] Council for Social Science Data Archives

CSSR [Roman Catholic Church] *Congregatio Sanctissimi Redemptoris* (Latin: Congregation of the Most Holy Redeemer, the Redemptorists)

CSSS Canadian Soil Science Society

CST [USA] Central Standard Time; College of Science and Technology; College of Speech Therapists; convulsive shock therapy

CSTA Canadian Society of Technical Agriculturists; [New Zealand] Canterbury Science Teachers' Association

CSTI Council of Science and Technology Institutes

CStJ Commander of the Most Venerable Order of the Hospital of St John of Jerusalem

CSU [medicine] catheter specimen of urine; Central Services Unit; Central Statistical Unit; *Christlich-Soziale Union* (German: Christian Social Union) (German political party); Civil Service Union; Colorado State University; [engineering] constant speed unit

CSV [computing] comma-separated variables; community service volunteer

CSW [USA] Certified Social Worker; continuous seismic wave

CSYS [Scotland] Certificate of Sixth Year Studies

CT cable transfer; Candidate in Theology; [UK postcode] Canterbury; Cape Town; [fishing port] Castletown; [medicine] cell therapy; [USA] Central Time; [medicine] cerebral thrombosis; [medicine] cerebral tumour; certifi(cat)ed teacher; Civic Trust; code telegrams; College of Technology; commercial traveller; *commissario tecnico* (Italian: sports coach); [medicine] compute(rize)d tomography (as in **CT scan**); [US postcode] Connecticut; [medicine] coronary thrombosis; corporation tax; counter trade; [electrical engineering] current transformer; cycle time; [vehicle registration] Lincoln

C/T Californian Terms (in grain trade)

Ct Count; Court

ct carat; caught; [currency] cent (hundredth of dollar etc.); [currency] centime (hundredth of franc etc.); circuit; *courant* (French: current, this month, inst.) (in formal correspondence); court; credit; current

Ct. Canton; Connecticut; [music] countertenor

ct. *centum* (Latin: hundred); certificate; crate

CTA Cable Television Association; Camping Trade Association; Canadian Tuberculosis Association; Caribbean Technical Assistance; Caribbean Tourist Association; Catering Teachers' Association; [chemistry] cellulose triacetate; Channel Tunnel Association; Chaplain Territorial Army; Chicago Transit Authority; Commercial Travellers' Association; [USA] commodities trading advisor; [medicine] compute(rize)d tomographic angiography; [medicine] compute(rize)d tomographic arteriography

c.t.a. [law] *cum testamento annexo* (Latin: with the will annexed)
CTAU Catholic Total Abstinence Union
CTB Commonwealth Telecommunications Board; comprehensive test ban
CTBT comprehensive test ban treaty
CTC Canadian Transport Commission; [chemistry] carbon tetrachloride; centralized traffic control; Central Training Council; [USA] Citizens' Training Corps; city technology college; Civil Technical Corps; Commando Training Centre; *Confederación de Trabajadores Cubanos* (Spanish: Confederation of Cuban Workers); *Congrès du travail du Canada* (French: Canadian Labour Congress); corn trade clauses; crushing, tearing and curling (machine); Cyclists' Touring Club
CTD central training depot; [electronics] charge-transfer device; classified telephone directory
ctd coated; continued; crated
CTE [physics] coefficient of thermal expansion
Cte *Comte* (French: Count)
CTEB Council of Technical Examining Bodies
Ctesse *Comtesse* (French: Countess)
CTETOC Council for Technical Education and Training for Overseas Countries
CText Chartered Textile Technologist
CTF Catholic Teachers' Federation; Chaplain to the Territorial Forces; coal-tar fuels
ctf. certificate; certify
ctge cartage; cartridge; cottage
CTH Corporation of Trinity House
CTI computer telephony integration
CTIO Cerro Tololo Inter-American Observatory (Chile)
CTL constant tensile load; [insurance] constructive total loss; [medicine] cytotoxic T-lymphocyte
ctl central
CTM [medicine] compute(rize)d tomographic myelography
CTMB Canal Transport Marketing Board
CTN confectioner, tobacconist and newsagent
ctn carton; [mathematics] cotangent
CTNC Committee on Transnational Corporations (in UN)
CTO [philately] cancelled to order; Central Telegraph Office; Central Treaty Organization; chief technical officer
CTOL [aeronautics] conventional take-off and landing
CTP *Confederación de Trabajadores del Peru* (Spanish: Peruvian Confederation of Labour)
ctpt [music] counterpoint
ctptal [music] contrapuntal
ctptst [music] contrapuntist
CTR certified test record; controlled thermonuclear reaction; controlled thermonuclear research
ctr. centre; contribution; contributor
CTRA Coal Tar Research Association
Ctrl [computing] control (key)
CTRP *Confederación de Trabajadores de la República de Panama* (Spanish: Confederation of Workers of the Republic of Panama)
CTS [medicine] carpal tunnel syndrome; Catholic Truth Society; characteristic time scale; [computing] clear to send; [medicine] compute(rize)d tomographic scanner; Consolidated Tin Smelters
cts cents; certificates; crates
CTSA Crucible and Tool Steel Association
CTT capital transfer tax
CTTB Central Trade Test Board (of RAF)
Cttee committee
CTTH Cathedrals Through Touch and Hearing
CTTSC Certificate in the Teaching and Training of Subnormal Children
CTU Conservative Trade Unionists
CTUC Commonwealth Trade Union Council
CTUS Carnegie Trust for the Universities of Scotland
CTV cable television; Canadian Television Network Limited; *Confederación de Trabajadores de Venezuela* (Spanish: Confederation of Venezuelan Workers)
CTVM Centre for Tropical Veterinary Medicine
CTZ control traffic zone (around airport)
CU Cambridge University; Christian Union; Church Union; [photography] close-up; Congregational Union (of England and Wales); [computing] control unit; Cooperative Union; [USA] Cornell University; [civil aircraft marking] Cuba;

Customs Union; [vehicle registration] Newcastle upon Tyne
Cu [chemical element] copper (from Latin *cuprum*)
Cu [meteorology] cumulus
cu. cubic
.cu Cuba (in Internet address)
CUA Canadian Underwriters' Association; Catholic University of America; Colour Users' Association; [computing] common user access; Conference of University Administrators
CUAC Cambridge University Athletic Club; Cambridge University Automobile Club
CUAFC Cambridge University Association Football Club
CUAS Cambridge University Agricultural Society; Cambridge University Air Squadron
cub. cubic
CUBC Cambridge University Boat Club; Cambridge University Boxing Club
CUC Canberra University College; Coal Utilization Council
CUCC Cambridge University Cricket Club
CUDAT Community Urban Development Assistance Team
CUDS Cambridge University Dramatic Society
CUEP Central Unit on Environmental Pollution
CUEW Congregational Union of England and Wales
CUF *Catholicarum Universitatum Foederatio* (Latin: Federation of Catholic Universities); common university fund
CUG closed user group
CUGC Cambridge University Golf Club
CUHC Cambridge University Hockey Club
cuis. cuisine
CUKT Carnegie United Kingdom Trust
CUL Cambridge University Library
cul. culinary
CULS [finance] convertible unsecured loan stock
CULTC Cambridge University Lawn Tennis Club
CUM Cambridge University Mission
cum. [finance] cumulative
Cumb. Cumberland
cum div. [finance] cum dividend (i.e. with dividend)
cum pref. [finance] cumulative preference (shares)
CUMS Cambridge University Musical Society
CUNA Credit Union National Association
CUNY City University of New York
CUOG Cambridge University Opera Group
CUP Cambridge University Press; [currency] Cuban peso
cur. currency; current
CURAC [Australia] Coal Utilization Research Advisory Committee
cur. adv. vult [law] *curia advisari vult* (Latin: the court wishes to consider it) (used in reports when judgment follows hearing)
CURE Care, Understanding and Research (drug addiction organization)
curt current (month)
CURUFC Cambridge University Rugby Union Football Club
CURV [US navy] cable-controlled undersea recovery vehicle
CUS Catholic University School
CUSO Canadian University Services Overseas
CUSRPG Canada–United States Regional Planning Group (in NATO)
cust. custard; custodian; custody
custod. custodian
CUTF Commonwealth Unit Trust Fund
CUTS [computing] cassette users' tape specification; [computing] computer users' tape system
CV calorific value; [medicine] cardiovascular; [astronomy] cataclysmic variable; *cavallo vapore* (Italian: horsepower); *cavalos vapor* (Portuguese: horsepower); [medicine] cerebrovascular; *cheval-vapeur* (French: horsepower); [statistics] coefficient of variation; [mathematics] collective vector; common valve; [Bible] Common Version; [medicine] contrast ventriculography; [finance] convertible; [UK postcode] Coventry; [Canada] Cross of Valour; [chemistry] crystal violet; curriculum vitae; [vehicle registration] Truro
cv. [botany] cultivar
.cv Cape Verde (in Internet address)
c.v. *cheval-vapeur* (French: horsepower); chief value; [medicine] *cras vespere* (Latin: tomorrow evening); curriculum

vitae; *cursus vitae* (Latin: course of life)
CVA [medicine] cerebrovascular accident (i.e. stroke); [USA] Columbia Valley Authority
CVC capacitance-voltage characteristics; current-voltage characteristics
CVCP Committee of Vice-Chancellors and Principals (of UK universities)
CVD [medicine] cerebrovascular disease; [electronics] chemical vapour deposition; common valve development
c.v.d. [commerce] cash versus documents
CVE Certificate of Vocational Education; Council for Visual Education
CVEsc [currency] Cape Verde escudo
CVI chemical vapour infiltration; [medicine] common variable immunodeficiency
CVJ [engineering] constant velocity joint (in motor vehicles)
CVK centre vertical keel
CVL Central Veterinary Laboratory
CVM Company of Veteran Motorists
CVn [astronomy] Canes Venatici
CVO Commander of the Royal Victorian Order
CVP [medicine] central venous pressure; [Belgium] *Christelijk Volkspartif* (Flemish: Christian Social Party)
CVS [medicine] cardiovascular system; [medicine] chorionic villus sampling; Council of Voluntary Service
CVSNA Council of Voluntary Service National Association
CVT [mathematics] canonical variational theory; [chemistry] chemical vapour transport; [engineering] continuously variable transmission (in motor vehicles)
cvt. [finance] convertible
Cvt Gdn Covent Garden
CVWS combat vehicle weapons system
CVWW Council of Voluntary Welfare Work
CW Canada West; [physics] carrier wave; cavity wall (in property advertisement); chemical warfare; chemical weapons; child welfare; clerk of works; cold-worked (metals); commercial weight; Commissions and Warrants (department of Admiralty); complete with; continuous wave (as in **CW radar**); [UK postcode] Crewe; [physics] Curie–Weiss (law); [vehicle registration] Preston
c/w [cycling] chainwheel
cw. clockwise
c.w. continuous weld
CWA Catering Wages Act; chemical warfare agent; [USA] Civil Works Administration; [USA] Clean Water Act; [Australia] Country Women's Association; Crime Writers' Association
CWB Canadian Wheat Board; Central Wages Board
CWBW chemical warfare/biological (or bacteriological) warfare
CWC Catering Wages Commission; Commonwealth of World Citizens
CWD civilian war dead
CWDE Centre for World Development Education
C'wealth Commonwealth
CWF coal–water fuel
CWG Cooperative Women's Guild
CWGC Commonwealth War Graves Commission (formerly IWGC)
CWINC [India] Central Waterways, Irrigation and Navigation Commission
CWIS [computing] campus-wide information service
CWL Catholic Women's League
Cwlth Commonwealth
CWM Council for World Mission
CWME Commission on World Mission and Evangelism
CWNA Canadian Weekly Newspapers Association
CWO Chief Warrant Officer
c.w.o. cash with order
CWOIH Conference of World Organizations Interested in the Handicapped
CWP Christian Workers' Party (in Malta); [USA] Communist Workers' Party
CWR continuous welded rail
CW radar continuous-wave radar
CWS coal–water slurry; Cooperative Wholesale Society; Court Welfare Service
CWT central war time
cwt hundredweight
CWU Chemical Workers' Union; Communication Workers' Union
CX [vehicle registration] Huddersfield; [civil aircraft marking] Uruguay
cx [medicine] cervix; convex

CXR chest X-ray
CXT Common External Tariff
CY calendar year; [fishing port] Castlebay; [international vehicle registration] Cyprus; [vehicle registration] Swansea
cy capacity; currency; cycle(s)
.cy Cyprus (in Internet address)
cyath. [medicine] *cyathus* (Latin: glassful)
cyath. vin. [medicine] *cyathus vinarius* (Latin: wineglassful)
cyber. cybernetics
cyc. cycle(s); cycling; cyclopedia; cyclopedic
CYCA Clyde Yacht Clubs Association
cyclo. cyclopedia
CYEE Central Youth Employment Executive
Cyg [astronomy] Cygnus
CYL Communist Youth League
cyl. cylinder; cylindrical
Cym. Cymric
CYMS Catholic Young Men's Society
CYO [USA] Catholic Youth Organization
Cyp. Cyprian; Cypriot; Cyprus
CYS Catholic Youth Services
CYSA Community Youth Services Association
CYWU Community Youth Workers' Union
CZ [vehicle registration] Belfast; Canal Zone; [international vehicle registration] Czech Republic
Cz [geology] Cenozoic
.cz Czech Republic (in Internet address)
CZMA [USA] Coastal Zone Management Act

D

D [currency] dalasi (used in Gambia); *Damen* (German: ladies); [geology] darcy (permeability coefficient of rock); December; defence (as in **D notice**); Democrat; Democratic; [paper size] demy; Department; destroyer; Detective; *Deus* (Latin: God); [chemistry] deuterium; [music] Deutsch (catalogue of Schubert's works); *Deutschland* (German: Germany); [geology] Devonian; [card games] diamonds; digital; dimension; dimensional (as in **3-D**); [currency] dinar; dioptre; director; *diretto* (Italian: through train); distinguished; doctor; *dogana* (Italian: customs); Dom (title of monks); *Dominus* (Latin: Lord, God, Christ); Don (Spanish title for men); [currency] dông (used in Vietnam); *douane* (French: customs); Dowager; [fishing port] Dublin; Duchess; Duke; Dutch; [Roman numeral] five hundred; [civil aircraft marking] Germany; [international vehicle registration] Germany (from German *Deutschland*); [music] note of scale; [medicine] rhesus antigen (as in **anti-D**); semiskilled or unskilled (occupational group)
D absorbed dose (of radiation); diameter; [chemistry] diffusion coefficient; [physics] dispersion; [aeronautics] drag; [physics] electric flux density; [physics] electric flux displacement
d day; deci- (indicates one-tenth, as in **dl** = decilitre); [physics] deuteron; [music] do(h) (in tonic sol-fa); [physics] down (quark flavour); [meteorology] drizzle; [Roman numeral] five hundred; (old) pence (from Latin *denarii*); (old) penny (from Latin *denarius*)
d [chemistry] dextrorotatory; diameter; relative density
d. dam (in animal pedigree); damn; date; daughter; day; deacon; dead; deceased; [dentistry] deciduous; decision; decree; degree; delete; deliver; delivery; delta; density; depart(s); departure; depth; deputy; desert; deserted; deserter; *destro* (Italian: right); diameter; died; dime (= ten cents); [currency] dinar; discharge; distance; dividend; [currency] dollar; [medicine] dose; [currency] drachma; drama; *droite* (French: right); dump
D2 [civil aircraft marking] Angola
D2T2 [computing] dye diffusion thermal transfer
D4 [civil aircraft marking] Cape Verde
D6 [civil aircraft marking] Comoros Islands
3D [civil aircraft marking] Swaziland

3-D three-dimensional
DA [currency] Algerian dinar; [vehicle registration] Birmingham; [UK postcode] Dartford; Daughters of America; deed of arrangement; Defence Act; delayed action (bomb); [USA] Department of Agriculture; Depressives Anonymous; deputy advocate; deputy assistant; design automation; destructive analysis; developmental age; Diploma in Anaesthetics (or Anaesthesia); Diploma in Art; direct action; [chemistry] dissolved acetylene; [USA] District Attorney; Doctor of Arts; doesn't answer; [medicine] dopamine; [fishing port] Drogheda; duck's arse (hairstyle)
D/A [commerce] days after acceptance; [commerce] delivery on acceptance; deposit account; digital-to-analogue (converter); [commerce] documents against acceptance
D-A digital–analogue (converter)
Da dalton (unit of atomic mass)
Da. Danish
da deca- (indicates 10, as in **dal** = decalitre)
d/a [commerce] days after acceptance; deposit account; discharge afloat; [commerce] documents against acceptance
DAA *défense anti-aérienne* (French: anti-aircraft defence); [chemistry] diacetone acrylamide; [chemistry] diacetone alcohol; Diploma of the Advertising Association
DAA&QMG Deputy Assistant Adjutant and Quartermaster-General
DAAG Deputy Assistant Adjutant-General
DA&QMG Deputy Adjutant and Quartermaster-General
DAAS data acquisition and analysis system
DAB daily audience barometer; *Deutsches Apothekerbuch* (German: German Pharmacopoeia); *Dictionary of American Biography*; digital audio broadcasting
DABN [medicine] diffuse acute bacterial nephritis
DAC data analysis and control; Development Assistance Committee (of OECD); [computing] digital–analogue converter
DAc Doctor of Acupuncture
d.a.c. [insurance] deductible average clause; direct air cycle
DACC Dangerous Air Cargoes Committee
DACG Deputy Assistant Chaplain-General
dachs. dachshund
DACOR data correction
dact. dactyl
DAD deputy assistant director
DADG Deputy Assistant Director-General
DAdmin Doctor of Administration
DAE [USA] Department of Atomic Energy; *Dictionary of American English*; differential algebraic equation; Diploma in Advanced Engineering; Director of Army Education
DAEP Division of Atomic Energy Production
DAER Department of Aeronautical and Engineering Research
DAF [USA] Department of the Air Force; dissolved air flotation; *Doorne Automobielfabriek* (Dutch vehicle manufacturer); dry ash-free (coal)
d.a.f. described as follows
DAFS Department of Agriculture and Fisheries for Scotland
DAG Deputy Adjutant-General; *Deutsche Angestellten-Gewerkschaft* (German: German Salaried Employees' Union); development assistance group; [Ireland] Divorce Action Group
dag decagram
DAGMAR [commerce] defining advertising goals for measured advertising results
DAgr Doctor of Agriculture
DAgrSc Doctor of Agricultural Science
DAH [medicine] disordered action of the heart
DAI disease activity index; distributed artificial intelligence
d.a.i. death from accidental injuries
DAJAG Deputy Assistant Judge Advocate-General
Dak. Dakota
DAL direct acid leaching
dal decalitre
DALR [meteorology] dry adiabatic lapse rate
dal S [music] *dal segno* (Italian: (repeat) from the sign)
DAM Diploma in Ayurvedic Medicine
dam decametre
dam. damage
DAMS [USA] defense against missiles

system(s); deputy assistant military secretary
DAN (People's) Direct Action Network
Dan. [Bible] Daniel; Danish
D&AD Designers and Art Directors Association
D&B discipline and bondage; Dun and Bradstreet (financial reports)
D&C dean and chapter; [medicine] dil(a-t)ation and curettage (of cervix and uterus)
D&D death and dying; drunk and disorderly
D&G Dolce e Gabbana
D&HAA Dock and Harbour Authorities' Association
d&p developing and printing
d&s demand and supply
D&V [medicine] diarrhoea and vomiting
DAO district advisory officer
DAOT Director of Air Organization and Training
DAP Director of Administrative Planning; [computing] distributed array processor; [electronics] donor–acceptor pair; Draw a Person (psychological test)
d.a.p. do anything possible; documents against payment
DAP&E Diploma in Applied Parasitology and Entomology
DAPM Deputy Assistant Provost-Marshal
DAppSc Doctor of Applied Science
DAPS Director of Army Postal Services
DAQMG Deputy Assistant Quartermaster-General
DAR Daughters of the American Revolution; [USA] Defense Aid Reports; direct absorption receiver (of solar radiation); [Canada] Directorate of Atomic Research
DArch Doctor of Architecture
DARD Directorate of Aircraft Research and Development
DARE demand and resource evaluation
DARPA [USA] Defense Advanced Research Projects Agency (formerly ARPA)
DArt Doctor of Art
DAS [computing] data-acquisition system; development advisory service; Director of Armament Supply; double algebraic sum; Dramatic Authors' Society
d.a.s. [commerce] delivered alongside ship
DASA [USA] Defense Atomic Support Agency; Domestic Appliance Service Association
DASC [USA] Direct Air Support Centre
DASc Doctor of Agricultural Science
DASD [computing] direct-access storage device; Director of Army Staff Duties
DASH drone antisubmarine helicopter
dash [short form] dashboard
DASM delayed-action space missile
Dass Depressives Associated
DAT [medicine] dementia of the Alzheimer type; digital audio tape
dat. [grammar] dative
DATA Draughtsmen's and Allied Technician's Association
Datacom data communications
Datanet data network
Datastor data storage
Datran data transmission
Datrec data recording
DATV digitally assisted television
dau. daughter
DAV Disabled American Veterans
DAvMed Diploma in Aviation Medicine
DAW Drama Association of Wales; [nuclear technology] dry active waste
DAWS Director of Army Welfare Services
DAX [stock exchange] *Deutsche Aktienindex* (German: German share price index)
DAyM Doctor of Ayurvedic Medicine
DB Bachelor of Divinity (from Latin *Divinitatis Baccalaureus*); dark blue; database; [book-keeping] daybook; deals and battens (timber); delayed broadcast (in radio and television); *Deutsche Bundesbahn* (German: German Federal Railway); *Deutsche Bundesbank* (German: German Federal Bank); dock brief; Domesday Book; double-barrelled; [vehicle registration] Manchester
D/B [book-keeping] daybook
Db [currency] dobra (used in São Tomé and Príncipe)
dB decibel
d.b. [book-keeping] daybook; [music] double bass; double bed; double-breasted; drawbar (on tractors etc.)
DBA [computing] database administration; [computing] database administrator; [medicine] dihydrodimethylbenzopyranbutyric acid (used to

treat sickle-cell anaemia); Doctor of Business Administration; doing business as (or at)
d.b.a. doing business as (or at)
DBB deals, battens and boards (timber); *Deutscher Beamtenbund* (German: German Civil Servants' Association) (trade union); dinner, bed and breakfast (in accommodation advertisement)
DBC Deaf Broadcasting Council
DBE Dame Commander of the Order of the British Empire; design-basis event
DBEATS dispatch payable both ends on all time saved
DBELTS dispatch payable both ends on lay time saved
DBH [forestry] diameter at breast height
DBib Douay Bible
DBIU [Canada] Dominion Board of Insurance Underwriters
dbk disembark; drawback
dbkn debarkation
dbl. double
dble double
DBM Diploma in Business Management
DBMC Danish Bacon and Meat Council
DBMS [computing] database management system
DBMT [medicine] displacement bone-marrow transplantation
Dbn Durban (South Africa)
DBO Diploma of the British Orthoptic Board
dbre *diciembre* (Spanish: December)
DBS direct broadcasting by satellite; direct-broadcast satellite
DBST Double British Summer Time
dbt debit
DBW desirable body weight
DC [music] *da capo* (Italian: from the head) (instruction to repeat from beginning); Daughters of Charity of St Vincent de Paul; death certificate; decimal currency; *Democrazia Cristiana* (Italian: Christian Democratic Party); [USA] Dental Corps; depth charge; deputy chief; deputy commissioner; deputy consul; deputy counsel; Detective Constable; [computing] device coordinates; diagnostic centre; diplomatic corps; [physics] direct current; Disarmament Conference; Disciples of Christ; district commissioner; district council; district court; District of Columbia; [US postcode] District of Columbia; Doctor of Chiropractic; [commerce] documents against cash; Douglas Commercial (aircraft) (as in **DC10**); [theatre] down centre (of stage); [vehicle registration] Middlesbrough
D/C [insurance] deviation clause
dC *depois de Cristo* (Portuguese: after Christ, AD); *dopo Cristo* (Italian: after Christ, AD)
d.c. dead centre; [physics] direct current; [printing] double column; [music] double crotchet; [navigation] drift correction
DCA [USA] Defense Communications Agency; [Australia] Department of Civil Aviation; [computing] document content architecture
DCAe Diploma of the College of Aeronautics
DCAO deputy county advisor officer
DCAS Deputy Chief of Air Staff; Divorce Conciliation and Advisory Service
DCB Dame Commander of the Order of the Bath; double cantilever beam
DCBE [medicine] double-contrast barium enema
DCC Deputy Chief Constable; digital compact cassette; Diocesan Consistory Court; Diploma of Chelsea College
DCCC Domestic Coal Consumers Council
DCD [USA] Department of Community Development; Diploma in Chest Diseases; [electronics] drain-current drift
dcdr decoder
DCE [computing] data communications equipment; design and construction error; Diploma in Chemical Engineering; Doctor of Civil Engineering; domestic credit expansion
DCEP Diploma in Child and Educational Psychology
DCF [accounting] discounted cash flow
DCG Deputy Chaplain-General; direct coal gasification
dcg dancing
DCGS Deputy Chief of the General Staff
DCh Diploma in Child Health; Doctor of Surgery (from Latin *Doctor Chirurgiae*)
DChD Doctor of Dental Surgery
DChE Doctor of Chemical Engineering
DCI Detective Chief Inspector; direct com-

puter interviewing; [computing] display control interface; [advertising] double column inch; ductile cast iron

d.c.i. [advertising] double column inch

DCJ [USA] district court judge

DCL Distillers' Company Limited; Doctor of Civil Law

dcl. [cricket] declaration; [cricket] declared

DCLI Duke of Cornwall's Light Infantry

DCLJ Dame Commander of the Order of St Lazarus of Jerusalem

DClSc Doctor of Clinical Science

DCM Diploma in Community Medicine; Distinguished Conduct Medal; district court martial; Doctor of Comparative Medicine

DCMG Dame Commander of the Order of St Michael and St George

DCMS Department for Culture, Media and Sport; Deputy Commissioner Medical Services

DCnL Doctor of Canon Law

DCNS Deputy Chief of Naval Staff

DCO Duke of Cambridge's Own (regiment)

DC of S Deputy Chief of Staff

d. col. [printing] double column

DComL Doctor of Commercial Law

DComm Doctor of Commerce

DCompL Doctor of Comparative Law

DCP Diploma in Clinical Pathology; Diploma in Clinical Psychology; Diploma in Conservation of Paintings

DCPA [USA] Defense Civil Preparedness Agency

DCPath Diploma of the College of Pathologists

DCR Diploma of the College of Radiographers

DCrim Doctor of Criminology

DCS Deputy Chief of Staff; Deputy Clerk of Session(s); [physics] differential cross section; digital camera system; Doctor of Christian Science; Doctor of Commercial Sciences; [medicine] dorsal column stimulator

DCSO deputy chief scientific officer

DCST Deputy Chief of Supplies and Transport

DCT [computing] discrete cosine transform; Doctor of Christian Theology; [medicine] dynamic compute(rize)d tomography

dct document

DCV [accounting] direct charge voucher

DCVO Dame Commander of the Royal Victorian Order

DCW dead carcass weight; domestic cold water

DD [insurance] damage done; dangerous drug; [banking] demand draft; [USA] Department of Defense; deputy director; deputy directorate; Diploma in Dermatology; [banking] direct debit; *direttissimo* (Italian: fast train); discharged dead; dishonourable discharge; Doctor of Divinity (from Latin *Divinitatis Doctor*); *dono dedit* (Latin: gave as a gift); [paper size] double demy; [computing] double density (disk); [medicine] Duchenne dystrophy; [UK postcode] Dundee; [vehicle registration] Gloucester

D/D [commerce] delivered at docks; [banking] demand draft; dock dues

D/d days after date; [commerce] delivered

Dd. *Deo dedit* (Latin: gave to God)

dd dated; dedicated; delivered; drilled

d.d. days after date; *de dato* (Latin: today's date); delayed delivery; [commerce] delivered at docks; [banking] demand draft; detergent dispersant; dry dock; due date; due day

DDA Dangerous Drugs Act; Disabled Drivers' Association

D-Day Day Day (i.e. specified day, esp. date of Allied invasion of Europe)

DDBMS distributed database management system

DDC Dewey Decimal Classification (for library books); [medicine] dideoxycytidine (used to treat Aids); [computing] direct digital control; [computing] display data channel

DDCMP [computing] digital data communication message protocol

DDD *dat, dicat, dedicat* (Latin: gives, devotes and dedicates); deadline delivery date; *dono dedit dedicavit* (Latin: gave and dedicated as a gift)

DDDS Deputy Director of Dental Services

DDE [computing] direct data entry; Dwight David Eisenhower (US president); dynamic data exchange

DDG Deputy Director-General

DDGAMS Deputy Director-General, Army Medical Services

DDH Diploma in Dental Health
DDI [medicine] dideoxyinosine (used to treat Aids); Divisional Detective Inspector
d.d. in d. [medicine] *de die in diem* (Latin: from day to day)
DDL [computing] data definition language; [computing] data description language; Deputy Director of Labour; digital data link
DDM Diploma in Dermatological Medicine; Doctor of Dental Medicine
DDME Deputy Director of Mechanical Engineering
DDMI Deputy Director of Military Intelligence
DDMOI Deputy Director of Military Operations and Intelligence
DDMS Deputy Director of Medical Services
DDMT Deputy Director of Military Training
DDNI Deputy Director of Naval Intelligence
DDO Diploma in Dental Orthopaedics; district dental officer
DDOS Deputy Director of Ordnance Services
DDP [computing] distributed data processing
DDPH Diploma in Dental Public Health
DDPR Deputy Director of Personal Services; Deputy Director of Postal Services; Deputy Director of Public Relations
DDR *Deutsche Demokratische Republik* (German: German Democratic Republic, the former East Germany); Diploma in Diagnostic Radiology
DDRA Deputy Director, Royal Artillery
DDRB Doctors' and Dentists' Review Body
DDRD Deputy Directorate of Research and Development
DDS deep diving system; Deputy Directorate of Science; Dewey Decimal System (for classifying library books); [pharmacology] diaminodiphenyl sulphone (= dapsone, drug used to treat skin disease); digital data storage; Director of Dental Services; Doctor of Dental Science; Doctor of Dental Surgery
dd/s delivered sound
DDSc Doctor of Dental Science
DDSD Deputy Director of Staff Duties
DDSM [USA] Defense Distinguished Service Medal
DDSR Deputy Director of Scientific Research
DDST Deputy Director of Supplies and Transport
DDT dichlorodiphenyltrichloroethane (insecticide)
DDTL dreary desk-top lunch
DDVS Deputy Director of Veterinary Services
DDWE&M Deputy Director of Works, Electrical and Mechanical
DE *Dáil Éireann* (Gaelic: Assembly of Ireland) (lower chamber of Irish parliament); deflection error; [US postcode] Delaware; Department of Employment; [UK postcode] Derby; [military] destroyer escort; destruction efficiency; diesel engine; direct electrolysis; Doctor of Engineering; Doctor of Entomology; [paper size] double elephant; [fishing port] Dundee; [vehicle registration] Haverfordwest
.de Germany (in Internet address)
d.e. deckle edge; diesel-electric; [fencing] direct elimination; [book-keeping] double entry
DEA [computing] data encryption algorithm; Department of Economic Affairs (former government department); Department of External Affairs; [USA] Drug Enforcement Administration; [USA] Drug Enforcement Agency
Dea. Deacon; Dean
deb [short form] debutante
deb. debenture; debit; debut
debil. debilitating; debilitation
deb. stk debenture stock
DEC dental examination centre; [USA] Department of Environmental Conservation; Digital Equipment Corporation; Disasters Emergency Committee; Dollar Export Council
DEc Doctor of Economics
Dec. *Decani* (Latin: of the dean) (side of church choir); *Decanus* (Latin: dean); December; [architecture] Decorated
dec [astronomy] declination
dec. deceased; decimal; declaration; declare; declared; [grammar] declension; decorated; decoration; decorative;

decrease; [music] *decrescendo* (Italian: with decreasing loudness)
déc. *décembre* (French: December)
decaf [short form] decaffeinated (coffee)
decasyll. decasyllabic; decasyllable
decd deceased
decel. deceleration
decid. deciduous
decis. decision
decl. [grammar] declension
decn decontamination
decom. decommission
DEcon Doctor of Economics
DEconSc Doctor of Economic Science
DECR [meteorology] decrease
decr. decrease
decresc. [music] *decrescendo* (Italian: with decreasing loudness)
decrim. decriminalization
DED Department of Economic Development (Northern Ireland)
DEd Doctor of Education
ded. dedicate; dedicated; dedication; deduce; deduct; deduction
de d. in d. [medicine] *de die in diem* (Latin: from day to day)
deduct. deduction; deductive
DEE Diploma in Electrical Engineering
DEED [USA] Department of Energy and Economic Development
DEEP Directly Elected European Parliament
def. defecate; defecation; defect; defection; defective; defector; defence; defendant; deferred; deficit; define; definite; definition; definitive; deflagrate; deflect; deflection; defoliate; defrost; defunct; *defunctus* (Latin: deceased)
def. art. [grammar] definite article
DEFCON [military] defence readiness condition
defect. defective
defl. deflate; deflation; deflect; deflection
deft defendant
DEG [meteorology] degrees
deg. degree
degen. degeneration
degr. degradation; degree
dehyd. dehydration
DEI Dutch East Indies (former name of Indonesia)
Del [computing] delete (key); [astronomy] Delphinus
Del. Delaware; Delhi
del. delegate; delegation; delete; deletion; *delineavit* (Latin: (he/she) drew it); deliver; delivered; delivery
deld delivered
deleg. delegate; delegation
deli [short form] delicatessen
delib. deliberate; deliberation
deliq. deliquescent
DElo Doctor of Elocution
delv. deliver; delivered; delivery
dely delivery
Dem. Democrat; Democratic
dem. demand; demerara; democracy; democratic; demolish; demolition; [grammar] demonstrative; demurrage
DEME Directorate of Electrical and Mechanical Engineering
demo [short form] demonstration
demob [short form] demobilization; [short form] demobilize
demon. demonstrate; [grammar] demonstrative
demons. [grammar] demonstrative
demonstr. [grammar] demonstrative
DEMS defensively equipped merchant ships
DemU [Northern Ireland] Democratic Unionist
demur. demurrage
DEN District Enrolled Nurse
DEn Department of Energy; Doctor of English
Den. Denbighshire; Denmark; Denver
den. denier; denotation; denote; denoted; dental; dentist; dentistry
DenD *Docteur en droit* (French: Doctor of Law)
dend. dendrology
dendrochron. dendrochronology
dendrol. dendrological; dendrology
DEng Doctor of Engineering
DEngS Doctor of Engineering Science
DenM *Docteur en médecine* (French: Doctor of Medicine)
DenMed *Docteur en médecine* (French: Doctor of Medicine)
denom. denomination
DENR [USA] Department of Energy and Natural Resources
dens. density
DEnt Doctor of Entomology
dent. dental; dentist; dentistry; denture

DEOVR Duke of Edinburgh's Own Volunteer Rifles
DEP Department of Employment and Productivity; [USA] Department of Environmental Protection
dep. depart(s); department; departure; dependant; dependency; dependent; deponent; depose; deposed; deposit; deposition; depositor; depot; deputize; deputized; deputy
dép. *département* (French: department, administrative division); *député* (French: deputy, member of parliament)
Depca International Study Group for the Detection and Prevention of Cancer
dept department; deponent
dept. deputy
deptn deputation
DER [USA] Department of Environmental Resources
der. *derecha* (Spanish: right); derivation; derivative; derive; derived; *dernier* (French: last)
Derby. Derbyshire
Derbys Derbyshire
dereg. deregulation
deriv. derivation; derivative; derive; derived
DERL derived emergency reference level (of radiation)
derm. dermatitis; dermatology
dermat. dermatology
dermatol. dermatology
derog. derogatory
DERR Duke of Edinburgh's Royal Regiment
derv diesel-engined road vehicle (diesel oil used as transport fuel)
DES [computing] data encryption standard; Department of Education and Science (former government department); [pharmacology] diethylstilboestrol (synthetic hormone); Director of Educational Services
Des Deaconess
des. desert; design; designate; designated; designation; designer; desirable; desire; dessert
desc. descend; descendant; descent; describe; description
descr. description
desid. *desideratum* (Latin: something wanted)
desig. designate
DèsL *Docteur ès lettres* (French: Doctor of Letters)
desp. despatch; despatched
DesRCA Designer of the Royal College of Art
des res [short form] desirable residence
DèsS *Docteur ès sciences* (French: Doctor of Science)
DèsSc *Docteur ès sciences* (French: Doctor of Science)
DèsScPol *Docteur ès sciences politiques* (French: Doctor of Political Science)
dest. destination; destroyer
destn destination
DET [linguistics] determiner; [pharmacology] diethyltryptamine (hallucinogen); direct energy transfer
Det Detective
det. detach; detached (in property advertisement); detachment; detail; determine; [grammar] determiner; [medicine] *detur* (Latin: let it be given)
Det. Con. Detective Constable
Det. Insp. Detective Inspector
detn detention; determination
detox [short form] detoxification
DETR Department of the Environment, Transport and the Regions
Det. Sgt Detective Sergeant
Det. Supt Detective Superintendent
Deut. [Bible] Deuteronomy
Dev. Devon(shire)
dev. develop; developed; developer; development; deviate; [navigation] deviation
Devon. Devonshire
devp develop
devpt development
devs devotions
DEW directed-energy weapon; distant early warning
Dez. *Dezember* (German: December)
DF Dean of Faculty; [nuclear technology] decontamination factor; Defender of the Faith; [telecommunications] direction finder; [telecommunications] direction-finding; [currency] Djibouti franc; Doctor of Forestry; [paper size] double foolscap; [vehicle registration] Gloucester
d-f double-fronted (in property advertisement)
df. draft

d.f. [commerce] dead freight; drinking fountain
DFA [USA] Department of Foreign Affairs; Diploma in Foreign Affairs; Doctor of Fine Arts
DFC Distinguished Flying Cross
DFD [computing] dataflow diagram; data function diagram
DFDS *Det Forende Dampskibs-Selskab* (Danish shipping company)
DfEE Department for Education and Employment
DFHom Diploma of the Faculty of Homoeopathy
DFID Department for International Development
Dfl [currency] Dutch guilder (from alternative name florin)
DFLP Democratic Front for the Liberation of Palestine
DFLS Day Fighter Leaders' School
DFM Diploma in Forensic Medicine; Distinguished Flying Medal
dfndt defendant
DFR [nuclear technology] Dounreay fast reactor
d.f.r. decreasing failure rate
DFS disease-free survival; [computing] disk filing system
DFSc Doctor of Financial Science
DFT dual-flow turbine
dft defendant; draft
DFW Director of Fortifications and Works
DG *Dei gratia* (Latin: by the grace of God); *Deo gratias* (Latin: thanks be to God); dependence graph; *Deutsche Grammophon* (German record company); differential geometry; [navigation] directional gyro; Directorate-General; Director-General; double glazed (in property advertisement); double glazing (in property advertisement); Dragoon Guards; [UK postcode] Dumfries; [vehicle registration] Gloucester
dg decigram
DGA Director-General, Aircraft; Directors' Guild of America
DGAA Distressed Gentlefolk's Aid Association
DGAME Director-General, Army Medical Services
DGAS Double Glazing Advisory Service
DGB *Deutscher Gewerkschaftsbund* (German: German Trade Union Federation)
DGC Diploma in Guidance and Counselling
DGCA Director-General of Civil Aviation
DGCE Directorate-General of Communications Equipment
DGD Director, Gunnery Division
DGD&M Director-General, Dockyards and Maintenance
DGE Directorate-General of Equipment
DGEME Director-General, Electrical and Mechanical Engineering
DGI Director-General of Information; Director-General of Inspection
DGLP(A) Director-General, Logistic Policy (Army)
DGM Diploma in General Medicine; Director-General of Manpower
DGMS Director-General of Medical Services
DGMT Director-General of Military Training
DGMW Director-General of Military Works
Dgn Dragoon
DGO Diploma in Gynaecology and Obstetrics
DGP Director-General of Personnel; Director-General of Production
DGPS Director-General of Personal Services
DGR Dante Gabriel Rossetti (British poet and painter); Director of Graves Registration
DGS Diploma in General Studies; Diploma in General Surgery; Diploma in Graduate Studies; Directorate-General of Signals; Director-General, Ships
DGSRD Directorate-General of Scientific Research and Development
DGT Director-General of Training
DGW Director-General of Weapons; Director-General of Works
DH [fishing port] Dartmouth; [sports] dead heat; De Havilland (aircraft); Department of Health; [baseball] designated hitter; [currency] dirham (used in Morocco); district heating; Doctor of Humanities; [electronics] double heterostructure; [vehicle registration] Dudley; [UK postcode] Durham

Dh [currency] dirham (used in United Arab Emirates)
d.h. *das heisst* (German: that is, i.e.); [sports] dead heat
DHA Department of Humanitarian Affairs (of UN); district health authority
DHC Domestic Heating Council
Dhc *Doctor honoris causa* (Latin: Honorary Doctor)
DHDS Dolmetsch Historical Dance Society
DHHS [USA] Department of Health and Human Services
DHL Doctor of Hebrew Letters; Doctor of Hebrew Literature; Doctor of Humane Letters
DHMSA Diploma in the History of Medicine (Society of Apothecaries)
DHO damped harmonic oscillator; district headquarters; divisional headquarters
DHR [nuclear technology] decay heat removal
DHS Diploma in Horticultural Science; Doctor of Health Sciences
DHSA Diploma in Health Service Administration
DHSS Department of Health and Social Security (former government department)
DHumLit Doctor of Humane Letters
DHW domestic hot water
DHyg Doctor of Hygiene
DI Defence Intelligence; Department of the Interior; Detective Inspector; [medicine] diabetes insipidus; direct injection; Director of Infantry; district inspector; divisional inspector; [medicine] donor insemination; [paper size] double imperial; drill instructor
Di didymium
Di. [currency] dinar
di. diameter
d.i. daily inspection; *das ist* (German: that is, i.e.); de-ice; diplomatic immunity; document identifier
DIA [USA] Defense Intelligence Agency; Design and Industries Association; Diploma in International Affairs; Driving Instructors Association
dia. diagnose; diagram; dialect; diameter
diag. diagnose; diagnosis; diagonal; diagram
dial. dialect; dialectal; dialectic; dialectical; dialogue
diam. diameter
diamat dialectical materialism (in philosophy and economics)
DIANE Direct Information Access Network for Europe
diap. [music] diapason
diaph. diaphragm
DIAS Dublin Institute of Advanced Science
DIC Diamond Information Centre; Diploma of (Membership of the) Imperial College (of Science and Technology); [medicine] disseminated intravascular coagulation; [chemistry] dissolved inorganic carbon; drunk in charge
dic. *dicembre* (Italian: December)
DIChem Diploma in Industrial Chemistry
dicot. dicotyledon
dict. dictate; dictated; dictation; dictator; dictionary
DICTA Diploma of Imperial College of Tropical Agriculture
DIDS [electronics] donor-impurity density of states
DIE Designated Investment Exchange; Diploma in Industrial Engineering; Diploma of the Institute of Engineering
dieb. alt. [medicine] *diebus alternis* (Latin: on alternate days)
DIEL (Advisory Committee on Telecommunications for) Disabled and Elderly People
DIEME Directorate of Inspection of Electrical and Mechanical Equipment
diet. dietary; dietetics; dietician
DIF [computing] data interchange format; District Inspector of Fisheries
dif. differ; differential
diff. differ; difference; different; differential
diff. calc. differential calculus
diffr. diffraction
diffu. diffusion
DIG Deputy Inspector-General; disablement income group
dig. digest (compilation); digestion; digestive; digit; digital
DIH Diploma in Industrial Health
DIIR digital image-intensifier radiography
Dij. Dijon
DIL [electronics] dual in-line

dil. dilute; diluted; dilution
diln dilution
DIM Diploma in Industrial Management
dim. *dimanche* (French: Sunday); dimension; *dimidium* (Latin: half); diminish; [music] *diminuendo* (Italian: with diminishing loudness); diminutive
dimin. [music] *diminuendo* (Italian: with diminishing loudness); diminutive
Dimm [computing, electronics] dual in-line memory module
DIMS [computing] data and information management system
DIN *Deutsches Industrie Normen* (German: German Industry Standard); *Deutsches Institut für Normung* (German: German Standards Institute); [computing] digital imaging network
Din [currency] dinar
din. dining car; dining room (in property advertisement); dinner
DIng Doctor of Engineering (from Latin *Doctor Ingeniariae*)
dinky [informal] double (or dual) income, no kids (yet)
DInstPA Diploma of the Institute of Park Administration
DIO district intelligence officer
dio. diocese
dioc. diocesan; diocese
dioc. syn. diocesan synod
DIP [computing] document image processing; [electronics] dual in-line package; [electronics] dual in-line pin
Dip. Diploma
dip. diploma
DipAD Diploma in Art and Design
DipAe Diploma in Aeronautics
DipAgr Diploma in Agriculture
DipALing Diploma in Applied Linguistics
DipAM Diploma in Applied Mechanics
DipAppSc Diploma in Applied Science
DipArch Diploma in Architecture
DipArts Diploma in Arts
DipASE Diploma in Advanced Study of Education, College of Preceptors
DipAvMed Diploma in Aviation Medicine
DipBA Diploma in Business Administration
DipBac Diploma in Bacteriology
DipBMS Diploma in Basic Medical Sciences
DipBS Diploma in Fine Art, Byam Shaw School
DipCAM Diploma in Communication, Advertising and Marketing (of CAM Foundation)
DipCC Diploma of the Central College
DipCD Diploma in Child Development; Diploma in Civic Design
DipCE Diploma in Civil Engineering
DipChemEng Diploma in Chemical Engineering
DipCom Diploma in Commerce
DipDHus Diploma in Dairy Husbandry
DipDP Diploma in Drawing and Painting
DipDS Diploma in Dental Surgery
DipEcon Diploma in Economics
DipEd Diploma in Education
DipEl Diploma in Electronics
DipEng Diploma in Engineering
DipESL Diploma in English as a Second Language
DipEth Diploma in Ethnology
DipFA Diploma in Fine Arts
DipFD Diploma in Funeral Directing
DipFE Diploma in Further Education
DipFor Diploma in Forestry
DipGSM Diploma in Music, Guildhall School of Music (and Drama)
DipGT Diploma in Glass Technology
DipHA Diploma in Hospital Administration
DipHE Diploma in Higher Education; Diploma in Highway Engineering
DipHSc Diploma in Home Science
diphth. diphthong
DipHum Diploma in Humanities
DipJ Diploma in Journalism
DipL Diploma in Languages
dipl. diploma; diplomacy; diplomat; diplomatic
DipLA Diploma in Landscape Architecture
DipLib Diploma in Librarianship
DipLSc Diploma in Library Science
DipM Diploma in Marketing
DipMechE Diploma in Mechanical Engineering
DipMet Diploma in Metallurgy
DipMFOS Diploma in Maxillofacial and Oral Surgery
DipMusEd Diploma in Musical Education
DipN Diploma in Nursing

DipNEd Diploma in Nursery School Education
DipO&G Diploma in Obstetrics and Gynaecology
DipOL Diploma in Oriental Learning
DipOrth Diploma in Orthodontics
DipPA Diploma in Public Administration
DipP&OT Diploma in Physiotherapy and Occupational Therapy
DipPharmMed Diploma in Pharmaceutical Medicine
DipPhysEd Diploma in Physical Education
DipQS Diploma in Quantity Surveying
DipRADA Diploma of the Royal Academy of Dramatic Art
DipREM Diploma in Rural Estate Management
DIPS digital image-processing system
DipS&PA Diploma in Social and Public Administration
DipSMS Diploma in School Management Studies
DipSoc Diploma in Sociology
DipSpEd Diploma in Special Education
DipSS Diploma in Social Studies
DipSW Diploma in Social Work
DipT Diploma in Teaching
DipTA Diploma in Tropical Agriculture
DipT&CP Diploma in Town and Country Planning
DipTech Diploma in Technology
DipTEFL Diploma in the Teaching of English as a Foreign Language
DipTh Diploma in Theology
DipTP Diploma in Town Planning
DipTPT Diploma in Theory and Practice of Teaching
DIR [photography] developer inhibitor release
dir. direct; directed; direction; director; [currency] dirham
Dir-Gen Director-General
DIS [USA] Defense Intelligence School; Development Information System
dis. disabled; discharge; disciple; discipline; disconnect; discontinue; discontinued; discount; dispense; distance; distant; distribute
disab. disability
disabil. disability
disag. disagreeable
disb. disbursement
disc. disciple; discipline; discount; discover; discovered; discoverer; discovery
disch. discharge
disco [short form] discotheque
discont. discontinued
discr. discretion
disemb. disembark; disembarkation
DISH [medicine] diffuse idiopathic skeletal hyperostosis
dishon. dishonest; dishonourable; dishonourably
disloc. dislocation
dismac [military] digital scene-matching area correlation sensors
disp. dispensary; dispensation; dispense; disperse; dispersion; disputed
displ. displacement
diss. dissenter; dissertation; dissolve
dist. distance; distant; distilled; distinguish; distinguished; distribute; distributor; district
Dist. Atty [USA] District Attorney
distr. distribution; distributor
distrib. distributive
DistTP Distinction in Town Planning
DIT [medicine] desferrioxamine infusion test; Detroit Institute of Technology; double income tax (as in **DIT relief**)
DITB Distributive Industry Training Board
Div. Divine; Divinity
div [mathematics] divergence
div. diversion; divide; divided; dividend; divine; [music] *divisi* (Italian: divided) (referring to musical parts); division; divisor; divorce; divorced
div. in par. aeq. [medicine] *dividatur in partes aequales* (Latin: let it be divided into equal parts) (in prescriptions)
divn division
divnl divisional
DIY do-it-yourself
DJ dinner jacket; Diploma in Journalism; disc jockey; [USA] district judge; divorce judge; Doctor of Law (from Latin *Doctor Juris*); [finance] Dow Jones; dust jacket (of book); [vehicle registration] Liverpool
d.J *der Jüngere* (German: the Younger, Junior); *dieses Jahres* (German: of this year)
.dj Djibouti (in Internet address)
DJAG Deputy Judge Advocate-General
DJF Disc Jockeys Federation
DJI [finance] Dow Jones Index

DJIA [finance] Dow Jones Industrial Average
DJS Doctor of Juridical Science
DJT Doctor of Jewish Theology
DJTA [finance] Dow Jones Transportation Average
DJUA [finance] Dow Jones Utilities Average
DJur Doctor of Law (from Latin *Doctor Juris*)
DK [international vehicle registration] Denmark and Greenland; Dorling Kindersley (publishing company); [fishing port] Dundalk; [vehicle registration] Manchester
dk dark; deck; dock; duck
.dk Denmark (in Internet address)
DKB [computing] distributed knowledge base
dkhse deckhouse
DKNY [trademark] Donna Karan New York
Dkr [currency] Danish krone
DKS Deputy Keeper of the Signet
dkt docket
dkyd dockyard
DL [UK postcode] Darlington; [fishing port] Deal; Deputy Lieutenant; [physics] detection limit; diesel; [psychology] difference limen; [electronics] distribution line; Doctor of Laws (from Latin *Doctor Legum*); dog licence; [physics] dose level; [book-keeping] double ledger; [theatre] down left (of stage); [computing] download (on Internet); driving licence; [vehicle registration] Portsmouth
D/L data link; demand loan
dl decilitre
DLA diffusion limited aggregation
DLC Diploma of Loughborough College; divisional land commissioner; Doctor of Celtic Literature; [theatre] down left centre (of stage)
d.l.c. direct lift control
DLCO-EA Desert Locust Control Organization for Eastern Africa
dld delivered
d.l.d. deadline date
DLE [medicine] discoid lupus erythematosus
DLES Doctor of Letters in Economic Studies
DLett *Docteur ès lettres* (French: Doctor of Letters)
DLF Disabled Living Foundation
DLG David Lloyd George (British statesman)
DLI Durham Light Infantry
D-Lib [USA] Liberal Democrat
DLit Doctor of Literature
DLitt Doctor of Letters (from Latin *Doctor Litterarum*)
DLittS Doctor of Sacred Letters
DLJ Dame of Justice of the Order of St Lazarus of Jerusalem
DLL [computing] dynamic link library
DLM [genetics] dominant lethal mutation
DLO dead letter office (former name of RLO); Diploma in Laryngology and Otology; Diploma in Laryngology and Otorhinolaryngology; dispatch loading only
DLOY Duke of Lancaster's Own Yeomanry
DLP Democratic Labour Party
DLR Docklands Light Railway
dlr dealer
DLS debt liquidation schedule; Doctor of Library Science; Dominion Land Surveyor
DLSc Doctor of Library Science
DLT Dave Lee Travis (British disc jockey)
dlvd delivered
dlvr deliver
dlvy delivery
DLW Diploma in Labour Welfare
dly daily
DM [vehicle registration] Chester; *Daily Mail*; [astronomy] dark matter; deputy master; design manual; [currency] Deutschmark; [medicine] diabetes mellitus; [medicine] diastolic murmur; [physics] dipole moment; direct mail; Director of Music; dispersion measures; [computing] distributed memory; district manager; *Docteur en médecine* (French: Doctor of Medicine); Doctor of Mathematics; Doctor of Medicine; Doctor of Music
d.M *dieses Monats* (German: this month, inst.)
dm decimetre
.dm Dominica (in Internet address)
DMA Defence Manufacturers' Association; Diploma in Municipal Administration; [computing] direct memory access
DMAC [computing] direct memory access

control; [television] duobinary multiplexed analogue component
DM&CW Diploma in Maternity and Child Welfare
DMath Doctor of Mathematics
DMC direct manufacturing costs; district medical committee
DMD [computing] digital micromirror device; Doctor of Dental Medicine; Doctor of Mathematics and Didactics; Doctor of Medical Dentistry; [medicine] Duchenne muscular dystrophy
dmd demand
DME Diploma in Mechanical Engineering; [computing] direct machine environment; [aeronautics] distance-measuring equipment; [computing] distributed management environment; [electronics] dropping mercury electrode
DMed Doctor of Medicine
DMet Doctor of Metallurgy; Doctor of Meteorology
DMF decayed, missing and filled (teeth); Disabled Motorists Federation; [electronics] dose-modifying factor
DMFOS Diploma in Maxillofacial and Oral Surgery
dmg. damage
DMGO Divisional Machine-Gun Officer
DMGT [genetics] DNA-mediated gene transfer
DMHS Director of Medical and Health Services
DMI [computing] desktop management interface; Director of Military Intelligence
DMin Doctor of Ministry
DMJ Diploma in Medical Jurisprudence
DMJ(Path) Diploma in Medical Jurisprudence (Pathology)
DML [computing] data-manipulation language; Defence Medal for Leningrad (former Soviet decoration); Doctor of Modern Languages
dml. demolish
DMLJ Dame of Merit of the Order of St Lazarus of Jerusalem
DMLS Doppler microwave landing system
DMLT Diploma in Medical Laboratory Technology
DMM Defence Medal for Moscow (former Soviet decoration); [medicine] diffuse malignant mesothelioma
dmn dimension
dmnl dimensional
DMO Defence Medal for Odessa (former Soviet decoration); [astronomy] diffuse massive object; Director of Military Operations; district medical officer
DMO&I Director, Military Operations and Intelligence
DMP Diploma in Medical Psychology; Director of Manpower Planning
DMPB Diploma in Medical Pathology and Bacteriology
DMR Diploma in Medical Radiology; Director of Materials Research
DMRD Diploma in Medical Radiological Diagnosis; Directorate of Materials Research and Development
DMRE Diploma in Medical Radiology and Electrology
DMRT Diploma in Medical Radiotherapy
DMS [computing] database management system; [computing] data management system; [mining] dense-medium separation; Diploma in Management Studies; Directorate of Military Survey; Director of Medical Services; *Dis manibus sacrum* (Latin: consecrated to the souls of the departed); Doctor of Medical Science; Doctor of Medicine and Surgery
DMs Doc(tor) Martens (trademark for brand of lace-up boots)
DMSA [medicine] dimercaptosuccinic acid (used in diagnosis)
DMSO [medicine] dimethylsulphoxide (used in ointments)
DMSSB Direct Mail Services Standard Board
dmst. demonstration; demonstrator
dmstn demonstration
dmstr demonstrator
DMSV Defence Medal for Sevastopol (former Soviet decoration)
DMT [pharmacology] dimethyltryptamine (hallucinogen); Director of Military Training
DMTF [computing] desktop management task force
DMU [commerce] decision-making unit; directly managed unit (of hospital in NHS)
DMus Doctor of Music
DMV [USA] Department of Motor Vehicles; *Docteur en médecine vétérinaire*

(French: Doctor of Veterinary Medicine)
DMZ demilitarized zone
DN [commerce] debit note; *de novo* (Latin: from the beginning); Diploma in Nursing; *Dominus noster* (Latin: our Lord); [UK postcode] Doncaster; [vehicle registration] Leeds
D/N [commerce] debit note
Dn Deacon; *Don* (Spanish: Mr); Dragoon
dn down; dozen
DNA [USA] Defense Nuclear Agency; [genetics] deoxyribonucleic acid; *Det Norske Arbeiderpartiet* (Norwegian: Norwegian Labour Party); *Deutscher Normenausschuss* (German: German Standards Committee); [medicine] did not attend; Director of Naval Accounts; District Nursing Association
Dna *Doña* (Spanish: Mrs)
DNAase [biochemistry] deoxyribonuclease
DNAD Director of Naval Air Division
DNase [biochemistry] deoxyribonuclease
DNB *Dictionary of National Biography*
DNC [nuclear technology] delayed-neutron counting; Director of Naval Construction; [computing] distributed numerical control
DND Director of Navigation and Direction
DNE Diploma in Nursing Education; Director of Naval Equipment; Director of Nurse Education; Dounreay Nuclear Establishment
dne *douane* (French: customs)
DNES Director of Naval Education Service
DNF [sports] did not finish (in race)
DNH Department of National Heritage
DNHW [USA] Department of National Health and Welfare
DNI Director of Naval Intelligence
DNJC *Dominus noster Jesus Christus* (Latin: Our Lord Jesus Christ)
DNMS Director of Naval Medical Services
DNO Director of Naval Ordnance; district naval officer; district nursing officer; divisional nursing officer
DNP declared national programme; dynamic nuclear polarization
DNPDE Dounreay Nuclear Power Development Establishment
DNPP *Dominus Noster Papa Pontifex* (Latin: Our Lord the Pope)
DNR [USA] Department of Natural Resources; Director of Naval Recruitment; [medicine] do not resuscitate
Dnr [currency] dinar
DNS Department for National Savings; [computing] domain name system
dns downs (on map)
DNSA Diploma in Nursing Service Administration
DNT Director of Naval Training
DNWA Director of Naval Weather Service
DO defence order; [finance] deferred ordinary (shares); [commerce] delivery order; Diploma in Ophthalmology; Diploma in Osteopathy; [grammar] direct object; [commerce] direct order; dissolved oxygen; district office; district officer; divisional office; divisional officer; Doctor of Optometry; Doctor of Oratory; Doctor of Osteopathy; [fishing port] Douglas; drawing office; [vehicle registration] Lincoln
D/O [commerce] direct order
d/o [commerce] delivery order
Do. *Donnerstag* (German: Thursday)
do. ditto
.do Dominican Republic (in Internet address)
DOA date of availability; [medicine] dead on arrival; [USA] Department of the Army; dissolved-oxygen analyser
DOAE Defence Operational Analysis Establishment (of MOD)
DOB date of birth
d.o.b. date of birth
DObstRCOG Diploma in Obstetrics of the Royal College of Obstetricians and Gynaecologists
DOC *denominazione di origine controllata* (Italian: name of origin controlled) (wine classification); [USA] Department of Commerce; direct operating cost; [chemistry] dissolved organic carbon; District Officer Commanding
Doc. Doctor
doc [short form] doctor
doc. document(s)
d.o.c.a. date of current appointment
d.o.c.e. date of current enlistment
DocEng Doctor of Engineering
DOCG *denominazione di origine controllata garantita* (Italian: name of origin guaranteed controlled) (wine classification)

docu. document; documentary; documentation
DOD date of death; [USA] Department of Defense; died of disease
d.o.d. date of death
DOE [USA] Department of Energy; Department of the Environment; depends on experience (in job advertisement); Director of Education
d.o.e. depends on experience (in job advertisement)
DOF [science] degrees of freedom
D of Corn. LI Duke of Cornwall's Light Infantry
D of H degree of honour
D of L Duchy of Lancaster
D of S Director of Stores
DOG Directory of Opportunities for Graduates
DOH Department of Health
DOHC double overhead cam(shaft); dual overhead cam(shaft)
DOHS [USA] Department of Health Services
DOI Department of Industry; [USA] Department of the Interior; died of injuries; Director of Information
DOJ [USA] Department of Justice
DOL [USA] Department of Labor; Doctor of Oriental Learning
dol. [music] *dolce* (Italian: sweetly, gently); [currency] dollar
dolciss. [music] *dolcissimo* (Italian: very sweetly, very gently)
DOM date of marriage; *Deo Optimo Maximo* (Latin: to God, the best, the greatest); *département d'outre mer* (French: overseas department); [informal] dirty old man; dispersed organic material; dissolved organic material; [international vehicle registration] Dominican Republic; *Dominus omnium magister* (Latin: God the master of all)
Dom. Dominica; Dominical; [Roman Catholic Church] Dominican; *Dominus* (Latin: Lord)
dom. domain; *domenica* (Italian: Sunday); domestic; domicile; dominant; *domingo* (Spanish: Sunday); dominion
d.o.m. date of marriage
Dom. Bk Domesday Book
Dom. Proc. [law] *Domus Procerum* (Latin: House of Lords)
DOMS Diploma in Ophthalmic Medicine and Surgery
Domsat domestic communications satellite
DON [USA] Department of the Navy; Diploma in Orthopaedic Nursing; [chemistry] dissolved organic nitrogen
Don. Donegal
don. *donec* (Latin: until)
Doneg. Donegal
DOpt Diploma in Ophthalmic Optics
DOR Director of Operational Requirements
Dor [astronomy] Dorado
Dor. Dorian; Doric
DORA Defence of the Realm Act
dorm [short form] dormitory
Dors. Dorset
DOrth Diploma in Orthodontics; Diploma in Orthoptics
DOS date of sale; day of sale; [USA] Department of State; Diploma in Orthopaedic Surgery; Directorate of Overseas Surveys; Director of Ordnance Services; [computing] disk-operating system; Doctor of Ocular Science
dos. dosage
DOSV deep ocean survey vehicle
DOT Department of Overseas Trade; Department of Transport; [USA] Department of Transportation; designated order turnaround (in New York Stock Exchange); [computing] digital optical tape; Diploma in Occupational Therapy; [medicine] directly observed therapy; [physiology] dissolved oxygen tension
dot. [law] dotation (= endowment)
dott. *dottore* (Italian: doctor)
DOV double oil of vitriol (sulphuric acid)
DOW died of wounds
Dow. Dowager
dow. dowager
doz. dozen
DP data processing; decimal pitch; [chemistry] degree of polymerization; delivery point; Democratic Party; diametral pitch; Diploma in Psychiatry; (by) direction of the president; Director of Photography; disabled person; displaced person; Doctor of Philosophy; domestic prelate; [law] *Domus Procerum* (Latin: House of Lords); durable press; duty

paid; [computing] dynamic programming; [vehicle registration] Reading
D/P delivery on payment; delivery papers; [commerce] documents against payment; [commerce] documents against presentation
dp deep
d.p. damp-proof; damp-proofed; damp-proofing; deep penetration; departure point; [finance] depreciation percentage; direct port; double paper; [baseball] double play; dry powder; dual purpose
DPA Data Protection Authority; *Deutsche Presse Agentur* (German news agency); Diploma in Public Administration; discharged prisoners' aid; [USA] Doctor of Public Administration
d.p.a. deferred payment account
DPAA Draught Proofing Advisory Association
DPAS Discharged Prisoners' Aid Society
DPath Diploma in Pathology
DPB [finance] deposit pass book
DPC Defence Planning Committee (in NATO)
d.p.c. damp-proof course
DPCM [telecommunications] differential pulse code modulation
DPCP Department of Prices and Consumer Protection
DPCS data personal communications service
DPD Data Protection Directive; Diploma in Public Dentistry; [statistics] discrete probability distributions
DPE Diploma in Physical Education
DPEc Doctor of Political Economy
DPed Doctor of Pedagogy
DPH Diploma in Public Health; Director of Public Health; [USA] Doctor of Public Health
DPh Doctor of Philosophy
DPharm Doctor of Pharmacy
DPHD Diploma in Public Health Dentistry
DPhil Doctor of Philosophy
DPHN Diploma in Public Health Nursing
DPhysMed Diploma in Physical Medicine
DPI Department of Public Information
dpi [computing] dots per inch
dpl. diploma; diplomat; duplex
DPM data processing manager; Deputy Prime Minister; Deputy Provost-Marshal; Diploma in Psychological Medicine
DPMI [computing] DOS/Protected Mode Interface
DPMS [computing] display power management system
DPO distributing post office; district pay office
d.p.o.b. date and place of birth
DPolSc Doctor of Political Science
DPP [insurance] deferred payment plan; Diploma in Plant Pathology; Director of Public Prosecutions; [US finance] direct participation program
DPR Data Protection Register; Director of Public Relations
DPRK Democratic People's Republic of Korea (North Korea)
DPS Dales Pony Society; Director of Personal Services; Director of Postal Services; Doctor of Public Service
dps dividend per share
DPSA Diploma in Public and Social Administration
DPSK [computing] differential phase shift keying
DPSN Diploma in Professional Studies in Nursing
DPsSc Doctor of Psychological Science
DPsy *Docteur en psychologie* (French: Doctor of Psychology)
DPsych Diploma in Psychiatry; Doctor of Psychology
DPT [medicine] dental pantomogram; [medicine] diphtheria, pertussis (whooping cough), tetanus (vaccine)
dpt department; deponent; deposit; depot
dpty deputy
DPU data processing unit
DPW Department of Public Works
dpx duplex
DQ dispersion quotient; [sports] disqualified; [sports] disqualify; [civil aircraft marking] Fiji
d.q. direct question
DQDB [computing] distributed queue dual bus
DQMG Deputy Quartermaster-General
DQMS Deputy Quartermaster-Sergeant
DR [USA] Daughters of the Revolution; [navigation] dead reckoning; [physics] decay ratio; defence regulation; *Deutsches Reich* (German: German

Empire); dining room (in property advertisement); Diploma in Radiology; discount rate; dispatch rider; dispersion relation; district railway; district registry; [paper size] double royal; [fishing port] Dover; [theatre] down right (of stage); dry riser (for firefighter's hose); Dutch Reformed (Church); dynamic relaxation; [vehicle registration] Exeter

D/R deposit receipt

Dr Director; Doctor; [currency] drachma

Dr. Drive (in road name)

dr debtor; door; dram; [meteorology] drizzle and rain

dr. debit; drachm; [currency] drachma; drama; draw; drawer; drawn; dresser; driver; drum; drummer

d.r. deficiency report; design requirements; development report; document report

DRA de-rating appeals

Dra *Doctora* (Spanish: Doctor (female)); *Doutora* (Portuguese: Doctor (female)); [astronomy] Draco

DRAC Director, Royal Armoured Corps

DrAgr Doctor of Agriculture

DRAM [computing] dynamic random-access memory

dram. drama; dramatic; dramatist

dram. pers. *dramatis personae* (Latin: characters in the play)

DRAO Dominion Radio Astrophysical Observatory

Drav. Dravidian (language)

DRAW [computing] direct read after write

draw. drawing room (in property advertisement)

DrBusAdmin Doctor of Business Administration

DRC [theatre] down right centre (of stage); Dutch Reformed Church

DrChem Doctor of Chemistry

DRCOG Diploma of the Royal College of Obstetricians and Gynaecologists

DRCPath Diploma of the Royal College of Pathologists

DRCS [computing] dynamically redefinable character set

DRCST Diploma of the Royal College of Science and Technology (Glasgow)

DRD Diploma in Restorative Dentistry

DRDW [computing] direct read during write

DRE [medicine] digital rectal examination; Director of Religious Education; Doctor of Religious Education

DRelEd Doctor of Religious Education

DrEng Doctor of Engineering

DRG [medicine] diagnosis-related group

drg drawing

DRK *Deutsches Rotes Kreuz* (German: German Red Cross)

DRLS dispatch-rider letter service

DRM Diploma in Radiation Medicine; Diploma in Resource Management

DrMed Doctor of Medicine

drn drawn

DrNatSci Doctor of Natural Science

DRO daily routine order; disablement resettlement officer; divisional routine order

DrOecPol Doctor of Political Economics (from Latin *Doctor Oeconomiae Politicae*)

DRP dividend reinvestment plan

DrPH Doctor of Public Health

DrPhil Doctor of Philosophy

DrPolSci Doctor of Political Science

DRS Diploma in Religious Studies

DRSAMD Diploma of the Royal Scottish Academy of Music and Drama

DRSE [medicine] drug-related side effects

DRSN [meteorology] drifting snow

DRT [psychology] diagnostic rhyme test

DrTheol Doctor of Theology

Dr. und Vrl. *Druck und Verlag* (German: printed and published (by))

DRurSc Doctor of Rural Science

DRV dietary reference values

DRW [computing] draw format

drx. [currency] drachma

DS [music] *dal segno* (Italian: (repeat) from the sign); [finance] debenture stock; defect score; [physics] defect size; dental surgeon; Department of State; deputy secretary; Detective Sergeant; [physics] diffractive system; Directing Staff; [medicine] disseminated sclerosis; Doctor of Science; Doctor of Surgery; [computing] double-sided (disk); [medicine] Down's syndrome; driver seated (vehicle); [fishing port] Dumfries; [vehicle registration] Glasgow

D/S [medicine] dextrose saline

Ds *Deus* (Latin: God); *Dominus* (Latin: Lord, Master)

ds. *destro* (Italian: right)

d.s. date of service; daylight saving; days after sight; day's sight; document signed
DSA [medicine] digital subtraction angiography; Diploma in Social Administration; *Docteur ès sciences agricoles* (French: Doctor of Agricultural Science); Down's Syndrome Association; Driving Standards Agency
DSAC Defence Scientific Advisory Council
DSAO Diplomatic Service Administration Office
DSASO Deputy Senior Air Staff Officer
DSB *Dansk Statsbaner* (Danish: Danish State Railways); Drug Supervisory Body (of UN)
DSC Discovery Channel; Distinguished Service Cross (replacement for CSC); Doctor of Surgical Chiropody
DSc Doctor of Science
DScA *Docteur ès sciences agricoles* (French: Doctor of Agricultural Science); *Docteur ès sciences appliquées* (French: Doctor of Applied Sciences)
DSc(Agr) Doctor of Science in Agriculture
DSc(Eng) Doctor of Science in Engineering
DSc(For) Doctor of Science in Forestry
DSCHE Diploma of the Scottish Council for Health Education
DScMil Doctor of Military Science
DScTech Doctor of Technical Science
DSD Director of Signals Division; Director of Staff Duties
dsDNA [biochemistry] double-stranded deoxyribonucleic acid
DSDP deep-sea drilling project
DSE Doctor of Science in Economics
Dsf Düsseldorf
dsgn design
dsgn. designer
DSIR [New Zealand] Department of Scientific and Industrial Research
DSL district Scout leader; Doctor of Sacred Letters
DSM deputy stage manager; *Diagnostic and Statistical Manual* (of American Psychiatric Association); [computing] digital storage medium; Directorate of Servicing and Maintenance; Distinguished Service Medal; Doctor of Sacred Music
dsmd dismissed
DSN [astronautics] Deep-Space Network
DSO (Companion of the) Distinguished Service Order; District Staff Officer
DSocSC Doctor of Social Science(s)
DSP Democratic Socialist Party; [electronics] digital signal processing; [electronics] digital signal processor; *Docteur ès sciences politiques* (French: Doctor of Political Science); dye sublimation printing
d.s.p. *decessit sine prole* (Latin: died without issue)
dspl disposal
d.s.p.l. *decessit sine prole legitima* (Latin: died without legitimate issue)
d.s.p.m. *decessit sine prole mascula* (Latin: died without male issue)
d.s.p.m.s. *decessit sine prole mascula superstite* (Latin: died without surviving male issue)
dspn disposition
d.s.p.s. *decessit sine prole superstite* (Latin: died without surviving issue)
d.s.p.v. *decessit sine prole virile* (Latin: died without male issue)
d.s.q. discharged to sick quarters
DSR [commerce] debt service ratio; [medicine] digital subtraction radiography; Director of Scientific Research; [medicine] dynamic spatial reconstructor
DSRD Directorate of Signals Research and Development
DSS [computing] decision support system; Department of Social Security; Director of Social Services; Doctor of Holy (or Sacred) Scripture (from Latin *Doctor Sacrae Scripturae*); Doctor of Social Science
Dss Deaconess
DSSc Diploma in Sanitary Science; Doctor of Social Science
DST Daylight Saving Time; deep-sleep therapy; Director of Supplies and Transport; Doctor of Sacred Theology; Double Summer Time; [mining] drill-stem test
dstn destination
D Surg. Dental Surgeon
DSW [New Zealand] Department of Social Welfare; Doctor of Social Welfare; Doctor of Social Work
DT *Daily Telegraph*; damage-tolerant; data transmission; daylight time; [medicine] dead from tumour; delirium tremens; dental technician; [USA] Department of

Transportation; [USA] Department of Treasury; destructive testing; [US informal] detective; [nuclear technology] deuterium–tritium; Director of Transport; Doctor of Divinity (or Theology) (from Latin *Doctor Theologiae*); [UK postcode] Dorchester; [vehicle registration] Sheffield

d.t. delirium tremens; double throw

DTA [physics] differential thermal analysis; Diploma in Tropical Agriculture; Distributive Trades' Alliance

DTAM data transfer, access and manipulation

d.t.b.a. [commerce] date to be advised

DTC Department of Technical Cooperation; [USA] Depository Trust Company; Diamond Trading Company; [medicine] differentiated thyroid carcinoma; Diploma in Textile Chemistry; Docklands Transportation Consortium

DTCD [USA] Department of Technical Cooperation for Development; Diploma in Tuberculosis and Chest Diseases

DTD Diploma in Tuberculous Diseases; Director of Technical Development; document type definition

dtd dated

d.t.d. [medicine] *detur talis dosis* (Latin: let such a dose be given) (in prescriptions)

DTDP ditridecyl phthalate (PVC plasticizer)

DTE [computing] data terminal equipment

DTech Doctor of Technology

DTF Dairy Trade Federation; Domestic Textiles Federation

Dtg *Dienstag* (German: Tuesday)

DTH [immunology] delayed-type hypersensitivity; Diploma in Tropical Hygiene

DTh Doctor of Divinity (or Theology) (from Latin *Doctor Theologiae*)

DTheol Doctor of Divinity (or Theology) (from Latin *Doctor Theologiae*)

DThPT Diploma in Theory and Practice of Teaching

DTI Department of Trade and Industry

DTIC [medicine] dacarbazine (used to treat cancer)

DTL [electronics] diode-transistor logic; down the line (in shooting)

DTM Diploma in Tropical Medicine

Dtm. Dortmund

DTMH Diploma in Tropical Medicine and Hygiene

dto *direito* (Portuguese: right)

DTOD Director of Trade and Operations Division

DTP [computing] desktop publishing

DTPA [medicine] diethylenetriaminepentaacetic acid (used in diagnosis)

DTPH Diploma in Tropical Public Health

DTR [photography] diffusion-transfer reversal; Diploma in Therapeutic Radiology; double taxation relief

DTRP Diploma in Town and Regional Planning

DTRT [meteorology] deteriorating

DTS [medicine] dual tracer scintigraphy

DTs [informal] delirium tremens

DTV digital television

DTVM Diploma in Tropical Veterinary Medicine

DU [vehicle registration] Coventry; [physics] depleted uranium; died unmarried; Doctor of the University; [medicine] duodenal ulcer

Du. Ducal; Duchy; Duke; Dutch

DUART [computing, electronics] dual universal asynchronous receiver transmitter

Dub. Dublin

dub. dubious; *dubitans* (Latin: doubting)

Dubl. Dublin

DUC [meteorology] dense upper cloud

DUI [USA] driving under the influence (of alcohol or drugs)

Dumf. Dumfries and Galloway

Dun. Dundee

Dunelm. *Dunelmensis* (Latin: (Bishop) of Durham)

DUniv Doctor of the University

duo. [paper size] duodecimo

DUP [Northern Ireland] Democratic Unionist Party; *Docteur de l'Université de Paris* (French: Doctor of the University of Paris)

dup. duplicate

Dur. Durban; Durham

DUS Diploma of the University of Southampton

DUSC [US air force] deep underground support center

Dut. Dutch

DUV damaging ultraviolet (radiation)

DV defective vision; *Deo volente* (Latin: God willing); Diploma in Venereology;

direct vision; distinguished visitor; district valuer; [Bible] Douay Version; double vision; [vehicle registration] Exeter

DVA [medicine] digital video angiography; Diploma in Veterinary Anaesthesia; Dunkirk Veterans' Association

DV&D Diploma in Venereology and Dermatology

DVC [microbiology] direct viable count

DVD [computing] digital versatile disc; digital video disc

DVD-R [computing] digital versatile disc recordable

DVE Diploma in Vocational Education

DVH Diploma in Veterinary Hygiene

DVI [computing] digital video imaging; [computing] digital video interactive

DVLA Driver and Vehicle Licensing Agency

DVLC Driver and Vehicle Licensing Centre (Swansea)

DVM digital voltmeter; Doctor of Veterinary Medicine

d.v.m. *decessit vita matris* (Latin: died in the lifetime of the mother)

DVMS Doctor of Veterinary Medicine and Surgery

DVO district veterinary officer

d.v.p. *decessit vita patris* (Latin: died in the lifetime of the father)

DVPH Diploma in Veterinary Public Health

DVR Diploma in Veterinary Radiology; [computing] discrete-variable representation

DVS Doctor of Veterinary Surgery

DVSc Doctor of Veterinary Science

DVSci Doctor of Veterinary Science

DVT [medicine] deep-vein thrombosis

DW [vehicle registration] Cardiff; [chemistry] deionized water; [commerce] dock warrant

D/W [commerce] dock warrant

d/w dust wrapper

d.w. dead weight; delivered weight

DWA driving without awareness

DWAS Doctor Who Appreciation Society

d.w.c. deadweight capacity

dwel. dwelling

DWEM [USA] dead white European male

dwg drawing; dwelling

DWI [USA] driving while intoxicated; Dutch West Indies (former name of Netherlands Antilles)

DWR Duke of Wellington's Regiment

dwr drawer

dwt pennyweight

d.w.t. deadweight tonnage

DWU [USA] Distillery, Wine and Allied Workers International Union

DX [photography] daylight exposure; [vehicle registration] Ipswich; [telecommunications] long-distance

DXF data exchange format

DXR [medicine] deep X-ray

DXRT [medicine] deep X-ray therapy

DXS diagnostic X-ray spectrometry

DY [international vehicle registration] Benin (from former name Dahomey); [vehicle registration] Brighton; dockyard; [UK postcode] Dudley

Dy [chemical element] dysprosium

dy delivery; [paper size] demy

DYB do your best (Scout motto)

Dyd dockyard

dyn dyne

dyn. dynamic; dynamics; dynamite; dynamo; dynasty

DYS Duke of York's Royal Military School

DZ [international vehicle registration] Algeria (from Arabic *Djazïr*); [vehicle registration] Antrim; Doctor of Zoology; [meteorology] drizzle; [military] drop zone

dz. dozen

.dz Algeria (in Internet address)

DZool Doctor of Zoology

D-Zug *Durchgangszug* (German: express train)

E

E casual workers (occupational group); Earl; [astronomy] earth; [electrical engineering] earth; east; Easter; eastern; [UK postcode] east London; [slang] ecstasy (drug); Edinburgh; efficiency; Egypt; Egyptian; [chemistry] electromeric effect; electronic (as in **E-commerce**); [chemistry] elimination reaction; [astronomy] elliptical galaxy; elocution; [currency] emalangeni (used in Swaziland); eminence; enemy; engineer; engineering; England; English; [numismatics] English shilling; envoy; equator; *España* (Spanish: Spain); EU-recognized food additive (as in **E120** = cochineal); European; evening; evensong; exa- (indicates 10^{18}, as in **Em** = exametre); [fishing port] Exeter; [music] note of scale; [international vehicle registration] Spain (from Spanish *España*); [logic] universal negative categorical proposition

E [physics] electric field strength; [chemistry] electrode potential; [physics] electromotive force; [physics] energy; [physics] illuminance; [physics] irradiance

e [mathematics] base of natural logarithm; electromotive; [physics] electron; electronic (as in **e-text**); [physics] positron; [meteorology] wet air

e [mathematics] eccentricity (of ellipse); [physics] electron charge; [chemistry] equatorial conformation (of molecules); [physics] proton charge

e. edition; educated; elder; eldest; electric; electricity; electromotive; engineer; engineering; Erlang (unit of traffic intensity in telephony); [baseball] error; evening; excellence; excellent

EA [vehicle registration] Dudley; early antigen; East Anglia; economic adviser; educational age; effective action; effective agent (as in **EA content**); electrical artificer; *Ente Autonomo* (Italian: Autonomous Corporation); [Freemasonry] Entered Apprentice; enterprise allowance; environmental assessment; Evangelical Alliance; experimental area; exposure age

E/A enemy aircraft; experimental aircraft

ea. each

EAA Edinburgh Architectural Association; Electrical Appliance Association; [USA] Engineer in Aeronautics and Astronautics; [chemistry] eth(yl)ene acrylic acid

EAAA European Association of Advertising Agencies

EAAC European Agricultural Aviation Centre

EAAFRO East African Agriculture and Forestry Research Organization

EAAP European Association for Animal Production

EAB [medicine] extra-anatomic bypass

EAC East African Community; Educational Advisory Committee; Engineering Advisory Council; European Atomic Commission

EACA East Africa Court of Appeal; [medicine] epsilon aminocaproic acid

EACC East Asia Christian Conference

EACSO East African Common Services Organization

ead. *eadem* (Latin: the same (woman))

eaed. *eaedem* (Latin: the same (women))

EAEG European Association of Exploration Geophysicists

EAES European Atomic Energy Society

EAF electric-arc furnace

e.a.f. emergency action file

EAFFRO East African Freshwater Fisheries Research Organization

EAG Economists Advisory Group

EAGGF European Agricultural Guidance and Guarantee Fund (in EU)

EAHF [medicine] eczema, asthma, hay fever

EAK [international vehicle registration] (East Africa) Kenya

EAM *Ethniko Apelentherotiko Metopo* (Greek: National Liberation Front) (in World War II)

EAMF European Association of Music Festivals

EAMFRO East African Marine Fisheries Research Organization

EAMTC European Association of Management Training Centres
EAN [chemistry] effective atomic number; [computing] European Academic Network; European Article Number (computer coding for retail goods)
e&e each and every
E&O errors and omissions
E&OE errors and omissions excepted
e.a.o.n. except as otherwise noted
EAP East Africa Protectorate; Edgar Allan Poe (US writer); [USA] employee-assistance program; English for academic purposes
EAPC Euro-Atlantic Partnership Council (in NATO, replacement for NACC)
EAPR European Association for Potato Research
EAPROM [computing] electrically alterable programmable read-only memory
EAR employee advisory resource; employee attitude research; [engineering] energy-absorbing resin
EARCCUS East African Regional Committee for Conservation and Utilization of Soil
EARN [computing] European Academic and Research Network
EAROM [computing] electrically alterable read-only memory
EAROPH East Asia Regional Organization for Planning and Housing
EAS electronic article surveillance; [medicine] endotoxin-activated serum; [aeronautics] equivalent air speed; [aeronautics] estimated air speed
EASA Entertainment Arts Socialist Association
EASEP [astronautics] Early Apollo Scientific Experiments Package
EASHP European Association of Senior Hospital Physicians
east. eastern
EASTROPAC Eastern Tropical Pacific
EAT earliest arrival time; [medicine] Ehrlich ascites tumour; Employment Appeals Tribunal; estimated arrival time; [medicine] experimental autoimmune thyroiditis; [international vehicle registration] (East Africa) Tanzania
EATRO East African Trypanosomiasis Research Organization
EAU [international vehicle registration] (East Africa) Uganda
EAVRO East African Veterinary Research Organization
EAW Electrical Association for Women; equivalent average words
EAX [telecommunications] electronic automatic exchange
EAZ [international vehicle registration] (East Africa) Tanzania (formerly Zanzibar)
EB electricity board; electron beam; electronic book; *Encyclopaedia Britannica*; [medicine] epidermolysis bullosa (skin disease); Epstein–Barr (virus); [currency] Ethiopian birr; Evans blue (dye); [vehicle registration] Peterborough
Eb [computing] exabyte
e-b estate-bottled
EBA English Bowling Association
EB&RA Engineer Buyers' and Representatives' Association
e.b.a.r. edited beyond all recognition
EBC English Benedictine Congregation; European Billiards Confederation; European Brewery Convention
EBCDIC [computing] extended binary-coded decimal-interchange code
e-beam electron beam
EBICON [physics] electron-bombardment-induced conductivity
EBIT [accounting] earnings before interest and tax
EBL electron-beam lithography; European Bridge League
EBM electron-beam machining; [medicine] expressed breast milk
EBMC English Butter Marketing Company
EbN east by north
EBNF [computing] extended Backus normal form
Ebor. *Eboracensis* (Latin: (Archbishop) of York); *Eboracum* (Latin: York)
EBR electron-beam recording; [nuclear technology] experimental breeder reactor
EBRA Engineer Buyers' and Representatives' Association
EBRD European Bank for Reconstruction and Development
EBS emergency bed service; emergency

broadcast system; engineered barrier system; English Bookplate Society
EbS east by south
EBT [medicine] electron-beam therapy
EBU English Bridge Union; European Badminton Union; European Boxing Union; European Broadcasting Union
EBV [medicine] Epstein–Barr virus
EBWR [nuclear technology] experimental boiling-water reactor
EC East Caribbean; [UK postcode] east central London; east coast; Eastern Command; Ecclesiastical Commissioner; [international vehicle registration] Ecuador; [physics] eddy current; educational committee; education committee; [chemistry] effective concentration; electricity council; electrolytic corrosion; electronic computer; emergency commission; [medicine] endothelial cell; Engineering Corps; [biochemistry] Enzyme Commission (in enzyme code number); Episcopal Church; Established Church; [chemistry] eth(yl)ene carbonate; [Canada] *Étoile du Courage* (French: Star of Courage); European Commission; European Community; executive committee; [vehicle registration] Preston; [civil aircraft marking] Spain
Ec. Ecuador
.ec Ecuador (in Internet address)
ec. earth closet; enamel-coated; enamel-covered; error correction; *exempli causa* (Latin: for example); extended coverage; extension course
ECA Early Closing Association; Economic Commission for Africa; [USA] Economic Cooperation Administration; Educational Centres Association; Electrical Contractors' Association; European Congress of Accountants
ECAC Engineering College Administrative Council; European Civil Aviation Conference
ECAFE Economic Commission for Asia and the Far East (former name of ESCAP)
ECAS Electrical Contractors' Association of Scotland
ECAT [medicine] emission compute(rize)d axial tomography
ECB electronic codebook; electronic components board; European Central Bank
ECBS engineering of computer-based systems
ECC [electrical engineering] earth continuity conductor; [physics] emergency core cooling (or coolant); energy-conscious construction; [computing] error-correction code; European Cultural Centre
Ecc. *Eccellenze* (Italian: Excellency)
ecc. *eccetera* (Italian: et cetera, etc.)
Ecc. Hom. *Ecce Homo* (Latin: behold the man)
ECCI European Confederation for Commerce and Industry plc
Eccl. [Bible] Ecclesiastes
eccl. ecclesiastic(al)
Eccles. [Bible] Ecclesiastes
eccles. ecclesiastic(al)
Ecclus. [Bible] Ecclesiasticus (book of Apocrypha)
ECCM [military] electronic counter-countermeasure(s)
ECCP European Committee on Crime Problems
ECCS [physics] emergency core cooling system
ECCU English Cross-Country Union
ECD early closing day; [electronics] electrostatic charge decay; [computing] enhanced colour display; estimated completion date
ECE Economic Commission for Europe
ECF [US medicine] extended-care facility; extracellular fluid
ECFA European Committee for Future Accelerators
ECFMG Educational Council for Foreign Medical Graduates
ECFMS Educational Council for Foreign Medical Students
ECG [medicine] electrocardiogram; [medicine] electrocardiograph; Export Credit Guarantee
ECGB East Coast of Great Britain
ECGC Empire Cotton Growing Corporation
ECGD Export Credits Guarantee Department
ech. echelon
ECHP [USA] Environmental Compliance and Health Protection

ECHR European Commission on Human Rights; European Court of Human Rights
ECI East Coast of Ireland; energy-cost indicator
ECIA European Committee of Interior Architects
ECITO European Central Inland Transport Organization
ECJ European Court of Justice
ECL [physics] emergency cooling limit; [electronics] emitter-coupled logic
ECLAC Economic Commission for Latin America and the Caribbean
eclec. eclectic; eclecticism
ecli. eclipse; ecliptic
ECLO [electronics] emitter-coupled logic operator
ECLOF Ecumenical Church Loan Fund
ECLSS environmental control and life-support system
ECM electric coding machine; electrochemical machining; [military] electronic countermeasure(s); energy conservation measure; environmental corrosion monitor; extended core memory
ECMA [geology] East Coast Magnetic Anomaly; European Computer Manufacturers' Association
ECME Economic Commission for the Middle East
ECMF Electric Cable Makers' Federation
ECMO [medicine] extracorporeal membrane oxygenation
ECMRA European Chemical Market Research Association
ECMT European Conference of Ministers of Transport
ECMWF European Centre for Medium-range Weather Forecast
ECN epoxy–cresol–novolak (synthetic resin)
ECNSW Electricity Commission of New South Wales
ECO energy conservation opportunity; English Chamber Orchestra; European Coal Organization
eco. ecological; ecology
ECODU European Control Data Users
ECoG [medicine] electrocochleography; electrocorticogram
ecol. ecological; ecology
E coli *Escherichia coli* (Latin: name of bacterium)
Ecol. Soc. Am. Ecological Society of America
ECOM electronic computer-originated mail
ECOMOG ECOWAS Monitoring Group (peacekeeping force)
econ. economic(al); economics; economist; economy
Econ. J *Economic Journal*
Econ. R *Economic Review*
ECOR [USA] Engineering Committee on Ocean Resources
ECOSOC Economic and Social Council (of UN)
ECOVAST European Council for the Village and Small Town
ECOWAS Economic Community of West African States
ECP [finance] Euro-commercial paper; European Committee on Crop Protection; *Evangelii Christi Praedicator* (Latin: Preacher of the Gospel of Christ)
ECPA Electric Consumers Protection Act
ECPD [USA] Engineers' Council for Professional Development
ECPS European Centre for Population Studies
ECQAC Electronic Components Quality Assurance Committee
ECR electronic cash register
ECS emergency cooling (or coolant) system; environmental control system; European Communications Satellite; European Components Service
ECSC European Coal and Steel Community (predecessor of EU)
ECST European Convention on the Suppression of Terrorism
ECT [medicine] electroconvulsive therapy; [medicine] emission-compute(rize)d tomography
ECTA Electrical Contractors' Trading Association
ECTD [USA] Emission Control Technology Division
ECTF Enterprise Computer Telephony Forum
ECU English Church Union; environmental control unit; European Chiropractic Union; European Currency Unit;

European Customs Union; [photography] extreme close-up
ecu European Currency Unit
Ecua. Ecuador; Ecuadorian
ECUK East Coast of the United Kingdom
ECUSA Episcopal Church of the United States of America
ECV [obstetrics] external cephalic version
ECWA Economic Commission for Western Asia
ECWEC European Community Wind Energy Conference and Exhibition
ECWS English Civil War Society
ECY European Conservation Year
ECYO European Community Youth Orchestra
ED [USA] Doctor of Engineering; economic dispatch; Education Department; [pharmacology] effective dose; Efficiency Decoration; election district; [physics] electromagnetic dissociation; [electronics] electron device; [physics, chemistry] electron diffraction; [medicine] embryonic day; Employment Department; [medicine] end-diastole; [medicine] end-diastolic; entertainments duty; equilibrium dialysis; equivalent dose (of radiation); European Democrat; evening dinner (in accommodation advertisement); [finance] ex dividend; existence doubtful; experimental detector; [medicine] extensive disease; [finance] extra dividend; [vehicle registration] Liverpool
Ed. Edinburgh; Editor
ed. *edile* (Italian: building); *edilizia* (Italian: building); edited; edition; editor; educated; education
éd. *édition* (French: edition)
e.d. edge distance; enemy dead; error detecting; excused duty; extra duty
EDA [USA] Economic Development Administration; Electrical Development Association; electronic design automation; *Eniea Dimokratiki Aristera* (Greek: Union of the Democratic Left) (political party)
e.d.a. early departure authorized
ED&S *English Dance and Song* (publication of EFDSS)
EDAS [computing] enhanced data-acquisition system
EDB ethene dibromide (fuel additive)
EdB Bachelor of Education
EDBS [computing] expert database system
EDC Economic Development Committee; Engineering Design Centre; [computing] error-detection code; ethylene dichloride; European Defence Community; [obstetrics] expected date of confinement
e.d.c. error detection and correction; extra dark colour
EDD *English Dialect Dictionary*; exactly delayed detonator; [obstetrics] expected date of delivery
EdD Doctor of Education
edd. *ediderunt* (Latin: published by); *editiones* (Latin: editions)
EDE effective dose equivalent (of radiation)
EDF *Électricité de France* (French electricity corporation); [USA] Environmental Defense Fund; European Development Fund
EDG emergency diesel generator; European Democratic Group
EDHE experimental data handling equipment
EDI [computing] electronic data interchange
Edin. Edinburgh
Ed. in Ch. Editor in Chief
EDIP European Defence Improvement Programme (in NATO)
EDIS Engineering Data Information System
edit. edited; edition; editor; *editore* (Italian: publisher); editorial
EDL economic discard limits; [chemistry] electrical double layer; electrodeless discharge lamp
e.d.l. edition de luxe
EDM [chemistry] electrical-discharge machining; electric dipole moment; [surveying] electronic distance measurement; [physics] energy-density model
EdM Master of Education
EDMA European Direct Marketing Association
Edm. & Ips. (Bishop of) St Edmundsbury and Ipswich
Edmn Edmonton
edn edition
Ednbgh Edinburgh

EDNS expected demand not supplied
EDO [computing] extended data out
e.d.o.c. effective date of change
EDO DRAM [computing] extended data out dynamic random-access memory
EDP [physics] electron-diffraction pattern; [computing] electronic data processing; emergency defence plan; [medicine] end-diastolic pressure
EDPS [computing] electronic data-processing system
EDPT [computing] enhanced-drive parameter table
EDR electronic decoy rocket; Electronic Dictionary Research; European Depository Receipts; except during rain (following pollen count)
EDRF [medicine] endothelium-derived relaxing factor
EDRP European Demonstration Reprocessing Plant (for nuclear fuel)
EDS electrically adjusted driver's seat (in car advertisement); Electronic Data Systems Corporation; English Dialect Society; [computing] exchangeable disk store
EdS Education Specialist
EDSAC [computing] Electronic Delay Storage Automatic Calculator
EDSAT Educational Television Satellite
EDSP Exchange Delivery Settlement Price
EDSS expert decision-support system
ED/st electrically adjusted driver's seat (in car advertisement)
EDT [USA, Canada] Eastern Daylight Time; energy design technique
EDTA European Dialysis and Transplant Association
EDU European Democratic Union
.edu US educational institution (in Internet address)
educ. educated; education; educational
educn education
EDV [medicine] end-diastolic volume
EDVAC Electronic Discrete Variable Automatic Computer
Edw. Edward
EE Early English; Eastern Electricity; edge-to-edge; electrical engineer; electrical engineering; electron emission; electronic engineer; electronic engineering; employment exchange; environmental education; environmental engineering; Envoy Extraordinary; errors excepted; explosive emission; expressed emotion; [vehicle registration] Lincoln
e.e. errors excepted; eye and ear
.ee Estonia (in Internet address)
EEA Electronic Engineering Association; European Economic Area
EEAIE Electrical, Electronic and Allied Industries, Europe
EE&MP Envoy Extraordinary and Minister Plenipotentiary
EEB European Environmental Bureau
EEC [physics] energy–energy correlation; English Electric Company; European Economic Community (predecessor of EU); [electronics] explosive-emission cathode
EECA European Electronic Component Manufacturers' Association
EECS electrical-energy conversion system
EED effective equivalent dose (of radiation); electro-explosive device
EEDC Economic Development Committee for the Electronics Industry
EEF Egyptian Expeditionary Force; Engineering Employers' Federation; equivalent-energy function
EEG [medicine] electroencephalogram; [medicine] electroencephalograph; Essence Export Group
EEI [USA] Edison Electric Institute; [USA] Environmental Equipment Institute
EEIBA Electrical and Electronic Industries Benevolent Association
EEMJEB Electrical and Electronic Manufacturers' Joint Education Board
EEMS [computing] enhanced expanded memory specification
EEMUA Engineering Equipment and Materials Users Association
E Eng. Early English
EENT [medicine] eye, ear, nose and throat
EEO Energy Efficiency Office; equal employment opportunity
EEOC [USA] Equal Employment Opportunities Commission
EEPLD [computing] electrically erasable programmable logic device
EEPROM [computing] electrically erasable programmable read-only memory
EER energy–efficiency ratio
EERI [USA] Earthquake Engineering Research Institute

EEROM [computing] electrically erasable read-only memory
EES European Exchange System
EET Eastern European Time
EETPU Electrical, Electronic, Telecommunications and Plumbing Union (became part of AEEU)
EETS Early English Text Society
EEZ exclusive economic zone
EF edge-to-face; educational foundation; education foundation; [genetics] elongation factor; emergency fleet; [physics] enrichment factor; expectant father; expeditionary force; experimental flight; extra fine; [vehicle registration] Middlesbrough
EFA engine fault analysis; [biochemistry] essential fatty acid; Eton Fives Association; European Fighter Aircraft
EFB energy from biomass
EFC European Federation of Corrosion; European Forestry Commission
EFCE European Federation of Chemical Engineering
EFCT European Federation of Conference Towns
EFD [engineering] early fault detection
EFDSS English Folk Dance and Song Society
EFF Electronic Frontier Foundation; European Furniture Federation
eff. *effetto* (Italian: bill, promissory note); efficiency; effigy
EFG electric-field gradient
EFGF [electronics] epitaxial ferrite-garnet film
EFI electronic fuel injection
EFIS [aeronautics] electronic flight-information system
EFL English as a foreign language; external financial limit
EFM [medicine] electronic fetal monitor; European Federalist Movement
EFNS Educational Foundation for Nuclear Science
EFP [mathematics] Einstein–Fokker–Planck (differential equation); [photography] electronic field production; [commerce] exchange of futures for physicals; explosively formed penetrator; explosively formed projectile
EFPD effective full-power day
EFPH effective full-power hour
EFPW European Federation for the Protection of Waters
EFPY effective full-power year
EFR [astronomy] emerging flux region; [telecommunications] Enhanced Full Rate (for voice quality on mobile phone); [nuclear technology] European Fast Reactor; [nuclear technology] experimental fast reactor
EFRC [USA] Edwards Flight Research Center
EFSA European Federation of Sea Anglers
EFSC European Federation of Soroptimist Clubs
EFT electronic funds transfer
EFTA European Free Trade Association
EFTC Electrical Fair Trading Council
EFTPOS electronic funds transfer at point of sale
EFTS electronic funds transfer system; elementary flying training school
EFTU Engineering and Fastener Trade Union
EFU energetic feed unit; European Football Union
EFVA Educational Foundation for Visual Aids
EFW electric front windows (in car advertisement); energy from waste
EG Engineers Guild; equivalent grade; [chemistry] ethylene glycol; [vehicle registration] Peterborough
Eg. Egypt; Egyptian; Egyptologist; Egyptology
.eg Egypt (in Internet address)
e.g. *ejusdem generis* (Latin: of a like kind); *exempli gratia* (Latin: for example)
EGA Elizabeth Garrett Anderson (women's hospital); [computing] enhanced graphics adapter; European Golf Association
EGARD environmental gamma-ray and radon detector
EGAS Educational Grants Advisory Service
EGCI Export Group for the Construction Industries
EGCS English Guernsey Cattle Society
EGD epithermal gold deposit
EGEAS Electric Generating Expansion Analysis System
EGF [medicine] epidermal growth factor

EGFR [medicine] epidermal growth factor receptor
EGIFO Edward Grey Institute of Field Ornithology (Oxford)
EGL Engineers Guild Limited
EGM Empire Gallantry Medal (replaced by GC); European Glass Container Manufacturers' Committee; extraordinary general meeting
EGmbH [commerce] *Eingetragene Gesellschaft mit beschränkter Haftung* (German: registered limited company)
EGO eccentric (orbit) geophysical observatory
EGR [finance] earned growth rate; exhaust gas recirculation (as in **EGR valve**)
EGSP electronics glossary and symbol panel
EGT [physics] Einstein-invariant gauge theory (of gravitation)
e.g.t. exhaust gas temperature
EGU English Golf Union; [chemistry] external gelation of uranium
EGYPT eager to grab your pretty tits (on envelope of love letter)
Egypt. Egyptian
Egyptol. Egyptologist; Egyptology
EH [UK postcode] Edinburgh; [music] English horn (= cor anglais); [medicine] essential hypertension; [vehicle registration] Stoke-on-Trent
eh. *ehrenhalber* (German: honorary)
EHC effective heat capacity (of building); European Hotel Corporation; [medicine] external heart compression
EHF European Hockey Federation; experimental husbandry farm; [radio] extremely high frequency
EHG electro-hydraulic governor
EHL [physics] effective half-life
EHO environmental health officer
EHP electric and hybrid propulsion
ehp effective horsepower; electric horsepower
EHR Environmental Hazard Ranking; [USA] Environmental Health Services; European hybrid spectrometer; extra-high strength
EHT [electronics] extra-high tension
EHV electric and hybrid vehicle; extra-high voltage
EHWS extreme high water springs (level of tide)
EI earth (atmosphere) interface; East Indian; East Indies; electrical insulation; electromagnetic interaction; electron impact; electron ionization; [finance] endorsement irregular; energy intake; environmentally induced illness; [photography] exposure index; external irradiation; [civil aircraft marking] (Republic of) Ireland
EIA East Indian Association; economic impact assessment; [USA] Electrical Industries Association; [USA] Electronic Industries Association; Engineering Industries Association; environmental impact analysis; environmental impact assessment; Environmental Investigation Agency; [medicine] enzyme immunoassay; [medicine] exercise-induced asthma
EIB European Investment Bank; Export–Import Bank
EIC East India Company; Electrical Industries' Club; Engineering Institute of Canada
EICM employer's inventory of critical manpower
EICS East India Company's Service
EID East India Dock; [military] Electrical Inspection Directorate
EIDCT Educational Institute of Design, Craft and Technology
E-IDE enhanced integrated-drive electronics
EIEE [medicine] early infantile epileptic encephalopathy
EIEMA Electrical Installation Equipment Manufacturers' Association
EIF Elderly Invalids Fund
EIFAC European Inland Fisheries Advisory Committee
EIIR *Elizabetha Secunda Regina* (Latin: Queen Elizabeth the Second)
E-in-C Engineer-in-Chief
E Ind. East Indies
einschl. *einschliesslich* (German: including, inclusive)
Einw. *Einwohner* (German: inhabitant)
EIO extended interaction oscillator
EIPC European Institute of Printed Circuits
EIR [taxation] earned income relief; [computing] error-indicating recording

EIRMA European Industrial Research Management Association
EIS economic information system; Educational Institute of Scotland; effluent information system; energy information system; Enterprise Investment Scheme (replacement for BES); environmental impact statement; epidemic intelligence service
EISA [computing] enhanced industry standard architecture; [computing] extended industry standard architecture
EITB Engineering Industry Training Board
EITF [USA] Emerging Issues Task Force
EIU Economist Intelligence Unit
EIVT European Institute for Vocational Training
EJ elbow jerk; exajoule; [vehicle registration] Haverfordwest; [civil aircraft marking] (Republic of) Ireland
ej. *ejemplo* (Spanish: example)
EJC [USA] Engineers' Joint Council
EJMA English Joinery Manufacturers' Association
ejusd. *ejusdem* (Latin: of the same)
EK [civil aircraft marking] Armenia; East Kilbride; *Enosis Kentron* (Greek: Centre Union) (political party); [vehicle registration] Liverpool
eK *etter Kristi* (Norwegian: after Christ, AD)
Ekco E. K. Cole (manufacturer of electrical goods)
EKD *Evangelische Kirche in Deutschland* (German: Protestant Church in Germany)
EKG [USA] electrocardiogram; [USA] electrocardiograph; *Elektrokardiogramme* (German: electrocardiogram)
EL [vehicle registration] Bournemouth; [music] easy listening; electrical laboratory; electroluminescent; electronics laboratory; Engineer Lieutenant; epitaxial layer; Everyman's Library; explosive limit; [medicine] extracorporeal lithotripsy; [civil aircraft marking] Liberia
el. elect; elected; electric(al); electricity; element; elevated; elevated railway; elevation; elongation
ELA electronic learning aid; Eritrean Liberation Army
ELAS *Ethnikos Laikos Apeleutherotikos Stratos* (Greek: Hellenic People's Army of Liberation) (in World War II)
elas. elasticity
ELB Bachelor of English Literature
ELBS English Language Book Society
ELC Early Learning Centre (chain of educational toyshops); Environment Liaison Centre (Nairobi)
ELD economic load distribution
eld. elder; eldest
ELDC economic load dispatching centre; equivalent load duration curve
ELDO [astronautics] European Launcher Development Organization (became part of ESA)
ELEC European League for Economic Cooperation
elec. election; elector; electoral; electric(al); electrician; electricity; electron; electronic; [medicine] electuary
elect. election; elector; electoral; electric(al); electrician; electricity; electron; electronic; [medicine] electuary
electr. electrical; electrically
Electra Electrical, Electronics and Communications Trades Association
electron. electronic; electronically; electronics
elem. element(s); elementary
elev. elevation; elevator
ELF Eritrean Liberation Front; European Landworkers' Federation; [radio] extra-low frequency; [radio] extremely low frequency
e.l.f. early lunar flare
ELG [astronomy] emission-line galaxy
ELH [biochemistry] egg-laying hormone
ELI [sports] electronic line indicator
Eli. Elias; Elijah
Elien. *Eliensis* (Latin: (Bishop) of Ely)
Elint [military] electronic intelligence
ELISA [medicine] enzyme-linked immunosorbent assay
elix. [medicine] elixir
Eliz. Elizabethan
ELLA European Long Lines Agency
ellipt. elliptical
ELMA electromechanical aid
Elmint [military] electromagnetic intelligence
elo. elocution; eloquence
ELOISE European Large Orbiting Instrumentation for Solar Experiments
E Long. east longitude
elong. elongate; elongated; elongation

ELP equivalent local potential
ELR [meteorology] environment lapse rate; exceptional leave to remain (for asylum-seekers); export licensing regulations
ELS Electronic Lodgement Service
elsewh. elsewhere
ELSIE electronic speech information equipment
ELSS emergency life support system
ELT English language teaching (for foreign learners); European letter telegram
ELU English Lacrosse Union
ELV expendable launch vehicle; extra-low voltage
ELWS extreme low water springs (level of tide)
ely easterly
EM Earl Marshal; Edward Medal; [physics] effective mass; Efficiency Medal; electrical and mechanical; electromagnetic; electromotive; electronic mail; electron microscope (or microscopy); emission measure; engineering model; Engineer of Mines; [genetics] enhanced mutagenesis; enlisted man; environmental modelling; equipment module; European Movement; evaluation model; evening meal (in accommodation advertisement); expectation maximization; [vehicle registration] Liverpool; Master of the Horse (from Latin *Equitum Magister*)
Em. Eminence
em. emanation; embargo; eminent
e.m. electromagnetic; emergency maintenance; expanded metal; external memorandum
EMA effective medium approximation; [immunology] epithelial membrane antigen; European Marketing Association; European Monetary Agreement; Evangelical Missionary Alliance
EMAD engine maintenance and disassembly
e-mail electronic mail
EMAS [computing] Edinburgh multiaccess system; Employment Medical Advisory Service
EMB [USA] Energy Mobilization Board
Emb. Embankment (London); Embassy
emb. embargo; embossed
EMBL European Molecular Biology Laboratory
EMBO European Molecular Biology Organization
embr. embroider; embroidery
embryol. embryological; embryology
EMC [USA] Einstein Medical Center; [computing] electromagnetic compatibility; Energy Management Centre; Energy Management Company; [USA] Engineering Manpower Commission; environmental monitoring and compliance
EMCB earth-mounded concrete bunker
EMCC European Municipal Credit Community
EMCCC European Military Communications Coordinating Committee
EMCOF European Monetary Cooperation Fund
EMCS energy monitoring and control system
EME East Midlands Electricity
Emer. Emeritus
emer. emergency
EMet Engineer of Metallurgy
EMEU East Midlands Educational Union
EMF electromagnetic force; electromotive force; European Metalworkers' Federation; European Motel Federation
emf electromotive force
EMFI [USA] Energy and Mineral Field Institute
EMG [medicine] electromyogram; [medicine] electromyograph
EMI [USA] Earth Mechanics Institute; Electric and Musical Industries (Limited) (recording company); [computing] electromagnetic interference; European Monetary Institute
EMIC emergency maternity and infant care
EMK *elektromotorische Kraft* (German: electromotive force)
EML Environmental Measurement(s) Laboratory; Everyman's Library
EMLA [medicine] eutectic mixture of local anaesthetics (as in **EMLA cream**)
E Mn E Early Modern English
EMNRD Energy, Minerals and Natural Resources Department
e.m.o.s. earth's mean orbital speed
EMP ecological monitoring programme; electromagnetic pulse; electronic

materials programme; environmental management (or monitoring) plan; environmental monitoring programme
Emp. Emperor; Empire; Empress
emp. [medicine] *emplastrum* (Latin: plaster); employed; employer; employment
emp. agcy employment agency
empld employed
EMR Eastern Mediterranean Region; electromagnetic radiation
EMRIC [USA] Educational Media Research Information Center
EMRS East Malling Research Station
EMS emergency management system; emergency medical service; energy management system; European Monetary System; [computing] expanded memory specification; [computing] expanded memory support
EMSA Electron Microscopy Society of America
EMSC [USA] Electrical Manufacturers' Standards Council
EMT [physics] effective-mass theory; emergency medical technician
EMTA Electro-Medical Trade Association
EMU electrical multiple unit; electromagnetic unit; European monetary union (in EU); [astronautics] extravehicular mobility unit
emu electromagnetic unit
EMV [accounting] expected monetary value
EMW energy from municipal waste
EN [meteorology] El Niño; *Emissora Nacional* (Portuguese: national broadcasting); [UK postcode] Enfield; English Nature (replacement for NCC); Enrolled Nurse; *Estrada Nacional* (Portuguese: national highway); Euro Norm (European standard); exceptions noted; extrapolation number; [vehicle registration] Manchester
En. Engineer; English
en. enemy
ENA Eastern News Agency (Bangladesh); Eastern North America; *École nationale d'administration* (French: national school of administration) (college for top civil servants); English Newspaper Association
ENAB Evening Newspaper Advertising Bureau
enam. enamel; enamelled
ENB English National Ballet; English National Board for Nursing, Midwifery and Health Visiting
ENC equivalent noise charge
enc. enclosed; enclosure
ENCA European Naval Communications Agency
Enc. Brit. *Encyclopaedia Britannica*
encl. enclosed; enclosure
ency. encyclopedia; encyclopedic; encyclopedism; encyclopedist
encyc. encyclopedia; encyclopedic
encycl. encyclopedia; encyclopedic
END European Nuclear Disarmament
ENDO Ethiopian National Democratic Organization
endow. endowment
endp. endpaper
ENDS Euratom Nuclear Documentation System
ENE east-northeast
ENEA European Nuclear Energy Agency
ENF European Nuclear Force
ENG [television] electronic news gathering; Enrolled Nurse (General) (formerly SEN)
Eng. England; English
eng. engine; engineer; engineering; engraved; engraver; engraving
EngD Doctor of Engineering
engg engineering
Eng. hn [music] English horn (= cor anglais)
engin. engineer; engineering
Engl. England; English
engr engineer; engraver
engr. engrave; engraved; engraving
EngScD Doctor of Engineering Science
EngTech Engineering Technician
ENIAC Electronic Numerical Integrator and Calculator (first electronic calculator)
ENIT *Ente Nazionale Industrie Turistiche* (Italian: National Tourist Authority)
enl. enlarge; enlarged; enlargement; enlisted
ENM Enrolled Nurse (Mental)
ENMH Enrolled Nurse (Mental Handicap)
ENO English National Opera
eno *enero* (Spanish: January)

ENP electronic number plate
ENR Energy and Natural Resources
ENS empty nest syndrome; European Nuclear Society
Ens. [music] Ensemble; Ensign
ens. [music] ensemble; en suite (in property or accommodation advertisement)
ENSA Entertainments National Service Association (in World War II)
ENSDF Evaluated Nuclear Structure Data File
ENSO [meteorology] El Niño southern oscillation
ENT [medicine] ear, nose and throat
Ent. [theatre] enter (stage direction)
ent. entertainment; entomological; entomology; entrance
entom. entomological; entomology
entomol. entomological; entomology
Ent. Sta. Hall entered at Stationers' Hall (registration of copyright pre-1924)
E-number code number of EU-recognized food additive
Env. Envoy
env. envelope; environment; environmental; environs
Env. Ext. Envoy Extraordinary
EO Eastern Orthodox (Church); education officer; [physics] electro-optic(al); emergency operation; employers' organization; Engineer Officer; entertainments officer; equal opportunities; executive officer; executive order; experimental officer; [vehicle registration] Preston
e.o. *ex officio* (Latin: by right of office)
EOA [USA] Essential Oil Association; examination, opinion and advice
EOARDC [USA] European Office of the Air Research and Development Command
EOB [computing] end of block; executive office building
EOC electron-optical camera; [USA] Emergency Operating Center; [USA] Emergency Operations Center; [physics] end of charge; end of cycle; Equal Opportunities Commission
Eoc [geology] Eocene
EOD [computing] end of data; [military] explosive ordnance demolition; [military] explosive ordnance disposal
e.o.d. entry on duty; every other day
EOE enemy-occupied Europe; equal opportunity employer; errors and omissions excepted; European Options Exchange
EOF [USA] Emergency Operating Facility; [USA] Emergency Operations Facility; [computing] end of file
EOG [medicine] electrooculogram
e.o.h.p. except otherwise herein provided
EOJ [computing] end of job
Eoka *Ethniki Organosis Kypriakou Agonos* (Greek: National Organization of the Cypriot Struggle)
EOL end of life
EOLM electro-optical light modulator
EOM Egyptian Order of Merit; [computing] end of message (on Internet); extractable organic material; extractable organic matter
e.o.m. [commerce] end of the month; every other month
EONR European Organization for Nuclear Research
e.o.o.e. [commerce] *erreur ou omission exceptée* (French: errors and omissions excepted)
EOP [microbiology] efficiency of plating; emergency operating procedure
EOPH Examined Officer of Public Health
EOQ [accounting] economic order quantity
EOQC European Organization for Quality Control
EOQL end of qualified life
EOR [astronautics] earth-orbit rendezvous; [computing] end of record; enhanced oil recovery
EORI [USA] Economic Opportunity Research Institute
EORTC European Organization for Research into the Treatment of Cancer
EOS [physics] equation of state; [computing] erasable optical storage; European Orthodontic Society
EOT [computing] end of tape; end of terrace (in property advertisement); [computing] end of transmission
e.o.t. enemy-occupied territory
EOTP European Organization for Trade Promotion
EP early picture; educational psychologist; [electronics] electrically conducting polymer; electroplate; electroplated; electrostatic precipitator; end point; environmental protection; [navigation]

estimated position; European Parliament; expanded polystyrene; extended-play (record); extraction procedure; Extraordinary and Plenipotentiary; [civil aircraft marking] Iran; [vehicle registration] Swansea

Ep. *Episcopus* (Latin: Bishop); [Bible] Epistle

e.p. easy projection; *editio princeps* (Latin: first edition); electrically polarized; endpaper; engineering personnel; [chess] *en passant* (French: in passing); [navigation] estimated position; extreme pressure

EPA educational priority area; Emergency Powers Act; Employment Protection Act; energy-performance assessment; [USA] Environmental Protection Agency; European Productivity Agency

EPAA [USA] Emergency Petroleum Allocation Act

EPACCI Economic Planning and Advisory Council for the Construction Industries

EPAQ electronic parts of assessed quality

EPB equivalent pension benefit

EPC Economic and Planning Council; Educational Publishers' Council; evaporative pattern-casting (in foundry)

EPCA [USA] Energy Policy and Conservation Act; energy production and consumption account; European Petro-Chemical Association

EPCOT Experimental Prototype Community of Tomorrow (Florida)

EPD earliest practicable date

EPDA Emergency Powers Defence Act

EPDC [USA] Electric Power Development Company

EPEA Electrical Power Engineers' Association

EPF emulsified petroleum fuel; European Packaging Federation

EPFM elastic-plastic fracture mechanics

EPG [USA] Electronic Proving Ground; [medicine] electropalatogram; [medicine] electropalatology; Emergency Procedure Guideline(s); Eminent Persons Group

EPGS electric power generating system

Eph. [Bible] Ephesians

Ephes. [Bible] Ephesians

EPI echo planar imaging; electronic position indicator

EPIC Engineering and Production Information Council; European Prospective Investigation into Cancer

Epict. Epictetus (ancient Greek philosopher)

epid. epidemic

epil. epilogue

Epiph. Epiphany

EPIRB [navigation] emergency position indicator radio beacon

Epis. Episcopal; Episcopalian; [Bible] Epistle

Episc. Episcopal; Episcopalian

Epist. [Bible] Epistle

epit. epitaph; epitome

EPL exact power law

EPLD [computing] erasable programmable logic device

EPLF Eritrean People's Liberation Front

EPM electron-probe microanalysis; extract of particulate matter

EPMA electron-probe microanalysis

EPMI Esso Production Malaysia Incorporated

EPN elemental point number

EPNdB effective perceived noise decibels

EPNG El Paso Natural Gas Company

EPNS electroplated nickel silver; English Place-Name Society

EPO [medicine] erythropoietin

EPOC Eastern Pacific Oceanic Conference

Epoch End Physical Punishment of Children

EPOS [commerce] electronic point of sale (as in **EPOS system**)

EPP [physiology] endplate potential; [computing] enhanced parallel port; European People's Party; executive pension plan; [computing] extended parallel port

EPPO European and Mediterranean Plant Protection Organization

EPPT [computing] European printer performance test

EPPV electropneumatic proportional valve

EPR electron paramagnetic resonance; ethylene–propylene rubber

EPRDF Ethiopian People's Revolutionary Democratic Front

EPRI [USA] Electric Power Research Institute

EPROM [computing] erasable programmable read-only memory

EPS electrically positioned seats (in car

advertisement); electric(al) power system; [USA] Environmental Protection Service
eps earnings per share
EPSP [physiology] excitatory postsynaptic potential
EPSRC Engineering and Physical Sciences Research Council
EPSS electrical power supervision system
EPT [medicine] early pregnancy test; Environmental Protection Technology; ethylene–propylene terpolymer (synthetic rubber); excess profits tax
EPTA Expanded Programme of Technical Assistance (in UN)
Ep. tm [law] Epiphany term
EPU European Payments Union
Epus *Episcopus* (Latin: Bishop)
EPW earth-penetrator weapon; enemy prisoner of war
EQ educational quotient; [electronics] equalize; equipment qualification; [electronics] equivalence (as in **EQ gate**)
Eq. Equerry
eq. equal; equate; equation; equator; equatorial; equipment; equitable; equity; equivalent
EQA [commerce] European Quality Award
EQC external quality control
EQD Electrical Quality Assurance Directorate
EQDB equipment qualification data bank
EQI exhaust quality index
eqn equation
eqn. equine
eqpt equipment
Equ [astronomy] Equuleus
equil. equilibrium
EQUIP equipment usage information programme
equip. equipment
equiv. equivalent
ER [railways] Eastern Region; East Riding (of Yorkshire); *Eduardus Rex* (Latin: King Edward); efficiency report; *Elizabetha Regina* (Latin: Queen Elizabeth); [medicine] emergency room; engine room; [computing] entity relationship; evaporation residue; [civil aircraft marking] Moldova; [vehicle registration] Peterborough
Er [chemical element] erbium
er elder
.er Eritrea (in Internet address)
e.r. echo ranging; effectiveness report; electronic reconnaissance; emergency request; emergency rescue; established reliability; external resistance
ERA [baseball] earned run average; [USA] Economic Regulatory Administration; Education Reform Act; Electrical Research Association; electronic reading automation; Electronic Rentals Association; [USA] Emergency Relief Administration; engine-room artificer; [computing] entity relationship attribute; [USA] Equal Rights Amendment; European Ramblers' Association; Evangelical Radio Alliance
ERAB Energy Research Advisory Board
ERAMS Environmental Radiation Ambients Monitoring System
Eras. (Desiderius) Erasmus (Dutch humanist)
Erasmus European Community Action Scheme for the Mobility of University Students
ERB electric roller blind
ERBM extended-range ballistic missile
ERC Economic Research Council; Electronics Research Council; Employment Rehabilitation Centre; [medicine] endoscopic retrograde cholangiography; [USA] Energy Research Corporation
ERC&I Economic Reform Club and Institute
ERCB [USA] Energy Resources Conservation Board
ERCP [medicine] endoscopic retrograde cholangiopancreatography
ERCS emergency response computer system
ERD elastic recoil detection; Emergency Reserve Decoration; emergency return device; environmental radiation data; equivalent residual dose (of radiation); extrapolated response dose
ERDA [electronics] elastic recoil detection analysis; [Australia] Electrical and Radio Development Association; [USA] Energy Research and Development Administration
ERDAF [USA] Energy Research and Development in Agriculture and Food
ERDE Engineering Research and Development Establishment; Explosives

Research and Development Establishment
ERDF European Regional Development Fund
ERDIC Energy Research, Development and Information Centre
ERDL Engineering Research and Development Laboratory
ERDS emergency response data system
ERE *Ethniki Rizospastiki Enosis* (Greek: National Radical Union) (political party); extent of reaction effect
erec. erection
ERFA European Radio Frequency Agency
ERG electrical resistance gauge; [medicine] electroretinogram
ERGOM European Research Group on Management
ergon. ergonomic; ergonomics
ERI *Eduardus Rex et Imperator* (Latin: Edward King and Emperor)
Eri [astronomy] Eridanus
ERIC [USA] Educational Resources Information Center; energy rate input controller
ERIM Environmental Research Institute of Michigan
ERIS Emergency Response Information System; [astronautics] Exo-atmospheric Re-entry Vehicle Interceptor Subsystem
ERISA [USA] Employee Retirement Income Security Act
Erit. Eritrea
ERL Energy Research Laboratory
Erl. *Erläuterung* (German: explanatory note)
ERLL [computing] enhanced run length limited
ERM [finance] Exchange Rate Mechanism
erm. ermine
Ernie electronic random number indicator equipment (selecting winning premium bonds)
ERO European Regional Organization of the International Confederation of Free Trade Unions
EROM [computing] erasable read-only memory
EROPA Eastern Regional Organization for Public Administration
EROS earth resources observation satellite; [astronautics] experimental reflection orbital shot
ERP [medicine] endoscopic retrograde pancreatography; [commerce] enterprise resource planning; [biochemistry] enzyme-releasing peptide; European Recovery Programme
e.r.p. effective radiated power
ERPF [medicine] effective renal plasma flow
ERR energy release rate
erron. erroneous; erroneously
ERS earnings-related supplement; earth resources satellite; emergency radio service; emergency response system; engine repair section; Ergonomics Research Society; [USA] Experimental Research Society
ERT *Elliniki Radiophonia Tileorasis* (Greek: Hellenic National Radio and Television); excess retention tax
ERTA [USA] Economic Recovery and Tax Act
ERTS Earth Resources Technology Satellite; European Rapid Train System
ERU English Rugby Union
ERV [Bible] English Revised Version; [medicine] exercise radionuclide ventriculography
ERW enhanced radiation weapon
erw. *erweitert* (German: enlarged, extended)
erweit. *erweitert* (German: enlarged, extended)
ES [vehicle registration] Dundee; Econometric Society; Education Specialist; [chemistry] electronic structure; electrostatic; [international vehicle registration] El Salvador; [medicine] endoscopic sphincterotomy; [medicine] end-systole; [medicine] end-systolic; energy spectrum; engine-sized (paper); Entomological Society; [civil aircraft marking] Estonia; [mining] exploratory shaft
Es [chemical element] einsteinium
e/s en suite (in property or accommodation advertisement)
es. *esempio* (Italian: example)
.es Spain (in Internet address)
e.s. eldest son; electrical sounding; electric starting; [medicine] *enema saponis* (Latin: soap enema)
ESA Ecological Society of America; Educational Supply Association; electrostatic

sector analyser; energy system analysis; Entomological Society of America; environmentally sensitive area; European Space Agency; Euthanasia Society of America

ESAAB [USA] Energy System Acquisition Advisory Board

ESAF enhanced structural adjustment facility (in IMF)

ESANZ Economic Society of Australia and New Zealand

ESAR electronically steerable array radar

ESB electrical stimulation of the brain; [USA] Electricity Supply Board; electric storage battery; Empire State Building; English Speaking Board; environmental specimen bank

ESBA English Schools' Badminton Association

ESBBA English Schools' Basket Ball Association

ESBTC [USA] European Space Battery Test Center

ESC Economic and Social Council (of UN); electric seat control (in car advertisement); electronic stills camera; electronic structural correlator; [USA] Energy Security Corporation; Energy Study Centre (Netherlands); English Stage Company; English Steel Corporation; Entomological Society of Canada; etched security code (in car advertisement); European Space Conference; [computing] extended core storage

Esc [computing] escape (key); [currency] escudo

esc. *escompte* (French: discount); escutcheon

ESCA [physical chemistry] electron spectroscopy for chemical analysis; English Schools' Cricket Association; English Schools' Cycling Association

ESCAP Economic and Social Commission for Asia and the Pacific (formerly ECAFE)

ESCB European System of Central Banks

ESCC [engineering] external stress corrosion cracking

ESCCD electrical short-circuit current decay

eschat. eschatology

ESCO Educational, Scientific and Cultural Organization (of UN)

ESCOM Electricity Supply Commission of South Africa

ESCR external standard channel ratio

ESD echo-sounding device; electromagnetic shower detector; [computing] electrostatic discharge; [USA] Environmental Sciences Division; Euratom Safeguards Directorate

Esd. [Bible] Esdras (books of Apocrypha)

Esda electrostatic deposition analysis; electrostatic document analysis

ESDAC European Space Data Centre

ESDI enhanced small-device interface

ESE east-southeast; engineers stores establishment

ESECA [USA] Energy Supply and Environmental Coordination Act

ESEF Electrotyping and Stereotyping Employers' Federation

ESES environmentally sound energy system

ESF European Science Foundation

ESG Education Support Grant; English Standard Gauge

ESH Environmental Safety and Health; equivalent standard hours; European Society of Haematology

ESI electricity supply industry; environment sensitivity index

ESITB Electricity Supply Industry Training Board

Esk. Eskimo

ESL English as a second language

e.s.l. expected significance level

ESLAB European Space Research Laboratory

ESMA Electrical Sign Manufacturers' Association

ESN educationally subnormal

esn. essential

ESNS educationally subnormal, serious

esntl essential

ESNZ Entomological Society of New Zealand

ESO Energy Services Operator; European Southern Observatory (Chile)

ESOC European Space Operations Centre

ESOL English for speakers of other languages

ESOMAR European Society for Opinion Surveys and Market Research

ESOP employee share-ownership plan; [USA] employee stock-option plan

ESOT employee share-ownership trust
ESP electric submersible pump(ing); [commerce] emotional selling proposition; English for special purposes; English for specific purposes; extrasensory perception
Esp. *Espagne* (French: Spain); *España* (Spanish: Spain); Esperanto
esp. especially; [music] *espressivo* (Italian: expressively)
espec. especially
espg. espionage
espr. [music] *espressivo* (Italian: expressively)
espress. [music] *espressivo* (Italian: expressively)
ESPRIT European strategic programme for research and development in information technology
Esq. Esquire
ESQA English Slate Quarries Association
esqo *esquerdo* (Portuguese: left)
Esqr. Esquire
ESR electric sunroof (in car advertisement); [physics] electron-spin resonance; [medicine] erythrocyte sedimentation rate
ESRC Economic and Social Research Council (formerly SSRC); Electricity Supply Research Council
ESRD [medicine] end-stage renal disease
ESRF [medicine] end-stage renal failure
ESRIN European Space Research Institute
ESRO European Space Research Organization (became part of ESA)
ESRS European Society for Rural Sociology
ESS energy storage system; evolutionarily stable strategy
Ess. Essex
ess. essence; [pharmacology] *essentia* (Latin: essence); essential
ESSA English Schools' Swimming Association; [USA] Environmental Science Services Administration
Esso Standard Oil (phonetic spelling of initials)
EST earliest start time; [USA, Canada] Eastern Standard Time; electric-shock treatment; electroshock therapy; [nuclear technology] ellipsoidal shell tokamak; [international vehicle registration] Estonia
Est. Established; Estonia; Estonian
est. establish; established; [law] estate; estimate; estimated; estimation; estimator; estuary
estab. establish; established; establishment
ESTEC European Space Technology Centre
estg estimating
Esth. [Bible] Esther
ESTI European Space Technology Institute
estn estimation
ESU electrostatic unit; English-Speaking Union
esu electrostatic unit
ESV [astronautics] earth satellite vehicle; [engineering] emergency shutdown valve; [medicine] end-systolic volume
ESWL [medicine] extracorporeal shockwave lithotripsy
ET [USA] Eastern Time; educational therapy; [international vehicle registration] (Arab Republic of) Egypt; [chemistry] electron transfer; [physics, chemistry] electron transition; [nuclear technology] elongated tokamak; [medicine] embryo transfer; emerging technology (in NATO); Employment Trainee; Employment Training (for unemployed); emptying time; English text; English translation; ephemeris time; [physics] equation of time; [civil aircraft marking] Ethiopia; [electronics] excitation transport; extraterrestrial; [vehicle registration] Sheffield
.et Ethiopia (in Internet address)
e.t. electric telegraph; engineering time; entertainment tax; exchange telegraph
ETA Entertainment Trades' Alliance; estimated time of arrival; European Teachers' Association; *Euzkadi ta Askatasuna* (Basque: Basque Nation and Liberty) (separatist organization)
Étab. *Établissement* (French: (business) establishment)
ETAC Education and Training Advisory Council
et al. *et alibi* (Latin: and elsewhere); *et alii* (Latin: and others)
ETB English Tourist Board
ETC Eastern Telegraph Company; European Translation Centre
etc. *et cetera* (Latin: and the other things)

ETCTA Electrical Trades Commercial Travellers' Association
ETD estimated time of departure; [telecommunications] extension trunk dialling
ETE estimated time en route; evacuation-time estimate; Experimental Tunnelling Establishment
ETF [banking] electronic transfer of funds
ETH [Switzerland] *Eidgenössische technische Hochschule* (German: Federal Institute of Technology); [international vehicle registration] Ethiopia
Eth. Ethiopia; Ethiopian; Ethiopic
eth. ether; ethical; ethics
ethnog. ethnographical; ethnography
ethnol. ethnological; ethnology
ETI estimated time of interception; extraterrestrial intelligence
e.t.i. elapsed time indicator
ETJC Engineering Trades Joint Council
e.t.k.m. every test known to man
ETMA English Timber Merchants' Association; European Television Magazine Association
ETO European Theatre of Operations (in World War II); European Transport Organization
e.t.o. estimated time off
ETOP [USA] Environmental Threat and Opportunity Profile
e.t.p. estimated turning (or turnaround) point
ETR [nuclear technology] engineering test reactor; estimated time of return; [nuclear technology] experimental test reactor; [nuclear technology] experimental thermonuclear reactor
Etr. Etruscan
ETS earth thermal storage; [USA] Educational Testing Service; [biochemistry] electron-transport system; estimated time of sailing; [US military] estimated time of separation (i.e. discharge); [medicine] exercise thallium scintigraphy; expiration of time of service
ETSA Electricity Trust of South Australia
et seq. *et sequens* (Latin: and the following); *et sequentia* (Latin: and those that follow)
et seqq. *et sequentia* (Latin: and those that follow)
ETSI European Telecommunications Standards Institute
e.t.s.p. entitled to severance pay
et sqq. *et sequentia* (Latin: and those that follow)
ETSU Energy Technology Support Unit
ETTA English Table Tennis Association
ETTU European Table Tennis Union
ETU Electrical Trades Union; experimental test unit
ETUC European Trade Union Confederation
ETUI European Trade Union Institute
et ux. *et uxor* (Latin: and wife)
ETV educational television; engine test vehicle
ety. etymological; etymologist; etymology
etym. etymological; etymologist; etymology
etymol. etymological; etymologist; etymology
EU [vehicle registration] Bristol; *Estados Unidos* (Portuguese or Spanish: United States); *États-Unis* (French: United States); European Union; Evangelical Union; [medicine] excretory urography; experimental unit
Eu [chemical element] europium
EUA *Estados Unidos da América* (Portuguese: United States of America); *Estados Unidos de América* (Spanish: United States of America); *États-Unis d'Amérique* (French: United States of America); [finance] European unit of account; [medicine] examination under anaesthesia
Euc. Euclid (ancient Greek mathematician)
Eucl. Euclid (ancient Greek mathematician)
EUCOM [US military] European Command
EUDISED European Documentation and Information Service for Education
EUFTT European Union of Film and Television Technicians
eugen. eugenics
EUI energy utilization index; energy utilization intensity
EUL Everyman's University Library
EUM *Estados Unidos Mexicanos* (Spanish: Mexico)
EUMETSAT European Meteorological Satellite System
EUP English Universities Press

euph. euphemism; euphemistic; euphemistically
EUR *Esposizione Universale di Roma* (Italian: Roman Universal Exhibition)
Eur. Europe; European
Euratom European Atomic Energy Authority (predecessor of EU)
Eureca [astronautics] European retrievable carrier
Eur. Ing. European Engineer (from the word for engineer in several European languages)
Eurip. Euripides (ancient Greek dramatist)
EURO European Regional Office
EUROCAE European Organization for Civil Aviation Electronics
EUROCEAN European Oceanographic Association
EUROCHEMIC European Company for the Chemical Processing of Irradiated Fuels
EUROCOM European Coal Merchants' Union
EUROM European Federation for Optics and Precision Mechanics
EURONET European data-transmission network
EUROP European Railway Wagon Pool
Europol European Police Office
EUROSPACE European Industrial Space Study Group
EUROTOX European Standing Committee for the Protection of Populations against the Risks of Chronic Toxicity
EUS Eastern United States
Eus. Eusebius of Caesarea (ecclesiastical historian)
Euseb. Eusebius of Caesarea (ecclesiastical historian)
EUV [physics] extreme ultraviolet
EUVE [astronomy] Extreme Ultraviolet Explorer
EUW European Union of Women
EV [vehicle registration] Chelmsford; electric vehicle; [Bible] English Version; [astronautics] entry vehicle; [medicine] equilibrium venography; [medicine] erythrocyte volume; [accounting] expected value; [image technology] exposure value
eV *eingetragener Verein* (German: registered society); electronvolt
ev. *evangelisch* (German: Protestant)
e.v. efficient vulcanization
EVA Electric Vehicle Association of Great Britain; Engineer Vice-Admiral; [chemistry] ethene and vinyl acetate; [astronautics] extravehicular activity
evac. evacuate; evacuated; evacuation
eval. evaluate; evaluated; evaluation
evan. evangelical; evangelist
evang. evangelical; evangelist
evap [short form] evaporated milk
evap. evaporate; evaporated; evaporation; evaporator
evce evidence
EVCS [astronautics] extravehicular communications system
EVFU [computing] electronic vertical format unit
evg evening
EVGA [computing] enhanced video graphics array
evid. evidence
evng evening
evol. evolution; evolutionary; evolutionist
EVR electronic video recording and reproduction
EVT Educational and Vocational Training
EVW European Voluntary Workers
evy every
EW [civil aircraft marking] Belarus; early warning; electric windows (in car advertisement); electronic warfare; [USA] enlisted woman; [vehicle registration] Peterborough
e.w. each way (in betting)
EWA [USA] Education Writers' Association
EWF Electrical Wholesalers' Federation; European Welding Federation
EWICS European Workshop for Industrial Computer Systems
EWL evaporative water loss
EWO educational welfare officer; essential work order; European Women's Orchestra
EWP emergency war plan
EWR early-warning radar
EWS emergency water supply; emergency welfare service
EWSF European Work Study Federation
EX [UK postcode] Exeter; [civil aircraft marking] Kyrgyzstan; [vehicle registration] Norwich
Ex. Exeter; [Bible] Exodus

ex. examination; examine; examined; examiner; example; excellent; except; excepted; exception; excess; exchange; exclude; excluding; exclusive; excursion; excursus (literary digression); execute; executed; executive; executor; exempt; exercise; export; express; extended; extension; extra; extract
exag. exaggerate; exaggerated; exaggeration
exam [short form] examination
exam. examine; examiner
examd examined
examg examining
examn examination
ex aq. [medicine] *ex aqua* (Latin: from water)
ex b. [finance] ex bonus (i.e. without bonus)
Exc. Excellency
exc. excellent; except; excepted; exception; exchange; excommunication; *excudit* (Latin: (he/she) engraved it); excursion
ex cap. [finance] ex capitalization (i.e. without capitalization)
excel. excellent
Exch. Exchequer
exch. exchange; exchequer
excl. exclamation; exclamatory; exclude; excluding; exclusive
exclam. exclamation; exclamatory
ex cp. [finance] ex coupon (i.e. without interest on coupon)
exd examined
ex div. [finance] ex dividend (i.e. without dividend)
exec. execute; execution; executive; executor
execx executrix
exempl. *exemplaire* (French: copy (of publication))
exes expenses
ex. g. *exempli gratia* (Latin: for example)
ex. gr. *exempli gratia* (Latin: for example)
exh. exhaust; exhibition
exhbn exhibition
exhib. exhibit; exhibition; exhibitioner; exhibitor
Ex-Im [USA] Export-Import Bank
Eximbank [USA] Export-Import Bank
ex int. [banking] ex interest (i.e. without interest)
ex lib. *ex libris* (Latin: from the books (of), from the library (of))
ex n. [stock exchange] ex new (of shares)
Exod. [Bible] Exodus
ex off. *ex officio* (Latin: by right of office)
Exon. *Exonia* (Latin: Exeter); *Exoniensis* (Latin: (Bishop) of Exeter)
exor executor
EXP Exchange of Persons Office (in UNESCO); [meteorology] expected
exp [mathematics] exponential
exp. expand; expansion; expedition; expense(s); experience; experiment; experimental; expiration; expire; expired; expiry; export; exportation; exported; exporter; exposed; express; expression; expurgated
ex p. [law] *ex parte* (Latin: on behalf of one party)
expdn expedition
exper. experimental
expl. explain; explanation; explanatory; explosion; explosive
exploit. exploitation
expn exposition
exp. o. experimental order
expr. express; expression
expt experiment
exptl experimental
exptr exporter
expurg. expurgate; expurgated
exr executor
exrx executrix
exs expenses
ext. extend; extension; extent; exterior; external; externally; extinct; extra; extract; extraction; [medicine] *extractum* (Latin: extract); extreme
EXTEL Exchange Telegraph (news agency)
exten. extension
EXTEND Exercise Training for the Elderly and/or Disabled
ext. liq. *extractum liquidum* (Latin: liquid extract)
extn extension
extr. extraordinary
extrad. extradition
EXW ex works (i.e. from the factory)
exx examples; executrix
EY [vehicle registration] Bangor; [civil aircraft marking] Tajikistan
EYC European Youth Campaign
EYR East Yorkshire Regiment

EZ [vehicle registration] Belfast; [US informal] easy; [civil aircraft marking] Turkmenistan

Ez. [Bible] Ezra

Ezek. [Bible] Ezekiel

Ezr. [Bible] Ezra

F

F Fahrenheit; fail; false; family; farad; fast (on clock or watch regulator); Father; fathom; [fishing port] Faversham; February; Federation; Fellow; female; [grammar] feminine; *ferrovia* (Italian: railway); [medicine] *fiat* (Latin: let it be made); fiction; [USA] fighter (aircraft) (as in **F-111**); [genetics] filial generation; [horseracing] filly; finance; fine; fleet; [chemical element] fluorine; [photography] f-number (as in **F16**); Fokker (aircraft); folio; foolscap; [sports] Formula (as in **F1**); [sports] foul; [currency] franc; [civil aircraft marking] France; [international vehicle registration] France; *Frauen* (German: women); *freddo* (Italian: cold); French; [ecclesiastical] *Frère* (French: Brother); Friday; *frio* (Portuguese or Spanish: cold); *froid* (French: cold); [music] note of scale

F [physics] Faraday constant; [physics] force

f [music] fa(h) (in tonic sol-fa); [numismatics] face value; femto- (indicates 10^{-15}, as in **fm** = femtometre); [photography] f-number (as in **f4**); [meteorology] fog; foreign

f [physics] focal length; [music] *forte* (Italian: loudly); [physics] frequency; [physical chemistry] fugacity; [mathematics] function; [biochemistry] furanose

f. facing; fair; farthing (quarter of old penny); father; fathom; feet; female; [grammar] feminine; [horseracing] filly; fine; [horseracing] firm; flat; fluid; folio; following (page); foot; for; forecastle; [botany] form (in classification of plants); formula; [sports] foul; founded; [currency] franc; freehold; from; front; fuck; furlong; furlough; furnished (in accommodation advertisement); [currency] guilder (from alternative name florin)

FA [statistics] factor analysis; Factory Act; Faculty of Actuaries; family allowance; [slang] Fanny Adams (i.e. nothing); farm adviser; [chemistry] fatty acid; field activities; field allowance; field ambulance; field artillery; filtered air; Finance Act; financial adviser; fine art; [immunology] fluorescent antibody; [building] fly ash; [biochemistry] folic acid; [biochemistry] folinic acid; Football Association; freight agent; [slang] fuck all (i.e. nothing); [building] fuel ash; [nuclear technology] fuel assembly; [metallurgy] furnace annealing; [vehicle registration] Stoke-on-Trent

Fa *Firma* (German: firm, business); Florida

Fa. Faeroes

fa *factura* (Spanish: invoice)

f.a. [slang] Fanny Adams (i.e. nothing); fire alarm; first aid; first attack; [commerce] free alongside; [optics] free aperture; freight agent; friendly aircraft; [slang] fuck all (i.e. nothing); fuel–air (ratio)

FAA [USA] Federal Aviation Administration; Fellow of the Australian Academy (of Science); Film Artistes' Association; Fleet Air Arm; [biochemistry] free amino acid; [insurance] free of all averages

FAAAS Fellow of the American Academy of Arts and Sciences; Fellow of the American Association for the Advancement of Science

FAAC Food Additives and Contaminants Committee

FAARM Fellow of the American Academy of Reproductive Medicine

FAAV Fellow of the Central Association of Agricultural Valuers

FAB [physics, electronics] fast-atom beam; [physics, electronics] fast-atom bombardment; Flour Advisory Bureau; French–American–British; fuel-air bomb

fab [short form] fabulous

fab. fabric; fabricate; [commerce] *fabrication* (French: make, manufacture)
f.a.b. first aid box
f. à b. [commerce] *franco à bord* (French: free on board)
fabbr. *fabbrica* (Italian: factory)
FABMDS [USA] field army ballistic missile defense system
fabr. fabricate; fabrication
Fab. Soc. Fabian Society
fabx fire alarm box
FAC Federation of Agricultural Cooperatives; [military] forward air controller
Fac. Faculty
fac. façade; facial; facility; facsimile; factor; factory; faculty
f.a.c. fast as can; [insurance] *franc d'avarie commune* (French: free of general average)
FACC [USA] Ford Aerospace and Communication Corporation
FACCP Fellow of the American College of Chest Physicians
FACD Fellow of the American College of Dentistry
FACE Fellow of the Australian College of Education; field artillery computer equipment; Fight Against Cuts in Education; [USA] Financial Advertising Code of Ethics
FACEM Federation of the Associations of Colliery Equipment Manufacturers
FACerS Fellow of the American Ceramic Society
facet. facetious
FACG Fellow of the American College of Gastroenterology
facil. facility
FACMTA [USA] Federal Advisory Council on Medical Training
FACOG Fellow of the American College of Obstetricians and Gynecologists
FACOM Fellow of the Australian College of Occupational Medicine
FACP Fellow of the American College of Physicians; Fellow of the American College of Radiology
FACRM Fellow of the Australian College of Reproductive Medicine
FACS Fellow of the American College of Surgeons; [immunology] fluorescence-activated cell sorter
facs. facsimile
facsim. facsimile
FACT Federation Against Copyright Theft; fully automatic compiler-translator
fact. *factura* (Spanish: invoice)
facta *factura* (Spanish: invoice)
FAD [biochemistry] flavin adenine dinucleotide
f.a.d. free air delivered
FADEC [computing] fully authorized digital engine control
FADO Fellow of the Association of Dispensing Opticians
FAE [military] fuel-air explosive(s)
Faer. Faeroes
FAGO Fellowship in Australia in Obstetrics and Gynaecology
FAGS Federation of Astronomical and Geophysical Services; Fellow of the American Geographical Society
Fah. Fahrenheit
Fahr. Fahrenheit
FAI *Fédération aéronautique internationale* (French: International Aeronautical Federation); Football Association of Ireland; fresh-air inlet
FAIA Fellow of the American Institute of Architects; Fellow of the Association of International Accountants; Fellow of the Australian Institute of Advertising
FAIAA Fellow of the American Institute of Aeronautics and Astronautics
FAIAS Fellow of the Australian Institute of Agricultural Science
FAIB Fellow of the Australian Institute of Builders
FAIC Fellow of the American Institute of Chemists
FAIE Fellow of the Australian Institute of Energy
FAII Fellow of the Australian Insurance Institute
FAIM Fellow of the Australian Institute of Management
FAK [shipping] freights all kinds
Fak. *Faktura* (German: invoice)
Falk. I Falkland Islands
Falk. Is. Falkland Islands
FALN *Fuerzas Armadas de Liberación Nacional* (Spanish: Armed Forces of National Liberation) (in Puerto Rico)
FAM Free and Accepted Masons
fam. familiar; family

FAMA Fellow of the American Medical Association; Fellow of the Australian Medical Association; Foundation for Mutual Assistance in Africa
FAMEME Fellow of the Association of Mining Electrical and Mechanical Engineers
FAmNucSoc Fellow of the American Nuclear Society
FAMS Fellow of the Ancient Monuments Society; Fellow of the Indian Academy of Medical Sciences
f&a fore and aft
F&AP [insurance] fire and allied perils
F&C full and change (tides)
F&D freight and demurrage
f&d fill and drain; freight and demurrage
f&f fixtures and fittings
F&Gs [bookbinding] folded and gathered pages
F&M [veterinary science] foot and mouth (disease)
F&T [insurance] fire and theft
FANY First Aid Nursing Yeomanry
FAO Fleet Accountant Officer; Food and Agriculture Organization (of the United Nations)
f.a.o. finish all over; for the attention of
FAP [USA] Family Assistance Program; fixed action pattern (in ethology); *Força Aérea Portuguesa* (Portuguese: Portuguese Air Force); [insurance] *franc d'avarie particulière* (French: free of particular average)
FAPA Fellow of the American Psychiatric Association; Fellow of the American Psychological Association
FAPHA Fellow of the American Public Health Association
FAQ [commerce] free alongside quay; [computing] frequently asked question (used on Internet)
f.a.q. [commerce] fair average quality; [commerce] free alongside quay
f.a.q.s. [commerce] fair average quality of season
FAR false alarm rate; [USA] Federal Aviation Regulation(s); [insurance] free (of claim) for accident reported; front arm rests (in car advertisement)
far. farriery; farthing (quarter of old penny)
FArborA Fellow of the Arboricultural Association
FARE Federation of Alcoholic Rehabilitation Establishments
FARELF Far East Land Forces
FAS Faculty of Architects and Surveyors; Federation of American Scientists; Fellow of the Anthropological Society; Fellow of the Antiquarian Society; [medicine] fetal alcohol syndrome; [commerce] free alongside ship
f.a.s. firsts and seconds; [commerce] free alongside ship
FASA Fellow of the Australian Society of Accountants
FASB [USA] Financial Accounting Standards Board
FASc Fellow of the Indian Academy of Sciences
fasc. [anatomy] fascicle (bundle of fibres); fascicule (instalment of printed work)
FASCE Fellow of the American Society of Civil Engineers
FASE Fellow of the Antiquarian Society, Edinburgh
FASEB Federation of American Societies for Experimental Biology
FASI Fellow of the Architects' and Surveyors' Institute
FASS Federation of the Associations of Specialists and Subcontractors
FAST factor analysis system; fast automatic shuttle transfer; Federation Against Software Theft; first atomic ship transport; forecasting and assessment in science and technology (in EU)
fastnr fastener
FAT [computing] file allocation table
fath. fathom
FATIS Food and Agriculture Technical Information Service (of OEEC)
FAU Friends' Ambulance Unit
FAusIMM Fellow of the Australasian Institute of Mining and Metallurgy
fav. favour; favourite
FAVO Fleet Aviation Officer
FAWA Federation of Asian Women's Associations
FAX fuel-air explosion
fax [short form] facsimile
FB [vehicle registration] Bristol; Fenian Brotherhood; film badge (for radiation protection); fire brigade; fisheries board; fishery board; [railways] flat bottom;

flying boat; [medicine] foreign body; Forth Bridge; Free Baptist; full board (in accommodation advertisement)

F-B full-bore

f.b. flat bar; fog bell; freight bill; full board (in accommodation advertisement); [sports] fullback

FBA Farm Buildings Association; [USA] Federal Bar Association; Federation of British Artists; Federation of British Astrologers; Fellow of the British Academy; fluorescent brightening agent (in detergent); Freshwater Biological Association

FBAA Fellow of the British Association of Accountants and Auditors

f 'ball football

f.b.c. [insurance] fallen building clause

FBCM Federation of British Carpet Manufacturers

FBCO Fellow of the British College of Optometrists (or Ophthalmic Opticians)

FBCS Fellow of the British Computer Society

f.b.c.w. [insurance] fallen building clause waiver

fbd freeboard

FBEA Fellow of the British Esperanto Association

FBEC(S) Fellow of the Business Education Council (Scotland)

FBFM Federation of British Film Makers

FBH fire brigade hydrant

FBHI Fellow of the British Horological Institute

FBHS Fellow of the British Horse Society

FBHTM Federation of British Hand Tool Manufacturers

FBI [USA] Federal Bureau of Investigation; Federation of British Industries

FBIBA Fellow of the British Insurance Brokers' Association

FBIM Fellow of the British Institute of Management

FBINZ Fellow of the Bankers' Institute of New Zealand

FBIPP Fellow of the British Institute of Professional Photography

FBIS Fellow of the British Interplanetary Society

FBL [aeronautics] fly-by-light (aircraft control using optical fibres)

FBM fleet ballistic missile

FBMA Food and Beverage Managers' Association

f.b.o. for the benefit of

FBOA Fellow of the British Optical Association

FBOU Fellow of the British Ornithologists' Union

FBP [chemistry] final boiling point; [biochemistry] folate-binding protein

FBPS Fellow of the British Phrenological Society

FBPsS Fellow of the British Psychological Society

FBR [nuclear technology] fast breeder reactor

fbr. fibre

FBRAM Federation of British Rubber and Allied Manufacturers

fbro *febrero* (Spanish: February)

FBS Fellow of the Botanical Society; [medicine] fetal bovine serum; [military] forward-based system

FBSC Fellow of the British Society of Commerce

FBSE Fellow of the Botanical Society, Edinburgh

FBSM Fellow of the Birmingham School of Music

FBSS [medicine] failed back-surgery syndrome

FBT *Fédération des bourses du travail* (French: Federation of Labour Exchanges) (French trade union); fringe benefit tax

FBU Fire Brigades Union

FBu [currency] Burundi franc

FBW [aeronautics] fly-by-wire (aircraft control using electronic circuits)

f.b.y. future budget year

FC [Australia] Federal Cabinet; [Freemasonry] fellow craft; fencing club; *ferrocarril* (Spanish: railway); *fidei commissum* (Latin: bequeathed in trust); *fieri curavit* (Latin: the donor directed this to be done) (on monuments); fifth column; Fighter Command; fire cock; fire control; Fishmongers' Company; football club; Forestry Commission; [medicine] free cholesterol; Free Church; fuel cell; [medicine] full course (of treatment); [meteorology] funnel cloud; [vehicle registration] Oxford

f.c. [baseball] fielder's choice; filing

cabinet; *fin courant* (French: at the end of this month); fixed charge; [printing] follow copy; for cash

FCA [USA] Farm Credit Administration; Federation of Canadian Artists; Fellow of the Institute of Chartered Accountants

FCAATSI [Australia] Federal Council for the Advancement of Aborigines and Torres Strait Islanders

FC-AL [computing] fibre channel arbitrated loop

FCAnaes Fellow of the College of Anaesthetists

fcap foolscap

FCAR [insurance] free of claim for accident reported

FCASI Fellow of the Canadian Aeronautics and Space Institute

FCB [computing] file control block

FCBA Federal Communications Bar Association; Fellow of the Canadian Bankers' Association

FCBSI Fellow of the Chartered Building Societies Institute

FCC [USA] Federal Communications Commission; Federal Council of Churches; first-class certificate

FCCA Fellow of the Chartered Association of Certified Accountants

FCCEA Fellow of the Commonwealth Council for Educational Administration

FCCEd Fellow of the College of Craft Education

FCCS Fellow of the Corporation of Secretaries (formerly Fellow of the Corporation of Certified Secretaries)

FCCSET [USA] Federal Coordinating Council on Science, Engineering and Technology

FCCT Fellow of the Canadian College of Teachers

FCD First Chief Directorate (of KGB)

FCDA [USA] Federal Civil Defense Administration

FCEC Federation of Civil Engineering Contractors

FCFC Free Church Federal Council

FCFI Fellow of the Clothing and Footwear Institute

fcg facing

FCGB Forestry Commission of Great Britain

FCGI Fellow of the City and Guilds (of London) Institute

FCH full central heating (in property advertisement)

FChS Fellow of the Society of Chiropodists

FCI *Fédération cynologique internationale* (French: International Federation of Kennel Clubs); Fellow of the Institute of Commerce

FCIA Fellow of the Corporation of Insurance Agents; Foreign Credit Insurance Association

FCIArb Fellow of the Chartered Institute of Arbitrators

FCIB Fellow of the Chartered Institute of Bankers; Fellow of the Corporation of Insurance Brokers

FCIBSE Fellow of the Chartered Institution of Building Services Engineers

FCIC [USA] Federal Crop Insurance Corporation; Fellow of the Chemical Institute of Canada

FCII Fellow of the Chartered Insurance Institute

FCILA Fellow of the Chartered Institute of Loss Adjusters

FCIM Fellow of the Chartered Institute of Marketing

FCIOB Fellow of the Chartered Institute of Building

FCIPA Fellow of the Chartered Institute of Patent Agents

FCIPS Fellow of the Chartered Institute of Purchasing and Supply

FCIS Fellow of the Institute of Chartered Secretaries and Administrators (formerly Fellow of the Chartered Institute of Secretaries)

FCIT Fellow of the Chartered Institute of Transport; Four Countries International Tournament (in basketball)

FCIV Fellow of the Commonwealth Institute of Valuers

FCMA Fellow of the Chartered Institute of Management Accountants

FCMS Fellow of the College of Medicine and Surgery

FCMSA Fellow of the College of Medicine of South Africa

FCNA Fellow of the College of Nursing, Australia

fcng facing

FCO Farmers' Central Organization; fire-control officer; Foreign and Commonwealth Office
fco [commerce] *franco* (French: free of charge)
f. co. [printing] fair copy
FCOG(SA) Fellow of the South African College of Obstetrics and Gynaecology
FCollP Fellow of the College of Preceptors
FCOphth Fellow of the College of Ophthalmologists
FCOT Fellow of the College of Occupational Therapists
FCP [engineering] fatigue-crack propagation; Fellow of the College of Clinical Pharmacology; Fellow of the College of Preceptors
fcp foolscap
FCPA Fellow of the Canadian Psychological Association; [USA] Foreign Corrupt Practices Act
FCPO Fleet Chief Petty Officer
FCPS Fellow of the College of Physicians and Surgeons
FCS Federation of Conservative Students; [medicine] fetal calf serum
fcs francs
f.c.s. [insurance] warranted free of capture, seizure, arrest, detainment and the consequences thereof
FCSA Fellow of the Institute of Chartered Secretaries and Administrators
FCSD Fellow of the Chartered Society of Designers
FCSP Fellow of the Chartered Society of Physiotherapy
f.c.s.r.c.c. [insurance] warranted free of capture, seizure, arrest, detainment and the consequences thereof, and damage caused by riots and civil commotions
FCST [USA] Federal Council for Science and Technology; Fellow of the College of Speech Therapists
FCT [Australia] Federal Capital Territory; Fellow of the Association of Corporate Treasurers
FCTB Fellow of the College of Teachers of the Blind
FCTU Federation of Associations of Catholic Trade Unionists
fcty factory
FCU fighter control unit
FD [vehicle registration] Dudley; *Fidei Defensor* (Latin: Defender of the Faith); financial director; [computing] finite difference; fire department; fleet duties; [fishing port] Fleetwood; [medicine] folate deficiency; free delivery; Free Democrat
fd field; fiord; ford; forward; found; founded; fund
f.d. flight deck; focal distance; free delivery; free discharge; free dispatch
FDA First Division Association (former name of AFDCS); [USA] Food and Drug Administration
FD&C [USA] Food, Drug and Color Regulations
FDC [USA] Fire Detection Center; [philately] first-day cover; [numismatics] *fleur de coin* (French: mint condition)
FDDI [computing] fibre distributed data interface
FDF Food and Drink Federation
fdg funding
FDHO Factory Department, Home Office
FDI *Fédération dentaire internationale* (French: International Dental Federation)
FDIC [USA] Federal Deposit Insurance Corporation; Food and Drink Industries Council
FDIF *Fédération démocratique internationale des femmes* (French: Women's International Democratic Federation)
FDM [computing] finite-difference method; [telecommunications] frequency-division multiplexing
FDO Fleet Dental Officer; [taxation] for declaration (purposes) only
FDP *Freie Demokratische Partei* (German: Free Democratic Party)
FDR Franklin Delano Roosevelt (US president); *Freie Demokratische Republik* (German: Free Democratic Republic, the former West Germany)
fdr founder
fdry foundry
FDS Fellow in Dental Surgery; [aeronautics] flight-director system
FDSRCPSGlas Fellow in Dental Surgery of the Royal College of Physicians and Surgeons of Glasgow
FDSRCS Fellow in Dental Surgery of the Royal College of Surgeons (of England)

FDSRCSE Fellow in Dental Surgery of the Royal College of Surgeons of Edinburgh
FE Far East; [fishing port] Folkestone; foreign editor; further education; [vehicle registration] Lincoln
Fe [chemical element] iron (from Latin *ferrum*)
f.e. first edition; for example
FEA [USA] Federal Energy Administration; [USA] Federal Executive Association; *Fédération internationale pour l'éducation artistique* (French: International Federation for Art Education); [mathematics] finite-element analysis
FEAF Far East Air Force
FEANI *Fédération européenne des associations nationales d'ingénieurs* (French: European Federation of National Associations of Engineers)
FEB [USA] Fair Employment Board; functional electronic block
Feb. February
febb. *febbraio* (Italian: February)
Febr. *Februar* (German: February)
FEBS Federation of European Biochemical Societies
Feby February
FEC [USA] Federal Election(s) Commission; First Edition Club; *Fondation européenne de la culture* (French: European Cultural Foundation)
fec. *fecit* (Latin: (he/she) made it)
FECB Foreign Exchange Control Board
FECDBA Foreign Exchange and Currency Deposit Brokers' Association
FECI Fellow of the Institute of Employment Consultants
FED Federal Reserve System
Fed. Federal; Federalist; Federated; Federation
fed. federal; federated
FEDC Federation of Engineering Design Consultants
FedEx [trademark] Federal Express
FEER [banking] fundamental equilibrium exchange rate
FEF Far East Fleet
FEI *Fédération équestre internationale* (French: International Equestrian Federation); [USA] Financial Executive Institute
FEIDCT Fellow of the Educational Institute of Design Craft and Technology
FEIS Fellow of the Educational Institute of Scotland
FEL free-electron laser
FELF Far East Land Forces
Fell. Fellow
FeLV [microbiology] feline leukaemia virus
FEM [physics] field-emission microscope (or microscopy); [mathematics] finite-element method
fem. female; [grammar] feminine
f. ém. *force électromotrice* (French: electromotive force, emf)
FEMA [USA] Federal Emergency Management Agency
fenc. fencing
FEng Fellow of the Fellowship of Engineering; Fellow of the Royal Academy of Engineering
FENSA Film Entertainments National Service Association
FEO Fleet Engineer Officer
FEOGA *Fonds européen d'orientation et de garantie agriculturel* (French: European Agricultural Guidance and Guarantee Fund) (in EU)
FEP fluorinated ethene propene (plastic)
FEPA [USA] Fair Employment Practices Act
FEPC [USA] Fair Employment Practices Committee
FEPEM Federation of European Petroleum Equipment Manufacturers
Fer. Fermanagh
FERA [USA] Federal Emergency Relief Administration
FERC [USA] Federal Energy Regulatory Commission
FERDU Further Education Review and Development Unit
Ferm. Fermanagh
ferr. *ferrovia* (Italian: railway)
ferv. [pharmacology] *fervens* (Latin: boiling)
FES Federation of Engineering Societies; Fellow of the Entomological Society; Fellow of the Ethnological Society; F(rederick) E(dwin) Smith, Earl of Birkenhead (British statesman); [fencing] foil, épée and sabre
Fest. Festival
FET [USA] federal estate tax; [USA] federal excise tax; field-effect transistor; fossil-energy technology

FEU Further Education Unit
feud. feudal; feudalism
FEV [medicine] forced expiratory volume
fév. *février* (French: February)
FEX [US navy] fleet exercise
FF [vehicle registration] Bangor; *Felicissimi Fratres* (Latin: Most Fortunate Brothers); Fellows; *Fianna Fáil* (Gaelic: Warriors of Ireland) (Irish political party); [military] field force; fixtures and fittings (in property advertisement); [USA] Ford Foundation; [currency] (French) franc; [military] frontier force; fully fitted (in property advertisement); fully furnished (in accommodation advertisement)
ff [music] *fortissimo* (Italian: very loudly)
f/f fully fitted (in property advertisement); fully furnished (in accommodation advertisement)
ff. *fecerunt* (Latin: (they) made it); folios; following (pages or lines); forms
f.f. factory fitted; fixed focus; fully fashioned
FFA Fellow of the Faculty of Actuaries; Fellow of the Institute of Financial Accountants; [biochemistry] free fatty acid; Future Farmers of America
f.f.a. free foreign agency; [commerce] free from alongside (ship)
FFARACS Fellow of the Faculty of Anaesthetists of the Royal Australasian College of Surgeons
FFARCS Fellow of the Faculty of Anaesthetists of the Royal College of Surgeons (of England)
FFARCSI Fellow of the Faculty of Anaesthetists of the Royal College of Surgeons in Ireland
FFAS Fellow of the Faculty of Architects and Surveyors
FFB Fellow of the Faculty of Building
FFC Foreign Funds Control
FFCM Fellow of the Faculty of Community Medicine
FFCMI Fellow of the Faculty of Community Medicine of Ireland
FFD Fellow of the Faculty of Dental Surgeons
FFDRCSI Fellow of the Faculty of Dentistry of the Royal College of Surgeons in Ireland
FFF Free French Forces
fff [music] *fortississimo* (Italian: as loudly as possible)
FFHC Freedom from Hunger Campaign
FFHom Fellow of the Faculty of Homoeopathy
FFI Fellow of the Faculty of Insurance; Finance for Industry; free from infection; French Forces of the Interior
FFJ Franciscan Familiar of Saint Joseph
FFL *Forces françaises libres* (French: Free French Forces)
ffly faithfully
FFOM Fellow of the Faculty of Occupational Medicine
FFPath Fellow of the Faculty of Pathologists
FFPHM Fellow of the Faculty of Public Health Medicine
FFPM Fellow of the Faculty of Pharmaceutical Medicine
FFPS Fauna and Flora Preservation Society; Fellow of the Faculty of Physicians and Surgeons
FFR Fellow of the Faculty of Radiologists
FFr [currency] French franc
Ffr [currency] French franc
FFRR full-frequency range recording
FFS [Algeria] *Front des Forces Socialistes* (French: Socialist Forces Front)
FFSS full-frequency stereophonic sound
FFT [computing] fast Fourier transform; [computing] final form text
f/furn fully furnished (in accommodation advertisement)
FFV [USA] First Families of Virginia
FFWM free-floating wave meter
FFY Fife and Forfar Yeomanry
ffy faithfully
FG [vehicle registration] Brighton; Federal Government; *Fine Gael* (Gaelic: Tribe of the Gaels) (Irish political party); fire guard; [engineering] flue gas; [meteorology] fog; foot guards; *frais généraux* (French: overheads); full gilt
fg fog
f.g. [sports] field goal; fine grain; [commerce] fully good
FGA Fellow of the Gemmological Association; [insurance] free of general average
FGCH full gas central heating (in property advertisement)
FGCM field general court martial
FGDS *Fédération de la gauche démocrate et*

socialiste (French: Federation of the Democratic and Socialist Left)
f.g.f. [commerce] fully good, fair
FGI *Fédération graphique internationale* (French: International Graphical Federation); Fellow of the Institute of Certificated Grocers
Fgn Foreign
FGO Fleet Gunnery Officer
Fg Off. Flying Officer
FGS Fellow of the Geological Society
FGSM Fellow of the Guildhall School of Music (and Drama)
FGT [USA] federal gift tax
fgt freight
FGTB *Fédération générale du travail de Belgique* (French: Belgian General Federation of Labour)
FH [fishing port] Falmouth; [medicine] family history; field hospital; fire hydrant; fly half (in rugby); [medicine] fetal heart; [vehicle registration] Gloucester
F/H freehold (in property advertisement)
f.h. [medicine] *fiat haustus* (Latin: let a draught be made); foghorn; forehatch; forward hatch
FHA [USA] Farmers' Home Administration; [USA] Federal Housing Administration; Finance Houses Association
FHAS Fellow of the Highland and Agricultural Society of Scotland
FHB [informal] family hold back
FHCIMA Fellow of the Hotel Catering and Institutional Management Association
FHH [medicine] fetal heart heard
FHI *Fédération haltérophile internationale* (French: International Weightlifting Federation)
FHLB [USA] Federal Home Loan Bank
FHLBA [USA] Federal Home Loan Bank Administration
FHLBB [USA] Federal Home Loan Bank Board
fhld freehold (in property advertisement)
FHLMC [USA] Federal Home Loan Mortgage Corporation
FHM *For Him Magazine*
FHNH [medicine] fetal heart not heard
f/hold freehold (in property advertisement)
fhp friction horsepower
FHR [Australia] Federal House of Representatives; [medicine] fetal heart rate
FHS Fellow of the Heraldry Society
FHSA Family Health Services Authority
FHSM Fellow of the Institute of Health Services Management
FHWA [USA] Federal Highway Administration
FI Faeroe Islands; Falkland Islands; Fiji Islands; fire insurance; [engineering] flow injection
.fi Finland (in Internet address)
f.i. for instance; [commerce] free in
FIA [USA] Federal Insurance Administration; *Fédération internationale de l'automobile* (French: International Automobile Federation); Fellow of the Institute of Actuaries; Fitness Industry Association; [commerce] full interest admitted
FIAA *Fédération internationale athlétique d'amateur* (French: International Amateur Athletic Federation)
FIAA&S Fellow of the Incorporated Association of Architects and Surveyors
FIAAS Fellow of the Institute of Australian Agricultural Science
FIAB *Fédération internationale des associations de bibliothécaires* (French: International Federation of Library Associations and Institutions); Fellow of the International Association of Bookkeepers
FIAF *Fédération internationale des archives du film* (French: International Federation of Film Archives)
FIAgrE Fellow of the Institution of Agricultural Engineers
FIAI *Fédération internationale des associations d'instituteurs* (French: International Federation of Teachers' Associations); Fellow of the Institute of Industrial and Commercial Accountants
FIAJ *Fédération internationale des auberges de la jeunesse* (French: International Youth Hostel Federation)
FIAL Fellow of the International Institute of Arts and Letters
FIAM Fellow of the Institute of Administrative Management; Fellow of the International Academy of Management
FIAP *Fédération internationale de l'art photographique* (French: International Federation of Photographic Art); Fellow of the Institution of Analysts and Programmers
FIAPF *Fédération internationale des associ-*

ations de producteurs de films (French: International Federation of Film Producers' Associations)

FIAS [USA] Fellow of the Institute of the Aerospace Sciences

FIASc Fellow of the Indian Academy of Sciences

Fiat *Fabbrica Italiana Automobili Torino* (Italian car manufacturer)

fib. [anatomy] fibula

f.i.b. free into barge; free into bond; free into bunker

FIBA *Fédération internationale de basketball amateur* (French: International Amateur Basketball Federation); Fellow of the Institute of Business Administration (Australia)

FIBD Fellow of the Institute of British Decorators

FIBiol Fellow of the Institute of Biology

FIBOR [finance] Frankfurt Inter-Bank Offered Rate

FIBOT Fair Isle Bird Observatory Trust

FIBP Fellow of the Institute of British Photographers

FIBScot Fellow of the Institute of Bankers in Scotland

FIBST Fellow of the Institute of British Surgical Technicians

FIC Falkland Islands Company; Fellow of Imperial College (London); Fellow of the Institute of Chemistry; frequency interference control

fic. fiction; fictional; fictitious

FICA [USA] Federal Insurance Contributions Act; Fellow of the Commonwealth Institute of Accountants; Food Industries Credit Association

FICAI Fellow of the Institute of Chartered Accountants in Ireland

FICC *Fédération internationale de camping et de caravanning* (French: International Federation of Camping and Caravanning); *Fédération internationale des ciné-clubs* (French: International Federation of Film Societies)

FICCI Federation of Indian Chambers of Commerce and Industry

FICD Fellow of the Indian College of Dentists; Fellow of the Institute of Civil Defence

FICE Fellow of the Institution of Civil Engineers

FICFor Fellow of the Institute of Chartered Foresters

FIChemE Fellow of the Institution of Chemical Engineers

FICI Fellow of the Institute of Chemistry in Ireland

FICM Fellow of the Institute of Credit Management

FICS Fellow of the Institute of Chartered Shipbrokers; Fellow of the International College of Surgeons

FICSA Federation of International Civil Servants' Associations

fict. *fictilis* (Latin: made of pottery); fiction; fictional; fictitious

FICW Fellow of the Institute of Clerks of Works of Great Britain

FID Falkland Islands Dependencies; *Fédération internationale de documentation* (French: International Federation for Documentation); *Fédération internationale du diabète* (French: International Diabetes Federation); Fellow of the Institute of Directors; field intelligence department

fid. fidelity; fiduciary

FIDA Fellow of the Institute of Directors, Australia

Fid. Def. *Fidei Defensor* (Latin: Defender of the Faith)

FIDDI [computing] fibre-distributed data interface

FIDE *Fédération internationale des échecs* (French: International Chess Federation); Fellow of the Institute of Design Engineers

FIDO Film Industry Defence Organization; [US astronautics] Flight Dynamics Officer; Fog Investigation Dispersal Operation (in World War II)

FIDP Fellow of the Institute of Data Processing

FIE *Fédération internationale d'escrime* (French: International Fencing Federation)

FIE(Aust) Fellow of the Institution of Engineers, Australia

FIED Fellow of the Institution of Engineering Designers

FIEE Fellow of the Institution of Electrical Engineers

FIEEE [USA] Fellow of the Institute of Electrical and Electronics Engineers

FIEI Fellow of the Institution of Engineers in Ireland
FIEJ *Fédération internationale des éditeurs de journaux* (French: International Federation of Newspaper Publishers)
FIET *Fédération internationale des employés, techniciens et cadres* (French: International Federation of Commercial, Clerical and Technical Employees)
FIEx Fellow of the Institute of Export
FIFA *Fédération internationale de football association* (French: International Federation of Association Football); *Fédération internationale du film d'art* (French: International Federation of Art Films); Fellow of the International Faculty of Arts
fi. fa. *fieri facias* (Latin: have it done) (writ of execution)
FIFCLC *Fédération internationale des femmes de carrières libérales et commerciales* (French: International Federation of Business and Professional Women)
FIFDU *Fédération internationale des femmes diplômées des universités* (French: International Federation of University Women)
FIFF Fellow of the Institute of Freight Forwarders
FIFireE Fellow of the Institution of Fire Engineers
FIFO first in, first out
FIFSP *Fédération internationale des fonctionnaires supérieurs de police* (French: International Federation of Senior Police Officers)
FIFST Fellow of the Institute of Food Science and Technology
FIG *Fédération internationale de gymnastique* (French: International Gymnastic Federation)
Fig. Figure (book illustration)
fig. figurative; figuratively; figure
FIGasE Fellow of the Institution of Gas Engineers
FIGC *Federazione Italiana Gioco Calcio* (Italian: Italian Football Association)
FIGCM Fellow of the Incorporated Guild of Church Musicians
FIGED *Fédération internationale des grandes entreprises de distribution* (French: International Federation of Distributors)
FIGO *Fédération internationale de gynécologie et d'obstétrique* (French: International Federation of Gynaecology and Obstetrics)
FIGRS Fellow of the Irish Genealogical Research Society
FIH *Fédération internationale de hockey* (French: International Hockey Federation); *Fédération internationale des hôpitaux* (French: International Hospital Federation); Fellow of the Institute of Hygiene; [image technology] focused-image holography
FIHE Fellow of the Institution of Health Education
FIHort Fellow of the Institute of Horticulture
FIHospE Fellow of the Institute of Hospital Engineering
FIHT Fellow of the Institution of Highways and Transportation
FII franked investment income
FIIA Fellow of the Institute of Internal Auditors
FIIC Fellow of the International Institute for Conservation of Historic and Artistic Works
FIIE Fellow of the Institution of Incorporated Engineers
FIIM Fellow of the Institution of Industrial Managers
FIInfSc Fellow of the Institute of Information Scientists
FIInst Fellow of the Imperial Institute
FIISec Fellow of the International Institute of Security
FIITech Fellow of the Institute of Industrial Technicians
FIJ *Fédération internationale de judo* (French: International Judo Federation); *Fédération internationale des journalistes* (French: International Federation of Journalists)
FIL *Fédération internationale de laiterie* (French: International Dairy Federation); Fellow of the Institute of Linguists
fil. filament; fillet; filter; filtrate
FILA *Fédération internationale de lutte amateur* (French: International Amateur Wrestling Federation)
FILE Fellow of the Institute of Legal Executives
FILO first in, last out
FILT *Fédération internationale de lawn*

tennis (French: International Lawn Tennis Federation)

FIM *Fédération internationale des musiciens* (French: International Federation of Musicians); *Fédération internationale motocycliste* (French: International Motorcycle Federation); Fellow of the Institute of Materials; field-ion microscope (or microscopy)

FIMA Fellow of the Institute of Mathematics and its Applications

FIMarE Fellow of the Institute of Marine Engineers

FIMBRA Financial Intermediaries, Managers and Brokers Regulatory Association

FIMC Fellow of the Institute of Management Consultants

FIMechE Fellow of the Institution of Mechanical Engineers

FIMGTechE Fellow of the Institution of Mechanical and General Technician Engineers

FIMH Fellow of the Institute of Military History

FIMI Fellow of the Institute of the Motor Industry

FIMIT Fellow of the Institute of Musical Instrument Technology

FIMM Fellow of the Institution of Mining and Metallurgy

FIMP *Fédération internationale de médecine physique* (French: International Federation of Physical Medicine)

FIMS *Fédération internationale de médecine sportive* (French: International Federation of Sporting Medicine); Fellow of the Institute of Mathematical Statistics

FIN [international vehicle registration] Finland

Fin. Finland; Finnish

fin. *ad finem* (Latin: at the end, towards the end); final; finance; financial; financier; *finis* (Latin: the end); finish

FINA *Fédération internationale de natation amateur* (French: International Amateur Swimming Federation)

f.i.n.a. following items not available

Findus Fruit Industries Limited

Finn. Finnish

Fin. Sec. financial secretary

FInstAM Fellow of the Institute of Administrative Management

FInstB Fellow of the Institution of Buyers

FInstCh Fellow of the Institute of Chiropodists

FInstD Fellow of the Institute of Directors

FInstE Fellow of the Institute of Energy

FInstF Fellow of the Institute of Fuel

FInstLEx Fellow of the Institute of Legal Executives

FInstMC Fellow of the Institute of Measurement and Control

FInstO Fellow of the Institute of Ophthalmology

FInstP Fellow of the Institute of Physics

FInstPet Fellow of the Institute of Petroleum

FInstPI Fellow of the Institute of Patentees and Inventors

FInstR Fellow of the Institute of Refrigeration

FInstSMM Fellow of the Institute Sales and Marketing Management

FINucE Fellow of the Institution of Nuclear Engineers

f.i.o. for information only; [commerce] free in and out

FIOA Fellow of the Institute of Acoustics

FIOP Fellow of the Institute of Printing

FIP *Fédération internationale de philatélie* (French: International Philatelic Federation); *Fédération internationale pharmaceutique* (French: International Pharmaceutical Federation); Fellow of the Institute of Plumbing

FIPA *Fédération internationale des producteurs agricoles* (French: International Federation of Agricultural Producers); Fellow of the Institute of Practitioners in Advertising

FIPENZ Fellow of the Institution of Professional Engineers, New Zealand

FIPG Fellow of the Institute of Professional Goldsmiths

FIPR Fellow of the Institute of Public Relations

FIPS [computing] Federal International Processing Standards

FIQ *Fédération internationale de quilleurs* (French: International Bowling Federation); Fellow of the Institute of Quarrying

FIQA Fellow of the Institute of Quality Assurance

FIQS Fellow of the Institute of Quantity Surveyors

FIR far-infrared radiation; fuel-indicator reading
fir. firkin
f.i.r. flight information region; floating-in rate; fuel-indicator reading
FIRA *Fédération internationale de rugby amateur* (French: International Amateur Rugby Federation); Furniture Industry Research Association
FIREE(Aust) Fellow of the Institute of Radio and Electronics Engineers (Australia)
FIRSE Fellow of the Institute of Railway Signalling Engineers
FIRST Far Infrared and Submillimetre Telescope; [computing] Forum of Incident and Response Teams
FIRTE Fellow of the Institute of Road Transport Engineers
FIS Family Income Supplement; farm improvement scheme; *Fédération internationale de sauvetage* (French: International Life Saving Federation); *Fédération internationale de ski* (French: International Ski Federation); Fellow of the Institute of Statisticians; [Algeria] *Front Islamique du Salut* (French: Islamic Salvation Front)
f.i.s. flight information service; free into store
FISA *Fédération internationale de sport automobile* (French: International Motor Sport Federation); *Fédération internationale des sociétés d'aviron* (French: International Rowing Federation); Fellow of the Incorporated Secretaries Association; Finance Industry Standards Association
FISE *Fédération internationale syndicale de l'enseignement* (French: International Federation of Teachers' Unions); Fellow of the Institution of Sales Engineers; *Fonds international de secours à l'enfance* (French: United Nations Children's Fund, UNICEF)
fish. fishery; fishes; fishing
FIST Fellow of the Institute of Science Technology
FISTC Fellow of the Institute of Scientific and Technical Communicators
FIStructE Fellow of the Institution of Structural Engineers
FISU *Fédération internationale du sport universitaire* (French: International University Sports Federation)
FISVA Fellow of the Incorporated Society of Valuers and Auctioneers
FISW Fellow of the Institute of Social Work
FIT [USA] federal income tax; *Fédération internationale des traducteurs* (French: International Federation of Translators)
f.i.t. [commerce] free in truck; free of income tax
FITA *Fédération internationale de tir à l'arc* (French: International Archery Federation)
FITCE *Fédération des ingénieurs des télécommunications de la CE* (French: Federation of Telecommunications Engineers in the EU)
FITD Fellow of the Institute of Training and Development
FITE Fellow of the Institution of Electrical and Electronics Technician Engineers
FITS [astronomy] flexible image transport system
FITT *Fédération internationale de tennis de table* (French: International Table Tennis Federation)
FITW [USA] federal income tax withholding
FIUO for internal use only
FIVB *Fédération internationale de volley-ball* (French: International Volleyball Federation)
f.i.w. [commerce] free in(to) wagon
FIWC Fiji Industrial Workers' Congress
FIWEM Fellow of the Institution of Water and Environmental Management
FIWSc Fellow of the Institute of Wood Science
fix. fixture(s)
fixt. fixture(s)
FJ [vehicle registration] Exeter
Fj. Fjord
.fj Fiji (in Internet address)
FJA Future Journalists of America
Fjd Fjord
FJI Fellow of the Institute of Journalists; [international vehicle registration] Fiji
FK [vehicle registration] Dudley; [UK postcode] Falkirk; [astronomy] *Fundamental Katalog* (German: Fundamental Catalogue)
fk fork

.fk Falkland Islands (in Internet address)
f.k. flat keel
FKC Fellow of King's College (London)
FKCHMS Fellow of King's College Hospital Medical School
Fkr [currency] Faeroese krone
FL Flag Lieutenant; Flight Lieutenant; [US postcode] Florida; football league; [international vehicle registration] Liechtenstein (from German *Fürstentum Liechtenstein*); [vehicle registration] Peterborough
Fl. Flanders; Flemish
fl. *fleuve* (French: river); floor; [medicine] *flores* (Latin: flowers) (powdered drug); [currency] florin; *floruit* (Latin: flourished) (of famous person whose dates (of birth and death) are not known); flourish; flourished; fluid; [music] flute; [currency] guilder (from alternative name florin)
f.l. *falsa lectio* (Latin: false reading)
FLA Fellow of the Library Association; *fiat lege artis* (Latin: let it be done by the rules of the art); Film Laboratory Association; Finance and Leasing Association; Future Large Aircraft (design project)
Fla Florida
flag. [music] flageolet
FLAI Fellow of the Library Association of Ireland
flak *Fliegerabwehrkanone* (German: aircraft defence gun)
FLCD [electronics] ferroelectric liquid-crystal display
FLCM Fellow of the London College of Music
FLCO Fellow of the London College of Osteopathy
fld failed; field; filed; fluid
fldg folding
fl. dr. fluid dram
Flem. Flemish
flex. flexible
flg flagging; flooring; flying; following
FLHS Fellow of the London Historical Society
FLI Fellow of the Landscape Institute
FLIA Fellow of the Life Insurance Association
Flint. Flintshire
FLIP [US navy] floating instrument platform
FLIR [military] forward-looking infrared
Flli *Fratelli* (Italian: Brothers)
FLN [Algeria] *Front de Libération Nationale* (French: National Liberation Front)
FLOOD [USA] fleet observation of oceanographic data
flops [computing] floating-point operations per second (measure of computer power)
Flor. Florence; Florentine; Florida
flor. [currency] florin; *floruit* (Latin: flourished) (of famous person whose dates (of birth and death) are not known)
fl. oz fluid ounce
f.l.p. [aeronautics] fault location panel
fl. pl. [botany] *flore pleno* (Latin: with double flowers)
FLQ [Canada] *Front de Libération du Québec* (French: Quebec Liberation Front) (French-speaking separatists)
flr floor
flr. failure; [currency] florin
FLRA [USA] Federal Labor Relations Authority
flrg flooring
fl. rt. flow rate
FLS Fellow of the Linnean Society
FLSA [USA] Fair Labor Standards Act
flst flautist
F/Lt Flight Lieutenant
Flt Flight (in air force rank)
flt flat; flight
Flt Cmdr Flight Commander
fltg floating
Flt Lt Flight Lieutenant
Flt Off. Flight Officer
Flt Sgt Flight Sergeant
flu [short form] influenza
fluc. fluctuant; fluctuate; fluctuated; fluctuating; fluctuation
fluor. fluorescent; fluoridation; fluoride; fluorspar
fly. [boxing] flyweight
FM [vehicle registration] Chester; [computing] facilities management; [electrical engineering] field magnet; Field Marshal; [aeronautics] figure of merit; Flight Mechanic; foreign mission; *Fraternitas Medicorum* (Latin: Fraternity of Physicians); *fraternité mondiale* (French: world brotherhood); freemason; [radio] frequency modulation; Friars Minor

Fm [chemical element] fermium
fm farm; fathom; femtometre; from
.fm Micronesia (in Internet address)
f.m. face measurement; facial measurement; [advertising] facing matter; *femmes mariées* (French: married women); [medicine] *fiat mistura* (Latin: let a mixture be made) (in prescriptions); fine measure; fine measurement; [radio] frequency modulation
FMA Farm Management Association; Fellow of the Museums Association; Food Machinery Association
fman foreman
FMANU *Fédération mondiale des associations pour les Nations Unies* (French: World Federation of United Nations Associations)
FMANZ Fellow of the Medical Association of New Zealand
FMAO farm machinery advisory officer
FMAS Foreign Marriage Advisory Service
FMB Farmers' Marketing Board (in Malawi); [USA] Federal Maritime Board; Federation of Master Builders
FMC [USA] Federal Maritime Commission; Fellow of the Medical Council; Forces Motoring Club; Ford Motor Company
FMCE Federation of Manufacturers of Construction Equipment
FMCG fast-moving consumer goods
FMCP Federation of Manufacturers of Contractors' Plant
FMCS [USA] Federal Mediation and Conciliation Service
FMCW [electronics] frequency modulated continuous wave
FMD [veterinary science] foot and mouth disease
fmd formed
FMDV [microbiology] foot and mouth disease virus
FMEA failure mode and effect analysis
FMES Fellow of the Minerals Engineering Society
FMF [medicine] Fiji Military Forces; Fleet Marine Force(s); fetal movements felt; Food Manufacturers' Federation
FMFPAC [USA] Fleet Marine Forces, Pacific
FMG Federal Military Government (in Nigeria); [currency] franc malgache (used in Madagascar)
FMI Fellow of the Motor Industry; *Filii Mariae Immaculatae* (Latin: Sons of Mary Immaculate)
FMIG Food Manufacturers' Industrial Group
FMk [currency] Finnish markka
Fmk Finnmark
fml formal
FMLN *Farabundo Martí Liberación Nacional* (Spanish: Farabundo Martí National Liberation Front) (guerrilla movement in El Salvador)
FMN [biochemistry] flavin mononucleotide
fmn formation
FMO Fleet Medical Officer; Flight Medical Officer
FMPA *Fédération mondiale pour la protection des animaux* (French: World Federation for the Protection of Animals)
fmr farmer; former
fmrly formerly
FMRS Foreign Member of the Royal Society
FMS Federated Malay States; *Fédération mondiale des sourds* (French: World Federation of the Deaf); Fellow of the Institute of Management Studies; Fellow of the Medical Society; [computing] flexible manufacturing system; [aeronautics] flight management system(s)
FMSA Fellow of the Mineralogical Society of America
FMTS field maintenance test station
FMV [computing] full-motion video
FMVSS [USA] Federal Motor Vehicle Safety Standards
FN [vehicle registration] Maidstone
f.n. footnote
FNA Fellow of the Indian National Science Academy; French North Africa
f.n.a. for necessary action
FNAEA Fellow of the National Association of Estate Agents
FNAL Fermi National Accelerator Laboratory
FNB Federal Narcotics Bureau
FNCB [USA] First National City Bank
FNCO Fleet Naval Constructor Officer
fnd found; foundered
fnd. foundation

fndd founded
fndr founder
fndry foundry
FNECInst Fellow of the North East Coast Institution of Engineers and Shipbuilders
FNI *Fédération naturiste internationale* (French: International Naturist Federation); Fellow of the Nautical Institute
FNIF Florence Nightingale International Foundation
FNILP Fellow of the National Institute of Licensing Practitioners
FNL Friends of the National Libraries
FNLA *Frente Nacional de Libertação de Angola* (Portuguese: National Front for the Liberation of Angola)
FNMA [USA] Federal National Mortgage Association
FNO Fleet Navigation Officer
FNU *Forces des Nations Unies* (French: United Nations Forces)
f-number [photography] ratio of focal length to aperture
FNWC [USA] Fleet Numerical Weather Center
FNZIA Fellow of the New Zealand Institute of Architects
FO federal official; Field Officer; [commerce] firm offer; First Officer; Flag Officer (in Royal Navy); Flying Officer; Foreign Office (became part of FCO); [commerce] formal offer; [military] forward observer; [music] full organ; [vehicle registration] Gloucester
Fo [physics] Fourier number
fo *firmato* (Italian: signed)
f/o [commerce] for orders; full out
fo. folio
.fo Faeroe Islands (in Internet address)
f.o. fast operating; [commerce] free overside; fuel oil
FOAF friend of a friend (used on Internet)
FOB [medicine] faecal occult blood; [commerce] free on board
FOBFO Federation of British Fire Organizations
FOBS [military] fractional orbital bombardment system
FOBTSU [military] forward observer target survey unit
FOC [commerce] free of charge; free of claims
FoC father of the chapel (in printing or publishing trade union)
FOCL fibre-optic communications line
FOCOL Federation of Coin-Operated Launderettes
FOCUS Focus on Computing in the United States
FOD finger of death (in computer game); [aeronautics] foreign object damage (of aircraft engine); free of damage
FODA Fellow of the Overseas Doctors' Association
FOE [USA] Fraternal Order of Eagles
FoE Friends of the Earth
FOF [stock exchange] Futures and Options Fund
FOFA follow-on forces attack
FOFATUSA Federation of Free African Trade Unions of South Africa
F of F Firth of Forth
FOH [theatre] front of house
FOHCL falls off her/his chair laughing (in Internet chat)
FOI [USA] freedom of information
FOIA [USA] Freedom of Information Act
FOIC Flag Officer in Charge
f.o.k. [stock exchange] fill or kill (i.e. carry out or cancel)
FOL [New Zealand] Federation of Labour
fol. folio; follow; followed; following
folg following
foll. followed; following
FOM [statistics] figure of merit
FOMC [USA] Federal Open Market Committee
FONA Flag Officer, Naval Aviation
FONAC Flag Officer, Naval Air Command
FOP forward observation post
FOQ [commerce] free on quay
FOR Fellowship of Operational Research; flying objects research; [commerce] free on rail
For [astronomy] Fornax
For. [currency] forint (used in Hungary)
for. foreign; foreigner; forensic; forest; forester; forestry; [music] *forte* (Italian: loudly)
FORATOM *Forum atomique européen* (French: European Atomic Forum)
FORES floor order routing and execution system (in Tokyo Stock Exchange)
FOREST Freedom Organization for the Right to Enjoy Smoking Tobacco

FOREX foreign exchange
formn formation
form. wt [chemistry] formula weight
for. rts foreign rights
fort. fortification; fortified; fortify
f.o.r.t. [commerce] full out rye terms
Fortran formula translation (computer programming language)
Forts. *Fortsetzung* (German: continuation)
forz. [music] *forzando* (Italian: with force)
FOS Fisheries Organization Society; [finance] free of stamp; [commerce] free on ship; [commerce] free on station; [commerce] free on steamer
FOSDIC [computing] film optical sensing device
FOT [commerce] free of tax; [commerce] free on truck
Found. Foundation
found. foundry
FOV field of view
FOW [commerce] first open water; [commerce] free on wagon
FOX Futures and Options Exchange
FP Federal Parliament; field punishment; filter paper; fireplug; [insurance] fire policy; [nuclear technology] fission product; [insurance] floating policy; [optics] focal plane; [Australia] forensic pathologist; former pupil; [veterinary science] fowl pest; Free Presbyterian; freezing point; fresh paragraph; fully paid; [computing] functional programming; [vehicle registration] Leicester
Fp. frontispiece
fp foolscap
fp [music] *forte-piano* (Italian: loudly (then) softly)
fp. fireplace
f.p. [medicine] *fiat pilula* (Latin: let a pill be made) (in prescriptions); [medicine] *fiat potio* (Latin: let a drink be made) (in prescriptions); fine paper; [cricket] fine point; fixed price; flameproof; [chemistry] flash point; footpath; foot-pound; [sports] forward pass; freezing point; fresh paragraph; full point; fully paid (shares)
FPA Family Planning Association; Film Production Association of Great Britain; Fire Protection Association; [astronomy] first point of Aries; [computing] floating-point accelerator; Foreign Press Association; [insurance] free of particular average
f.p.b. fast patrol boat
f.p.b.g. fast patrol boat with guided missiles
FPC family planning clinic; Family Practitioner Committee; [USA] Federal Power Commission; Federation of Painting Contractors; fish protein concentrate; Flowers Publicity Council
f.p.c. for private circulation
FPEA Fellow of the Physical Education Association
FPF *Federação Portuguesa de Futebol* (Portuguese: Portuguese Football Federation)
FPGA [computing] field-programmable gate array
FPHA [USA] Federal Public Housing Authority
FPhyS Fellow of the Physical Society
FPI [USA] Federal Prison Industries
FPIA Fellow of the Plastics Institute of Australia
FPLA [computing, electronics] field-programmable logic array
fpm feet per minute
FPMI Fellow of the Pensions Management Institute
FPMR [USA] Federal Property Management Regulation
FPO field post office; fire prevention officer; [US navy] fleet post office
FPRC Flying Personnel Research Committee
FPROM [computing] field-programmable read-only memory; [computing] fusible-link programmable read-only memory
FPS Fellow of the Pharmaceutical Society; Fellow of the Philharmonic Society; Fellow of the Philological Society; Fellow of the Philosophical Society; Fellow of the Physical Society; [USA] Fluid Power Society
fps feet per second; foot-pound-second (as in **fps units**); [photography] frames per second
fpsps feet per second per second
FPT [commerce] fixed price tender; [nautical] forepeak tank
FPU [computing] floating point unit
f.q. [finance] fiscal quarter
FQDN [computing] fully qualified domain name

FQS [USA] Federal Quarantine Service
FR [international vehicle registration] Faeroe Islands; Federal Republic; Federal Reserve (System); fighter reconnaissance; [chemistry] fluorine rubber; *Forum Romanum* (Latin: Roman Forum); [fishing port] Fraserburgh; freight release; frequency rate; [nuclear technology] fusion reactor; [vehicle registration] Preston
F/R folio reference
Fr [ecclesiastical] Father; [chemical element] francium; [Roman Catholic Church] *Frater* (Latin: Brother)
Fr. France; *Fratelli* (Italian: Brothers); *Frau* (German: Mrs); French; Friar; Friday
fr. fragment; frame; [currency] franc; free; frequent; frequently; from; front; fruit; [botany] fruiting
.fr France (in Internet address)
f.r. *folio recto* (Latin: on the right-hand page)
FRA [finance] forward rate agreement
Fra [Roman Catholic Church] *Frate* (Italian: Brother)
f.r.a. flame retardant additive
FRACDS Fellow of the Royal Australian College of Dental Surgeons
FRACGP Fellow of the Royal Australian College of General Practitioners
FRACI Fellow of the Royal Australian Chemical Institute
FRACMA Fellow of the Royal Australian College of Medical Administrators
FRACO Fellow of the Royal Australian College of Ophthalmologists
FRACOG Fellow of the Royal Australian College of Obstetricians and Gynaecologists
FRACP Fellow of the Royal Australasian College of Physicians
FRACS Fellow of the Royal Australasian College of Surgeons
FRAD Fellow of the Royal Academy of Dancing
FRAeS Fellow of the Royal Aeronautical Society
FRAgSs Fellow of the Royal Agricultural Societies
FRAHS Fellow of the Royal Australian Historical Society
FRAI Fellow of the Royal Anthropological Institute
FRAIA Fellow of the Royal Australian Institute of Architects
FRAIC Fellow of the Royal Architectural Institute of Canada
FRAM Fellow of the Royal Academy of Music; [computing] ferroelectric random-access memory
FRAME Fund for the Replacement of Animals in Medical Experiments
Franc. Franciscan
f.r. & c.c. [insurance] free of riot and civil commotions
Frank. Frankish
FRAP *Frente de Acción Popular* (Spanish: Popular Action Front) (in Chile)
FRAPI Fellow of the Royal Australian Planning Institute
FRAS Fellow of the Royal Asiatic Society; Fellow of the Royal Astronomical Society
FRASE Fellow of the Royal Agricultural Society of England
frat. fraternity; fraternize
FRATE [railways] formulae for routes and technical equipment
fraud. fraudulent
FRB [USA] Federal Reserve Bank; [USA] Federal Reserve Board; Fisheries Research Board of Canada; *Frente de la Revolución Boliviana* (Spanish: Bolivian Revolutionary Front)
FRBS Fellow of the Royal Botanic Society; Fellow of the Royal Society of British Sculptors
FRC [USA] Federal Radiation Council; [USA] Federal Radio Commission; Financial Reporting Council; Flight Research Center (at NASA)
FRCA Fellow of the Royal College of Art
Fr-Can French-Canadian
FRCD Fellow of the Royal College of Dentists of Canada; [banking] floating-rate certificate of deposit
FRCGP Fellow of the Royal College of General Practitioners
FRCM Fellow of the Royal College of Music
FRCN Fellow of the Royal College of Nursing
FRCO Fellow of the Royal College of Organists
FRCO(CHM) Fellow of the Royal College

of Organists with Diploma in Choir Training
FRCOG Fellow of the Royal College of Obstetricians and Gynaecologists
FRCP Fellow of the Royal College of Physicians
FRCPA Fellow of the Royal College of Pathologists of Australasia
FRCPath Fellow of the Royal College of Pathologists
FRCPE Fellow of the Royal College of Physicians of Edinburgh
FRCPI Fellow of the Royal College of Physicians of Ireland
FRCPSGlas Fellow of the Royal College of Physicians and Surgeons of Glasgow
FRCPsych Fellow of the Royal College of Psychiatrists
FRCR Fellow of the Royal College of Radiologists
FRCS Fellow of the Royal College of Surgeons (of England)
FRCSE Fellow of the Royal College of Surgeons of Edinburgh
FRCSEd Fellow of the Royal College of Surgeons of Edinburgh
FRCSI Fellow of the Royal College of Surgeons in Ireland
FRCSoc Fellow of the Royal Commonwealth Society
FRCVS Fellow of the Royal College of Veterinary Surgeons
frd friend
FR Dist. [USA] Federal Reserve District
Fre. *Freitag* (German: Friday); French
fre *facture* (French: invoice)
FREconS Fellow of the Royal Economic Society
FRED Fast Reactor Experiment, Dounreay; figure reading electronic device; financial reporting exposure draft
Free. [USA] freeway
FREGG Free Range Egg Association
FREI Fellow of the Real Estate Institute (Australia)
Frelimo *Frente de Libertação de Moçambique* (Portuguese: Mozambique Liberation Front)
freq. frequency; frequent; [grammar] frequentative; frequently
FRES Federation of Recruitment and Employment Services; Fellow of the Royal Entomological Society
FRESH foil research hydrofoil
FRG Federal Republic of Germany
Fr. G French Guiana
FRGS Fellow of the Royal Geographical Society; Fellow of the Royal Geographical Society of Australasia
frgt freight
FRHB Federation of Registered House Builders
FRHistS Fellow of the Royal Historical Society
Frhr *Freiherr* (German: Baron)
FRHS Fellow of the Royal Horticultural Society
FRI Fellow of the Royal Institution; Food Research Institute
Fri. Fribourg; Friday
FRIA Fellow of the Royal Irish Academy
FRIAI Fellow of the Royal Institute of the Architects of Ireland
FRIAS Fellow of the Royal Incorporation of Architects in Scotland; Fellow of the Royal Institute for the Advancement of Science
FRIBA Fellow of the Royal Institute of British Architects
fric. friction; frictional
FRICS Fellow of the Royal Institution of Chartered Surveyors
frict. friction; frictional
fridge [short form] refrigerator
FRIH [New Zealand] Fellow of the Royal Institute of Horticulture
FRIIA Fellow of the Royal Institute of International Affairs
FRIN Fellow of the Royal Institute of Navigation
FRINA Fellow of the Royal Institution of Naval Architects
FRIPA Fellow of the Royal Institute of Public Administration
FRIPHH Fellow of the Royal Institute of Public Health and Hygiene
Fris. Friesland; Frisian
Frk. *Fröken* (Swedish: Miss); *Frøken* (Danish or Norwegian: Miss)
FRL full repairing lease
Frl. *Fräulein* (German: Miss)
frld foreland; freehold (in property advertisement)
frm from
FRMCM Fellow of the Royal Manchester College of Music

FRMCS Fellow of the Royal Medical and Chirurgical Society
FRMedSoc Fellow of the Royal Medical Society
FRMetS Fellow of the Royal Meteorological Society
FRMS Fellow of the Royal Microscopical Society
FRN [finance] floating-rate note
FRNCM Fellow of the Royal Northern College of Music
FRNS Fellow of the Royal Numismatic Society
FRNSA Fellow of the Royal Navy School of Architects
FRO Fellow of the Register of Osteopaths; Fire Research Organization; [insurance] fire risk only
f.r.o.f. [insurance] fire risk on freight
Frolinat *Front de Libération Nationale Tchadienne* (French: Chad National Liberation Front)
front. frontispiece
frontis. frontispiece
FRP fibreglass-reinforced plastic; fibre-reinforced plastic; fuel-reprocessing plant
frpf fireproof
FRPharmS Fellow of the Royal Pharmaceutical Society
FRPS Fellow of the Royal Photographic Society
FRPSL Fellow of the Royal Philatelic Society, London
FRQ [meteorology] frequent
frq. frequent
FRR Financial Reporting Release
FRRP Financial Reporting Review Panel
FRS [USA] Federal Reserve System; Fellow of the Royal Society; Ffestiniog Railway Society; Financial Reporting Standard; fuel research station
Frs. Frisian
FRSA Fellow of the Royal Society of Arts
FRSAI Fellow of the Royal Society of Antiquaries of Ireland
FRSAMD Fellow of the Royal Scottish Academy of Music and Drama
FRSC Fellow of the Royal Society of Canada; Fellow of the Royal Society of Chemistry
FRSCan Fellow of the Royal Society of Canada
FRSCM Fellow of the Royal School of Church Music
FRSE Fellow of the Royal Society of Edinburgh
FRSGS Fellow of the Royal Scottish Geographical Society
FRSH Fellow of the Royal Society of Health
FRSL Fellow of the Royal Society of Literature
FRSM Fellow of the Royal Society of Medicine
FRSNZ Fellow of the Royal Society of New Zealand
FRSS Fellow of the Royal Statistical Society
FRSSA Fellow of the Royal Scottish Society of Arts; Fellow of the Royal Society of South Africa
FRSSI Fellow of the Royal Statistical Society of Ireland
FRSSS Fellow of the Royal Statistical Society of Scotland
FRST Fellow of the Royal Society of Teachers
FRSTM&H Fellow of the Royal Society of Tropical Medicine and Hygiene
frt freight
frt fwd freight forward
FRTPI Fellow of the Royal Town Planning Institute
frt ppd freight prepaid
FRTS Fellow of the Royal Television Society
Fru [biochemistry] fructose
frum *fratrum* (Latin: of the brothers)
frust. [medicine] *frustillatim* (Latin: in small portions)
FRVA Fellow of the Rating and Valuation Association
FRVC Fellow of the Royal Veterinary College
frwk framework
frwy freeway
FRZSScot Fellow of the Royal Zoological Society of Scotland
FS [vehicle registration] Edinburgh; Fabian Society; Faraday Society; feasibility study; *Ferrovie dello Stato* (Italian: State Railways); field security; financial secretary; financial statement; Fleet Surgeon; Flight Sergeant; Foreign Service; [USA] Forest Service; Free State; Friendly Society

fs. facsimile

f.s. factor of safety; *faire suivre* (French: please forward); far side; film strip; fire station; flight service; flying saucer; flying status; foot-second

FSA [USA] Farm Security Agency; [USA] Federal Security Agency; [USA] Fellow of the Society of Actuaries; Fellow of the Society of Antiquaries; Field Survey Association; Financial Services Act; Financial Services Authority; [computing] finite-state automaton; foreign service allowance; Friendly Societies Act

f.s.a. fuel storage area

FSAA Fellow of the Society of Incorporated Accountants and Auditors

FSAE Fellow of the Society of Art Education; Fellow of the Society of Automotive Engineers

FSAI Fellow of the Society of Architectural Illustrators

FSAM Fellow of the Society of Art Masters

FSAScot Fellow of the Society of Antiquaries of Scotland

FSB Federation of Small Businesses

FSBI Fellow of the Savings Bank Institute

FSBR Financial Statement and Budget Report

FSC [USA] Federal Supreme Court; Field Studies Council; [Roman Catholic Church] *Fratres Scholarum Christianorum* (Latin: Brothers of the Christian Schools, Christian Brothers); Friends Service Council

FSCA Fellow of the Society of Company and Commercial Accountants

FSD full-scale deflection (of measuring instrument)

FSDC Fellow of the Society of Dyers and Colourists

FSE Fellow of the Society of Engineers; field support equipment

FSF Fellow of the Institute of Shipping and Forwarding Agents; Free Software Foundation

FSFMV [computing] full-screen, full-motion video

FSG Fellow of the Society of Genealogists

FSGT Fellow of the Society of Glass Technology

FSgt Flight Sergeant

FSH [biochemistry] follicle-stimulating hormone; full service history (in car advertisement)

FSHM Fellow of the Society of Housing Managers

FSI *Fédération spirite internationale* (French: International Spiritualist Federation); Free Sons of Israel

FSK [telecommunications] frequency shift keying

FSL First Sea Lord; Folger Shakespeare Library

FSLAET Fellow of the Society of Licensed Aircraft Engineers and Technologists

FSLIC [USA] Federal Savings and Loan Insurance Corporation

FSLN *Frente Sandinista de Liberación Nacional* (Spanish: Sandinista National Liberation Front) (in Nicaragua)

FSLTC Fellow of the Society of Leather Technologists and Chemists

FSM *Fédération syndicale mondiale* (French: World Federation of Trade Unions); [electronics] flying-spot microscope; [USA] Free Speech Movement

FSMC Freeman of the Spectacle-Makers' Company

FSME Fellow of the Society of Manufacturing Engineers

FSN federal stock number

FSO field security officer; Fleet Signals Officer; Foreign Service Officer

FSP field security police; foreign service pay

FSR Field Service Regulations; *Fleet Street Patent Law Reports*

FSRP Fellow of the Society for Radiological Protection

FSS Fellow of the Royal Statistical Society; [Algeria] *Front des forces socialistes* (French: Socialist Forces Front)

FSSI Fellow of the Statistical Society of Ireland

FSSU Federated Superannuation Scheme for Universities

FST flatter squarer tube (for computer or TV screen)

FSTD Fellow of the Society of Typographic Designers

FSU family service unit

FSUC Federal Statistics Unit Conference

FSVA Fellow of the Incorporated Society of Valuers and Auctioneers

FT *Financial Times*; [obstetrics] full term

(of pregnancy); [vehicle registration] Newcastle upon Tyne
Ft [currency] forint (used in Hungary); Fort
ft feet (unit of length); feint; [medicine] *fiat* (Latin: let there be made); foot (unit of length); fort
ft. fortification; fortify
f.t. formal training; full term(s)
FTA [medicine] fluorescent treponemal antibody; Free Trade Agreement; Free Trade Area; Freight Transport Association; Future Teachers of America
FTA Index Financial Times Actuaries Share Index
FTAM [computing] file transfer, access and management
FTASI Financial Times Actuaries All-Share Index
FTAT Furniture, Timber and Allied Trades Union
FTB first-time buyer (in property advertisement); fleet torpedo bomber
FTBD [obstetrics] full term, born dead
ftbrg. footbridge
FTC [USA] Federal Trade Commission; [USA] flight test center; flying training command; Full Technological Certificate (of City and Guilds Institute)
FTCD Fellow of Trinity College, Dublin
FTCL Fellow of Trinity College of Music, London
FTD foreign technology division
FTDA Fellow of the Theatrical Designers and Craftsmen's Association
f.t.e. full-time equivalent
FTESA Foundry Trades Equipment and Supplies Association
FTFL [computing] fixed-to-fixed-length (code)
FTG Fuji Texaco Gas
ftg fitting
fth. fathom
fthm fathom
FTI Fellow of the Textile Institute
FT Index Financial Times Ordinary Share Index
ft-lb foot-pound
Ft Lieut. Flight Lieutenant
FTM flying training manual; [medicine] fractional test meal
ft mist. [medicine] *fiat mistura* (Latin: let a mixture be made) (in prescriptions)
FTND [obstetrics] full term, normal delivery
FTO Fleet Torpedo Officer
FT Ord. Financial Times (Industrial) Ordinary Share Index
FTP [computing] file-transfer protocol (used on Internet)
FTPA Fellow of the Town and Country Planning Association
ft pulv. [medicine] *fiat pulvis* (Latin: let a powder be made) (in prescriptions)
FTS Fellow of the Tourism Society
FTS flying training school
ft/s feet per second
ft/s² feet per second per second
FTSC Fellow of the Tonic Sol-Fa College
FTSE 100 Financial Times Stock Exchange 100 Index (also called Footsie)
FTT [medicine] failure to thrive
fttgs fittings (in property advertisement)
fttr fitter
FTU Federation of Trade Unions (in Hong Kong); [photography] Freeman time-unit
FTVL [computing] fixed-to-variable-length (code)
FTW [commerce] tree-trade wharf
FTZ Free Trade Zone
FU Farmers' Union; [photography] Freeman time-unit; *Freie Universität* (German: Free University (of Berlin)); [vehicle registration] Lincoln
f.u. follow-up
FUACE *Fédération universelle des associations chrétiennes d'étudiants* (French: World Student Christian Federation)
FUEN Federal Union of European Nationalities
FUMIST Fellow of the University of Manchester Institute of Science and Technology
fund. fundamental
FUO [medicine] fever of uncertain origin
fur. furlong; furnished (in accommodation advertisement); further
furn. furnace; furnish; furnished (in accommodation advertisement); furniture
fus. fuselage; fusilier
fut. future; [finance] futures
FUW Farmers' Union of Wales
FV [vehicle registration] Preston
f.v. fire vent; fishing vessel; flush valve; *folio verso* (Latin: on the left-hand page)

FVC [medicine] forced vital capacity (in breathing tests)
FVRDE Fighting Vehicle Research and Development Establishment
FW [chemistry] formula weight; fresh water; [vehicle registration] Lincoln
FWA Factories and Workshops Act; Family Welfare Association; [USA] Federal Works Agency; Fellow of the World Academy of Arts and Sciences; Free Wales Army
FWAG Farming and Wildlife Advisory Group
FWB Free Will Baptists
f.w.b. four-wheel brake; four-wheel braking
FWCC Friends' World Committee for Consultation
fwd forward
f.w.d. four-wheel drive; fresh water damage; front-wheel drive
fwdg forwarding
FWeldI Fellow of the Welding Institute
FWFM Federation of Wholesale Fish Merchants
f.w.h. flexible working hours
FWI Federation of West Indies; French West Indies
FWIW for what it's worth (in Internet chat and e-mail)
FWL Foundation of World Literacy
FWO Federation of Wholesale Organizations; Fleet Wireless Officer
FWPCA [USA] Federal Water Pollution Control Administration
FWS fighter weapons school; fleet work study
FWSG farm water supply grant
fwt [boxing] featherweight
f.w.t. fair wear and tear
FX [vehicle registration] Bournemouth; foreign exchange; Francis Xavier (Spanish Jesuit missionary); [theatre] sound effects (phonetic spelling of 'effects'); [cinema] special effects (phonetic spelling of 'effects')
fxd fixed; foxed
fxg fixing
fxle [nautical] forecastle
FY [UK postcode] Blackpool; [USA, Canada] fiscal year; [fishing port] Fowey; [vehicle registration] Liverpool
f.y.a. first-year allowance
FYC Family and Youth Concern
FYI for your information
FYM farmyard manure
FYP [economics] Five-Year Plan
FYROM Former Yugoslav Republic of Macedonia
FZ [vehicle registration] Belfast; [meteorology] freezing; Free Zone; French Zone
fz. [music] *forzando* (Italian: accentuating strongly); [music] *forzato* (Italian: accentuated strongly)
FZA [USA] Fellow of the Zoological Academy
FZGB Federation of Zoological Gardens of Great Britain and Ireland
FZS Fellow of the Zoological Society
F-Zug *Fernschnellzug* (German: long-distance express train)

G

G [international vehicle registration] Gabon; [fishing port] Galway; gauss (unit of magnetic flux density); [cinema] general exhibition (film classification in Australia and USA); German; Germany; giga- (indicates 10^9, as in **GW** = gigawatt); [computing] giga- (indicates 2^{30}, as in **GB** = gigabyte); [UK postcode] Glasgow; [biochemistry] glycine; good; [currency] gourde (used in Haiti); [slang] grand (= 1,000 (pounds, dollars, etc.)); gravity (as in **G-force**); Great; green; Group; [biochemistry] guanine; [biochemistry] guanosine; [currency] guaraní (used in Paraguay); Guernsey; Gulf; [botany] gynoecium (in floral formula); [music] note of scale; [civil aircraft marking] United Kingdom
G [physics] conductance; [physics] gravitational constant

g [physics] acceleration of free fall; [meteorology] gale; gallon; gas; [chemistry] gaseous; [physics] gluon; [mathematics] grade; gram; grav (unit of acceleration); [physics] gravitational acceleration; gravity

g [physics] degeneracy

g. garage; *gauche* (French: left); gauge; gelding; gender; general; [grammar] genitive; geographical; gilt; goal; goalkeeper; gold; good; government; grand; great; green; grey; *gros(se)* (French: large); guardian; guide; [currency] guilder; [currency] guinea; gunnery

G3 [economics] Group of Three (most powerful western industrialized nations)

G^3 [electronics] gadolinium gallium garnet

G5 [finance] Group of Five (nations stabilizing exchange rates)

G7 [economics] Group of Seven (leading industrialized nations)

G10 [finance] Group of Ten (nations lending money to IMF)

G24 [economics] Group of Twenty-Four (richest industrialized nations)

G77 [economics] Group of Seventy-Seven (developing nations)

9G [civil aircraft marking] Ghana

GA Gaelic Athletic (Club); Gamblers Anonymous; garrison artillery; General Accident (property and insurance company); general administrator; general agent; [linguistics] General American; [medicine] general anaesthesia; [medicine] general anaesthetic; General Assembly (of UN); general assignment; [insurance] general average; Geographical Association; Geologists' Association; [US postcode] Georgia; [obstetrics] gestational age; [vehicle registration] Glasgow; [netball] goal attack; government actuary; graphic arts

G/A [insurance] general average; ground-to-air

Ga [chemical element] gallium; Georgia

Ga. Gallic

g/a ground-to-air

.ga Gabon (in Internet address)

g.a. [insurance] general average

GAA [Ireland] Gaelic Athletic Association

GAAP generally accepted accounting principles

GAAR [taxation] general anti-avoidance rule

GAAS generally accepted auditing standards

GAB general arrangements to borrow (in IMF)

Gab. Gabon

GABA [biochemistry] gamma-aminobutyric acid (neurotransmitter)

Gae. Gaelic

Gael. Gaelic

GAFTA Grain and Free Trade Association

GAI General Assembly of International Sports Federations; [USA] guaranteed annual income; Guild of Architectural Ironmongers

Gal. [Bible] Galatians; Galicia; Galway

gal. gallon

gall. gallery; gallon

GALT [medicine] gut-associated lymphoid tissue

galv. galvanic; galvanize; galvanized; galvanometer

GAM guided aircraft missile

Gam. Gambia

G&AE [accounting] general and administrative expense(s)

G&O [medicine] gas and oxygen (in anaesthetic)

G&S (William Schwenck) Gilbert and (Arthur) Sullivan (British writers of comic operettas)

G&T gin and tonic

GAO [USA] General Accounting Office

GAP general assembly programme; great American public; [economics] gross agricultural product

GAPAN Guild of Air Pilots and Air Navigators

GAR Grand Army of the Republic (in American Civil War); guided aircraft rocket

gar. garage; garrison

gard. garden

GARIOA government aid and relief in occupied areas

GARP Global Atmospheric Research Programme

GASC German-American Securities Corporation

GASCO General Aviation Safety Committee

GASP Group Against Smokers' Pollution

gast. gastric
gastroent. gastroenterological; gastroenterology
GATB General Aptitude Test Battery
GATCO Guild of Air Traffic Control Officers
GATT General Agreement on Tariffs and Trade (replaced by WTO)
GAUFCC General Assembly of Unitarian and Free Christian Churches
GAV [accounting] gross annual value
GAW Global Atmosphere Watch; guaranteed annual wage
GAWF Greek Animal Welfare Fund
GAYE give as you earn
gaz. gazette; gazetteer
GB [medicine] gall bladder; gas board; [computing] gigabyte; Girls' Brigade; [vehicle registration] Glasgow; government and binding; Great Britain; [international vehicle registration] Great Britain; guide book; gunboat
Gb [computing] gigabyte; gilbert (unit of magnetomotive force)
GBA [international vehicle registration] Alderney; Governing Bodies Association
GB&I Great Britain and Ireland
GBCW Governing Body of the Church in Wales
GBDO Guild of British Dispensing Opticians
GBE (Dame or Knight) Grand Cross of the Order of the British Empire
g.b.e. gilt bevelled edge
GBF gay black female
GBG [international vehicle registration] Guernsey
GBGSA Governing Bodies of Girls' Schools Association
GBH grievous bodily harm
GBJ [international vehicle registration] Jersey
GBM gay black male; [international vehicle registration] Isle of Man
GBNE Guild of British Newspaper Editors
g.b.o. goods in bad order
g/box gearbox (in car advertisement)
GBP British pounds; [biochemistry] glutamate-binding protein; great British public
GBRE General Board of Religious Education
GBS George Bernard Shaw (Irish dramatist); [computing] Gragg–Burlisch–Stoer (method)
GBSM Graduate of Birmingham and Midland Institute School of Music
GBT Green Bank Telescope
GBTA Guild of Business Travel Agents
GBZ [international vehicle registration] Gibraltar
GC [astronomy] galactic centre; gas chromatography; gas council; [chemistry] gel chromatography; [astronomy] General Catalogue; George Cross (replacement for EGM); gliding club; Goldsmiths' College; golf club; good conduct; government chemist; Grand Chancellor; Grand Chaplain; Grand Chapter; Grand Conductor; Grand Cross; [vehicle registration] southwest London
g.c. going concern; good condition (in advertisement)
GCA Girls' Clubs of America; Global Commission on Aids; [aeronautics] ground-controlled approach; [international vehicle registration] Guatemala (Central America)
G Capt. Group Captain
GCB (Dame or Knight) Grand Cross of the Order of the Bath
GCBS General Council of British Shipping
GCC Game Conservancy Council; Gas Consumers' Council; Gulf Cooperation Council
GCD general and complete disarmament; [mathematics] greatest common divisor
GCE General Certificate of Education; [USA] General College Entrance
GCF [mathematics] greatest common factor
GCFR [nuclear technology] gas-cooled fast reactor
GCH gas central heating (in property advertisement); Guild Certificate of Hairdressing
GCHQ Government Communications Headquarters
GCI [aeronautics] ground-controlled interception
GCIE (Knight) Grand Commander of the Order of the Indian Empire
GCIU [USA] Graphic Communications International Union
GCL [aeronautics] ground-controlled

landing; Guild of Cleaners and Launderers

GCLH Grand Cross of the Legion of Honour

GCLJ (Knight) Grand Cross of the Order of St Lazarus of Jerusalem

GCM [meteorology] general circulation model; general court martial; Good Conduct Medal; [statistics] greatest common measure; [mathematics] greatest common multiple

GCMG (Dame or Knight) Grand Cross of the Order of St Michael and St George

GCO Gun Control Officer (in Royal Navy)

GCON Grand Cross of the Order of the Niger

GCR [nuclear technology] gas-cooled reactor; [computing] grey component replacement; ground-controlled radar; [computing] group code recording

GCRN General Council and Register of Naturopaths

GCRO General Council and Register of Osteopaths

GCSE General Certificate of Secondary Education (replacement for CSE and GCE O level)

GCSG (Knight) Grand Cross of the Order of St Gregory the Great

GCSI (Knight) Grand Commander of the Order of the Star of India

GCSJ (Knight) Grand Cross of the Order of St John of Jerusalem

GCStJ (Bailiff or Dame) Grand Cross of the Order of St John of Jerusalem

GCVO (Dame or Knight) Grand Cross of the Royal Victorian Order

GD [obstetrics] gestational day; [vehicle registration] Glasgow; [electronics] glow discharge; [netball] goal defence; Graduate in Divinity; Grand Duchess; Grand Duchy; Grand Duke; Gunnery Division

Gd [chemical element] gadolinium

gd good; granddaughter; ground

.gd Grenada (in Internet address)

g.d. general duties; gravimetric density

GDA Glasgow Development Agency

GDBA Guide Dogs for the Blind Association

GDC General Dental Council; General Dynamics Corporation

Gde [currency] gourde (used in Haiti)

GDI [computing] graphical device interface; [economics] gross domestic income

Gdk Gdansk

gdn garden; guardian

Gdns Gardens

GDP [economics] gross domestic product

GDPA General Dental Practitioners' Association

GDR German Democratic Republic (the former East Germany)

Gds Guards

gds goods

Gdsm. Guardsman

GDT graphic display terminal

GDU graphic display unit

GE garrison engineer; gastroenterology; general election; [USA] General Electric (Company); [international vehicle registration] Georgia; [vehicle registration] Glasgow; [fishing port] Goole; [astronomy] greatest elongation; gross energy

Ge [chemical element] germanium

.ge Georgia (in Internet address)

g.e. [bookbinding] gilt edges

GEA Garage Equipment Association

geb. *geboren* (German: born); *gebunden* (German: bound)

GEBCO general bathymetric chart of the oceans

Gebr. *Gebrüder* (German: brothers)

GEC General Electric Company

GED general educational development

Gedcom [computing] genealogical data communications

GEF Global Environment Facility

gegr. *gegründet* (German: founded)

gel. gelatin(e); gelatinous

GEM genetically engineered microorganism; [computing] graphics environment manager; ground effect machine; guidance evaluation missile; Guild of Experienced Motorists

Gem [astronomy] Gemini

GEMS Global Environmental Monitoring System (in UN)

Gen. General; [Bible] Genesis; Geneva; Genoa

gen [short form] (general) information

gen. gender; genealogy; general; generally; generator; generic; genetic; gen-

etics; genital; [grammar] genitive; genuine; [biology] genus
gen. av. [insurance] general average
gend. *gendarme* (French: police officer)
geneal. genealogy
genit. genital; [grammar] genitive
Genl General
genn. *gennaio* (Italian: January)
gent [short form] gentleman
GEO geostationary earth orbit; geosynchronous earth orbit
Geo. George
geod. geodesy; geodetic
geog. geographer; geographic(al); geography
geol. geologic(al); geologist; geology
geom. geometer; geometric(al); geometry
GEON gyro-erected optical navigation
geophys. geophysical; geophysics
geopol. geopolitical; geopolitics
GEOREF World Geographic Reference System
GEOS geodetic orbiting satellite
GER gross energy requirement
Ger. German; Germany
ger. [grammar] gerund; [grammar] gerundive
Gerbil Great Education Reform Bill
GES Global Epidemiological Surveillance and Health Situation (of WHO)
Ges. [commerce] *Gesellschaft* (German: company, society)
GESP generalized extrasensory perception
GEST Grants for Education, Support and Training
gest. *gestorben* (German: deceased)
Gestapo *Geheime Staatspolizei* (German: secret state police) (in Nazi Germany)
GET [medicine] gastric emptying time
GETT [USA] Grants Equal To Tax
GeV gigaelectronvolt
GEW gram-equivalent weight
gez. *gezeichnet* (German: signed)
GF General Foods Limited; girlfriend; glass fibre; government form; gradient freezing; growth factor; Guggenheim Foundation; [currency] Guinea franc; [vehicle registration] southwest London
g/f ground floor (in property advertisement)
g.f.a. [commerce] good fair average; [commerce] good freight agent
GFCH gas-fired central heating (in property advertisement)
GFCM General Fisheries Council for the Mediterranean
GFD geophysical fluid dynamics
GFG *Good Food Guide*
GFH George Frederick Handel (German composer)
GFOF [stock exchange] Geared Futures and Options Fund
GFR German Federal Republic; [medicine] glomerular filtration rate
GFS Girls' Friendly Society
GFT Glasgow Film Theatre
GFTU [USA] General Federation of Trade Unions
GFWC General Federation of Women's Clubs
GG [medicine] gamma globulin; Girl Guides; [vehicle registration] Glasgow; Governor-General; great gross (= 144 dozen); Grenadier Guards
g.g. gas generator
GGA Girl Guides Association
GGC generalized genetic code
ggd great-granddaughter
gge garage (in property advertisement)
GGF Glass and Glazing Federation
GGG [electronics] gadolinium gallium garnet
g.gr. great gross (= 144 dozen)
ggs great-grandson
GGSM Graduate of the Guildhall School of Music (and Drama)
GH general hospital; [international vehicle registration] Ghana; [fishing port] Grangemouth; [military] Green Howards; Greenwich Hospital; [biochemistry] growth hormone; [vehicle registration] southwest London
.gh Ghana (in Internet address)
GHA [astronomy] Greenwich hour angle
GHB gamma hydroxybutyrate (bodybuilding drug)
GHCIMA Graduate of the Hotel Catering and Institutional Management Association
g.h.e. ground handling equipment
GHI Good Housekeeping Institute
GHMS Graduate in Homoeopathic Medicine and Surgery

GHOST global horizontal sounding technique (for collection of atmospheric data)
GHQ [military] General Headquarters
GHRH [biochemistry] growth-hormone-releasing hormone
GHS girls' high school
GHz gigahertz
GI galvanized iron; gastrointestinal; [USA] general issue; generic issue; Gideons International; (Royal) Glasgow Institute (of the Fine Arts); [USA] government issue; Government of India; [biochemistry] growth inhibitor; US soldier (from government (or general) issue)
Gi gilbert (unit of magnetomotive force)
gi. gill (unit of liquid measure)
.gi Gibraltar (in Internet address)
g.i. galvanized iron
GIA Garuda Indonesian Airways
GIB Gulf International Bank
Gib. Gibraltar
GIBiol Graduate of the Institute of Biology
GIC *Guilde internationale des coopératrices* (French: International Cooperative Women's Guild)
GIEE Graduate of the Institute of Electrical Engineers
GIF [computing] graphics interchange format; [biochemistry] growth-hormone inhibiting factor
GIFT [medicine] gamete intrafallopian transfer (infertility treatment)
gig [short form, computing] gigabyte
GIGO [computing] garbage in, garbage out
GIMechE Graduate of the Institution of Mechanical Engineers
GINO [computing] graphical input output
GInstAEA Graduate of the Institute of Automotive Engineer Assessors
GINucE Graduate of the Institution of Nuclear Engineers
gio. *giovedì* (Italian: Thursday)
GIP glazed imitation parchment (paper)
GIPME Global Investigation of Pollution in the Marine Environment
GIS [computing] geographical information system; [computing] geological information system; Global Information Solutions
GISS Goddard Institute for Space Studies
GITB Gas Industry Training Board
giu. *giugno* (Italian: June)
GIUK Greenland, Iceland, United Kingdom
GJ [vehicle registration] southwest London
GJD [Freemasonry] Grand Junior Deacon
GK goalkeeper; [fishing port] Greenock; [vehicle registration] southwest London
Gk Greek
GKA Garter King of Arms
GKC G(ilbert) K(eith) Chesterton (British writer)
GKN Guest, Keen and Nettlefold (engineering company)
GKS [computing] graphical kernel system
GL [shipping] *Germanischer Lloyd* (German shipping classification society); [UK postcode] Gloucester; good-looking (in personal advertisement); [printing] gothic letter; government laboratory; [Freemasonry] Grand Lodge; Grand Luxe (car); ground level; gun licence; [vehicle registration] Truro
Gl. Gloria (doxology)
gl gill (unit of liquid measure)
g/l grams per litre
gl. glass; gloss
.gl Greenland (in Internet address)
4GL [computing] fourth-generation language
GLAB Greater London Arts Board
glab. [botany] glabrous
Glam. Glamorgan
glam [informal] greying, leisured, affluent, married
gland. glandular
Glas. Glasgow; Glaswegian
glau. [botany] glaucous
glauc. [medicine] glaucoma
glaz. glazed; glazing
GLB gay, lesbian, bisexual; Girls' Life Brigade
GLC [chemistry] gas–liquid chromatography; Greater London Council (former local authority); ground-level concentration (of radioactive material); Guild of Lettering Craftsmen
GLCM Graduate of the London College of Music; ground-launched cruise missile
gld. [currency] guilder
GLDP Greater London Development Plan
GLM graduated length method (in skiing)

GLOBECOM [US air force] Global Communications System
GLOMEX Global Oceanographic and Meteorological Experiment
GLORIA Geological Long Range ASDIC
Glos Gloucestershire
gloss. glossary
Gloucestr. *Gloucestriensis* (Latin: (Bishop) of Gloucester)
GLS [Freemasonry] Grand Lodge of Scotland
GLT greetings letter telegram
glt [bookbinding] gilt
GM [physics] Geiger–Müller (as in **GM counter**); general manager; general merchandise; [computing] General Midi; general mortgage; General Motors Corporation; genetically modified; Geological Museum; geometric mean; George Medal; gold medal; gold medallist; Grand Marshal; Grand Master; [education] grant maintained; guided missile; [vehicle registration] Reading
gm gram
.gm Gambia (in Internet address)
gm² grams per square metre (unit of weight of paper)
GMAG Genetic Manipulation Advisory Group
G-man [USA] government man (FBI agent)
GMB General, Municipal, Boilermakers and Allied Trades Union; Grand Master Bowman (in archery); Grand Master of the Order of the Bath
g.m.b. good merchantable brand
GMBE Grand Master of the Order of the British Empire
GmbH [commerce] *Gesellschaft mit beschränkter Haftung* (German: limited company, Ltd)
GMC general management committee; General Medical Council; [astronomy] giant molecular cloud; Guild of Memorial Craftsmen
Gmc Germanic
GMF Glass Manufacturers' Federation
GMIE Grand Master of the Order of the Indian Empire
GMKP Grand Master of the Knights of St Patrick
GMMG Grand Master of the Order of St Michael and St George
GMO genetically modified organism
GMP [USA] Glass, Molders, Pottery, Plastics and Allied Workers International Union; Grand Master of the Order of St Patrick; [economics] gross material product; Gurkha Military Police
g.m.q. good merchantable quality
GMR ground-mapping radar
GMRT Giant Metre-wave Radio Telescope
GMS [education] grant-maintained status
GMSC General Medical Services Committee
GMSI Grand Master of the Order of the Star of India
GMST Grant-Maintained Schools Trust; [astronomy] Greenwich Mean Sidereal Time
GMT Greenwich Mean Time
GMTA great minds think alike (in Internet chat)
GMTV Good Morning Television
GMV [microbiology] golden mosaic virus
GMW gram-molecular weight
GN [USA] Graduate Nurse; [fishing port] Granton; [vehicle registration] southwest London
gn grandnephew; grandniece
gn. [currency] guinea
.gn Guinea (in Internet address)
GNA Ghana News Agency; Guinea News Agency; Guyana News Agency
GNAS Grand National Archery Society
GNC General Nursing Council (replaced by UKCC)
gnd ground
GNMA [USA] Government National Mortgage Association
GNP [economics] gross national product
GNR *Guarda Nacional Republicana* (Portuguese: National Republican Guard)
Gnr Gunner
GnRH [biochemistry] gonadotrophin-releasing hormone
gns guineas
GNTC Girls' Nautical Training Corps
GNVQ General National Vocational Qualification
GO gas operated; General Office; General Officer; [military] general order; [music] great organ; Group Officer; [vehicle registration] southwest London
g.o.a. gone on arrival

g.o.b. good ordinary brand
GOC General Officer Commanding; General Optical Council; Greek Orthodox Church
GOC-in-C General Officer Commanding-in-Chief
GOCO government-owned, contractor-operated
GOE General Ordination Examination
GOES [USA] Geostationary Operational Environmental Satellite
GOM Grand Old Man
GONG [astronomy] Global Oscillations Network Group
GOP *Girls' Own Paper*; [USA] Grand Old Party (i.e. the Republican Party)
Gopa Government Oil and Pipeline Agency
GORD [medicine] gastro-oesophageal reflux disease
Gos. *Gosudarstvo* (Russian: state) (in former USSR)
GOSIP [computing] government open systems interconnection profile
Gosplan *Gosudarstvennaya Planovaya Comissiya* (Russian: State Planning Commission) (in former USSR)
Gosud. *Gosudarstvo* (Russian: state) (in former USSR)
Goth. Gothic
gou. [currency] gourde (used in Haiti)
Gov. Government; Governor
gov. government; governor
.gov government (in Internet address)
Gov-Gen Governor-General
Govt Government
govt government
.gov.uk UK government (in Internet address)
GOX gaseous oxygen
GP Gallup Poll; gas-permeable (contact lenses); [medicine] general paralysis; [music] general pause; general practitioner; general purpose; general-purpose computer; *Gloria Patri* (Latin: Glory to the Father); government property; graduated pension; Graduate in Pharmacy; *grande passion* (French: great passion); grand passion; Grand Prix; gross profit; [vehicle registration] south-west London
gp group
g.p. [printing] galley proofs; [mathematics] geometrical progression; [printing] great primer
GPA General Practitioners' Association; [US education] grade point average
GPALS Global Protection Against Limited Strikes (reduced form of SDI)
GPC general purposes committee
g.p.c. good physical condition (in advertisement)
Gp Capt Group Captain
gpcd gallons per caput per day
Gp Comdr Group Commander
gpd gallons per day
GPDST Girls' Public Day School Trust
GPh Graduate in Pharmacy
gph gallons per hour
GPHI Guild of Public Health Inspectors
GPI [medicine] general paralysis of the insane
GPIB [computing] general-purpose interface bus
GPKT Grand Priory of the Knights of the Temple
GPM [USA] graduated payment mortgage; [Freemasonry] Grand Past Master
gpm gallons per minute
GPMU Graphical, Paper and Media Union (became part of NATSOPA)
GPO General Post Office; [USA] Government Printing Office
GPR *genio populi Romani* (Latin: to the genius of the Roman people); ground-penetrating radar
GPS Global Positioning System; Graduated Pension Scheme; [Australia] Great Public Schools
gps gallons per second
GPSS General Purpose System Simulator
GPT Guild of Professional Toastmasters
GPU General Postal Union (former name of UPU); [USA] General Public Utilities Corporation; *Gosudarstvennoye Politicheskoye Upravlenie* (Russian: State Political Administration) (former Soviet secret police)
GQ [military] general quarters
.gq Equatorial Guinea (in Internet address)
GQG *Grand Quartier Général* (French: General Headquarters)
GR gamma ray; general reconnaissance; [physics] general relativity; general reserve; *Georgius Rex* (Latin: King

George); [fishing port] Gloucester; grand recorder; [international vehicle registration] Greece; ground rent; *Gulielmus Rex* (Latin: King William); Gurkha Rifles; [vehicle registration] Newcastle upon Tyne

Gr Gunner

Gr. Great; Greater; Grecian; Greece; Greek; Grove (in road name)

gr. grade; grain (unit of weight); gram; grammar; grand; great; greater; grey; gross; ground; group

.gr Greece (in Internet address)

GRA Game Research Association; Greyhound Racing Association

GRACE group routing and charging equipment

grad. gradient; grading; gradual; graduate; graduated

GradIAE Graduate of the Institution of Automobile Engineers

GradInstBE Graduate of the Institution of British Engineers

GradInstP Graduate of the Institute of Physics

GradInstR Graduate of the Institute of Refrigeration

GradSE Graduate of the Society of Engineers

gram. grammar; grammarian; grammatical

GRAS [USA] generally regarded as safe

GRB [astronomy] gamma-ray burst; Gas Research Board

GRBI Gardeners' Royal Benevolent Institution

Gr. Br. Great Britain

Gr. Brit. Great Britain

GRBS Gardeners' Royal Benevolent Society

GRC General Research Corporation

Gr. Capt Group Captain

GRCM Graduate of the Royal College of Music

GRDF Gulf Rapid Deployment Force

GRE [USA] Graduate Record Examination; grant-related expenditure; Guardian Royal Exchange Assurance plc

GRF [biochemistry] growth-hormone releasing factor

gr.f. [horseracing] grey filly

GRI *Georgius Rex Imperator* (Latin: George King and Emperor); [New Zealand] guaranteed retirement income

GRID gay-related immunodeficiency; Global Resource Information Database

Gr-L Graeco-Latin

grm gram

GRN goods received note

Grn Green (in road name)

grn green

GRO Gamma Ray Observatory; General Register Office; Greenwich Royal Observatory

Gro. Grove

gro. gross

GROBDM General Register Office for Births, Deaths and Marriages

gro. t. gross ton; gross tonnage

GRP glass(fibre)-reinforced plastic (or polyester)

grp group

GRS [astronomy] Great Red Spot (on Jupiter)

grs grains; gross

GRSC Graduate of the Royal Society of Chemistry

GRSE Guild of Radio Service Engineers

GRSM Graduate of the Royal Schools of Music

gr. t. gross ton

g.r.t. gross registered tonnage

GRU *Glavnoye Razvedyvatelnoye Upravleniye* (Russian: Central Intelligence Office) (in former USSR)

Gru [astronomy] Grus

gr. wt gross weight

g.r.y. [finance] gross redemption yield

GS General Schedule (in US civil service); general secretary; general service; [military] General Staff; geographical survey; geological survey; [netball] goal shooter; gold standard; grammar school; [aeronautics] ground speed; [vehicle registration] Luton

Gs gauss (unit of magnetic flux density); [currency] guaraní (used in Paraguay)

gs grandson; guineas

GSA [USA] General Services Administration; Girl Scouts of America; Girls' Schools Association; Glasgow School of Art

GS&WR [Ireland] Great Southern and Western Railway

GSB Government Savings Bank

GSC [chemistry] gas–solid chromatography; General Service Corps; [USA] General Staff Corps
GSD general supply depot; [astronomy] Greenwich sidereal gate
GSE ground service equipment; ground support equipment
GSEE *Geniki Synomospondia Ergaton Hellados* (Greek: Greek General Confederation of Labour)
GSGB Geological Survey of Great Britain; Golf Society of Great Britain
GSI [medicine] genuine stress incontinence
GSL Geological Society of London; group Scout leader; [USA] guaranteed student loan
GSM Garrison Sergeant-Major; general sales manager; General Service Medal; global system for mobile communications; (Member of the) Guildhall School of Music (and Drama)
gsm grams per square metre (unit of weight of paper)
g.s.m. [commerce] good sound merchantable (quality)
GSMD (Member of the) Guildhall School of Music and Drama
GSO General Staff Officer
GSOH good sense of humour (in personal advertisement)
GSP glass(fibre)-strengthened polyester; Good Service Pension; [economics] gross social product
G-spot Gräfenburg spot (erogenous zone)
GSR galvanic skin reflex; galvanic skin response
GSS geostationary satellite; global surveillance system; Government Statistical Service
GST [Canada, New Zealand] goods and services tax; [astronomy] Greenwich Sidereal Time
g. st. [knitting] garter stitch
GSVQ General Scottish Vocational Qualification
GSW gunshot wound
GT gas turbine; [physics] gauge theory; Good Templar; [Freemasonry] Grand Tiler; *Gran Turismo* (Italian: Grand Touring) (sports car); greetings telegram; [vehicle registration] southwest London
gt [bookbinding] gilt; great
gt. [medicine] *gutta* (Latin: a drop)
.gt Guatemala (in Internet address)
g.t. gas tight; [bookbinding] gilt top; gross tonnage
GTA gas–tungsten arc
Gt Br. Great Britain
Gt Brit. Great Britain
GTC [Scotland] General Teaching Council; Girls' Training Corps; [commerce] good till cancelled (or countermanded); Government Training Centre
GTCL Graduate of Trinity College of Music, London
gtd guaranteed
g.t.e. [bookbinding] gilt top edge
gtee guarantee
GTH [biochemistry] gonadotrophic hormone
GTI GT Injection (sports car)
gtm good this month
GTO *Gran Turismo Omologato* (Italian: homologated GT) (sports car)
GTR general theory of relativity
gtr greater
GTS gas turbine ship; [USA] General Theological Seminary
GTT [medicine] glucose tolerance test
gtt. [medicine] *guttae* (Latin: drops); [medicine] *guttatim* (Latin: drop by drop)
g.t.w. good this week
GU [medicine] gastric ulcer; [medicine] genitourinary; [fishing port] Guernsey; [UK postcode] Guildford; [vehicle registration] southeast London
Gu. Guinea
gu. [currency] guinea; [heraldry] gules (= red)
guar. guarantee; guaranteed
Guat. Guatemala
GUI Golfing Union of Ireland; [computing] graphical user interface
gui. guitar
GUIDO [US astronautics] Guidance Officer
guil. [currency] guilder
Guin. Guinea
Gulag *Glavnoye Upravleniye Lagerei* (Russian: Central Administration for Camps) (former Soviet labour camp system)
GUM [medicine] genitourinary medicine; *Gosudarstvenni Universalni Magazin* (Russian: Universal State Store)

gun. gunnery; gunpowder
GUR [medicine] glucose utilization rate
GUS Great Universal Stores
GUT [physics] grand unified theory
guttat. [medicine] *guttatim* (Latin: drop by drop)
guv [short form] governor
g.u.v. *gerecht und vollkommen* (German: correct and complete)
GUY [international vehicle registration] Guyana
GV *grande vitesse* (French: high speed (train)); [vehicle registration] Ipswich
g.v. gravimetric volume; gross valuation
GVH [medicine] graft versus host
GVHD [medicine] graft-versus-host disease
gvt government
GVW gross vehicle weight
GW George Washington (US president); gigawatt; [fishing port] Glasgow; gross weight; guided weapon(s); [vehicle registration] southeast London
.gw Guinea-Bissau (in Internet address)
GW-Basic [computing] gee whizz beginners' all-purpose symbolic instruction code
GWF gay white female
GWH gigawatt-hour
GWM gay white male
GWP Government White Paper; [economics] gross world product
GWR Great Western Railway
Gwyn. Gwynedd
GX [vehicle registration] southeast London
GY [fishing port] Grimsby; [UK postcode] Guernsey; [vehicle registration] southeast London
Gy gray (unit of radiation dose)
.gy Guyana (in Internet address)
gym [short form] gymnasium; [short form] gymnastics
gyn. gynaecological; gynaecology
gynaecol. gynaecological; gynaecology
GZ [vehicle registration] Belfast; ground zero
G-Z [astronomy] Giacobini–Zinner (comet)

H

H [advertising] half page; harbour; hard (pencil lead); hardness; [card games] hearts; [immunology] heavy; height; henry (unit of electric inductance); herbaceous; [slang] heroin; [medicine] histamine receptor; [biochemistry] histidine; Holy; [music] horn; hospital; hour; [fishing port] Hull; [international vehicle registration] Hungary; hydrant; [chemical element] hydrogen
H [physics, medicine] dose equivalent; [physics] Hamiltonian; [physics, photography] light exposure; [physics] magnetic field strength
h [meteorology] hail; hecto- (indicates 100, as in **hg** = hectogram); hour
h [physics] heat transfer coefficient; height; [physics] Planck constant
h. hand; harbour; hard; hardness; heat; height; high; hip; [sports] hit; horizontal; [music] horn; horse; hot; hour; house; hundred; husband
H4 [civil aircraft marking] Solomon Islands
2H double hard (pencil lead)
3H treble hard (pencil lead)
5H [civil aircraft marking] Tanzania
9H [civil aircraft marking] Malta
HA [vehicle registration] Dudley; [medicine] haemagglutination; [horticulture] hardy annual; [UK postcode] Harrow; Hautes-Alpes (French department); health authority; heavy artillery; high altitude; Highway(s) Act; [biochemistry] histamine; Historical Association; Hockey Association; [astronomy] hour angle; [geology] humic acid; [civil aircraft marking] Hungary; Hydraulic Association of Great Britain
Ha [chemical element] hahnium
Ha. Haiti; Haitian; Hawaii; Hawaiian
ha hectare
h.a. heir apparent; high angle (in gunnery); *hoc anno* (Latin: in this year)
HAA heavy anti-aircraft; [immunology] hepatitis-associated antigen

HA&M *Hymns Ancient and Modern*
HAB high-altitude bombing
Hab. [Bible] Habakkuk
hab. habitat; habitation
hab. corp. [law] habeas corpus (type of writ)
habt *habeat* (Latin: let him have)
HAC high-alumina cement; Honourable Artillery Company
HACSG Hyperactive Children's Support Group
h.a.d. hereinafter described
haem. haemoglobin; haemorrhage
HAF Hellenic Air Force
Hag. [Bible] Haggai
hagiol. hagiology
HAI [medicine] haemagglutination inhibition; Health Action International; [medicine] hospital-acquired infection
HAIL Hague Academy of International Law
Hak. Soc. Hakluyt Society
Hal [computing] hard-array logic
hal. halogen
Hal. Orch. Hallé Orchestra
Ham. Hamburg
Han. Hanover; Hanoverian
H&C hot and cold (water)
H&E *Health and Efficiency*; heredity and environment
h&f heated and filtered (swimming pool)
h&j [printing] hyphenation and justification
h&t hardened and tempered; hospitalization and treatment
H&W Harland and Wolff (shipbuilding company); Hereford and Worcester
Hants Hampshire (from Old English name of county)
HAO hydrogenated anthracene oil
HAP hazardous air pollutant
HAPA Handicapped Adventure Playground Association
h. app. heir apparent
HAPPA Horses and Ponies Protection Association
HaPV [microbiology] hamster polyomavirus
har. harbour
HARCVS Honorary Associate of the Royal College of Veterinary Surgeons
HARM high-speed anti-radiation missile
harm. harmonic; harmony
harp. harpoon; harpsichord
HART [New Zealand] Halt All Racist Tours (sports organization)
Harv. [USA] Harvard University
HAS Headmasters' Association of Scotland; Health Advisory Service; Helicopter Air Service; Hospital Advisory Service
HASAWA Health and Safety at Work Act
HASTE Helicopter Ambulance Service to Emergencies
HAT housing action trust; housing association trust
haust. [medicine] *haustus* (Latin: draught)
HAV [medicine] hepatitis A virus
HAWT horizontal-axis wind turbine
haz. hazard; hazardous
HAZOP [computing] hazard and operability study
HB [vehicle registration] Cardiff; hard black (pencil lead softer than H); [horticulture] hardy biennial; His Beatitude; House of Bishops; [civil aircraft marking] Switzerland and Liechtenstein
Hb [biochemistry] haemoglobin
h.b. [sports] halfback; handbook; hardback (of books); homing beacon; human being
HbA [biochemistry] adult haemoglobin
HBAB [medicine] hepatitis B antibody
h'back hatchback (in car advertisement)
HBAg [medicine] hepatitis B antigen
HBC [electrical engineering] high breaking capacity; Historic Buildings Council; Hudson's Bay Company
HBCU [USA] Historically Black Colleges and Universities
HBD had (or has) been drinking
hbd hardboard; headboard
h.b.d. hereinbefore described
HBF [medicine] hepatic blood flow; House-Builders' Federation
HbF [biochemistry] fetal haemoglobin
Hbf. *Hauptbahnhof* (German: central station)
HBIG [medicine] hepatitis B immunoglobulin
HBJ Harcourt Brace Jovanovich
hbk hardback (of books)
HBLV [medicine] human B-lymphotropic virus
HBM Her/His Britannic Majesty('s)

HBMC Historic Buildings and Monuments Commission for England
HBO hyperbaric oxygen
h/board hardboard; headboard
H-bomb hydrogen bomb
HBP [medicine] high blood pressure
HBPF High Blood Pressure Foundation
hbr harbour
HBS Harvard Business School
HbS [biochemistry] sickle-cell haemoglobin
HBT [electronics] heterojunction bipolar transistor
Hbt Hobart
HBV [medicine] hepatitis B virus
HBWTA Home Brewing and Winemaking Trade Association
hby hereby
HC [vehicle registration] Brighton; [civil aircraft marking] Ecuador; Hague Convention; Hairdressing Council; hard copy; Headmasters' Conference; Headteachers' Conference; health certificate; Heralds' College; High Church; High Commission; High Commissioner; High Court; higher certificate; highly commended; [computing] high-speed CMOS; *Highway Code*; hockey club; Holy Communion; home counties; *hors concours* (French: outside the competition); House of Clergy; House of Commons; house of correction; housing centre; housing corporation
H/C [insurance] held covered; hot and cold (water)
h.c. habitual criminal; hand control; heating cabinet; high capacity; *honoris causa* (Latin: for the sake of honour, honorary); hot and cold (water)
HCA Hospital Caterers' Association
HCAAS Homeless Children's Aid and Adoption Society
hcap handicap
HCB House of Commons Bill
HCBA Hotel and Catering Benevolent Association
HCC Housing Consultative Council for England
h.c.c. hydraulic cement concrete
h.c.d. high current density
h.c.e. human-caused error
HCEC Hospital Committee of the European Community
HCF high-calorific fuel; high carbohydrate and fibre; [mathematics] highest common factor; Honorary Chaplain to the Forces
h.c.f. hundred cubic feet
HCFC hydrochlorofluorocarbon
HCG [biochemistry] human chorionic gonadotrophin
HCH Herbert Clark Hoover (US president); hexachlorocyclohexane (insecticide)
HCI Hotel and Catering Institute; human–computer interaction (or interface)
HCIL Hague Conference on International Law
HCIMA Hotel Catering and Institutional Management Association
HCITB Hotel and Catering Industry Training Board
HCJ High Court of Justice; Holy Child Jesus
h.c.l. high cost of living
HCM Her Catholic Majesty; High Court Master; His Catholic Majesty
HCO Harvard College Observatory; higher clerical officer
HCOPIL Hague Conference on Private International Law
HCP House of Commons Paper
hcp handicap
HCPT Historic Churches Preservation Trust
hcptr helicopter
HCR High Chief Ranger; [USA] highway contract route
HCS Home Civil Service
h.c.s. high-carbon steel
HCSA Hospital Consultants and Specialists Association
HCT [computing] high-speed CMOS with TTL inputs
HCVC Historic Commercial Vehicle Club
HCVD [medicine] hypertensive cardiovascular disease
h.c.w. hot and cold water
HD heavy duty; [medicine] herniated disc; high density; high dose (of radiation); (51st) Highland Division; Hilda Doolittle (US poet); [medicine] Hodgkin's disease; home defence; honourable discharge; Hoover Dam; [UK postcode] Huddersfield; [vehicle registration] Huddersfield; [chemistry] hydrogen–deuterium

H/D [shipping] Havre–Dunkirk
hd hand; head
h.d. heavy duty; high density; [medicine] *hora decubitus* (Latin: at bedtime) (in prescriptions)
HDA [Australia] Hawkesbury Diploma in Agriculture; high-duty alloy; Hospital Doctors' Association
HDATZ high-density air traffic zone
hdbk handbook; hardback (of books)
HDC [medicine] high-dose chemotherapy; [law] holder in due course
HDCD high-density CD-ROM
HDCR Higher Diploma of the College of Radiographers
HDD [computing] hard disk drive; [aeronautics, computing] head-down display; heavy-duty diesel; Higher Dental Diploma
hdg heading
HDipEd Higher Diploma in Education
HDK husbands don't know
hdkf handkerchief
HDL [computing] hardware description language; [biochemistry] high-density lipoprotein
hdl. handle
HDLC [biochemistry] high-density lipoprotein cholesterol; [computing] high-level data link control
hdle handle; [horseracing] hurdle
hdlg handling
hdlr handler
HDM high-duty metal
HDN [medicine] haemolytic disease of the newborn
hdn harden
HDP heavy-duty petrol; [chemistry] high-density polyeth(yl)ene
HDPE [chemistry] high-density polyeth(yl)ene
hdqrs headquarters
HDR high dose rate (of radiation); hot dry rock
HDRA Henry Doubleday Research Association
HDTV high-definition television
HDU haemodialysis unit
HDV heavy-duty vehicle; [medicine] hepatitis delta virus
hdw. [computing] hardware
hdwd hardwood; headword
HE [medicine] hepatic encephalopathy; Her Excellency; high energy; higher education; high explosive; His Eminence; His Excellency; home establishment; horizontal equivalent; hydraulic engineer; [vehicle registration] Sheffield
He [chemical element] helium
He. Hebrew
h.e. heat engine; *hic est* (Latin: this is); hub end
HEA Health Education Authority; Horticultural Education Association
HEAO High Energy Astronomy Observatory; High Energy Astrophysical Observatory
Heb. Hebraic; Hebrew; [Bible] Hebrews
Hebr. Hebrew; [Bible] Hebrews; Hebridean; Hebrides
HEC (*école des*) *hautes études commerciales* (French: (college of) higher commercial studies); Health Education Council; Higher Education Corporation; [chemistry] hydroxyethyl cellulose
HECTOR [nuclear technology] heated experimental carbon thermal oscillator reactor
HEDCOM [US air force] headquarters command
HEF high-energy fuel
HEFA Human Embryo and Fertilization Authority
HEFC Higher Education Funding Council
HEH Her/His Exalted Highness
h.e.i. high-explosive incendiary
HEIC Honourable East India Company
HEICS Honourable East India Company's Service
heir app. heir apparent
heir pres. heir presumptive
HEL high-energy laser
hel. helicopter
heli. helicopter
Hellen. Hellenic; Hellenism; Hellenistic
HELLP [medicine] haemolysis, elevated liver enzymes, low platelet count (as in **HELLP syndrome**)
helo [short form] helicopter; [short form] heliport
HELP helicopter electronic landing path; Help Establish Lasting Peace
HEMM heavy earth-moving machinery
HEMS helicopter-based emergency medical services

HEMT [electronics] high-electron-mobility transistor
HEO [astronautics] high earth orbit; higher executive officer
HEP [statistics] human error probability; hydroelectric power
HEPC [USA] hydroelectric power commission
HEPCAT helicopter pilot control and training
Her [astronomy] Hercules
Her. Hereford(shire)
her. heraldic; heraldry; [law] *heres* (Latin: heir)
HERA high-explosive rocket-assisted
HERALD [nuclear technology] Highly Enriched Reactor, Aldermaston
herb. herbaceous; herbalist; herbarium
hered. hereditary; heredity
HERI Higher Education Research Institute
herm. hermetic; hermetically
Herod. Herodotus (ancient Greek historian)
herp. herpetologist; herpetology
herpet. herpetologist; herpetology
herpetol. herpetologist; herpetology
Herts Hertfordshire
HERU Higher Education Research Unit
HET heavy-equipment transporter
heterocl. heteroclite
heterog. heterogeneous
HEU highly enriched uranium
heur. heuristic
HEW [USA] Department of Health, Education and Welfare (replaced by HHS)
hex [computing] hexadecimal (notation)
hex. hexachord; hexagon; hexagonal
hexa. hexamethylene tetramine (synthetic rubber)
hexag. hexagonal
HF hard firm (pencil lead); [radio] high frequency; Holy Father; home fleet; home forces; [vehicle registration] Liverpool
H/F [commerce] *Hlutafjelagid* (Icelandic: limited company, Ltd)
Hf [chemical element] hafnium
hf half
h.f. hold fire; [military] horse and foot
Hfa Haifa (Israel)
HFARA Honorary Foreign Associate of the Royal Academy
hf bd [bookbinding] half bound
HFC high-frequency current; [chemistry] hydrofluorocarbon
hf cf [bookbinding] half calf
hf cl. [bookbinding] half cloth
HFDF high-frequency direction-finder
HFEA Human Fertility and Embryology Authority
h.f.m. hold for money
hf mor. [bookbinding] half morocco
HFO heavy fuel oil; high-frequency oscillator
HFR [nuclear technology] high-flux reactor
hfr heifer
HFRA Honorary Foreign Member of the Royal Academy
HFRO Hill Farming Research Organization
HFS heated front seats (in car advertisement)
Hft *Heft* (German: part (of book))
HG [UK postcode] Harrogate; Haute-Garonne (French department); Her Grace; High German; high grade; His Grace; Holy Ghost; Home Guard; Horse Guards; [vehicle registration] Preston
Hg [chemical element] mercury (from Latin *hydrargyrum*)
hg hectogram
hgb. haemoglobin
HGC [computing] Hercules graphics card
HGCA Home Grown Cereals Authority
hgd hogshead
HGDH Her/His Grand Ducal Highness
HGG [biochemistry] human gamma-globulin; [medicine] hypogammaglobulinaemia
HGH [biochemistry] human growth hormone
HGHSC Home Grown Herbage Seeds Committee
HGMM Hereditary Grand Master Mason
hgr hangar; hanger
hgt height
HGTAC Home Grown Timber Advisory Committee
HGTMC Home Grown Timber Marketing Corporation
HGV heavy goods vehicle (replaced by LGV)
HGW heat-generating water; H(erbert) G(eorge) Wells (British writer)
hgwy highway
HH [vehicle registration] Carlisle; double hard (pencil lead); [civil aircraft marking]

Haiti; [fishing port] Harwich; [physics, chemistry] heavy hydrogen; Her Highness; Her Honour; (Member of the) Hesketh Hubbard Art Society; His Highness; His Holiness; His Honour

hh hands (unit of height of horses)

HHA [horticulture] half-hardy annual; Historic Houses Association

HHB [horticulture] half-hardy biennial

HHD [USA] Doctor of Humanities (from Latin *Humanitatum Doctor*); [medicine] hypertensive heart disease

hhd hogshead

HHDWS heavy handy deadweight scrap

HHFA [USA] Housing and Home Finance Agency

HHH treble hard (pencil lead)

HHI Highland Home Industries

hhld household

HHNK [medicine] hyperglycaemic hyperosmolar nonketoacidotic (diabetic coma)

H-Hour Hour Hour (i.e. specified time, esp. of commencement of operation)

HHP [horticulture] half-hardy perennial

HHS [USA] Department of Health and Human Services (replacement for HEW)

HHV [medicine] human herpes virus

HHW household hazardous waste

HI [civil aircraft marking] Dominican Republic; [US postcode] Hawaii; Hawaiian Islands; hearing impaired; [surveying] height of instrument; *hic iacet* (Latin: here lies) (on tombstone); high intensity

Hi. Hindi

HIA Housing Improvement Association

h.i.a. hold in abeyance

hi. ac. high accuracy

HIAS [USA] Hebrew Immigrant Aid Society

HIB Herring Industry Board

Hib [medicine] *Haemophilus influenzae* type B (as in **Hib vaccine**)

Hib. Hibernia; Hibernian

HICAT high-altitude clear air turbulence

Hi. Com. High Command; High Commission; High Commissioner

HIDB Highlands and Islands Development Board

HIE Highlands and Islands Enterprise

hier. hieroglyphics

hi-fi [short form] high fidelity (equipment)

HIH Her/His Imperial Highness

HIL [chemistry] hazardous immiscible liquid

HILAC [nuclear technology] heavy-ion linear accelerator

HILAT high-latitude (satellite)

HIM Her/His Imperial Majesty

Hind. Hindi; Hindu; Hindustan; Hindustani

HIP [USA] health-insurance plan; [accounting] human information processing

HIPAR high-power acquisition radar

hipot high potential

Hipp. Hippocrates (ancient Greek physician)

HIPPI [computing] high-performance parallel processor interface

HIPS high-impact polystyrene (synthetic plastic)

hi-rel high reliability

hi-res [physics] high resolution

HIS *hic iacet sepultus* (or *sepulta*) (Latin: here lies buried) (on tombstone)

hist. histology; historian; historic(al); history

histn historian

histol. histological; histologist; histology

hi-tech [short form] high technology

Hitt. Hittite

HIUS Hispanic Institute of the United States

HIV [medicine] human immunodeficiency virus (formerly LAV)

HIV-P [medicine] HIV-positive

HJ [vehicle registration] Chelmsford; *hic jacet* (Latin: here lies) (on tombstone); high jump; Hilal-e-Jurat (Pakistani honour); *Hitler Jugend* (German: Hitler Youth)

HJBT [electronics] heterojunction bipolar transistor

HJS *hic jacet sepultus* (or *sepulta*) (Latin: here lies buried) (on tombstone)

HJSC Hospital Junior Staff Council

HK [vehicle registration] Chelmsford; [civil aircraft marking] Colombia; Hong Kong; [international vehicle registration] Hong Kong; House of Keys (parliament of Isle of Man); [taxation] housekeeper allowance

.hk Hong Kong (in Internet address)

hkf handkerchief

HKI Helen Keller International
HKJ [international vehicle registration] (Hashemite Kingdom of) Jordan
HL hard labour; [fishing port] Hartlepool; Haute-Loire (French department); honours list; House of Laity; House of Lords; [civil aircraft marking] Republic of Korea; [vehicle registration] Sheffield
Hl. *Heilige(r)* (German: Saint)
hl hectolitre
h.l. *hoc loco* (Latin: in this place)
HLA [immunology] human lymphocyte antigen
HLBB [USA] Home Loan Bank Board
HLD Doctor of Humane Letters
HLE [physics] high-level exposure (to radiation)
HLG Historic Landscapes Group
HLHSR [computing] hidden-line/hidden-surface removal
HLI Highland Light Infantry
HLL [computing] high-level language
h/lmp headlamp
HLNW high-level nuclear waste
HLPR Howard League for Penal Reform
hlpr helper
HLRW high-level radioactive waste
HLS Harvard Law School
HLW headlamp wipers (in car advertisement); high-level waste
HLWN highest low water neaps (level of tide)
HLWW headlamp wash and wipe (in car advertisement)
HM [vehicle registration] central London; harbour master; [music] harmonic mean; Haute-Marne (French department); [chemistry] hazardous material; headmaster; headmistress; heavy metal; Her Majesty('s); His Majesty('s); home mission
hm hectometre
h.m. hallmark; *hoc mense* (Latin: in this month)
HMA Head Masters' Association; [computing] high-memory area
HMAC Her/His Majesty's Aircraft Carrier
HMAS Her/His Majesty's Australian Ship
HMBDV Her/His Majesty's Boom Defence Vessel
HMC Headmasters' and Headmistresses' Conference; Her/His Majesty's Customs; Historical Manuscripts Commission; Horticultural Marketing Council; Hospital Management Committee; Household Mortgage Corporation
HMCA Hospital and Medical Care Association
HMCG Her/His Majesty's Coast Guard
HMCIC Her/His Majesty's Chief Inspector of Constabulary
HMCIF Her/His Majesty's Chief Inspector of Factories
HMCN Her/His Majesty's Canadian Navy
HMCS Her/His Majesty's Canadian Ship
HMCSC Her/His Majesty's Civil Service Commissioners
HMD [computing] head-mounted display; Her/His Majesty's Destroyer
hmd humid
HMF [chemistry] heavy-metal fluoride; Her/His Majesty's Forces
HMFI Her/His Majesty's Factory Inspectorate
HMG heavy machine gun; Her/His Majesty's Government; [medicine] human menopausal gonadotrophin
HMHS Her/His Majesty's Hospital Ship
HMI Her/His Majesty's Inspector (of schools); Her/His Majesty's Inspectorate (of schools); [computing] human–machine interface
HMIC Her/His Majesty's Inspectorate of Constabulary
HMIED Honorary Member of the Institution of Engineering Designers
HMIP Her/His Majesty's Inspectorate of Pollution
HMIT Her/His Majesty's Inspector of Taxes
HML Her/His Majesty's Lieutenant
HMLR Her/His Majesty's Land Registry
HMML Her/His Majesty's Motor Launch
HMMS Her/His Majesty's Mine Sweeper
HMNZS Her/His Majesty's New Zealand Ship
HMO [USA] health maintenance organization
HMOCS Her/His Majesty's Overseas Civil Service
HMP Her/His Majesty's Prison; *hoc monumentum posuit* (Latin: (he/she) erected this monument)
h.m.p. handmade paper
HMRT Her/His Majesty's Rescue Tug
HMS [mining] heavy media separation;

Her/His Majesty's Service; Her/His Majesty's Ship
h.m.s. hours, minutes, seconds
HMSO Her/His Majesty's Stationery Office (replaced by The Stationery Office)
hmstd homestead
HMT Her/His Majesty's Trawler; Her/His Majesty's Treasury; Her/His Majesty's Tug
HMV His Master's Voice (music company)
HMW high molecular weight
HMWA Hairdressing Manufacturers' and Wholesalers' Association
HMXB [astronomy] high-mass X-ray binary
HN [vehicle registration] Middlesbrough
hn [music] horn
.hn Honduras (in Internet address)
h.n. [medicine] *hac nocte* (Latin: tonight)
HNC [education] Higher National Certificate
HND [education] Higher National Diploma
hndbk handbook
hndlg handling
hndlr handler
HNL [physics] helium–neon laser
hnRNA [biochemistry] heterogeneous nuclear ribonucleic acid
hnRNP [biochemistry] heterogeneous nuclear ribonucleoprotein
Hnrs Honours
HO [vehicle registration] Bournemouth; [law] habitual offender; head office; Home Office; hostilities only; Hydrographic Office
Ho [chemical element] holmium
ho. house
h.o. hold over
hobgoblin [informal] help, our budget's gone beyond the limits of our income
HOC heavy organic chemical
HoC House of Commons
h.o.c. held on charge
HOCRE Home Office Central Research Establishment
HoD head of department
H of C House of Commons
H of K House of Keys
H of L House of Lords
H of R [USA] House of Representatives
HoL House of Lords
Hol [geology] Holocene
Hol. Holland
hol. holiday
HOLC [USA] Home Owners' Loan Corporation
Holl. Holland
HOLLAND hope our love lasts and never dies (on envelope of love letter)
Holmes Home Office Large Major Enquiry System (crime-investigation computer)
hols [short form] holidays
Hom. Homer (ancient Greek poet)
homoeo. homoeopath; homoeopathic; homoeopathy
Hon. Honorary; Honorary Member; Honourable
hon. honorary; honour; honourable
Hond. Honduran; Honduras
Hono. Honolulu
Hons Honours
Hon. Sec. honorary secretary
HOOD [computing] hierarchical object-oriented design
hopeful [informal] hard-up old person expecting full useful life
Hor [astronomy] Horologium
Hor. Horace (Roman poet)
hor. horizon; horizontal; horology
hor. decub. [medicine] *hora decubitus* (Latin: at bedtime) (in prescriptions)
HoReCa (International Union of National Associations of) Hotel, Restaurant and Café Keepers
horol. horological; horologist; horology
hort. horticultural; horticulturalist; horticulture
hortic. horticultural; horticulture
HORU Home Office Research Unit
Hos. [Bible] Hosea
hosp. hospital
HOT Hawk and Owl Trust
HOTOL [astronautics] horizontal take-off and landing
HOV high-occupancy vehicle
how. howitzer
HP [vehicle registration] Coventry; Handley Page (aircraft); [horticulture] hardy perennial; Hautes-Pyrénées (French department); [UK postcode] Hemel Hempstead; [trademark] Hewlett-Packard (computer manufacturer); high performance; high power; high pressure; high priest; Himachal Pradesh; hire purchase; hot-pressed (paper); house phys-

ician; Houses of Parliament; [horticulture] hybrid perpetual (rose); [civil aircraft marking] Panama

hp horsepower

h.p. half pay; heir presumptive; high power (electricity); hire purchase; horizontally polarized

HPA Hospital Physicists' Association

HPC [medicine] history of present complaint

hpch. harpsichord

hpd harpsichord

HPF [computing] highest priority first

HPFS [computing] high-performance filing system

HPGL [trademark, computing] Hewlett-Packard graphics language

HPIB [trademark, computing] Hewlett-Packard interface bus

HPk Hilal-e-Pakistan (Pakistani honour)

HPLC [chemistry] high-performance liquid chromatography; [chemistry] high-pressure liquid chromatography

HPPA Horses and Ponies Protection Association

HPRU Handicapped Persons Research Unit

HPS Highland Pony Society; high-pressure steam; high-protein supplement

HPT high-pressure turbine

HPTA Hire Purchase Trade Association

HPV [medicine] human papilloma virus

HQ headquarters

h.q. headquarters; *hoc quaere* (Latin: look for this)

HQA Hilal-i-Quaid-i-Azam (Pakistani honour)

HQBA headquarters base area

HQMC [USA] Headquarters, Marine Corps

HR [international vehicle registration] Croatia (from Croatian *Hrvatska*); [medicine] heart rate; [UK postcode] Hereford; Highland Regiment; [optics] high resolution; Home Rule; Home Ruler; [baseball] home run; [civil aircraft marking] Honduras; [USA] House of Representatives; human resources; [vehicle registration] Swindon

H-R [astronomy] Hertzsprung–Russell (diagram)

Hr *Herr* (German: Mr, Sir); Hussar

hr [meteorology] hail and rain; hour

.hr Croatia (in Internet address)

h.r. [baseball] home run

HRA [USA] Health Resources Administration

HRC [chemistry] high-resolution chromatography; Holy Roman Church

HRCA Honorary Royal Cambrian Academician

HRCT [medicine] high-resolution compute(rize)d tomography

HRE Holy Roman Emperor; Holy Roman Empire

HREM high-resolution electron microscope (or microscopy)

HRG high-resolution graphics

HRGC [chemistry] high-resolution gas chromatography

HRGI Honorary Member of the Royal Glasgow Institute of the Fine Arts

HRH Her/His Royal Highness

HRHA Honorary Member of the Royal Hibernian Academy

HRI Honorary Member of the Royal Institute of Painters in Water Colours

HRIP *hic requiescit in pace* (Latin: here rests in peace) (on tombstone)

HRM human resource management

Hrn *Herren* (German: Messrs, Sirs, Gentlemen)

HROI Honorary Member of the Royal Institute of Oil Painters

HRP Home Responsibilities Protection; [military] human remains pouch

HRR [taxation] higher reduced rate

HRS Human Rights Society

hrs hours

HRSA Honorary Member of the Royal Scottish Academy

hrsg. *herausgegeben* (German: edited, published)

HRSW Honorary Member of the Royal Scottish Water Colour Society

HRT [medicine] hormone replacement therapy

HRTEM high-resolution transmission electron microscope (or microscopy)

HRW heated rear window (in car advertisement)

HS [vehicle registration] Glasgow; Haute-Saône (French department); Hawker Siddeley (aircraft); *hic sepultus* (or *sepulta*) (Latin: here is buried) (on tombstone); high school; Home Secretary; hospital

ship; house surgeon; [numismatics] sesterce (Roman coin); [civil aircraft marking] Thailand
Hs [chemical element] hassium
Hs. *Handschrift* (German: manuscript)
hs [medicine] hail and snow
h.s. highest score; *hoc sensu* (Latin: in this sense); [medicine] *hora somni* (Latin: at bedtime) (in prescriptions)
HSA [USA] Health Systems Agency; [medicine] human serum albumin; Humane Slaughter Association
HSAB [chemistry] hard and soft acids and bases
HSB [computing] hue, saturation, brightness
HSBC Hongkong and Shanghai Banking Corporation
HSC [medicine] haemopoietic stem cell; Health and Safety Commission; [Australia] Higher School Certificate
HSD heat-storage device; high-speed diesel
HSDU hospital sterilization and disinfection unit
HSE Health and Safety Executive; *hic sepultus* (or *sepulta*) *est* (Latin: here is buried) (on tombstone)
hse house
hsekpr housekeeper
hsg housing
HSH Her/His Serene Highness
HSI [computing] human–system interaction (or interface)
HSL [computing] hue, saturation, lightness; Huguenot Society of London
HSLA high strength, low alloy (steel)
HSM Her Serene Majesty; [computing] hierarchical storage management; His Serene Majesty
HSO Hamburg Symphony Orchestra
HSP [medicine] heat-shock protein
HSR [genetics] homogeneously staining region
HSS high-speed steel; *Historicae Societatis Socius* (Latin: Fellow of the Historical Society)
Hss. *Handschriften* (German: manuscripts)
HSSU hospital sterile supply unit
HST Harry S Truman (US president); Hawaii Standard Time; highest spring tide; high-speed train; Hubble Space Telescope; hypersonic transport
HSV [medicine] herpes simplex virus
HSWA [USA] Hazardous and Solid Waste Act; [USA] Hazardous and Solid Waste Amendments
HT [vehicle registration] Bristol; [sports] half time; Hawaii Time; heat-treated; heat treatment; high temperature; [electrical engineering] high tension; high tide; high treason; [horticulture] hybrid tea (rose)
ht heat; height
h/t [printing] half-title
.ht Haiti (in Internet address)
h.t. [sports] half time; halftone; heavy tank; *hoc tempore* (Latin: at this time); *hoc titulo* (Latin: under this title)
HTA Help the Aged; Horticultural Traders' Association; Household Textile Association
h.t.b. high-tension battery
HTC [physics] heat-transfer coefficient
htd heated
Hte *Haute* (French: high) (in place-names)
htg heating
HTGR [nuclear technology] high-temperature gas-cooled reactor
HTLV [medicine] human T-cell lymphotropic virus
HTM heat-transfer medium
HTML [computing] hypertext markup language (used on Internet)
HTOL [astronautics] horizontal take-off and landing
HTR [nuclear technology] high-temperature reactor
htr heater
H Trin. Holy Trinity
HTS high-temperature superconductivity; high-temperature superconductor; high-tensile steel
Hts Heights (in place-names)
h.t.s. half-time survey; high-tensile steel
HTT heavy tactical transport
HTTP [computing] hypertext transfer protocol (used on Internet)
HTTR [nuclear technology] high-temperature test reactor
HTV Harlech Television
ht wkt [cricket] hit wicket
HU [vehicle registration] Bristol; Harvard University; [UK postcode] Hull
.hu Hungary (in Internet address)

HUAC House (of Representatives) Un-American Activities Committee
HUD [aeronautics, computing] head-up display; [USA] (Department of) Housing and Urban Development
Hugo Human Genome Organization
HUJ Hebrew University of Jerusalem
HUKFORLANT [US navy] hunter-killer forces, Atlantic
HUKS [US navy] hunter-killer submarine
Hum. humanities (academic subject)
hum. human; humane; humanism; humanity; humble; humorous
HUMINT [military] human intelligence
HUMRRO Human Resources Research Office
HUMV [military] human light vehicle
hund. hundred
Hung. Hungarian; Hungary
Hunts Huntingdonshire
HUP Harvard University Press
hur. hurricane
Huridocs International Human Rights Information and Documentation System
hurr. hurricane
Husat Human Science and Advanced Technology Research Institute
husb. husband; husbandry
HV [vehicle registration] central London; health visitor; [anatomy] hepatic vein; high velocity; high voltage; *hoc verbum* (Latin: this word); [civil aircraft marking] Vatican City State
HVAC heating, ventilation and air conditioning; high-voltage alternating current
HVAR high-velocity aircraft rocket
HVCA Heating and Ventilating Contractors' Association
HVCert Health Visitor's Certificate
HVDC high-voltage direct current
HVEM high-voltage electron microscope (or microscopy)
HVP hydrolysed vegetable protein
HVT [physics] half-value thickness; health visitor teacher
hvy heavy
HW [vehicle registration] Bristol; hazardous waste; high water; hot water
h/w herewith; husband and wife
h.w. [cricket] hit wicket
HWL Henry Wadsworth Longfellow (US poet); high-water line
HWLB high water, London Bridge
HWM high-water mark
HWONT high water, ordinary neap tides
HWOST high water, ordinary spring tides
HWR [nuclear technology] heavy-water reactor
HWS hot water system; hurricane warning system
HWW headlamp wash and wipe (in car advertisement); [engineering] hot-and-warm worked
hwy highway
HX [vehicle registration] central London; [UK postcode] Halifax
HXR hard X-ray
HY [vehicle registration] Bristol
Hy. Henry
hy heavy; highway
Hya [astronomy] Hydra
hyb. hybrid
HyCoSy [medicine] hysterosalpingo-contrast sonography
hyd. hydrate; hydraulic; hydrographic
hydrog. hydrographic
hydt hydrant
hyg. hygiene; hygienic
Hyi [astronomy] Hydrus
hyp. hypodermic; [mathematics] hypotenuse; hypothesis; hypothetical
hyperb. hyperbole; hyperbolic
hypo [short form] hypodermic (syringe)
hypoth. hypothesis; hypothetical
HZ [civil aircraft marking] Saudi Arabia; [vehicle registration] Tyrone
Hz hertz

I

I *Iesus* (Latin: Jesus); *Imperator* (Latin: Emperor); *Imperatrix* (Latin: Empress); Imperial; *Imperium* (Latin: Empire); [advertising] (single column) inch; incumbent; Independence; Independent; India; Indian; [chemistry] inductive effect; *Infidelis* (Latin: infidel); information; inspector; Institute; instructor; intelligence; interceptor; International; interpreter; [chemical element] iodine; Ireland; Irish; Island; Isle; issue; Italian; [civil aircraft marking] Italy; [international vehicle registration] Italy; [Roman numeral] one

I [physics] electric current; [chemistry] ionic strength; [physics, chemistry] ionization potential; [physics] luminous intensity; [physics] moment of inertia (in mechanics); [physics] radiant intensity; [mathematics] unit matrix

i [mathematics] imaginary number (square root of –1); [Roman numeral] one

i [physics] instantaneous current

i. *id* (Latin: that); incisor (tooth); indicate; [banking] interest; [grammar] intransitive; island

3i Investors in Industry

IA [vehicle registration] Antrim; Incorporated Accountant; Indian Army; infected area; information anxiety; [taxation] initial allowance; Institute of Actuaries; Inter-American; [computing] International Alphabet (as in **IA5**); [medicine] intra-arterial; [US postcode] Iowa

I/A Isle of Anglesey

Ia Iowa

i.A *im Auftrage* (German: by order of)

i.a. immediately available; *in absentia* (Latin: while absent); [aeronautics] indicated altitude; initial appearance

IAA indoleacetic acid (plant hormone); Institute of Industrial Administration; International Academy of Astronautics; International Actuarial Association; International Advertising Association

IAAA Irish Amateur Athletic Association; Irish Association of Advertising Agencies

IAAE [USA] Institution of Automotive and Aeronautical Engineers

IAAF International Amateur Athletic Federation

IAAP International Association of Applied Psychology

IAAS Incorporated Association of Architects and Surveyors

IAB Industrial Advisory Board; Industrial Arbitration Board; Inter-American Bank; Internet architecture board

IABA International Association of Aircraft Brokers and Agents

IABO International Association of Biological Oceanography

IAC [USA] Industrial Advisory Council; Institute of Amateur Cinematographers

i.a.c. integration, assembly and checkout

IACA Independent Air Carriers' Association

IACB International Advisory Committee on Bibliography (in UNESCO)

IACCP Inter-American Council of Commerce and Production

IACOMS International Advisory Committee on Marine Sciences

IACP International Association for Child Psychiatry and Allied Professions; International Association of Chiefs of Police; [USA] International Association of Computer Programmers

IACR Institute of Arable Crops Research

IACS International Annealed Copper Standard

IADB Inter-American Defense Board; Inter-American Development Bank

IADR International Association for Dental Research

IAE [USA] Institute of Atomic Energy; Institute of Automotive Engineers; Institution of Automobile Engineers

IAEA International Atomic Energy Agency

IAEC Israel Atomic Energy Commission

IAECOSOC Inter-American Economic and Social Council

IAEE International Association of Energy Economists

IAF Indian Air Force; Indian Auxiliary Force; International Archery Federation; International Astronautical Federation

i.a.f. [aeronautics] interview after flight

IAFD International Association on Food Distribution

IAG International Association of Geodesy; International Association of Geology; International Association of Gerontology

IAGB&I Ileostomy Association of Great Britain and Ireland

IAgrE Institution of Agricultural Engineers

IAH International Association of Hydro-

geologists; International Association of Hydrology
IAHA Inter-American Hotel Association
IAHM Incorporated Association of Headmasters
IAHP International Association of Horticultural Producers
IAHR International Association for Hydraulic Research; International Association for the History of Religions
IAI International African Institute
IAL Imperial Airways Limited; Imperial Arts League; [computing] international algorithmic language; Irish Academy of Letters
IALA International African Law Association; International Association of Lighthouse Authorities
IALL International Association of Law Libraries
IALS International Association of Legal Science
IAM Institute of Administrative Management; Institute of Advanced Motorists; Institute of Aviation Medicine; [anatomy] internal auditory meatus; [USA] International Association of Machinists and Aerospace Workers; International Association of Meteorology; International Association of Microbiologists
IAMA Incorporated Advertising Managers' Association
IAMAP International Association of Meteorology and Atmospheric Physics
IAMC Indian Army Medical Corps
IAML International Association of Music Libraries
IAMS International Association of Microbiological Societies; International Association of Microbiological Studies
IANC International Airline Navigators' Council
I&D [medicine] incision and drainage
I&O intake and output
IANE Institute of Advanced Nursing Education
IANEC Inter-American Nuclear Energy Commission
IAO Incorporated Association of Organists
IAOC Indian Army Ordnance Corps
IAOS Irish Agricultural Organization Society
IAP International Academy of Pathology; Internet access provider
IAPA Inter-American Press Association
IAPB International Association for the Prevention of Blindness
IAPC International Auditing Practices Committee
IAPG International Association of Physical Geography
IAPH International Association of Ports and Harbours
IAPO International Association of Physical Oceanography
IAPS Incorporated Association of Preparatory Schools
IAPSO International Association for the Physical Sciences of the Oceans
IAPT International Association for Plant Taxonomy
IAR instruction address register
IARA Inter-Allied Reparations Agency
IARC Indian Agricultural Research Council; International Agency for Research on Cancer
IARD International Association for Rural Development
IARF International Association for Religious Freedom
IARI Indian Agricultural Research Institute
IARO Indian Army Reserve of Officers
IARU International Amateur Radio Union
IAS [computing] immediate access store; Indian Administrative Service (formerly ICS); [aeronautics] indicated air speed; [USA] Institute for Advanced Studies; [USA] Institute of the Aerospace Sciences; [aeronautics] instrument approach system; International Accounting Standard
IASA International Air Safety Association
IASC Indian Army Service Corps; International Accounting Standards Committee
IASH International Association of Scientific Hydrology
IASI Inter-American Statistical Institute
i.a.s.o.r. ice and snow on runway
IASS International Association for Scandinavian Studies; International Association of Soil Science
IAT International Atomic Time
i.a.t. inside air temperature

IATA International Air Transport Association; International Amateur Theatre Association
IATUL International Association of Technological University Libraries
IAU International Association of Universities; International Astronomical Union
IAUPL International Association of University Professors and Lecturers
IAV International Association of Vulcanology
IAVG International Association for Vocational Guidance
IAW International Alliance of Women
i.a.w. in accordance with
IAWPRC International Association on Water Pollution Research and Control
IB [vehicle registration] Armagh; in bond; incendiary bomb; industrial business; information bureau; instruction book; intelligence branch; International Baccalaureate; International Bank (for Reconstruction and Development); invoice book
ib. *ibidem* (Latin: in the same place) (indicating reference cited earlier)
IBA Independent Bankers' Association; Independent Broadcasting Authority (replacement for ITA); Industrial Bankers' Association; [taxation] industrial buildings allowances; International Bar Association; International Bowling Association; Investment Bankers' Association
IBAA Investment Bankers' Association of America
IBAE Institution of British Agricultural Engineers
IBB Institute of British Bakers; International Bowling Board; Invest in Britain Bureau
IBBR [finance] interbank bid rate
IBC International Broadcasting Corporation
IBD Incorporated Institute of British Decorators and Interior Designers; [medicine] inflammatory bowel disease; [electronics] ion-beam deposition
IBE Institution of British Engineers; International Bureau of Education (became part of UNESCO)
IBEL [finance] interest-bearing eligible liability
IBEW [USA] International Brotherhood of Electrical Workers
IBF Institute of British Foundrymen; International Badminton Federation; international banking facility; International Boxing Federation
IBG Incorporated Brewers Guild; Institute of British Geographers; [computing] interblock gap
IBI [book-keeping] invoice book inwards
IBID international bibliographical description
ibid. *ibidem* (Latin: in the same place) (indicating reference cited earlier)
IBiol Institute of Biology
IBK Institute of Book-keepers
IBM intercontinental ballistic missile; International Business Machines (Corporation) (computer manufacturer)
IBMBR [finance] interbank market bid rate
IBO [book-keeping] invoice book outwards
IBP initial boiling point; Institute of British Photographers; International Biological Programme
IBPAT [USA] International Brotherhood of Painters and Allied Trades
IBRC Insurance Brokers Registration Council
IBRD International Bank for Reconstruction and Development (World Bank)
IBRO International Bank Research Organization; International Brain Research Organization
IBS Institute of Bankers in Scotland; [medicine] irritable bowel syndrome
IBScot Institute of Bankers in Scotland
IBST Institute of British Surgical Technicians
IBT International Brotherhood of Teamsters, Chauffeurs, Warehousemen and Helpers of America
IBTE Institute of British Telecommunications Engineers
IBWM International Bureau of Weights and Measures
IC identity card; *Iesus Christus* (Latin: Jesus Christ); [grammar] immediate constituent; [immunology] immune complex; Imperial College (of Science and Technology, London); [astronomy] Index Catalogue; industrial court; information centre; [electronics] integrated

circuit; Intelligence Corps; [engineering] internal-combustion (engine); [chemistry] ion chromatography; [physics] ionization chamber

I-C Indo-China

i/c in charge; in command

i.c. index correction; instrument correction; internal communication

ICA ignition control additive (for motor vehicles); Industrial Caterers' Association; Institute of Chartered Accountants (in England and Wales); Institute of Company Accountants; Institute of Contemporary Arts; [medicine] internal carotid artery; International Cartographic Association; International Chefs' Association; International Coffee Agreement; International Colour Authority; International Commercial Arbitration; International Commission on Acoustics; International Commodity Agreement; International Cooperation Administration; International Cooperative Alliance; International Council on Archives; International Court of Arbitration; International Cyclist Association; invalid care allowance

ICAA Invalid Children's Aid Association

ICAE International Commission on Agricultural Engineering

ICAEW Institute of Chartered Accountants in England and Wales

ICAI Institute of Chartered Accountants in Ireland; International Commission for Agricultural Industries

ICAM Institute of Corn and Agricultural Merchants

ICAN International Commission for Air Navigation

IC&CY Inns of Court and City Yeomanry

ICAO International Civil Aviation Organization

ICAP Institute of Certified Ambulance Personnel; International Congress of Applied Psychology

ICAR Indian Council of Agricultural Research

ICAS Institute of Chartered Accountants of Scotland; International Council of Aeronautical Sciences; International Council of Aerospace Sciences

ICB Institute of Comparative Biology

ICBA International Community of Booksellers' Associations

ICBD International Council of Ballroom Dancing

ICBHI Industrial Craft (Member) of the British Horological Institute

ICBM intercontinental ballistic missile

ICBN International Code of Botanical Nomenclature

ICBP International Council for Bird Preservation

ICC [USA] Indian Claims Commission; intercounty championship; International Chamber of Commerce; International Children's Centre; International Congregational Council; International Convention Centre (Birmingham); International Correspondence Colleges; International Cricket Conference (formerly Imperial Cricket Conference); [USA] Interstate Commerce Commission

ICCB Intergovernmental Consultation and Coordination Board

ICCC International Conference of Catholic Charities

ICCE International Council of Commerce Employers

ICCF International Correspondence Chess Federation

ICCH International Commodities Clearing House

ICCPR International Covenant on Civil and Political Rights (of UN)

ICCROM International Centre for Conservation at Rome

ICCS International Centre of Criminological Studies

ICD Institute of Cooperative Directors; International Classification of Diseases (published by WHO)

ICDO International Civil Defence Organization

ICE [medicine] ice, compress, elevation (treatment for bruised limbs); [computing] in-circuit emulator; Institute of Chartered Engineers; Institution of Civil Engineers; internal-combustion engine; International Cultural Exchange

Ice. Iceland; Icelander; Icelandic

ICED International Council for Educational Development

ICEF International Council for Educational Films
ICEI Institution of Civil Engineers of Ireland
Icel. Iceland; Icelander; Icelandic
ICeram Institute of Ceramics (became part of Institute of Materials)
ICES International Council for the Exploration of the Sea
ICETT Industrial Council for Educational and Training Technology
ICF Industrial and Commercial Finance Corporation; [nuclear technology] inertial-confinement fusion; International Canoe Federation; International Chess Federation
ICFTU International Confederation of Free Trade Unions
icg icing
ICGS interactive computer-graphics system; International Catholic Girls' Society
ich. ichthyology
ICHCA International Cargo Handling Coordination Association
IChemE Institution of Chemical Engineers
ICHEO Inter-University Council for Higher Education Overseas
ICHPER International Council for Health, Physical Education and Recreation
ichth. ichthyology
ichthyol. ichthyologist; ichthyology
ICI Imperial Chemical Industries; International Commission on Illumination; [USA] Investment Casting Institute
ICIA International Credit Insurance Association
ICIANZ Imperial Chemical Industries, Australia and New Zealand
ICID International Commission on Irrigation and Drainage
ICIDH International Classification of Impairments, Disabilities and Handicaps (published by WHO)
ICJ International Commission of Jurists; International Court of Justice
ICJW International Council of Jewish Women
ICL International Computers Limited; International Confederation of Labour
ICLA International Committee on Laboratory Animals
ICM Institute for Complementary Medicine; Institute of Credit Management; Intergovernmental Committee for Migrations (of UN); International Confederation of Midwives; [astronomy] intracluster medium; Irish Church Missions
ICMMP International Committee of Military Medicine and Pharmacy
ICMS International Centre for Mathematical Sciences (Edinburgh)
ICN *in Christi nomine* (Latin: in Christ's name); infection control nurse; International Council of Nurses
ICNA Infection Control Nurses' Association
ICNB International Code of Nomenclature of Bacteria
ICNCP International Code of Nomenclature of Cultivated Plants
ICNV International Code of Nomenclature of Viruses
ICO Institute of Careers Officers; International Coffee Organization; Islamic Conference Organization
ICOM International Council of Museums
ICOMOS International Council of Monuments and Sites
ICON indexed currency option note
icon. iconographical; iconography
ICOR Intergovernmental Conference on Oceanic Research (in UNESCO)
ICorrST Institution of Corrosion Science and Technology
ICP [medicine] intracranial pressure
ICPA International Commission for the Prevention of Alcoholism; International Cooperative Petroleum Association
ICPHS International Council for Philosophy and Humanistic Studies
ICPO International Criminal Police Organization (= Interpol)
ICPU International Catholic Press Union
ICQ [accounting] internal control questionnaire
ICR [computing] intelligent character recognition
ICRC International Committee of the Red Cross
ICRF Imperial Cancer Research Fund
ICRP International Commission on Radiological Protection

ICRU International Commission on Radiation Units (and Measurements)
ICRUM International Commission on Radiation Units and Measurements
ICS Imperial College of Science and Technology (London); Indian Civil Service (former name of IAS); instalment credit selling; Institute of Chartered Shipbrokers; International Chamber of Shipping; International College of Surgeons; international consultancy service; [finance] investors' compensation scheme
ICSA Institute of Chartered Secretaries and Administrators (formerly CIS)
ICSB International Congress of Small Businesses
ICSH [biochemistry] interstitial-cell-stimulating hormone
ICSI [medicine] intracytoplasmic sperm injection (infertility treatment)
ICSID International Council of Societies of Industrial Design
ICSLS International Convention for Safety of Life at Sea
ICSPE International Council of Sport and Physical Education
ICST Imperial College of Science and Technology (London)
ICSU International Council of Scientific Unions (in UNESCO)
ICTA International Council of Travel Agents
ICTP International Centre for Theoretical Physics
ICTU Irish Congress of Trade Unions
ICTV International Committee on Taxonomy of Viruses
ICU [medicine] intensive care unit; international code use (in signalling)
ICVA International Council of Voluntary Agencies
ICW Institute of Clerks of Works of Great Britain; International Congress of Women; [telecommunications] interrupted continuous wave
i.c.w. in connection with
ICWA Indian Council of World Affairs; Institute of Cost and Works Accountants
ICWG International Cooperative Women's Guild
ICWU [USA] International Chemical Workers Union
ICYF International Catholic Youth Federation
ICZN International Code of Zoological Nomenclature
ID [US postcode] Idaho; identification; identify; identity; infectious disease(s); information department; inside diameter; Institute of Directors; intelligence department; [medicine] intradermal; [currency] Iraqi dinar
Id. Idaho
id. *idem* (Latin: the same (man))
.id Indonesia (in Internet address)
i.d. inside diameter
IDA Industrial Diamond Association; International Development Association (affiliate of World Bank); Irish Dental Association; Islamic Democratic Association
IDB illicit diamond buyer; illicit diamond buying; Industrial Development Bank; [Northern Ireland] Industrial Development Board; Inter-American Development Bank; Internal Drainage Board
IDC industrial development certificate; insulation displacement connector
ID card identification card
IDD [medicine] insulin-dependent diabetes; [telecommunications] international direct dialling
IDDA Interior Decorators and Designers Association
IDDD [telecommunications] international direct distance dialling
IDDM [medicine] insulin-dependent diabetes mellitus
IDE [computing] integrated drive electronics; [computing] intelligent drive electronics; [computing] interactive development environment
iden. identification; identify; identity
ident. identification; identify; identity
IDF International Dairy Federation; International Democratic Fellowship; International Dental Federation; International Diabetes Federation
IDIB Industrial Diamond Information Bureau
IDL [biochemistry] intermediate-density lipoprotein; international date line; international driver's licence
IDLH immediately dangerous to life and health

IDMS [computing] integrated data-management system
IDN *in Dei nomine* (Latin: in God's name); [computing] integrated data network
IDP Institute of Data Processing; [computing] integrated data processing; International Driving Permit; [astronomy] interplanetary dust particle(s)
IDPM Institute of Data Processing Management
IDR [finance] International Depository Receipt
IDRC International Development Research Centre
IDS Income Data Services; Industry Department for Scotland; Institute of Development Studies
IDSM Indian Distinguished Service Medal
IDT industrial design technology
IDV International Distillers and Vintners
IE [medicine] immunoelectrophoresis; index error; Indian Empire; Indo-European (languages); Institute of Engineers and Technicians (became part of IIE); [chemistry] ion exchange; [chemistry] ionization energy; [fishing port] Irvine
.ie Ireland (in Internet address)
i.e. *id est* (Latin: that is); inside edge
IEA Institute of Economic Affairs; Institution of Engineers, Australia; International Economic Association; International Energy Agency; International Ergonomics Association
IE(Aust) Institution of Engineers, Australia
IEC industrial energy conservation; integrated environmental control; International Electrotechnical Commission
IED improvised explosive device; Information Engineering Directorate; Institution of Engineering Designers
IEDD improvised explosive device disposal
IEE [USA] Institute of Energy Economics; Institution of Electrical Engineers
IEEE Institute of Electrical and Electronics Engineers
IEEIE Institution of Electrical and Electronics Incorporated Engineers (became part of IIE)
IEF Indian Expeditionary Force
IEHO Institution of Environmental Health Officers
IEI Industrial Engineering Institute; Institution of Engineers of Ireland
IEM inborn error of metabolism
IEME Inspectorate of Electrical and Mechanical Engineering
IEng Incorporated Engineer
IER Institute of Environmental Research
IERE Institution of Electronic and Radio Engineers (became part of IEE)
IES Indian Educational Service; Institution of Engineers and Shipbuilders in Scotland
IET interest equalization tax
IETF Internet Engineering Task Force
IEW intelligence and electronic warfare
IExpE Institute of Explosives Engineers
IF [nuclear technology] inertial fusion; [baseball] infield; [biochemistry] inhibitory factor; [genetics] initiation factor; [sports] inside forward; Institute of Fuel; [medicine] interferon; [electronics] intermediate frequency
i-f in-flight
i.f. information feedback; *ipse fecit* (Latin: (he) did it himself)
IFA [medicine] immunofluorescence assay; Incorporated Faculty of Arts; independent financial adviser; instrumented fuel assembly; International Federation of Actors; International Fertility Association; International Fiscal Association; Irish Football Association
IFAA Independent Financial Advisers Association
IFAC International Federation of Automatic Control
IFAD International Fund for Agricultural Development
IFALPA International Federation of Air Line Pilots' Associations
IFAP International Federation of Agricultural Producers
IFATCA International Federation of Air Traffic Controllers' Associations
IFAW International Fund for Animal Welfare
IFB [finance] invitation for bid
IFBPW International Federation of Business and Professional Women
IFC International Finance Corporation

(affiliate of World Bank); [USA, Canada] International Fisheries Commission
IFCATI International Federation of Cotton and Allied Textile Industries
IFCC International Federation of Camping and Caravanning; International Federation of Children's Communities
IFCCPTE International Federation of Commercial, Clerical, Professional and Technical Employees
IFCO International Fisheries Cooperative Organization
IFCTU International Federation of Christian Trade Unions
IFE [computing] intelligent front end
IFF [radar] Identification, Friend or Foe; [computing] image file format; Institute of Freight Forwarders; [computing] interchange file format
iff [logic, mathematics] if and only if
IFFA International Federation of Film Archives
IFFPA International Federation of Film Producers' Associations
IFFS International Federation of Film Societies
IFFTU International Federation of Free Teachers' Unions
IFGA International Federation of Grocers' Associations
IFGO International Federation of Gynaecology and Obstetrics
IFHE International Federation of Home Economics
IFHP International Federation for Housing and Planning
IFIP International Federation for Information Processing
IFireE Institution of Fire Engineers
IFJ International Federation of Journalists
IFL International Friendship League
IFLA International Federation of Landscape Architects; International Federation of Library Associations
IFM International Falcon Movement
IFMC International Folk Music Council
IFMSA International Federation of Medical Students' Associations
IFOR Implementation Force (NATO-led peacekeeping force in Bosnia, replaced by SFOR); International Fellowship of Reconciliation
IFORS International Federation of Operational Research Societies
Ifox Irish Futures and Options Exchange
IFP [South Africa] Inkatha Freedom Party
IFPA Industrial Film Producers' Association
IFPAAW International Federation of Plantation, Agricultural and Allied Workers
IFPCS International Federation of Unions of Employees in Public and Civil Services
IFPM International Federation of Physical Medicine
IFPW International Federation of Petroleum (and Chemical) Workers
IFR [aeronautics] instrument flying regulations; [nuclear technology] integral fast reactor
IFRB International Frequency Registration Board
IFS Indian Forest Service; Institute for Fiscal Studies; International Federation of Surveyors; Irish Free State; [computing] iterated function system
IFSPO International Federation of Senior Police Officers
IFST Institute of Food Science and Technology
IFSW International Federation of Social Workers
IFTA International Federation of Teachers' Associations; International Federation of Travel Agencies
IFTC International Film and Television Council
IFTU International Federation of Trade Unions (replaced by WFTU)
IFUW International Federation of University Women
IFWEA International Federation of Workers' Educational Associations
IFWL International Federation of Women Lawyers
IG [UK postcode] Ilford; imperial gallon; Indo-Germanic (languages); industrial group; [astronomy] inertial guidance; inner guard; Inspector-General; Instructor in Gunnery; Irish Guards
Ig [immunology] immunoglobulin
ig. ignition
IGA International Geographical Association; International Golf Association

IGADD Intergovernmental Authority on Drought and Development
IGasE Institution of Gas Engineers
IGBT [computing] insulated-gate bipolar transistor
IGC Intergovernmental Conference
IGCM Incorporated Guild of Church Musicians
IGD illicit gold dealer
IGES [computing] initial graphics exchange specification
IGF Inspector-General of Fortifications; [medicine] insulin-like growth factor; International Gymnastic Federation
IGFA International Game Fish Association
IGFET [electronics] insulated-gate field-effect transistor
IGH Incorporated Guild of Hairdressers
IGM [chess] International Grandmaster
ign. ignite(s); ignition; *ignotus* (Latin: unknown)
IGO intergovernmental organization
IGPP Institute of Geophysics and Planetary Physics
IGRS Irish Genealogical Research Society
IGS Imperial General Staff; independent grammar school
IGU International Gas Union; International Geographical Union
IGWF International Garment Workers' Federation
IGY International Geophysical Year
IH *iacet hic* (Latin: here lies) (on tombstone); industrial hygiene; [computing] interrupt handler; [fishing port] Ipswich
IHA International Hotel Association
IHAB International Horticultural Advisory Bureau
IHB International Hydrographic Bureau
IHC [New Zealand] intellectually handicapped child; Intercontinental Hotels Corporation
IHCA International Hebrew Christian Alliance
IHD [medicine] ischaemic heart disease
IHEU International Humanist and Ethical Union
IHF Industrial Hygiene Foundation; International Hockey Federation; International Hospitals Federation
IHospE Institute of Hospital Engineering
ihp indicated horsepower
IHR Institute of Historical Research
IHRB International Hockey Rules Board
IHS *Iesous* (Greek: Jesus) (from first three letters of name in Greek alphabet); *Iesus Hominum Salvator* (Latin: Jesus Saviour of Mankind); *in hoc signo* (Latin: in this sign)
IHSM Institute of Health Services Management
IHT inheritance tax; Institution of Highways and Transportation
IHU Irish Hockey Union
IHVE Institute of Heating and Ventilation Engineers
II [electronics] image intensifier; [electronics] ion implantation
IIA International Institute of Agriculture
IIAC Industrial Injuries Advisory Council
IIAL International Institute of Arts and Letters
IIAS International Institute of Administrative Sciences
IIB *Institut international des brevets* (French: International Patent Institute)
IIBD&ID Incorporated Institute of British Decorators and Interior Designers
IID [medicine] insulin-independent diabetes; [electronics] ion-implantation doping
iid. *iidem* (Latin: the same (men))
i.i.d. [statistics] independent identically distributed (random variables)
IIE Institute for International Education; Institution of Incorporated Engineers (in Electronic, Electrical and Mechanical Engineering); International Institute of Embryology
IIEP International Institute of Educational Planning
IIExE Institution of Incorporated Executive Engineers
IIF [computing] image interchange facility
IIHF International Ice Hockey Federation
III International Institute of Interpreters
IIL [electronics] integrated injection logic
IIM Institution of Industrial Managers
IInfSc Institute of Information Scientists
IIP *Institut international de la presse* (French: International Press Institute); International Ice Patrol; International Institute of Philosophy
IIR [chemistry] isobutylene-isoprene rubber

IIRS [Ireland] Institute for Industrial Research and Standards
IIS Institute of Information Scientists; International Institute of Sociology
IISO Institution of Industrial Safety Officers
IISS International Institute of Strategic Studies
IIT Indian Institute of Technology
IIW International Institute of Welding
IJ [vehicle registration] Down
i.J *im Jahre* (German: in the year)
IKBS [computing] intelligent knowledge-based system
IL [vehicle registration] Fermanagh; [US postcode] Illinois; Ilyushin (aircraft); [sports] inside left; Institute of Linguists; [aeronautics] instrument landing; [immunology] interleukin; [international vehicle registration] Israel
I/L import licence
.il Israel (in Internet address)
i.l. inside leg
ILA Individual Learning Account (for vocational training); [physics] induction linear accelerator; Institute of Landscape Architects; [aeronautics] instrument landing approach; International Law Association; International Longshoremen's Association
ILAA International Legal Aid Association
ILAB International League of Antiquarian Booksellers
ILAE International League Against Epilepsy
ILBM [computing] interleaved bit map
ILC International Law Commission (of UN)
ILD [medicine] interstitial lung disease
ILE Institution of Locomotive Engineers
ILEA Inner London Education Authority
ILEC Inner London Education Committee
ILF International Landworkers' Federation
ILGA Institute of Local Government Administration
ILGWU [USA] International Ladies' Garment Workers' Union
Ill. Illinois
ill. illustrate; illustrated; illustration; illustrator; *illustrissimus* (Latin: most distinguished)
illegit. illegitimate
illit. illiterate
illum. illuminate; illuminated; illumination
illus. illustrate; illustrated; illustration; illustrator
illust. illustrate; illustrated; illustration; illustrator
ILN *Illustrated London News*
ILO industrial liaison officer; International Labour Office (of UN); International Labour Organization
i.l.o. in lieu of
ILocoE Institution of Locomotive Engineers
ILP Independent Labour Party
ILR Independent Law Reports; independent local radio
ILRM International League for the Rights of Man
ILS Incorporated Law Society; [aeronautics] instrument landing system; [statistics] inverse least-squares
i.l.t. in lieu thereof
ILTF International Lawn Tennis Federation
ILU Institute of London Underwriters
ILW [nuclear technology] intermediate-level waste
ILY I love you
IM Indian Marines; Institute of Materials; Institute of Metals (became part of Institute of Materials); interceptor missile; [chess] International Master; [medicine] intramuscular; [UK postcode] Isle of Man
Im. Imperial
IMA Indian Military Academy; Institute of Mathematics and its Applications; International Music Association; Irish Medical Association
imag. imaginary; imagination; imagine
IM&AWU [USA] International Molders' and Allied Workers' Union
IMarE Institute of Marine Engineers
IMAS International Marine and Shipping Conference
IMB Institute of Marine Biology
IMC [photography] image motion compensation; Institute of Management Consultants; Institute of Measurement and Control; [aeronautics] instrument meteorological conditions; International Maritime Committee; International Missionary Council; International Music Council

IMCO Intergovernmental Maritime Consultative Organization (former name of IMO)
IME Institute of Medical Ethics
IMEA Incorporated Municipal Electrical Association
IMechE Institution of Mechanical Engineers
I Meth. Independent Methodist
IMF International Monetary Fund; International Motorcycle Federation; interplanetary magnetic field (in astrophysics)
IMG [computing] image file format
IMGTechE Institution of Mechanical and General Technician Engineers
IMHO in my humble opinion (in Internet chat and e-mail)
IMinE Institution of Mining Engineers (became part of IMM)
IMINT [military] image intelligence (from aerial photographs)
imit. imitate; imitation; imitative
IMM Institution of Mining and Metallurgy; International Mercantile Marine; International Monetary Market
imm. immediately
immac. immaculate (in advertisement)
immed. immediate
IMMTS Indian Mercantile Marine Training Ship
immun. immunity; immunization; immunology
IMO in my opinion (in Internet chat and e-mail); International Maritime Organization (formerly IMCO); International Meteorological Organization; International Miners' Organization
IMP [computing] interface message processor (in network); [card games] International Match Point (in bridge); interplanetary measurement probe
Imp. *Imperator* (Latin: Emperor); *Imperatrix* (Latin: Empress); Imperial
imp. imperative; imperfect; imperial; impersonal; implement; import; important; imported; importer; impression; imprimatur; *imprimeur* (French: printer); *imprimé* (French: printed); imprint; improved; improvement
IMPA International Master Printers' Association
IMPACT implementation, planning and control technique
impce importance
imper. imperative
imperf. imperfect; [philately] imperforate (of stamps)
impers. impersonal
impf. imperfect
impft imperfect
imp. gal. imperial gallon
imposs. impossible
IMPR [meteorology] improving
impreg. impregnate; impregnated; impregnation
improp. improper; improperly
impt important
imptd imported
imptr importer
IMR individual medical report; infant mortality rate; Institute of Medical Research
IMRA Industrial Marketing Research Association
IMRAN international marine radio aids to navigation
IMRO Investment Management Regulatory Organization
IMS Indian Medical Service; industrial methylated spirit; [trademark, computing] Information Management System; Institute of Management Services; International Musicological Society
IMT International Military Tribunal
IMU International Mathematical Union
IMunE Institution of Municipal Engineers (became part of Institution of Civil Engineers)
IMVS [Australia] Institute of Medical and Veterinary Science
IMW Institute of Masters of Wine; intermediate molecular weight
IN [US postcode] Indiana; Indian Navy
In [chemical element] indium
In. India; Indian; Instructor
in. inch
.in India (in Internet address)
INA Indian National Army; Institution of Naval Architects; International Newsreel Association; Iraqi News Agency
INAO *Institut national des appellations d'origine des vins et eaux-de-vie* (French authority controlling wine production)
inaud. inaudible

inaug. inaugural; inaugurate; inaugurated; inauguration
inbd inboard
Inbucon International Business Consultants
INC *in nomine Christi* (Latin: in the name of Christ); Indian National Congress; International Numismatic Commission
Inc. Incorporated (after US company name)
inc. include; included; including; inclusive; income; incomplete; incorporate; incorporated; increase; increment; incumbent
INCA International Newspaper Colour Association
incalz. [music] *incalzando* (Italian: hastening)
INCB International Narcotics Control Board (of UN)
incho. [law] inchoate
incid. incidental
incl. inclination; incline; include(s); included; including; inclusive
incldg including
incls. inclusive
incog. incognito
incomp. incomplete
incompat. incompatibility; incompatible
incorp. incorporated; incorporation
incorr. incorrect
INCPEN Industry Committee for Packaging and the Environment
INCR [meteorology] increase
incr. increase; increased; increasing; increment
incumb. incumbent
incun. incunabula
IND [international vehicle registration] India; *in nomine Dei* (Latin: in the name of God); [US pharmacology] investigational (or investigative) new drug
Ind [astronomy] Indus
Ind. Independent; India; Indian; Indiana; Indies
ind. independence; independent; index; indicate; indication; indicative; indigenous; indigo; indirect; indirectly; industrial; industry
in d. [medicine] *in dies* (Latin: daily)
indecl. [grammar] indeclinable
indef. indefinite
indep. independence; independent
indic. indicating; indicative; indicator
Ind. Imp. *Indiae Imperator* (Latin: Emperor of India); *Indiae Imperatrix* (Latin: Empress of India)
indiv. individual
individ. individual
Ind. Meth. Independent Methodist
Indo-Eur. Indo-European
Indo-Ger. Indo-Germanic
Indon. Indonesia; Indonesian
indre indenture
induc. inductance; induction
indust. industrial; industrialized; industrious; industry
ined. *ineditus* (Latin: unpublished)
INER Institute of Nuclear Energy Research
INET Institute of Nuclear Energy Technology
in ex. *in extenso* (Latin: in full)
INF intermediate-range nuclear forces; International Naturist Federation; International Nuclear Force
Inf. Infantry
inf. infant; infectious; inferior; [grammar] infinitive; influence; informal; information; *infra* (Latin: below); [medicine] *infusum* (Latin: infusion)
infin. [grammar] infinitive
infirm. infirmary
infl. inflammable; inflated; inflect; inflection; [botany] inflorescence; influence; influenced
infm. information
info [short form] information
infra dig [short form] *infra dignitatem* (Latin: beneath one's dignity, undignified)
Ing. *Ingenieur* (German: engineer)
Ingl. *Inghilterra* (Italian: England)
INGO international nongovernmental organization
INH [pharmacology] isonicotinic acid hydrazide (= isoniazid, drug used to treat tuberculosis)
Inh. *Inhaber* (German: proprietor); *Inhalt* (German: contents)
inhab. inhabitant
INI *in nomine Iesu* (Latin: in the name of Jesus)
init. initial; initially; *initio* (Latin: in the beginning)
INJ *in nomine Jesu* (Latin: in the name of Jesus)

inj. injection; injury
INLA International Nuclear Law Association; Irish National Liberation Army
in lim. *in limine* (Latin: at the outset)
in loc. *in loco* (Latin: in the place (of))
in loc. cit. *in loco citato* (Latin: in the place cited)
Inmarsat International Maritime Satellite Organization
in mem. *in memoriam* (Latin: to the memory (of))
inn. [cricket] innings
INO Inspectorate of Naval Ordnance
inorg. inorganic
INP Institute of Nuclear Physics
in pr. *in principio* (Latin: in the beginning)
in pro. in proportion
inq. inquest; inquiry; inquisition
INR independent national radio (as in **INR licence**); Index of Nursing Research
INRI *Iesus Nazarenus Rex Iudaeorum* (Latin: Jesus of Nazareth King of the Jews)
INS [USA] Immigration and Naturalization Service; Indian Naval Ship; inertial navigation system; International News Service; [fishing port] Inverness
Ins [computing] insert (key)
ins. inches; inscribe; inscription; insert; inspection; inspector; insular; insulate; insulated; insulation; insurance
in s. in situ
INSA Indian National Science Academy
INSAG International Nuclear Safety Advisory Group
insce insurance
inscr. inscribe; inscription
INSEA International Society for Education through Art
INSEAD *Institut européen d'administration des affaires* (French: European Institute of Administrative Affairs)
insep. inseparable
INSET [education] in-service (education and) training
insol. insoluble
insolv. insolvent
Insp. Inspector; Inspectorate
insp. inspect; inspected; inspection; inspector
Insp-Gen Inspector-General
INST *in nomine Sanctae Trinitatis* (Latin: in the name of the Holy Trinity)
Inst. Institute; Institution
inst. instance; instant; instant (= this month, used in formal correspondence); instantaneous; institute; institution; instruct; instruction; instructor; instrument; instrumental
INSTAB Information Service on Toxicity and Biodegradability (relating to water pollution)
InstAct Institute of Actuaries
InstBE Institution of British Engineers
InstCE Institution of Civil Engineers
InstD Institute of Directors
InstE Institute of Energy
InstEE Institution of Electrical Engineers
InstF Institute of Fuel
instl. installation
InstMM Institution of Mining and Metallurgy
Instn Institution
instn institution
InstP Institute of Physics
InstPet Institute of Petroleum
InstPI Institute of Patentees and Inventors
InstR Institute of Refrigeration
instr. instruction; instructor; instrument; instrumental
INSTRAW United Nations International Research and Training Institute for the Advancement of Women
InstSMM Institute of Sales and Marketing Management
InstT Institute of Transport
INT Isaac Newton Telescope (La Palma)
int. intelligence; intercept; interest; interim; interior; [grammar] interjection; intermediate; internal; international; interpret; interpretation; interpreter; interval; [grammar] intransitive; [music] introit
.int international (in Internet address)
INTAL Institute for Latin American Integration (Buenos Aires)
int. al. *inter alia* (Latin: among other things)
int. comb. internal combustion
Intelsat International Telecommunications Satellite Organization
intens. intensifier; intensify; intensive
inter. intermediate
intercom [short form] intercommunication (system)

interj. [grammar] interjection
internat. international
interp. interpreter
Interpol International Criminal Police Organization
interrog. interrogate; interrogation; [grammar] interrogative; interrogatively
intl international
INTO Irish National (Primary) Teachers' Organization
intr. [grammar] intransitive
intrans. [grammar] intransitive
in trans. in transit
intro [short form] introduction
intro. introduce; introduction; introductory
introd. introduce; introduction; introductory
INTUC Indian National Trade Union Congress
INucE Institution of Nuclear Engineers
Inv. Inverness
inv. *invenit* (Latin: (he/she) designed it); invent; invented; invention; inventor; inventory; inverse; inversion; invert; investment; invoice
inv. et del. *invenit et delineavit* (Latin: (he/she) designed and drew it)
invty inventory
IO India Office; [grammar] indirect object; inspecting officer; integrated optics; intelligence officer
I/O [computing] input/output; inspecting order
Io. Iowa
IOA Institute of Acoustics
IOB Institute of Bankers (former name of CIB); Institute of Biology; Institute of Book-keepers; Institute of Brewing; Institute of Building (former name of CIOB)
IOC Intergovernmental Oceanographic Commission; International Olympic Committee
IOCU International Organization of Consumers' Unions
IOD injured on duty; Institute of Directors
IODE [Canada] Imperial Order of Daughters of the Empire
IOE International Organization of Employers
IOF Independent Order of Foresters; Institute of Fuel; International Oceanographic Foundation; International Orienteering Federation
IOFB [medicine] intraocular foreign body
I of E Institute of Export
I of M Isle of Man
I of W Isle of Wight
IOGT International Order of Good Templars
IOJ Institute of Journalists; International Organization of Journalists
IOM Indian Order of Merit; Institute of Materials; Institute of Medicine; Isle of Man
IOMTR International Office for Motor Trades and Repairs
Ion. Ionic
IONARC Indian Ocean National Association for Regional Cooperation
IOO Inspecting Ordnance Officer
IOOF Independent Order of Oddfellows
IOP [computing] input/output processor; Institute of Painters in Oil Colours; Institute of Petroleum; Institute of Physics; Institute of Plumbing; Institute of Printing; [medicine] intraocular pressure
IOPAB International Organization for Pure and Applied Biophysics
IOPCW International Organization for the Prohibition of Chemical Weapons
IOR Independent Order of Rechabites
IOS [computing] integrated office system
IoS *Independent on Sunday*
IOSCO International Organization of Securities Commissions
IOSM Independent Order of the Sons of Malta
IOT Institute of Transport
IOU Industrial Operations Unit; I owe you
IOW in other words (in Internet chat and e-mail); Isle of Wight
IP [electronics] image processing; Imperial Preference; India Paper; [baseball] innings pitched; [medicine] in-patient; [electrical engineering] input primary; instalment plan; Institute of Petroleum; Institute of Plumbing; International Pharmacopoeia; [computing] Internet protocol; [chemistry] ionization potential; [UK postcode] Ipswich
i.p. identification point; incentive pay; indexed and paged; initial phase; [electrical engineering] input primary
IPA India Pale Ale; Insolvency Prac-

titioners' Association; Institute of Park Administration; Institute of Practitioners in Advertising; International Phonetic Alphabet; International Phonetic Association; International Poetry Archives (Manchester); International Police Academy; International Police Association; International Publishers' Association

IPAA International Petroleum Association of America; International Prisoners' Aid Association

IPARS International Programmed Airline Reservation System

IPBM interplanetary ballistic missile (in computer game)

IPC [astronomy] imaging proportional counter; International Petroleum Company; International Polar Commission; International Publishing Corporation; [computing] interprocess communication; Iraq Petroleum Company

IPCA International Pest Control Association

IPCC Intergovernmental Panel on Climatic Change (of UN)

IPCS Institution of Professional Civil Servants; [computing] intelligent process-control system

IPD individual package delivery; [law] *in praesentia dominorum* (Latin: in the presence of the Lords (of Session)) (Scotland); Institute of Personnel and Development; [medicine] intermittent peritoneal dialysis

IPE Institution of Plant Engineers; International Petroleum Exchange

IPF [medicine] interstitial pulmonary fibrosis; Irish Printing Federation

IPFC Indo-Pacific Fisheries Council

IPG Independent Publishers' Guild; Industrial Painters' Group

IPH [medicine] idiopathic portal hypertension; industrial process heat(ing)

iph impressions per hour

IPHE Institution of Public Health Engineers

IPI [computing] image processing and interchange; Institute of Patentees and Inventors; Institute of Professional Investigators; International Press Institute

i.p.i. *in partibus infidelium* (Latin: in the regions of unbelievers)

IPL [computing] information processing language; [computing] initial program load

IPlantE Institution of Plant Engineers

IPLO Irish People's Liberation Organization

IPM [Freemasonry] immediate past master; Institute of Personnel Management

ipm inches per minute; inches per month

IPMS Institute of Professionals, Managers and Specialists

IPO [US stock exchange] initial public offering (flotation on market); [computing] input-process-output; Israel Philharmonic Orchestra

IPP Institute for Plasma Physics; [medicine] intermittent positive pressure (in ventilation)

IPPF International Planned Parenthood Federation

IPPR Institute for Public Policy Research

IPPS Institute of Physics and the Physical Society

IPPV [medicine] intermittent positive-pressure ventilation

IPR Institute of Public Relations

IPRA International Public Relations Association

IPRE Incorporated Practitioners in Radio and Electronics

IProdE Institution of Production Engineers (became part of IEE)

IPS Indian Police Service; Indian Political Service; International Confederation for Plastic Surgery; [astronomy] interplanetary scintillations; Inter Press Service (Italian news agency); [computing] interpretative programming system

Ips. Ipswich

ips inches per second; [computing] instructions per second

IPSA International Political Science Association

IPSE [computing] integrated project support environment

IPSP [physiology] inhibitory post-synaptic potential

IPT Institute of Petroleum Technologies; interpersonal therapy

IPTO [astronautics] independent power take-off

IPTPA International Professional Tennis Players' Association
IPTS [physics] International Practical Temperature Scale
IPU Inter-Parliamentary Union
IPX Internet package exchange
ipy inches per year
IQ Institute of Quarrying; intelligence quota; international quota
.iq Iraq (in Internet address)
i.q. *idem quod* (Latin: the same as)
IQA Institute of Quality Assurance
IQS Institute of Quantity Surveyors
IR [meteorology] ice on runway; incidence rate; index register; industrial relations; informal report; information retrieval; infrared (radiation); Inland Revenue; [sports] inside right; inspector's report; Institute of Refrigeration; instrument reading; international registration; [international vehicle registration] Iran; [currency] Iranian rial; [chemistry] isoprene rubber
Ir [chemical element] iridium
Ir. Ireland; Irish
i.R *im Ruhestand* (German: retired, emeritus)
.ir Iran (in Internet address)
i.r. inside radius
IRA [USA] individual retirement account; Institute of Registered Architects; Irish Republican Army
IRAD Institute for Research on Animal Diseases
IRAF [astronomy] image reduction and analysis facility
IRAM *Institut de radioastronomie millimétrique* (French: Institute of Millimetre Radioastronomy)
Iran. Iranian
i.r.a.n. inspect and repair as necessary
IRAS Infrared Astronomical Satellite
IRB industrial revenue bond; Irish Republican Brotherhood
IRBM intermediate-range ballistic missile
IRC Industrial Reorganization Corporation; Infantry Reserve Corps; interdisciplinary research centre (of EPSRC); International Red Cross; international reply coupon; International Research Council; Internet relay chat
IRCert Industrial Relations Certificate
IRD International Research and Development Company
IRDA Industrial Research and Development Authority; Infra-Red Data Association
IRE [USA] Institute of Radio Engineers
Ire. Ireland
IREE(Aust) Institution of Radio and Electronics Engineers (Australia)
Irel. Ireland
IRF International Road Federation; International Rowing Federation
IRFB International Rugby Football Board
IRFU Irish Rugby Football Union
IRI Institution of the Rubber Industry (became part of Institute of Materials); *Istituto per la Ricostruzione Industriale* (Italian: Industrial Reconstruction Institute)
irid. iridescent
IRIS International Research and Information Service
Iris infrared intruder system
IRL in real life (in Internet chat); infrared (remote) locking (in car advertisement); [international vehicle registration] Ireland
IRLS [navigation] interrogation recording location system
IRM Islamic Republic of Mauritania; [geology] isothermal remanent magnetization
IRN Independent Radio News
IRO industrial relations officer; Inland Revenue Office; International Refugee Organization; International Relief Organization
iron. ironic(al)
IRPA International Radiation Protection Association
IRQ [computing] interrupt request; [international vehicle registration] Iraq
IRR infrared radiation; Institute of Race Relations; [finance] internal rate of return
irr. [finance] irredeemable; irregular
irreg. irregular; irregularly
IRRI International Rice Research Institute
IRRV Institute of Revenues, Rating and Valuation
IRS [computing] information retrieval system; [USA] Internal Revenue Service
IRSF Inland Revenue Staff Federation (became part of PTC)

IRTE Institute of Road Transport Engineers

IRTF Infrared Telescope Facility (Mauna Kea, Hawaii)

IRU industrial rehabilitation unit; International Relief Union; International Road Transport Union

IRWC International Registry of World Citizens

IS [international vehicle registration] Iceland (from Icelandic *Ísland*); independent suspension (in car advertisement); Industrial Society; information science; information system; [electrical engineering] input secondary; [genetics] insertion sequence; internal security; International Society of Sculptors, Painters and Gravers; Irish Society

Is. [Bible] Isaiah; Islam; Islamic; Island(s); Isle(s); Israel; Israeli

.is Iceland (in Internet address)

i.s. [electrical engineering] input secondary

ISA Independent Schools' Association; Individual Savings Account (replacement for TESSA); [computing] Industry Standard Architecture; International Sociological Association; [aeronautics] International Standard Atmosphere (formerly Interim Standard Atmosphere); International Standards in Auditing

Isa. [Bible] Isaiah

ISAB Institute for the Study of Animal Behaviour

ISAC Industrial Safety Advisory Council

ISAM [computing] indexed sequential access method

ISAS [Japan] Institute of Space and Astronautical Science

ISBA Incorporated Society of British Advertisers

ISBN International Standard Book Number (replacement for SBN)

ISC Imperial Service College (Haileybury); Imperial Staff College; Indian Staff Corps; [medicine] intermittent self-catheterization; International Seismological Centre; International Student Conference; International Sugar Council; [Freemasonry] International Supreme Council

ISCE International Society of Christian Endeavour

ISCM International Society for Contemporary Music

ISCO Independent Schools Careers Organization; International Standard Classification of Occupations

ISD international standard depth; international subscriber dialling

ISDA International Swaps and Derivatives Association

ISDN [computing, telecommunications] Integrated Services Digital Network

ISE Indian Service of Engineers; Institution of Structural Engineers; International Stock Exchange

ISEE [astronomy] International Sun–Earth Explorer

ISF [computing] integrated systems factory; International Shipping Federation; International Spiritualist Federation

ISGE International Society of Gastroenterology

ISH International Society of Haematology

ISHS International Society for Horticultural Science

ISI Indian Standards Institution; International Statistical Institute; Iron and Steel Institute (became part of Institute of Materials)

ISIS Independent Schools Information Service; International Shipping Information Services

ISJC Independent Schools Joint Council

ISK [currency] Icelandic króna

isl. island; isle

ISM *Iesus Salvator Mundi* (Latin: Jesus Saviour of the World); Imperial Service Medal; Incorporated Society of Musicians; [astronomy] interstellar medium

ISMA International Securities Market Association

ISME International Society for Musical Education

ISMRC Inter-Services Metallurgical Research Council

ISO Imperial Service Order; Infrared Space Observatory; International Organization for Standardization (from Greek *iso-* meaning 'equal', chosen as a multilingual abbreviation); International Sugar Organization

ISOL [meteorology] isolated

isol. isolate; isolated; isolation

ISP Institute of Sales Promotion; [computing] instruction set processor; International Study Programme; Internet service provider
ISPA International Society for the Protection of Animals; International Sporting Press Association
ISPEMA Industrial Safety (Personal Equipment) Manufacturers' Association
ISQ *in statu quo* (Latin: in the same state)
ISR information storage and retrieval; Institute of Social Research; International Society for Radiology; [computing] interrupt service routine
ISRB Inter-Services Research Bureau
ISRD International Society for Rehabilitation of the Disabled
ISRO International Securities Regulatory Organization
ISS Institute for Strategic Studies; Institute of Space Sciences; Institute of Space Studies; International Social Service(s); interstellar scintillations
iss. issue; issued
ISSA International Social Security Association
ISSC International Social Science Council
ISSN International Standard Serial Number
ISSS International Society of Soil Science
IST Indian Standard Time; information sciences technology; Institute of Science Technology; [medicine] insulin shock therapy
ISTC Institute of Scientific and Technical Communicators; Iron and Steel Trades Confederation
ISTD Imperial Society of Teachers of Dancing
ISTEA Iron and Steel Trades Employers' Association
isth. isthmus
IStructE Institution of Structural Engineers
ISU International Seamen's Union; International Shooting Union; International Skating Union
ISV independent software vendor; International Scientific Vocabulary
ISVA Incorporated Society of Valuers and Auctioneers
ISWG Imperial Standard Wire Gauge
IT ignition temperature; income tax; [USA] Indian Territory; industrial tribunal; infantry training; information technology; [law] Inner Temple; [physics] International Table (as in **IT calorie**); Investment Trust
It [short form] Italian vermouth
It. Italian; Italy
it. italic (type)
.it Italy (in Internet address)
i.t. in transit; inspection tag; internal thread (of tool)
ITA Independent Television Authority (replaced by IBA); industrial and technical assistance; Industrial Transport Association; Information Technology Agreement; Initial Teaching Alphabet; Institute of Air Transport; Institute of Travel Agents
ITAI Institution of Technical Authors and Illustrators
Ital. Italian; Italy
ital. italic (type)
ITALY I trust and love you (on envelope of love letter)
ITAR Information Telegraph Agency of Russia
ITB Industry Training Board; International Time Bureau; Irish Tourist Board
ITC Imperial Tobacco Company; Independent Television Commission; Industrial Training Council; International Tin Council; International Trade Centre; [meteorology] intertropical confluence; [USA] investment tax credit
i.t.c. installation time and cost
ITCA Independent Television Contractors' Association
ITCZ [meteorology] intertropical convergence zone
ITDA [military] indirect target damage assessment
ITE Institute of Terrestrial Ecology
ITEME Institution of Technician Engineers in Mechanical Engineering
ITER [nuclear technology] international thermonuclear engineering reactor; [nuclear technology] international tokamak engineering reactor
ITF [accounting] integrated test facility; International Tennis Federation; International Trade Federations; International Transport Workers' Federation

ITGWF International Textile and Garment Workers' Federation
itin. itinerary
ITMA Institute of Trade Mark Agents; *It's That Man Again* (former radio comedy series)
ITN Independent Television News
ITO [electronics] indium–tin oxide; International Trade Organization
ITS Industrial Training Service; [USA] Intermarket Trading System; International Trade Secretariat
ITT [medicine] insulin tolerance test; International Telephone and Telegraph Corporation
ITTF International Table Tennis Federation
ITU [computing] intelligent thermal update; [medicine] intensive therapy unit; International Telecommunication Union; International Temperance Union; International Typographical Union
ITV Independent Television; [USA] instructional television
ITVA International Television Association
ITWF International Transport Workers' Federation
IU immunizing unit; [pharmacology] international unit(s); *Izquierda Unida* (Spanish: United Left) (political party)
IUA International Union against Alcoholism; International Union of Architects
IUAA International Union of Advertisers' Associations
IUAES International Union of Anthropological and Ethnological Sciences
IUAI International Union of Aviation Insurers
IUAO International Union for Applied Ornithology
IUAPPA International Union of Air Pollution Prevention Associations
IUB International Union of Biochemistry; International Universities Bureau
IUBS International Union of Biological Sciences
IUCD [medicine] intrauterine contraceptive device
IUCN International Union for the Conservation of Nature and Natural Resources
IUCr International Union of Crystallography
IUCW International Union for Child Welfare
IUD [medicine] intrauterine death; [medicine] intrauterine (contraceptive) device
IUE [astronomy] International Ultraviolet Explorer; [USA] International Union of Electronic, Electrical, Salaried, Machine and Furniture Workers
IUF International Union of Food and Allied Workers' Associations
IUFO International Union of Family Organizations
IUFRO International Union of Forest Research Organizations
IUGG International Union of Geodesy and Geophysics
IUGR [medicine] intrauterine growth retardation
IUGS International Union of Geological Sciences
IUHPS International Union of the History and Philosophy of Science
IUI [medicine] intrauterine insemination
IULA International Union of Local Authorities
IUMF *institut universitaire de formation des maîtres* (French: university institute for advanced teacher education)
IUMI International Union of Marine Insurance
IUMSWA Industrial Union of Marine and Shipbuilding Workers of America
IUNS International Union of Nutritional Sciences
IUOE [USA] International Union of Operating Engineers
IUP *institut universitaire professionnel* (French: vocational university institute); [medicine] intrauterine pressure
IUPAB International Union of Pure and Applied Biophysics
IUPAC International Union of Pure and Applied Chemistry
IUPAP International Union of Pure and Applied Physics
IUPS International Union of Physiological Sciences
IUS [astronautics] inertial upper stage; International Union of Students; [medi-

cine] intrauterine system (contraceptive device)

IUSP International Union of Scientific Psychology

IUSY International Union of Socialist Youth

IUT *institut universitaire de technologie* (French: university institute of technology); [medicine] intrauterine transfusion

IUTAM International Union of Theoretical and Applied Mechanics

IV interactive video; [chemistry] intermediate valency; [medicine] intravenous; [medicine] intravenously; [UK postcode] Inverness; invoice value

i.V *in Vertretung* (German: by proxy)

i.v. increased value; initial velocity; [medicine] intravenous; [medicine] intravenously; invoice value

IVA individual voluntary arrangement (in bankruptcy proceedings); invalidity allowance

IVB invalidity benefit

IVBF International Volleyball Federation

IVC [medicine] inferior vena cava; intervarsity club

IVF [medicine] in vitro fertilization

IVL in virtual life (in Internet chat)

IVM illuminated vanity mirror

IVP [medicine] intravenous pyelogram

IVR international vehicle registration

IVS International Voluntary Service

IVT [astronautics] intravehicular transfer; [medicine] intravenous transfusion

IVU International Vegetarian Union

IW inspector of works; Isle of Wight; [vehicle registration] Londonderry

i.w. indirect waste; inside width

IWA Inland Waterways Association; Institute of World Affairs

IWC International Whaling Commission; International Wheat Council

IWD Inland Waterways and Docks

IWEM Institution of Water and Environmental Management (replacement for IWPC)

IWGC Imperial War Graves Commission (former name of CWGC)

IWM Imperial War Museum

IWO Institute of Welfare Officers; Institution of Water Officers

IWPC Institute of Water Pollution Control (replaced by IWEM)

IWS International Wool Secretariat

IWTA Inland Water Transport Association

IWW Industrial Workers of the World; International Workers of the World

IX *Iesous Christos* (Greek: Jesus Christ) (from initial letters in Greek alphabet)

IY Imperial Yeomanry

IYHF International Youth Hostels Federation

IYRU International Yacht Racing Union

iyswim if you see what I mean

IZ I Zingari (cricket club)

IZS [medicine] insulin zinc suspension (used to treat diabetes)

J

J [engineering] advance ratio; [vehicle registration] Durham; [card games] jack; Jacobean; [mathematics] Jacobian determinant; *Jahr* (German: year); January; [international vehicle registration] Japan; [fishing port] Jersey; Jesus; jet; Jew; Jewish; [immunology] joining region (of immunoglobulin chain); [slang] joint (of cannabis); joule; Journal; Judaic; Judaism; *judex* (Latin: judge); Judge; July; June; [geology] Jurassic; Justice

J [physics] angular momentum; [physics] magnetic polarization; [physics] sound intensity

j imaginary number (square root of –1)

j. *jour* (French: day); *juris* (Latin: of law); *jus* (Latin: law)

J2 [civil aircraft marking] Djibouti

J3 [civil aircraft marking] Grenada

J5 [civil aircraft marking] Guinea-Bissau

J6 [civil aircraft marking] St Lucia

J7 [civil aircraft marking] Dominica

9J [civil aircraft marking] Zambia

JA [international vehicle registration] Jamaica; [civil aircraft marking] Japan; joint account; Judge Advocate; Justice of Appeal; [vehicle registration] Manchester
J/A joint account
Ja. January
JAA Japan Aeronautic Association; Jewish Athletic Association
Jaat [military] joint air attack team
JAC Joint Advisory Committee (of UN); [USA] Joint Apprenticeship Committee; [USA] Junior Association of Commerce
Jac. Jacobean
JACARI Joint Action Commission Against Racial Interference
JACNE Joint Advisory Committee on Nutritional Education
JACT Joint Association of Classical Teachers
JAD Julian Astronomical Day
JADB [USA] Joint Air Defense Board
JAEC Japan Atomic Energy Commission; Joint Atomic Energy Committee (of US Congress)
JAF Judge Advocate of the Fleet
JAFC Japan Atomic Fuel Corporation
Jafo [military slang] just another fucking observer
JAG Judge Advocate-General
Jag [short form] Jaguar (car)
JAIEG Joint Atomic Information Exchange Group
JAL jet approach and landing (chart)
Jam. Jamaica; Jamaican; [Bible] James
JAMA *Journal of the American Medical Association*
Jan. *Januar* (German: January); January
jan. janitor
J&K Jammu and Kashmir
j. & w.o. [insurance] jettisoning and washing overboard
JANET [computing] Joint Academic Network
janv. *janvier* (French: January)
Jap. Japan; Japanese
jap. japanned
jar. jargon
JARE Japanese Antarctic Research Expedition
JAS Jamaica Agricultural Society; Junior Astronomical Society
Jas. [Bible] James
jastop [aeronautics] jet-assisted stop
JAT *Jugoslovenski Aero-Transport* (Yugoslav airline company)
JATCC Joint Aviation Telecommunications Coordination Committee
JATCRU joint air traffic control radar unit
JATO [aeronautics] jet-assisted take-off
JATS joint air transportation service
jaund. jaundice
Jav. Java; Javanese
jav. [athletics] javelin
JB Bachelor of Laws (from Latin *Juris Baccalaureus*); junior beadle; [vehicle registration] Reading
Jb. *Jahrbuch* (German: yearbook, annual)
j.b. jet bomb; joint board; junction box
JBAA *Journal of the British Archaeological Association*
JBC Jamaica Broadcasting Corporation; Japan Broadcasting Corporation
JBCNS Joint Board of Clinical Nursing Studies
Jber. *Jahresbericht* (German: annual report)
JBES Jodrell Bank Experimental Station
JBL *Journal of Business Law*
JBS [USA] John Birch Society
JC [vehicle registration] Bangor; Jesus Christ; *Jewish Chronicle*; Jockey Club; Julius Caesar (Roman emperor); [USA] Junior Chamber (of Commerce) (applied to members); [USA] junior college; [law] jurisconsult (legal adviser); Justice Clerk; justiciary case; juvenile court
J-C *Jésus-Christ* (French: Jesus Christ)
j.c. joint compound
JCAC [USA] Joint Civil Affairs Committee
JCAR Joint Commission on Applied Radioactivity
JCB Bachelor of Canon Law (from Latin *Juris Canonici Baccalaureus*); Bachelor of Civil Law (from Latin *Juris Civilis Baccalaureus*); Joseph Cyril Bamford (manufacturer of excavating machines)
JCC Joint Consultants' Committee; Joint Consultative Committee; Junior Chamber of Commerce
JCD Doctor of Canon Law (from Latin *Juris Canonici Doctor*); Doctor of Civil Law (from Latin *Juris Civilis Doctor*)
JCHMT Joint Committee on Higher Medical Training
JCHST Joint Committee on Higher Surgical Training

JCI Junior Chamber International
JCL [computing] job-control language; Licentiate in Canon Law (from Latin *Juris Canonici Licentiatus*); Licentiate in Civil Law (from Latin *Juris Civilis Licentiatus*)
JCMC Joint Conference on Medical Conventions
JCMD Joint Committee on Mobility for the Disabled
JCMT James Clerk Maxwell Telescope
JCNAAF Joint Canadian Navy-Army-Air Force
JC of C Junior Chamber of Commerce
JCP Japan Communist Party
JCR junior combination room (in university or college); junior common room (in university or college)
JCS Jersey Cattle Society of the United Kingdom; Joint Chiefs of Staff; Joint Commonwealth Societies; *Journal of the Chemical Society*
jct. junction
jctn junction
JCWI Joint Council for the Welfare of Immigrants
JD [vehicle registration] central London; Diploma in Journalism; Doctor of Jurisprudence (or Laws) (from Latin *Jurum Doctor*); [currency] Jordanian dinar; [astronomy] Julian date; junior deacon; junior dean; jury duty; [USA] Justice Department; juvenile delinquent
jd joined
JDA Japan Defence Agency
JDB Japan Development Bank
JDipMA Joint Diploma in Management Accounting Services
JDL [USA] Jewish Defense League
JDM [medicine] juvenile diabetes mellitus
JDS [accounting] Joint Disciplinary Scheme
j.d.s. job data sheet
JE [UK postcode] Jersey; [vehicle registration] Peterborough
JEA Jesuit Educational Association; Joint Engineering Association
j.e.a. joint export agent
JEB Joint Examining Board
JEC Joint Economic Committee (of US Congress)
JECFI Joint Expert Committee on Food Irradiation
JECI *Jeunesse étudiante catholique internationale* (French: International Young Catholic Students)
JEDEC Joint Electronic Devices Engineering Council
JEIDA Japanese Electronic Industry Development Association
Jer. [Bible] Jeremiah; Jersey; Jerusalem
JERC Joint Electronic Research Committee
JERI Japan Economic Research Institute
jerob. jeroboam (large wine bottle)
Jes. Jesus
JESA Japanese Engineering Standards Association
JESSI Joint European Submicron Silicon Initiative
JET [nuclear technology] Joint European Torus (Culham, Oxfordshire); Joint European Transport
jet. jetsam; jettison
JETCO Jamaican Export Trading Company; Japan Export Trading Company
JETP *Journal of Experimental and Theoretical Physics*
JETRO Japan External Trade Organization
jett. jettison
jeu. *jeudi* (French: Thursday)
JF [vehicle registration] Leicester
J/F [book-keeping] journal folio
JFET [electronics] junction field-effect transistor
JFK John Fitzgerald Kennedy (US president)
JFM *Jeunesse fédéraliste mondiale* (French: Young World Federalists)
JFTC Joint Fur Trade Committee
JFU Jersey Farmers' Union
JG [vehicle registration] Maidstone
Jg. *Jahrgang* (German: year's issues (of magazine))
j.g. junior grade
JGTC Junior Girls' Training Corps
JGW [Freemasonry] Junior Grand Warden
JH [numismatics] Jubilee head (of Queen Victoria); [biochemistry] juvenile hormone; [vehicle registration] Reading
Jh. *Jahresheft* (German: annual volume); *Jahrhundert* (German: century)
j.h.a. job hazard analysis
JHDA Junior Hospital Doctors' Association
JHMO junior hospital medical officer
JHS *Jesus Hominum Salvator* (Latin: Jesus

Saviour of Men); [USA] junior high school
JHU [USA] Johns Hopkins University
JI Journalists' Institute; [vehicle registration] Tyrone
JIB joint intelligence bureau
JIC joint industrial council; [USA] joint intelligence center; [USA] joint intelligence committee; just in case
JICNARS Joint Industry Committee for National Readership Surveys
JICRAR Joint Industry Committee for Radio Audience Research
JICTAR Joint Industry Committee for Television Advertising Research
JIE Junior Institute of Engineers
JIM Japan Institute of Metals
JINS [USA] juvenile(s) in need of supervision
JINucE Junior Member of the Institution of Nuclear Engineers
JIOA joint intelligence objectives agency
JIS Jamaica Information Service; Japan Industrial Standard; Jewish Information Society; joint intelligence staff
JIT [commerce] just-in-time (manufacturing system)
JIU joint inspection unit
JJ jaw jerk; (Sir) Joseph John Thomson (British physicist); [electronics] Josephson junction; Judges; Justices; [vehicle registration] Maidstone
JK [vehicle registration] Brighton
JKG John Kenneth Galbraith (US economist)
jkt jacket
j.k.t. job knowledge test
JL [vehicle registration] Lincoln
Jl. July
jl journal
JLA Jewish Lads' Brigade; Jewish Librarians' Association
JLC [USA] Jewish Labor Committee
JLP Jamaica Labour Party
JM [vehicle registration] Reading
.jm Jamaica (in Internet address)
JMA Japanese Meteorological Agency
JMB J(ames) M(atthew) Barrie (Scottish writer); Joint Matriculation Board
JMBA *Journal of the Marine Biological Association*
JMC Joint Mathematical Council of the United Kingdom
JMCS Junior Mountaineering Club of Scotland
JMJ [Roman Catholic Church] Jesus, Mary and Joseph
JMPR Joint Meeting on Pesticide Residues (of WHO)
JMSAC Joint Meteorological Satellite Advisory Committee
JN [vehicle registration] Chelmsford
Jn Junction
jn join; junction
jn. junior
JNA Jordan News Agency
JNC joint negotiating committee
jnc. junction
JND just noticeable difference
JNEC Jamaican National Export Corporation
JNF Jewish National Fund
Jnl Journal
jnl journal
jnlst journalist
JNR Japanese National Railways
Jnr Junior
jnr junior
j.n.s. just noticeable shift
jnt joint
JNTO Japan National Tourist Organization
jnt stk joint stock
JO job order; *Journal Officiel* (French: Official Gazette); junior officer; [vehicle registration] Oxford
.jo Jordan (in Internet address)
Jo. Bapt. John the Baptist
Joburg [short form] Johannesburg
JOC *Jeunesse ouvrière chrétienne* (French: Young Christian Workers); [USA] joint operations center
joc. jocose; jocular
JOD [medicine] juvenile onset diabetes
j.o.d. joint occupancy date
J of E *Journal of Education*
JOG junior offshore group (in yachting)
Johan. Johannesburg
join. joinery
Jon. [Bible] Jonah
Jos. Joseph
Josh. [Bible] Joshua
JOT joint observer team
jour. journal; journalist; journey; journeyman
JOVIAL [computing] Jules' own version of

international algorithmic language (named after Jules Schwarz)
JP jet-propelled; jet propulsion; Justice of the Peace; [vehicle registration] Liverpool
.jp Japan (in Internet address)
JPA Jamaica Press Association
JPC joint planning council; joint production council; Judge of the Prize Court
JPCAC Joint Production, Consultative and Advisory Committee
JPEG Joint Photographic Expert Group
JPL Jet Propulsion Laboratory (California); *Journal of Planning Law*
JPMO Jersey Potato Marketing Organization
Jpn Japan
JPRS [USA] Joint Publications Research Service
JPS jet-propulsion system; [USA] Jewish Publications Society; Joint Parliamentary Secretary; joint planning staff; Junior Philatelic Society
JPTO [astronautics] jet-propelled take-off
JR *Jacobus Rex* (Latin: King James); joint resolution; Judges' Rules; Jurist Reports; [vehicle registration] Newcastle upon Tyne
Jr Junior; juror
jr *jour* (French: day); junior
jr. journal
JRA [medicine] juvenile rheumatoid arthritis
JRAI *Journal of the Royal Anthropological Institute*
JRC Junior Red Cross
JS [vehicle registration] Inverness; [USA] Japan Society; [law] judgment summons; [law] judicial separation
JSA jobseekers' allowance
JSAWC Joint Services Amphibious Warfare Centre
JSB joint-stock bank
JSC Johnson Space Center (Texas)
JSD Doctor of Juristic Science; [computing] Jackson system development
JSDC Joint Service Defence College
JSE Johannesburg Stock Exchange
Jsey Jersey
JSLS Joint Services Liaison Staff
JSP [trademark, computing] Jackson Structured Programming; Japan Socialist Party
JSPS Japan Society for the Promotion of Science
JSS Jacob Sheep Society; joint services standard
JSSC Joint Services Staff College; joint shop stewards' committee
J-stars joint surveillance and targeting acquisition radar system
JT [vehicle registration] Bournemouth
jt joint
j.t. [law] joint tenancy
JTC Junior Training Corps
Jt Ed. joint editor
JTIDS Joint Tactical Information Distribution Systems
jtly jointly
JTMP [computing] job transfer and manipulation protocol
JTO [aeronautics] jump take-off
JTS job training standards
JTUAC Joint Trade Union Advisory Committee
JU [vehicle registration] Leicester
Ju. June
j.u. joint use
JUD Doctor of Canon and Civil Law (from Latin *Juris Utriusque Doctor*)
Jud. Judaea; [Bible] Judah; Judaism; Judge; [Bible] Judges; [Bible] Judith (book of Apocrypha)
jud. judgment; judicial; judo
Judg. [Bible] Judges
judgt judgment
juev. *jueves* (Spanish: Thursday)
JUGFET [electronics] junction-gate field-effect transistor
juil. *juillet* (French: July)
Jul. July
jul. *julio* (Spanish: July)
Jun. June; Junior
jun. *junio* (Spanish: June); junior
junc. junction
jun. part. junior partner
Junr Junior
JurD Doctor of Law (from Latin *Juris Doctor*)
jurisd. jurisdiction
jurisp. jurisprudence
jus. justice
JUSMAG Joint United States Military Advisory Group
juss. [grammar] jussive
Just. Justinian (Byzantine emperor)

just. justice
Juv. (Decimus Junius) Juvenal(is) (Roman poet)
juv. juvenile
JUWTFA Joint Unconventional Warfare Task Force, Atlantic
jux. juxtaposed; juxtaposition
JV [commerce] joint venture; [anatomy] jugular vein; [USA] junior varsity; [vehicle registration] Lincoln
Jv. Java; Javanese
JVS Jewish Vegetarian and Natural Health Society
JW [vehicle registration] Birmingham; Jehovah's Witness(es); junior warden
JWB Jewish Welfare Board; joint wages board
JWEF Joinery and Woodwork Employers' Federation
JWG joint working group
jwlr jeweller
j.w.o. [insurance] jettisoning and washing overboard
JWPAC Joint Waste Paper Advisory Council
JWS Joint Warfare Staff
JWV Jewish War Veterans
JX [vehicle registration] Huddersfield; Jesus Christ
JY [vehicle registration] Exeter; [civil aircraft marking] Jordan
Jy jansky (unit used in astronomy); July; jury
JZ [vehicle registration] Down

K

K [botany] calyx (in floral formula); [international vehicle registration] Cambodia (from former name Kampuchea); [geology] Cretaceous; *Kalt* (German: cold); [physics] kaon; kelvin (unit of thermodynamic temperature); [immunology] killer (as in **K-cell**); [computing] kilo- (indicates 1,024, as in **KB** = kilobyte); [currency] kina (used in Papua New Guinea); King('s); [chess, card games] king; [currency] kip (used in Laos); [music] Kirkpatrick (catalogue of Domenico Scarlatti's works); [fishing port] Kirkwall; kitchen (in property advertisement); Knight; knighthood; [music] Köchel (catalogue of Mozart's works); *koel* (Dutch: cold); [currency] krona (used in Sweden); [currency] króna (used in Iceland); [currency] krone (used in Denmark and Norway); [currency] kwacha (used in Zambia); [currency] kyat (used in Myanmar); [vehicle registration] Liverpool; [chemical element] potassium (from Latin *kalium*); [astronomy] solar constant; [baseball] strikeout; thousand (from prefix kilo-)
K [physics] bulk modulus; [ecology] carrying capacity; [chemistry] equilibrium constant; [physics] kinetic energy; [physics] luminous efficacy
k [mathematics] constant; [mathematics] curvature; kilo- (indicates 1,000, as in **kg** = kilogram); [computing] kilo- (indicates 1,024, as in **kbyte** = kilobyte)
k radius of gyration (in mechanics); [chemistry] rate coefficient; [chemistry] rate constant; [physics] thermal conductivity
k. [USA] karat; keel; killed; king; kingdom; knight; [knitting] knit; knot; [currency] kopek (hundredth of rouble); kosher
K9 [military] canine (referring to army dogs)
9K [civil aircraft marking] Kuwait
KA [UK postcode] Kilmarnock; King of Arms; Knight of St Andrew, Order of Barbados; [vehicle registration] Liverpool
KADU Kenya African Democratic Union (became part of KANU)
KAI Keep America Independent
KAK *Kungliga Automobil Klubben* (Swedish: Royal Automobile Club)
Kal. *Kalendae* (Latin: calends, first day of month)
Kan. Kansas
k&b kitchen and bathroom (in property advertisement)
Kans. Kansas

KANTAFU Kenya African National Traders' and Farmers' Union
KANU Kenya African National Union
KANUPP Karachi Nuclear Power Plant
KAO Kuiper Airborne Observatory
kao. kaolin
Kap. [finance] *Kapital* (German: capital); *Kapitel* (German: chapter)
KAR King's African Rifles
Kar. Karachi
Karel. Karelia; Karelian
Kash. Kashmir
KB [computing] kilobyte; King's Bench; [chess] kings' bishop; Knight Bachelor; [knitting] knit into back of stitch; [computing] knowledge base; *Koninkrijk België* (Flemish: Kingdom of Belgium); [vehicle registration] Liverpool
kb kilobar (unit of pressure)
KBC [law] King's Bench Court
KBD [law] King's Bench Division
kbd keyboard
KBE Knight Commander of the Order of the British Empire
KBES [computing] knowledge-based expert system
Kbhvn *København* (Danish: Copenhagen)
Kbl Kabul
KBP [chess] king's bishop's pawn
KBS Knight of the Blessed Sacrament; [computing] knowledge-based system
KBW King's Bench Walk (Temple, London)
kbyte [computing] kilobyte
KC Kansas City; Kennel Club; King's College; King's Counsel; King's Cross (London); Knight Commander; Knight of the Crescent (in Turkey); Knights of Columbus; [vehicle registration] Liverpool
kc kilocycle(s per second) (unit of frequency)
KCA *Keesing's Contemporary Archives*
kcal kilocalorie
KCB Knight Commander of the Order of the Bath
KCC (Knight) Commander of the Order of the Crown (Belgium and the Congo Free State)
K-cell [immunology] killer cell
KCH King's College Hospital (London); Knight Commander of the Hanoverian Order
KCHS Knight Commander of the Order of the Holy Sepulchre
KCIE Knight Commander of the Order of the Indian Empire
KCL King's College, London
KCLJ Knight Commander of the Order of St Lazarus of Jerusalem
KCMG Knight Commander of the Order of St Michael and St George
KCMS [trademark] Kodak colour management system
KCNA Korean Central News Agency
Kcs [currency] koruna (used in Czech Republic)
kc/s kilocycles per second (unit of frequency)
KCSA Knight Commander of the Military Order of the Collar of St Agatha of Paterna
KCSG Knight Commander of the Order of St Gregory the Great
KCSI Knight Commander of the Order of the Star of India
KCSJ Knight Commander of the Order of St John of Jerusalem (Knights Hospitallers)
KCSS Knight Commander of the Order of St Silvester
KCVO Knight Commander of the Royal Victorian Order
KD kiln dried; knock down (at auction); [commerce] knocked down (of goods sold in parts); *Kongeriget Danmark* (Danish: Kingdom of Denmark); [currency] Kuwaiti dinar; [vehicle registration] Liverpool
kd killed
KDC [computing] key distribution centre; [commerce] knocked-down condition (of goods sold in parts)
KDD [computing] knowledge discovery in databases
KDF *Kraft durch Freude* (German: Strength through Joy) (Nazi holiday scheme)
KDG King's Dragoon Guards
KDM *Kongelige Danske Marine* (Danish: Royal Danish Navy)
KE kinetic energy; kinetic equation; [vehicle registration] Maidstone
.ke Kenya (in Internet address)
KEAS [aeronautics] knots equivalent air speed
Kef. Keflavik (Iceland)

KEH King Edward's Horse
Ken. Kensington; Kentucky; Kenya
Kent. Kentucky
KEO King Edward's Own
Ker. Kerry
keV kiloelectronvolt
KEY keep extending yourself
KF [vehicle registration] Liverpool
KFA Keep-Fit Association; Kenya Farmers' Association
KFAED Kuwait Fund for Arab Economic Development
KFAT National Union of Knitwear, Footwear and Apparel Trades
KFC [trademark] Kentucky Fried Chicken
KFL Kenya Federation of Labour
Kfm. *Kaufmann* (German: merchant)
kfm. *kaufmännisch* (German: commercial)
KFOR Kosovo Force (NATO-led peace-keeping force)
Kfz. *Kraftfahrzeug* (German: motor vehicle)
KG [vehicle registration] Cardiff; Knight of the Order of the Garter; [commerce] *Kommanditgesellschaft* (German: limited partnership)
kg keg; kilogram
.kg Kyrgyzstan (in Internet address)
KGB *Komitet Gosudarstvennoi Bezopasnosti* (Russian: Committee of State Security) (former Soviet secret police)
KGC Knights of the Golden Circle (US antifederal organization)
Kgf. *Kriegsgefangener* (German: prisoner-of-war)
kgf [physics] kilogram-force
KGFR [medicine] kidney glomerular filtration rate
Kgl. *Königlich* (German: Royal)
Kgn Kingston (Jamaica)
KGS known geological structure
Kgs [Bible] Kings
KGV Knight of Gustavus Vasa (Swedish decoration)
KH [vehicle registration] Hull; kennel huntsman; [astronautics] keyhole (as in **KH-11**, name of NASA satellite); King's Hussars; Knight of the Hanoverian Order
.kh Cambodia (in Internet address)
KHC King's Honorary Chaplain
KHDS King's Honorary Dental Surgeon
KHM King's Harbour Master
KHNS King's Honorary Nursing Sister
KHP King's Honorary Physician
KHS King's Honorary Surgeon; Knight of the Order of the Holy Sepulchre
kHz kilohertz
.ki Kiribati (in Internet address)
KIA killed in action
KIAS [aeronautics] knots indicated air speed
kid. kidney
kil. kilderkin (brewing cask size)
Kild. Kildare
kild. kilderkin (brewing cask size)
Kilk. Kilkenny
Kinc. Kincardineshire
kind. kindergarten
kingd. kingdom
Kinr. Kinross
KIO Kuwait Investment Office
Kirk. Kirkcudbrightshire
KISS keep it short and simple; [informal] keep it simple, stupid; [stock exchange] Kurs Information Service System
kit. kitchen (in property advertisement)
kitch. kitchen (in property advertisement)
KJ [medicine] knee jerk; Knight of St Joachim; [vehicle registration] Maidstone
kJ kilojoule
KJV [Bible] King James Version
KK [commerce] *Kabushiki Kaisha* (Japanese: joint-stock company); [vehicle registration] Maidstone
KKK Ku Klux Klan
KKt [chess] king's knight
KKtP [chess] king's knight's pawn
KL [astronomy] Kleinmann–Low (as in **KL nebula**); Kuala Lumpur; [vehicle registration] Maidstone
kl kilolitre
KLA Kosovo Liberation Army
klax. klaxon
KLH Knight of the Legion of Honour
KLJ Knight of the Order of St Lazarus of Jerusalem
KLM *Koninklijke Luchtvaart Maatschappij* (Dutch airline company)
KLS [medicine] kidney, liver, spleen
KLSE Kuala Lumpur Stock Exchange
KM King's Medal; Knight of Malta; [vehicle registration] Maidstone
km kilometre
.km Comoros (in Internet address)

KMF [currency] Comorian franc
km/h kilometres per hour
KMO Kobe Marine Observatory (Japan)
KMP [computing] Knuth–Morris–Pratt (algorithm)
kmph kilometres per hour
KMT Kuomintang (Chinese Nationalist Party)
KN [chess] king's knight; [numismatics] King's Norton (Birmingham mint mark); *Kongeriket Norge* (Norwegian: Kingdom of Norway); [vehicle registration] Maidstone
kn knot (unit of speed); [currency] krona (used in Sweden); [currency] krone (used in Denmark and Norway)
KNA Kenya News Agency; *Kongelig Norsk Automobil-klubb* (Norwegian: Royal Norwegian Automobile Club)
KNM *Kongelige Norske Marine* (Norwegian: Royal Norwegian Navy)
KNP [chess] king's knight's pawn; Kruger National Park (South Africa)
KNPC Kuwait National Petroleum Company
Knt Knight
KO [informal] knock out; [informal] knockout; [vehicle registration] Maidstone
k.o. keep off; keep out; kick-off (in football); [informal] knock out; [informal] knockout
KOC Kuwait Oil Company
KOD [navigation] kick-off drift
K of C Knights of Columbus
K of K (Lord) Kitchener of Khartoum (British field marshal)
K of P [USA] Knights of Pythias
KOM Knight of the Order of Malta
Komintern *Kommunisticheskii Internatsionál* (Russian: Communist International)
Komp. [commerce] *Kompanie* (German: company)
Komsomol *Kommunisticheskii Soyuz Molodezhi* (Russian: Communist Union of Youth)
kop. [currency] kopek (hundredth of rouble)
Kor. Koran; Korea; Korean
KORR King's Own Royal Regiment
KOSB King's Own Scottish Borderers
KOYLI King's Own Yorkshire Light Infantry
KP King's Parade; [chess] king's pawn; [US military] kitchen police; Knight of the Order of St Patrick; [vehicle registration] Maidstone
.kp North Korea (in Internet address)
k.p. key personnel
kpc kiloparsec (unit of astronomical distance)
KPD *Kommunistische Partei Deutschlands* (German: German Communist Party)
KPDR Korean People's Democratic Party
KPFSM King's Police and Fire Service Medal
kpg kilometres per gallon
kph kilometres per hour
KPM King's Police Medal
KPMG (Piet) Klynveld, (William Barclay) Peat, (James) Marwick, (Reinhard) Goerdeler (founding members of international accounting group)
Kpmtr [music] *Kapellmeister* (German: conductor)
KPNLF Khmer People's National Liberation Front
KPNO Kitt Peak National Observatory (Arizona)
KPP Keeper of the Privy Purse
kpr keeper
KPTT [medicine] kaolin partial thromboplastin time
KPU Kenya People's Union
KR King's Regiment; [military] King's Regulations; [chess] king's rook; [vehicle registration] Maidstone
Kr [currency] króna (used in Iceland); [chemical element] krypton
kr. [currency] krona (used in Sweden); [currency] krone (used in Denmark and Norway)
.kr Republic of Korea (in Internet address)
KRC Knight of the Red Cross
KRE Knight of the Order of the Red Eagle
KRL [computing] knowledge representation language
KRP [chess] king's rook's pawn
KRR King's Royal Rifles
KRRC King's Royal Rifle Corps
KS [vehicle registration] Edinburgh; [US postcode] Kansas; [medicine] Kaposi's sarcoma; King's Scholar; King's School; Kipling Society; Kitchener Scholar;

Konungariket Sverige (Swedish: Kingdom of Sweden); [international vehicle registration] Kyrgyzstan

KSA Kitchen Specialists Association

KSC Kennedy Space Center (Florida); King's School, Canterbury; Knight of St Columba

KSF key success factor

KSG Knight of the Order of St Gregory the Great

Ksh [currency] Kenya shilling

KSI Knight of the Order of the Star of India

KSJ Knight of the Order of St John of Jerusalem (Knights Hospitallers)

KSL [medicine] kidney, spleen, liver

KSLI King's Shropshire Light Infantry

KSM Korean Service Medal; *Kungliga Svenska Marinen* (Swedish: Royal Swedish Navy)

KSS Knight of the Order of St Silvester

KSSU KLM, SAS, Swissair, UTA (international airline organization)

KStJ Knight of the Order of St John of Jerusalem (Knights Hospitallers)

KSU Kansas State University

KT [UK postcode] Kingston-upon-Thames; Knight of the Order of the Thistle; Knight Templar; [meteorology] knot; [vehicle registration] Maidstone

Kt knight

kt [USA] karat; kilotonne; knot (unit of speed)

Kt Bach. Knight Bachelor

Kto [banking] *Konto* (German: account)

KU [vehicle registration] Sheffield

Ku [chemical element] kurchatovium (alternative name for rutherfordium)

KUB [medicine] kidney, ureter, bladder

KUTD keep up to date

Kuw. Kuwait

KV [vehicle registration] Coventry; [music] *Köchel Verzeichnis* (German: Köchel catalogue) (catalogue of Mozart's works)

kV kilovolt

KW [UK postcode] Kirkwall (Orkney); [vehicle registration] Sheffield

kW kilowatt

.kw Kuwait (in Internet address)

KWAC key word and context

kWh kilowatt hour

KWIC key word in context

KWOC key word out of context

KWP Korean Workers' Party

KWT [international vehicle registration] Kuwait

KX [vehicle registration] Luton

KY [US postcode] Kentucky; [fishing port] Kirkcaldy; [UK postcode] Kirkcaldy; *Kol Yisrael* (Israeli broadcasting station); [vehicle registration] Sheffield

Ky Kentucky

ky. [currency] kyat (used in Myanmar)

kybd keyboard

Kyr. *Kyrie eleison* (Greek: Lord have mercy) (ecclesiastical invocation)

KZ [vehicle registration] Antrim; [international vehicle registration] Kazakhstan; [military] killing zone

.kz Kazakhstan (in Internet address)

Kzrl [currency] kwanza (used in Angola)

L

L [Roman numeral] fifty; [electrical engineering] inductor; [politics] Labour; Lady; Lake; lambert (former unit of luminance); [military] Lancers; [linguistics] language; large; Latin; law; League; learner (driver) (as in **L-plate**); lecturer; left; [currency] lempira (used in Honduras); lethal; *liber* (Latin: book); [politics] Liberal; Licentiate; Lieutenant; [aeronautics] lift; [immunology] light; [fishing port] Limerick; line (of text); linear; link; [currency] lira; litre; [electrical engineering] live; [UK postcode] Liverpool; Loch; *locus* (Latin: place); Lodge (of fraternal organization); London; Lord; [sports] lost; Lough; low; [international vehicle registration] Luxembourg; [currency] pound sterling (from Latin *libra*); [theatre] stage left

L [physics] angular momentum; [chemistry] Avogadro constant; [physics] Lagrangian function; [physics] latent heat;

length; [biochemistry] linking number; longitude; [physics] luminance; [astronomy] luminosity; [physics] radiance; [electrical engineering] self-inductance; [physics] sound intensity

l [Roman numeral] fifty; [music] la(h) (in tonic sol-fa); [meteorology] lightning; [chemistry] liquid; [currency] lira; litre; [currency] pound sterling (from Latin *libra*)

l [chemistry] laevorotatory; length; [physics] lepton number

l. lake; land; large; late; lateral; latitude; law; leaf; league; leasehold; left; legitimate; length; light; line (of text); link; literate; little; loch; long; lost; lough; low

4L [civil aircraft marking] Georgia

9L [civil aircraft marking] Sierra Leone

LA [UK postcode] Lancaster; [photography] large aperture; Latin America; Latin American; law agent; leave allowance; [medicine] left atrial; [medicine] left atrium; legal adviser; Legislative Assembly; letter of authority; Library Association; Licensing Act; licensing authority; Lieutenant-at-Arms; [physics] linear accelerator; [computing] linear arithmetic; Literate in Arts; Liverpool Academy; [fishing port] Llanelly; Lloyd's agent; local agent; local anaesthetic; local association; local authority; long acting; Los Angeles; [US postcode] Louisiana; low altitude; [vehicle registration] northwest London

La [chemical element] lanthanum; Louisiana

La. Lancastrian; Lane

la. last

.la Laos (in Internet address)

l.a. landing account; leading article; [medicine] *lege artis* (Latin: as directed) (in prescriptions); lighter than air

LAA [USA] League of Advertising Agencies; Library Association of Australia; Libyan Arab Airlines; Lieutenant-at-Arms; [USA] Life Assurance Advertisers; light anti-aircraft

LAADS [USA] Los Angeles Air Defense Sector

LAAOH Ladies' Auxiliary, Ancient Order of Hibernians

LAAR liquid-air accumulator rocket

LAB Legal Aid Board; [chemistry] linear alkyl benzene; load aboard barge; low-altitude bombing

Lab. [USA] Laborite; [politics] Labour; Labrador

lab [short form] laboratory; [short form] labrador (dog)

lab. label; laboratory; labour; labourer

LABA [USA] Laboratory Animal Breeders' Association

LABBS Ladies' Association of British Barbershop Singers

LAC Laboratory Animals Centre; Landscape Advisory Committee; leading aircraftman; Licentiate of the Apothecaries' Company; London Athletic Club; [finance] long-run average cost

Lac [astronomy] Lacerta

lac. lacquer; lactation

LACES London Airport cargo electronic processing scheme; [USA] Los Angeles Council of Engineering Societies

LACONIQ [computing] laboratory computer online inquiry

LACS League Against Cruel Sports

LACSA *Lineas Aéreas Costarricenses* (Costa Rican airline company)

LACSAB Local Authorities' Conditions of Service Advisory Board

LACW leading aircraftwoman

LAD [linguistics] language acquisition device; light aid detachment

ladar laser detection and ranging

Ladp Ladyship

L Adv. Lord Advocate

LAE [mathematics] linear algebraic equation

laev. [medicine] *laevus* (Latin: left)

LAF *L'Académie française* (French: the French Academy)

LaF Louisiana French

LAFC Latin American Forestry Commission

La Font. (Jean de) La Fontaine (French writer)

LAFTA Latin American Free Trade Association (former name of LAIA)

lag. lagoon

LAH Licentiate of the Apothecaries' Hall (Dublin)

Lah. Lahore

LAHS low altitude, high speed

LAI [botany] leaf area index; Library

Association of Ireland; *Logos Agencia de Información* (Spanish news agency)
LAIA Latin American Integration Association (formerly LAFTA)
LAK [medicine] lymphokine-activated killer (cell) (used to treat cancer)
LAL *Laboratoire de l'accélérateur linéaire* (French: Linear Accelerator Laboratory)
lali [informal] lonely aged low income
LAM London Academy of Music (and Dramatic Art); Master of the Liberal Arts (from Latin *Liberalium Artium Magister*)
Lam. Lamarck (French naturalist); [Bible] Lamentations
lam. laminate; laminated; lamination
LAMA Locomotive and Allied Manufacturers' Association of Great Britain
Lamb. Lambeth
LAMC Livestock Auctioneers' Market Committee of England and Wales
LAMCO Liberian-American-Swedish Mineral Corporation
LAMDA London Academy of Music and Dramatic Art
LAMIDA Lancashire and Merseyside Industrial Development Association
LAMP low-altitude manned penetration; [USA] Lunar Analysis and Mapping Program
LAMS launch acoustic measuring system
LAMSAC Local Authorities' Management Services and Computer Committee
LAN *Linea Aérea Nacional (de Chile)* (Chilean airline company); local apparent noon; [computing] local area network
LANBY large automatic navigation buoy
Lanc. Lancaster; [military] Lancers
Lancs Lancashire
L&D loans and discounts; loss and damage
L&ID London and India Docks
L&NRR [USA] Louisville and Nashville Railroad
L&NWR London and North-Western Railway
L&SWR London and South-Western Railway
l&w living and well
L&YR Lancashire and Yorkshire Railway
Lan. Fus. Lancashire Fusiliers
Lang. Languedoc
lang. language
LANICA *Lineas Aéreas de Nicaragua* (Nicaraguan airline company)
LANL [USA] Los Alamos National Laboratory
LANRAC Land Army Reunion Association Committee
LanR(PWV) Lancashire Regiment (Prince of Wales' Volunteers)
LANSA *Lineas Aéreas Nacionales SA* (Peruvian airline company)
Lantirn [military] low-altitude navigation and targeting infrared system
LAO [international vehicle registration] Laos; Licentiate in the Art of Obstetrics
LAOAR [US air force] Latin American Office of Aerospace Research
LAP [USA] Laboratory of Aviation Psychology; *Lineas Aéreas Paraguayas* (Paraguayan airline company); [computing] link access protocol
Lap. Lapland; Lappish
LAPD Los Angeles Police Department
LAPES low-altitude parachute extraction system
LAPO Los Angeles Philharmonic Orchestra
LAPT London Association for the Protection of Trade
LAR [botany] leaf area ratio; [international vehicle registration] Libya (Arab Republic); [taxation] life assurance relief; [computing] limit address register
LARA light armed reconnaissance aircraft
larg. [music] *largamente* (Italian: broadly); *largeur* (French: width); [music] *largo* (Italian: broad, slow)
LARO Latin American Regional Office
LARSP Language Assessment, Remediation and Screening Procedure
laryngol. laryngologist; laryngology
LAS Land Agents' Society; large astronomical satellite; League of Arab States; Legal Aid Society; London Archaeological Service; Lord Advocate of Scotland; low-altitude satellite; lower airspace
LASER London and South Eastern Library Region
laser light amplification by stimulated emission of radiation
LASH [commerce] lighter aboard ship
LASL [USA] Los Alamos Scientific Laboratory

LASMO London and Scottish Marine Oil
LASP low-altitude space platform
LASS lighter-than-air submarine simulator
LAT local apparent time; *Los Angeles Times*
Lat. Latin; Latvia; Latvian
lat. latent; lateral; latitude; *latus* (Latin: wide)
LATCC London air traffic control centre
LATCRS London air traffic control radar station
lat. ht latent heat
LATS [medicine] long-acting thyroid stimulator
Latv. Latvia
Latvn Latvian
lau. laundry
LAUK Library Association of the United Kingdom
laun. launched
LAUTRO Life Assurance and Unit Trust Regulatory Organization
LAV light armoured vehicle; *Lineas Aéreas Venezolanas* (Venezuelan airline company); [medicine] lymphadenopathy-associated virus (former name of HIV)
lav [short form] lavatory
LAW League of American Writers; light anti-tank weapon
law. lawyer
Lawn [computing] local area wireless network
LAWRS limited airport weather reporting system
lax. laxative
LB Bachelor of Letters (or Literature) (from Latin *Litterarum Baccalaureus*); late bottled (wine); [international vehicle registration] Liberia; light bomber; local board; [vehicle registration] northwest London
L.b. *Lectori benevolo* (Latin: to the kind reader)
lb binary logarithm; pound (unit of weight, from Latin *libra*)
.lb Lebanon (in Internet address)
l.b. landing barge; [sports] left back; [cricket] leg bye; letter box; link belt
LBA late booking agent (= ticket tout); linear-bounded automaton; [computing] logical block address
LB&SCR London, Brighton and South Coast Railway
LBB [engineering] leak before break
LBBB [medicine] left bundle branch block
LBC Land Bank Commission; London Broadcasting Company
Lbc. Lübeck
LBCH London Bankers' Clearing House
LBCM Licentiate of the Bandsmen's College of Music; London Board of Congregational Ministers
LBD League of British Dramatists
L/Bdr Lance-Bombardier
LBF [medicine] liver blood flow
lbf pound-force
lb-ft pound-foot
LBH length, breadth, height
LBI [astronomy] long baseline interferometry
LBJ Lyndon Baines Johnson (US president)
LBL [medicine] lymphoblastic lymphoma
LBO [commerce] leveraged buyout
LBP length between perpendiculars
lbr labour; lumber
LBS Libyan Broadcasting Service; lifeboat station; London Business School
L.b.s. *Lectori benevolo salutem* (Latin: to the kind reader, greeting)
LBSM Licentiate of Birmingham and Midland Institute School of Music
LBV landing barge vehicle; late bottled vintage (port); [astronomy] luminous blue variable
LBW live body weight
lbw [cricket] leg before wicket
LC Cross of Leo; landing craft; [medicine] Langerhans cells; Leander Club; Legislative Council; letter of credit; level crossing (on map); [USA] Library of Congress; Lieutenant-Commander; [chemistry] linear chain; [electronics] linear contact; [military slang] line crosser (i.e. defector); [chemistry] liquid chromatography; [electronics] liquid crystal; livestock commissioner; Lord Chamberlain; Lord Chancellor; Lower Canada; Lutheran Council of Great Britain; [vehicle registration] northwest London
L/C letter of credit
l/c letter of credit
.lc St Lucia (in Internet address)
l.c. label clause; law courts; lead covered;

leading cases; left centre; legal currency; letter card; letter of credit; *loco citato* (Latin: in the place (already) cited); low-calorie; low-carbon; [printing] lower case

LCA Library Club of America; Licensed Company Auditor; [computing] logic cell array; low-cost automation

LCAD London Certificate in Art and Design

LCAP [computing] loosely coupled array of processors

LCB [theatre] left centre back (of stage); [USA] Liquor Control Board; London Convention Bureau; Lord Chief Baron

l.c.b. longitudinal centre of buoyancy

LCC [electronics] leadless chip carrier; Legalize Cannabis Campaign; [accounting] life-cycle cost(ing); load-carrying capability; London Chamber of Commerce; London County Council (former local authority)

LCCC [USA] Library of Congress Catalog Card

LCD [electronics] liquid-crystal display; Lord Chamberlain's Department; Lord Chancellor's Department; lower court decisions; [mathematics] lowest common denominator

LCDT London Contemporary Dance Theatre

LCE Licentiate in Civil Engineering; London Commodity Exchange

lce lance

LCF Law Centres Federation; [mathematics] lowest common factor

l.c.f. longitudinal centre of flotation

l.c.g. longitudinal centre of gravity

LCGB Locomotive Club of Great Britain

LCH London Clearing House

LCh Licentiate in Surgery (from Latin *Licentiatus Chirurgiae*); Lord Chancellor

LChir Licentiate in Surgery (from Latin *Licentiatus Chirurgiae*)

LCIGB Locomotive and Carriage Institution of Great Britain and Ireland

LCIOB Licentiate of the Chartered Institute of Building

LCJ Lord Chief Justice

LCL [US commerce] less-than-carload lot; [commerce] less-than-container load; Licentiate in Canon Law

l.c.l. lower control limit

LCLS Livestock Commission Levy Scheme

LCM landing craft mechanized; [mathematics] least common multiple; [computing] life-cycle management; London College of Music; [mathematics] lowest common multiple

LCN [aeronautics] load classification number; local civil noon

Lcn Lincoln

LCO landing craft officer; launch control officer

L/Corp. Lance-Corporal

LCP last complete programme; least-cost planning; Licentiate of the College of Preceptors; [chemistry] liquid-crystal polymer; London College of Printing; low-cost production

LCP&SA Licentiate of the College of Physicians and Surgeons of America

LCP&SO Licentiate of the College of Physicians and Surgeons of Ontario

L/Cpl Lance-Corporal

LCPS Licentiate of the College of Physicians and Surgeons

l/cr. *lettre de crédit* (French: letter of credit)

LCS London Cooperative Society

LCSAJ [computing] linear code sequence and jump

LCSP London and Counties Society of Physiologists

LCST Licentiate of the College of Speech Therapists

LCT landing craft tank; local civil time

LCU [photography] large close-up

LCV Licentiate of the College of Violinists

LD Doctor of Letters (or Literature) (from Latin *Litterarum Doctor*); Lady Day; *laus Deo* (Latin: praise be to God); [education, psychology] learning difficulties; [education, psychology] learning-disabled; legal dose (or dosage); *lepide dictum* (Latin: wittily said); [pharmacology] lethal dose (as in $\mathbf{LD}_{50}$, dose killing 50% of test group); Liberal and Democratic; Liberal Democrat(s); [currency] Libyan dinar; Licentiate in Divinity; Light Dragoons; *Litera Dominicalis* (Latin: Dominical letter); [UK postcode] Llandrindod Wells; London Docks; low density; Low Dutch; [vehicle registration] northwest London

L/D letter of deposit

Ld Limited (company); Lord (in titles)

ld land; [printing] lead; load
l.d. light difference; line of departure; line of duty
LDA Lead Development Association
Lda [commerce] *Sociedade de responsabilidade limitada* (Portuguese: limited company, Ltd)
l.d.b. light distribution box
LDC less developed country; local distribution company
l.d.c. long-distance call; lower dead centre
LDDC London Docklands' Development Corporation
LDEF [astronomy] long duration exposure facility
LDEG *laus Deo et gloria* (Latin: praise and glory be to God)
LDentSc Licentiate in Dental Science
L'derry Londonderry
Ldg Leading (in military rank)
ldg landing; leading; loading; lodging
Ldge Lodge
Ld'H *Légion d'Honneur* (French: Legion of Honour)
LDiv Licentiate in Divinity
ldk lower deck
LDL [biochemistry] low-density lipoprotein
ldmk landmark
LDN less developed nation
Ldn London
LDOS Lord's Day Observance Society
LDP Liberal Democratic Party; [finance] London daily price; long-distance path
Ldp Ladyship; Lordship
LDPE low-density polyethylene (packaging material)
LDR Liberal, Democratic and Reform Goup (in European Parliament); low dose rate
ldr leader; ledger; lodger
ldry laundry
LDS Latter-Day Saints; *laus Deo semper* (Latin: praise be to God for ever); Licentiate in Dental Surgery
lds loads
LDSc Licentiate in Dental Science
LDT [finance] licensed deposit taker
LDV Local Defence Volunteers (i.e. Home Guard)
LDWA Long Distance Walkers' Association
LDX long-distance xerography
LDY Leicestershire and Derbyshire Yeomanry
LE labour exchange (former name for jobcentre); [UK postcode] Leicester; London Electricity; low energy; [medicine] lupus erythematosus; [vehicle registration] northwest London
Le [currency] leone (used in Sierra Leone)
Le. Lebanese; Lebanon
l.e. leading edge; left eye; library edition; light equipment; limited edition; low explosive
LEA local education authority
lea. league; leather; leave
LEAJ [USA] Law Enforcement and Administration of Justice
LEAP Life Education for the Autistic Person; lift-off elevation and azimuth programmer; Loan and Educational Aid Programme
LEB London Electricity Board; [astronautics] low-energy booster
Leb. Lebanese; Lebanon
LEC Local Employment Committee; Local Enterprise Company
lect. *lectio* (Latin: lesson); lecture; lecturer
lectr lecturer
LED [electronics] light-emitting diode
led. ledger
LEDC Lighting Equipment Development Council
LEFM linear elastic fracture mechanics
leg. legal; legate; legation; [music] *legato* (Italian: bound, smoothly); legion; legislation; legislative; legislature; legitimate
legg. [music] *legg(i)ero* (Italian: light, rapid)
legis. legislation; legislative; legislature
legit [short form] legitimate
Leics Leicestershire
Leip. Leipzig
Leit. Leitrim
LEL Laureate in English Literature; [physics] linear energy loss
LEM [astronautics] lunar excursion module
LEMA Lifting Equipment Manufacturers' Association
LENTA London Enterprise Agency
LEO [astronautics] low earth orbit; Lyons Electronic Office (early computer)
LEP [physics] large electron-positron (collider) (at CERN)

Lep [astronomy] Lepus
LEPMA [USA] Lithographic Engravers' and Plate Makers' Association
LEPORE [USA] long-term and expanded program of oceanic research and exploration
LEPRA Leprosy Relief Association
LEPT long-endurance patrolling torpedo
LES launch escape system; Liverpool Engineering Society
LèsL *Licencié ès lettres* (French: Bachelor of Arts)
LESS least-cost estimating and scheduling
LèsS *Licencié ès sciences* (French: Bachelor of Science)
LEST large earth-based solar telescope
LET [physics] linear energy transfer
let. letter
LETS Local Employment and Trade System; Local Exchange and Trading System (community bartering system)
LEU [physics] low-enriched uranium
LEV [astronautics] lunar excursion vehicle
Lev. Levant; [Bible] Leviticus
Levit. [Bible] Leviticus
LEX land exercise
lex. lexicon
lexicog. lexicographer; lexicographical; lexicography
LEY Liberal European Youth
LF Lancashire Fusiliers; line feed; [radio] low frequency; [astronomy] luminosity function; [currency] Luxembourg franc; [vehicle registration] northwest London
Lf limit of flocculation (in toxicology)
lf leaf
l.f. ledger folio; life float; [printing] light face
LFA less favoured area; local freight agent
LFB London Fire Brigade
LFBC London Federation of Boys' Clubs
LFC low-frequency current; Lutheran Free Church
LFCDA London Fire and Civil Defence Authority
LFD least fatal dose; low-fat diet
LFE laboratory for electronics
Lfg *Lieferung* (German: delivery)
LFO low-frequency oscillator
lft leaflet
LFTU landing force training unit
LG [vehicle registration] Chester; Lady Companion of the Order of the Garter; landing ground; Lewis gun; Lieutenant-General; Life Guards; (David) Lloyd George (British statesman); *London Gazette*; Low German
lg common logarithm; long
lg. lagoon; large
LGAR [USA] Ladies of the Grand Army of the Republic
LGB Local Government Board
LGBC Local Government Boundary Commission for England
LGC lunar (module) guidance computer
lge large; league; lounge (in property advertisement)
LGEB Local Government Examination Board
L-Gen Lieutenant-General
LGer Low German
LGIO Local Government Information Office
LGk Late Greek
LGM little green men; Lloyd's Gold Medal
LGO [USA] Lamont Geological Observatory
LGPRA Local Government Public Relations Association
LGR leasehold ground rent; local government reports
LGr Late Greek
LGSM Licentiate of the Guildhall School of Music (and Drama)
LGTB Local Government Training Board
lgth length
lg tn long ton
LGU Ladies' Golf Union
LGV large goods vehicle (replacement for HGV)
LH left hand; left handed; [fishing port] Leith; licensing hours; Licentiate in Hygiene; [military] Light Horse; [biochemistry] luteinizing hormone; [vehicle registration] northwest London
L/H leasehold (in property advertisement)
l.h. [sports] left half; left hand; left handed
LHA landing helicopter assault; local health authority; local hour angle; Lord High Admiral; lower hour angle
l.h.b. [sports] left halfback
LHC [physics] Large Hadron Collider (at CERN); Lord High Chancellor

LHCIMA Licentiate of the Hotel Catering and Institutional Management Association
LHD Doctor of Humanities (or Literature) (from Latin *Litterarum Humaniorum Doctor*)
l.h.d. left-hand drive (in car advertisement)
LHDC lateral homing depth charge
LHeb Late Hebrew
lhld leasehold (in property advertisement)
LHMC London Hospital Medical College
LHO livestock husbandry officer
lhr lumen-hour
LHRC Light and Health Research Council
LH-RH [biochemistry] luteinizing-hormone-releasing hormone
LHS left hand side
LHSM Licentiate of the Institute of Health Services Management
LHT Lord High Treasurer
LHWN lowest high water neaps (level of tide)
LI Leeward Islands; Liberal International; [USA] Licentiate in Instruction; Light Infantry; [law] Lincoln's Inn; [fishing port] Littlehampton; Long Island (New York)
Li [chemical element] lithium
li. link; [currency] lira
.li Liechtenstein (in Internet address)
l.i. letter of introduction; longitudinal interval
LIA [USA] Laser Industry Association; [USA] Lead Industries Association; Leather Industries of America; Lebanese International Airways; Life Insurance Association
LIAB Licentiate of the International Association of Book-keepers
LIAT London International Arbitration Trust
Lib [astronomy] Libra
Lib. [politics] Liberal; Liberia; Liberian; Libya; Libyan
lib. *liber* (Latin: book); liberation; liberty; librarian; library; libretto
LIBA Lloyd's Insurance Brokers' Association
lib. cat. library catalogue
Lib. Cong. [USA] Library of Congress
Lib Dem [short form] Liberal Democrat
LIBER *Ligue des bibliothèques européennes de recherche* (French: League of European Research Libraries)
LIBID [finance] London Inter-Bank Bid Rate
LIBOR [finance] London Inter-Bank Offered Rate
libst librettist
LIC Lands Improvement Company; [electronics] linear integrated circuit
Lic. *Licenciado* (Spanish: Bachelor) (in academic degrees); Licentiate (in academic degrees)
lic. licence; licensed
LicAc Licentiate of Acupuncture
LicMed Licentiate in Medicine
LicTheol Licentiate in Theology
LICW Licentiate of the Institute of Clerks of Works of Great Britain
lidar light detection and ranging
LIDC Lead Industries Development Council
LIE loss of independent existence
Lieut. Lieutenant
Lieut-Cdr Lieutenant-Commander
Lieut-Col Lieutenant-Colonel
Lieut-Com Lieutenant-Commander
Lieut-Gen Lieutenant-General
Lieut-Gov Lieutenant-Governor
LIF [medicine] left iliac fossa; [computing] low insertion force
LIFFE London International Financial Futures (and Options) Exchange
LIFireE Licentiate of the Institution of Fire Engineers
LIFO last in, first out
Lig. Liguria; Limoges
LIHG *Ligue internationale de hockey sur glace* (French: International Ice Hockey Federation)
LILO last in, last out
LIM linear-induction motor; [computing] Lotus, Intel, Microsoft
Lim. Limerick
lim. limit; limited
LIMEAN [finance] London Inter-Bank Mean Rate
limo [short form] limousine
lin. lineal; linear; liniment
linac [physics] linear accelerator
Lincs Lincolnshire
ling. linguistic; linguistics
Linn. (Carolus) Linnaeus (Swedish botanist); Linnean

lino [short form] linoleum
LInstP Licentiate of the Institute of Physics
LIOB Licentiate of the Institute of Building
LIP life insurance policy; [medicine] lymphocytic interstitial pneumonitis
LIPA Liverpool Institute for the Performing Arts
LIPM Lister Institute of Preventive Medicine
lips [computing] logical inferences per second
liq. liquid; liquor
LIRA Linen Industry Research Association
LIRMA London International Insurance and Reinsurance Market Association
LIS laser isotope separation
Lis. Lisbon
LISA *Library and Information Science Abstracts*
LISC Library and Information Services Council
LISM Licentiate of the Incorporated Society of Musicians
LISP list processing (computer programming language)
Lit [currency] Italian lira
lit. literal; literally; literary; literature; litre; litter; little; liturgy
LitB Bachelor of Letters (or Literature) (from Latin *Litterarum Baccalaureus*)
lit crit [short form] literary criticism
LitD Doctor of Letters (or Literature) (from Latin *Litterarum Doctor*)
Lith. Lithuania; Lithuanian
lith. lithograph; lithography
litho. lithograph; lithographic; lithography
lithog. lithograph; lithographic; lithography
lithol. lithology
Lit. Hum. *Literae Humaniores* (Latin: Humane Letters) (classics degree at Oxford University)
LitM Master of Letters (or Literature) (from Latin *Litterarum Magister*)
Lit. Sup. (*Times*) *Literary Supplement*
LittB Bachelor of Letters (or Literature) (from Latin *Litterarum Baccalaureus*)
LittD Doctor of Letters (or Literature) (from Latin *Litterarum Doctor*)
LittM Master of Letters (or Literature) (from Latin *Litterarum Magister*)
liturg. liturgical; liturgy
LIUNA Laborers' International Union of North America
Liv. Liverpool; Livy (Roman historian)
liv. [commerce] *livraison* (French: delivery)
liv. st. *livre sterling* (French: pound sterling)
Lix [computing] legal information exchange
LJ [vehicle registration] Bournemouth; *Library Journal*; [athletics] long jump; Lord Justice
l.j. life jacket
LJA Lady Jockeys' Association
LJC London Juvenile Courts
LJJ Lords Justices
LK [fishing port] Lerwick; [vehicle registration] northwest London
Lk [currency] lek (used in Albania)
.lk Sri Lanka (in Internet address)
lkd locked
lkg locking
lkge leakage
lkr locker
LL Late Latin; Law Latin; *Law List*; laws; lending library; lend-lease; limited liability; [mathematics, physics] linear-linear; lines (of text); [fishing port] Liverpool; [UK postcode] Llandudno; London Library; Lord Lieutenant; Lords; [medicine] lower limb; Low Latin; [vehicle registration] northwest London
L/L [commerce] *Lutlang* (Norwegian: limited company, Ltd)
ll. leaves; *leges* (Latin: laws); lines (of text)
l.l. live load; *loco laudato* (Latin: in the place cited with approval); lower left; lower limit
LLA Lady Literate in Arts
LL.AA.II. *Leurs Altesses Impériales* (French: Their Imperial Highnesses)
LL.AA.RR. *Leurs Altesses Royales* (French: Their Royal Highnesses)
LLB Bachelor of Laws (from Latin *Legum Baccalaureus*)
l.l.c. lower left centre
LLCM Licentiate of the London College of Music
LLCO Licentiate of the London College of Osteopathy

LLD Doctor of Laws (from Latin *Legum Doctor*)
Llds [insurance] Lloyd's
LLE low-level exposure (to radiation)
LL.EE. *Leurs Éminences* (French: Their Eminences); *Leurs Excellences* (French: Their Excellencies)
LLett Licentiate of Letters
LLI Lord Lieutenant of Ireland
l.l.i. latitude and longitude indicator
LLL Licentiate in Laws; loose leaf ledger; [computing] low-level language; [computing] low-level logic
LLLW [nuclear technology] liquid low-level waste
LLM Master of Laws (from Latin *Legum Magister*)
LLMCom Master of Laws in Commercial Law
LL.MM. *Leurs Majestés* (French: Their Majesties)
LLN [USA] League for Less Noise
LLNL [USA] Lawrence Livermore National Laboratory
LLNW low-level nuclear waste
LLRW low-level radioactive waste
LLS [astronautics] lunar logistics system
LLSV [astronautics] lunar logistics system vehicle
LLU lending library unit
LLV [astronautics] lunar logistics vehicle
LLW [nuclear technology] low-level waste
LM Legion of Merit; Licentiate in Medicine; Licentiate in Midwifery; Licentiate in Music; light microscopy; liquid metal; [electrical engineering] load management; London Museum; [music, prosody] long metre; [Scotland] Lord Marquis; Lord Mayor; [astronautics] lunar module; [currency] Maltese lira; [vehicle registration] northwest London
l.M *laufenden Monats* (German: of the current month)
lm lumen (unit of luminous flux)
l.m. land mine; light metal; *locus monumenti* (Latin: place of the monument)
LMA Linoleum Manufacturers' Association; low moisture avidity
LMBC Liverpool Marine Biological Committee
LMC [astronomy] Large Magellanic Cloud; [nuclear technology] liquid-metal coolant; Lloyd's Machinery Certificate; local medical committee
LMCC Licentiate of the Medical Council of Canada
LMD local medical doctor; [music, prosody] long metre double
lmd leafmould
LME London Metal Exchange
LMed Licentiate in Medicine
LMFBR [nuclear technology] liquid-metal-cooled fast breeder reactor
LMG light machine gun
LMI [USA] Logistics Management Institute
LMi [astronomy] Leo Minor
LMO lens-modulated oscillator; light machine oil
LMP [medicine] last menstrual period; [astronautics] lunar module pilot
LMR [nuclear technology] liquid-metal reactor; [railways] London Midland Region
LMRCP Licentiate in Midwifery of the Royal College of Physicians
LMRSH Licentiate Member of the Royal Society of Health
LMRTPI Legal Member of the Royal Town Planning Institute
LMS Latin Mass Society; Licentiate in Medicine and Surgery; [education] local management of schools; London Mathematical Society; London Medical Schools; London Missionary Society; London, Midland and Scottish (Railway); [medicine] loss of memory syndrome
LMSR London, Midland and Scottish Railway
LMSSA Licentiate in Medicine and Surgery of the Society of Apothecaries
LMT [physics] length, mass, time; [astronomy] local mean time
LMus Licentiate in Music
LMVD [New Zealand] Licensed Motor Vehicle Dealer
LMW low molecular weight
LMX [insurance] London Market Excess of Loss (at Lloyd's)
LMXB [astronomy] low-mass X-ray binary
LN [fishing port] King's Lynn; [UK postcode] Lincoln; liquid nitrogen; [medicine] lymph node; [vehicle registration]

northwest London; [civil aircraft marking] Norway
Ln. Lane
ln natural logarithm (from Latin *logarithmus naturalis*)
LNat Liberal National
LNB low noise blocker (on satellite dish)
LNC League of Nations Covenant
LNER London and North Eastern Railway
LNG liquefied natural gas
lnge lounge (in property advertisement)
LNLC Ladies' Naval Luncheon Club
Lnrk Lanark
LNS land navigation system
LNT liquid-nitrogen temperature
LNU League of Nations Union
LNWR London and North Western Railway
LO *Landsorganisationen i Sverige* (Swedish: General Federation of Swedish Trade Unions); launch operator; liaison officer; [fishing port] London; London office; [vehicle registration] northwest London
Lo. Lord
l/o [commerce] *leur ordre* (French: their order)
lo. loam; local
l.o. lubricating oil
LOA leave of absence; length over all; light observation aircraft
l.o.a. length over all
LOB [baseball] left on base; line of balance; Location of Offices Bureau
LOBAL long-base-line buoy
LOBAR long-base-line radar
LOC launch operations centre; [USA] Library of Congress; [meteorology] locally
loc. local; location; [grammar] locative
l.o.c. letter of credit; line(s) of communication
LOCA [nuclear technology] loss-of-coolant accident
loc. cit. *loco citato* (Latin: in the place (already) cited)
loc. laud. *loco laudato* (Latin: in the place cited with approval)
locn location
loco. locomotion; locomotive
loc. primo cit. *loco primo citato* (Latin: in the place first cited)
LOD limit(s) of detection
LOF loss of flow; loss of fluid; loss of function
L of C [USA] Library of Congress; line(s) of communication
L of N League of Nations
LOFT low-frequency radio telescope
log [short form] logarithm
log. logic; logical; logistic
LOH light observation helicopter
LOI [Northern Ireland] Loyal Orange Institution; lunar orbit insertion
LOL laughs out loud (in Internet chat); [Northern Ireland] Loyal Orange Lodge
LOLA library on-line acquisition; lunar orbit landing approach
LOM [USA] Loyal Order of Moose
LOMA [USA] Life Office Management Association
Lomb. Lombard; Lombardy
lombard [informal] loads of money but a right dickhead
Lon. London; Londonderry
lon. longitude
Lond. London; Londonderry
Londin. *Londiniensis* (Latin: (Bishop) of London)
Long. Longford
long. longitude
longl longitudinal
Lonrho [finance] London Rhodesian
LOOM [USA] Loyal Order of Moose
l.o.p. [navigation] line of position
LOPAR low-power acquisition radar
loq. *loquitur* (Latin: (he/she) speaks)
LOR light output ratio; lunar orbit rendezvous
LORAC long-range accuracy
LORAD long-range active detection
LORAN long-range navigation
LORAPH long-range passive homing system
LORCS League of Red Cross and Red Crescent Societies
LORV low observable re-entry vehicle
LOS Latin Old Style; Law of the Seas; line of sight; loss of signal
LOSS large-object salvage system
LOT large orbital telescope; *Polskie Linie Lotnicze* (Polish airline company)
lot. lotion
LOTC [finance] London over-the-counter market
Lou. Louisiana
LOX liquid oxygen
loy. loyal; loyalty

LOYA League of Young Adventurers

LP Labour Party; Lady Provost; large paper (edition of book); [paper size] large post; last post; legal procurator; Liberal Party; life policy; limited partnership; [computing] linear programming; liquid petroleum; liquid propellant; long play (on video recorder); long-playing (record); Lord Provost; low pressure; [medicine] lumbar puncture; [vehicle registration] northwest London

Lp Ladyship; Lordship

L/P letterpress; life policy

lp limp

l.p. last paid; latent period; launch platform; [printing] long primer (type size); low pressure

LPA Leather Producers' Association for England; Local Productivity Association

LPC leaf protein concentrate (in nutrition); Legal Practice Course; Lord President of the Council

l.p.c. low pressure chamber

LPE [electronics] liquid-phase epitaxy; London Press Exchange

LPEA Licentiate of the Physical Education Association

LPed Licentiate in Pedagogy

LPF [computing] League for Programming Freedom

LPG liquefied petroleum gas

LPGA Ladies' Professional Golf Association

LPh Licentiate in Philosophy

lpi lines per inch

LPLC low-pressure liquid chromatography

lpm lines per millimetre; lines per minute

LPN [USA] Licensed Practical Nurse

LPNA [USA] Lithographers' and Printers' National Association

LPO local post office; local purchasing officer; London Philharmonic Orchestra

L'pool Liverpool

LPRP Laotian People's Revolutionary Party

LPS London Philharmonic Society; Lord Privy Seal

LPSO Lloyd's Policy Signing Office

LPU low pay unit

lpw lumens per watt

Lpz. Leipzig

LQ [civil aircraft marking] Argentina; [computing] letter quality (of printing); [mathematics] linear-quadratic

l.q. *lege quaeso* (Latin: please read)

lqdr liquidator

LQR *Law Quarterly Review*

LQT [commerce] Liverpool quay terms

LR [fishing port] Lancaster; Land Registry; Law Report; left-(to-)right; Lloyd's Register (of Shipping); Lowland Regiment; Loyal Regiment; [vehicle registration] northwest London

Lr Lancer; [chemical element] lawrencium; ledger; [currency] lira

l.R *laufen der Rechnung* (German: current account)

lr ledger; [currency] lira; lower

.lr Liberia (in Internet address)

l.r. landing report; log run; long range; long run

LRA Local Radio Association

LRAC Law Reports, Appeal Cases; [finance] long-run average cost

LRAD Licentiate of the Royal Academy of Dancing

LRAM Licentiate of the Royal Academy of Music

LRB London Residuary Body; London Rifle Brigade

LRC Labour Representation Committee; Langley Research Center (in NASA); Leander Rowing Club; London Rowing Club; [computing] longitudinal redundancy check

LRCh Law Reports, Chancery Division

LRCM Licentiate of the Royal College of Music

LRCP Licentiate of the Royal College of Physicians

LRCPE Licentiate of the Royal College of Physicians of Edinburgh

LRCPI Licentiate of the Royal College of Physicians of Ireland

LRCPSGlas Licentiate of the Royal College of Physicians and Surgeons of Glasgow

LRCS League of Red Cross Societies; Licentiate of the Royal College of Surgeons (of England)

LRCSE Licentiate of the Royal College of Surgeons of Edinburgh

LRCSI Licentiate of the Royal College of Surgeons in Ireland

LRCVS Licentiate of the Royal College of Veterinary Surgeons
LREC [medicine] Local Research Ethics Committee
LRHL Law Reports, House of Lords
LRIBA Licentiate of the Royal Institute of British Architects
LRKB Law Reports, King's Bench
LRM language reference manual
LRP Law Reports, Probate Division; long-range planning
LRPS Licentiate of the Royal Photographic Society
LRQB Law Reports, Queen's Bench
LRR [taxation] lower reduced rate
LRS Land Registry Stamp; Lloyd's Register of Shipping
Lrs Lancers
LRSC Licentiate of the Royal Society of Chemistry
LRSM Licentiate of the Royal Schools of Music
LRT light rail transit; London Regional Transport; long-range transport
LRTF long-range theatre nuclear forces
LRTI [medicine] lower respiratory tract infection
LRU least recently used; line replaceable unit
LRV light rail vehicle; lunar roving vehicle
LRWES long-range weapons experimental station
LS [vehicle registration] Edinburgh; Law Society; leading seaman; [UK postcode] Leeds; legal seal; [international vehicle registration] Lesotho; letter service; Licensed Surveyor; Licentiate in Surgery; [psychology] liminal sensitivity; Linnean Society; [law] *locus sigilli* (Latin: the place of the seal); London Scottish; London Sinfonietta; [cinema] long shot; loudspeaker
ls litres per second
.ls Lesotho (in Internet address)
l.s. landing ship; left side; letter signed; local sunset; [law] *locus sigilli* (Latin: the place of the seal); long sight; low speed; lump sum
LSA Land Settlement Association; leading supply assistant; learning support assistant; Licence in Agricultural Sciences; Licentiate of the Society of Apothecaries
LSAA Linen Supply Association of America
LS&GCM Long Service and Good Conduct Medal
LSB [computing] least significant bit; London School Board
LSC Licentiate in Sciences; [chemistry] liquid–solid chromatography; London Salvage Corps; Lower School Certificate
l.s.c. *loco supra citato* (Latin: in the place cited above)
LScAct Licentiate in Actuarial Science
LSCF [statistics] least squares curve fitting
LSCS [obstetrics] lower segment Caesarean section
LSD League of Safe Drivers; [computing] least significant digit; *librae, solidi, denarii* (Latin: pounds, shillings, pence); Lightermen, Stevedores and Dockers; [pharmacology] lysergic acid diethylamide (hallucinogen, from German *Lysergsäure-Diäthylamid*)
l.s.d. *librae, solidi, denarii* (Latin: pounds, shillings, pence)
lsd li. leased line
LSE [chemistry] liquid–solid extraction; [chemistry] liquid–solvent extraction; London School of Economics and Political Science; London Stock Exchange
lse lease
l.s.e. limited signed edition
L/Sgt Lance-Sergeant
LSHTM London School of Hygiene and Tropical Medicine
LSI Labour and Socialist International; [electronics] large-scale integration
LSJ London School of Journalism
LSJM *laus sit Jesu et Mariae* (Latin: praise be to Jesus and Mary)
LSL landing ship logistic; low-speed logic
LSM laser scanning microscope; [mathematics, physics] least-squares method; [electrical engineering] linear synchronous motor
l.s.m. *litera scripta manet* (Latin: the written word remains)
LSO London Symphony Orchestra
LSS large-scale structure; large-scale system; Licentiate in Sacred Scripture; life-saving station (or service); life-support system
LSSc Licentiate in Sanitary Science

LST landing ship (for) tanks; landing ship (for) transport; Licentiate in Sacred Theology; [astronomy] local sidereal time; local standard time
l.s.t. local standard time
LSU Louisiana State University
LSW lights spray and wipe (in car advertisement)
LSZ [New Zealand] limited speed zone
LT lawn tennis; leading telegraphist; letter telegram; [medicine] leukotriene; Licentiate in Teaching; Licentiate in Theology; [international vehicle registration] Lithuania; London Transport; [fishing port] Lowestoft; low temperature; [electrical engineering] low tension; [vehicle registration] northwest London; [currency] Turkish lira
Lt Lieutenant; [military] Light
lt light
.lt Lithuania (in Internet address)
l.t. landed terms; landing team; large tug; local time; locum tenens (person standing in for another); long ton; loop test
LTA Lawn Tennis Association; lighter than air (of aircraft); London Teachers' Association
LTAA Lawn Tennis Association of Australia
LT&SR London, Tilbury and Southend Railway
LTB London Tourist Board; London Transport Board
l.t.b. low-tension battery
LTBT Limited Test Ban Treaty
LTC lawn tennis club
Lt-Cdr Lieutenant-Commander
LTCL Licentiate of Trinity College of Music, London
Lt-Col Lieutenant-Colonel
Lt-Com Lieutenant-Commander
Ltd Limited (after company name)
LTDP long-term defence programme
LTE [astronomy] local thermodynamic equilibrium; London Transport Executive
LTF Lithographic Technical Foundation
ltg lettering; lighting
ltge [commerce] lighterage
Lt-Gen Lieutenant-General
Lt-Gov Lieutenant-Governor
LTH light training helicopter; [biochemistry] luteotrophic hormone
LTh Licentiate in Theology
LTheol Licentiate in Theology
lthr leather
LTI Licentiate of the Textile Institute
LTIB Lead Technical Information Bureau
Lt Inf. Light Infantry
LTL [US commerce] less-than-truckload lot
LTM Licentiate in Tropical Medicine; London Terminal Market; long-term memory
ltn. lightning
LTO leading torpedo operator
LTOM London Traded Options Market
LTP [biochemistry] lipid-transfer protein; [science] long-term potentiation
LTR [genetics] long terminal repeat
ltr letter; lighter; litre
LTRA Lands Tribunal Rating Appeals
LtRN Lieutenant, Royal Navy
LTRS Low Temperature Research Station
LTSC Licentiate of Tonic Sol-Fa College
LTTE Liberation Tigers of Tamil Eelam (in Sri Lanka)
LTU *Lufttransport-Unternehmen GmbH* (German airline company)
LU Liberal Unionist; lock-up (in property advertisement); loudness unit; [UK postcode] Luton; [vehicle registration] northwest London
Lu [chemical element] lutetium
Lu. Lucerne
l/u [shipping] laid up; [shipping] lying up
lu. *luglio* (Italian: July)
.lu Luxembourg (in Internet address)
LUA Liverpool Underwriting Association
lub. lubricant; lubricate; lubrication
lubr. lubricant; lubricate; lubrication
LUC London Underwriting Centre
LUCOM lunar communication system
LUD leather-upholstered dashboard (in car advertisement)
LUG light utility glider; [computing] local users group
lug. luggage; lugger
LUHF [electronics] lowest useful high frequency
LULOP *London Union List of Periodicals*
LUM lunar excursion module
lum. lumbago; lumber; luminous
LUMAS lunar mapping system
lun. *lundi* (French: Monday); *lunedì*

(Italian: Monday); *lunes* (Spanish: Monday)
LUNCO Lloyd's Underwriters Non-Marine Claims Office
LUOTC London University Officers' Training Corps
Lup [astronomy] Lupus
l/up lock-up
LUS Land Utilization Survey
LUSCS [obstetrics] lower uterine segment Caesarean section
LUSI lunar surface inspection
lusing. [music] *lusingando* (Italian: coaxing, caressing)
LUT [computing] look-up table
Luth. Lutheran
Lux. Luxembourg; Luxembourger
lux. luxurious; luxury
LV [civil aircraft marking] Argentina; [international vehicle registration] Latvia; [medicine] left ventricle; [medicine] left ventricular; licensed victualler; [meteorology] light and variable; [vehicle registration] Liverpool; luncheon voucher
Lv [currency] lev (used in Bulgaria)
lv. leave (of absence); *livre* (French: book)
.lv Latvia (in Internet address)
l.v. low voltage
LVA Licensed Victuallers' Association
LVF [medicine] left ventricular function
LVI *laus Verbo Incarnato* (Latin: praise to the Incarnate Word); low viscosity index
LVLO Local Vehicle Licensing Office
LVN [USA] Licensed Vocational Nurse
LVO Lieutenant of the Royal Victorian Order
LVS Licentiate in Veterinary Science
lvs leaves
LVT landing vehicle, tracked
LW light weight; [radio] long wave; low water; [vehicle registration] northwest London
Lw [chemical element] lawrencium (former symbol, replaced by Lr)
lw lumens per watt
l.w. [sports] left wing
LWA London Weighting Allowance; London Welsh Association
LW&S lights wipe and spray (in car advertisement)
l.w.b. long wheelbase (in car advertisement)
LWEST low water equinoctial spring tide
LWF Lutheran World Federation
LWL length at waterline (of boat or ship); [shipping] load waterline
LWM low water mark
LWONT low water ordinary neap tides
LWOST low water ordinary spring tides
LWR [nuclear technology] light-water reactor
LWRA London Waste Regulation Authority
LWT London Weekend Television
LWV [USA] League of Women Voters
LX electricians (phonetic spelling of 'elecs'); electrics (phonetic spelling of 'elecs'); [civil aircraft marking] Luxembourg; [vehicle registration] northwest London
lx lux (unit of light)
Lxmbrg Luxembourg
LXX [Bible] Septuagint (Roman numeral for 70)
LY [civil aircraft marking] Lithuania; [fishing port] Londonderry; [vehicle registration] northwest London
Ly. Lyon
.ly Libya (in Internet address)
l.y. light year
Lyn [astronomy] Lynx
Lyr [astronomy] Lyra
lyr. lyric; lyrical; lyrics
LZ [vehicle registration] Armagh; [civil aircraft marking] Bulgaria

M

M [printing] em; [currency] (ma)loti (used in Lesotho); [aeronautics] Mach (followed by number); *Magister* (Latin: Master); magistrate; Majesty; [international vehicle registration] Malta; [UK postcode] Manchester; Manitoba; March; [currency] mark; Marquess; Marquis; martyr; [grammar] masculine;

Master; [cinema] mature audience (film classification in Australia); May; medal; medieval; medium (size); mega- (indicates one million, as in **MHz** = megahertz); [computing] mega- (indicates 2^{20}, as in **MB** = megabyte); Member; [chemistry] mesomeric effect; [astronomy] Messier Catalogue; [chemistry] metal (in chemical formula); Methodist; [music] metronome; metropolitan; *mezzo* (Italian: half); Middle; [fishing port] Milford; militia; million; minesweeper; minim (unit of liquid measure); Monday; [economics] monetary aggregate (in measures of money supply); *Monsieur* (French: Mr, Sir); *Monte* (Italian: Mount); mother; motorway (as in **M6**); mountain; mud (on chart); [Roman numeral] thousand

M [astronomy] absolute magnitude; [physics] magnetic quantum number; [physics] magnetization; mass; molar mass; [physics] moment (of a force); [electrical engineering] mutual inductance

m [printing] em; [music] me (in tonic sol-fa); metre; milli- (indicates one-thousandth, as in **mm** = millimetre); million; [meteorology] mist; [Roman numeral] thousand

m [astronomy] apparent magnitude; [physics] magnetic moment; [physics] magnetic quantum number; [chemistry] mass; [chemistry] molality

m. [cricket] maiden (over); male; *manipulus* (Latin: handful); mare; [currency] mark; married; [grammar] masculine; master; mate; measure; medical; medicine; medium; memorandum; meridian; *meridies* (Latin: noon); meridional; midday; middle; mile; [currency] mill (thousandth of dollar); *mille* (French: thousand); minim (unit of liquid measure); minor; minute; [medicine] *misce* (Latin: mix); mixture; moderate; *mois* (French: month); molar (tooth); month; moon; morning; *mort(e)* (French: dead); *morto* (Italian: dead); mountain

3M Minnesota Mining and Manufacturing Company

9M [civil aircraft marking] Malaysia

MA [vehicle registration] Chester; Magistrates' Association; [USA] Manpower Administration; [USA] Maritime Administration; [US postcode] Massachusetts; Master of Arts; Mathematical Association; medieval archaeology; [psychology] mental age; Middle Ages; Military Academy; military assistant; military attaché; *Missionarius Apostolicus* (Latin: Apostolic Missionary); mobility allowance; [international vehicle registration] Morocco; Mountaineering Association; Museums Association

Ma [aeronautics] Mach number

Ma. *Mater* (Latin: Mother)

mA milliampere

m/a [book-keeping] my account

.ma Morocco (in Internet address)

m.a. manufacturing assembly; map analysis; menstrual age

MAA Manufacturers' Agents Association of Great Britain; Master-at-Arms; Mathematical Association of America; Member of the Architectural Association; Motor Agents' Association; [USA] Mutual Aid Association; [USA] Mutual Assurance Association

MAAAS Member of the American Academy of Arts and Sciences

MAAF Mediterranean Allied Air Forces

ma'am madam

MAAT Member of the Association of Accounting Technicians

MAB monoclonal antibody

MABP [medicine] mean arterial blood pressure

MABS [USA] marine air base squadron

MAC maximum allowable concentration; [computing] media access control; [television] multiplexed analogue component(s); [USA] Municipal Assistance Corporation

MAc Master of Accountancy

Mac. Macao; [Bible] Maccabees (books of Apocrypha)

mac [short form] mackintosh

MACA Mental After Care Association

MACC military aid to the civilian community

Macc. [Bible] Maccabees (books of Apocrypha)

MACE Member of the Association of Conference Executives; Member of the Australian College of Education

Maced. Macedonia; Macedonian

mach. machine; machinery; machinist
MACHO [astronomy] massive astrophysical compact halo object
MACM Member of the Association of Computing Machines
macroecon. macroeconomics
MACS Member of the American Chemical Society
MAD magnetic anomaly detection; maintenance, assembly and disassembly; [psychology] major affective disorder; [commerce] mean absolute deviation; [military] mutual assured destruction
Mad. Madeira
Madag. Madagascar
MADD Mothers Against Drunk Driving
MADO Member of the Association of Dispensing Opticians
Madr. Madras; Madrid
MAE Master of Aeronautical Engineering; Master of Art Education; Master of Arts in Education
m.a.e. mean absolute error
MA(Econ) Master of Arts in Economics
MA(Ed) Master of Arts in Education
MAEE Marine Aircraft Experimental Establishment
maesto. [music] *maestoso* (Italian: majestic)
MAFA Manchester Academy of Fine Arts
MAFF Ministry of Agriculture, Fisheries and Food
MAG Motorcycle Action Group
MAg Master of Agriculture
Mag. Magnificat (canticle); Magyar
mag [short form] magazine
mag. magazine; magnesium; magnet; magnetic; magnetism; magneto; magnitude; magnum
MAgEc Master of Agricultural Economics
magg. *maggio* (Italian: May); [music] *maggiore* (Italian: major) (key or scale)
maglev magnetic levitation (for high-speed train)
magn. magnetic; magnetism
magnif. magnificent (in property advertisement)
MAGPI [medicine] meatal advancement and glanuloplasty (surgical operation)
MAgr Master of Agriculture
MAgrSc Master of Agricultural Science
mah. mahogany
mahog. mahogany
MAI Master of Engineering (from Latin *Magister in Arte Ingeniaria*); [forestry] mean annual increment; Member of the Anthropological Institute
MAIAA Member of the American Institute of Aeronautics and Astronautics
MAIB Marine Accidents Investigation Branch
MAICE Master of the American Institute of Consulting Engineers
MAIChE Master of the American Institute of Chemical Engineers
maint. maintenance
mais. maisonette (in property advertisement)
MAISE Member of the Association of Iron and Steel Engineers
Maj. [military] Major
maj. major; majority
Maj-Gen Major-General
MAL [international vehicle registration] Malaysia
Mal *Maréchal* (French: Field Marshal)
Mal. [Bible] Malachi; Malay; Malaya; Malayan; Malaysia; Malaysian; Malta; Maltese
MALD Master of Arts in Law and Diplomacy
mall. malleable
MAM [computing] multiple allocation memory
MAMBO Mediterranean Association for Marine Biology and Oceanography
MAMEME Member of the Association of Mining Electrical and Mechanical Engineers
MAN [computing] metropolitan area network
Man. Manchester; Manila; Manitoba
man. management; manager; managing; manual; manually; manufacture; manufacturer; manufacturing
MAnaes Master of Anaesthesiology
Manch. Manchester; Manchuria
mand. [law] mandamus (High Court order); mandatory; mandolin
M&A [finance] mergers and acquisitions
M&B May and Baker (pharmaceutical company); mild and bitter (beer); Mills and Boon (publishing company)
M&E music and effects
M&G Mercantile and General (insurance company)

Man. Dir. managing director
m&r maintenance and repairs
M&S Marks and Spencer plc (chain store)
m&s maintenance and supply
Man. Ed. managing editor
MANF May, August, November, February (end of financial quarters)
manf. manufacture; manufactured; manufacturer
mang. B manganese bronze
Manit. Manitoba
man. op. manually operated
man. pr. [medicine] *mane primo* (Latin: first thing in the morning)
Mans. Mansion(s)
manuf. manufacture; manufactured; manufacturer; manufacturing
manufac. manufacture; manufactured; manufacturer; manufacturing
Manweb Merseyside and North Wales Electricity Board
MAO Master of Arts in Obstetrics; [biochemistry] monoamine oxidase
MAOI [pharmacology] monoamine oxidase inhibitor (antidepressant)
MAOT Member of the Association of Occupational Therapists
MAOU Member of the American Ornithologists' Union
MAP major air pollutant; [computing] manufacturing automation protocol; maximum average price; [medicine] mean arterial (blood) pressure; medical aid post; Member of the Association of Project Managers; Ministry of Aircraft Production; [USA] modified American plan (for payment of hotel bills)
MAPI [computing] messaging application program interface
MAppArts Master of Applied Arts
MAppSc Master of Applied Science
MAPsS Member of the Australian Psychological Society
MAR [taxation] marginal age relief; Master of Arts in Religion; [computing] memory address register
Mar. March
mar. *mardi* (French: Tuesday); [music] marimba; marine; maritime; marriage; married; *martedì* (Italian: Tuesday); *martes* (Spanish: Tuesday); *marzo* (Italian: March); *marzo* (Spanish: March)
MARAC Member of the Australasian Register of Agricultural Consultants
MARC [bibliography] machine-readable cataloguing
marc. [music] *marcato* (Italian: marked, emphasizing each note)
MArch Master of Architecture
March. Marchioness
MArchE Master of Architectural Engineering
marg [short form] margarine
marg. margin; marginal
marit. maritime
mar. lic. marriage licence
MARMAP [USA] Marine Resources Monitoring Assessment and Prediction
Marq. Marquess; Marquis
MARS meteorological automatic reporting station (or system)
mart market
mart. martyr
MARV [military] manœuvrable re-entry vehicle
MAS Malaysian Airline System; Master of Agricultural Science; Master of Applied Science; Medical Advisory Service; Military Agency for Standardization
mas. [grammar] masculine
MASC Member of the Australian Society of Calligraphers
MASc Master of Applied Science
masc. [grammar] masculine
MASCE Member of the American Society of Civil Engineers
mascon [astronomy] mass concentration
maser microwave amplification by stimulated emission of radiation
MASH [USA] mobile army surgical hospital
MASI Member of the Architects' and Surveyors' Institute
MASME Member of the American Society of Mechanical Engineers
MA(SS) Master of Arts in Social Sciences
Mass. Massachusetts
MASTA Medical Advisory Service for Travellers Abroad
MAT [insurance] marine, aviation and transport; Master of Arts in Teaching
mat. maternity; matinée; matins; [printing] matrix; mature; [finance] maturity
MATA multiple answering teaching aid

MATh Master of Arts in Theology
math [US and Canadian short form] mathematics
math. mathematical; mathematically; mathematician; mathematics
maths [short form] mathematics
MATIF *marché à terme des instruments financiers* (French: financial futures market)
matr. matrimonial; *matrimonium* (Latin: marriage)
matric [short form] matriculation (former school examination)
MATS [US air force] Military Air Transport Service
MATSA Managerial Administrative Technical Staff Association
Matt. [Bible] Matthew
MATTS [military] multiple airborne target trajectory system
MATV master antenna television
MAU [computing] multi-station access unit
Maur. Mauritian; Mauritius
Mau Rs [currency] Mauritian rupee
MAusIMM Member of the Australasian Institute of Mining and Metallurgy
MAW [USA] marine air wing; [military] medium assault weapon
MAX maximum
max. maxim; maximum
MAYC Methodist Association of Youth Clubs
MB Bachelor of Medicine (from Latin *Medicinae Baccalaureus*); Bachelor of Music (from Latin *Musicae Baccalaureus*); [vehicle registration] Chester; Manitoba; maritime board; marketing board; mark of the Beast; maternity benefit; [Canada] Medal of Bravery; medical board; [computing] megabit; [computing] megabyte; metropolitan borough; millibar (unit of atmospheric pressure); motor barge; motorboat; municipal borough
mb millibar (unit of atmospheric pressure)
m.b. magnetic bearing; main battery; medium bomber; [medicine] *misce bene* (Latin: mix well); motor barge; motorboat
MBA Master of Business Administration
Mba Mombasa
MBAC Member of the British Association of Chemists
MBAcC Member of the British Acupuncture Council
mbar millibar (unit of atmospheric pressure)
MBASW Member of the British Association of Social Workers
MBC metropolitan borough council; mountain bike club; municipal borough council
m.b.c. [medicine] maximum breathing capacity
MBCO Member of the British College of Optometrists (or Ophthalmic Opticians)
MBCPE Member of the British College of Physical Education
MBCS Member of the British Computer Society
MBD [medicine] minimal brain dysfunction
MBdgSc Master of Building Science
MBE Member of the Order of the British Empire; [electronics] molecular-beam epitaxy
MBF Musicians Benevolent Fund
MBG microemulsion-based gel
MBH [astronomy] massive black hole
mbH [commerce] *mit beschränkter Haftung* (German: with limited liability) (of company)
MBHI Member of the British Horological Institute
MBI [finance] management buy-in
MBIAT Member of the British Institute of Architectural Technologists
MBIFD Member of the British Institute of Funeral Directors
MBIM Member of the British Institute of Management
MBK [military] missing, believed killed
MBKSTS Member of the British Kinematograph, Sound and Television Society
MBL [medicine] menstrual blood loss
MBM Master of Business Management
MBNOA Member of the British Naturopathic and Osteopathic Association
MBNQA [commerce] Malcolm Baldridge National Quality Award
MBO [finance] management buyout; [commerce] management by objectives
MBOU Member of the British Ornithologists' Union
MBP [medicine] mean blood pressure
MBPICS Member of the British

Production and Inventory Control Society

MBPsS Member of the British Psychological Society

MBR [astronomy] microwave background radiation

mbr member

MBRF [military] mutual and balanced force reduction

MBS Manchester Business School

MBSc Master of Business Science

MBT [military] main battle tank; [medicine] mean body temperature

MBuild Master of Building

MBWA [commerce] management by wandering around

Mbyte [computing] megabyte

MC machinery certificate; magistrates' court; [navigation] magnetic course; marginal cost; [USA] Marine Corps; [USA] Maritime Commission; marriage certificate; Master of Ceremonies; Master of Surgery (from Latin *Magister Chirurgiae*); medical certificate; [USA] Medical Corps; [astrology] *Medium Caeli* (Latin: Midheaven); [USA] Member of Congress; Member of Council; mess committee; Methodist Church; military college; Military Cross; Missionaries of Charity; [astronomy] molecular cloud; [chemistry] molecular cluster; [international vehicle registration] Monaco; [politics] Monday Club; Monte Carlo; Morse code; motor contact; [vehicle registration] northeast London

M/C Manchester; [finance] marginal credit

Mc megacycle

m/c machine; motorcycle

.mc Monaco (in Internet address)

m.c. *mois courant* (French: current month); motorcycle

MCA Management Consultants' Association; Manufacturing Chemists' Association; Maritime and Coastguard Agency; Master of Commerce and Administration; Matrimonial Causes Act; [trademark, computing] micro channel architecture; monetary compensatory amount(s); Motor Cycle Association; [electronics] multichannel analyser; multicriteria analysis; [electronics] multiple channel analyser; multiple classification analysis

MCAB [USA] Marine Corps air base

MCAM Member of the CAM Foundation

MC&G mapping, charting and geodesy

MCANW Medical Campaign Against Nuclear Weapons

MCAV [computing] modified constant angular velocity

MCB [USA] Marine Corps Base; Master of Clinical Biochemistry; [computing] memory control block; Metric Conversion Board; miniature circuit breaker; [military] multiple-cratering bomblets

MCBSI Member of the Chartered Building Societies Institute

MCC Manchester Computer Centre; Marylebone Cricket Club; Maxwell Communications Corporation; Melbourne Cricket Club; member of the county council; metropolitan county council; [navigation] mid-course correction; Motor Caravanners' Club

MCCA Minor Counties Cricket Association

MCCC Middlesex County Cricket Club

MCCD RCS Member in Clinical Community Dentistry of the Royal College of Surgeons (of England)

MCCU [medicine] mobile coronary care unit

MCD Master of Civic Design; [medicine] mean cell diameter; [medicine] mean corpuscular diameter; Movement for Christian Democracy

MCDS management control data system

MCE Master of Chemical Engineering; Master of Civil Engineering

MCFP [Canada] Member of the College of Family Physicians

MCG Melbourne Cricket Ground

MCGA [computing] multicolour graphics array

MCGB Master Chef of Great Britain

McGU McGill University (Canada)

MCH [medicine] mean cell haemoglobin; [medicine] mean corpuscular haemoglobin; [biochemistry] melanin-concentrating hormone

MCh Master of Surgery (from Latin *Magister Chirurgiae*)

Mch. Manchester

MCHC [medicine] mean cell haemoglobin concentration; [medicine] mean corpuscular haemoglobin concentration

MChD Master of Dental Surgery (from Latin *Magister Chirurgiae Dentalis*)
MChE Master of Chemical Engineering
MChemA Master in Chemical Analysis
MChemEng Master of Chemical Engineering
MChir Master of Surgery (from Latin *Magister Chirurgiae*)
MChOrth Master of Orthopaedic Surgery (from Latin *Magister Chirurgiae Orthopaedicae*)
MChS Member of the Society of Chiropodists
mcht merchant
mchy machinery
mCi millicurie (unit of radioactivity)
m.c.i. malleable cast iron
MCIBSE Member of the Chartered Institution of Building Services Engineers
MCIM Member of the Chartered Institute of Marketing
MCIOB Member of the Chartered Institute of Building
MCIS Member of the Institute of Chartered Secretaries and Administrators (formerly Member of the Chartered Institute of Secretaries)
MCIT Member of the Chartered Institute of Transport
MCL Master of Civil Law; maximum contamination levels
MClinPsychol Master of Clinical Psychology
MClSc Master of Clinical Science
MCLV [computing] modified constant linear velocity
MCM [mathematics] Monte Carlo method; [computing] multichip module; multistage conventional munitions
MCMES Member of the Civil and Mechanical Engineers' Society
MCO Managed Care Organization
Mco Morocco
mcol. musicological; musicologist; musicology
MCollH Member of the College of Handicrafts
MCom Master of Commerce
MCommH Master of Community Health
MConsE Member of the Association of Consulting Engineers
MCOphth Member of the College of Ophthalmologists
MCP male chauvinist pig; [USA] Master of City Planning; Member of Colonial Parliament; Member of the College of Preceptors
MCPO Master Chief Petty Officer
MCPP Member of the College of Pharmacy Practice
MCPS Mechanical Copyright Protection Society; Member of the College of Physicians and Surgeons
m.c.q. multiple-choice question
MCR mass communications research; [engineering] maximum continuous rating; [medicine] metabolic clearance rate; middle common room (in university or college); mobile control room
MCS Madras Civil Service; Malayan Civil Service; Marine Conservation Society; Master of Commercial Science; Military College of Science; monitoring and control system; [electronics] multichannel scaler
Mc/s megacycles per second
MCSD [computing] Microsoft Certified Solutions Developer
MCSE Microsoft Certified Systems Engineer
MCSP Member of the Chartered Society of Physiotherapy
MCST Member of the College of Speech Therapists
MCT mainstream corporation tax; Member of the Association of Corporate Treasurers
MCU main control unit; [photography] medium close-up
MCV [medicine] mean cell volume; [medicine] mean corpuscular volume
MCW [telecommunications] modulated continuous wave
MD Doctor of Medicine (from Latin *Medicinae Doctor*); [music] *main droite* (French: right hand); malicious damage; managing director; [music] *mano destra* (Italian: right hand); map distance; market day; [US postcode] Maryland; medical department; [banking] memorandum of deposit; mentally deficient; mess deck; Middle Dutch; military district; minidisc (audio recording); [international vehicle registration] Moldova; molecular dynamics; Monroe Doctrine; [medicine] muscular dystrophy; musical

director; [vehicle registration] northeast London
Md Maryland; [chemical element] mendelevium
M/d [commerce] months after date
.md Moldova (in Internet address)
MDA [pharmacology] methylenedioxyamphetamine (= ice, hallucinogenic drug); minimum detectable activity; minimum detectable amount; [computing] monochrome display adapter; [finance] multiple discriminant analysis; Muscular Dystrophy Association
MDAM [computing] multidimensional access memory
MD&A [commerce] management discussion and analysis
MDAP [USA] Mutual Defense Assistance Program
M-day [USA] mobilization day
MDB *Movimento Democrático Brasileiro* (Portuguese: Brazilian Democratic Movement)
MdB *Mitglied des Bundestages* (German: Member of the Bundestag)
MDC metropolitan district council; minimum detectable concentration; modification and design control; more developed country
MDD minimum detectable dose
Mddx Middlesex
MDentSc Master of Dental Science
MDes Master of Design
MDF Manic Depression Fellowship; medium-density fibreboard
MDG Medical Director-General
MDHB Mersey Docks and Harbour Board
m. dict. [medicine] *more dicto* (Latin: in the manner directed) (in prescriptions)
MDip Master of Diplomacy
mdise merchandise
MDiv Master of Divinity
MDL minimum detectable level
mdl model
Mdlle *Mademoiselle* (French: Miss)
Mdm Madam
MDMA [pharmacology] methylenedioxymethamphetamine (= ecstasy, hallucinogenic drug)
Mdme *Madame* (French: Mrs)
mdn median
MDNS [computing] managed data network service
mdnt midnight
MDP Mongolian Democratic Party
MDQ minimum detectable quantity
MDR [computing] memory data register; minimum daily requirement
MDRAM [computing] multibank dynamic random-access memory
MDS main dressing station; Master of Dental Surgery; memory-adjusted driver's seat (in car advertisement); microprocessor development system
MDSc Master of Dental Science
mdse merchandise
MD/st memory-adjusted driver's seat (in car advertisement)
MDT [computing] mean downtime; [USA] Mountain Daylight Time
MDU Medical Defence Union
MDu Middle Dutch
MDV Doctor of Veterinary Medicine
MDW Military Defence Works
Mdx Middlesex
ME [US postcode] Maine; managing editor; marine engineer; marine engineering; [USA] marriage encounter; Master of Education; Master of Engineering; mechanical engineer; mechanical engineering; [USA] Medical Examiner; [UK postcode] Medway; [medicine] metabolizable energy; Methodist Episcopal; Middle East; Middle Eastern; Middle English; military engineer; milled edge; mining engineer; mining engineering; [fishing port] Montrose; [physics] Mössbauer effect; Most Excellent; [medicine] myalgic encephalomyelitis; [vehicle registration] northeast London
Me Maine; *Maître* (French: Master) (title of lawyer); Messerschmitt (German aircraft); [chemistry] methyl (used in formulae)
m.e. [bookbinding] marbled edges; maximum effort; mobility equipment; [bookbinding] mottled edges
MEA Member of the European Assembly; Middle East Airlines
MEAF Middle East Air Force
meas. measurable; measure; measurement
MEB Midlands Electricity Board
MEC [finance] marginal efficiency of capital; Master of Engineering Chemistry; Member of the Executive Council;

Methodist Episcopal Church; Middle East Command; minimum effective concentration
MEc Master of Economics
MECAS Middle East Centre for Arab Studies
mech. mechanic; mechanical; mechanically; mechanics; mechanism; mechanize; mechanized
MechE mechanical engineer
ME(Chem) Master of Chemical Engineering
MECI Member of the Institute of Employment Consultants
MECO [astronautics] main engine cut off
MEcon Master of Economics
MED maximum equivalent dose; [pharmacology] minimum effective dose; [chemistry] molecular electronic device; [New Zealand] Municipal Electricity Department
MEd Master of Education
Med [short form] Mediterranean
Med. Mediterranean
med. medal; medallist; median; medical; medicine; medieval; medium
Medit. Mediterranean
med. jur. medical jurisprudence
MEDLARS [USA] Medical Literature Analysis and Retrieval System
Med. Lat. Medieval Latin
MedRC Medical Reserve Corps
MedScD Doctor of Medical Science
med. tech. medical technician; medical technology
MEE Master of Electrical Engineering
ME(Elec) Master of Electrical Engineering
MEF Mediterranean Expeditionary Force; Middle East Force
meg [short form, computing] megabyte
MEIC Member of the Engineering Institute of Canada
Mej. *Mejuffrouw* (Dutch: Miss)
MEK methyl ethyl ketone (solvent)
Melan. Melanesia; Melanesian
Melb. Melbourne
MELF Middle East Land Forces
Mem. Member
mem. member; *memento* (Latin: remember); memoir(s); memorandum; memorial; memory
ME(Mech) Master of Mechanical Engineering
memo [short form] memorandum
MEN [medicine] multiple endocrine neoplasia
Men [astronomy] Mensa
MENA Middle East News Agency
Mencap Royal Society for Mentally Handicapped Children and Adults
MEng Master of Engineering
MENS [medicine] multiple endocrine neoplasia syndromes
menst. menstrual; menstruation
mensur. mensuration
ment. mental; mention; mentioned
mentd mentioned
MEO Marine Engineering Officer
MEP *Mahajana Eksath Peramuna* (Sinhalese: People's United Front) (in Sri Lanka); Master of Engineering Physics; mean effective pressure; Member of the European Parliament
MEPA Master of Engineering and Public Administration
Mer. Merionethshire
mer. mercantile; merchandise; *mercoledì* (Italian: Wednesday); *mercredi* (French: Wednesday); mercury; meridian; meridional
Merc [short form] Mercedes (car)
merc. mercantile; mercury
MERCOSUR *Mercado Común del Sur* (Spanish: Southern (American) Common Market)
MERLIN [astronomy] Multi-Element Radio-linked Interferometer Network
MERU Maharishi European Research University
MèsA *Maître ès arts* (French: Master of Arts)
MESc Master of Engineering Science
MESFET [electronics] metal-semiconductor field-effect transistor
Messrs *Messieurs* (French: gentlemen, sirs) (plural of Mr in English)
Met [short form] Metropolitan Opera House (New York); [short form] Metropolitan Police
Met. Meteorological (as in **Met. Office**)
met. metallurgical; metallurgist; metallurgy; metaphor; metaphoric(al); metaphysical; metaphysics; meteorological; meteorology; metronome; metropolitan
metall. metallurgical; metallurgist; metallurgy

metaph. metaphor; metaphoric(al); metaphysical; metaphysics
METAR Meteorological Airfield Report
met. bor. metropolitan borough
MetE metallurgical engineer
meteor. meteorological; meteorology
meteorol. meteorological; meteorology
Meth. Methodist
meths [short form] methylated spirits
M-et-L Maine-et-Loire (French department)
M-et-M Meurthe-et-Moselle (French department)
m. et n. [medicine] *mane et nocte* (Latin: morning and night) (in prescriptions)
MetR Metropolitan Railway (London)
metro [short form] metropolitan railway
metrol. metrological; metrology
metrop. metropolis; metropolitan
metropol. metropolis; metropolitan
metsat meteorological satellite
MeV megaelectronvolt
Mev. *Mevrouw* (Dutch: Mrs)
MEW [finance] measure of economic welfare; [military] microwave early warning (system)
MEX [international vehicle registration] Mexico
Mex. Mexican; Mexico
MEXE Military Engineering Experimental Establishment
Mex. Sp. Mexican Spanish
MEZ *Mitteleuropäische Zeit* (German: Central European Time)
mez. [music] *mezza* (Italian: half, medium); [music] *mezzo* (Italian: half, medium)
mezzo. mezzotint
MF machine finish (on paper); machine finished (paper); magnetic field; Master of Forestry; [radio] medium frequency; melamine-formaldehyde (as in **MF resin**); Middle French; mill finish; [US slang] motherfucker; [telecommunications] multifrequency; [vehicle registration] northeast London
M/F male or female
mF millifarad
mf [music] *mezzo forte* (Italian: moderately loudly)
MFA Master of Fine Arts; Multi-Fibre Arrangement
MFAMus Master of Fine Arts in Music
MFARCS Member of the Faculty of Anaesthetists of the Royal College of Surgeons (of England)
MFB Metropolitan Fire Brigade
MFC Mastership in Food Control; motor-fuel consumption
MFCM Member of the Faculty of Community Medicine
MFD minimum fatal dose
mfd manufactured
mfg manufacturing
MFH Master of Foxhounds; mobile field hospital
MFHom Member of the Faculty of Homoeopathy
MFlem Middle Flemish
mflops [computing] millions of floating-point operations per second (measure of computer power)
MFM [computing] modified frequency modulation
MFN most favoured nation (in trade agreement)
MFOM Member of the Faculty of Occupational Medicine
MFP [physics] mean free path
MFPA Mouth and Foot Painting Artists
MFr Middle French
mfr manufacturer
mfr. manufacture
mfre manufacture
MFS Master of Food Science; Master of Foreign Study
mfst manifest
MFT [computing] master file table
m. ft [medicine] *mistura fiat* (Latin: let a mixture be made) (in prescriptions)
m.f.t. motor freight tariff
MFV motor fleet vehicle; motor fleet vessel
MG machine glazed (paper); machine gun; [music] *main gauche* (French: left hand); Major-General; [building] make good; Morris Garages (sports car manufacturer); motor generator; [medicine] myasthenia gravis; [vehicle registration] northeast London
Mg [chemical element] magnesium
mg milligram
.mg Madagascar (in Internet address)
MGA Major-General in charge of Administration

m.g.a.w.d. make good all works disturbed (in commercial contract)
MGB metropolitan green belt; *Ministerstvo Gosudarstvennoi Bezopasnosti* (Russian: Ministry of State Security) (former Soviet secret police); motor gunboat
MGC Machine Gun Corps; Marriage Guidance Council (former name of Relate)
mgd million gallons per day
MGDS RCS Member in General Dental Surgery of the Royal College of Surgeons (of England)
mge message
MGGS Major-General, General Staff
MGI Member of the Institute of Certificated Grocers
MGk Medieval Greek; Modern Greek
M Glam. Mid Glamorgan
MGM Metro-Goldwyn-Mayer (film studio); mobile guided missile
mgmt management
MGN Mirror Group Newspapers
MGO Master General of the Ordnance; Master of Gynaecology and Obstetrics
MGP manufactured-gas plant
MGR [nuclear technology] modular gas-cooled reactor
MGr Medieval Greek; Modern Greek
Mgr Manager; *Monseigneur* (French: my lord); [Roman Catholic Church] Monsignor
mgr manager
Mgrs Managers; *Monseigneurs* (French: my lords); [Roman Catholic Church] Monsignors
mgs metre-gram-second
mgt management
MH [navigation] magnetic heading; [nautical] main hatch; marital history; Master of Horse; Master of Horticulture; Master of Hounds; Master of Hygiene; [USA] Medal of Honor; medical history; mental health; [fishing port] Middlesbrough; military hospital; Ministry of Health; [vehicle registration] northeast London
mH millihenry (unit of electric inductance)
.mh Marshall Islands (in Internet address)
MHA [USA] Master of Hospital Administration; [Australia, Canada] Member of the House of Assembly; [USA] Mental Health Administration; Methodist Homes for the Aged
MHC [immunology] major histocompatibility complex
MHCIMA Member of the Hotel Catering and Institutional Management Association
MHD [physics] magnetohydrodynamics
MHE Master of Home Economics
MHeb Middle Hebrew
MHF massive hydraulic fracture (or fracturing); [radio] medium high frequency
MHG Middle High German
MHK Member of the House of Keys (in Isle of Man)
MHLG Ministry of Housing and Local Government
M Hon. Most Honourable
MHortSc Master of Horticultural Science
MHR [USA, Australia] Member of the House of Representatives
MHRA Modern Humanities Research Association
MHRF Mental Health Research Fund
MHS medical history sheet; Member of the Historical Society; [computing] message-handling service (or system)
MHTGR [nuclear technology] modular high-temperature gas-cooled reactor
MHum Master of Humanities
MHW mean high water (level of tide)
MHWN mean high water neaps (level of tide)
MHWS mean high water springs (level of tide)
MHy Master of Hygiene
MHz megahertz
MI malleable iron; [civil aircraft marking] Marshall Islands; medical inspection; [US postcode] Michigan; Military Intelligence (as in **MI5**); Ministry of Information; [biology] mitotic index; moment of inertia; mounted infantry; [medicine] myocardial infarction
Mi. Minor; Mississippi
mi. mile; [currency] mill (thousandth of dollar); minute
MI5 Military Intelligence, section five (popular name for UK counterintelligence agency)
MI6 Military Intelligence, section six (popular name for UK intelligence and espionage agency)
MIA Master of International Affairs; [mili-

tary] missing in action; [Australia] Murrumbidgee Irrigation Area
MIAA&S Member of the Incorporated Association of Architects and Surveyors
MIAgrE Member of the Institution of Agricultural Engineers
MIAM Member of the Institute of Administrative Management
MIAP Member of the Institution of Analysts and Programmers
MIAS Member of the Institute of Accounting Staff
MIB [computing] management information base
MIBE Member of the Institution of British Engineers
MIBF Member of the Institute of British Foundrymen
MIBiol Member of the Institute of Biology
MIBK methyl isobutyl ketone (solvent)
MIBritE Member of the Institution of British Engineers
MIBScot Member of the Institute of Bankers in Scotland
Mic [astronomy] Microscopium
Mic. [Bible] Micah
MICE Member of the Institution of Civil Engineers
MICEI Member of the Institution of Civil Engineers of Ireland
MICFor Member of the Institute of Chartered Foresters
Mich. Michaelmas; Michigan
MIChemE Member of the Institution of Chemical Engineers
MICorrST Member of the Institution of Corrosion Science and Technology
MICR [computing] magnetic ink character recognition
Micro Micronesia; Micronesian; Multinational Initiative for the Use of Computers in Research Organizations
micro. microscope; microscopic; microscopist; microscopy
microbiol. microbiology
micros. microscope; microscopic; microscopist; microscopy
MICS Member of the Institute of Chartered Shipbrokers
MICU [medicine] mobile intensive care unit
MICV [military] mechanized infantry combat vehicle
MID minimum infective dose
Mid. Midlands; Midshipman
mid. middle; midnight
MIDAS [computing] measurement information and data analysis system; missile defence alarm system
Middx Middlesex
MIDELEC Midlands Electricity Board
Midi musical instrument digital interface
Midl. Midlands; Midlothian
Mid. Lat. Middle Latin
MIDPM Member of the Institute of Data Processing Management
midw. midwest; midwestern
MIE(Aust) Member of the Institution of Engineers, Australia
MIED Member of the Institution of Engineering Designers
MIEE Member of the Institution of Electrical Engineers
MIEEE [USA] Member of the Institute of Electrical and Electronics Engineers
MIEI Member of the Institution of Engineering Inspection
MIE(Ind) Member of the Institution of Engineers, India
miér. *miércoles* (Spanish: Wednesday)
MIES Member of the Institution of Engineers and Shipbuilders, Scotland
MIEx Member of the Institute of Export
MIExpE Member of the Institute of Explosives Engineers
MIF [computing] management information format; [immunology] migration inhibition factor; milk in first (in pouring tea); Miners' International Federation
MIFA Member of the Institute of Field Archaeologists
MIFF Member of the Institute of Freight Forwarders
MIFireE Member of the Institute of Fire Engineers
MIG metal-inert gas (as in **MIG welding**); mortgage indemnity guarantee
MiG Mikoyan and Gurevich (designers of Soviet fighter aircraft)
MIGA Multilateral Investment Guarantee Agency (affiliate of World Bank)
MIGasE Member of the Institution of Gas Engineers

MIGeol Member of the Institution of Geologists
MIH Master of Industrial Health
MIHort Member of the Institute of Horticulture
MIHT Member of the Institution of Highways and Transportation
MIIE Member of the Institution of Industrial Engineers
MIIM Member of the Institution of Industrial Managers
MIInfSc Member of the Institute of Information Sciences
MIISec Member of the International Institute of Security
MIL Member of the Institute of Linguists; [USA] one million
Mil. Milan
mil. mileage; military; militia
.mil US military (in Internet address)
Mil. Att. Military Attaché
MILGA Member of the Institute of Local Government Administrators
milit. military
mill. million
MILocoE Member of the Institution of Locomotive Engineers
Milw. Milwaukee
MIM Member of the Institute of Materials
MIMarE Member of the Institute of Marine Engineers
MIMC Member of the Institute of Management Consultants
MIMD [computing] multiple instruction, multiple data
MIME multipurpose Internet mail extension
MIMechE Member of the Institution of Mechanical Engineers
MIMGTechE Member of the Institution of Mechanical and General Technician Engineers
MIMI Member of the Institute of the Motor Industry
MIMM Member of the Institution of Mining and Metallurgy
MIMS *Monthly Index of Medical Specialities*
MIN minimum
Min. Minister; Ministry
min. mineralogical; mineralogy; minim (unit of liquid measure); minimum; mining; ministerial; minor; minute
mineral. mineralogical; mineralogy
Minn. Minnesota
Min. Plen. Minister Plenipotentiary
Min. Res. Minister Resident(iary)
MINS [USA] minor(s) in need of supervision
MInstAM Member of the Institute of Administrative Management
MInstBE Member of the Institution of British Engineers
MInstD Member of the Institute of Directors
MInstE Member of the Institute of Energy
MInstEnvSci Member of the Institute of Environmental Sciences
MInstMC Member of the Institute of Measurement and Control
MInstMM Member of the Institution of Mining and Metallurgy
MInstP Member of the Institute of Physics
MInstPet Member of the Institute of Petroleum
MInstPI Member of the Institute of Patentees and Inventors
MInstPkg Member of the Institute of Packaging
MInstR Member of the Institute of Refrigeration
MInstRA Member of the Institute of Registered Architects
MInstTM Member of the Institute of Travel Managers in Industry and Commerce
MInstWM Member of the Institute of Wastes Management
MINucE Member of the Institution of Nuclear Engineers
Mio [geology] Miocene
MIOSH Member of the Institution of Occupational Safety and Health
MIP marine insurance policy; maximum investment plan; Member of the Institute of Plumbing; monthly investment plan
m.i.p. mean indicated pressure
MIPA Member of the Institute of Practitioners in Advertising
MIPD Member of the Institute of Personnel and Development
MIPR Member of the Institute of Public Relations
mips [computing] millions of instructions per second

MIQ Member of the Institute of Quarrying
MIQA Member of the Institute of Quality Assurance
MIR [taxation] mortgage interest relief
MIr Middle Irish
MIRA Member of the Institute of Registered Architects; Motor Industry Research Association
MIRAS [taxation] mortgage interest relief at source
MIRD medical internal radiation dose
MIRT Member of the Institute of Reprographic Technicians
MIRTE Member of the Institute of Road Transport Engineers
MIRV [military] multiple independently targeted re-entry vehicle
MIS management information system; manufacturing information system; marketing information system; Member of the Institute of Statisticians; meteorological information system; Mining Institute of Scotland
Mis [geology] Mississippian
misc. miscellaneous; miscellany
MISD [computing] multiple instruction, single data
MISFET [electronics] metal-insulator-semiconductor field-effect transistor
Miss. Mission; Missionary; Mississippi
mist. *mistura* (Latin: mixture)
mistrans. mistranslation
MIStructE Member of the Institution of Structural Engineers
MIT Massachusetts Institute of Technology
Mit. *Mittwoch* (German: Wednesday)
MITA Member of the Industrial Transport Association
MITD Member of the Institute of Training and Development
MITE Member of the Institution of Electrical and Electronics Technician Engineers
MITI [Japan] Ministry of International Trade and Industry
MITL magnetically insulated transmission line
MITT Member of the Institute of Travel and Tourism
mitts minutes of telecommunications traffic
MIU Maharishi International University
MIWEM Member of the Institution of Water and Environmental Management
mixt. mixture
MJ [vehicle registration] Luton; megajoule; Ministry of Justice
MJA Medical Journalists' Association
MJD management job description
MJI Member of the Institute of Journalists
MJQ Modern Jazz Quartet
MJS Member of the Japan Society
MJSD March, June, September, December (end of financial quarters)
MJur Master of Law (from Latin *Magister Juris*)
MK [international vehicle registration] Macedonia; [currency] Malawi kwacha; [UK postcode] Milton Keynes; [vehicle registration] northeast London
Mk mark (model of car etc.); Mark; [currency] markka (used in Finland)
mk [currency] mark
.mk Macedonia (in Internet address)
mkd marked
MKO Mauna Kea Observatory (Hawaii)
mks [currency] marks; metre-kilogram-second (as in **mks units**)
mksA metre-kilogram-second-ampere (as in **mksA system**)
mkt market
ML Licentiate in Medicine (from Latin *Medicinae Licentiatus*); Licentiate in Midwifery; Master of Law(s); Master of Letters; [statistics] maximum likelihood; Medieval Latin; [fishing port] Methil (Scotland); [UK postcode] Motherwell; motor launch; muzzle-loading (gun); [vehicle registration] northeast London
ml mail; millilitre
.ml Mali (in Internet address)
m.l. machine language; mean level; minelayer
MLA [accounting] mandatory liquid assets; Master Locksmiths Association; Master of Landscape Architecture; Master of the Liberal Arts; Medical Library Association; Member of the Legislative Assembly; [USA] Modern Language Association
MLArch Master of Landscape Architecture
MLC Meat and Livestock Commission; [Australia, India] Member of the Legisla-

tive Council; [medicine] mixed lymphocyte culture
MLCOM Member of the London College of Osteopathic Medicine
MLD Master of Landscape Design; [pharmacology] mean lethal dose; [pharmacology] minimum lethal dose
mld mould; moulded
mldg moulding
m.l.e. maximum loss expectancy
MLF *Mouvement de libération des femmes* (French: Women's Liberation Movement); [military] multilateral (nuclear) force
MLG Middle Low German
mlg. mileage (in car advertisement)
MLib Master of Library Science
MLibSc Master of Library Science
MLitt Master of Letters (from Latin *Magister Litterarum*)
MLK Martin Luther King (US civil-rights leader)
Mlle *Mademoiselle* (French: Miss)
MLNS [medicine] mucocutaneous lymph node syndrome
MLO military liaison officer; [microbiology] mycoplasma-like organism(s)
MLR [banking] minimum lending rate; [medicine] mixed lymphocyte reaction; *Modern Language Review*; [statistics] multiple linear regression
MLRS multiple-launch rocket system
MLS main-line station; Master of Library Science; [cinema] medium long shot; Member of the Linnean Society; [aeronautics] microwave landing system; mixed language system; multi-language system
MLSO medical laboratory scientific officer
MLV [microbiology] murine leukaemia virus
MLW mean low water (level of tide)
MLWN mean low water neaps (level of tide)
MLWS mean low water springs (level of tide)
MM [music] Maelzel's metronome (indication of tempo); maintenance manual; Majesties; [medicine] malignant melanoma; Martyrs; [Freemasonry] Master Mason; Master Mechanic; Master of Music; Medal of Merit; mercantile marine; *Messieurs* (French: gentlemen, sirs) (plural of M (Monsieur) in French); Military Medal; [medicine] mucus membrane; music master; [vehicle registration] northeast London
mm millimetre
.mm Myanmar (in Internet address)
m.m. made merchantable; *mutatis mutandis* (Latin: with the necessary changes)
MMA Metropolitan Museum of Art; [astronomy] Millimeter Array; Music Masters' Association
MMath Master of Mathematics
MMB Milk Marketing Board (replaced by Milk Marque)
MMC metal-matrix composite; Monopolies and Mergers Commission
MMD Movement for Multiparty Democracy (in Zambia)
MMDA [USA] money market deposit account
MMDS [radio] multipoint microwave distribution system
MME Master of Mechanical Engineering; Master of Mining Engineering; Master of Music Education
Mme *Madame* (French: Mrs)
MMechE Master of Mechanical Engineering
MMed Master of Medicine
MMedSci Master of Medical Science
Mmes *Mesdames* (French: plural of Mme)
MMet Master of Metallurgy
MMetE Master of Metallurgical Engineering
mmf [physics] magnetomotive force
MMG [military] medium machine gun
MMGI Member of the Mining, Geological and Metallurgical Institute of India
mmHg millimetre(s) of mercury (unit of pressure)
MMI [computing] man–machine interface; Municipal Mutual Insurance
MMin Master of Ministry
MMM [Canada] Member of the Order of Military Merit
mmol millimole
MMP [biochemistry] matrix metalloproteinase (enzyme); Military Mounted Police; mixed member proportional (system of proportional representation)
m.m.p. [chemistry] mixture melting point
MMPI [psychology] Minnesota Multiphasic Personality Inventory

MMQ minimum manufacturing quantity
MMR [medicine] mass miniature radiography; [medicine] measles, mumps and rubella (vaccine)
MMRBM mobile medium-range ballistic missile
MMS Marine Meteorological Services; Member of the Institute of Management Services; Methodist Missionary Society; Moravian Missionary Society; multimission modular spacecraft
MMSA Master of Midwifery of the Society of Apothecaries
MMSc Master of Medical Science
MMT methylcyclopentadienyl manganese tricarbonyl (fuel additive); Multiple Mirror Telescope (Arizona)
MMU [computing] memory management unit; [finance] million monetary units
MMus Master of Music
MMusEd Master of Musical Education
MMX multimedia extension
MN magnetic north; [fishing port] Maldon; Master of Nursing; Merchant Navy; [US postcode] Minnesota
Mn [chemical element] manganese; Modern (language)
mn *maison* (French: house); million
mn. midnight
.mn Mongolia (in Internet address)
m.n. *mutato nomine* (Latin: with the name changed)
MNA Master of Nursing Administration; Member of the National Assembly (of Quebec)
MNAD Multinational Airmobile Division (of NATO)
MNAEA Member of the National Association of Estate Agents
MNAS [USA] Member of the National Academy of Sciences
MNC major NATO command; multinational company
MND Ministry of National Defence; [medicine] motor neurone disease
MNE multinational enterprise
MnE Modern English
MNECInst Member of the North East Coast Institution of Engineers and Shipbuilders
mng managing
MnGk Modern Greek
mngmt management
MnGr Modern Greek
mngr manager
MNI Member of the Nautical Institute
MNIMH Member of the National Institute of Medical Herbalists
Mnl. Manila
mnm minimum
MNOS [electronics] metal-nitride-oxide semiconductor
MNP microcomputer networking protocol
MNR marine nature reserve; mean neap rise (of tide); Mozambique National Resistance
Mnr *Mijnheer* (Dutch: Mr, Sir)
MNSc Master of Nursing Science
MNT mean neap tide
MNurs Master of Nursing
MO mail order; manually operated; mass observation; Master of Obstetrics; Master of Oratory; medical officer; medical orderly; Meteorological Office; military operations; [US postcode] Missouri; *modus operandi* (Latin: method of operating); [chemistry] molecular orbital; money order; monthly order; motor-operated; municipal officer; [vehicle registration] Reading
Mo [computing] magneto-optical; [chemical element] molybdenum
Mo. Missouri; Monday
m-o months old
mo. moment; month; mouth
m.o. mail order; *modus operandi* (Latin: method of operating); money order
MOA memorandum of agreement; Ministry of Aviation
MO&G Master of Obstetrics and Gynaecology
MOB movable object block
mob. mobile; mobilization; mobilize
MOBS multiple orbit bombardment system (nuclear weapons)
MOC management and operating contractor; [international vehicle registration] Mozambique (from Portuguese *Moçambique*)
MoC mother of the chapel (in printing or publishing trade union)
MOD mail-order department; Ministry of Defence; Ministry of Overseas Development
mod [computing, mathematics] modulo

mod. model; moderate; [music] *moderato* (Italian: at a moderate tempo); modern; modernization; modernized (in property advertisement); modification; modified; [mathematics] modulus
mod cons [short form] modern conveniences
mod. dict. [medicine] *modo dicto* (Latin: as directed) (in prescriptions)
modem [computing] modulator demodulator
MODFET [electronics] modulation-doped field-effect transistor
modif. modification; modified
mod. praes. [medicine] *modo praescripto* (Latin: as directed) (in prescriptions)
Mods [short form] Honour Moderations (at Oxford University)
modto [music] *moderato* (Italian: at a moderate tempo)
MODU mobile offshore drilling unit
.mod.uk Ministry of Defence (in Internet address)
MOEH Medical Officer for Environmental Health
MOF [medicine] multiple organ failure
M of A Ministry of Agriculture, Fisheries and Food
M of W Ministry of Works
MOH Master of Otter Hounds; Medical Officer of Health; Ministry of Housing (and Local Government)
MOHLG Ministry of Housing and Local Government
MOHLL [computing] machine-oriented high-level language
MOI military operations and intelligence; Ministry of Information; Ministry of the Interior
MOL [astronautics] manned orbital laboratory; Ministry of Labour
mol mole (unit of amount of substance)
mol. molecular; molecule
Mold. Moldavia; Moldavian; Moldova
Moldv. Moldavia; Moldavian; Moldova
mol. wt molecular weight
MOM milk of magnesia
m.o.m. middle of month
MOMA Museum of Modern Art
MOMI Museum of the Moving Image
MOMIMTS Military and Orchestral Instrument Makers' Trade Society
moms *mervaerdiomsaetningsskat* (Danish: value-added tax); *mervardesomsattningsskatt* (Swedish: value-added tax)
Mon [astronomy] Monoceros
Mon. Monaco; Monaghan; Monday; Monegasque; Monmouth(shire); *Montag* (German: Monday); Montana
mon. monastery; monastic; monetary; monitor; monsoon; month
Monag. Monaghan
MONEP *Marché des options négotiables de Paris* (French: Paris traded option market)
Mong. Mongolia; Mongolian
Mongol. Mongolia; Mongolian
Monm. Monmouth(shire)
monog. monogram; monograph
Mons. *Monsieur* (French: Mr)
Mont. Montana; Montgomeryshire
Montgom. Montgomeryshire
Montr. Montreal
MOO [computing] multiuser object-oriented
m.o.p. mother-of-pearl
MOPA [electronics] master oscillator power amplifier
MOPH [USA] Military Order of the Purple Heart
MOPS Mail Order Protection Scheme
MOR middle-of-the-road; [engineering] modulus of rupture
Mor. Moroccan; Morocco
mor. [music] *morendo* (Italian: dying away); [bookbinding] morocco
MORC Medical Officer Reserve Corps
mor. dict. [medicine] *more dicto* (Latin: as directed) (in prescriptions)
Mori Market and Opinion Research Institute (as in **Mori poll**)
morn. morning
morph. morphological; morphology
morphol. morphological; morphology
mor. sol. [medicine] *more solito* (Latin: in the usual way) (in prescriptions)
mort. mortal; mortality; mortar; mortgage; mortuary
MOS magneto-optical system; [electronics] metal oxide semiconductor; [electronics] metal oxide silicon; Ministry of Supply
Mos. Moscow; Moselle
mos. months
MOSFET [electronics] metal-oxide-silicon field-effect transistor

MOST [electronics] metal-oxide-silicon transistor
MOT Ministry of Transport (as in **MOT test**)
mot. motor; motorized
MOTNE meteorological operational telecommunications network
MOU memorandum of understanding
MOUS [medicine] multiple occurrence of unexplained symptoms
MOUSE [military] minimum orbital unmanned satellite of the earth (used to gather information)
MOV [engineering] motor-operated valve
mov. [music] *movimento* (Italian: movement, motion)
MOVE Men Over Violence (organization counselling wife-batterers)
movt movement
MOW [New Zealand] Ministry of Works; Movement for the Ordination of Women
MOX mixed oxide (as in **MOX fuel**)
Moz. Mozambique
MP Madhya Pradesh; [metallurgy] martensitic phase; medium pressure; melting point; Member of Parliament; [physiology] membrane potential; [cartography] Mercator's projection; metal pollutant; Methodist Protestant; Metropolitan Police; mile post (on map); Military Police; Military Policeman; *mille passuum* (Latin: 1,000 paces) (Roman mile); Minister Plenipotentiary; miscellaneous papers; miscellaneous publications; Mounted Police; Mounted Policeman; [vehicle registration] north-east London
M/P memorandum of partnership
mp [music] *mezzo piano* (Italian: moderately softly)
m.p. meeting point; melting point; mile post (on map); months after payment; mooring post
MPA Master of Professional Accounting; Master of Public Administration; Master Printers Association; Member of the Parliamentary Assembly of Northern Ireland; Music Publishers' Association
MPAA Motion Picture Association of America
MPAGB Modern Pentathlon Association of Great Britain
MPB male pattern baldness; [USA] Missing Persons Bureau
MPC mathematics, physics, chemistry; maximum permissible concentration; Metropolitan Police College; Metropolitan Police Commissioner; multimedia personal computer
MPD maximum permissible dose
MPE Master of Physical Education; maximum permissible exposure (to radiation); maximum possible error
MPEA Member of the Physical Education Association
MPEG [computing] Moving Picture Expert Group
MPer Middle Persian
MPF [medicine] maturation-promoting factor
MPG [education] main professional grade (basic salary); *Max-Planck-Gesellschaft zur Förderung der Wissenschaften* (German: Max Planck Society for the Advancement of Science)
mpg miles per gallon
MPH Master of Public Health
MPh Master of Philosophy
mph miles per hour
MPharm Master of Pharmacy
MPhil Master of Philosophy
MPI Max Planck Institute; maximum permissible intake
m.p.i. mean point of impact
MPIA Master of Public and International Affairs
MPIR Max Planck Institute for Radio Astronomy
MPL maximum permissible level
MPLA *Movimento Popular de Libertação de Angola* (Portuguese: Popular Movement for the Liberation of Angola)
mpm metres per minute
MPO management and personnel office; Metropolitan Police Office; military post office; mobile printing office; mobile publishing office
MPP [computing] massively parallel processor; Member of the Provincial Parliament (of Ontario)
m.p.p. most probable position
MPR *Majelis Permusyawaratan Rakyat* (Bahasa Indonesian: People's Consultative Assembly); maximum permitted

radiation; Mongolian People's Republic
MPRISA Member of the Public Relations Institute of South Africa
MPRP Mongolian People's Revolutionary Party
MPS manufacturer's part specification; marginal propensity to save; master production schedule; Medical Protection Society; Member of the Pharmaceutical Society; Member of the Philological Society; Member of the Physical Society; [medicine] mucopolysaccharide (as in **MPS disease**)
MPs Master of Psychology
mps metres per second
MPsSc Master of Psychological Science
MPsych Master of Psychology
MPsyMed Master of Psychological Medicine
MPTA Municipal Passenger Transport Association
MPU Medical Practitioners Union; [computing] microprocessor unit
MPV multipurpose vehicle
Mpy [commerce] *Maatschappij* (Dutch: company, Co.)
MQ [photography] metol-quinol (developing fluid)
mq. mosque
Mqe Martinique
MR magnetic resonance (as in **MR scan**); [computing] magneto-resistive; [fishing port] Manchester; map reference; [law] Master of the Rolls; match rifle; [commerce] mate's receipt; mental retardation; metabolic rate; Middlesex Regiment; Minister Resident(iary); motivation(al) research; motorways regulations; municipal reform; [vehicle registration] Swindon
Mr Master; Mister
.mr Mauritania (in Internet address)
m.r. memorandum receipt
MRA Maritime Royal Artillery; Moral Rearmament
MRAC Member of the Royal Agricultural College
MRACP Member of the Royal Australasian College of Physicians
MRACS Member of the Royal Australasian College of Surgeons
MRadA Member of the Radionic Association
MRAeS Member of the Royal Aeronautical Society
MRAF Marshal of the Royal Air Force
MRAIC Member of the Royal Architectural Institute of Canada
MRAO Mullard Radio Astronomy Observatory
MRAS Member of the Royal Academy of Science; Member of the Royal Asiatic Society; Member of the Royal Astronomical Society
MRB Mersey River Board
MRBM medium-range ballistic missile
MRBS Member of the Royal Botanic Society
MRC Medical Registration Council; Medical Research Council; Medical Reserve Corps; Model Railway Club
MRCA multirole combat aircraft
MRCGP Member of the Royal College of General Practitioners
MRC-LMB Medical Research Council Laboratory of Molecular Biology
MRCO Member of the Royal College of Organists
MRCOG Member of the Royal College of Obstetricians and Gynaecologists
MRCP Member of the Royal College of Physicians
MRCPA Member of the Royal College of Pathologists of Australia
MRCPath Member of the Royal College of Pathologists
MRCPE Member of the Royal College of Physicians of Edinburgh
MRCPI Member of the Royal College of Physicians of Ireland
MRCPSGlas Member of the Royal College of Physicians and Surgeons of Glasgow
MRCPsych Member of the Royal College of Psychiatrists
MRCS Member of the Royal College of Surgeons (of England)
MRCSE Member of the Royal College of Surgeons of Edinburgh
MRCSI Member of the Royal College of Surgeons in Ireland
MRCVS Member of the Royal College of Veterinary Surgeons
MRD machine-readable dictionary; minimal residual disease
MRE Master of Religious Education; [mili-

tary] meal(s) ready to eat; Member of the Royal Society of Painter-Printmakers (formerly Member of the Royal Society of Painter-Etchers and Engravers); Microbiological Research Establishment; Mining Research Establishment

MRes Master of Research

MRG Minority Rights Group

MRGS Member of the Royal Geographical Society

MRH Member of the Royal Household

MRHS Member of the Royal Horticultural Society

MRI [medicine] magnetic resonance image; [medicine] magnetic resonance imaging; Member of the Royal Institution

MRIA Member of the Royal Irish Academy

MRIAI Member of the Royal Institute of the Architects of Ireland

MRICS Member of the Royal Institution of Chartered Surveyors

MRIN Member of the Royal Institute of Navigation

MRINA Member of the Royal Institution of Naval Architects

MRIPHH Member of the Royal Institute of Public Health and Hygiene

mrkr marker

MRM mechanically recovered meat (in food processing)

MRMetS Member of the Royal Meteorological Society

MRN materials return note

mRNA [biochemistry] messenger ribonucleic acid

mrng morning

MRO Member of the Register of Osteopaths

MRP manufacturer's recommended price; Master of Regional Planning; [commerce] material requirements planning

MRPharmS Member of the Royal Pharmaceutical Society

MRRP manufacturer's recommended retail price

MRS Market Research Society; [computing] monitored retrievable storage

MRs [currency] Mauritian rupee

Mrs Mistress

MRSC Member of the Royal Society of Chemistry

MRSH Member of the Royal Society of Health

MRSL Member of the Royal Society of Literature

MRSM Member of the Royal Society of Medicine; Member of the Royal Society of Musicians of Great Britain

MRSPP Member of the Royal Society of Portrait Painters

MRST Member of the Royal Society of Teachers

MRT [medicine] magnetic resonance tomography; mass rapid transit

MRTPI Member of the Royal Town Planning Institute

MRU manpower research unit; mobile repair unit

MRUSI Member of the Royal United Service Institution

MRV [military] multiple re-entry vehicle

MRVA Member of the Rating and Valuation Association

MS [vehicle registration] Edinburgh; [physics] magnetic susceptibility; mail steamer; [astronomy] main sequence; [music] *mano sinistra* (Italian: left hand); manuscript; [physics, chemistry] mass spectrometer; [physics, chemistry] mass spectrometry; [USA] Master of Science; Master of Surgery; [international vehicle registration] Mauritius; media studies; medical staff; [photography] medium shot; *memoriae sacrum* (Latin: sacred to the memory of) (on tombstone); Mess Sergeant; [photography] mid-shot; milestone (on map); minesweeper; Ministry of Supply; [US postcode] Mississippi; [medicine] mitral stenosis; [USA] motor ship; [medicine] multiple sclerosis; municipal surveyor

Ms Miss or Mrs

ms millisecond

m/s metres per second; [finance] months after sight

ms. manuscript

m.s. mail steamer; margin of safety; maximum stress; mild steel

m/s^2 metres per second per second (unit of acceleration)

MSA Malaysia-Singapore Airways; Master of Science and Arts; Master of Science in Agriculture; Media Studies Association; Member of the Society of Apothecaries;

Merchant Shipping Act; metropolitan statistical area; Mineralogical Society of America; Motor Schools Association of Great Britain Limited; motorway service area; [USA] Mutual Security Agency

MSAE [USA] Master of Science in Aeronautical Engineering; [USA] Member of the Society of Automotive Engineers

MSAgr Master of Science in Agriculture

MS&R Merchant Shipbuilding and Repairs

MSArch Master of Science in Architecture

MSB Maritime Safety Board; Metropolitan Society for the Blind; [computing] most significant bit

MSBA Master of Science in Business Administration

MSBus Master of Science in Business

MSByte [computing] most significant byte

MSC major subordinate command (in NATO); Manchester Ship Canal; Manpower Services Commission; medical staff corps; Metropolitan Special Constabulary

MSc Master of Science

msc. miscellaneous

m.s.c. moved, seconded and carried

MSc(Ag) Master of Science in Agriculture

MScApp Master of Applied Science

MSc(Arch) Master of Science in Architecture

MSc(ChemE) Master of Science in Chemical Engineering

MScD [USA] Doctor of Medical Science; Master of Dental Science

MSCE Master of Science in Civil Engineering

MSc(Econ) Master of Science in Economics

MSc(Ed) Master of Science in Education

MSChE Master of Science in Chemical Engineering

MSc(Hort) Master of Science in Horticulture

MSCI Index [finance] Morgan Stanley Capital International World Index

MScMed Master of Medical Science

MSc(Nutr) Master of Science in Nutrition

MSCP Master of Science in Community Planning

MScTech Master of Technical Science

MSD Doctor of Medical Science; Master of Science in Dentistry; Master Surgeon Dentist; [computing] most significant digit

MSDent Master of Science in Dentistry

MS-DOS [trademark, computing] Microsoft Disk Operating System

MSE Master of Science in Education; Master of Science in Engineering; Member of the Society of Engineers

MSEd Master of Science in Education

MSEE Master of Science in Electrical Engineering

MSEM Master of Science in Engineering Mechanics; Master of Science in Engineering of Mines

MSF Manufacturing, Science and Finance (Union); Master of Science in Forestry; *Médecins sans frontières* (French: Doctors Without Frontiers) (charity); minesweeping flotilla

MSFC [USA] Marshall Space Flight Center

MSG monosodium glutamate (food additive)

msg. message

Msgr *Monseigneur* (French: my lord); [Roman Catholic Church] Monsignor

msgr messenger

MSgt [US military] Master Sergeant

MSH Master of Staghounds; [biochemistry] melanocyte-stimulating hormone

MSHE Master of Science in Home Economics

MSHEc Master of Science in Home Economics

Mshl Marshal

MSHyg Master of Science in Hygiene

MSI [electronics] medium-scale integration; Member of the Securities Institute; *Movimento Sociale Italiano* (Italian: Italian Social Movement)

MSIE Master of Science in Industrial Engineering

MSJ Master of Science in Journalism

MSL Master of Science in Linguistics; mean sea level

MSLS Master of Science in Library Science

MSM Master of Sacred Music; Master of Science in Music; Meritorious Service Medal

MSME Master of Science in Mechanical Engineering

MSMed Master of Medical Science

MSMetE Master of Science in Metallurgical Engineering
MSMus Master of Science in Music
MSN Master of Science in Nursing; [trademark, computing] Microsoft Network
MSO Member of the Society of Osteopaths
MSocIS *Membre de la société des ingénieurs et scientifiques de France* (French: Member of the Society of Engineers and Scientists of France)
MSocSc Master of Social Science(s)
MSP matched sale–purchase agreement; [trademark, computing] Microsoft Paint
MSPE Master of Science in Physical Education
MSPH Master of Science in Public Health
MSPhar Master of Science in Pharmacy
MSPharm Master of Science in Pharmacy
MSPHE Master of Science in Public Health Engineering
MSQ managing service quality
MSR [computing] magnetic stripe reader; main supply route; manual sunroof (in car advertisement); mean spring rise (of tide); Member of the Society of Radiographers; [military] missile-site radar
MSRP [USA] manufacturer's suggested retail price
MSS manuscripts; [computing] mass storage system; Master of Social Science; Master of Social Service; Member of the Royal Statistical Society; [medicine] midstream specimen (of urine)
mss manuscripts
MSSc Master of Social Science
MSSE [USA] Master of Science in Sanitary Engineering
MST Master of Sacred Theology; Master of Science in Teaching; mean spring tide; mean survival time; [USA] Mountain Standard Time
MSt Master of Studies
mst measurement
MStat Master of Statistics
MSTD Member of the Society of Typographic Designers
Mstr Master
MSTS [US navy] Military Sea Transportation Service
MSU [medicine] midstream specimen of urine
MSUL Medical Schools of the University of London
MSurv Master of Surveying
MSurvSc Master of Surveying Science
MSW magnetic surface wave(s); Master of Social Welfare; Master of Social Work; medical social worker; municipal solid waste
MSw Middle Swedish
MSX [trademark, computing] Microsoft extended Basic
MSY maximum sustainable yield (of natural resource)
MT machine translation; magnetic tape; mail transfer; [medicine] malignant tumour; mandated territory; [fishing port] Maryport; mass transport; mean time; mechanical transport; megaton (unit of explosive power); [currency] metical (used in Mozambique); [law] Middle Temple; [US postcode] Montana; motor tanker; motor transport; [USA] Mountain Time; [vehicle registration] northeast London
M/T empty; mail transfer
Mt [chemical element] meitnerium; Mount
Mt. Mountain
mt. megaton (unit of explosive power); mountain
.mt Malta (in Internet address)
m.t. metric ton; missile test
MTA [computing] message transfer agent; minimum terms agreement; Music Teachers' Association; Music Trades' Association
MTB motor torpedo boat; mountain bike
MTBE methyl tertiary-butyl ether (fuel additive)
MTBF [computing] mean time between failures
MTBI [computing] mean time between incidents
MTC Mechanized Transport Corps; Music Teacher's Certificate
MTCA Ministry of Transport and Civil Aviation
MTD maximum tolerated dose; mean temperature difference; Midwife Teacher's Diploma; moving target detector
mtd mounted
mtDNA [biochemistry] mitochondrial deoxyribonucleic acid

MTech Master of Technology
MTEFL Master in the Teaching of English as a Foreign Language
MTFA medium-term financial assistance
MTG [USA] methanol to gasoline
mtg meeting; mounting
mtg. mortgage
mtgd mortgaged
mtge mortgage
mtgee mortgagee
mtgor mortgagor
MTh Master of Theology
mth month
MTI [radar] moving target indicator (or indication)
MTL mean tide level
mtl material
mtl. *monatlich* (German: monthly)
MTM methods-time measurement
MTN [finance] medium-term note; multilateral trade negotiations
mtn motion; mountain
MTNA Music Teachers' National Association
MTO made to order; mechanical transport officer
MTP Master of Town Planning
MTR minimum time rate
mtr meter
Mt Rev. Most Reverend (title of archbishop)
MTS Master of Theological Studies; Merchant Taylors' School; [computing] Michigan terminal system; motor transport service; [USA] multichannel television sound
Mts Mountains; Mounts
MTT [electronics] mean transit time
MTTR mean time to repair; mean time to restore
MTU [computing] magnetic tape unit; [computing] maximum transfer unit; [US air force] missile training unit
MTV motor torpedo vessel; [USA] music television
MU maintenance unit; marginal utility; monetary unit; Mothers' Union; Musicians' Union; [vehicle registration] northeast London
m/u make-up
.mu Mauritius (in Internet address)
MUC Missionary Union of the Clergy
MU car [US railways] multiple-unit car
MUD [computing] multi-user dungeon (or dimension) (in game)
MUF [telecommunications] maximum usable frequency
MUFTI [military] minimum use of force tactical intervention
MUG [computing] multi-user game
MUGA [medicine] multiple-gated arteriography (as in **MUGA scan**)
Multics [trademark] Multiplexed Information and Computing Service
mun. municipal; municipality; munitions
munic. municipal; municipality
MUniv Master of the University
Mus [astronomy] Musca
mus. museum; music; musical; musician
musa multiple unit steerable aerial (or antenna)
MusB Bachelor of Music (from Latin *Musicae Baccalaureus*)
MusD Doctor of Music (from Latin *Musicae Doctor*)
MusM Master of Music (from Latin *Musicae Magister*)
musn musician
mut. mutilate; mutilated; mutual
MUX multiplexer
MV market value; megavolt; merchant vessel; [chemistry] mixed valence; motor vessel; muzzle velocity (of gun); [vehicle registration] southeast London
mV millivolt
mv [music] *mezza voce* (Italian: half voice, softly)
.mv Maldives (in Internet address)
m.v. market value; mean variation; merchant vessel; motor vessel
MVB Bachelor of Veterinary Medicine
MVD Doctor of Veterinary Medicine; *Ministerstvo Vnutrennikh Del* (Russian: Ministry of Internal Affairs) (former Soviet police organization); [medicine] mitral valve disease
MVEE Military Vehicles and Engineering Establishment
MVetMed Master of Veterinary Medicine
MVetSc Master of Veterinary Science
MVL motor-vehicle licence
mvmt movement
MVO Member of the Royal Victorian Order
MVP most valuable player; most valued player

MVRA Motor Vehicle Repairers Association
MVS Master of Veterinary Science
MVSc Master of Veterinary Science
mvt movement
MW [international vehicle registration] Malawi; Master of Wine; [radio] medium wave; megawatt; Middle Welsh; [nuclear technology] mixed waste; molecular weight; Most Worshipful; Most Worthy; [vehicle registration] Swindon
mW milliwatt
.mw Malawi (in Internet address)
MWA Mystery Writers of America
MWC municipal waste combustion
MWeldI Member of the Welding Institute
MWF Medical Women's Federation
MWG music wire gauge
MWGM [Freemasonry] Most Worshipful Grand Master; [Freemasonry] Most Worthy Grand Master
MWh megawatt hour
MWI municipal waste incineration; municipal waste incinerator
MWIA Medical Women's International Association
MWO Meteorological Watch Office
MWP mechanical wood pulp
MWPA Married Women's Property Act
MX missile-experimental; [vehicle registration] southeast London
Mx maxwell (unit of magnetic flux); Middlesex
.mx Mexico (in Internet address)
mxd mixed
mxm maximum
MY motor yacht; [vehicle registration] southeast London
my. myopia; myopic
.my Malaysia (in Internet address)
m.y. million years
myc. mycological; mycology
mycol. mycological; mycology
MYOB [informal] mind your own business
MYRA [finance] multiyear rescheduling agreement
myst. mysteries; mystery
myth. mythical; mythological; mythology
mythol. mythological; mythology
MZ [vehicle registration] Belfast
Mz [geology] Mesozoic
.mz Mozambique (in Internet address)

N

N [printing] en; [chess] knight; [currency] naira (used in Nigeria); National; Nationalist; navigation; Navy; neap (tide); near; [electrical engineering] neutral; New; [fishing port] Newry; newton (unit of force); [currency] ngultrum (used in Bhutan); [chemical element] nitrogen; Norse; north; northern; [UK postcode] north London; [international vehicle registration] Norway; November; nuclear; [physics] nucleon; [law] nullity; nurse; nursing; [civil aircraft marking] United States of America
N [physics] neutron number; [physics, chemistry] number (of molecules etc.)
n [printing] en; nano- (indicates 10^{-9}, as in **nm** = nanometre); [physics] neutron
n [genetics] haploid chromosome number; [mathematics] indefinite number; [chemistry] normal; [physics, chemistry] number density (of atoms etc.); [physics] principal quantum number; [optics] refractive index; [physics] rotational frequency
n. nail (former unit of length); name; nasal; *natus* (Latin: born); nautical; naval; near; negative; nephew; nerve; [commerce] net; [grammar] neuter; neutral; new; night; [grammar] nominative; noon; norm; normal; *nostro* (Italian: our); note; *notre* (French: our); [grammar] noun; *nous* (French: we, us); number
'n' and (as in **fish 'n' chips**)
5N [civil aircraft marking] Nigeria
9N [civil aircraft marking] Nepal
NA [vehicle registration] Manchester; Narcotics Anonymous; [USA] National Academician; National Academy; National Airlines; National Archives; National Army; National Assembly; nautical almanac; naval architect; naval attaché;

naval auxiliary; [international vehicle registration] Netherlands Antilles; [engineering] neutral axis; [banking] new account; [medicine] *Nomina Anatomica* (Latin: Anatomical Names) (official terminology); [biochemistry] noradrenaline; North America; North American; [optics] numerical aperture; nursing auxiliary

N/A [banking] new account; no account; [banking] no advice; [banking] non-acceptance; not applicable; not available

Na Nebraska; [chemical element] sodium (from Latin *natrium*)

n/a not applicable; not available

.na Namibia (in Internet address)

NAA [USA] National Aeronautic Association; National Association of Accountants; [USA] National Automobile Association; Nursing Auxiliaries' Association

n.a.a. [shipping] not always afloat

NAAA National Alliance of Athletic Associations

NAACP [USA] National Association for the Advancement of Colored People

NAAFA National Association to Aid Fat Americans

NAAFI Navy, Army and Air Force Institutes

NAAQS [USA] National Ambient Air Quality Standard

NAAS National Agricultural Advisory Service

NAB National Advisory Body for Public Sector Higher Education; National Alliance of Businessmen; National Assistance Board (former government department); [USA] National Association of Broadcasters; National Australia Bank; naval air base; naval amphibious base; New American Bible; News Agency of Burma

NABC National Association of Boys' Clubs

NABS National Advertising Benevolent Society

NAC National Advisory Council; National Agricultural Centre; [USA] National Airways Corporation; National Anglers' Council; National Archives Council; National Association for the Childless; [geology] North American craton; North Atlantic Council (in NATO)

NACA [USA] National Advisory Committee for Aeronautics

NACAB National Association of Citizens' Advice Bureaux

NACC North Atlantic Cooperation Council (in NATO, replaced by EAPC)

NACCAM National Coordinating Committee for Aviation Meteorology

NACCB National Accreditation Council for Certification Bodies

NACEIC National Advisory Council on Education for Industry and Commerce

NACF National Art Collections Fund

NACM National Association of Colliery Managers

NACNE National Advisory Committee on Nutrition Education

NACO National Association of Cooperative Officials

NACODS National Association of Colliery Overmen, Deputies and Shotfirers

NACOSS National Approval Council for Security Systems

NACRO National Association for the Care and Resettlement of Offenders

NACS National Association of Chimney Sweeps

NACST National Advisory Council on the Training and Supply of Teachers

NAD [USA] National Academy of Design; naval aircraft department; naval air division; [medicine] no abnormality detected; no appreciable difference; not on active duty

nad. nadir

NADC naval aide-de-camp

NADEC National Association of Development Education Centres

NADFAS National Association of Decorative and Fine Arts Societies

NADGE NATO Air Defence Ground Environment

NADOP [USA] North American Defense Operational Plan

NADW North Atlantic deep water

NADWARN [USA] Natural Disaster Warning System

NAE [USA] National Academy of Engineering; naval aircraft establishment

NAEA National Association of Estate Agents

NAEP [USA] National Assessment of Educational Progress

NAEW NATO Airborne Early Warning
NAf [currency] Netherlands Antilles guilder (from alternative name florin)
NAFD National Association of Funeral Directors
NAFO National Association of Fire Officers; Northwest Atlantic Fisheries Organization
NAFTA New Zealand and Australia Free Trade Agreement; North American Free Trade Agreement; North Atlantic Free Trade Area
NAG National Association of Goldsmiths
Nag. Nagasaki
n.a.g. net annual gain
NAGC National Association for Gifted Children
NAGS National Allotments and Gardens Society
Nah. [Bible] Nahum
NAHA National Association of Health Authorities
Nahal *No'ar Halutzi Lohem* (Hebrew: Pioneer and Military Youth) (in Israel)
NAHAT National Association of Health Authorities and Trusts
NAHB [USA] National Association of Home Builders
NAHT National Association of Head Teachers
NAI nonaccidental injury
NAIR [USA] national arrangements for incidents involving radioactivity
NAIRU [economics] nonaccelerating inflation rate of unemployment
NAITA National Association of Independent Travel Agents
NAK [telecommunications] negative acknowledgment
NAL [USA] National Aerospace Laboratory
NALC [USA] National Association of Letter Carriers
NALGO National and Local Government Officers' Association (became part of Unison)
NALHM National Association of Licensed House Managers
NAM [international vehicle registration] Namibia; [USA] National Association of Manufacturers
N Am. North America; North American
NAMAS National Measurement and Accreditation Service
NAMB National Association of Master Bakers
NAMCW National Association of Maternal and Child Welfare
NAMH National Association for Mental Health (former name of MIND)
NAMMA NATO MRCA Management Agency
NAMS [USA] national air-monitoring sites
NAN News Agency of Nigeria
NANC non-adrenergic non-cholinergic
N&Q notes and queries
n&v [medicine] nausea and vomiting
NAO National Audit Office
NAP National Association for the Paralysed
Nap. Naples; Napoleon (Bonaparte) (French emperor); Napoleonic
NAPA [USA] National Association of Performing Artists
NAPF National Association of Pension Funds
naph. [chemistry] naphtha
NAPLPS [computing] North American presentation level protocol syntax
NAPO National Association of Probation Officers; National Association of Property Owners
NAPT National Association for the Prevention of Tuberculosis
NAPV National Association of Prison Visitors
NAR [botany] net assimilation rate
nar. narrow
narc. narcotic; narcotics
NARM natural and accelerator-produced radioactive material
NAS [USA] National Academy of Sciences; National Adoption Society; National Association of Schoolmasters (became part of NAS/UWT); naval air station; Noise Abatement Society; nursing auxiliary service
NASA [USA] National Aeronautics and Space Administration
NASCAR [USA] National Association for Stock Car Auto Racing
NASD National Amalgamated Stevedores and Dockers; [USA] National Association of Securities Dealers
NASDA [Japan] National Space Development Agency

NASDAQ [USA] National Association of Securities Dealers Automated Quotations (system)
Nash. Nashville
NASL North American Soccer League
Nass. Nassau
NAS/UWT National Association of Schoolmasters/Union of Women Teachers
NASW [USA] National Association of Social Workers
NAT National Arbitration Tribunal
Nat. Natal; National; Nationalist
nat. national; nationalist; native; natural; naturalize; naturalized; nature; naturist; *natus* (Latin: born)
N At. North Atlantic
n.a.t. normal allowed time
NATCS National Air Traffic Control Service
NATE National Association for the Teaching of English
NATFHE National Association of Teachers in Further and Higher Education
nat. hist. natural history
Nativ. Nativity
natl national
NATLAS National Testing Laboratory Accreditation Scheme
NATM New Austrian Tunnelling Method
NATO North Atlantic Treaty Organization
nat. phil. natural philosophy
NATS National Air Traffic Services; [USA] Naval Air Transport Service
NatScD Doctor of Natural Science
nat. sci. natural science(s)
NATSOPA National Society of Operative Printers, Graphical and Media Personnel (formerly National Society of Operative Printers and Assistants)
N Att. naval attaché
NATTKE National Association of Theatrical, Television and Kinematographic Employees
NATTS National Association of Trade and Technical Schools
natur. naturalist
NatWest National Westminster Bank plc
NAU [international vehicle registration] Nauru
naut. nautical
NAV [finance] net asset value (of organization)
nav. naval; navigable; navigation; navigator
NAVAIR [USA] Naval Air Systems Command
Nav. E naval engineer
navig. navigable; navigation; navigator
NAVS National Anti-Vivisection Society
NAVSAT navigational satellite
NAWB National Association of Workshops for the Blind
NAWC National Association of Women's Clubs
NAWO National Alliance of Women's Organizations
NAYC Youth Clubs UK (formerly National Association of Youth Clubs)
NAYPIC National Association of Young People in Care
NAYT National Association of Youth Theatres
naz. *nazionale* (Italian: national)
Nazi *Nationalsozialisten* (German: National Socialist)
NB [vehicle registration] Manchester; narrow bore; naval base; Nebraska; [medicine] needle biopsy; [physics] neutral beam; New Brunswick; North Britain (i.e. Scotland); *nota bene* (Latin: note well)
Nb [chemical element] niobium
Nb [meteorology] nimbus
n.b. [cricket] no ball; *nota bene* (Latin: note well)
NBA [USA] National Basketball Association; [USA] National Book Award; [USA] National Boxing Association; National Building Agency; Net Book Agreement; North British Academy
NBC [USA] National Basketball Committee; National Book Council (former name of NBL); National Boys' Club; [USA] National Broadcasting Company; National Bus Company; nuclear, biological and chemical (weapons or warfare)
NBCD [computing] natural binary-coded decimal
NBD [statistics] negative binomial distribution
NbE north by east
NBER [USA] National Bureau of Economic Research
n.b.g. [informal] no bloody good

NBI National Benevolent Institution; [medicine] no bone injury
NBK National Bank of Kuwait
NBL National Book League (formerly NBC)
n.b.l. [informal] not bloody likely
NBP [chemistry] normal boiling point
NBPI National Board for Prices and Incomes (replacement for PIB)
NBR National Buildings Record; [chemistry] nitrile-butadiene rubber
nbre *noviembre* (Spanish: November)
NBRI National Building Research Institute
NBS [USA] National Bureau of Standards; Newcastle Business School
NBTS National Blood Transfusion Service
NBV [accounting] net book value (of asset)
NbW north by west
NC [vehicle registration] Manchester; National Certificate; National Congress; National Council; [education] National Curriculum; Nature Conservancy; New Caledonia; New Church; nickel–cadmium (battery); nitrocellulose; [chemistry] nitrogen compound; [meteorology] no change; no charge; normally closed; North Carolina; [US postcode] North Carolina; Northern Command; numerical control; numerically controlled; [USA] Nurse Corps
N/C new charter; nitrocellulose; no charge
NCA National Certificate of Agriculture; National Childminding Association; National Cricket Association; no copies available
NCAA [USA] National Collegiate Athletic Association; Northern Counties Athletic Association
NCACC National Civil Aviation Consultative Committee
NCAR [USA] National Center for Atmospheric Research (Colorado)
NCARB [USA] National Council of Architectural Registration Boards
NCB National Children's Bureau; National Coal Board (replaced by BCC); Nippon Credit Bank; [insurance] no-claim(s) bonus
NCBA National Cattle Breeders' Association
NCBAE [insurance] no-claim(s) bonus as earned
NCBW nuclear, chemical and biological warfare
NCC [USA] National Climatic Center; National Computing Centre; National Consumer Council; [USA] National Council of Churches; [education] National Curriculum Council; Nature Conservancy Council (replaced by EN)
NCCA National Carpet Cleaners Association
NCCI National Committee for Commonwealth Immigrants
NCCJ National Conference of Christians and Jews
NCCL National Council for Civil Liberties (former name of Liberty)
NCCS national command and control system; National Council for Civic Responsibility
NCCVD National Council for Combating Venereal Diseases
NCD naval construction department
n.c.d. [informal] no can do
NCDAD National Council for Diplomas in Art and Design
NCDL National Canine Defence League
NCERT National Council for Educational Research and Training
NCET National Council for Educational Technology
NCFT National College of Food Technology
NCH National Children's Home; National Clearing House
n.Chr. *nach Christus* (German: after Christ, AD)
NCI [USA] National Cancer Institute; [finance] New Community Instrument
n.c.i. no common interest
NCIC National Cancer Institute of Canada; [USA] National Crime Information Center
NCIS National Criminal Intelligence Service
NCL National Carriers Limited; National Central Library; National Chemical Laboratory; National Church League
NCLC National Council of Labour Colleges
NCN National Council of Nurses
NCNA New China News Agency
NCNC National Convention of Nigeria and the Cameroons; National Conven-

tion of Nigerian Citizens (political party)
NCO noncommissioned officer
NCP National Car Parks (Limited); [Australia] National Country Party (former name of National Party); national cycling proficiency; [computing] network control protocol
n.c.p. [engineering] normal circular pitch
NCPL National Centre for Programmed Learning
NCPS noncontributory pension scheme
NCPT [USA] National Congress of Parents and Teachers
NCR National Cash Register (Company Limited); no carbon required (of paper)
NCRE Naval Construction Research Establishment
NCRL National Chemical Research Laboratory
NCRP [USA] National Council on Radiation Protection and Measurement
NCS [USA] National Communications System
NCSC [Australia] National Companies and Securities Commission; [USA] National Computer Security Center
NCSE National Council for Special Education
NCSS National Council of Social Service
NCT National Chamber of Trade; National Childbirth Trust; [medicine] neutron-capture therapy; [medicine] neutron compute(rize)d tomography
NCTA [USA] National Community Television Association
NCTE [USA] National Council of Teachers of English
NCU National Communications Union (became part of CWU); National Cyclists' Union
n.c.u.p. no commission until paid
NCV no commercial value
NCVCCO National Council of Voluntary Child Care Organizations
NCVO National Council of Voluntary Organizations
NCVQ National Council for Vocational Qualifications
NCW National Council of Women (of Great Britain)
ND [vehicle registration] Manchester; national debt; National Diploma; Naturopathic Diploma; [photography] neutral density; no date; nondelivery; North Dakota; [US postcode] North Dakota
N-D *Notre-Dame* (French: Our Lady) (in church names)
Nd [chemical element] neodymium
n.d. [photography] neutral density; next day (delivery); no date; no decision; no deed; no delay; no demand; nondelivery; not dated; not deeded; [banking] not drawn; [informal] nothing doing
NDA National Dairymen's Association; National Diploma in Agriculture; [engineering] nondestructive analysis; [engineering] nondestructive assay
NDAC [USA] National Defense Advisory Commission
N Dak. North Dakota
NDB [aeronautics] nondirectional beacon
NDC National Dairy Council; NATO Defence College; [computing] normalized device coordinates
NDCS National Deaf Children's Society
NDD National Diploma in Dairying; National Diploma in Design
NDE near-death experience; [engineering] nondestructive evaluation; [engineering] nondestructive examination
NDF National Diploma in Forestry
NDH National Diploma in Horticulture
NDIC National Defence Industries Council
Ndl. Netherlands
NDN National District Nurse Certificate
NDP National Democratic Party; [economics] net domestic product; [Canada] New Democratic Party
n.d.p. [engineering] normal diametric pitch
NDPB nondepartmental public body
NDPS National Data Processing Service
NDR [electronics] negative differential resistance; [electronics] negative differential resistivity; nondomestic rates; *Norddeutscher Rundfunk* (German: North German Radio)
NDRC National Defence Research Committee
NDSB Narcotic Drugs Supervisory Body (of UN)
NDT [engineering] nondestructive testing; [commerce] nondistributive trade

NDTA [USA] National Defense Transportation Association
NDU Nursing Development Unit
NDV [microbiology] Newcastle disease virus
NE [vehicle registration] Manchester; national emergency; National Executive; naval engineer; [US postcode] Nebraska; [fishing port] Newcastle upon Tyne; [UK postcode] Newcastle upon Tyne; new edition; New England; news editor; [banking] no effects (= no funds); northeast; northeastern; nuclear energy; nuclear explosion; nuclear explosive
Ne [chemical element] neon
Ne. Nepal; Nepalese; Nepali; Netherlands
n/e new edition; [banking] no effects (= no funds); [accounting] not entered
.ne Niger (in Internet address)
n.e. not essential; not exceeding
NEA [USA] National Education Association; [USA] National Endowment for the Arts; North East Airlines
NEAC New English Art Club
NEACP [USA] National Emergency Airborne Command Post (pronounced 'kneecap')
NEAF Near East Air Force
NEAFC North-East Atlantic Fisheries Commission
Neapol. Neapolitan
NEARELF Near East Land Forces
NEB [USA] National Electricity Board; [USA] National Energy Board; National Enterprise Board; New English Bible
Neb. Nebraska
NEBOSH National Examination Board in Occupational Safety and Health
Nebr. Nebraska
NEBSS National Examinations Board for Supervisory Studies
NEC [USA] National Economic Council; [USA] National Electric Code; National Electronics Council; National Equestrian Centre; National Executive Committee; National Exhibition Centre (Birmingham); National Extension College (Cambridge); [medicine] necrotizing enterocolitis; [Japan] Nippon Electric Company
nec. necessary
n.e.c. not elsewhere classified
NECCTA National Educational Closed Circuit Television Association
NECInst North East Coast Institution of Engineers and Shipbuilders
necr. necrosis
necrol. necrology
NED [medicine] no evidence of disease
NEDC National Economic Development Council (also called Neddy); North East Development Council
NEDO National Economic Development Office
NEEB North Eastern Electricity Board
NEF National Energy Foundation; [acoustics] noise exposure forecast (value)
neg. negation; negative; negatively; negligence; negotiable (in job advertisement); negotiate; negotiation
NEH National Endowment for the Humanities
Neh. [Bible] Nehemiah
NEI Netherlands East Indies
n.e.i. *non est inventa* (Latin: (she) has not been found); *non est inventum* (Latin: (it) has not been found); *non est inventus* (Latin: (he) has not been found); not elsewhere indicated
NEL [USA] National Electronics Laboratory; National Engineering Laboratory
nem. con. *nemine contradicente* (Latin: nobody opposing, unanimously)
nem. dis. *nemine dissentiente* (Latin: nobody opposing, unanimously)
NE/n.d. [bibliography] new edition, no date given
N Eng. New England; northern England
neol. neologism
NEP [international vehicle registration] Nepal; New Economic Policy (in USSR in 1920s)
Nep. Nepal; Nepalese; Nepali; Neptune
n.e.p. new edition pending
NEPA [USA] National Environmental Policy Act
NEPP [USA] National Energy Policy Plan
NEQ [computing] nonequivalence (as in **NEQ gate**)
NERA [USA] National Emergency Relief Administration
NERC National English Rabbit Club; Natural Environment Research Council
NERIS National Educational Resources Information Service

NES National Eczema Society
n.e.s. not elsewhere specified
NESC [USA] National Electric Safety Code
NESTOR [nuclear technology] neutron source thermal reactor
NET [USA] National Educational Television; [nuclear technology] Next European Torus
.net network (in Internet address)
n.e.t. not earlier than
Neth. Netherlands
Neth. Ant. Netherlands Antilles
n. et m. [medicine] *nocte et mane* (Latin: night and morning) (in prescriptions)
neurol. neurological; neurology
neut. [grammar] neuter; neutral; neutralize; neutralized; neutralizer
Nev. Nevada
NEW [US economics] net economic welfare
Newf. Newfoundland
New M New Mexico
news. newsagency; newsagent
New Test. New Testament
NF [vehicle registration] Manchester; *Nationale Front* (German: National Front); [US pharmacology] National Formulary; National Front; [medicine] neurofibromatosis; New Forest; Newfoundland; New French; [banking] no funds; [telecommunications] noise factor; [telecommunications] noise figure; Norman French (language)
N/F [banking] no funds
n.f. [engineering] near face; [informal] no fool; [grammar] noun feminine
NFA National Farmers' Association; National Federation of Anglers; [USA] National Food Administration; [USA] National Futures Association; no fixed abode; no fixed address
n.f.a. no further action
NFAL National Foundation of Arts and Letters
NFB National Film Board (of Canada)
NFBPM National Federation of Builders' and Plumbers' Merchants
NFBTE National Federation of Building Trades Employers
NFC [USA] National Football Conference; National Freight Consortium
n.f.c. not favourably considered
NFCO National Federation of Community Organizations
NFD Newfoundland; no fixed date
Nfd Newfoundland
NFDM nonfat dry milk
NFER National Foundation for Educational Research
NFFC National Film Finance Corporation
NFFE [USA] National Federation of Federal Employees
NFFO non-fossil-fuel obligation (for electricity companies)
NFFPT National Federation of Fruit and Potato Trades
NFHA National Federation of Housing Associations
NFI National Federation of Ironmongers
NFL [USA, Canada] National Football League
Nfld Newfoundland
n.f.m. nearest full moon; next full moon
NFMPS National Federation of Master Printers in Scotland
NFMS National Federation of Music Societies
NFO National Freight Organization
NFPW National Federation of Professional Workers
n.f.r. no further requirements
NFRC National Federation of Roofing Contractors
NFRN National Federation of Retail Newsagents
NFS National Fire Service; National Flying Services; National Forest Service; [computing] network filing service; [computing] network filing system; not for sale
NFSE National Federation of the Self-Employed
NFT National Film Theatre
NFTS National Film and Television School
NFU National Farmers' Union
NFUW National Farmers' Union of Wales
NFWI National Federation of Women's Institutes
NFYFC National Federation of Young Farmers' Clubs
NG [railways] narrow gauge; National Gallery; National Government; [USA] National Guard; National Guardsman; New Granada; [medicine] new growth; New Guinea; nitroglycerine; [Free-

masonry] Noble Grand; [Freemasonry] Noble Guard; no go; no good; North Germanic; [vehicle registration] Norwich; [UK postcode] Nottingham

Ng [geology] Neogene

Ng. Norwegian

.ng Nigeria (in Internet address)

n.g. no good; not given

NGA National Glider Association; National Graphical Association (became part of GPMU)

NGC [USA] National Grid Company; [astronomy] New General Catalogue

NGF [biochemistry] nerve growth factor

NGk New Greek

NGL [chemistry] natural-gas liquid(s)

NGNP [economics] nominal gross national product

NGO [USA] National Gas Outlet; [India] nongazetted officer; nongovernmental organization

NGR [international vehicle registration] Nigeria

NGr New Greek

NGRC National Greyhound Racing Club

NGRS Narrow Gauge Railway Society

NGS National Galleries of Scotland; National Geographic Society; nuclear generating station

NGT National Guild of Telephonists

ngt *négociant* (French: merchant)

NGTE National Gas Turbine Establishment

NGU [medicine] nongonococcal urethritis

NGV natural-gas vehicle

NH National Hunt; naval hospital; New Hampshire; [US postcode] New Hampshire; [vehicle registration] Northampton; northern hemisphere; Northumberland Hussars

NHA National Horse Association of Great Britain; [USA] National Housing Agency

NHBC National Housebuilding Council

NHBRC National House-Builders' Registration Certificate

NHC National Hunt Committee

NHD Doctor of Natural History

NHeb New Hebrew

N Heb. New Hebrides

NHF National Hairdressers' Federation

NHG New High German

NHI National Health Insurance

NHK *Nippon Hoso Kyokai* (Japanese: Japanese Broadcasting Corporation)

NHL [USA] National Hockey League; [medicine] non-Hodgkin lymphoma

NHLBI [USA] National Heart, Lung and Blood Institute

NHMF National Heritage Memorial Fund

NHMRCA National Health and Medical Research Council of Australia

NHO Navy Hydrographic Office

nhp nominal horsepower

NHR National Housewives Register; National Hunt Rules

NHS National Health Service

NHSTA National Health Service Training Authority

NHTPC National Housing and Town Planning Council

NI National Insurance; Native Infantry; naval instructor; Naval Intelligence; new impression; News International; [computing] noninterfaced; Northern Ireland; North Island (New Zealand)

Ni [chemical element] nickel

.ni Nicaragua (in Internet address)

NIA [USA] National Intelligence Authority; Newspaper Institute of America

NIAAA Northern Ireland Amateur Athletic Association

NIAB National Institute of Agricultural Botany

NIACRO Northern Ireland Association for the Care and Resettlement of Offenders

NIAE National Institute of Agricultural Engineering

NIAID National Institute of Allergy and Infectious Diseases

Nibmar no independence before majority African rule

NIBSC National Institute for Biological Standards Control

NIC National Incomes Commission; National Insurance contribution(s); network interface card; newly industrialized country; [international vehicle registration] Nicaragua

Nic. Nicaragua; Nicaraguan

n.i.c. not in contract

Nica. Nicaragua; Nicaraguan

NiCad nickel–cadmium (battery)

NICAM [electronics] near-instantaneous companded audio multiplex (for coding sound signals digitally)

Nicar. Nicaragua; Nicaraguan
NiCd nickel–cadmium (battery)
NICEC National Institute for Careers Education and Counselling
NICEIC National Inspection Council for Electrical Installation Contracting
NICF Northern Ireland Cycling Federation
NICG Nationalized Industries Chairmen's Group
NICRA Northern Ireland Civil Rights Association
NICS Northern Ireland Civil Service
NICU [medicine] neonatal intensive care unit
NID National Institute for the Deaf; [India] National Institute of Design; Naval Intelligence Division; Northern Ireland District
NIDC Northern Ireland Development Council
NIDD [medicine] non-insulin-dependent diabetes
NIES Northern Ireland Electricity Service
NIESR National Institute of Economic and Social Research
NIF [finance] note issuance facility
NIFES National Industrial Fuel Efficiency Service
NIFO next in, first out
NIFTP [computing] network independent file transfer protocol
Nig. Nigeria; Nigerian
NIH [USA] National Institutes of Health; North Irish Horse (former regiment)
NIHCA Northern Ireland Hotels and Caterers Association
NIHE [Ireland] National Institute for Higher Education
NII Nuclear Installations Inspectorate
NIIP National Institute of Industrial Psychology
NILP Northern Ireland Labour Party
NIMA National Infomercial Marketing Association
nimby [informal] not in my back yard
NIMH National Institute of Medical Herbalists; [USA] National Institute of Mental Health
n. imp. new impression
NIMR National Institute for Medical Research
NIN national information network
NINO no inspector, no operator (system)
NIO National Institute of Oceanography
NIOSH [USA] National Institute for Occupational Safety and Health
Nip. Nippon; Nipponese
nip. [engineering] nipple
ni. pri. *nisi prius* (Latin: unless previously)
NIR non-ionizing radiation; Northern Ireland Railways
N Ir. Northern Ireland
NIRA [USA] National Industrial Recovery Act
NIRC National Industrial Relations Court
N Ire. Northern Ireland
NIREX Nuclear Industry Radioactive Waste Executive
NIRS [USA] National Institute of Radiological Sciences
NIS [currency] (new) Israeli shekel
n.i.s. not in stock
NISA National Independent Supermarkets' Association
NISC National Industrial Safety Committee
NIST [USA] National Institute of Standards and Technology
NISTRO Northern Ireland Science and Technology Regional Organization
NISW National Institute for Social Workers
NIT national intelligence test; negative income tax
NITB Northern Ireland Tourist Board
NIV New International Version (of Bible)
NIWAAA Northern Ireland Women's Amateur Athletic Association
NJ [vehicle registration] Brighton; New Jersey; [US postcode] New Jersey; [informal] nose job
n.J *nächsten Jahres* (German: next year)
NJA National Jewellers' Association
NJAC National Joint Advisory Council
NJC National Joint Council
NJCC National Joint Consultative Committee
NJNC National Joint Negotiating Committee
NK [vehicle registration] Luton; [immunology] natural killer (as in **NK-cell**); not known
NKC [immunology] natural killer cell
NKGB *Narodny Komissariat Gosudarstvennoi Bezopasnosti* (Russian: People's

Commissariat of State Security) (former Soviet secret police)
NKr [currency] Norwegian krone
NKVD *Narodny Komissariat Vnutrennikh Del* (Russian: People's Commissariat of Internal Affairs) (former Soviet police organization)
NL National Labour; [USA] National League (baseball); National Liberal; Navy League; Navy List; [international vehicle registration] Netherlands; [vehicle registration] Newcastle upon Tyne; New Latin; no liability (after Australian company name); north latitude
Nl National
.nl Netherlands (in Internet address)
n.l. [printing] new line; *non licet* (Latin: it is not permitted); *non liquet* (Latin: it is not clear)
N Lat. north latitude
NLB National Library for the Blind
NLBD National League for the Blind and Disabled
NLC National Liberal Club; National Library of Canada
NLCB National Lottery Charities Board
NLCS North London Collegiate School
NLD National League for Democracy (in Myanmar)
NLF National Labour Federation; National Liberal Federation; National Liberation Front; National Loans Fund
n.l.f. nearest landing field
NLI National Library of Ireland
NLLST National Lending Library for Science and Technology
NLM National Library of Medicine
NLMC National Labour Management Council
NLN National League for Nursing
n.l.n. no longer needed
NLO naval liaison officer
NLP [computing] natural language processing; Natural Law Party; [USA] neighborhood loan program; [computing] neurolinguistic programming
NLQ [computing] near letter quality (of printing)
NLR [astronomy] narrow-line region
NLRB [USA] National Labor Relations Board
NLS National Library of Scotland
n.l.t. not later than; not less than
NLW National Library of Wales
nly northerly
NLYL National League of Young Liberals
NM [vehicle registration] Luton; national marketing; nautical mile; New Mexico; [US postcode] New Mexico; nuclear medicine
N/m [commerce] no mark(s) (on bill of lading)
Nm. *Nachmittag* (German: afternoon); [advertising] next matter
n.M *nächsten Monats* (German: next month)
nm nanometre
n/m not married (in personal advertisement)
nm. nutmeg
n.m. nautical mile; new moon; [medicine] *nocte et mane* (Latin: night and morning) (in prescriptions); nonmetallic; [grammar] noun masculine
NMA National Management Association; National Medical Association
NMB National Maritime Board
NMC National Marketing Council; [USA] National Meteorological Center
n.m.c. no more credit
N Mex. New Mexico
NMFS [USA] National Marine Fisheries Service
NMHA National Mental Health Association
NMHF [USA] National Mental Health Foundation
NMI [computing] non-maskable interrupt
n mile nautical mile
NMP [economics] net material product
NMR nuclear magnetic resonance
NMRI [medicine] nuclear magnetic resonance imaging
NMS [USA] National Market System; National Museums of Scotland; [stock exchange] Normal Market Size
NMSQT [USA] National Merit Scholarship Qualifying Test
NMSS [USA] National Multiple Sclerosis Society
n.m.t. not more than
NMTF National Market Traders' Federation
NMU National Maritime Union
NMW national minimum wage
NN [fishing port] Newhaven; no name;

[UK postcode] Northampton; [vehicle registration] Nottingham
N/N [banking] not to be noted
nn. names; notes; nouns
NND [medicine] neonatal death
NNE north-northeast
NNEB National Nursery Examination Board
NNF Northern Nurses' Federation
NNHT Nuffield Nursing Homes Trust
NNI noise and number index (for aircraft noise); noise nuisance index
NNMA Nigerian National Merit Award
NNOM Nigerian National Order of Merit
NNP [economics] net national product
NNR national nature reserve
NNSA [USA] National Nuclear Safety Administration
NNT nuclear nonproliferation treaty
NNTP [computing] net(work) news transfer protocol
NNTR no need to return
NNW north-northwest
NO [vehicle registration] Chelmsford; natural order; naval officer; naval operations; navigation officer; New Orleans; Nuffield Observatory (Jodrell Bank, Cheshire); nursing officer
N/O [banking] no orders
No [chemical element] nobelium
No. north; northern; Norway; Norwegian; number (from Latin *numero*, ablative of *numerus*, or French *numéro*)
no. north; northern; number (from Latin *numero*, ablative of *numerus*, or French *numéro*)
.no Norway (in Internet address)
n.o. normally open; [cricket] not out
NOA National Opera Association; National Orchestral Association; not otherwise authorized
NOAA [USA] National Oceanic and Atmospheric Administration
NOAO [USA] National Optical Astronomy Observatories
NOB naval operating base
nob. *nobis* (Latin: for our part, on our part); noble
NOC National Olympic Committee; not otherwise classified
n.o.c. notation of content; not otherwise classified
NOCD [informal] not our class, dear
No. Co. northern counties
noct. [medicine] *nocte* (Latin: at night) (in prescriptions)
NOD Naval Ordnance Department; night observation device
NODA National Operatic and Dramatic Association
NODC non-OPEC developing country
NOE nuclear Overhauser effect
n.o.e. notice of exception; not otherwise enumerated
NOERC North of England Regional Consortium
n.o.h.p. not otherwise herein provided
n.o.i.b.n. not otherwise indexed by name
NOIC Naval Officer in Charge
NOISE [USA] National Organization to Insure a Sound-controlled Environment
n.o.k. next of kin
NOL [USA] Naval Ordnance Laboratory
nol. con. [law] *nolo contendere* (Latin: I do not wish to contend)
nol. pros. [law] *nolle prosequi* (Latin: to be unwilling to prosecute)
nom. nomenclature; nominal; nominated; nomination; [grammar] nominative
nom. cap. [finance] nominal capital
nomen. nomenclature
nomin. nominal; nominated; nomination; [grammar] nominative
nom. nov. *nomen novum* (Latin: new name)
NOMSS [USA] National Operational Meteorological Satellite System
noncom. noncommissioned
Noncon. Nonconformist
non cul. *non culpabilis* (Latin: not guilty)
non obst. *non obstante* (Latin: notwithstanding)
non pros. [law] *non prosequitur* (Latin: he does not prosecute)
non rep. [medicine] *non repetatur* (Latin: do not repeat) (in prescriptions)
non seq. *non sequitur* (Latin: it does not follow (logically))
nonstand. nonstandard
nonstd nonstandard
non-U not upper-class
NOP National Opinion Poll; not our publication
n.o.p. not otherwise provided (for)

NOPWC National Old People's Welfare Council
NOR [biology] nucleolar-organizing region
Nor [astronomy] Norma
Nor. Norman; Normandy; north; northern; Norway; Norwegian; Norwich
nor. normal; north; northern
NORAD North American Air Defense Command
Norf. Norfolk
NORM not operationally ready maintenance
Norm. Norman; Normandy
norm. normal; normalized
NORML [USA] National Organization for the Reform of Marijuana Laws
NORS not operationally ready supply (or supplies)
Northants Northamptonshire
Northd Northumberland
Northumb. Northumberland
Norvic. *Norvicensis* (Latin: (Bishop) of Norwich)
Norw. Norway; Norwegian
Norweb North Western Electricity Board
NORWICH knickers off ready when I come home (on envelope of love letter)
NOS *Nederlandse Omroep Stichting* (Dutch: Netherlands Broadcasting Corporation); [computing] network operating system
Nos. numbers
nos. numbers
n.o.s. not otherwise specified
NOSC [US navy] Naval Ordnance Systems Command
Not. Notary
not. notice
NOTAR no-tail rotor (of aircraft)
NOTB National Ophthalmic Treatment Board
Nottm Nottingham
Notts Nottinghamshire
notwg notwithstanding
nouv. *nouveau* (French: new); *nouvelle* (French: new)
Nov. November; *November* (German: November)
nov. novel; novelist; *novembre* (Italian: November); *novembre* (French: November); novice; novitiate
NOW [USA] National Organization for Women; [US banking] negotiable order of withdrawal; New Opportunities for Women
NoW *News of the World*
NOX nitrogen oxide(s)
n.o.y. not out yet
noz. nozzle
NP Nationalist Party; national park; National Party; National Power plc; net profit; neuropsychiatric; neuropsychiatry; [UK postcode] Newport; New Providence (Bahamas); nitro proof (in firearms); Nobel Prize; [chemistry] nonpolar; Notary Public; [grammar] noun phrase; nurse practitioner; [vehicle registration] Worcester
Np napalm; neap (tide); neper (unit used in telecommunications); [chemical element] neptunium
np neap (tide); new pence (used in 1970s, after decimalization)
n/p net proceeds
.np Nepal (in Internet address)
n.p. near point; [law] net personalty; net proceeds; [printing] new paragraph; new pattern; nickel-plated; *nisi prius* (Latin: unless previously); [medicine] *nomen proprium* (Latin: its own name) (in prescriptions); nonparticipating; [bibliography] no place of publication (given); no printer; no publisher; normal pitch; not paginated; nursing procedure
NPA National Park Authority; National Pigeon Association; New People's Army (in Philippines); Newspaper Publishers' Association
NPACI National Production Advisory Council on Industry
NPBA National Pig Breeders' Association
NPC [China] National People's Congress; [USA] National Petroleum Council; National Ports Council; [USA] National Press Club; no-player character (in computer game); [computing] normalized projection coordinates; Northern People's Congress (in Nigeria)
NPCS Narrowband Personal Communications Service
NPD *Nationaldemokratische Partei Deutschlands* (German: National Democratic Party of Germany); [marketing] new product development; [astronomy] north polar distance

NPF National Progressive Front (in Syria); Newspaper Press Fund
n.p.f. not provided for
NPFA National Playing Fields Association
NPG National Portrait Gallery; Nuclear Planning Group (in NATO)
NPGH [education] National Professional Qualification for Headship
NPH [chemistry] normal paraffin hydrocarbon
NPh nuclear physics
NPHT Nuffield Provincial Hospitals Trust
NPK nitrogen, phosphorus and potassium (in fertilizers, from chemical symbols)
NPL National Physical Laboratory (Teddington, Middlesex)
n. pl. [grammar] noun plural
NPN [medicine] nonprotein nitrogen
n.p.n.a. [commerce] no protest for nonacceptance
NPO New Philharmonia Orchestra
n.p.o. [medicine] *ne per oris* (Latin: not by mouth)
n.p. or d. no place or date
NPP nuclear power plant
n.p.p. no passed proof
NPR [USA] National Public Radio; noise power ratio
NPRA National Petroleum Refiners Association
NPS National Portrait Society; nuclear power source; nuclear power station
n.p.s. nominal pipe size; no prior service
NPT (Nuclear) Non-Proliferation Treaty
NPTA National Pest Technicians' Association
NPU National Pharmaceutical Union; National Postal Union; [medicine] not passed urine
n.p.u. *ne plus ultra* (Latin: not more beyond) (i.e. extremity, culmination or perfection)
NPV [finance] net present value; [finance] no par value (of shares)
NPW nuclear-powered warship
n.q.a. [finance] net quick assets
NQOC [informal] not quite our class
NR [vehicle registration] Leicester; National Register; natural rubber; naval rating; Navy Regulations; [insurance] no risk; North Riding (former division of Yorkshire); [UK postcode] Norwich
Nr *Nummer* (German: number)
nr near; number
.nr Nauru (in Internet address)
n.r. net register; [insurance] no risk
NRA National Reclamation Association; [USA] National Recovery Administration; National Recreation Area; [USA] National Rehabilitation Association; National Rifle Association; National Rivers Authority; nuclear-reaction analysis
n.r.a. never refuse anything
NRAA National Rifle Association of America
NRAO [USA] National Radio Astronomy Observatory
NRC National Redemption Council (in Ghana); National Research Council; [USA] Nuclear Regulatory Commission
NRCA National Retail Credit Association
NRCC National Research Council of Canada
NRD National Registered Designer; National Register of Designers
NRDC National Research Development Corporation; [USA] Natural Resources Defense Council
NRDS [medicine] neonatal respiratory distress syndrome
NREM [physiology] non-rapid eye movement (as in **NREM sleep**)
NREN [computing] National Research and Education Network
NRF National Relief Fund
NRFL Northern Rugby Football League
NRI National Resources Institute
NRK *Norsk Rikskringkasting* (Norwegian broadcasting company)
NRL National Reference Library; [USA] Naval Research Laboratory
NRM National Resistance Movement (in Uganda)
NRMA [Australia] National Roads and Motorists Association
nrml normal
NROR [finance] normal rate of return
NROTC Naval Reserve Officer Training Corps
NRP nuclear reprocessing plant
NRPB National Radiological Protection Board
NRR net reproduction rate (of populations); Northern Rhodesia Regiment

NRS National Readership Survey; National Rose Society
NRs [currency] Nepalese rupee
n.r.t. net registered tonnage
NRTA [USA] National Retired Teachers Association
NRV [finance] net realizable value; non-return valve
Nrw. Norwegian
NRZ [computing] nonreturn to zero
NS [vehicle registration] Glasgow; *Nachschrift* (German: postscript, PS); [computing] Nassi–Schneidermann (as in **NS chart**); National Service; National Society; natural science; naval service; [fishing port] New Ross; new series; Newspaper Society; New Style (in dates); nonsmoker (in personal advertisement); Nova Scotia; nuclear science; nuclear ship; Numismatic Society
N/S nonsmoker (in personal advertisement)
N-S *Notre-Seigneur* (French: Our Lord)
Ns [meteorology] nimbostratus
ns nanosecond
n/s news-sheet; nonsmoker (in personal advertisement); [banking] not sufficient (funds)
n.s. near side; new series; nickel steel; not satisfactory; not significant; not specified; [banking] not sufficient (funds)
NSA [USA] National Security Agency; [USA] National Shipping Authority; National Skating Association; [USA] National Standards Association; [USA] National Student Association; New Society of Artists; non-sterling area
NSACS National Society for the Abolition of Cruel Sports
NSAE National Society of Art Education
NSAFA National Service Armed Forces Act
NSAID [pharmacology] nonsteroidal anti-inflammatory drug
NSB National Savings Bank; [USA] National Science Board
NSBA National Sheep Breeders' Association
NSC National Safety Council; National Savings Certificate(s); [USA] National Security Council; National Sporting Club; National Steel Corporation
NSCA National Society for Clean Air
NSCC [USA] National Securities Clearing Corporation
NSCR National Society for Cancer Relief
NSD naval supply depot; nominal standard dose; normal spontaneous delivery
NSDAP *Nationalsozialistische Deutsche Arbeiterpartei* (German: National Socialist German Workers' Party, Nazis)
NSERC [USA] Natural Sciences and Engineering Research Council
NSF [USA] National Science Foundation; [banking] not sufficient funds; Nuclear Structure Facility (Daresbury, Cheshire)
n.s.f. [banking] not sufficient funds
NSFGB National Ski Federation of Great Britain
NSG [education] nonstatutory guidelines (relating to National Curriculum)
NSGT non-self-governing territory (or territories)
NSHEB North of Scotland Hydroelectric Board
NSI [USA] National Security Information
n. sing. [grammar] noun singular
NSL National Sporting League
NSM new smoking material; non-stipendiary minister
NSO National Solar Observatory; Naval Staff Officer
NSP nonsmoker preferred (in personal advertisement)
NSPCC National Society for the Prevention of Cruelty to Children
NSPE [USA] National Society of Professional Engineers
n.s.p.f. not specifically (or specially) provided for
NSRA National Small-Bore Rifle Association
NSS national sample survey; National Secular Society; New Shakespeare Society; [medicine] normal saline solution
NSSA National School Sailing Association
NSSU National Sunday School Union
NST Newfoundland Standard Time
NSTC Nova Scotia Technical College
NSTP Nuffield Science Teaching Project
NSU [medicine] nonspecific urethritis
NSW New South Wales
NSY New Scotland Yard
NT [Ireland] National Teacher; National Theatre; National Trust; neap tide(s);

[fishing port] Newport; new technology; New Testament; New Translation; Northern Territory (Australia); not titled; [card games] no-trump(s) (in bridge); Nurse Teacher; [vehicle registration] Shrewsbury

n.t. net terms; net tonnage; normal temperature

NTA [USA] National Technical Association; National Training Award; net tangible assets

NTB [economics] non-tariff barrier

NTC [physics] negative temperature coefficient

NTD [informal] not top drawer

NTDA National Trade Development Association

NTEU [USA] National Treasury Employees Union

NTFS new technology filing system

ntfy notify

NTG North Thames Gas

NTGB North Thames Gas Board

NTGk New Testament Greek

Nth North

Nthb. Northumberland

nthn northern

NTI noise transmission impairment

NTIA [USA] National Telecommunications and Information Administration

NTL [electronics] non-threshold logic

n.t.l. no time lost

NTM [economics] non-tariff measure

NTO naval transport officer

n.t.o. not taken out

NTP normal temperature and pressure

n.t.p. normal temperature and pressure; no title page

NTS National Trust for Scotland; Nevada Test Site; not to scale

NTSB [USA] National Transportation Safety Board

NTSC [USA] National Television System Committee (US broadcasting system)

NTT New Technology Telescope

NTUC National Trades Union Congress (in Singapore)

NTV Nippon Television

NTVLRO National Television Licence Records Office

NTW no time wasters (in personal advertisement)

nt wt net weight

NU name unknown; National Union; *Nations Unies* (French: United Nations, UN); natural uranium; Northern Union; [vehicle registration] Nottingham; number unobtainable

Nu [currency] ngultrum (used in Bhutan)

n.u. name unknown; number unobtainable

NUAAW National Union of Agricultural and Allied Workers

NUBE National Union of Bank Employees

nuc. nuclear

nucl. nuclear

NUCPS National Union of Civil and Public Servants (became part of PTC)

NUCUA National Union of Conservative and Unionist Associations

nud. nudism; nudist

NUDAGO National Union of Domestic Appliances and General Operatives

NUDETS nuclear detection system

NUI National University of Ireland

NUIW National Union of Insurance Workers

NUJ National Union of Journalists

NUJMB Northern Universities Joint Matriculation Board

NUKFAT National Union of Knitwear, Footwear and Apparel Trades

NUL [USA] National Urban League

NULMW National Union of Lock and Metal Workers

NUM National Union of Mineworkers; New Ulster Movement

Num. [Bible] Numbers

num. number; numeral(s); numerical; numerological; numerologist; numerology; numerous

NUMAST National Union of Marine, Aviation and Shipping Transport Officers

Numb. [Bible] Numbers

numis. numismatic; numismatics; numismatist

numism. numismatic; numismatics; numismatist

NUOS Naval Underwater Ordnance Station

NUPE National Union of Public Employees (became part of Unison)

NUR National Union of Railwaymen (became part of RMT)

NURBS [computing] nonuniform rational B-splines

NUS National Union of Seamen (became part of RMT); National Union of Students
NUT National Union of Teachers
N-u-T Newcastle-upon-Tyne
NUTG National Union of Townswomen's Guilds
NUTN National Union of Trained Nurses
nutr. nutrition
NUU New University of Ulster
NV [commerce] *Naamloze Vennootschap* (Dutch: public limited company, plc); needle valve; [US postcode] Nevada; New Version; nonvintage (wine); [finance] nonvoting (shares); [shipping] *Norske Veritas* (Norwegian shipping classification society); [vehicle registration] Northampton
N/V nonvintage (wine); [banking] no value
n.v. nonvoting
NVALA National Viewers' and Listeners' Association
NVB National Volunteer Brigade
NVC nonverbal communication
n.v.d. no value declared
NVG [military] night-vision goggles
NVGA [USA] National Vocational Guidance Association
NVI nonvalue indicator (postage stamp)
NVM Nativity of the Virgin Mary; [chemistry] nonvolatile matter
NVQ National Vocational Qualification
NVRAM [computing] nonvolatile random-access memory
NVRS National Vegetable Research Station
NW [vehicle registration] Leeds; net worth; North Wales; northwest; northwestern; [UK postcode] northwest London
n.w. net weight; no wind
NWC National War College
NWEB North Western Electricity Board
Nwfld Newfoundland
NWFP North-West Frontier Province (Pakistan)
NWG national wire gauge
NWGA National Wool Growers' Association
NWI Netherlands West Indies (former name of Netherlands Antilles)
NWIDA North West Industrial Development Association
NWS [USA] National Weather Service; normal water surface
NWT Northwest Territories (Canada)
nwt nonwatertight
n. wt net weight
NWTV North West Television
NX [vehicle registration] Dudley
NY [vehicle registration] Cardiff; new year; New York; [US postcode] New York
NYA [USA] National Youth Administration
NYC New York City
NYCSCE New York Coffee, Sugar and Cocoa Exchange
NYD [medicine] not yet diagnosed
NYFE New York Futures Exchange
nyl. nylon
NYMEX New York Mercantile Exchange
NYMT National Youth Music Theatre
NYO National Youth Orchestra
NYOS National Youth Orchestra of Scotland
NYP not yet published
NYPD New York Police Department
NYR not yet returned
NYS New York State
NYSE New York Stock Exchange
NYT National Youth Theatre; *New York Times*
NYU New York University
NZ [vehicle registration] Londonderry; neutral(ity) zone; New Zealand; [international vehicle registration] New Zealand
.nz New Zealand (in Internet address)
NZBC New Zealand Broadcasting Corporation
NZDSIR New Zealand Department of Scientific and Industrial Research
N Zeal. New Zealand
NZEF New Zealand Employers' Federation; New Zealand Expeditionary Force (in both world wars)
NZEFIP New Zealand Expeditionary Force in the Pacific (in World War II)
NZEI New Zealand Educational Institute
NZFL New Zealand Federation of Labour
NZIA New Zealand Institute of Architects
NZLR New Zealand Law Reports
NZMA New Zealand Medical Association
NZPA New Zealand Press Association
NZRFU New Zealand Rugby Football Union
NZRN New Zealand Registered Nurse

O

O [medicine] blood group; observe; observer; [obstetrics] occiput; occupation; Ocean; [pharmacology] *octarius* (Latin: pint); [printing] octavo; October; [medicine] *oculus* (Latin: eye); Oddfellows; *oeste* (Portuguese or Spanish: west); office; officer; Ohio; old; operation; [genetics] operator; [slang] opium; orange; [computing, mathematics] order; Order (of monks, knights, etc.); ordinary; [geology] Ordovician; Orient; *Osten* (German: east); [music] *ottava* (Italian: octave); *ouest* (French: west); [cricket] over; *ovest* (Italian: west); owner; [chemical element] oxygen

o [computing, mathematics] order; [meteorology] overcast

o' of

o. occasional; [printing] octavo; off; old; only; *optimus* (Latin: best); order; organ; [music] *ottava* (Italian: octave); [baseball] out; over; overseer; owner

6O [civil aircraft marking] Somalia

7O [civil aircraft marking] Yemen

OA [vehicle registration] Birmingham; objective analysis; office address; office automation; Officers' Association; *Officier d'Académie* (French: Officer of the Academy); [banking] old account; [chemistry] oleic acid; operational analysis; [medicine] osteoarthritis; overall

O/A [banking] old account

o/a on account (of); on or about

o.a. overall

OAA *Organisation pour l'alimentation et l'agriculture* (French: Food and Agriculture Organization, FAO); Outdoor Advertising Association of Great Britain

OACI *Organisation de l'aviation civile internationale* (French: International Civil Aviation Organization, ICAO)

OAD [medicine] obstructive airways disease

o.a.d. overall depth

OAG [USA] Official Airline Guide

o.a.h. overall height

o. alt. hor. [medicine] *omnibus alternis horis* (Latin: every other hour)

OAMDV *omnia ad majorem Dei gloriam* (Latin: all to the greater glory of God)

OANA Organization of Asian News Agencies

O&A October and April (on bills)

O&C Oxford and Cambridge (Schools Examination Board)

o&c onset and course

O&E [USA] Operations and Engineers (or Engineering)

O&G obstetrics and gynaecology

O&M Ogilvie and Mather (advertising agency); organization and method(s)

O&O Oriental and Occidental Steamship Company; owned and operated

OAO one and only; Orbiting Astronomical Observatory

o.a.o. off and on

OAP old age pension; old age pensioner

OAPC [USA] Office of Alien Property Custodian

OAPEC Organization of Arab Petroleum Exporting Countries

OAR [Roman Catholic Church] Order of Augustinian Recollects

OAr Old Arabic

OAS [military] offensive air support; on active service; *Organisation de l'armée secrète* (French: Secret Army Organization); Organization of American States

OASIS optimal aircraft sequencing using intelligent systems

OAT outside air temperature

OATC Oceanic Air Traffic Control

OATG outside air temperature gauge

OATUU Organization of African Trade Union Unity (replacement for AATUF)

OAU Organization of African Unity

OB [vehicle registration] Birmingham; [fishing port] Oban; observed bearing; [USA] obstetric; [USA] obstetrician; [USA] obstetrics; [theatre] off-Broadway; official board; Old Bailey; old bonded (whisky); old boy; Order of Barbados; order of battle; Order of the Bath;

[insurance] ordinary business (in life assurance); ordnance board; outside broadcast; [civil aircraft marking] Peru
Ob. [Bible] Obadiah
o/b on or before
ob. *obiit* (Latin: (he/she) died); *obiter* (Latin: incidentally); obligation; oboe; observation; obsolete; obstetric; obstetrics
o.b. ordinary building (grade of timber)
OBA optical bleaching agent (in detergent)
Obad. [Bible] Obadiah
ÖBB *Österreichische Bundesbahnen* (German: Federal Railways of Austria)
obb. [music] *obbligato* (Italian: essential (part))
obbl. [music] *obbligato* (Italian: essential (part))
OBC old boys' club; on-board computer (in car advertisement)
OBD [medicine] organic brain disease
ob. dk observation deck
obdt obedient
OBE (Officer of the) Order of the British Empire; out-of-the-body experience
OBEV *Oxford Book of English Verse*
ob-gyn obstetrics-gynaecology
OBI Order of British India
obit [short form] obituary
obj. object; objection; objective
objn objection
obl. obligation; oblige; oblique; oblong
OBLI Oxford and Buckinghamshire Light Infantry
OBM [surveying] Ordnance benchmark
OBO ore-bulk-oil (ship)
o.b.o. or best offer (in advertisement)
Obogs [military] on-board oxygen-generating system
ob. ph. [surveying] oblique photograph (or photography)
obre *octobre* (French: October)
OBS [medicine] organic brain syndrome
Obs. Observatory
Obs. *The Observer*
obs. obscure; observation; observatory; observe; observed; observer; obsolete; obstacle; obstetric; obstetrician; obstetrics; obstruction
obsc. obscure
obscd obscured
OBSF [accounting] off balance sheet finance
obsol. obsolescent; obsolete
ob.s.p. *obiit sine prole* (Latin: died without issue)
obst oboist
obstet. obstetric; obstetrician; obstetrics
obstn obstruction
obt obedient
obtd obtained
OBU offshore banking unit; One Big Union
OBV ocean boarding vessel
obv. obverse
OC [vehicle registration] Birmingham; Observer Corps; [USA] Office of Censorship; officer commanding; Officer in Charge; [electrical engineering] operating characteristic; operations centre; [pharmacology] oral contraceptive; Order in Council; (Officer of the) Order of Canada; orienteering club; [philately] original cover; Oslo Convention; Ottawa Convention; overseas command; overseas country
Oc. Ocean
o/c officer commanding; overcharge
o.c. office copy; official classification; [architecture] on centre; only child; [shipping] open charter; open cover; *opere citato* (Latin: in the work cited); over-the-counter
OCA Old Comrades Association
oca. [music] ocarina
OCAM *Organisation commune africaine et malgache* (French: African and Malagasy Common Organization)
OCarm. Order of Carmelites
OCart. Order of Carthusians
OCAS Organization of Central American States
OCAW [USA] Oil, Chemical and Atomic Workers International Union
occ. occasion; occasional; occasionally; occident; occidental; occupation; occupied; occurrence
occas. occasional; occasionally
occn occasion
OCD [medicine] obsessive compulsive disorder; [USA] Office of Civil Defense; [computing] on-line communications driver; *Ordinis Carmelitarum Discalceatorum* (Latin: of the Order of Discalced

Carmelites); *Ordo Carmelitarum Discalceatorum* (Latin: Order of Discalced Carmelites)
OCDE *Organisation de coopération et de développement economiques* (French: Organization for Economic Cooperation and Development, OECD)
OCDM [USA] Office of Civil Defense Mobilization
OCDS [Canada] Overseas College of Defence Studies
O/Cdt Officer-Cadet
oceanog. oceanography
OCelt Old Celtic
OCF Officiating Chaplain to the Forces
OCH oil central heating (in property advertisement)
och. ochre
OCNL [meteorology] occasional
OCorn Old Cornish
OCPSF organic chemicals, plastics and synthetic fibres
OCR [computing] optical character reader; [computing] optical character recognition; *Ordinis Cisterciensium Reformatorum* (Latin: of the Order of Reformed Cistercians); *Ordo Cisterciensium Reformatorum* (Latin: Order of Reformed Cistercians, Trappists)
OCS [USA] Officer Candidate School; Old Church Slavonic; outer continental shelf
OCSC Office of the Civil Service Commissioners
OCSO Order of Cistercians of the Strict Observance (= Trappists)
ocst [meteorology] overcast
Oct [astronomy] Octans
Oct. October
oct. [music] octave; [printing] octavo; *octubre* (Spanish: October)
OCTU Officer Cadet Training Unit
OCTV open-circuit television
OCU Operational Conversion Unit
OCUC Oxford and Cambridge University Club
OCV open-circuit voltage
OD Doctor of Ophthalmology; Doctor of Optometry; Doctor of Osteopathy; [vehicle registration] Exeter; [civil aircraft marking] Lebanon; [medicine] *oculus dexter* (Latin: right eye); officer of the day; Old Dutch; [military] olive drab; operations division; [Jamaica] (Officer of the) Order of Distinction; ordinary seaman; ordnance datum (standard sea level); ordnance department; ordnance depot; organization development; other denominations; outside diameter; overdose
O/D on deck; [banking] on demand; [banking] overdraft; [banking] overdrawn
o/d on deck; overdose
od. *oder* (German: or)
o.d. [medicine] *oculus dexter* (Latin: right eye); [military] olive drab; optical density; outside diameter
ODA [computing] office document architecture; [computing] open (or office) document architecture; [medicine] operating department assistant; Overseas Development Administration (former government department)
ODan Old Danish
ODAS Ocean Data Station
ODC Order of Discalced Carmelites
ODCh Chaplain for Other Denominations
ODE [mathematics] ordinary differential equation
ODECA *Organización de estados centroamericanos* (Spanish: Organization of Central American States, OCAS)
ODESSA Ocean Data Environmental Sciences Services Acquisition; *Organisation der SS-Angehörigen* (German: Organization of SS Members)
ODETTE Organization for Data Exchange through Tele-Transmission in Europe
ODI [computing] open datalink interface; Overseas Development Institute
ODLQC Open and Distance Learning Quality Council (formerly CACC)
ODO outdoor officer (at customs)
ODP official development planning; [computing] open distributed processing; open-door policy; overall development planning
ODV [informal] brandy (phonetic spelling of French name *eau de vie*)
OE [civil aircraft marking] Austria; [vehicle registration] Birmingham; [USA] Office of Education; Old English; Old Etonian; [medicine] on examination; Order of Excellence (in Guyana); original error; outboard engine

Oe oersted (unit of magnetic field strength)
o.e. omissions excepted; open end
OEA Overseas Education Association; oxygen-enriched air
OEC oxygen-enriched combustion
OECD Organization for Economic Cooperation and Development (replacement for OEEC)
OECS Organization of Eastern Caribbean States
OED *Oxford English Dictionary*
OEEC Organization for European Economic Cooperation (replaced by OECD)
OEF Organization of Employers' Federations and Employers in Developing Countries
OEIC open-ended investment company
OEL occupational exposure limit (of radiation)
OEM [computing] original equipment manufacturer
OEO [USA] Office of Economic Opportunity
OEP [USA] Office of Economic Preparedness
OER Officers' Emergency Reserve; Organization for European Research
OES ocean energy system(s); [USA] Office of Economic Stabilization; Order of the Eastern Star; Organization of European States
OET Office of Education and Training
OF [vehicle registration] Birmingham; Oddfellows; oil-filled; oil-fired; [printing] old face (type); Old French; operating forces; operational forces; Order of the Founder (of Salvation Army); oxidizing flame
o.f. optional form; outside face
OFA [medicine] oncofetal antigen
O factor [psychology] oscillation factor
OFB [computing] output feedback
OFEMA *Office français d'exportation de matériel aéronautique* (French: French Office for the Export of Aeronautical Material)
Off. Offaly
off. offer; offered; offering; office; officer; official; officinal
Offer Office of Electricity Regulation
offg offering; officiating
offic. official; officially
offl official
offr officer
Ofgas Office of Gas Supply
OFHC [engineering] oxygen-free high-conductivity copper
Oflag *Offizierslager* (German: officers' (prisoner-of-war) camp)
OFlem Old Flemish
Oflot Office of the National Lottery
OFM Order of Friars Minor (= Franciscans); *Ordo Fratrum Minorum* (Latin: Order of Friars Minor)
OFMCap. Order of Friars Minor Capuchin
OFMConv. Order of Friars Minor Conventual
OFR Order of the Federal Republic of Nigeria
OFr Old French
OFris Old Frisian
OFS Orange Free State
Ofsted Office for Standards in Education
OFT Office of Fair Trading
Oftel Office of Telecommunications
Ofwat Office of Water Services
OG [vehicle registration] Birmingham; [astronomy] object glass; officer of the guard; [architecture] ogee; Olympic Games; [US slang] original gangster (criminals' term of respect); original gravity (in brewing); [philately] original gum; outside guard
o.g. [philately] original gum; [sports] own goal
OGael Old Gaelic
ÖGB *Österreichischer Gewerkschaftsbund* (German: Austrian Federation of Trade Unions)
OGCM [meteorology] ocean general circulation model
OGD [medicine] oesophagogastroduodenoscopy
OGL [commerce] open general licence
OGM ordinary general meeting
OGO Orbiting Geophysical Observatory
OGPU *Obyedinyonnoye Gosudarstvennoye Politicheskoye Upravleniye* (Russian: United State Political Administration) (former Soviet police organization)
OGS Oratory of the Good Shepherd; [electronics] oxide glassy (or glasslike) semiconductor
OH [vehicle registration] Birmingham; [civil aircraft marking] Finland; [US post-

code] Ohio; [numismatics] old head (of Queen Victoria)

o.h. observation helicopter; office hours; [medicine] *omni hora* (Latin: hourly); on hand; open hearth; overhead

OHAC own house and car (in personal advertisement)

OHBMS On Her/His Britannic Majesty's Service

OHC overhead cam(shaft) (in car advertisement)

OHD [medicine] organic heart disease

OHDETS over-horizon detection system

OHG [commerce] *Offene Handelsgesellschaft* (German: partnership); Old High German

OHMS On Her/His Majesty's Service

OHN occupational health nurse

OHNC occupational health nursing certificate

OHP overhead projector

OHS occupational health service; [metallurgy] open-hearth steel

OHV overhead valve

OI [vehicle registration] Belfast; office instruction; Old Irish; operating instructions; [medicine] osteogenesis imperfecta

OIC Officer in Charge; *Organisation internationale du commerce* (French: International Trade Organization, ITO); Organization of the Islamic Conference

OIcel Old Icelandic

OIEO offers in excess of (in advertisement)

OIG *organisation intergouvernementale* (French: intergovernmental organization)

OII [physics] optical imaging instrument

OILC Offshore Industry Liaison Committee

OIPC *Organisation internationale de police criminelle* (French: International Criminal Police Organization, Interpol)

OIr Old Irish

OIRO offers in the region of (in advertisement)

OIRT *Organisation internationale de radiodiffusion et télévision* (French: International Radio and Television Organization)

OIS organizer industrial safety; overnight indexed swap

OIT *Organisation internationale du travail* (French: International Labour Organization, ILO)

OIt Old Italian

OJ [vehicle registration] Birmingham; *Official Journal* (of EU); orange juice; Order of Jamaica

o.j. open joint; open joist

OJAJ October, January, April, July (end of financial quarters)

OJCS Office of the Joint Chiefs of Staff

Ojocs [horseracing] overnight declaration of jockeys

OJR old Jamaica rum

OJT on-the-job training

OK all correct (perhaps from facetious misspelling 'oll korrekt'); [vehicle registration] Birmingham; [civil aircraft marking] Czech Republic; [US postcode] Oklahoma

o.k.a. otherwise known as

OKH *Oberkommando der Heeres* (German: Army High Command) (in World War II)

Okla Oklahoma

Okt. *Oktober* (German: October)

OL [vehicle registration] Birmingham; [medicine] *oculus laevus* (Latin: left eye); [UK postcode] Oldham; Old Latin; [computing] on-line; operating licence; (Officer of the) Order of Leopold; Ordnance Lieutenant; [sports] outside left; overflow level; overhead line

Ol. Olympiad; Olympic

ol. [medicine] *oleum* (Latin: oil)

o.l. [medicine] *oculus laevus* (Latin: left eye)

OLC oak-leaf cluster (US military decoration)

Old Test. Old Testament

OLE [computing] object linking and embedding

O level [education] Ordinary level (replaced by GCSE)

OLG Old Low German

Oli [geology] Oligocene

o'lkng overlooking (in property advertisement)

OLQ officer-like qualities

OLR off-line reader

OLRT [computing] on-line real time

OLS [statistics] ordinary least squares

OM [vehicle registration] Birmingham; old man; optical microscopy; *Optimus*

Maximus (Latin: greatest and best) (Roman title for Jupiter); Order of Merit; ordnance map; organic matter; [civil aircraft marking] Slovakia
Om. Oman
.om Oman (in Internet address)
o.m. old measurement; [medicine] *omni mane* (Latin: every morning)
OMA [US finance] orderly marketing agreement
OMB [USA] Office of Management and Budget
OMC operation and maintenance costs
OMCS Office of the Minister for the Civil Service
OMI Oblate(s) of Mary Immaculate
OMM [Canada] (Officer of the) Order of Military Merit
omn. hor. [medicine] *omni hora* (Latin: every hour)
omn. noct. [medicine] *omni nocte* (Latin: every night)
OMO one-man operation (or operator) (of bus)
OMR [computing] optical mark reading (or reader)
OMRS Orders and Medals Research Society
OMS [computing] object management system; [astronautics] orbital manœuvring system; *Organisation mondiale de la santé* (French: World Health Organization, WHO)
o.m.s. output per man shift
OMT [computing] object modelling technique
OMV open-market value
ON [vehicle registration] Birmingham; octane number; Old Norse; Ontario; [Jamaica] Order of the Nation; orthopaedic nurse
o.n. [medicine] *omni nocte* (Latin: every night)
ONC Ordinary National Certificate; Orthopaedic Nursing Certificate
OND Ophthalmic Nursing Diploma; Ordinary National Diploma; [medicine] other neurological disorders
ONERA *Office national d'études et de recherches aérospatiales* (French: National Office of Aerospace Study and Research)
ONF Old Norman French; Old Northern French
ONG *organisation non-gouvernementale* (French: nongovernmental organization)
ONGC [USA] Oil and Natural Gas Commission
ONI Office of Naval Intelligence
o.n.o. or near(est) offer (in advertisement)
onomat. onomatopoeia; onomatopoeic
ONorw Old Norwegian
ONR [USA] Office of Naval Research
ONS Office for National Statistics
ONT ordinary neap tide
Ont. Ontario
ONZ Order of New Zealand
OO [civil aircraft marking] Belgium; [vehicle registration] Chelmsford; observation officer; [informal] once-over; operation order; orderly officer
o/o offers over (in advertisement); on order; order of
OOBE out-of-the-body experience
OOD [computing] object-oriented design; officer of the day; officer of the deck
OODBMS [computing] object-oriented database management system
OOG officer of the guard
OOL [computing] object-oriented language
OON Officer of the Order of the Niger
o/o/o out of order
o.o.o. of obscure origin
OOP [computing] object-oriented programming; out-of-pocket (expenses)
OOT out of town
OOW officer of the watch
OP [vehicle registration] Birmingham; observation point; observation post; old people; Old Persian; old prices; [insurance] open policy; [theatre] opposite prompt (side); *Ordinis Praedictatorum* (Latin: of the Order of Preachers); *Ordo Praedictatorum* (Latin: Order of Preachers, Dominicans); organophosphate; osmotic pressure; [informal] other people('s); out of print; [medicine] outpatient; over proof (of alcohol)
Op. [music] Opus (piece by composer)
op [short form] operation
op. opaque; opera; *opera* (Latin: works); operation; operational; operator; opinion; opposite; optical; *optimus* (Latin: best, excellent); *opus* (Latin: work)

o.p. old pattern; open pattern; open-plan (in property advertisement); [theatre] opposite prompt (side); out of print; over proof (of alcohol)
OPA [USA] Office of Price Administration (in World War II); Orbis Press Agency (Czech news agency)
op art [short form] optical art
OPAS Occupational Pensions Advisory Board
OPB Occupational Pensions Board
OPC [computing] optical photoconductor; ordinary Portland cement; [medicine] outpatient(s') clinic; Overseas Press Club of America
op. cit. *opere citato* (Latin: in the work cited)
OPCON operational control
OPCS Office of Population Censuses and Surveys
OPD [medicine] outpatient(s') department
OPDAR optical detection and ranging
OPE out-of-pocket expenses
OPEC Organization of (the) Petroleum Exporting Countries
Op-Ed [USA] opposite editorial (page) (in newspaper)
OPEIU [USA] Office and Professional Employees International Union
OPEP *Organisation des pays exportateurs de pétrole* (French: Organization of Petroleum Exporting Countries, OPEC)
OPers Old Persian
OPEX operational, executive and administrative personnel (in UN)
OPG [dentistry] orthopantomogram
OPg Old Portuguese
opg opening
Oph [astronomy] Ophiuchus
oph. ophthalmic
ophthal. ophthalmic; ophthalmologist; ophthalmology
ophthalmol. ophthalmologist; ophthalmology
OPIC [USA] Overseas Private Investment Corporation
opl operational
OPM [USA] Office of Personnel Management; [informal] other people's money; output per man
opm operations per minute
OPMA Overseas Press and Media Association
opn operation; opinion; option
o.p.n. *ora pro nobis* (Latin: pray for us)
OPO one-person operation (of bus); one-person operator (of bus)
OPol Old Polish
OPP oriented polypropene (film); out of print at present
Opp. [music] Opuses (pieces by composer)
opp. *opera* (Latin: works); opportunity; oppose; opposed; opposite; opposition
oppy opportunity
OPQ occupational personality questionnaire
OPr Old Provençal
opr operator
opr. operate
OPRAF Office of Passenger Rail Franchising
OProv Old Provençal
OPruss Old Prussian
OPS Office of Public Service
ops [short form] operations
OPT optimized production technology
opt. [grammar] optative; optic(al); optician; optics; optimal; *optime* (Latin: best, excellently); optimum; option; optional
OptD Doctor of Optometry
OPV [medicine] oral poliomyelitis vaccine
OQ (Officer of the) National Order of Quebec
OR [statistics] odds ratio; official receiver; official referee; Old Roman; [currency] Omani rial; [US medicine] operating room; operational (or operations) requirement; operational (or operations) research; orderly room; [US postcode] Oregon; [military] other ranks; [sports] outside right; [insurance] owner's risk; [vehicle registration] Portsmouth
ÖR *Österreichischer Rundfunk* (German: Austrian Radio) (broadcasting service)
or other
or. orange; oratorio; orient; oriental; orientalist; original
o.r. operationally risky; operational (or operations) requirement; operations room; out of range; overhaul and repair; [insurance] owner's risk
Oracle [trademark] optional reception of announcements by coded line electronics (teletext service)
orat. oration; orator; oratorical; oratorically; oratorio; oratory

ORB oceanographic research buoy; omnidirectional radio beacon
o.r.b. [insurance] owner's risk of breakage
ORBIS orbiting radio beacon ionospheric satellite
ORBIT on-line retrieval of bibliographical information
ORC [USA] Officers' Reserve Corps; Overseas Research Council
ORCA Ocean Resources Conservation Association
orch. orchestra; orchestral; orchestrated (by); orchestration
orchd orchestrated (by)
orchid [informal] one recent child, heavily in debt
ord. ordain; ordained; order; ordinal; ordinance; ordinary; ordnance
o.r.d. [insurance] owner's risk of damage
ordn. ordnance
ORE occupational radiation exposure
Ore. Oregon
Oreg. Oregon
ORELA Oak Ridge Electron Linear Accelerator
ORESCO Overseas Research Council
ORF [genetics] open reading frame
o.r.f. [insurance] owner's risk of fire
org. organ; organic; organism; organist; organization; organize; organized; organizer
.org noncommercial organization (in Internet address)
ORGALIME *Organisme de liaison des industries métalliques européennes* (French: Liaison Group for the European Metal Industries)
organ. organic; organization
orgst organist
orgzn organization
Ori [astronomy] Orion
orient. oriental; orientalist
orig. origami; origin; original; originally; originate; originated
ORIT *Organización regional interamericana de trabajadores* (Spanish: Inter-American Regional Organization of Workers)
Ork. Orkney (Islands)
Orkn. Orkney (Islands)
ORL [medicine] otorhinolaryngology (= ear, nose and throat (ENT))
o.r.l. [insurance] owner's risk of leakage
orn. ornament; ornamental; ornithology
ornith. ornithological; ornithology
ornithol. ornithological; ornithology
ORNL Oak Ridge National Laboratory
OROM [computing] optical read-only memory
ORP off-road parking (in property advertisement)
orph. orphan; orphanage
ORR Office of the Rail Regulator
o.r.r. owner's risk rates
ORS [geology] Old Red Sandstone; Operational Research Society
ors others
ORSL Order of the Republic of Sierra Leone
ORSORT Oak Ridge School of Reactor Technology
ORT [medicine] oral rehydration therapy; [USA] Organization for Rehabilitation by Training
ORTF *Office de radiodiffusion-télévision française* (French: French Radio and Television Organization) (former state broadcasting service)
Orth. Orthodox
orth. orthographic(al); orthography; orthopaedic; orthopaedics
ORuss Old Russian
ORV off-road vehicle
OS [vehicle registration] Glasgow; [medicine] *oculus sinister* (Latin: left eye); Old Saxon; Old School; old series; Old Side; Old Style (in dates); [computing] operating system; Ordinary Seaman; Ordnance Survey; out of stock; outsize (clothing)
Os [chemical element] osmium
o/s on sale; out of service; out of stock; outsize (clothing); [banking] outstanding
o.s. ocean station; [medicine] *oculus sinister* (Latin: left eye); oil switch; old series; only son; on station; outside
OSA [USA] Office of the Secretary of the Army; Official Secrets Act; [printing] old style antique (type); Order of St Augustine (= Augustinians); *Ordinis Sancti Augustini* (Latin: of the Order of St Augustine); *Ordo Sancti Augustini* (Latin: Order of St Augustine, Augustinians); Overseas Sterling Area
OSAF [USA] Office of the Secretary of the Air Force

OS&W [building] oak, sunk and weathered
OSax Old Saxon
OSB Order of St Benedict (= Benedictines); *Ordinis Sancti Benedicti* (Latin: of the Order of St Benedict); *Ordo Sancti Benedicti* (Latin: Order of St Benedict, Benedictines)
OSC on-site cover; Order of St Clare (= Poor Clares)
osc. oscillator
OScan Old Scandinavian
OScand Old Scandinavian
OSCAR Orbital Satellites Carrying Amateur Radio; Organization for Sickle Cell Anaemia Research
OSCE Organization for Security and Cooperation in Europe (formerly CSCE)
OSCH off-peak (or overnight) storage central heating (in property advertisement)
OSD [USA] Office of the Secretary of Defense; Order of St Dominic (= Dominicans)
OSE operational support equipment
OSerb Old Serbian
OSF [computing] Open Software Federation; Order of St Francis (= Franciscans); *Ordinis Sancti Francisci* (Latin: of the Order of St Francis); *Ordo Sancti Francisci* (Latin: Order of St Francis, Franciscans)
OSFC Order of St Francis, Capuchin
OSHA [USA] Occupational Safety and Health Administration
OSI [USA] Office of Scientific Integrity; on-site inspection; [computing] open systems interconnection
O/Sig Ordinary Signalman
OSJ on a secret journey
OSL Old Style Latin
OSl Old Slavonic
Osl. Oslo
OSlav Old Slavonic
OSM Order of the Servants of Mary (= Servites)
OSN [USA] Office of the Secretary of the Navy
OSNC Orient Steam Navigation Company
OSO orbiting solar observatory
OSP off-street parking (in property advertisement)
OSp Old Spanish
o.s.p. *obiit sine prole* (Latin: died without issue)
OSR [USA] Office of Science and Research
OSRB Overseas Service Resettlement Bureau
OSRD [USA] Office of Scientific Research and Development
OSRO Office for Special Relief Operations
OSS Office for the Supervision of Solicitors; [USA] Office of Space Sciences (in NASA); [USA] Office of Strategic Services (in World War II)
O.SS.S. *Ordinis Sanctissimi Salvatoris* (Latin: of the Order of the Most Holy Saviour); *Ordo Sanctissimi Salvatoris* (Latin: Order of the Most Holy Saviour, Bridgettines)
O.SS.T. *Ordinis Sanctissimae Trinitatis Redemptionis Captivorum* (Latin: of the Order of the Most Holy Trinity for the Redemption of Captives); *Ordo Sanctissimae Trinitatis Redemptionis Captivorum* (Latin: Order of the Most Holy Trinity for the Redemption of Captives, Trinitarians)
OST [USA] Office of Science and Technology; ordinary spring tide
osteo. osteopath; osteopathic; osteopathy
OSTI [USA] Office of Scientific and Technical Information; [USA] Organization for Social and Technological Innovation
OStJ (Officer of the) Order of St John of Jerusalem
OSU Order of St Ursula (= Ursulines)
OSUK Ophthalmological Society of the United Kingdom
OSV ocean station vessel
OSw Old Swedish
OT occupational therapist; occupational therapy; off time; Old Testament; Old Teutonic; [medicine] operating theatre; [Australia] Overland Telegraph (from Adelaide to Darwin); overseas trade; overtime; [vehicle registration] Portsmouth
OTA Office of Technology Assessment
OTAN *Organisation du traité de l'Atlantique nord* (French: North Atlantic Treaty Organization, NATO)
OTASE *Organisation du traité de défense collective pour l'Asie du sud-est* (French: South-East Asia Treaty Organization, SEATO)
OTB [USA] off-track betting; oxide titanium bronze
otbd outboard

OTC [USA] officer in tactical command; Officers' Training Corps; Officers' Transit Camp; one-stop-inclusive tour charter; Organization for Trade Cooperation; over-the-counter (as in **OTC medicines**); [pharmacology] oxytetracycline (antibiotic)
OTE on-target earnings (in job advertisement); or the equivalent
OTEC ocean thermal-energy conversion
OTeut Old Teutonic
OTF [photography] off the film
OTG outside temperature gauge (in car advertisement)
OTH [telecommunications] over the horizon
OTOH on the other hand (in Internet chat and e-mail)
otol. otological; otology
OTP [computing] one-time programmable (EPROM)
OTS Office of Technical Services; Officers' Training School; [advertising] opportunities to see
OTT [medicine] oesophageal transit test; [informal] over the top
Ott. Ottawa
ott. [music] *ottava* (Italian: octave); *ottobre* (Italian: October)
OTU [biology] operational taxonomic unit; operation training unit
OTurk Old Turkish
OU [vehicle registration] Bristol; official use; Open University; Oxford University
OUAC Oxford University Appointments Committee; Oxford University Athletic Club
OUAFC Oxford University Association Football Club
OUBC Oxford University Boat Club
OUCC Oxford University Cricket Club
OUDS Oxford University Dramatic Society
OUP [Northern Ireland] Official Unionist Party; Oxford University Press
OURC Oxford University Rifle Club
OURFC Oxford University Rugby Football Club
OURT Order of the United Republic of Tanzania
out. outlet
outbd outboard
OV [vehicle registration] Birmingham
Ov. Ovid (Roman poet)
ov. ovary; over; overture
ovbd overboard
o.v.c. [law] other valuable consideration
overlkg overlooking (in property advertisement)
ovfl. overflow
OVH overhead projector
ovhd overhead
ovld overload
OVNI *objet volant non identifié* (French: unidentified flying object, UFO)
o.v.n.o. or very near offer (in advertisement)
ÖVP *Österreichische Volkspartei* (German: Austrian People's Party)
ovpd overpaid
ovrd. override
OW Office of Works; Old Welsh; old woman; [vehicle registration] Portsmouth
O/W oil in water (emulsion)
o.w. one way; out of wedlock
OWC Ordnance Weapons Command
OWF optimum working frequency
OWI [USA] Office of War Information (in World War II); [USA] operating (a motor vehicle) while intoxicated
own. owner
OWRS [USA] Office of Water Regulations and Standards
OWS ocean weather service; ocean weather ship; ocean weather station
OX [vehicle registration] Birmingham; [UK postcode] Oxford
Ox. Oxford
Oxf. Oxford(shire)
Oxfam Oxford Committee for Famine Relief
Oxon. Oxfordshire (from Latin *Oxonia*); *Oxoniensis* (Latin: of Oxford)
OY [civil aircraft marking] Denmark; [vehicle registration] northwest London
oys. oysters
OZ [vehicle registration] Belfast
oz ounce (from Italian *onza*)
oz ap apothecaries' ounce
oz av avoirdupois ounce
oz avdp avoirdupois ounce
oz T troy ounce

P

P [civil aircraft marking] North Korea; [Roman Catholic Church] *Papa* (Latin: Pope); [genetics] parental generation; park; parking; parson; pass; passed; [US education] passing; pastor; *pater* (Latin: father); [chess] pawn; [music] pedal; pedestrian; pedestrian crossing; [horticulture] perennial; [ecclesiastical] *Père* (French: Father); [botany] perianth (in floral formula); period; [geology] Permian; personnel; peta- (indicates 10^{15}, as in **Pm** = petametre); pharmacy (on non-prescription medicine); [currency] Philippine peso; [biochemistry] phosphate; [chemical element] phosphorus; [botany] phytochrome; pitch; [physics] poise; [computing] polynomial; [Roman Catholic Church] Pope; *populus* (Latin: people); port; [fishing port] Portsmouth; [international vehicle registration] Portugal; positive; post; postage; posterior; post office (on map); Presbyterian; President; priest; Prince; probate; pro-consul; [politics] Progressive; [theatre] prompt (side); proprietary (product); Protestant; public; [currency] pula (used in Botswana); pupil

P [physics] dielectric polarization; [physics] parity; [physics] power; [physics] pressure; [genetics] promoter

p page; [currency] pence; [currency] penny; per; pico- (indicates 10^{-12}, as in **ps** = picosecond); [physics] proton; [meteorology] shower

p [physics] electric dipole moment; [physics] momentum (in vector equations); [chemistry] permanent dipole moment (of molecule); [music] *piano* (Italian: softly); [physics] pressure; [biochemistry] pyranose

p. page; pamphlet; paragraph; part; [grammar] participle; particle; *partim* (Latin: in part); pass; passed; [grammar] passive; [grammar] past; peak; pectoral (fin); per; *per* (Latin: by, for); perch (unit of measure for stone); [music] percussion; perennial; [grammar] person; [currency] peseta; [currency] peso; [currency] piastre; *pied* (French: foot); pint; pipe; *pius* (Latin: holy); plaster; polar; pole; *pondere* (Latin: by weight); population; port; positive; *post* (Latin: after); *pouce* (French: inch); *pour* (French: for, per); power; [grammar] present; *primus* (Latin: first); *pro* (Latin: for, in favour of); professional; [knitting] purl

P2 [civil aircraft marking] Papua New Guinea

P4 [civil aircraft marking] Aruba

7P [civil aircraft marking] Lesotho

8P [civil aircraft marking] Barbados

PA [vehicle registration] Guildford; [UK postcode] Paisley; Pakistan Army; [international vehicle registration] Panama; [chemistry] parent atom; Parents' Association; [insurance] particular average; Patients' Association; Pedestrians' Association; [US postcode] Pennsylvania; performance assessment; [medicine] pernicious anaemia; [insurance] personal accident; personal account; [taxation] personal allowance; personal appearance; personal assistant; [chemistry] phosphoric acid; photograph appreciated (in personal advertisement); [USA] physician assistant; Pierre Allain (brand of climbing boot); Piper Aircraft; [engineering] pitch angle; [medicine] plasminogen activator; political agent; *por autorización* (Spanish: by authority of); [astronomy] position angle; power amplifier; power of attorney; [Roman Catholic Church] Prefect Apostolic; press agent; Press Association; press attaché; private account; product analysis; programme assistant; [USA] prosecuting attorney; Protestant Alliance; [medicine] psoriatic arthritis; [USA] public accountant; public address (system); publicity agent; Publishers Association; [medicine] pulmonary artery; [engineering] pulsed annealing; purchasing agent

P/A [insurance] particular average; per-

sonal account; power of attorney; private account
Pa pascal (unit of pressure); Pennsylvania; [chemical element] protactinium
p.A *per Adresse* (German: care of, c/o) (in postal addresses)
pa. past
.pa Panama (in Internet address)
p.a. [grammar] participial adjective; *per annum* (Latin: yearly); permanent address; personal appearance
PAA Pan American Airways; [chemistry] peracetic acid; [chemistry] polyacrylic acid
PAADC Principal Air Aide-de-camp
PABIAC Paper and Board Industry Advisory Committee
PABLA problem analysis by logical approach
PABX [telecommunications] private automatic branch exchange
PAC [US air force] Pacific Air Command; Pan-African(ist) Congress; Pan-American Congress; [building] passive air cycle; Permanent Agricultural Committee (of ILO); [USA] political action committee; polymer–asphalt composite; [chemistry] powdered activated carbon; Public Accounts Committee; Public Assistance Committee; [stock exchange] put-and-call (option)
P-A-C [psychology] parent, adult, child
Pac. Pacific
PACA Public Art Commissions Agency
PACAF [US air force] Pacific Air Forces
PACE Parental Alliance for Choice in Education; performance and cost evaluation; Police and Criminal Evidence Act; precision analogue computing equipment; Protestant and Catholic Encounter
Pacif. Pacific
PACOM [USA] Pacific Command
PACS Pacific area communications system; [medicine] picture archiving and communication system
PACT Producers' Alliance for Cinema and Television
PAD [computing] packet assembler/disassembler; passive air defence; payable after death
PaD Pennsylvania Dutch
pad. padding; paddock; padlock
PADAR [military] passive detection and ranging
PADLOC [military] passive detection and location of countermeasures
p. Adr. *per Adresse* (German: care of, c/o) (in postal addresses)
PADT Public Art Development Trust
p. ae. [pharmacology] *partes aequales* (Latin: equal parts)
paediat. paediatrician; paediatrics
PAF [computing] peripheral address field; [medicine] platelet-activating factor; [Northern Ireland] Protestant Action Force
p.a.f. *puissance au frein* (French: brake horsepower)
PAFC phosphoric acid fuel cell
PAg Professional Agronomist
PaG Pennsylvania German
PAGB Poultry and Egg Producers' Association of Great Britain; Proprietary Association of Great Britain
PAHO Pan-American Health Organization
PAI [medicine] platelet accumulation index
PAICV *Partido Africano da Independencia de Cabo Verde* (Portuguese: African Party for the Independence of Cape Verde)
PAIN Parents Against Injustice
paint. painter; painting
PAIS [USA] Public Affairs Information Service
PAISLEY pants away if sexual liaison expected – yes! (on envelope of love letter)
Pak. Pakistan; Pakistani
PakRs [currency] Pakistan rupee
PAL [USA] Parcel Air Lift; [computing] peripheral availability list; [television] phase alternation line (European broadcasting system); Philippine Airlines; [USA] Police Athletic League; present atmospheric level; [computing, electronics] programmable array logic
Pal [geology] Palaeocene
Pal. Palace; Palestine; Palestinian
pal. palace; palaeography; palaeontology
palaeob. palaeobotanical; palaeobotany
palaeobot. palaeobotanical; palaeobotany
palaeog. palaeographic(al); palaeography
palaeontol. palaeontological; palaeontology

PALS [computing] permissive action link systems
PAM [telecommunications] pulse-amplitude modulation
pam. pamphlet
PAMA Pan-American Medical Association; Press Advertisement Managers' Association
pamph. pamphlet
PAMR Public Access Mobile Radio
PAN [Mexico] *Partido Acción Nacional* (Spanish: National Action Party); peroxyacetyl nitrate (pollutant of atmosphere); Pesticides Action Network; polyacrylonitrile (polymer)
Pan. Panama; Panamanian
pan. panchromatic; panoramic; pantomime; pantry
PANA Pan-African News Agency
PANAFTEL Pan-African Telecommunications Network
Pan. Can. Panama Canal
P&E plant and equipment
P&F chart point-and-figure chart
P&G Procter and Gamble
P&L profit and loss
P&O Peninsular and Oriental (shipping company)
p&p postage and packing
P&RT physical and recreational training
P&S [US stock exchange] purchase and sales
PANN Professional Association of Nursery Nurses
PANS procedures for air navigation services
panto [short form] pantomime
PAO [medicine] peak acid output; Prince Albert's Own (regiment); public affairs officer
PAP People's Action Party (in Singapore); *Polska Agencja Prasowa* (Polish news agency); [medicine] pulmonary arterial pressure
Pap. Papua; Papuan
PAPS periodic armaments planning system
PAR [military] perimeter acquisition radar; phased-array radar; [botany] photosynthetically active radiation; [computing] positive acknowledgment and retransmission; [aeronautics] precision approach radar; programme analysis review; [electronics] pulse acquisition radar
Par. Paraguay; Paraguayan
par. paragraph; parallax; parallel; paraphrase; parenthesis; parish; parochial
p.a.r. planed all round (in woodworking)
Para. Paraguay; Paraguayan
para [short form] paratrooper
para. parachute; paragraph
parab. parabola
par. aff. [pharmacology] *pars affecta* (Latin: to the affected part)
Par. Ch. parish church
parch. parchment
paren. parenthesis
parens. parentheses
park. parking
Parl. Parliament; Parliamentary
parl. parliament; parliamentary
parl. agt parliamentary agent
parl. proc. parliamentary procedure
Parly Sec. Parliamentary Secretary
PARM programme analysis for resource management
part. partial; participate; participation; [grammar] participial; [grammar] participle; particle; particular; partition; [grammar] partitive; partner; partnership
part. aeq. [pharmacology] *partes aequales* (Latin: in equal parts)
PARU [medicine] post-anaesthetic recovery unit
PAS public address system
pas. [grammar] passive
p.a.s. power-assisted steering (in car advertisement)
PASCAL *programme appliqué à la sélection et la compilation automatique de la littérature* (French: program applied to the selection and automatic compilation of literature)
Pasok *Panellenion Sozialistikon Kinema* (Greek: Panhellenic Socialist Movement)
Pass. Passover
pass. passage; passenger; *passim* (Latin: here and there throughout); [grammar] passive
PASSIM [USA] Presidential Advisory Staff on Scientific Management
PAT planned activities time; [banking] preauthorized automatic transfer; Professional Association of Teachers

pat. patent; patented; pattern
p.a.t. *poids atomique* (French: atomic weight)
PATA Pacific Air Travel Association
Pata. Patagonia; Patagonian
patd patented
path. pathological; pathology
pathol. pathological; pathology
Pat. Off. Patent Office
pat. pend. patent pending
PAU Pan American Union; programmes analysis unit
Pav [astronomy] Pavo
pav. pavilion
PAW plasma-arc welding; powered all the way
PAWA Pan American World Airways
PAWC Pan-African Workers' Congress
PAWR [USA] Public Authority for Water Resources
PAX [telecommunications] private automatic exchange
p.a.x. per annum, exclusive (in accommodation advertisement)
PAYE [taxation] pay as you earn; pay as you enter
paymr paymaster
PAYP pay as you play (at golf club)
payt payment
PAYV pay as you view
PB Bachelor of Philosophy (from Latin *Philosophiae Baccalaureus*); [vehicle registration] Guildford; passbook; permanent base; [athletics] personal best; *Pharmacopoeia Britannica* (Latin: British Pharmacopoeia); [pharmacology] phenobarbitone; plastic-bonded; Plymouth Brethren; pocket book; power brakes; Prayer Book; premium bond; Primitive Baptists; [USA] Publications Board; [knitting] purl into back of stitch
Pb [chemical element] lead (from Latin *plumbum*); [computing] petabyte
p/b purpose-built (in property advertisement); push-button
p.b. paperback (of books); [baseball] passed ball(s)
PBA [informal] poor bloody assistant; [USA] Professional Bowlers Association; [USA] Public Buildings Administration
PBAB please bring a bottle
PBB [chemistry] polybrominated biphenyl (constituent of plastics)
PBC powerboat club
PBI Peace Brigades International; [informal] poor bloody infantry; [medicine] protein-bound iodine
pbk paperback (of books)
PBM [surveying] permanent benchmark; play by mail (of games)
PBMA Plastic Bath Manufacturers' Association
PBR payment by results
PBS [medicine] phosphate-buffered saline; Public Broadcasting Service
PBT [accounting] pay-back time
p.b.t. [finance] profit before tax
p.b.u.h. peace be upon him
PBX [telecommunications] private branch exchange
PC [vehicle registration] Guildford; Panama Canal; [chemistry] paper chromatography; [chemistry] paraffin concentration; parish council; parish councillor; Parliamentary Commissioner (= ombudsman); *Partie Communiste* (French: Communist Party); Past Commander; Paymaster Captain; [Ireland] Peace Commissioner; [USA] Peace Corps; perpetual curate; personal computer; [military] pioneer corps; [engineering] pitch circle; *Plaid Cymru* (Welsh: Party of Wales); Police Constable; politically correct; political correctness; polo club; [chemistry] polycarbonate; polymer concrete; polyprop(yl)ene carbonate (plastic); Poor Clares (religious order); Portland cement; port of call; postcard; Post Commander; potentially correct; preparatory commission; Press Council; prestressed concrete; Prince Consort; [electronics] printed circuit; Prison Commission; Privy Council; Privy Counsellor; process control; [USA] professional corporation; [Canada] Progressive Conservative; [chemistry] prop(yl)ene carbonate; propositional calculus; public convenience (on map); pulverized coal; [microbiology] pure culture
P/C petty cash; photocopy; price(s) current
pc parsec (unit of astronomical distance)
pc. percentage; [printing] pica; piece; price
p.c. per cent; postcard; [medicine] *post*

cibum (Latin: after meals) (in prescriptions)
PCA Parliamentary Commissioner for Administration (= ombudsman); Parochial Clergy Association; [medicine] patient-controlled analgesia; Permanent Court of Arbitration; Police Complaints Authority; [statistics] principal component analysis; Professional Cycling Association
PCAS Polytechnics Central Admissions System (became part of UCAS)
PC-AT personal computer, advanced technologies
PCB petty cash book; [chemistry] polychlorinated biphenyl (constituent of plastics); [medicine] post-coital bleeding; [electronics] printed-circuit board; [insurance] private car benefits
PCC parochial church council; *Partido Comunista de Cuba* (Spanish: Communist Party of Cuba); political consultative committee; Press Complaints Commission; Privy Council cases; Professional Conduct Committee (disciplinary body of BMA)
PCCS Primate Captive Care Society
PCD [electronics] photo compact disc
PC-DOS [trademark, computing] Personal Computer Disk Operating System
PCE *Partido Comunista de España* (Spanish: Communist Party of Spain); Postgraduate Certificate of Education; [engineering] pyrometric cone equivalent
pce piece
PCF *Parti Communiste Français* (French: French Communist Party); pistol, centre fire (gun calibre)
pcf pounds per cubic foot
PCFRE Professional Council for Religious Education
PCGC pulverized coal gasification and combustion
PCGG Primary Care Group in Gynaecology
PCGN Permanent Committee on Geographical Names
P Ch. parish church
PCI *Partito Comunista Italiano* (Italian: Italian Communist Party) (former name of PDS); Pax Christi International; [computing] peripheral component interconnect; [computing] personal computer interface
p.c.i. pounds per cubic inch
PCID Pontifical Council for Inter-Religious Dialogue
PCIFC Permanent Commission of the International Fisheries Convention
PCIJ Permanent Court of International Justice
PCIS Period Cottage Improvement Society
PCIUG personal computer independent user group
PCL [computing] printer control language
pcl parcel
PCM photochemical machinery; [USA] plug-compatible manufacturer; polyatomic ceramic material; protein-calorie malnutrition; [telecommunications] pulse-code modulation
pcm per calendar month
PCMA Plastic Crate Manufacturers' Association; Potato Chip Manufacturers' Association
PCMCIA Personal Computer Memory Card International Association
PCMI photochromic microimage
PCMO Principal Colonial Medical Officer
PCN *Partido de Conciliación Nacional* (Spanish: National Conciliation Party) (in El Salvador); [computing] personal communications network
PCOB Permanent Central Opium Board (in UN)
PCOD [medicine] polycystic ovary disease
PCP Past Chief Patriarch; pentachlorophenol (wood preservative); [finance] permissible capital payment; [trademark, pharmacology] phencycl(ohexylpiper)idine (= angel dust, hallucinogenic drug); [medicine] *Pneumocystis carinii* pneumonia; polychloroprene (rubber); prime commercial paper
PCPCU Pontifical Council for Promoting Christian Unity
PCPI Parent Cooperative Preschools International; Permanent Committee on Patent Information (of WIPO)
PCR Pedestrian Crossings Regulations; [medicine] plasma clearance rate; politically correct retailing; [biochemistry] polymerase chain reaction
PCRS Poor Clergy Relief Society

PCS [electronics] plasma-current switch; [Scotland] Principal Clerk of Session
pcs. pieces; prices
PCSP Permanent Commission for the South Pacific
PCT [medicine] positron compute(rize)d tomography; product consistency test
pct per cent
PCTCT [accounting] profit chargeable to corporation tax
PCTE [computing] portable common tool environment
PCTFE polychlorotrifluoroeth(yl)ene (plastic coating)
PCU plant control unit; power control unit; power conversion unit; pressurization control unit
p.c.u. passenger car unit
PCV [medicine] packed cell volume; passenger-carrying vehicle; passenger-controlled vehicle; [USA] Peace Corps Volunteers; positive crankcase ventilation (in car); pressure containment vessel
PCWPC Permanent Committee of the World Petroleum Congress
PCX [computing] picture exchange format
PC-XT personal computer extended
PCZ Panama Canal Zone
PCZST Panama Canal Zone Standard Time
PD Doctor of Pharmacy (from Latin *Pharmaciae Doctor*); [vehicle registration] Guildford; [fishing port] Peterhead; *Pharmacopoeia Dublinensis* (Latin: Dublin Pharmacopoeia); polar distance; [USA] Police Department; port dues; *posdata* (Spanish: postscript, PS); postal district; preventive detainee; preventive detention; *Privatdozent* (German: unsalaried university teacher); probability of detection; production department; [Ireland] Progressive Democrat(s); progressive disease; [insurance] property damage; [USA] Public Defender; [computing] public domain (software)
P/D price–dividend (ratio)
Pd [chemical element] palladium
pd paid; passed
p/d postdated
p.d. *per diem* (Latin: daily); [engineering] pitch diameter; poop deck; postage due; postdated; [physics] potential difference; preliminary design; printer's devil
PDA [medicine] patent ductus arteriosus; [computing] personal digital assistant; *pour dire adieu* (French: to say goodbye); [navigation] predicted drift angle
PDAD Probate, Divorce and Admiralty Division (former High Court division)
PdB [USA] Bachelor of Pedagogy (from Latin *Pedagogiae Baccalaureus*)
PDC *Partido Demócrata Cristiano* (Spanish: Christian Democratic Party) (in El Salvador); personnel dispatch centre; personnel dispersal centre; Programme Delivery Control (for video recording); [engineering] pulse-discharge cleaning
PDCI *Parti Démocratique de la Côte d'Ivoire* (French: Democratic Party of Côte d'Ivoire)
PDD precise delay detonator
PdD [USA] Doctor of Pedagogy (from Latin *Pedagogiae Doctor*)
PDE [mathematics] partial differential equation; Projectile Development Establishment
P-de-C Pas-de-Calais (French department)
P-de-D Puy-de-Dôme (French department)
PDF [statistics] probability density function
PDFLP Popular Democratic Front for the Liberation of Palestine
PDG *Parti Démocratique de Guinée* (French: Democratic Party of Guinea); Paymaster Director-General; *président directeur général* (French: chairman and managing director)
PDGF [medicine] platelet-derived growth factor
PDH [computing] plesiochronous digital hierarchy
PDI [astronautics] powered descent initiation; product data interchange
p.d.i. predelivery inspection
PDL [computing] page definition language; [computing] page description language; poverty datum line; [computing] program design language
pdl poundal (unit of force)
PDM physical distribution management; [telecommunications] pulse-duration modulation
PdM [USA] Master of Pedagogy (from Latin *Pedagogiae Magister*)

PDN public data network
pdn production
PDP [computing] parallel distributed processing; program development plan (in NASA); programmed data processor (or processing)
PDPA People's Democratic Party of Afghanistan
PDQ [informal] pretty damn quick
PDR People's Democratic Republic; [astronomy] photodissociation region; [engineering] pitch-to-diameter ratio; precision depth recorder; price–dividend ratio
PDRA postdoctoral research assistant
P/D ratio price–dividend ratio
PDRE People's Democratic Republic of Ethiopia
PDRY People's Democratic Republic of Yemen
PDS Parkinson's Disease Society; *Partei Demokratischen Sozialismus* (German: Party of Democratic Socialism); *Partito Democratico della Sinistra* (Italian: Democratic Party of the Left) (formerly PCI); previously digested sludge; [computing] programming documentation standards
PDSA People's Dispensary for Sick Animals
PDSR Principal Director of Scientific Research
PDT Pacific Daylight Time; personal development technology; [medicine] photodynamic therapy
PDTC Professional Dancer's Training Course (Diploma)
PDU process-development unit
PE [vehicle registration] Guildford; peat extract; permissible error; [insurance] personal effects; [international vehicle registration] Peru; [UK postcode] Peterborough; [USA] petroleum engineer; *Pharmacopoeia Edinburgensis* (Latin: Edinburgh Pharmacopoeia); [computing] phase-encoded (tape format); physical education; plastic explosive; pocket edition; polyeth(yl)ene; [fishing port] Poole; Port Elizabeth (South Africa); [physics] potential energy; Presiding Elder; printer's error; [statistics] probable error; [computing] processing element; procurement executive; [USA] Professional Engineer; Protestant Episcopal; [medicine] pulmonary embolism
P/E part exchange (in advertisement); port of embarkation; price–earnings (ratio)
.pe Peru (in Internet address)
p.e. [law] personal estate; printer's error
PEA Physical Education Association of Great Britain and Northern Ireland
PEAB Professional Engineers' Appointments Bureau
PEC photoelectric cell; photoelectrochemical cell; Protestant Episcopal Church
pec [short form] pectoral (muscle)
PECD [electronics] photoelectric conversion device
ped. pedal; pedestal; pedestrian
PedD [USA] Doctor of Pedagogy (from Latin *Pedagogiae Doctor*)
PEDir Director of Physical Education
Peeb. Peebles(shire)
PEEP pilot's electronic eye-level presentation
PEF Palestine Exploration Fund; [US insurance] personal effects floater; [electronics] pulsed electric field
PEFCO Private Export Funding Corporation
Peg [astronomy] Pegasus
PEI [Canada] Prince Edward Island
pej. pejorative
p.ej. *por ejemplo* (Spanish: for example)
Pek. Peking
PEL permissible exposure level; permissible exposure limit
Pembs Pembrokeshire
Pemex *Petróleos Mexicanos* (Mexican oil company)
PEN International Association of Poets, Playwrights, Editors, Essayists and Novelists
Pen [geology] Pennsylvanian
Pen. Peninsula; Penitentiary
pen. penal; penetrate; penetration; peninsula; peninsular
PEng Member of the Society of Professional Engineers; [Canada] (Registered) Professional Engineer
Penn. Pennsylvania
penol. penology
Pent. [Bible] Pentateuch; Pentecost

pent. pentagon
penthse penthouse (in accommodation advertisement)
PEO [USA] Philanthropic Educational Organization
PEP [radio] peak envelope power; personal equity plan (savings scheme); political and economic planning
PEPP [USA] Professional Engineers in Private Practice
PER price–earnings ratio; Professional and Executive Recruitment; Professional Employment Register
Per [astronomy] Perseus
Per. Persia; Persian
per. percentile; period; person
PERA Production Engineering Research Association of Great Britain
per an. *per annum* (Latin: yearly)
per ann. *per annum* (Latin: yearly)
P/E ratio price–earnings ratio
perc. [music] percussion
per con. [book-keeping] *per contra* (Latin: on the other side)
perd. [music] *perdendosi* (Italian: dying away)
perf. perfect; perfection; perforate; perforated; perforation; performance; performed (by); performer
perh. perhaps
peri. perigee
perig. perigee
perjy perjury
perk [short form] percolate; [short form] perquisite
PERL [computing] practical extraction and report language; [medicine] pupils equal and react(ive) to light
Perm pre-embossed rigid magnetic technology
perm [short form] permanent wave; [short form] permutation
perm. permanent; permission
PERME Propellants, Explosives and Rocket Motor Establishment
perp. perpendicular; perpetual
per pro. *per procurationem* (Latin: through the agency of)
Pers. Persia; Persian
pers. person; personal; personally; perspective
persp. perspective
PERT [commerce] performance evaluation and review technique; [computing] program evaluation and review technique; programme evaluation and review technique; project evaluation and review technique
pert. pertaining
Peruv. Peruvian
PES [computing] programmable electronic system
Pes. [currency] peseta
PESA [medicine] percutaneous epididymal sperm aspiration
PESC Public Expenditure Survey Committee
PESGB Petroleum Exploration Society of Great Britain
Pesh. Peshawar (Pakistan)
PEST political, environmental, social and technological; Pressure for Economic and Social Toryism
PET polyeth(yl)ene terephthalate (packaging plastic); [medicine] positron emission tomography (as in **PET scanner**); [taxation] potentially exempt transfer; [medicine] pre-eclamptic toxaemia
Pet. [Bible] Peter; (Gaius) Petronius (Roman satirist)
pet. petrol; petroleum; petrological; petrologist; petrology
PETA People for Ethical Treatment of Animals
Pet.E [USA] petroleum engineer
PETN pentaerythritol tetranitrate (explosive)
petn petition
PETP [chemistry] polyeth(yl)ene terephthalate (polyester)
petr. petrification; petrify; petrology
Petriburg. *Petriburgensis* (Latin: (Bishop) of Peterborough)
petro. petrochemical
petrochem. petrochemical
petrog. petrography
petrol. petrological; petrology
PETS [computing] posting and enquiry terminal system
P/Ex part exchange (in advertisement)
p.ex. *par exemple* (French: for example, e.g.)
PF [vehicle registration] Guildford; Pagan Federation; panchromatic film; Patriotic Front; phenol–formaldehyde (as in **PF resin**); [building] plain face; power

factor; Procurator Fiscal; [finance] public funding; pulverized fuel
Pf [currency] Pfennig (hundredth of Deutschmark)
pF picofarad (unit of electrical capacitance)
pf [music] piano(forte); proof
pf [music] *piano e forte* (Italian: softly and (then) loudly); [music] *più forte* (Italian: louder)
pf. perfect; [finance] preferred (stock)
p.f. pneumatic float; pro forma (invoice)
PFA Popular Flying Association; [USA] Private Fliers' Association; Professional Footballers' Association; pulverized fuel ash
P factor [psychology] preservation factor
PFB [building] preformed beam(s)
PFBR [nuclear technology] prototype fast breeder reactor
PFC polychlorinated fluorocarbon (synthetic resin); [US informal] poor foolish (or forlorn) civilian
Pfc [US military] Private first class
pfce performance
PFD personal flotation device; position fixing device
Pfd *Pfund* (German: pound)
pfd preferred
pfd sp. preferred spelling
PFF pathfinder force
pfg [currency] Pfennig (hundredth of Deutschmark)
PFLO Popular Front for the Liberation of Oman
PFLP Popular Front for the Liberation of Palestine
PFLT People's Front of Liberation Tigers (Sri Lankan separatist group)
PFM [telecommunications] pulse-frequency modulation
PFMA Pet Food Manufacturers Association
PFP Partnership for Peace (in NATO); personal financial planning; [South Africa] Progressive Federal Party
PFPUT Pension Fund Property Unit Trust
PFR [nuclear technology] prototype fast reactor
PFRT preliminary flight rating test
PFSA *pour faire ses adieux* (French: to say goodbye)
PFSF Parents for Safe Food
PFT [medicine] pulmonary function test
PFV *pour faire visite* (French: to make a call)
pfx [grammar] prefix
PG [vehicle registration] Guildford; [cinema] parental guidance (film classification); [Freemasonry] Past Grand; paying guest; postgraduate; Preacher-General; [US informal] pregnant; *prisonnier de guerre* (French: prisoner of war); Procurator-General; [pharmacology] prostaglandin
Pg [geology] Palaeocene
Pg. Portugal; Portuguese
pg. page
.pg Papua New Guinea (in Internet address)
p.g. pay group; paying guest; *persona grata* (Latin: acceptable person); proof gallon (of alcohol); proving ground
PGA [electronics] pin grid array; Power Generation Association; Prison Governors' Association; Professional Golfers' Association; [computing] programmable gate array; [biochemistry] pteroylglutamic acid (folic acid)
p.g.c. [navigation] per gyrocompass
PGCE Postgraduate Certificate of Education
PGCert Postgraduate Certificate
PGD [Freemasonry] Past Grand Deacon
PGDip Postgraduate Diploma
PgDn [computing] page down (key)
PGDRS psychogeriatric dependency rating scale
PGF [medicine] polypeptide growth factor
PGG Professional Gardeners' Guild
PGJD [Freemasonry] Past Grand Junior Deacon
PGL [medicine] persistent generalized lymphadenopathy (stage of Aids); [Freemasonry] Provincial Grand Lodge
PGM [Freemasonry] Past Grand Master; precision-guided missile (or munition)
pgn pigeon
PGP [computing] pretty good privacy
PGR [cinema] parental guidance recommended (film classification in Australia); population growth rate; [psychology] psychogalvanic response
PGSD [Freemasonry] Past Grand Senior Deacon
p.g.t. per gross ton

PgUp [computing] page up (key)
PH [vehicle registration] Guildford; [civil aircraft marking] Netherlands; [UK postcode] Perth; petroleum hydrocarbon; [fishing port] Plymouth; previous (medical) history; public health; public house (on map); [medicine] pulmonary hypertension; Purple Heart (US military decoration)
Ph [geology] Phanerozoic
Ph. Philosophy (in academic degrees)
pH [chemistry] potential of hydrogen ions (measure of acidity or alkalinity)
ph phot (unit of illumination)
ph. phase; philosopher; philosophy; phone
.ph Philippines (in Internet address)
p.h. [engineering] precipitation hardening
PHA [immunology] phytohaemagglutinin; Public Health Act; [USA] Public Housing Administration; [USA] public housing authority
PHAB Physically Handicapped and Able Bodied
phal. phalanx
phar. pharmaceutical; pharmacist; pharmacology; pharmacopoeia; pharmacy
PharB Bachelor of Pharmacy (from Latin *Pharmaciae Baccalaureus*)
PharD Doctor of Pharmacy (from Latin *Pharmaciae Doctor*)
PharM Master of Pharmacy (from Latin *Pharmaciae Magister*)
pharm. pharmaceutical; pharmacist; pharmacology; pharmacopoeia; pharmacy
pharmacol. pharmacological; pharmacology
PharmB Bachelor of Pharmacy (from Latin *Pharmaciae Baccalaureus*)
pharm. chem. pharmaceutical chemistry
PharmD Doctor of Pharmacy (from Latin *Pharmaciae Doctor*)
PharmM Master of Pharmacy (from Latin *Pharmaciae Magister*)
PhB Bachelor of Philosophy (from Latin *Philosophiae Baccalaureus*)
ph. brz. phosphor bronze
PHC pharmaceutical chemist; primary health care
PHCA Private Hire Car Association
PHD Doctor of Public Health
PhD Doctor of Philosophy (from Latin *Philosophiae Doctor*)
PhDEd Doctor of Philosophy in Education
PHE public health engineer
Phe [astronomy] Phoenix
PhG [USA] Graduate in Pharmacy
PHI permanent health insurance; public health inspector
PHIBLANT [US navy] Amphibious Forces, Atlantic
PHIBPAC [US navy] Amphibious Forces, Pacific
PHIGS [computing] programmers' hierarchical interactive graphics standard
Phil. Philadelphia; Philharmonic; [Bible] Philippians; Philippines
phil. philological; philology; philosopher; philosophical; philosophy
Phila. Philadelphia
Philem. [Bible] Philemon
Phil. I Philippine Islands
Phil. Is. Philippine Islands
philol. philological; philology
philos. philosopher; philosophical; philosophy
Phil. Soc. Philharmonic Society
Phil. Trans. *Philosophical Transactions of the Royal Society of London*
PhL Licentiate in Philosophy (from Latin *Philosophiae Licentiatus*)
PHLS Public Health Laboratory Service
PHLSB Public Health Laboratory Service Board
PhM Master of Philosophy (from Latin *Philosophiae Magister*)
PHN public health nurse
Phoen. Phoenician; Phoenix
phon. phonetic; phonetically; phonetics; phonological; phonology
phone [short form] telephone
phonet. phonetic; phonetically; phonetics
phonog. phonography
phonol. phonological; phonology
phot. photograph; photographer; photographic; photography
photog. photograph; photographer; photographic; photography
photom. photometric(al); photometry
php pounds per horsepower; pump horsepower
PHR [engineering] power-to-heat ratio
phr. phrase; phraseology
phren. phrenological; phrenology

phrenol. phrenological; phrenology
PHRG Parliamentary Human Rights Group
PHS [USA] Public Health Service
PHSA Provincial Hospital Services Association
PHTS [USA] Psychiatric Home Treatment Service
PHWR [nuclear technology] pressurized heavy-water reactor
phys. physical; physically; physician; physicist; physics; physiological; physiology
phys. ed. physical education
physio [short form] physiotherapy
physiog. physiognomy; physiography
physiol. physiological; physiologist; physiology
phys. sc. physical science
PI [medicine] parainfluenza virus; Pasteur Institute; [mathematics] path integral; per inquiry; [US law] personal injury; petrol-injected; *Pharmacopoeia Internationalis* (Latin: International Pharmacopoeia); Philippine Islands; [civil aircraft marking] (Republic of the) Philippines; photographic interpretation; photographic interpreter; [US informal] pimp; [USA] principal investigator; Privacy International; private investigator; [accounting] profitability index; [computing] programmed instruction
p.i. [insurance] professional indemnity
PIA Pakistan International Airlines Corporation; [computing] peripheral interface adapter; Personal Investment Authority
PIAC Petroleum Industry Advisory Council
piang. [music] *piangendo* (Italian: plaintively)
pianiss. [music] *pianissimo* (Italian: very softly)
piano [short form] pianoforte
PIARC Permanent International Association of Road Congresses
PIAT [military] projector infantry antitank (weapon)
PIB Petroleum Information Bureau; Prices and Incomes Board (replaced by NBPI)
PIBOR [finance] Paris Inter-Bank Offered Rate
PIBS permanent interest-bearing share
PIC [computing] picture format; Poultry Industry Conference; [computing] problem isolation code; product of incomplete combustion; [computing] programmable interrupt controller
Pic [astronomy] Pictor
pic [short form] picture
pic. [music] piccolo; pictorial; picture
PICC Provisional International Computation Centre
PICS [computing] platform for Internet content selection
pict. pictorial; picture
PICUTPC Permanent and International Committee of Underground Town Planning and Construction
PICV Permanent International Commission of Viticulture
PID [medicine] pelvic inflammatory disease; [computing] personal identification device; [medicine] prolapsed intervertebral disc (= slipped disc)
PIDE *Polícia Internacional e de Defesa do Estado* (Portuguese: International Police for the Defence of the State) (former state security system)
PIDS [medicine] primary immune deficiency syndrome
PIE Proto-Indo-European
PIF [computing] program information file
PIFA Packaging and Industrial Films Association
pigmt pigment
pigmtn pigmentation
PIH Paintings in Hospitals; [medicine] pregnancy-induced hypertension
PIK payment in kind
PIL [computing] paper interchange language; payment in lieu; Pest Infestation Laboratory
pil. [medicine] *pilula* (Latin: pill) (in prescriptions)
PILL [computing] programmed instruction language learning
PILOT [computing] programmed inquiry, learning or teaching
PIM [computing] personal information manager; [telecommunications] pulse-interval modulation
PIME *Pontificium Institutum pro Missionibus Externis* (Latin: Pontifical Institute for Foreign Missions)
PIMS profit impact of market strategy

PIN personal identification number
PINC property income certificate
P-in-C Priest-in-Charge
Pind. Pindar (ancient Greek poet)
PING [computing] Packet Internet Groper
PINS [USA] person(s) in need of supervision
pinx. *pinxit* (Latin: (he/she) painted it)
PIO [computing] parallel input/output; photographic interpretation officer; [US military] public information office; [US military] public information officer
PIPO [computing] parallel in, parallel out
pippy [informal] person inheriting parent's property
PIR passive infrared
PIRA Paper Industries Research Association; Provisional Irish Republican Army
PISO [computing] parallel in, serial out
PITB Petroleum Industry Training Board
PITCOM Parliamentary Information Technology Committee
PIX [computing] picture exchange format
pix [short form] pictures
pixel [computing] picture element
pizz. [music] *pizzicato* (Italian: plucked)
PJ [vehicle registration] Guildford; [civil aircraft marking] Netherlands Antilles; petajoule; Presiding Judge; Probate Judge; [informal] pyjama(s)
p.j. physical jerks; [informal] pyjama(s)
PK [vehicle registration] Guildford; [civil aircraft marking] Indonesia and West Irian; [international vehicle registration] Pakistan; personal knowledge; psychokinesis
pk pack; park; peak; peck (unit of dry measure)
pk. package
.pk Pakistan (in Internet address)
pkg packing; parking
pkg. package
pkge package
PKI *Partai Komunis Indonésia* (Bahasa Indonesian: Indonesian Communist Party)
PKP *Polskie Koleje Państwowe* (Polish: Polish State Railways)
pkt packet; pocket
PKTF Printing and Kindred Trades Federation
PKU [medicine] phenylketonuria
pkwy [USA] parkway
PL [vehicle registration] Guildford; [insurance] partial loss; [insurance] passenger liability; patrol leader (in Scouts or Guides); Paymaster Lieutenant; [fishing port] Peel; *Pharmacopoeia Londiniensis* (Latin: Pharmacopoeia of London); [shipping] Plimsoll line; [UK postcode] Plymouth; Poet Laureate; [international vehicle registration] Poland; position line; Primrose League; [law] product liability; product licence (on medicinal product); programmed learning; [computing] programming language; public law; public library
P/L [insurance] partial loss; [law] product liability
P-L [astronomy] period–luminosity
Pl. Place (in road name); Plate(s) (book illustration); *Platz* (German: Square) (in road name)
p/l profit and loss
pl. place; plain; plate; platoon; [grammar] plural; pole (unit of length)
.pl Poland (in Internet address)
PLA [China] People's Liberation Army; Port of London Authority; Private Libraries Association; [computing, electronics] programmable logic array; [computing, electronics] programmed logic array
Pla. Plaza
p.l.a. passengers' luggage in advance
PLAN People's Liberation Army of Namibia
plan. planet; planetarium
plas. plaster; plastic
plat. plateau; platform; platinum; platonic; platoon
platf. platform
PLATO [computing] programmed logic for automatic teaching operation
Plaut. (Titus Maccius) Plautus (Roman dramatist)
PLC Poor Law Commissioners; [marketing] product life cycle; [computing] programmable logic controller; public limited company
plc public limited company
PLCC [computing] plastic leadless chip carrier
PLCWTWU Power Loom Carpet Weavers' and Textile Workers' Union
plcy policy
PLD potentially lethal damage; [computing] programmable logic device

pld payload
Ple [geology] Pleistocene
pleb [short form] plebeian
Plen. Plenipotentiary
PLF Palestine Liberation Front; [medicine] (serum) placental fementin
plf plaintiff
plff plaintiff
PLG private/light goods (vehicle)
PLI *Partito Liberale Italiano* (Italian: Italian Liberal Party); President of the Landscape Institute
Pli [geology] Pliocene
PLJ [trademark] pure lemon juice
PLL [computing] phase-locked loop
PLM Paris–Lyons–Mediterranean (railway); [telecommunications] pulse-length modulation
PL/M [computing] Programming Language for Microcomputers
plmb. plumber; plumbing
plng planning
PLO Palestine Liberation Organization
PLP Parliamentary Labour Party; Progressive Labour Party (in Bermuda); Progressive Liberal Party (in Bahamas)
PLR public lending right
PLS [statistics] partial least-squares; [computing] programmable logic sequencer
Pls. Plates (book illustrations)
Pl. Sgt Platoon Sergeant
plsnt pleasant
PLSS [astronautics] personal life-support system; [astronautics] portable life-support system
plstc plastic
plstr plasterer
PLT Princeton Large Torus (nuclear reactor)
plt pilot
pltc. political
pltf plaintiff
PLU [informal] people like us
plu. [grammar] plural
PLUNA *Primeras Lineas Uruguayas de Navegación Aérea* (Uruguayan airline company)
plup. [grammar] pluperfect
plupf. [grammar] pluperfect
plur. [grammar] plural; plurality
Pluto pipe line under the ocean (for fuel in World War II)
Ply. Plymouth
plywd plywood
PL/Z [computing] Programming Language Zilog
PM [vehicle registration] Guildford; Pacific mail; parachute mine; [music] particular metre; Past Master (of fraternity); Paymaster; [music] peculiar metre; [telecommunications] phase modulation; *piae memoriae* (Latin: of pious memory); Pipe Major; police magistrate; *polícia militar* (Portuguese: military police); *polizia militare* (Italian: military police); Pope and Martyr; Postmaster; *post meridiem* (Latin: after noon); postmortem (examination); powder metallurgy; predictive maintenance; preventive maintenance; Prime Minister; product manager; [music] proper metre; Provost Marshal
Pm [chemical element] promethium
pm. premium
p.m. permanent magnet; *post meridiem* (Latin: after noon); postmortem (examination); premolar (tooth)
PMA Pakistan Medical Association; [dentistry] papillary, marginal, attached (gingivitis); [pharmacology] paramethoxyamphetamine (hallucinogen); personal military assistant; [chemistry] phenylmercuric acetate; [chemistry] polymethyl acrylate; [USA] Purchasing Management Association
PMAF [USA] Pharmaceutical Manufacturers' Association Foundation
PM&ATA Paint Manufacturers' and Allied Trades Association
PM&R physical medicine and rehabilitation
PMB Potato Marketing Board
PMBX [telecommunications] private manual branch exchange
PMC Personnel Management Centre; [building] plaster-moulded cornice
PMD [USA] Program for Management Development
PMDA Pianoforte Manufacturers' and Distributors' Association
PME [electronics] protective multiple earthing
PMF probable maximum flood; [physics] pulsating magnetic field
PMG *Pall Mall Gazette*; Paymaster-General; [electrical engineering] permanent-magnet generator;

Postmaster-General; Provost Marshal-General
PMH previous medical history
p.m.h. per man-hour
PMI Pensions Management Institute
pmk postmark
PML Prime Minister's list; [insurance] probable maximum loss
PMM platinum-metal minerals; [telecommunications] pulse-mode multiplex
PMMA polymethylmethacrylate (synthetic resin)
PMMS Plainsong and Medieval Music Society
PMN [medicine] polymorphonuclear
PMO principal medical officer
PMR Pacific missile range; [medicine] polymyalgia rheumatica
pmr paymaster
PMRAFNS Princess Mary's Royal Air Force Nursing Service
PMS [printing] Pantone Matching System; [medicine] pregnant mare's serum; [medicine] premenstrual syndrome; President of the Miniature Society; [computing] processor-memory-switch (notation); project management system
PMSG [medicine] pregnant mare's serum gonadotrophin
PMT [photography] photomechanical transfer; [US finance] post-market trading; [medicine] premenstrual tension; project management team
pmt payment
PMTS [commerce] predetermined motion-time standards
PMU Pontifical Missionary Unit
PMV predicted mean vote
PMX [telecommunications] private manual exchange
PN [vehicle registration] Brighton; Pakistan Navy; [medicine] parenteral nutrition; [engineering] performance number; [astronomy] planetary nebula; [medicine] postnatal; [physics] post-Newtonian; [fishing port] Preston; [commerce] promissory note; [computing] pseudonoise; psychoneurotic
P/N part number; [commerce] promissory note
p.n. percussion note; percussive note; please note; [commerce] promissory note; [physics] proton number
PNA Pakistan National Alliance; paranitroaniline (dye); Philippines News Agency; Psychiatric Nurses Association
Pna Panama
PNB Philippine National Bank
PNC Palestinian National Council; People's National Congress (in Guyana)
PND [medicine] postnatal depression
PNdB perceived noise decibel
pndg pending
PNEU Parents' National Education Union
pneu. pneumatic
pneum. pneumatic
PNG Papua New Guinea; [international vehicle registration] Papua New Guinea
p.n.g. *persona non grata* (Latin: unacceptable person)
PNI [medicine] psychoneuroimmunology
PNL Pacific Northwest Laboratory
pnl panel
PNLA Palestine National Liberation Army
PNLM Palestine National Liberation Movement
PNM People's National Movement (in Trinidad and Tobago)
PNO principal nursing officer
PNP *Partido Nuevo Progresista* (Spanish: New Progressive Party) (in Puerto Rico); [Jamaica] People's National Party
PnP [computing] plug and play
PNR [physics] prompt nuclear reaction
pnr pioneer
p.n.r. prior notice required
PNS [anatomy] parasympathetic nervous system
PNSB [microbiology] purple nonsulphur bacteria
Pnt. [USA] Pentagon
PNTO principal naval transport officer
pntr painter
PNV *Partido Nacional Vasco* (Spanish: Basque National Party)
pnxt *pinxit* (Latin: (he/she) painted it)
PNYA Port of New York Authority
Pnz. Penzance
PO parcels office; parole officer; *par ordre* (French: by order); Passport Office; Patent Office; personnel officer; petty officer; philharmonic orchestra; pilot officer; [UK postcode] Portsmouth; [vehicle registration] Portsmouth; postal order; post office; power-operated; power oscillator; Province of Ontario;

public office; public officer; Pyrénées-Orientales (French department)
Po [chemical element] polonium
p/o printout
p.o. part of; [medicine] *per os* (Latin: by mouth) (in prescriptions); postal order; previous order(s)
POA price on application (in advertisement); primary optical area (in graphic design); Prison Officers' Association
POAC Post Office Advisory Council
POB Post Office Box
PO Box Post Office Box
POC port of call; [chemistry] product of combustion
POD payment on delivery; pay on death; pay on delivery; *Pocket Oxford Dictionary*; port of debarkation; [USA] Post Office Department
POE port of embarkation; port of entry
POED Post Office Engineering Department
poet. poetic(al); poetry
POETS day [slang] piss off early tomorrow's Saturday (facetious name for Friday)
POEU Post Office Engineering Union
P of W Prince of Wales
POG passion fruit, orange and guava (juice)
POGO Polar Orbiting Geophysical Observatory
poi. poison; poisonous
POL Patent Office Library; petrol(eum), oil and lubricants; [computing] problem-oriented language
Pol. Poland; Polish
pol. polar; polarize; polarized; police; political; politician; politics
pol. ad. political adviser
pol. econ. political economy
pol. ind. pollen index
Polis Parliamentary On-Line Information Service
polit. political; politics
poll. pollution
pol. sci. political science
poly [short form] polytechnic
Poly. Polynesia; Polynesian; Polytechnic
Polyb. Polybius (ancient Greek historian)
Polyn. Polynesia; Polynesian
POM particulate organic matter; prescription-only medicine (or medication)
POMEF Political Office Middle East Force
PON [computing] passive optical network
PONI product of Northern Ireland
Ponsi [military slang] person of no strategical importance
pont. br. pontoon bridge
Ponti [military slang] person of no tactical importance
POO Post Office order
POOF [computing] peripheral on-line oriented function
POP plaster of Paris; [computing] point of presence; point of purchase; Post Office preferred (size of stationery); [computing] post office protocol; [photography] printing-out paper; [pharmacology] progestogen-only pill; proof of purchase
pop. popular; popularly; population
p.o.p. point of purchase
POPA Property Owners Protection Association
POPIN Population Information Network
POPL [computing] principles of programming languages
por. porosity; porous; portion; portrait
p.o.r. pay(able) on receipt; pay(able) on return; port of refuge
PORIS Post Office Radio Interference Station
porn [short form] pornography
Port. Portugal; Portuguese
port. portable; portrait; portraiture
POS [grammar] part of speech; point of sale; [medicine] polycystic ovary syndrome; Port of Spain (Trinidad); [computing] product of sums
pos. position; positive; possession; [grammar] possessive
POSAS Patent Office Search and Advisory Service
posn position
POSS Palomar Observatory Sky Survey; passive optical surveillance system; prototype optical surveillance system
poss. possession; [grammar] possessive; possible; possibly
POSSLQ [US informal] person of the opposite sex sharing living quarters
Possum patient-operated selector mechanism (phonetic spelling of initials)
POST Parliamentary Office of Science and

Technology; point-of-sale terminal; [computing] power-on self test
postgrad [short form] postgraduate
posth. posthumous; posthumously
posthum. posthumous; posthumously
pot. potash; potassium; potential; potentiometer
poul. poultry
POUM *Partido Obrero de Unificación Marxista* (Spanish: Workers' Party of Marxist Unity)
POUNC Post Ofice Users' National Council
POV point of view
p.o.v. point of view; privately owned vehicle
POW please oblige with; Prince of Wales; prisoner of war
POWAGOD Prince of Wales' Advisory Group on Disability
powd. powder
POY [textiles] partially oriented yarn
PP [civil aircraft marking] Brazil; [vehicle registration] Luton; [geology] Pacific plate; parcel post; parish priest; parliamentary papers; *Partido Popular* (Spanish: Popular Party); *Pastor Pastorum* (Latin: Shepherd of the Shepherds); Past President; *Pater Patriae* (Latin: Father of his Country); *Patres* (Latin: Fathers); [medicine] pellagra-preventive; permanent pass; petrol point; [chemistry] phenolphthalein (alkalinity test); pilot plant; [chemistry] polyprop(yl)ene; [grammar] prepositional phrase; present pupil
pp [music] *pianissimo* (Italian: very softly)
pp. pages
p.p. parcel post; [grammar] past participle; per person; *per procurationem* (Latin: through the agency of); planning permission (in property advertisement); play or pay; post(age) paid; [medicine] *post prandium* (Latin: after meals) (in prescriptions); prepaid; present position; privately printed
PPA Pakistan Press Association; *Parti Populaire Algérien* (French: Popular Party of Algeria); Periodical Publishers' Association; Pools Proprietors' Association; Pre-School Playgroups Association
PPARC Particle Physics and Astronomy Research Council
PPB paper, printing and binding; party political broadcast; planning-programming-budgeting (system); private posting box
ppb parts per billion
PPBAS planning-programming-budgeting-accounting system
PPBS planning-programming-budgeting system
PPC *Patres Conscripti* (Latin: Conscript Fathers) (members of Roman Senate); *pour prendre congé* (French: to take leave); Professional Purposes Committee; [medicine] progressive patient care; prospective parliamentary candidate; [USA] Public Power Corporation
PPCLI Princess Patricia's Canadian Light Infantry
PPCS [New Zealand] Primary Producers' Cooperation Society
PPD *Partido Popular Democrático* (Spanish: Popular Democratic Party) (in Puerto Rico); [medicine] purified protein derivative (of tuberculin)
ppd post(age) paid; prepaid
PPE personal protective equipment; philosophy, politics and economics (academic course)
PPF [US insurance] personal property floater
PPFA Planned Parenthood Federation of America
PPG Pacific proving grounds
PPH [USA] paid personal holidays; [medicine] postpartum haemorrhage
pph. pamphlet
PPI Pakistan Press International; [USA] patient package insert (instructions with prescribed medication); [radar] plan-position indicator; [insurance] policy proof of interest; [economics] producer price index
p.p.i. parcel post insured
PPITB Printing and Publishing Industry Training Board
PPK *Polizei Pistole Kriminal* (German: police criminal pistol)
PPL private pilot's licence
pple [grammar] participle
PPLO [microbiology] pleuropneumonia-like organism(s)
PPM [electronics] peak programme meter;

[telecommunications] pulse-position modulation
ppm pages per minute; parts per million
PPMA Produce Packaging and Marketing Association
PPN [computing] public packet network
PPO [US medicine] preferred-provider organization
PPP Pakistan People's Party; People's Progressive Party (in Gambia and Guyana); personal pension plan; [computing] point-to-point protocol; Private Patients Plan; psychology, philosophy and physiology (academic course); [economics] purchasing power parity
ppp [music] *pianississimo* (Italian: as softly as possible)
pppm per person per month
pppn per person per night
PPPS *post post postscriptum* (Latin: third postscript)
PPR printed paper rate (of postage)
ppr paper; proper
p.pr. [grammar] participle present
PPRA Past President of the Royal Academy
PPRBA Past President of the Royal Society of British Artists
PPRBS Past President of the Royal Society of British Sculptors
p.pro. *per procurationem* (Latin: through the agency of)
PPS Parliamentary Private Secretary; [medicine] pelvic pain syndrome; *post postscriptum* (Latin: second postscript); [Australia] prescribed payments system; Principal Private Secretary; *Proceedings of the Prehistoric Society*; purchasing power standard
PPT *Parti Progressiste Tchadien* (French: Chad Progressive Party); [electrical engineering] peak power transfer
ppt. [chemistry] precipitate
pptd [chemistry] precipitated
pptg [chemistry] precipitating
pptn [chemistry] precipitation
ppty property
PPU Peace Pledge Union; Primary Producers' Union
PQ parliamentary question; [Canada] *Parti Québecois* (French: Quebec Party); personality quotient; Province of Quebec
p.q. preceding question; previous question
PR [vehicle registration] Bournemouth; parliamentary report; [medicine] partial remission; partial response; *Partido Radical* (Spanish: Radical Party) (in Chile); *Parti Républicain* (French: Republican Party); [computing] pattern recognition; payroll; percentile rank; performance ratio; [law] personal representative; photographic reconnaissance; Pipe Rolls (former public records); plotting and radar; *Populus Romanus* (Latin: the Roman people); postal regulations; preliminary report; Pre-Raphaelite; press release; press representative; [UK postcode] Preston; [boxing] prize ring; production rate; profit rate; progress report; project report; [politics] proportional representation; public relations; Puerto Rican; Puerto Rico; purchase request
P/R payroll
Pr [chemical element] praseodymium
Pr. *Praça* (Portuguese: Square) (in road name); Prince; Protestant; Provençal
pr painter; pair; paper; per; power
pr. prayer; [US finance] preferred (stock); [grammar] present; pressure; price; priest; print; printed; printer; printing; [grammar] pronoun; proof; proper; prove; provincial
p.r. parcel receipt; [medicine] *per rectum* (Latin: by the rectum) (in prescriptions)
PRA [medicine] plasma renin activity; President of the Royal Academy; probabilistic risk analysis; probabilistic risk assessment; [USA] Public Roads Administration
prag. pragmatic; pragmatism
pram [short form] perambulator
PRB People's Republic of Bulgaria; Pre-Raphaelite Brotherhood
PRBS President of the Royal Society of British Sculptors
PRC People's Republic of China; [medicine] plasma renin concentration; [USA] Postal Rate Commission; *post Romam conditam* (Latin: after the foundation of Rome); [USA] Price Regulation Committee
PRCA President of the Royal Cambrian Academy; Public Relations Consultants' Association

prchst parachutist
PRCP President of the Royal College of Physicians
PRCS President of the Royal College of Surgeons (of England)
prcs process
prcst precast
PRE petroleum refining engineer; President of the Royal Society of Painter-Printmakers (formerly President of the Royal Society of Painter-Etchers and Engravers)
Preb. Prebend(ary)
Prec. Precentor
prec. preceding; precision
PRECIS preserved context index system
pred. [grammar] predicate; predicative; predicatively
predic. [grammar] predicate; predicative; predicatively
Pref. Prefect
pref. preface; prefatory; preferably; preference; preferred; [grammar] prefix
prefab [short form] prefabricated (building)
prehist. prehistoric(al); prehistory
prej. prejudice
prel. prelude
Prela *Prensa Latina* (Cuban news agency)
prelim. preliminary
prem. premature; premium
premed [short form] premedical (student); [short form] premedication
prems premises
PrEng [USA] Professional Engineer
prep [short form] preparation (for schoolwork); [short form] preparatory (school); [short form] prepare
prep. preparation; preparatory; [grammar] preposition
prepd prepared
prepg preparing
prepn preparation
PREPP Post-Registration Education and Practice Project (in nursing)
Pres. Presbyterian; President
pres. present; presentation; presidency; presidential; presumed; presumptive
Presb. Presbyterian
press. pressure
PRESTO [USA] program reporting and evaluation system for total operation
presv. preservation; preservative; preserve
pret. [grammar] preterite
prev. previous; previously
PRF Petroleum Research Fund; [electronics] pulse recurrence frequency; [electronics] pulse repetition frequency
prf proof
prfnl professional
prfr proofreader
PRHA President of the Royal Hibernian Academy
PRI [Mexico] *Partido Revolucionario Institucional* (Spanish: Institutional Revolutionary Party); *Partito Repubblicano Italiano* (Italian: Italian Republican Party); Penal Reform International; Plastics and Rubber Institute (became part of Institute of Materials); President of the Royal Institute of Painters in Water Colours; [computing] primary-rate ISDN
pri. primary; primate; primer; priority; private
PRIA President of the Royal Irish Academy
PRIAS President of the Royal Incorporation of Architects in Scotland
PRIBA President of the Royal Institute of British Architects
PRII Public Relations Institute of Ireland
prim. primary; primate; primer; primitive
primip. [obstetrics] primipara (woman who has given birth once)
Prin. Principal; Principality
prin. principal; principle
Princ. Principal; Principality
princ. principal; principle
print. printed; printer; printing
PRISA Public Relations Institute of South Africa
PRISM [USA] program reliability information system for management
prism. prismatic
priv. private; privative
PRM personal radiation monitor
prm premium
PRML [computing] partial-response maximum-likelihood
prn [medicine] *pro re nata* (Latin: when required) (in prescriptions)
PRO Public Record Office; public relations officer
Pr. O press officer
Pro. Provost

pro [short form] professional; [short form] prostitute
pro. procedure; proceed; procure; profession; professional; [finance] promissory (note)
pro-am [sports] professional–amateur
prob. probability; probable; probably; probate; probation; problem
prob. off. probation
Proc. Proceedings; Proctor
proc. procedure; proceedings; process; processed; processing
Proc. Roy. Soc. *Proceedings of the Royal Society*
prod. produce; produced; producer; product; production
Prof. Professor
prof. profession; professional
Prof. Eng. [USA] Professional Engineer
Pr. of Man. [Bible] Prayer of Manasseh (book of Apocrypha)
Prog. [politics] Progressive
prog [short form] programme
prog. prognosis; [computing] program; programme; progress; progressive
PROI President of the Royal Institute of Oil Painters
proj. project; projectile; projection; projector
prol. prologue
prole [short form] proletarian
PROLOG programming in logic (computer programming language)
PROM [computing] programmable read-only memory
prom [short form] promenade
prom. prominent; promontory; promote; promoter; promotion
pron. [grammar] pronominal; [grammar] pronoun; pronounce; pronounceable; pronounced; pronouncement; pronouncing; pronunciation
PRONED Promotion of Non-Executive Directors
pronunc. pronunciation
PROP Preservation of the Rights of Prisoners
prop [short form] propeller; [short form] property (in theatre)
prop. proper; properly; property; proportion; proportional; proposition; proprietary; proprietor
propl proportional
propn proportion
propr proprietor
props [short form] properties (in theatre)
PRORM Pay and Records Office, Royal Marines
PROS preventive maintenance, repair and operational services
pros. prosecution; prosodical; prosody; [advertising] prospectus rate
Pros. Atty [USA] prosecuting attorney
prosc. proscenium
prost. [medicine] prostate; prostitution
Prot. Protectorate; Protestant
pro tem. *pro tempore* (Latin: for the time being)
Prov. Provençal; Provence; [Bible] Proverbs; Province; Provost
prov. proverb; proverbial; proverbially; province; provincial; provision; provisional
Prov. GM [Freemasonry] Provincial Grand Master
prox. *proximo* (Latin: in the next (month)) (used in formal correspondence)
prox. acc. *proxime accessit* (Latin: (he/she) came nearest (to the winner)) (referring to runner-up in competition)
prox. luc. *proxima luce* (Latin: on the day before)
PRP performance-related pay; petrol refilling point; profit-related pay
pr.p. [grammar] present participle
pr. pr. *praeter propter* (Latin: about, nearly)
PRR [electronics] pulse repetition rate
PRS Performing Right Society Limited; President of the Royal Society; Protestant Reformation Society
PRs [currency] Pakistan rupee
prs pairs
PRSA President of the Royal Scottish Academy; Public Relations Society of America
prsd pressed
PRSE President of the Royal Society of Edinburgh
PRSH President of the Royal Society of Health
PRST please return some time
Pr.ST [USA] Prairie Standard Time
PRSW President of the Royal Scottish Water Colour Society

PRT [USA] personal rapid transit; petroleum revenue tax
PRTC Princess Royal Trust for Carers
prtg printing
PRU photographic reconnaissance unit(s) (in RAF)
PRUAA President of the Royal Ulster Academy of Arts
Prus. Prussia; Prussian
PRV *pour rendre visite* (French: to return a call); pressure-reducing valve
PRWA President of the Royal West of England Academy
PRWS President of the Royal Watercolour Society
PS [vehicle registration] Aberdeen; paddle steamer; Parliamentary Secretary; *Partido Socialista* (Portuguese: Socialist Party); *Parti Socialiste* (French: Socialist Party); passenger steamer; Pastel Society; penal servitude; Permanent Secretary; [computing] personal system; Pharmaceutical Society; Philological Society; [linguistics] phrase structure; Physical Society; [electronics] plasma switch; Police Sergeant; [chemistry] polystyrene; postscript; power steering (in car advertisement); press secretary; private secretary; Privy Seal; [theatre] prompt side; [biochemistry] protein synthesis; Provost Sergeant; *Pubblica Sicurezza* (Italian: police); [USA] public school; [Australia] public service
Ps. Psalm; [Bible] Psalms
ps picosecond
ps. pieces; pseudonym
p.s. particle size; pull switch
PSA Passenger Shipping Association; Petty Sessions Area; Photographic Society of America; pleasant Sunday afternoon; Political Studies Association of the United Kingdom; President of the Society of Antiquaries; [Australia] Prices Surveillance Authority; probabilistic safety analysis; probabilistic safety assessment; Property Services Agency; [medicine] prostatic specific antigen; [New Zealand] Public Service Association; Public Services Authority
PsA [astronomy] Piscis Austrinus
Psa. Psalm; [Bible] Psalms
PSAB Public Schools Appointments Bureau
PSAC [USA] President's Science Advisory Committee; Production Statistics Advisory Committee
PSAT [USA] Preliminary Scholastic Aptitude Test
PSB pistol, small-bore; [Japan] Postal Savings Bureau; Prayer Book Society; Premium Savings Bond
PSBA Public School Bursars' Association
PSBR public sector borrowing requirement
PSC [Belgium] *Parti Social Chrétien* (French: Christian Social Party); Pipe Smokers' Council; [meteorology] polar stratospheric clouds; Professional Services Committee; [USA] Public Service Commission
Psc [astronomy] Pisces
PSCD patrol service central depot
PSD *Partido Social Democrata* (Portuguese: Social Democratic Party); *Parti Social Démocrate* (French: Social Democratic Party) (in Madagascar); pay supply depot; [law] Petty Sessional Division; [physics] position-sensitive detector; [USA] prevention of significant deterioration
PSDI *Partito Socialista Democratico Italiano* (Italian: Italian Democratic Socialist Party)
PSDR public sector debt requirement
PSE Pacific Stock Exchange; pale soft exudate (in meat processing); Pidgin Sign English; [computing] programming support environment; [computing] project support environment; psychological stress evaluator (lie detector)
pseud. pseudonym
PSF [image technology] point spread function
psf pounds per square foot
PSG [linguistics] phrase-structure grammar
PSGB Pharmaceutical Society of Great Britain
PSHFA Public Servants Housing Finance Association
PSI *Partito Socialista Italiano* (Italian: Italian Socialist Party); [education] personalized system of instruction; Pharmaceutical Society of Ireland; Policy Studies Institute
psi pounds per square inch
psia pounds per square inch, absolute

psid pounds per square inch, differential
PSIF Prison Service Industries and Farms
psig pounds per square inch, gauge
PSIS Permanent Secretaries Commission on the Intelligence Services
PSIUP *Partito Socialista Italiano di Unità Proletaria* (Italian: Italian Socialist Party of Proletarian Unity)
PSK [telecommunications] phase shift keying
PSL Paymaster Sublieutenant; [USA] Primary Standards Laboratory; [economics] private-sector liquidity; public-sector loan(s)
PSL/PSA [computing] problem statement language/problem statement analyser
PSM product sales manager
PSMA President of the Society of Marine Artists
PSN [computing] packet-switching network; [computing] packet switch node; [computing] public switched network
PSNC Pacific Steam Navigation Company
PSO Personal Staff Officer; principal scientific officer
PSOE *Partido Socialista Obrero Español* (Spanish: Spanish Workers Socialist Party)
PSP *Pacifistisch Socialistische Partij* (Dutch: Pacifist Socialist Party); [medicine] phenolsulphonphthalein (in kidney function test)
PSPS Paddle Steamer Preservation Society
PSR [commerce] profit-sharing ratio
PSRAM [computing] pseudo static random-access memory
PSRO [USA] Professional Standards Review Organization
PSS [computing] packet switching service; Palomar Sky Survey; Partially Sighted Society; [medicine] physiological saline solution; postscripts; power-system stabilizer; Printing and Stationery Service; professional services section
Pss. Psalms
PSSC Personal Social Services Council
p.s.s.o. [knitting] pass slipped stitch(es) over
PST [USA, Canada] Pacific Standard Time
pstl postal
PSTN [telecommunications] public switched telephone network
PSU *Partito Socialista Unitario* (Italian: Unitary Socialist Party); police support unit; [computing] power supply unit; process support unit
p. surg. plastic surgery
PSV public service vehicle
PSW [computing] processor status word; [computing] program status word; psychiatric social worker
psych. psychiatric; psychiatry; psychic(al); psychological; psychologist; psychology
psychiat. psychiatric; psychiatry
psychoanal. psychoanalysis; psychoanalytic(al)
psychol. psychological; psychologist; psychology
PT [civil aircraft marking] Brazil; [vehicle registration] Newcastle upon Tyne; [USA] Pacific Time; [USA] patrol torpedo (as in **PT boat**); [insurance] *perte totale* (French: total loss); [physics] perturbation theory; [physics] phase transition; physical therapist; physical therapy; physical training; physiotherapist; physiotherapy; [fishing port] Port Talbot; postal telegraph; post town; preferential treatment; [medicine] previously treated; Public Trustee; pupil teacher; purchase tax
Pt [chemical element] platinum; Point (in place-names); Port (in place-names)
pt part; patient; payment; pint; point; port
pt. [grammar] preterite
.pt Portugal (in Internet address)
p.t. part time; [grammar] past tense; point of turn(ing); primary target; *pro tempore* (Latin: for the time being)
PTA Parent–Teacher Association; Passenger Transport Authority; [medicine] percutaneous transluminal angioplasty; Pet Traders' Association; Piano Tuners' Association; [medicine] plasma thromboplastin antecedent; [medicine] post-traumatic amnesia; preferential trade area; Printing Trades Alliance; [medicine] prior to admission
Pta [currency] peseta; Pretoria
ptbl. portable; potable (= drinkable)
PT boat [USA] patrol torpedo boat
PTBT partial test-ban treaty
PTC [medicine] percutaneous transhepatic

cholangiography; personnel transfer capsule (in diving); photographic type composition; [medicine] plasma thromboplastin component; primary training centre; Public Services, Tax and Commerce Union

Ptc [geology] Pleistocene

PTCA [medicine] percutaneous transluminal coronary angioplasty

PTD permanent total disability

ptd painted; printed

PTE Passenger Transport Executive; post-test examination

Pte Plate (book illustration); [military] Private; [commerce] private (equivalent of Ltd after company name in India and elsewhere)

pt ex. part exchange (in advertisement)

pt exch. part exchange (in advertisement)

PTFE polytetrafluoroeth(yl)ene

Ptg. Portugal; Portuguese

ptg painting; printing

PTH [biochemistry] parathyroid hormone; [USA] public teaching hospital

PTI physical training instructor; Press Trust of India; [computing] public tool interface

PTIA Pet Trade and Industry Association

PTM [telecommunications] pulse-time modulation

PTMA phosphotungstomolybdic acid (used in pigments)

PTN [informal] pay through the nose; public telephone network; public transport(ation) network

ptn partition; portion

ptnr partner

PTO [USA] Patent and Trademark Office; please turn over; [astronautics] power take-off; public telecommunications operator; Public Trustee Office

p.t.o. please turn over

ptp. [grammar] past participle

ptpg participating

pt/pt [horseracing] point-to-point

ptr porter (in property advertisement); printer

PTS Philatelic Traders' Society; pressurized thermal shock; printing technical school

Pts. Portsmouth

pts parts; payments; pints; points; ports

PTSD [medicine] post-traumatic stress disorder

pts/hr parts per hour

Ptsmth Portsmouth

PTT [medicine] partial thromboplastin time; Postal, Telegraph and Telephone Administration; *Postes, télécommunications et télédiffusion* (French post office and telephone service)

pt-tm part-time

PTU Plumbing Trades Union

PTUF Professional Tennis Umpires' Federation

PTV [USA] public television

p.t.w. per thousand words

Pty [commerce] proprietary (equivalent of Ltd after company name in Australia, South Africa and elsewhere)

pty party

PU [vehicle registration] Chelmsford; [medicine] passed urine; [medicine] peptic ulcer; pick-up; [chemistry] polyurethane; [computing] processing unit; public utility

Pu [chemical element] plutonium

p.u. paid up

pub [short form] public house

pub. public; publican; publication; publicity; publish; published; publisher; publishing

pubd published

pub. doc. public document

publ. public; publican; publication; publicity; publish; published; publisher; publishing

pubn publication

pubr publisher

pub. wks public works

PUC papers under consideration; pick-up car; [USA] Public Utilities Commission

PUD pick-up and deliver; pick-up and delivery; [USA] planned unit development (large condominium)

pud [short form] pudding

PUFA polyunsaturated fatty acids

pug. pugilist

PUHCA [USA] Public Utility Holding Company Act

pulv. [pharmacology] *pulvis* (Latin: powder)

p.u.m.s. permanently unfit for military service

pun. punish; punishment

punc. punctuation
punct. punctuation
Punj. Punjab
PUO [medicine] pyrexia (fever) of unknown origin
PUP People's United Party; [USA] Princeton University Press; [Northern Ireland] Progressive Unionist Party
Pup [astronomy] Puppis
pur. purchase; purchased; purchaser; purification; purified; purify; purity; purple; pursuit
purch. purchase; purchased; purchaser
purp. purple
PURV powered underwater research vehicle
PUS Parliamentary Undersecretary; Permanent Undersecretary
p.u.s. permanently unfit for service
PUVA [medicine] psoralen ultraviolet A (used to treat psoriasis)
PUWP Polish United Workers' Party
PV [vehicle registration] Ipswich; patrol vessel; *petite vitesse* (French: low speed (train)); [sports] pole vault; positive vetting; [microbiology] potato virus; power voltage; pressure vessel; pressure–volume; profit–volume
pv. [microbiology] pathovar
p.v. [medicine] *per vaginam* (Latin: by the vagina) (in prescriptions)
PVA polyvinyl acetate (synthetic resin)
PVC [computing] permanent virtual circuit; polyvinyl chloride
p.v.c. pigment volume concentration (in paint)
PVCu polyvinyl chloride unplasticized
PVD [medicine] peripheral vascular disease; physical vapour deposition
PVDA *Partij van de Arbeid* (Dutch: Labour Party)
PVF polyvinyl fluoride (synthetic resin)
PVFS [medicine] postviral fatigue syndrome
PVO principal veterinary officer
PVOA Passenger Vehicle Operators' Association
PVP polyvinyl pyrrolidone (synthetic resin)
PVR premature voluntary retirement
PVS [medicine] persistent vegetative state; [USA] post-Vietnam syndrome; [medicine] postviral (fatigue) syndrome
PVSM [India] Param Vishisht Seva Medal
PVT pressure, volume, temperature
Pvt. [military] Private
p.v.t. *par voie télégraphique* (French: by telegraph)
pvte private
PW [vehicle registration] Norwich; [fishing port] Padstow; policewoman; power windows (in car advertisement); prisoner of war; public works; [electronics] pulse width
p.w. per week
PWA [medicine] person with Aids; [USA] Public Works Administration
PWC [USA] personal watercraft; postwar credits
PWD Public Works Department
pwd powered
PWE Political Welfare Executive
PWG Permanent Working Group (of European Junior Hospital Doctors)
PWLB Public Works Loan Board
PWM [telecommunications] pulse-width modulation
PWO Prince of Wales's Own (regiment)
p.w.p. price when perfect
PWPS Pure Water Preservation Society
PWR [nuclear technology] pressurized-water reactor
pwr power
pwr sup. power supply
pwt pennyweight
PWV Pretoria-Witwatersrand-Vereeniging (former name of Gauteng province)
PX part exchange (in advertisement); physical examination; please exchange; [vehicle registration] Portsmouth; [USA] Post Exchange (army or navy retail store); [telecommunications] private exchange
pxt *pinxit* (Latin: (he/she) painted it)
PY [vehicle registration] Middlesbrough; [international vehicle registration] Paraguay
.py Paraguay (in Internet address)
PYB [accounting] preceding-year basis
PYO pick your own (fresh produce)
pyro. pyrotechnics
pyrotech. pyrotechnical; pyrotechnics
Pyx [astronomy] Pyxis
PZ [vehicle registration] Belfast; [fishing port] Penzance; [civil aircraft marking] Suriname

Pz [geology] Palaeozoic
PZI [medicine] protamine zinc insulin (used to treat diabetes)
PZS President of the Zoological Society
PZT [astronomy] photographic zenith tube

Q

Q [international vehicle registration] Qatar; quality; quantity; [nautical] quarantine; quarterly; Quartermaster; [advertising] quarter-page; Quarto (early Shakespearean text); [geology] Quaternary; Quebec; Queen('s); [chess] queen; Queensland; query; question; [currency] quetzal (used in Guatemala); queue; (Sir Arthur Thomas) Quiller-Couch (British writer)
Q [electrical engineering] quality factor; [physics] quantity of electricity (i.e. electric charge); [physics] quantity of heat; [physics] quantity of light; [electrical engineering] reactive power; [chemical engineering] throughput
q [physics] quark; quintal (= 100 lb or 100 kg); [meteorology] squall
q [physics] density of heat flow rate; [physics] electric charge
q. *quaere* (Latin: inquire); *quaque* (Latin: every); quart; quarter; quarterly; quarto; *quasi* (Latin: almost); queen; quench; query; question; quick; quire
8Q [civil aircraft marking] Maldives
9Q [civil aircraft marking] Democratic Republic of Congo (formerly Zaïre)
QA qualification approval; quality assurance; quarters allowance
Q/A qualification approval
.qa Qatar (in Internet address)
q.a. quick assembly
QAB Queen Anne's Bounty (in Church of England)
QADS quality-assurance data system
QAIMNS Queen Alexandra's Imperial Military Nursing Service
QALY quality-adjusted life year (used in assessment of treatment)
QAM [telecommunications] quadrature amplitude modulation
Q&A question and answer
Qantas Queensland and Northern Territory Aerial Service (Australian airline company)
QARANC Queen Alexandra's Royal Army Nursing Corps
QARNNS Queen Alexandra's Royal Naval Nursing Service
QB [USA, Canada] quarterback (in American and Canadian football); [law] Queen's Bench; [chess] queen's bishop
Qbc Quebec
QBD Queen's Bench Division
QBE [computing] query by example
QBI [informal] quite bloody impossible
QBO [meteorology] quasi-biennial oscillation
Q-boat query-boat (vessel of uncertain status, with concealed guns)
QBP [chess] queen's bishop's pawn
QC quality control; Quartermaster Corps; Queen's College; Queen's Consort; Queen's Counsel; [law] quit claim
QCD [physics] quantum chromodynamics
QCE quality-control engineering
QCH Queen Charlotte's Hospital
QC Is. Queen Charlotte Islands (Canada)
qck quick
QCR quality-control reliability
QCT quality-control technology; [medicine] quantitative compute(rize)d tomography
QCVSA Queen's Commendation for Valuable Service in the Air
q.d. [medicine] *quaque die* (Latin: every day) (in prescriptions); *quasi dicat* (Latin: as if one should say); *quasi dictum* (Latin: as if said); [medicine] *quater (in) die* (Latin: four times a day) (in prescriptions)
QDRI [USA] qualitative development requirement information
q.d.s. [medicine] *quater (in) die sumendus* (Latin: to be taken four times a day) (in prescriptions)
QE quantum electronics

q.e. *quod est* (Latin: which is)
QE2 Queen Elizabeth II (passenger ship)
QED [physics] quantum electrodynamics; *quod erat demonstrandum* (Latin: which was to be proved)
QEF *quod erat faciendum* (Latin: which was to be done)
QEH Queen Elizabeth Hall (London)
QEI *quod erat inveniendum* (Latin: which was to be found out)
QEO Queen Elizabeth's Own (regiment)
QER *Quarterly Economic Review*
QF [electronics] quality factor; quick-firing
QFA [computing] quick file access
QFD [commerce] quality function deployment; [physics] quantum flavour-dynamics
QFSM Queen's Fire Service Medal
QFT [physics] quantum field theory
QG Quartermaster-General; *quartiere generale* (Italian: headquarters); *quartier-général* (French: headquarters)
QGM Queen's Gallantry Medal
q.h. [medicine] *quaque hora* (Latin: every hour) (in prescriptions)
QHC Queen's Honorary Chaplain
QHDS Queen's Honorary Dental Surgeon
QHM Queen's Harbour Master
QHNS Queen's Honorary Nursing Sister
QHP Queen's Honorary Physician
QHS Queen's Honorary Surgeon
QI quartz–iodine (as in **QI lamp**)
QIC [computing] Quarter Inch (Cartridge Standards) Committee; [computing] quarter inch cartridge
q.i.d. [medicine] *quater in die* (Latin: four times a day) (in prescriptions)
QIP *quiescat in pace* (Latin: may he/she rest in peace)
QISAM [computing] queued indexed sequential access method
qk quick
QKt [chess] queen's knight
QKtP [chess] queen's knight's pawn
QL Queen's Lancers; [computing] query language
ql quarrel; quintal (= 100 lb or 100 kg)
q.l. [medicine] *quantum libet* (Latin: as much as you please) (in prescriptions)
Qld Queensland
QLF [commerce] quality loss function
q.lib. [medicine] *quantum libet* (Latin: as much as you please) (in prescriptions)
qlty quality
qly quarterly
QM [physics] quantum mechanics; [physics] quark model; Quartermaster; Queen's Messenger
qm. *quomodo* (Latin: by what means)
q.m. [medicine] *quaque mane* (Latin: every morning) (in prescriptions)
QMAAC Queen Mary's Army Auxiliary Corps
QMC Quartermaster Corps; Queen Mary College (London) (became part of QMW)
Q Mess. Queen's Messenger
QMG Quartermaster-General
QMGF Quartermaster-General to the Forces
QMR qualitative material requirement
Qmr Quartermaster
QMS Quartermaster-Sergeant
QMW Queen Mary and Westfield College (London)
QN [chess] queen's knight
Qn Queen
qn question; quotation
q.n. [medicine] *quaque nocte* (Latin: every night) (in prescriptions)
QNI Queen's Nursing Institute
QNP [chess] queen's knight's pawn
QNS quantity not sufficient
qnt quintet
qnty quantity
QO qualified in ordnance (in Royal Navy); qualified officer
QOCH Queen's Own Cameron Highlanders
QOOH Queen's Own Oxfordshire Hussars
QOR qualitative operational requirement
QP qualification pay; [chess] queen's pawn; [computing] query processing
q.p. [medicine] *quantum placet* (Latin: as much as seems good) (in prescriptions)
QPC Qatar Petroleum Company
q.pl. [medicine] *quantum placet* (Latin: as much as seems good) (in prescriptions)
QPM Queen's Police Medal
QPO [astronomy] quasi-periodic oscillation
QPR Queen's Park Rangers (football club)
QPS Quaker Peace and Service
Qq. Quartos (early Shakespearian texts)
qq. questions

qq.v. *quae vide* (Latin: which (items) see) (multiple cross-reference)
QR [currency] Qatari riyal; *Quarterly Review*; [chess] queen's rook; [marketing] quick response
qr quarter
qr. quarterly; quire
QRA [military] quick reaction alert (of aircraft)
QRIH Queen's Royal Irish Hussars
QRP [chess] queen's rook's pawn
QRR Queen's Royal Rifles
qrs quarters
QS quadraphonic-stereophonic (audio equipment); quantity surveyor; quarantine station; quarter sessions; Queen's Scholar; [building] quick sweep
q.s. [medicine] *quantum sufficit* (Latin: as much as will suffice) (in prescriptions); quarter section (of land)
QSAR quantitative structure–activity relationship
QSE qualified scientist and engineer
Q-ship query-ship (vessel of uncertain status, with concealed guns)
QSM [New Zealand] Queen's Service Medal
QSMR quantitative structure–metabolism relationship
QSO [astronomy] quasi-stellar object; [New Zealand] Queen's Service Order
QSS [astronomy] quasi-stellar source
QSTOL [aeronautics] quiet short take-off and landing
QSTS quadruple screw turbine ship
qt quart; quartet
qt. quantity
q.t. [informal] quiet (as in **on the q.t.**)
qtly quarterly
qto quarto
QTOL [aeronautics] quiet take-off and landing
qtr quarter
QTS Qualified Teacher Status
qty quantity
Qu. Queen
qu. quart; quarter; quarterly; queen; query; question
quad [short form] quadrangle; [short form] quadraphonic; [short form] quadruplet
quad. quadrant; quadrilateral; quadruple; quadruplicate
quadr. quadruplicate
quadrupl. quadruplicate
qual. qualification; qualified; qualitative; quality
qualgo quasi-autonomous local government organization
qualn qualification
quango quasi-autonomous national government organization; quasi-autonomous nongovernmental organization
quant. quantitative; quantity
quant. suff. [medicine] *quantum sufficit* (Latin: as much as will suffice) (in prescriptions)
quar. quarter; quarterly
quart. quarter; quarterly
quasar [astronomy] quasi-stellar object
quat. quaternary; [medicine] *quattuor* (Latin: four) (in prescriptions)
QUB Queen's University, Belfast
Que. Quebec
ques. question
questn. questionnaire
quin [short form] quintuplet
quint. quintuplicate
QUIP [computing] query interactive processor
quor. quorum
quot. quotation; quoted
quotid. [medicine] *quotidie* (Latin: daily)
q.v. [medicine] *quantum vis* (Latin: as much as you wish) (in prescriptions); *quod vide* (Latin: which see) (cross-reference)
QVR Queen Victoria Rifles
QWERTY standard keyboard layout (from first six letters on upper row)
QWL quality of working life
qy quay; query
qz quartz

R

R rabbi; [politics] Radical; [chemistry] radical (in formulae); radiology; radius; [USA] railroad; railway; [fishing port] Ramsgate; [currency] rand (used in South Africa); *rapido* (Italian: express train); [mathematics] ratio; [physics] Réaumur (temperature scale); *Recht* (German: law); [medicine] *recipe* (Latin: take) (in prescriptions); recommendation; rector; red; redactor; Regiment; *Regina* (Latin: Queen); registered; Regius (Professor); regular (clothing size); [navigation] relative; reliability; reply; report; Republic; Republican; reserve; [electrical engineering] resistance; [genetics] resistance; [chemistry] resonance effect; response (in liturgy); *Respublica* (Latin: Republic); [cinema] restricted (film classification in Australia and USA); *retarder* (French: slow down) (on clock or watch regulator); return (fare or ticket); reverse (in car); reward; *Rex* (Latin: King); [military] Rifles; right; river; road; roentgen (unit of electromagnetic radiation dose); Roman; Romania; Romanian; Rome; [chess] rook; rosary; [currency] rouble; route; Royal; *Rue* (French: Street); [sports] run(s); [currency] rupee; [theatre] stage right

® registered trademark

r [meteorology] rain; [music] ray (or re) (in tonic sol-fa); [biochemistry] ribonucleoside

r internal resistance (in electricity); [mathematics, physics] position vector; radius; [mathematics] radius vector; [ecology] rate of increase

r. radius; [USA] railroad; railway; rain; range; rare; ratio; rear; [commerce] received; [medicine] *recipe* (Latin: take) (in prescriptions); [printing] recto (right-hand page); red; replacing; reply; reserve; residence; resides; response; retired; right; rises (referring to the sun); river; road; rod (unit of length); [currency] rouble; [card games] rubber; ruled; [sports] run(s); [currency] rupee

4R [civil aircraft marking] Sri Lanka

5R [civil aircraft marking] Madagascar

8R [civil aircraft marking] Guyana

RA [international vehicle registration] (Republic of) Argentina; [vehicle registration] Nottingham; Racecourse Association; [meteorology] rain; Ramblers' Association; Rear-Admiral; reduction of area; Referees' Association (in football); [USA] Regular Army; *República Argentina* (Spanish: Argentine Republic); [USA] Resettlement Administration; [medicine] rheumatoid arthritis; [astronomy] right ascension; [medicine] right atrium; Road Association; Royal Academician; Royal Academy; Royal Artillery; Rural Action; [civil aircraft marking] Russia

R/A [finance] refer to acceptor (on bill of exchange); return to author

Ra [chemical element] radium

ra. radio

RAA Rabbinical Alliance of America; Regional Arts Association; Royal Academy of Arts; Royal Artillery Association; Royal Australian Artillery

RAAF Royal Australian Air Force; Royal Auxiliary Air Force

RAAFNS Royal Australian Air Force Nursing Service

RAAMC Royal Australian Army Medical Corps

RAANC Royal Australian Army Nursing Corps

Rab. Rabat (Morocco)

Rabb. Rabbinate; Rabbinic(al)

RABDF Royal Association of British Dairy Farmers

RABI Royal Agricultural Benevolent Institution

RAC Railway Association of Canada; Regional Advisory Committee (of TUC); Regional Advisory Council; Royal Aero Club (of the United Kingdom); Royal Agricultural College; Royal Armoured Corps; Royal Automobile Club

RACA Royal Automobile Club of Australia

RACE rapid automatic checkout equipment; Research and Development in

Advanced Communication Technologies for Europe
RACGP Royal Australian College of General Practitioners
RAChD Royal Army Chaplains' Department
RACI Royal Australian Chemical Institute
RACO Royal Australian College of Ophthalmologists
RACOG Royal Australian College of Obstetricians and Gynaecologists
RACP Royal Australasian College of Physicians
RACS Royal Arsenal Cooperative Society; Royal Australasian College of Surgeons
RAD radiation absorbed dose; [medicine] reflex anal dilation; Royal Academy of Dancing; Royal Albert Docks
Rad. [politics] Radical; Radnor(shire)
rad radian (unit of angle)
rad. radar; radiator; radical; radio; radiologist; radiology; radiotherapist; radiotherapy; radius; [mathematics, anatomy] radix
r.a.d. rapid automatic drill
RADA Royal Academy of Dramatic Art
RADAR Royal Association for Disability and Rehabilitation
radar radio detection and ranging
RADAS random access discrete address system
RADC Royal Army Dental Corps
RADCM radar countermeasure
raddol. [music] *raddolcendo* (Italian: becoming calmer)
RAdm Rear-Admiral
radmon radiological monitor(ing)
radn radiation
RAE Royal Aerospace Establishment (formerly Royal Aircraft Establishment); Royal Australian Engineers
r.a.e. radio astronomy explorer
RAEC Royal Army Educational Corps
RAeroC Royal Aero Club (of the United Kingdom)
RAeS Royal Aeronautical Society
RAF *Rote Armee Faktion* (German: Red Army Faction) (terrorist group); Royal Aircraft Factory; Royal Air Force
RAFA Royal Air Forces Association; Royal Australian Field Artillery
RAFBF Royal Air Force Benevolent Fund
RAFES Royal Air Force Educational Service
RAFG Royal Air Force Germany
RAFMS Royal Air Force Medical Services
RAFR Royal Air Force Regiment
RAFRO Royal Air Force Reserve of Officers
RAFSAA Royal Air Force Small Arms Association
RAFSC Royal Air Force Staff College; Royal Air Force Strike Command
RAFT [banking] revolving acceptance facility by transfer
RAFTC Royal Air Force Transport Command
RAFVR Royal Air Force Volunteer Reserve
r.a.g. river assault group
RAGA Royal Australian Garrison Artillery
RAH Royal Albert Hall
RAHS Royal Australian Historical Society
RAI *Radiotelevisione Italiana* (Italian broadcasting company, formerly *Radio Audizioni Italiane*); Royal Anthropological Institute; Royal Archaeological Institute
RAIA Royal Australian Institute of Architects
RAIC Royal Architectural Institute of Canada
RAID [computing] redundant array of independent (or inexpensive) disks
Raj. Rajasthan
RAJAR Radio Joint Audience Research
RAK random act of kindness
RAL Rutherford Appleton Laboratory (Harwell, Oxfordshire)
rall. [music] *rallentando* (Italian: slowing down)
RALS [aeronautics] remote augmented lift system
RAM [aeronautics] radar absorbing material; [computing] random-access memory; [USA] reverse-annuity mortgage; rocket-assisted motor; Royal Academy of Music; Royal Air Maroc (Moroccan airline company); [Freemasonry] Royal Arch Masons
r.a.m. relative atomic mass
RAMAC Radio Marine Associated Companies
ramb. rambler (rose)
RAMC Royal Army Medical Corps
RAN request for authority to negotiate; Royal Australian Navy
RANC Royal Australian Naval College

RANCOM random communication satellite
R&A Royal and Ancient (Golf Club) (St Andrews)
R&B rhythm and blues; ring and ball (game)
R&CC [insurance] riot and civil commotion
R&D research and development
R&E research and engineering
R&I *Regina et Imperatrix* (Latin: Queen and Empress); *Rex et Imperator* (Latin: King and Emperor)
R&M reliability and marketing
r&m reports and memoranda
R&R [medicine] rescue and resuscitation; rest and recreation; rock and roll
R&T research and technology
RANN [USA] Research Applied to National Needs
RANR Royal Australian Naval Reserve
RANVR Royal Australian Naval Volunteer Reserve
RAOB Royal Antediluvian Order of Buffaloes
RAOC Royal Army Ordnance Corps
RAOU Royal Australian Ornithologists' Union
RAP ready-assembled price; Regimental Aid Post; remedial action plan (or programme); [medicine] right atrial pressure
rap. rapid
RAPC Royal Army Pay Corps
RAPID Register for the Ascertainment and Prevention of Inherited Diseases
RAPRA Rubber and Plastics Research Association of Great Britain
RAR Royal Australian Regiment
RARDE Royal Armament Research and Development Establishment
RARE [computing] *Réseaux associés pour la recherche européenne* (French: Associated Networks for European Research)
RARO Regular Army Reserve of Officers
RAS [aeronautics] rectified air speed; Royal Agricultural Society; Royal Asiatic Society; Royal Astronomical Society
RASC Royal Army Service Corps (former name of RCT)
RASE Royal Agricultural Society of England
raser radio-frequency amplification by stimulated emission of radiation
RAT rocket-assisted torpedo
rat. rateable; rating; ration
RATAN radar and television aid to navigation
RATO rocket-assisted take-off
RATP *Régie autonome des transports parisiens* (French: Paris transport authority)
RAuxAF Royal Auxiliary Air Force
RAVC Royal Army Veterinary Corps
RAWC Radioactive Waste Coordinating Committee
RAX [telecommunications] rural automatic exchange
RB [international vehicle registration] (Republic of) Botswana; [vehicle registration] Nottingham; [astronomy] radiation belt; radiation burn; reconnaissance bomber (aircraft); representative body; *República Boliviana* (Spanish: Republic of Bolivia); review body; Rifle Brigade; *Ritzaus Bureau* (Danish news agency); Royal Ballet (formerly SWRB)
Rb [chemical element] rubidium
r.b. [sports] right back; rubber band
RBA Retail Book, Stationery and Allied Trades Employees Association; Royal Society of British Artists
RBAF Royal Belgian Air Force
RBC [medicine] red blood cell; [medicine] red blood (cell) count; Royal British Colonial Society of Artists
RBE relative biological effectiveness (of radiation)
r/belt rear seat belt (in car advertisement)
RBerks Royal Berkshire Regiment
RBG Royal Botanic Gardens (Kew)
RBI resource-based industry; right back inside (of skate); [baseball] run(s) batted in
r.b.i. require better information; [baseball] run(s) batted in
RBK&C Royal Borough of Kensington and Chelsea
RBL Royal British Legion
rbl. [currency] rouble
RBN Registry of Business Names
RBn radio beacon
RBNA Royal British Nurses' Association
RBO right back outside (of skate)
RBP [biochemistry] retinol-binding protein

RBS [medicine] radionuclide bone scintigraphy; Rare Breeds Society; Royal Botanical Society; Royal Society of British Sculptors
RBSA Royal Birmingham Society of Artists
RBT random breath-testing; [computing] remote batch terminal
rbt roundabout
RBY Royal Bucks Yeomanry
RC [vehicle registration] Nottingham; [cycling] racing club; radio/cassette (player); [medicine] red (blood) cell; [medicine] red corpuscle; Red Cross; Reformed Church; reinforced concrete; remote control; reproductive capacity; [USA] Republican Convention; research centre; reserve corps; [photography] resin-coated; [electronics] resistance-capacitance; [electronics] resistor-capacitor; [telecommunications] reversed charge; rifle club; [cycling] road club; Roman Catholic; [building] rough cutting; Royal College; Royal Commission; [international vehicle registration] Taiwan (Republic of China)
R/C recredited
r.c. radio code; radio coding; reinforced concrete; release clause; reverse course; right centre; rotary combustion; rubber-cushioned
RCA [international vehicle registration] Central African Republic (from French *République Centrafricaine*); Rabbinical Council of America; Racecourse Association; Radio Corporation of America; [medicine] right coronary artery; Royal Cambrian Academy; Royal Canadian Academy of Arts; Royal College of Art; Royal Company of Archers; Rural Crafts Association
RCAC Royal Canadian Armoured Corps
RCAF Royal Canadian Air Force
RCamA Royal Cambrian Academy
RCAMC Royal Canadian Army Medical Corps
RCASC Royal Canadian Army Service Corps
RCB [international vehicle registration] (Republic of) Congo (from former name Congo-Brazzaville); [theatre] right centre back (of stage)
RCC recovery control centre; [medicine] renal cell carcinoma; rescue coordination centre; Roman Catholic Chaplain; Roman Catholic Church; Rural Community Council
RCCh Roman Catholic Church
RCD *Rassemblement Constitutionnel Démocratique* (French: Democratic Constitutional Rally) (Tunisian political party); Regional Cooperation for Development (association of Asian countries); [electronics] residual current device
rcd received
RCDC Royal Canadian Dental Corps
RCDS Royal College of Defence Studies
RCE [engineering] rotary combustion engine
RCF Redundant Churches Fund
r.c.f. relative centrifugal force
RCFCA Royal Canadian Flying Clubs' Association
RCGA Royal Canadian Golf Association
RCGP Royal College of General Practitioners
RCGS Royal Canadian Geographical Society
RCH [international vehicle registration] (Republic of) Chile; railway clearing house
RCHA Royal Canadian Horse Artillery
RCHM Royal Commission on Historical Manuscripts; Royal Commission on Historical Monuments
RCI Radiochemical Inspectorate; Royal Canadian Institute
r.c.i. radar coverage indicator
RCJ Royal Courts of Justice
RCL Royal Canadian Legion; ruling case law
RCM radar countermeasures; radio countermeasures; [medicine] radiological contrast medium; regimental court martial; Royal College of Midwives; Royal College of Music
RCMP Royal Canadian Mounted Police (formerly RNWMP)
RCN Royal Canadian Navy; Royal College of Nursing
RCNC Royal Corps of Naval Constructors
RCNR Royal Canadian Naval Reserve
RCNT Registered Clinical Nurse Teacher
RCNVR Royal Canadian Naval Volunteer Reserve
RCO Royal College of Organists

RCOG Royal College of Obstetricians and Gynaecologists
RCP Revolutionary Communist Party; Royal College of Physicians; Royal College of Preceptors
RCPath Royal College of Pathologists
RCPB Revolutionary Communist Party of Great Britain
RCPE Royal College of Physicians of Edinburgh
RCPEd Royal College of Physicians of Edinburgh
RCPI Royal College of Physicians of Ireland
RCPSG Royal College of Physicians and Surgeons of Glasgow
RCPsych Royal College of Psychiatrists
rcpt receipt
RCR Royal College of Radiologists
RCRP Rape Counselling and Research Project
RCS reaction control system (in spacecraft); [nuclear technology] reactor cooling system; remote control system; Royal Choral Society; Royal College of Science; Royal College of Surgeons (of England); Royal Commonwealth Society; Royal Corps of Signals; Royal Counties Show
RCSB Royal Commonwealth Society for the Blind
RCSC Radio Components Standardization Committee
RCSE Royal College of Surgeons of Edinburgh
RCSEd Royal College of Surgeons of Edinburgh
RCSI Royal College of Surgeons in Ireland
RCSLT Royal College of Speech and Language Therapists
RCSS random communications satellite system
RCT randomized clinical trial; regimental combat team; Registered Clinical Teacher; remote control transmitter; Royal Corps of Transport (formerly RASC)
rct receipt; recruit
RCU remote control unit; road-construction unit; rocket-countermeasure unit
rcvr receiver
RCVS Royal College of Veterinary Surgeons
RD radiation dose; [metallurgy] radiation-induced defect; [vehicle registration] Reading; *récemment dégorgé* (French: recently disgorged) (in winemaking); [banking] refer to drawer (on cheque); [USA] Registered Dietician; *República Dominicana* (Spanish: Dominican Republic); research department; (Royal Naval and Royal Marine Forces) Reserve Decoration; Royal Dragoons; Rural Dean; [New Zealand] Rural Delivery
R/D [banking] refer to drawer (on cheque)
Rd Road
rd rendered; road; rod (unit of length); round; rutherford (unit of radioactivity)
r.d. [physics] relative density; *rive droite* (French: right bank); [shipping] running days
RDA *Rassemblement Démocratique Africain* (French: African Democratic Rally) (political party); recommended daily allowance (of nutrients etc.); recommended dietary allowance; Retail Distributors' Association; Riding for the Disabled Association; Royal Defence Academy; Royal Docks Association
RD&D research, development and demonstration
RD&E research, development and engineering
RDAT rotary-head digital audio tape
RDB [military] Research and Development Board; Royal Danish Ballet; Rural Development Board
RDBMS [computing] relational database management system
RDC Royal Defence Corps; [insurance] running-down clause; Rural Development Commission; rural district council
RDCA Rural District Councils' Association
RDD [US marketing] random digital dialing
r.d.d. required delivery date
RDE Research and Development Establishment; [chemistry] rotating-disc electrode
RDF radio direction finder (or finding); [US military] Rapid Deployment Force; refuse-derived fuel; Royal Dublin Fusiliers
RDI Royal Designer for Industry
RDP [South Africa] Reconstruction and Development Programme
RDPL [civil aircraft marking] Laos

rdr radar
RDS radio data system (for automatic tuning); Research Defence Society; [medicine] respiratory distress syndrome; Royal Drawing Society; Royal Dublin Society
rds. [shipping] roadstead
RDT&E research, development, testing and engineering
RDV rendezvous
RDX Research Department Explosive (= cyclonite)
RDY Royal Dockyard
rdy ready
RDZ radiation danger zone
RE [chemistry] rare earth; [USA] real estate; Reformed Episcopal; religious education; renewable energy; revised edition; Right Excellent; Royal Engineers; Royal Exchange; Royal Society of Painter-Printmakers (formerly Royal Society of Painter-Etchers and Engravers); [vehicle registration] Stoke-on-Trent
R/E [USA] real estate
Re [chemical element] rhenium; [currency] rupee
r.e. right eye
REA Radar and Electronics Association; request for engineer's authorization; Rubber Export Association; [USA] Rural Electrification Administration
REAC Regional Education Advisory Committee (of TUC)
reac. reactor
REACH Retired Executives' Action Clearing House
REACT research education and aid for children with potentially terminal illness
Rear-Adm Rear-Admiral
reasm. reassemble
Réau. Réaumur (temperature scale)
REB regional examining body
REC Railway Executive Committee; regional electricity company
rec [short form] recreation ground
rec. receipt; receive; received; [medicine] *recens* (Latin: fresh) (in prescriptions); recent; reception; reception room (in property advertisement); recipe; recognized; recommended; record; recorded; recorder; recording; recreation
recap [short form] recapitulate; [short form] recapitulation
recce [short form] reconnaissance; [short form] reconnoitre
recd received
recep. reception; reception room (in property advertisement)
recept. reception; reception room (in property advertisement)
RECHAR *Reconversion de bassins charbonniers* (French: Reconversion of Coal Fields) (EU funding programme)
recip. reciprocal; reciprocity
recirc. recirculate
recit. recitation; [music] recitative
reclam. reclamation
recm. recommend
recmd recommended
RECMF Radio and Electronic Component Manufacturers' Federation
recog. recognition; recognize
recom. recommend
recon. reconciliation; recondition; reconditioned; reconnaissance; reconnoitre; reconsign; reconsignment; reconstruct; reconstruction
recond. recondition; reconditioned
REconS Royal Economic Society
reconst. reconstruct; reconstruction
recpt receipt; reception; reception room (in property advertisement)
recr receiver
rec. sec. recording secretary
Rect. Rector; Rectory
rect receipt
rect. rectangle; rectangular; [medicine] *rectificatus* (Latin: rectified) (in prescriptions); rectify
red. [finance] redeemable; reduce; reduced; reduction
redox [chemistry] reduction–oxidation
redup. reduplicate; reduplication; reduplicative
redupl. reduplicate; reduplication; reduplicative
REE [chemistry] rare-earth element
Ref. Reformation; Reformatory; Reformed
ref [short form] referee
ref. refer; referee; reference; referred; refined; refining; reform; reformation; reformed; reformer; refrigerated ship; refund; refunding; refuse
refash. refashion; refashioned

Ref. Ch. Reformed Church
refd referred; refund
refl. reflect; reflection; reflective; reflex; [grammar] reflexive
Reform. Reformatory
Ref. Pres. Reformed Presbyterian
refrig. refrigerate; refrigerated; refrigeration; refrigerator
Ref. Sp. Reformed Spelling
refurb. refurbished
Reg. Regent; *Regina* (Latin: Queen); Regius (Professor)
reg. regiment; region; regional; register; registered; registrar; registration; registry; regular; regularly; regulation; regulator
REGAL [aeronautics] range and elevation guidance for approach and landing
regd registered
Reg-Gen Registrar-General
Reg. Prof. Regius Professor
regr registrar
Regt Regent; Regiment
regtl regimental
Reg. TM registered trademark
REHAB [medicine] Rehabilitation Evaluation of Hall and Baker
rehab [short form] rehabilitation
reinf. reinforce; reinforced
reinfmt reinforcement
REIT [USA] real-estate investment trust
reit. [printing] reiteration
rej. reject
REL recommended exposure limit (to radiation)
rel. relate; related; relating; relation; relative; relatively; release; released; relic; [bibliography] *relié* (French: bound); religion; religious; *reliquiae* (Latin: relics)
relig. religion; religious
rel. pron. [grammar] relative pronoun
REM [physiology] rapid eye movement (as in **REM sleep**); [chemistry] rare-earth metal
rem roentgen equivalent man (former unit of radioactivity)
rem. remainder; remains; remark(s); remission; remit; remittance
REMC Radio and Electronics Measurements Committee
REME Royal Electrical and Mechanical Engineers
remitt. remittance
Ren. Renaissance
Renf. Renfrew(shire)
RENFE *Red Nacional de Ferrocarriles Españoles* (Spanish: Spanish National Railway Network)
REngDes Registered Engineering Designer
renv. renovate; renovation
REO regional education officer
REP [USA] Recovery and Evacuation Program
Rep. Repertory (Theatre); [USA] Representative; Republic; Republican
rep [short form] repertory (theatre); [short form] representative
rep. repair; repeat; [theatre] repertory (company); [medicine] *repetatur* (Latin: let it be repeated) (in prescriptions); repetition; report; reported; reporter; represent; representative; representing; reprint
REPC Regional Economic Planning Council
repl. replace; replaced; replacement; replica; replicate
repo. repossess; repossession
repr. represent; representative; represented; representing; reprint; reprinted; reprinting
repres. represent; representative; represented; representing
repro. reproduced; reproduction
rept receipt; report
Repub. Republic; Republican
repub. republish; republished
req. request; require; required; requirement; requisition
reqd required
reqn requisition
reqs requires
RER renewable energy resource(s)
RERO Royal Engineers Reserve of Officers
RES renewable energy source; renewable energy system; [physiology] reticuloendothelial system; Royal Entomological Society of London
res. rescue; research; researcher; reservation; reserve; reserved; reservoir; reside; residence; resident; residential; resides; resigned; resolution
resgnd resigned
resid. residential; residual
resig. resignation

resp. respective; respectively; respiration; respondent; response; responsibility
res. phys. resident physician
res. sec. resident secretary
Rest. Restoration (historical period)
rest. restaurant; restoration; restored (in property advertisement); restraint; restrict; restricted; restriction
RET [computing] resolution enhancement technology
Ret [astronomy] Reticulum
ret. retain; retained; retainer; retire; retired; return; returned
retd retained; retired; returned
R et I *Regina et Imperatrix* (Latin: Queen and Empress); *Rex et Imperator* (Latin: King and Emperor)
retnr retainer
RETRA Radio, Electrical and Television Retailers' Association
REV [astronautics] re-entry vehicle
Rev. [Bible] Revelation; Revenue; Reverend; Review; Revised; Revolution
rev [short form] revolution
rev. revenue; reverse; reversed; review; reviewed; reviewer; revise; revised; revision; revolution; revolve; revolver; revolving
rev. ac. revenue account(s)
Revd Reverend
rev. ed. revised edition
Rev. Stat. Revised Statutes
Rev. Ver. Revised Version (of Bible)
rew. reward; rewind; rewired; rewiring
REXX [computing] restructured extended executor
RF radio frequency; reconnaissance fighter (aircraft); [military] regular forces; [genetics] release factor; [cartography] representative fraction; *République française* (French: French Republic); research foundation; [military] reserve force; Rockefeller Foundation; Royal Fusiliers; rugby football; [currency] Rwanda franc; [vehicle registration] Stoke-on-Trent
Rf [currency] rufiyaa (used in Maldives); [chemical element] rutherfordium
rf reef; [music] *rinforzando* (Italian: reinforcing)
r.f. radio frequency; range finder; rapid fire; [telecommunications] reception fair; relative flow; [medicine] rheumatic fever; [baseball] right field; [baseball] right fielder; rough finish (of paper)
RFA Royal Field Artillery; Royal Fleet Auxiliary; Rugby Fives Association
RFAC Royal Fine Art Commission
RFC [USA] Reconstruction Finance Corporation; [computing] request for comments; Royal Flying Corps; rugby football club
RFD radio-frequency device; reporting for duty; [USA] rural free delivery (postal service)
RFDS [Australia] Royal Flying Doctor Service
RFE Radio Free Europe
RFH Royal Festival Hall (London)
RFI radio-frequency interference; request for information; right forward inside (of skate)
RFL Rugby Football League
RFN Registered Fever Nurse
Rfn Rifleman
RFO right forward outside (of skate)
RFP [nuclear technology] reversed-field pinch
r.f.p. retired on full pay
RFPC [electronics] radio-frequency pulse compression
RFQ [commerce] request for quotation
RFR Royal Fleet Reserve
rfrd referred
RFS rear-facing seat; Registry of Friendly Societies; Royal Forestry Society
RFSU Rugby Football Schools' Union
RFT [computing] revisable form text; [astronomy] richest-field telescope
RFTF Retail Fruit Trade Federation
RFU Rugby Football Union
rfz. [music] *rinforzando* (Italian: reinforcing)
RG [international vehicle registration] (Republic of) Guinea; [vehicle registration] Newcastle upon Tyne; [UK postcode] Reading; reserve guard
r.g. *rive gauche* (French: left bank)
RGA remote geological analysis; residual-gas analyser; Royal Garrison Artillery; Royal Guernsey Artillery
RGB red, green, blue (in colour transmission etc.)
RGBI red, green, blue intensity
rgd registered; reigned
rge range

R-Gen Registrar-General
RGG Royal Grenadier Guards
RGH Royal Gloucestershire Hussars
RGI Royal Glasgow Institute of the Fine Arts
RGJ Royal Green Jackets
RGN Registered General Nurse (formerly SRN)
Rgn Rangoon
rgn region
RGNP [economics] real gross national product
RGO Royal Greenwich Observatory
RGS Royal Geographical Society
RGSA Royal Geographical Society of Australasia
RGT [physics] relativistic gravitational theory
Rgt Regiment
rgtl regimental
RH [international vehicle registration] (Republic of) Haiti; [vehicle registration] Hull; [UK postcode] Redhill; [meteorology] relative humidity; remote handling; right hand; right handed; [fishing port] Rochester; Royal Highlanders; Royal Highness; Royal Hospital
Rh [medicine] rhesus (factor) (as in **Rh negative**); [chemical element] rhodium
r.h. [sports] right half; right hand; right handed
RHA regional health authority; Road Haulage Association; Royal Hibernian Academy; Royal Horse Artillery
RHAF Royal Hellenic Air Force
RHamps Royal Hampshire Regiment
rhap. rhapsody
RHAS Royal Highland and Agricultural Society of Scotland
RHB regional hospital board
r.h.b. [sports] right halfback
RHBNC Royal Holloway and Bedford New College (London)
r.h.d. right-hand drive (in car advertisement)
RHEL Rutherford High Energy Laboratory
rheo. rheostat
rheol. rheological; rheology
rhet. rhetoric; rhetorical
RHF Royal Highland Fusiliers
RHG Royal Horse Guards
RHHI Royal Hospital and Home for Incurables
RHistS Royal Historical Society
RHM Ranks Hovis McDougall
RHMS Royal Hibernian Military School
rhomb. rhombic; rhomboid; rhombus
rhp rated horsepower
RHQ regimental headquarters
RHR rear head restraints (in car advertisement); Royal Highland Regiment
r/h/r rear head restraints (in car advertisement)
RHS Robin Hood Society; Royal Highland Show; Royal Historical Society; Royal Horticultural Society; Royal Humane Society
r.h.s. right-hand side; round-headed screw
RHSI Royal Horticultural Society of Ireland
RHT Railway Heritage Trust
RHV Registered Health Visitor
RI [international vehicle registration] (Republic of) Indonesia; radio interference; radioisotope; Railway Inspectorate; refractive index; Regimental Institute; *Regina et Imperatrix* (Latin: Queen and Empress); reinsurance; religious instruction; report of investigation; *Rex et Imperator* (Latin: King and Emperor); Rhode Island; [US postcode] Rhode Island; Rockwell International Corporation; Rotary International; Royal Institute of Painters in Water Colours; Royal Institution
R/I reinsurance
r.i. reflective insulation; rubber insulation
RIA [medicine] radioimmunoassay; Royal Irish Academy
RIAA Recording Industry Association of America
RIAC Royal Irish Automobile Club
RIAF Royal Indian Air Force
RIAI Royal Institute of the Architects of Ireland
RIAM Royal Irish Academy of Music
RIAS Royal Incorporation of Architects in Scotland
RIASC Royal Indian Army Service Corps
RIB Racing Information Bureau; rigid-hull inflatable boat; Rural Industries Bureau
RIBA Royal Institute of British Architects
RIBI Rotary International in Great Britain and Ireland
RIC [chemistry] radiation-induced change;

[physics] radiation-induced conductivity; Radio Industry Council; Royal Institute of Chemistry (former name of RSC); Royal Irish Constabulary

RICA Research Institute for Consumer Affairs

RICE rest, ice, compression, elevation (treatment for sports injuries)

RICO [USA] Racketeer Influenced and Corrupt Organizations Act

RICS Royal Institution of Chartered Surveyors

RID [physics] radiation-induced defect; [physics] radiation-induced diffusion

RIE [commerce] recognized investment exchange; Royal Indian Engineering College

RIF [military] reduction in force; Royal Inniskilling Fusiliers

Rif. Brig. Rifle Brigade

RIFF [computing] raster image file format

RIGS regionally important geological site

RIIA Royal Institute of International Affairs

RILC Racing Industry Liaison Committee

RILKO Research into Lost Knowledge Organization

RIM [international vehicle registration] (Islamic Republic of) Mauritania (from French *République Islamique de Mauritanie*); Royal Indian Marines

RIMB [South Africa] Research Institute for Medical Biophysics

RIMNET Radioactive Incident Monitoring Network

RIN [aeronautics] reference indicator number; Royal Indian Navy

RINA Royal Institution of Naval Architects

rinf. [music] *rinforzando* (Italian: reinforcing)

RINVR Royal Indian Naval Volunteer Reserve

RIO reporting in and out

RIOP Royal Institute of Oil Painters

RIP [computing] raster input processor; *requiescant in pace* (Latin: may they rest in peace); *requiescat in pace* (Latin: may he/she rest in peace); rest in peace

rip. [music] *ripieno* (Italian: filled, for all players)

RIPA Royal Institute of Public Administration

RIPHH Royal Institute of Public Health and Hygiene

RIR Royal Irish Regiment

RIrF Royal Irish Fusiliers

RIS Research Information Service

RISC reduced-instruction-set computer

RIT [psychology] Rorschach inkblot test

rit. [music] *ritardando* (Italian: slowing down); [music] *ritenuto* (Italian: held back)

RITA reusable interplanetary transport approach (vehicle)

ritard. [music] *ritardando* (Italian: slowing down)

riten. [music] *ritenuto* (Italian: held back)

riv. river

RJ [vehicle registration] Manchester; ramjet; road junction

RJA Royal Jersey Artillery

RJE [computing] remote job entry

RJET [computing] remote job entry terminal

RJF Reformed Jokers' Federation

RJLI Royal Jersey Light Infantry

RJM Royal Jersey Militia

RK [vehicle registration] northwest London; [medicine] radical keratotomy (used to treat myopia); religious knowledge

RKKA *Rabochekrest'yanshi Krasny* (Russian: Red Army of Workers and Peasants)

RKO Radio-Keith-Orpheum (US broadcasting and former film company)

rky rocky

RL [international vehicle registration] (Republic of) Lebanon; reference library; research laboratory; rocket launcher; Rugby League; [vehicle registration] Truro

Rl [currency] rouble; Royal

RLC Royal Logistic Corps

RLD [USA] retail liquor dealer

RLF Royal Literary Fund

RLL [computing] run length limited

RLO railway liaison officer; returned letter office (formerly DLO)

RLPAS Royal London Prisoners' Aid Society

RLPO Royal Liverpool Philharmonic Orchestra

RLPS Royal Liverpool Philharmonic Society

RLS Robert Louis Stevenson (Scottish writer)

Rls [currency] rial (used in Iran)
RLSS Royal Life Saving Society
rlwy railway
rly railway; relay
RM [vehicle registration] Carlisle; [international vehicle registration] (Republic of) Madagascar; radiation monitoring; radio monitoring; [computing] Reed-Muller (code); Registered Midwife (replacement for SCM); [currency] Reichsmark (formerly used in Germany); remote monitoring; resident magistrate; riding master; [UK postcode] Romford; Royal Mail; Royal Marines
rm ream; room
RMA Royal Marine Artillery; Royal Marines Association; Royal Military Academy (formerly RMC); Royal Musical Association
RMC regional meteorological centre; Royal Military College (former name of RMA)
RMCC Royal Military College of Canada
RMCM Royal Manchester College of Music
RMCS Royal Military College of Science
r.m.d. ready money down
RMedSoc Royal Medical Society (Edinburgh)
RMetS Royal Meteorological Society
RMFVR Royal Marine Forces Volunteer Reserves
RMH Royal Marsden Hospital (London)
RMI Resource Management Initiative (for NHS)
RMIT Royal Melbourne Institute of Technology
RMLI Royal Marine Light Infantry
RMM [international vehicle registration] (Republic of) Mali
r.m.m. [chemistry] relative molecular mass
RMN Registered Mental Nurse
RMO Regimental Medical Officer; regional medical officer; resident medical officer; Royal Marine Office
RMP Royal Marine Police; Royal Military Police
RMPA Royal Medico-Psychological Association
RMR Royal Marines Reserve
RMRA Royal Marines Rifle Association
RMS radiation-monitoring system; remote monitoring system; [mathematics] root mean square; Royal Mail Service; Royal Mail Ship; Royal Mail Steamer; Royal Medical Society; Royal Microscopical Society; Royal Society of Miniature Painters
rms [mathematics] root mean square; rooms (in property advertisement)
RMSchMus Royal Marines School of Music
RMSM Royal Military School of Music
RMT National Union of Rail, Maritime and Transport Workers
RN [international vehicle registration] (Republic of) Niger; [vehicle registration] Preston; Registered Nurse; *route nationale* (French: trunk road); Royal Naval; Royal Navy; [fishing port] Runcorn
Rn [chemical element] radon
r.n. [telecommunications] reception nil
RNA [biochemistry] ribonucleic acid; Romantic Novelists' Association; Royal Naval Association
RNAS Royal Naval Air Service; Royal Naval Air Station
RNase [biochemistry] ribonuclease
RNAW Royal Naval Aircraft Workshop
RNAY Royal Naval Aircraft Yard
RNB Royal Naval Barracks
R 'n' B rhythm and blues
RNBS Royal Naval Benevolent Society
RNBT Royal Naval Benevolent Trust
RNC [USA] Republican National Committee
RNC Royal Naval College
RNCM Royal Northern College of Music
RND Royal Naval Division
rnd round
RNEC Royal Naval Engineering College
RNF Royal Northumberland Fusiliers
RNHA Registered Nursing Home Association
RNIB Royal National Institute for the Blind
RNID Royal National Institute for the Deaf
RNLAF Royal Netherlands Air Force
RNLI Royal National Lifeboat Institution
RNLO Royal Naval Liaison Officer
RNMDSF Royal National Mission to Deep Sea Fishermen
RNMH Registered Nurse for the Mentally Handicapped

RNMS Royal Naval Medical School
RNoN Royal Norwegian Navy
RNP [biochemistry] ribonucleoprotein
RNPFN Royal National Pension Fund for Nurses
RNR Royal Naval Reserve
R 'n' R rock and roll
RNRA Royal Naval Rifle Association
RNRS Royal National Rose Society
RNS [stock exchange] Regulatory News Service; [mathematics] residue number system; Royal Numismatic Society
rns runs
RNSA Royal Naval Sailing Association
RNSC Royal Naval Staff College
RNSR Royal Naval Special Reserve
RNSS Royal Naval Scientific Service
RNT Registered Nurse Tutor; Royal National Theatre
RNTE Royal Naval Training Establishment
RNTNEH Royal National Throat, Nose and Ear Hospital
RNTU Royal Naval Training Unit
RNVR Royal Naval Volunteer Reserve
RNVSR Royal Naval Volunteer Supplementary Reserve
RNWMP [Canada] Royal Northwest Mounted Police (former name of RCMP)
rnwy runway
RNXS Royal Naval Auxiliary Service
RNZAC Royal New Zealand Armoured Corps
RNZAF Royal New Zealand Air Force
RNZIR Royal New Zealand Infantry Regiment
RNZN Royal New Zealand Navy
RNZNVR Royal New Zealand Naval Volunteer Reserve
RO [vehicle registration] Luton; radar observer; radar operator; radio operator; Radio Orchestra; [psychology] reality orientation; receiving office; receiving officer; receiving order; record(s) office; recruiting officer; regimental order; registered office; relieving officer; reserved occupation; returning officer; [chemistry] reverse osmosis; [currency] rial Omani; [international vehicle registration] Romania; [fishing port] Rothesay; Royal Observatory
ro. [printing] recto (right-hand page); roan
.ro Romania (in Internet address)
r.o. [rowing] rowed over; [cricket] run out
ROA Racehorse Owners' Association; [education] record of achievement; Reserve Officers' Association; [finance] return on assets
ROAM [finance] return on assets managed
ROAR right of admission reserved
ROB remaining on board
ROC [finance] return on capital; Royal Observer Corps
ROCE [finance] return on capital employed
ROE [finance] return on equity; Royal Observatory, Edinburgh
ROF Royal Ordnance Factory
Roffen. *Roffensis* (Latin: (Bishop) of Rochester)
R of O Reserve of Officers
ROG receipt of goods
ROH Royal Opera House (Covent Garden)
ROI region of interest; [finance] return on investment; Royal Institute of Oil Painters
ROK [international vehicle registration] (Republic of) Korea
Rolls [short form] Rolls-Royce (car)
ROM [computing] read-only memory; [medicine] rupture of membranes
Rom. Roman; Romance (language); Romania; Romanian; Romanic (language); [Bible] Romans
rom. roman (type)
Rom. Cath. Roman Catholic
RONA [finance] return on net assets
ROP [advertising] run of paper
RORC Royal Ocean Racing Club
ro-ro roll on, roll off (ferry)
ROS [computing] remote operations service
Ros. Roscommon
Rosa [computing] recognition of open systems achievement
ROSAT [astronomy] *Röntgenstrahlen Satellit* (German: X-ray satellite)
Rosco Road Operators' Safety Council
ROSE [computing] Research Open Systems in Europe
ROSL Royal Overseas League
ROSLA raising of school-leaving age
RoSPA Royal Society for the Prevention of Accidents
ROT Registered Occupational Therapist; remedial occupational therapy; rule of thumb

Rot. Rotterdam
rot. rotary; rotating; rotation; rotor
ROTC [USA] Reserve Officers' Training Corps
ROTFL rolls on the floor laughing (in Internet chat)
ROU [international vehicle registration] (Republic of) Uruguay
rout. routine
ROV remotely operated vehicle
ROW right of way; Rights of Women
ROWPU reverse osmosis water purification unit
Rox. Roxburghshire
Roy. Royal
RP [vehicle registration] Northampton; [civil aircraft marking] (Republic of the) Philippines; [international vehicle registration] (Republic of the) Philippines; radiation protection; [chemistry] reaction product; Received Pronunciation; recommended practice; recommended price; recovery phase; redundancy payment; Reformed Presbyterian; regimental police; regimental policeman; Registered Plumber; Regius Professor; reinforced plastic; reply paid; reprint; reprinting; *República Portuguesa* (Portuguese: Republic of Portugal); [US finance] repurchase agreement; research paper; [medicine] retinitis pigmentosa; [insurance] return (of) premium; *Révérend Père* (French: Reverend Father); rocket projectile; Royal Society of Portrait Painters; rules of procedure
R/P reprint; reprinting
Rp [currency] rupiah (used in Indonesia)
r.p. [telecommunications] reception poor; regimental policeman; reply paid
RPA radiation protection adviser; Rationalist Press Association; [education] record of personal achievement; Registered Plumbers' Association
RPB recognized professional body
RPC rapid Portland cement; [computing] remote procedure call; [USA] Republican Party Conference; request the pleasure of your company; Royal Pioneer Corps
RPD Doctor of Political Science (from Latin *Rerum Politicarum Doctor*); regional port director
RPE radio production executive; Reformed Protestant Episcopal; [medicine] retinal pigment epithelium (of eye)
RPF [medicine] renal plasma flow; [medicine] retroperitoneal fibrosis; Rwanda Patriotic Front
RPG [computing] report program generator; [military] rocket-propelled grenade; role-playing game
rpg rounds per gun
rph revolutions per hour
RPhilS Royal Philharmonic Society
RPI retail price index
rplca replica
RPM reliability performance measure; resale price maintenance; retail price maintenance
rpm revolutions per minute
RPMS Royal Postgraduate Medical School
RPN Registered Psychiatric Nurse; [computing, mathematics] reverse Polish notation
RP/ND reprinting, no date
RPO railway post office; regional personnel officer; Royal Philharmonic Orchestra
RPQ [commerce] request for price quotation
RPR *Rassemblement pour la République* (French: Rally for the Republic) (= Gaullists, formerly UDR)
RPRA Royal Pigeon Racing Association
RPS radiological protection service; rapid processing system; Royal Philharmonic Society; Royal Photographic Society
rps revolutions per second
RPSGB Royal Pharmaceutical Society of Great Britain
RPSL Royal Philatelic Society, London
RPT Registered Physiotherapist
rpt repeat; report; reprint
RPV [nuclear technology] reactor pressure vessel; [military] remotely piloted vehicle
RQ regraded quality (of tyre); remoulded quality (of tyre); [commerce] request for quotation; [medicine] respiratory quotient
R/Q [commerce] request for quotation
RQL reference quality level
RQMS Regimental Quartermaster-Sergeant
rqmt requirement
rqr. require; requirement
RR [vehicle registration] Nottingham; radiation resistance; [USA] railroad; Rem-

ington Rand (manufacturing company); research report; return rate; Right Reverend; [cycling] road race; [fishing port] Rochester; Rolls-Royce; [USA] rural route
rr. rare
r.r. ready reckoner
RRA Royal Regiment of Artillery
RRB Race Relations Board
RRC [cycling] Road Racing Club; Road Runners' Club; Royal Red Cross
RRE Royal Radar Establishment (former name of RSRE)
RRF [military] Rapid Reaction Force; Royal Regiment of Fusiliers
RRI Rowett Research Institute (Aberdeen)
RRL Registered Record Librarian; Road Research Laboratory
RRM [USA] renegotiable-rate mortgage
rRNA [biochemistry] ribosomal ribonucleic acid
RRP recommended retail price
RR.PP. *Révérends Pères* (French: Reverend Fathers)
RRR [USA] return receipt requested (of registered mail)
RRS Royal Research Ship
RRT rail rapid transit
RS [vehicle registration] Aberdeen; Rallye Sport; Received Standard (English); reconnaissance squadron; reconnaissance strike; recording secretary; recruiting service; [computing] Reed–Solomon (as in **RS code**); Reformed Spelling; remote sensing; research station; [medicine] respiratory system; [law] Revised Statutes; Royal Scots (regiment); Royal Society
R/S rejection slip
Rs [currency] rupee
rs [meteorology] rain and snow (i.e. sleet)
r.s. right side
3Rs reading, (w)riting and (a)rithmetic
RSA Republic of South Africa; [New Zealand] Returned Services Association; [computing] Rivest, Shamir and Adelman (as in **RSA cipher**); Road Safety Act; Royal Scottish Academician; Royal Scottish Academy; Royal Society for the Encouragement of Arts, Manufactures and Commerce; Royal Society of Arts; Royal Society of Australia
RSAA Royal Society for Asian Affairs
RSAD Royal Surgical Aid Society
RSAF Royal Small Arms Factory
RSAI Royal Society of Antiquaries of Ireland
RSAMD Royal Scottish Academy of Music and Drama
RSAS Royal Surgical Aid Society
r.s.b. range safety beacon
RSC Royal Shakespeare Company; Royal Society of Canada; Royal Society of Chemistry (formerly RIC); Rules of the Supreme Court
RSCDS Royal Scottish Country Dance Society
rsch research
RSCJ *Religiosae Sacratissimi Cordis Jesus* (Latin: Nuns of the Most Sacred Heart of Jesus, Sacred Heart Society)
RSCM Royal School of Church Music
RSCN Registered Sick Children's Nurse (formerly SRCN)
RSD recovery, salvage and disposal; Royal Society of Dublin
rsdntl residential
RSE Received Standard English; Royal Society of Edinburgh
RSF [building] rough sunk face; Royal Scots Fusiliers
RSFS Royal Scottish Forestry Society
RSFSR Russian Soviet Federative Socialist Republic (former official Soviet name of Russia)
RSG rate-support grant; recirculating steam generator; regional seat of government (in civil defence); Royal Scots Greys
RSGB Radio Society of Great Britain
RSGS Royal Scottish Geographical Society
RSH Royal Society of Health
RSHA *Reichssicherheitshauptamt* (German: Reich Security Central Office) (in Nazi Germany)
RSI regional staff inspector; [medicine] repetitive strain (or stress) injury; Royal Sanitary Institute
RSJ [building] rolled-steel joist
RSL [Australia] Returned Services League; Royal Society of Literature
RSLA raising of school-leaving age
RSM Regimental Sergeant-Major; regional sales manager; Royal School of Mines; Royal Society of Medicine; Royal Society of Musicians of Great Britain; [inter-

national vehicle registration] (Republic of) San Marino
RSMA Royal Society of Marine Artists
RSME Royal School of Military Engineering
rsn reason
RSNA Radiological Society of North America
RSNC Royal Society for Nature Conservation
RSNO Royal Scottish National Orchestra
RSNT Railway Staffs National Tribunal
RSNZ Royal Society of New Zealand
RSO Radio Symphony Orchestra; radiological safety officer; railway sorting office; railway suboffice; [military] range safety officer; Recruiting Staff Officer; resident surgical officer; Royal Scottish Orchestra (formerly SNO); rural suboffice
RSocMed Royal Society of Medicine
r.s.p. [cricket] rain stopped play
RSPB Royal Society for the Protection of Birds
RSPBA Royal Scottish Pipe Band Association
RSPCA Royal Society for the Prevention of Cruelty to Animals
RSPE Royal Society of Painter-Printmakers (formerly Royal Society of Painter-Etchers and Engravers)
RSPP Royal Society of Portrait Painters
RSPS Royal Scottish Pipers' Society
rsq. rescue
RSRE Royal Signals and Radar Establishment (formerly RRE)
RSS *Regiae Societatis Socius* (Latin: Fellow of the Royal Society); Royal Statistical Society
RSSA Royal Scottish Society of Arts
RSSPCC Royal Scottish Society for the Prevention of Cruelty to Children
RSTM&H Royal Society of Tropical Medicine and Hygiene
rstr. restricted
RSU road safety unit
RSUA Royal Society of Ulster Architects
RSV [medicine] respiratory syncytial virus; Revised Standard Version (of Bible); [microbiology] Rous sarcoma virus
RSVP *répondez s'il vous plaît* (French: please reply)
rsvr reservoir
RSW Royal Scottish Water Colour Society
RSWC right side up with care
RSwN Royal Swedish Navy
RT [vehicle registration] Ipswich; [medicine] radiation therapy; radio telegraph; radio telegraphy; radio telephone; radio telephony; reaction time; reading test; received text; return ticket; room temperature; round table; round trip
R/T radio telegraph; radio telegraphy; radio telephone; radio telephony
rt right
RTA reciprocal trade agreement(s); road traffic accident; Road Traffic Act
RTB return to base (as in **RTB warranty**)
RTBA rate to be agreed
RTBF *Radio-Télévision Belge de la Communauté Française* (Belgian broadcasting company)
RTC [computing] real-time clock; [India] Road Transport Corporation; Round Table Conference
rtc. ratchet
rtd retired; returned
rtd ht [cricket] retired hurt
RTDS [computing] real-time data system
RTE *Radio Telefis Éireann* (Irish broadcasting company); [computing] real-time execution
rte route
RTECS Registry of Toxic Effects of Chemical Substances
RTF *Radiodiffusion-Télévision Française* (European broadcasting company); [computing] rich text format
RTFM [slang, computing] read the fucking manual
RTG [astronomy] radioisotope thermoelectric generator; [physics] relativistic theory of gravitation
rtg rating
Rt Hon. Right Honourable
RTI [medicine] respiratory tract infection; Round Table International
RTITB Road Transport Industry Training Board
RTK right to know
RTL *Radio-Télé Luxembourg* (European broadcasting company); [computing] real-time language; [electronics] resistor-transistor logic

RTM [computing] read the manual; registered trademark
rtn retain; return
rtng returning
RTO [USA] railroad transportation officer; railway transport officer
RTOL [aeronautics] reduced take-off and landing
RTP [engineering] rated thermal power; [physics] room temperature and pressure
RTPI Royal Town Planning Institute
RTR Royal Tank Regiment
RTRA Road Traffic Regulation Act
Rt Rev. Right Reverend
Rt Revd Right Reverend
RTS Religious Tract Society; [computing] request to send; reserve tug service; Royal Television Society; Royal Toxophilite Society
RTSA Retail Trading Standards Association
RTT radioteletype
RTTC [cycling] Road Time Trials Council
RTU [military] return(ed) to unit
RTV real-time video
RTW ready to wear
Rt W Right Worshipful
rty rarity
RTYC Royal Thames Yacht Club
RTZ Rio Tinto Zinc Corporation Limited
RU [vehicle registration] Bournemouth; [international vehicle registration] (Republic of) Burundi (from former name Urundi); Readers' Union; [computing] registered user; reprocessed uranium; Rugby Union
Ru [chemical element] ruthenium
Ru. Russia; Russian
.ru Russia (in Internet address)
RUA Royal Ulster Academy of Painting, Sculpture and Architecture
RUAS Royal Ulster Agricultural Society
rub. rubber
RUC Royal Ulster Constabulary
RUCR Royal Ulster Constabulary Reserve
rud. rudder
RUF [banking] revolving underwriting facility
RUG [computing] restricted users group
RUI Royal University of Ireland
RUKBA Royal United Kingdom Beneficent Association
rumpie [informal] rural upwardly mobile professional
RUPP road used as public path
RUR Royal Ulster Regiment
RURAL Society for the Responsible Use of Resources in Agriculture and on the Land
RUS [international vehicle registration] Russia
Rus. Russia; Russian
RUSI Royal United Services Institute for Defence Studies (formerly Royal United Service Institution)
RUSM Royal United Service Museum
Russ. Russia; Russian
Rut. Rutland
Rutd Rutland
RV [vehicle registration] Portsmouth; rateable value; [USA] recreational vehicle; [astronautics] re-entry vehicle; rendezvous; research vessel; [medicine] residual volume; Revised Version (of Bible); Rifle Volunteers; [medicine] right ventricle; [medicine] right ventricular
r.v. [statistics] random variable; rendezvous
RVA Rating and Valuation Association
RVC Rifle Volunteer Corps; Royal Veterinary College
RVCI Royal Veterinary College of Ireland
RVLR Road Vehicles Lighting Regulations
RVM Royal Victorian Medal
RVO Royal Victorian Order
RVR runway visual range
RVSVP *répondez vite, s'il vous plaît* (French: please reply quickly)
RVU research vessel unit
RW [vehicle registration] Coventry; rainwater; right of way; Right Worshipful; Right Worthy; Royal Warrant; runway
R/W right of way
Rw. Rwanda; Rwandan
r/w read/write
.rw Rwanda (in Internet address)
r.w. [sports] right wing
RWA Race Walking Association; Royal West of England Academy; [international vehicle registration] Rwanda
RWAFF Royal West African Frontier Force
R War. R Royal Warwickshire Regiment
RWAS Royal Welsh Agricultural Society
RWD radioactive waste disposal
r.w.d. rear-wheel drive

RWEA Royal West of England Academy
RWF Radio Wholesalers' Federation; Royal Welch Fusiliers
RWFCS Red and White Friesian Cattle Society
RwFr [currency] Rwanda franc
RWGM [Freemasonry] Right Worshipful Grand Master
RWGR [Freemasonry] Right Worthy Grand Representative
RWGS [Freemasonry] Right Worthy Grand Secretary
RWGT [Freemasonry] Right Worthy Grand Templar; [Freemasonry] Right Worthy Grand Treasurer
RWGW [Freemasonry] Right Worthy Grand Warden
RWIC Rioja Wine Information Centre
RWK Queen's Own Royal West Kent Regiment
RWM radioactive waste management; [computing] read–write memory
RWMAC Radioactive Waste Management Advisory Committee
RWP rainwater pipe
RWS Royal Watercolour Society
rwy railway
RX [vehicle registration] Reading; [fishing port] Rye
Rx recording (in broadcasting)
RY [vehicle registration] Leicester; [fishing port] Ramsey
ry railway
RYA Royal Yachting Association
RYC in reply to your cable
RYS Royal Yacht Squadron
RZ [vehicle registration] Antrim
r.z. return to zero
RZS Royal Zoological Society
RZSI Royal Zoological Society of Ireland
RZSS Royal Zoological Society of Scotland
RZSScot Royal Zoological Society of Scotland

S

S Sabbath; [heraldry] sable; [anatomy] sacral (of vertebrae); Saint; *San* (Italian: Saint); *Sankt* (German: Saint); *Santa* (Italian: Saint); *Santo* (Italian: Saint); *São* (Portuguese: Saint); satisfactory; Saturday; Saxon; [currency] Schilling; School; Scotland; Scottish; Sea; secondary; secret; secretary; section; *Seite* (German: page); Senate; *Señor* (Spanish: Mr); sentence; September; *sepultus* (Latin: buried); series; [UK postcode] Sheffield; ship; siemens (unit of electric conductance); signaller; signature; *Signor* (Italian: Mr); *Signora* (Italian: Mrs); [geology] Silurian; silver; [fishing port] Skibbereen; slow (on clock or watch regulator); small; [microbiology] smooth; Socialist; Society; *Socius* (Latin: Fellow) (used in titles); solar; [astronomy] solar mass; [music] soprano; south; southern; [card games] spades; [astronomy] spiral galaxy; square; staff; [law] statute; [microbiology] strain; submarine; [chemistry] substitution reaction; [currency] sucre (used in Ecuador); [chemical element] sulphur; summer; [shipping] summer (load line); sun; Sunday; Sweden; [international vehicle registration] Sweden
S [electrical engineering] apparent power; [physics] entropy; [music] *segno* (Italian: sign); [chemistry] sinister; [physics] spin quantum number (of system); [physics] strangeness quantum number
s second; shilling(s) (from Latin *solidus*); [meteorology] snow; [music] soh (in tonic sol-fa); [chemistry] solid; [physics] strange (quark flavour)
s [chemistry] secondary (isomer); [chemistry] sedimentation coefficient; [physics] specific entropy; [physics] spin quantum number; [chemistry] symmetric
s/ *sur* (French: on) (in place-names)
s. school; sea; seaman; section; see; semi-; series; sermon; set; sets (referring to the sun); *siècle* (French: century); *siehe* (German: see); sign; signed; *sine* (Latin: without); single; [grammar] singular; *sinister* (Latin: left); *sinistra* (Italian: left); sire; sister; small; snow; society; solo; son; [music] soprano; spherical; steamer;

steel; stem; stock; [grammar] substantive; succeeded; suit; summer; sun; sunny; surplus

S2 [civil aircraft marking] Bangladesh

S4C *Sianel 4 Cymru* (Welsh: Channel 4 Wales)

S5 [civil aircraft marking] Slovenia

S7 [civil aircraft marking] Seychelles

SA [vehicle registration] Aberdeen; Salvation Army; Saudi Arabia; [international vehicle registration] Saudi Arabia; Saudi Arabian; seaman apprentice; secret agent; [USA] Secretary of the Army; [horticulture] semiannual; senior administrator; sex appeal; [microbiology] simian agent; [medicine] sinoatrial (as in **SA node**); small arms; [commerce] *sociedad anónima* (Spanish: (public) limited company, plc or Ltd); [commerce] *sociedade anónima* (Portuguese: (public) limited company, plc or Ltd); [commerce] *società anonima* (Italian: (public) limited company, plc or Ltd); [commerce] *société anonyme* (French: (public) limited company, plc or Ltd); Society of Antiquaries; Society of Arts; Society of Authors; Soil Association; *Son Altesse* (French: Her/His Highness); South Africa; South African; South America; South American; South Australia; South Australian; special agent; spherical aberration; [computing] structured systems analysis; *Sturmabteilung* (German: storm troopers) (Nazi militia); subsistence allowance; surface area; surface-to-air (missile); [fishing port] Swansea; [UK postcode] Swansea; systems analysis; systems analyst

S/A subject to acceptance; subject to approval; [US banking] survivorship agreement

Sa. Saturday

sa. [heraldry] sable

.sa Saudi Arabia (in Internet address)

s.a. safe arrival; *secundum artem* (Latin: by skill, scientifically, in the standard way); see also; [horticulture] semiannual; sex appeal; *siehe auch* (German: see also); *sine anno* (Latin: without year, undated); [chemistry] soluble in alkali; storage area; subject to acceptance; subject to approval; subsistence allowance

SAA Scottish Archery Association; small arms ammunition; South African Airways; Speech Association of America; Standards Association of Australia; [chemistry] surface-active agent; [computing] systems application architecture

SAAA Scottish Amateur Athletic Association

SAAAU South African Amateur Athletic Union

Saab *Svensk Aeroplan Aktiebolag* (Swedish car and aircraft manufacturer)

SAABS Scottish Action Against Blood Sports

SAAD small arms ammunition depot

SAAF South African Air Force

SAAFA Special Arab Assistance Fund for Africa

SAAO South African Astronomical Observatory

SAARC South Asian Association for Regional Cooperation

SAAU South African Agricultural Union

SAB Science Advisory Board; Scientific Advisory Board; Society of American Bacteriologists; [music] soprano, alto, bass; South Atlantic Bight

Sab. Sabbath

sab. *sabato* (Italian: Saturday); sabbatical

sáb. *sábado* (Spanish: Saturday)

SABA Scottish Amateur Boxing Association

Sabbat. Sabbatical

SABC Scottish Association of Boys' Clubs; South African Broadcasting Corporation

Sabena *Société anonyme belge d'exploitation de la navigation aérienne* (Belgian airline company)

SABIC Society for the Advancement of Brain-Injured Children

SABMIS seaborne antiballistic missile intercept system

sabo. sabotage

SABRA South African Bureau of Racial Affairs

SABS South African Bureau of Standards

SAC Scientific Advisory Committee; Scottish Arts Council; Scottish Automobile Club; Senior Aircraftman; [finance] short-run average cost; small-arms club; South Atlantic Coast; (Post Office) Stamp Advisory Committee; [USA] State Athletic Commission; [USA] Strategic Air Command

SACAB Scottish Association of Citizens' Advice Bureaux
SACEUR Supreme Allied Commander Europe
SACHR Standing Advisory Commission on Human Rights
SACL South African Confederation of Labour
SACLANT Supreme Allied Commander Atlantic
SACO *Sveriges Akademikers Centralorganisation* (Swedish: Swedish Confederation of Professional Associations)
SACP South African Communist Party
Sacr. Sacramento; Sacrist
SACRO Scottish Association for the Care and Resettlement of Offenders
SACSEA Supreme Allied Command, Southeast Asia
SACSIR South African Council for Scientific and Industrial Research
SACU single-application computer user; Society for the Promotion of Anglo-Chinese Understanding; Southern African Customs Union
SACW Senior Aircraftwoman
SAD Scottish Action on Dementia; Scottish Association for the Deaf; [psychology] seasonal affective disorder; systems analysis and design
SADC Southern African Development Community
SADCC Southern African Development Coordination Conference
SADF South African Defence Force
SADG *Société des architectes diplômés par le gouvernement* (French: Society of Government-Certified Architects)
SADI Society of Approved Driving Instructors
SADIE scanning analogue to digital input equipment
SADT [trademark, computing] structured analysis and design technique
SAE self-addressed envelope; [USA] Society of Automotive Engineers (motor-oil viscosity scale); stamped addressed envelope
s.a.e. self-addressed envelope; stamped addressed envelope
SAEF Stock Exchange Automatic Execution Facility
SAF Scottish Athletic Federation; [USA] Secretary of the Air Force; Society of American Foresters; [USA] Strategic Air Force; structural adjustment facility (in IMF)
SAFA Scottish Amateur Football Association; South Africa Freedom Association
s.a.f.e. stamped addressed foolscap envelope
S Afr. South Africa; South African
SAfrD South African Dutch
SAFU Scottish Amateur Fencing Union
SAG [USA] Screen Actors' Guild
SAGA Scottish Amateur Gymnastics Association; Society of American Graphic Artists
SAGB Schizophrenia Association of Great Britain; Spiritualist Association of Great Britain
SAGE [military] semiautomatic ground environment
SAGGA Scout and Guide Graduate Association
SAH [medicine] subarachnoid haemorrhage; Supreme Allied Headquarters
SAHC Scottish Association of Health Councils
SAHGB Society of Architectural Historians of Great Britain
SAHR Society of Army Historical Research
Sai. Saigon
SAIC Scottish Agricultural Improvement Council
SAID sexual allegations in divorce
SAIDS simian acquired immune deficiency syndrome
SAIF South African Industrial Federation
SAIMR South African Institute of Medical Research
SAIRR South African Institute of Race Relations
SAISSA Scottish Amateur Ice Speed Skating Association
SAL South Arabian League; surface air-lifted (mail)
sal. salary
SALA South African Library Association
SALC symmetry-adapted linear combinations
Salop Shropshire (from old name of county)
SALP South African Labour Party
SALR [meteorology] saturated adiabatic lapse rate; South African Law Reports

SALT Scottish Association for Language Teaching; Strategic Arms Limitation Talks; Strategic Arms Limitation Treaty
Salv. Salvador; Salvadorian
salv. salvage
SAM Scottish Aids Monitor; [USA] shared-appreciation mortgage; [USA] Space Available Mail; surface-to-air missile
S Am. South America; South American
Sam. Samaria; Samaritan; Samoa; Samoan; *Samstag* (German: Saturday); [Bible] Samuel
sam. *samedi* (French: Saturday)
SAMA Saudi Arabian Monetary Agency; Scottish Amateur Music Association
Samar. Samaritan
SAMC South African Medical Corps
S Amer. South America; South American
SAMH Scottish Association for Mental Health
SAMU *Service d'assistance médicale d'urgence* (French: emergency medical assistance service)
SAN styrene–acrylonitrile (polymer)
san. sanitary
SANA Scottish Anglers' National Association
sanat. sanatorium
SANCAD Scottish Association for National Certificates and Diplomas
SAND Scotland Against Nuclear Dumping
sand. sandwich
s&d search and destroy; song and dance
S&F [insurance] stock and fixtures
s&f [informal] shopping and fucking (popular fiction genre)
S&FA shipping and forwarding agents
S&H shipping and handling (charges)
S&L [USA] savings and loan association
S&M sadism and masochism; [insurance] stock and machinery
s&m sausages and mash
S&P 500 [USA] Standard and Poors 500 Stock Index
Sands Stillbirth and Neonatal Death Society
s&s [informal] sex and shopping (popular fiction genre)
s&sc sized and supercalendered (paper)
S&T signalling and telecommunications; supply and transport
S&TA Salmon and Trout Association
Sane Schizophrenia – A National Emergency
SANFP Scottish Association for Natural Family Planning
sanit. sanitary; sanitation
s.a.n.r. subject to approval, no risk
Sans. Sanskrit
sans. [printing] sanserif
Sansk. Sanskrit
SANZ Standards Association of New Zealand
SAO Scottish Association of Opticians
SAOS Scottish Agricultural Organization Society
SAP South African Police
s.a.p. soon as possible
SAPA South African Press Association; South African Publishers' Association
SAPC Scottish Accident Prevention Council
sapfu [slang] surpassing all previous foul-ups
sapl [shipping] sailed as per list (referring to Lloyd's List)
SAPT Scottish Association for Public Transport
SAR search and rescue; *Son Altesse Royale* (French: Her/His Royal Highness); Sons of the American Revolution; South African Republic; [China] Special Administrative Region; [physics] specific absorption rate; synthetic aperture radar
Sar. Sarawak; Sardinia; Sardinian
SARA Scottish Amateur Rowing Association; Scottish Anti-Racist Alliance
SARAH search and rescue homing (radar system); [medicine] surgery assistant robot acting on the head (in brain surgery)
SARBE search and rescue beacon equipment
Sarl [commerce] *société à responsabilité limitée* (French: limited company, Ltd)
SARM Scottish Anti-Racist Movement
SARs Substantial Acquisition Rules (for mergers and takeovers)
SARSAT search and rescue satellite(-aided tracking)
SA/RT [computing] structured systems analysis for real time
Sarum. *Sarumensis* (Latin: (Bishop) of Salisbury)
SAS Scandinavian Airlines System; Small

Astronomical Satellite; *Societatis Antiquariorum Socius* (Latin: Fellow of the Society of Antiquaries); *Son Altesse Sérénissime* (French: Her/His Most Serene Highness); [military] Special Air Service; Statement of Auditing Standards

Sas [commerce] *società in accomàndita semplice* (Italian: limited partnership)

SASA Scottish Amateur Snooker Association; Scottish Amateur Swimming Association

SASC Small Arms School Corps

SASE [USA] self-addressed stamped envelope

SASF Salvation Army Students' Fellowship

Sask. Saskatchewan

SASO Senior Air Staff Officer; South African Students' Organization

SASR Special Air Service Regiment

SASV Scottish Association for the Speaking of Verse

SAT [USA] scholastic aptitude test; Senior Member of the Association of Accounting Technicians; ship's apparent time; South Australian Time; [education] standard assessment task

S At. South Atlantic

Sat. Saturday

sat. satellite; saturate; saturated

SATB [music] soprano, alto, tenor, bass

SATCO signal automatic air traffic control system

SATEX semiautomatic telegraph exchange

SATIPS Society of Assistant Teachers in Preparatory Schools

satn saturation

SATRA Shoe and Allied Trades Research Association

SATRO Science and Technology Regional Organization

SATS South African Transport Services

S Aus. South Australia; South Australian

S Austral. South Australia; South Australian

SAV [microbiology] simian adenovirus

s.a.v. sale at valuation; stock at valuation

SAVS Scottish Anti-Vivisection Society

SAW Scottish Association of Writers; [advertising] space at will; submerged arc welding; [telecommunications] surface acoustic wave

SAWA Scottish Amateur Wrestling Association

SAWS synoptic automatic weather station

Sax. Saxon; Saxony

sax [short form] saxophone

sax. saxophone

SAYC Scottish Association of Youth Clubs

SAYE save as you earn

SB Bachelor of Science (from Latin *Scientiae Baccalaureus*); [astronomy] barred spiral galaxy; [vehicle registration] Glasgow; sales book; [military] Sam Browne (officer's belt with diagonal strap); savings bank; selection board; Serving Brother (of order); [commerce] short bill (of exchange); sick bay; Signal Boatswain; signal book; simultaneous broadcast(ing); [chemical engineering] slurry bed; small business; [chemistry] sodium borate; South Britain (i.e. England and Wales); Special Branch; statute book; [medicine] stillborn; stretcher bearer; sub-branch

Sb [chemical element] antimony (from Latin *stibium*)

sb stilb (unit of luminance)

sb. [grammar] substantive

.sb Solomon Islands (in Internet address)

s.b. single-breasted; small bore (rifle); smooth bore; [baseball] stolen base(s)

SBA School of Business Administration; Scottish Basketball Association; sick-bay (or -berth) attendant; [USA] Small Business Administration; [aeronautics] standard beam approach

SBAA Sovereign Base Areas Administration

SBAC Society of British Aerospace Companies (formerly Society of British Aircraft Constructors)

SBB *Schweizerische Bundesbahnen* (German: Swiss Federal Railways)

SBBNF Ship and Boat Builders' National Federation

SBC School Broadcasting Council; single-board computer; [electrical engineering] small bayonet cap

SBD [slang] silent but deadly (breaking of wind); Soviet Block Division (of CIA); [electronics] surface-barrier diode

SBE Southern British English

SbE south by east

SBGI Society of British Gas Industries
SBH Scottish Board of Health
SBIC [USA] small business investment company
SBL Society of Biblical Literature; [electronics] surface boundary layer
SBLI [USA] savings bank life insurance
SBM single buoy mooring
SBN Standard Book Number (replaced by ISBN)
SBNO Senior British Naval Officer
s'board starboard
SBOT Sacred Books of the Old Testament
SBP [medicine] systolic blood pressure
SBPR Society for Back Pain Research
SBR [medicine] strict bed rest; styrene–butadiene rubber
sbre *septiembre* (Spanish: September)
SBS [medicine] sick building syndrome; [military] Special Boat Service
SBSA Scottish Board Sailing Association
SBStJ Serving Brother of the Order of St John of Jerusalem
SBT [shipping] segregated ballast tanks
SBTD Society of British Theatre Designers
SBU Scottish Badminton Union; strategic business unit
SBV seabed vehicle
SbW south by west
SC [vehicle registration] Edinburgh; safe custody; sailing club; Salvage Corps; [law] same case; [US military] Sanitary Corps; [Australia, New Zealand] School Certificate; Schools Council; [fishing port] Scilly; Security Council (of UN); self-contained (in accommodation advertisement); *Senatus Consultum* (Latin: decree of the Senate); Senior Counsel; service certificate; [law] Sessions Cases; shooting club; short course; Signal Corps; [printing] single column; [chemistry] single crystal; skating club; skiing club; small craft; social club; solar cell; South Carolina; [US postcode] South Carolina; [military] Southern Command; special case; Special Constable; Special Constabulary; sports club; Staff Captain; staff college; Staff Corps; standing committee; standing conference; [Canada] Star of Courage; statutory committee; [engineering] stress corrosion; [grammar] structural change; [medicine] subcutaneous; Suffolk and Cambridgeshire (regiment); supercalendered (paper); Supreme Court; surface contamination; swimming club
Sc [chemical element] scandium
Sc [meteorology] stratocumulus
Sc. Scandinavia; Scandinavian; Science; Scotch; Scotland; Scots; Scottish; sculptor
s/c self-catering (in accommodation advertisement); self-contained (in accommodation advertisement); [commerce] *son compte* (French: (on) her/his account)
sc. scale; scene; science; scientific; *scilicet* (= namely, that is, from Latin *scire licet*); screw; scruple (unit of weight); *sculpsit* (Latin: (he/she) carved it); sculptor
.sc Seychelles (in Internet address)
s.c. salvage charges; self-contained (in property or accommodation advertisement); [printing] single column; [printing] small capital(s); steel casting; supercalendered (paper)
SCA Scottish Canoe Association; Scottish Chess Association; Scottish Council on Alcohol; Scottish Croquet Association; [medicine] sickle-cell anaemia; Suez Canal Authority; [computing] synchronous concurrent algorithm
SCAAA Southern Counties Amateur Athletic Association
SCAARF Scottish Combined Action Against Racism and Fascism
Scada system control and data acquisition
SCAFA Scottish Child and Family Alliance
SCAHT Scottish Churches Architectural Heritage Trust
SCAN suspected child abuse and neglect
Scan. Scandinavia; Scandinavian
Scand. Scandinavia; Scandinavian
SCAO Senior Civil Affairs Officer
SCAP Supreme Command Allied Powers; Supreme Commander Allied Powers
SCAPA Society for Checking the Abuses of Public Advertising
s. caps [printing] small capitals
SCAR Scientific Committee on Antarctic Research; Special Committee on Antarctic Research
SCARA selective compliance assembly robot arm
Scarab submerged craft assisting repair and burial

SCARF Sickle Cell Anaemia Research Foundation; [accounting] systems control and review file
SCART *Syndicat des constructeurs des appareils radio récepteurs et téléviseurs* (French: Syndicate of Radio and Television Manufacturers) (designers of plug-and-socket system used in home entertainment equipment)
SCAT [medicine] sheep-cell agglutination test
SCB Solicitors Complaints Bureau; [medicine] special-care baby; Speedway Control Board (in motorcycle racing)
ScB Bachelor of Science (from Latin *Scientiae Baccalaureus*)
ScBC Bachelor of Science in Chemistry
ScBE Bachelor of Science in Engineering
SCBU [medicine] special-care baby unit
SCC Scottish Churches Council; Scottish Consumer Council; Sea Cadet Corps; Society of Church Craftsmen; [medicine] squamous-cell carcinoma; [engineering] stress-corrosion cracking
s.c.c. [printing] single column centimetre; [electrical engineering] single cotton-covered (wire)
SCCA Scottish Consumer Credit Association; Society of Company and Commercial Accountants; Sports Car Club of America
SCCAPE Scottish Council for Commercial, Administrative and Professional Education
SCCL Scottish Council for Civil Liberties
SCD Scottish Council on Disability; [medicine] sickle-cell disease
ScD Doctor of Science (from Latin *Scientiae Doctor*)
scd scheduled
SCDA Scottish Community Drama Association
SCDC Schools Curriculum Development Committee
ScDHyg Doctor of Science in Hygiene
ScDMed Doctor of Science in Medicine
SCE schedule compliance evaluation; Scottish Certificate of Education; [genetics] sister-chromatid exchange
sce. scenario
SCEC Scottish Community Education Council
SCET Scottish Council for Educational Technology
SCF Save the Children Fund; Senior Chaplain to the Forces
scf standard cubic feet
scfd standard cubic feet per day
scfh standard cubic feet per hour
scfm standard cubic feet per minute
SCG Sydney Cricket Ground
scg scoring
SCGB Ski Club of Great Britain
Sch. [taxation] schedule; [currency] Schilling; School
sch. schedule; scholar; scholarship; scholastic; scholiast; *scholium* (Latin: note); school; schooner
sched. schedule
schem. schematic
scherz. [music] *scherzando* (Italian: joking, playfully)
SchMusB Bachelor of School Music
schol. scholar; scholarship; scholastic; scholiast; *scholium* (Latin: note)
schr schooner
SCI Scottish Central Institutions; Society of the Chemical Industry
sci. science; scientific
s.c.i. [printing] single-column inch
SCIAF Scottish Catholic International Aid Fund
SCID Scotland's Campaign against Irresponsible Drivers; [medicine] severe combined immune deficiency
sci. fa. *scire facias* (Latin: cause it to be known) (judicial writ)
sci-fi [short form] science fiction
scil. *scilicet* (= namely, that is, from Latin *scire licet*)
SCIT Special Commissioners of Income Tax
SCK Servants of Christ the King
SCL Scottish Central Library; Student of Civil Law
Scl [astronomy] Sculptor
SCLC Scottish Child Law Centre; [medicine] small-cell lung cancer (or carcinoma); Southern Christian Leadership Conference
SCLI Somerset and Cornwall Light Infantry
SCM [stock exchange] smaller companies market; State Certified Midwife (replaced

by RM); Student Christian Movement; summary court martial
ScM Master of Science (from Latin *Scientiae Magister*)
SCMA Society of Cinema Managers of Great Britain and Ireland (Amalgamated); Stilton Cheese Manufacturers' Association
SCMAC Scottish Catholic Marriage Advisory Council
SCMES Society of Consulting Marine Engineers and Ship Surveyors
ScMHyg Master of Science in Hygiene
SCNE Select Committee on National Expenditure
SCNI Sports Council for Northern Ireland
SCNO Senior Canadian Naval Officer
Sco [astronomy] Scorpius
SCOBEC Scottish Business Education Council
SCODL [computing] scan conversion object description language
SCOFF Society for the Conquest of Flight Fear
Scolag Scottish Legal Action Group
S Con. Res. [USA] Senate concurrent resolution
SCONUL Standing Conference of National and University Libraries
SCOR Scientific Committee on Oceanic Research; Standing Committee on Refugees
Scot. Scotch; Scotland; Scottish
ScotBIC Scottish Business in the Community
SCOTEC Scottish Technical Education Council
SCOTUS Supreme Court of the United States
SCOTVEC Scottish Vocational Educational Council (became part of SQA)
SCOUT [commerce] shared currency option under tender
SCP single-cell protein (in food technology); [Canada] Social Credit Party
SCPC [telecommunications] single channel per carrier
SCPR Scottish Council of Physical Recreation
SCPS Society of Civil and Public Servants
SCR [chemical engineering] selective catalytic reactor; senior combination room (in university or college); senior common room (in university or college); sequence control register; [electronics] silicon-controlled rectifier; small companies rate (of corporation tax)
scr. [finance] scrip; script; scruple (unit of weight)
SCRAM Scottish Campaign to Resist the Atomic Menace
SCRE Scottish Council for Racial Equality; Scottish Council for Research in Education
SCREAM Society for the Control and Registration of Estate Agents and Mortgage Brokers
Script. Scriptural; Scripture(s)
SCS Scottish Crime Squad; [USA] Soil Conservation Service; space communications system
SCSA signal computing system achitecture; Soil Conservation Society of America
SCSI small computer systems interface (pronounced 'scuzzy')
SCSS Scottish Council of Social Service
Sct [astronomy] Scutum
SCTR Standing Conference on Telecommunications Research
SCU Scottish Cricket Union; Scottish Cyclists' Union; [medicine] special care unit
SCUA Scottish Conservative and Unionist Association; Suez Canal Users' Association
scuba self-contained underwater breathing apparatus
sculp. *sculpsit* (Latin: (he/she) carved it); sculptor; sculptural; sculpture
sculps. *sculpsit* (Latin: (he/she) carved it)
sculpt *sculpsit* (Latin: (he/she) carved it)
sculpt. sculptor; sculptural; sculpture
SCV *Stato della Città del Vaticano* (Italian: Vatican City State)
SCWS Scottish Cooperative Wholesale Society
SCY [vehicle registration] Truro (Isles of Scilly)
SCYA Scottish Christian Youth Assembly
SD Diploma in Statistics; Doctor of Science (from Latin *Scientiae Doctor*); [vehicle registration] Glasgow; *salutem dicit* (Latin: (he/she) sends greeting); sea-damaged; [USA] Secretary of Defense; semi-detached (in property advertisement); *Senatus Decreto* (Latin: by decree

of the Senate); send direct; [medicine] senile dementia; senior deacon; sequence date; [military] service dress; [commerce] short delivery; *Sicherheitsdienst* (German: Security Service) (in Nazi Germany); [finance] sight draft; Signal Department; Signal Division; [computing] single density (disk); South Dakota; [US postcode] South Dakota; special delivery; special duty; spin dryer (in accommodation advertisement); staff duties; stage door; [statistics] standard deviation; [USA] State Department; [grammar] structural description; submarine detector; [currency] Sudanese dinar; [fishing port] Sunderland; supply depot; [international vehicle registration] Swaziland

S/D [USA] school district; [finance] sight draft

sd said; sailed; [bookbinding] sewed; signed; sound

.sd Sudan (in Internet address)

s.d. safe deposit; same date; *sans date* (French: no date); semi-detached (in property advertisement); sense datum (in philosophy); several dates; [commerce] short delivery; *siehe dies* (German: see this); *sine die* (Latin: without a day (being fixed)); [statistics] standard deviation

SDA Scottish Darts Association; Scottish Development Agency; Scottish Dinghy Association; Scottish Diploma in Agriculture; Seventh Day Adventist(s); Social Democratic Alliance; spray-drying absorption (or absorber)

S Dak. South Dakota

SD&T staff duties and training

SDAT [medicine] senile dementia of the Alzheimer type

S-DAT stationary digital audio tape

SDC Society of Dyers and Colourists; submersible decompression chamber

SDCGB Square Dance Callers of Great Britain

SDD Scottish Development Department; [telecommunications] subscriber direct dialling

SDECE *Service de documentation étrangère et de contre-espionnage* (French counterintelligence agency)

SDF Social Democratic Federation

SDG *Soli Deo Gloria* (Latin: Glory to God Alone)

SDH [computing] synchronous digital hierarchy

SDHE spacecraft data-handling equipment

SDI selective dissemination of information; Strategic Defense Initiative (US Star Wars programme)

SDIO [USA] Strategic Defense Initiative Office

SDL special duties list

sdl. saddle

SDLC [computing] synchronous data link control

SDLP [Northern Ireland] Social Democratic and Labour Party

SDMJ September, December, March, June (end of financial quarters)

SDO senior dental officer; senior duty officer; station duty officer; subdivisional officer

S Doc. [USA] Senate document

SDP Social Democratic Party (former political party); [insurance] social, domestic and pleasure

SDPM [computing] software development process model

SDR special dispatch rider; *Suddeutscher Rundfunk* (German: South German Radio)

SDRAM [computing] synchronous dynamic random-access memory

SDRs [finance] special drawing rights (in IMF)

SDRT stamp duty reserve tax

SDS scientific data system; Sisters of the Divine Saviour; sodium dodecyl sulphate (detergent); *Sozialistischer Deutscher Studentenbund* (German: Federation of Socialist Students); [USA] strategic defense system; [USA] Students for a Democratic Society

SDT Society of Dairy Technology

SDTU Sign and Display Trades Union

SDUK Society for the Diffusion of Useful Knowledge

SE [vehicle registration] Aberdeen; [fishing port] Salcombe; sanitary engineering; Scottish Enterprise; Society of Engineers; [computing] software engineering; *Son Éminence* (French: His Eminence); *Son Excellence* (French: Her/His Excellency);

southeast; southeastern; [UK postcode] southeast London; Staff Engineer; Standard English; Stirling engine; stock exchange; [building] stopped end; [civil aircraft marking] Sweden

S/E stock exchange

Se [chemical element] selenium

.se Sweden (in Internet address)

s.e. single end; single ended; single engine; [book-keeping] single entry; special equipment; [statistics] standard error; straight edge

SEA Southeast Asia

SEAAC Southeast Asia Air Command

SEAC School Examination and Assessment Council; Southeast Asia Command; Standard Eastern Automatic Computer

SEAL [US navy] sea-air-land

SEALF Southeast Asia Land Forces

SE&CR South Eastern and Chatham Railway

SEAQ Stock Exchange Automated Quotations (System)

SEAT *Sociedad Española de Automoviles de Tourismo* (Spanish vehicle manufacturer)

SEATO Southeast Asia Treaty Organization

SEATS Stock Exchange Alternative Trading Service

SEB Scottish Education Board (became part of SQA); Southern Electricity Board

SEC Scottish Evangelistic Crusade; Secondary Examinations Council; [USA] Securities and Exchange Commission; [military] Southeastern Command

Sec. Secretary

sec [mathematics] secant; [short form] second

sec. second; secondary; seconded; secretary; section; sector; *secundum* (Latin: according to); security

SECAM [television] *séquentiel couleur à mémoire* (French: colour sequence by memory) (broadcasting system)

SECC Scottish Exhibition and Conference Centre

Sec-Gen Secretary-General

sech [mathematics] hyperbolic secant

Sec. Leg. Secretary of the Legation

sec. leg. *secundum legem* (Latin: according to law)

sec. nat. *secundum naturam* (Latin: according to nature, naturally)

sec. reg. *secundum regulam* (Latin: according to rule)

sect. section

secy secretary

SED Scottish Education Department; shipper's export declaration; *Sozialistische Einheitspartei Deutschlands* (German: Socialist Unity Party) (former East German Communist Party)

sed. sedative; sediment

SEDAR [navigation] submerged electrode detection and ranging

sedt sediment

sedtn sedimentation

SEE senior electrical engineer; Society of Environment Engineers

Seeboard Southeastern Electricity Board

SEF Shipbuilding Employers' Federation

SEG [taxation] Self Employment Group; socioeconomic grade

seg. segment; segregate; [music] *segue* (Italian: follows, comes after)

SEIF *Secretaria de Estado da Informação e Turismo* (Portuguese: State Information and Tourist Board)

SEIS submarine escape immersion suit

seismol. seismological; seismology

SEIU [USA] Service Employees International Union

sel. select; selected; selection; *selig* (German: deceased)

Selk. Selkirk

SELNEC Southeast Lancashire, Northeast Cheshire

SEM scanning electron microscope (or microscopy)

Sem. Seminary; Semitic

sem. semester; semicolon; seminary

s.e.m. [statistics] standard error of the mean

semi [short form] semi-detached house

semp. [music] *sempre* (Italian: always, still)

s/empl. self-employed

SEN special educational needs; State Enrolled Nurse (former name of ENG)

Sen. Senate; Senator; (Marcus Annaeus) Seneca (Roman writer); Senior

sen. senior; [music] *senza* (Italian: without)

S en C [commerce] *sociedad en comandita* (Spanish: limited partnership); [commerce] *société en commandite* (French: limited partnership)

Sennac Special Educational Needs National Advisory Council

S en NC [commerce] *société en nom collectif* (French: partnership)

Senr Senior

sent. sentence

SEO senior executive officer; senior experimental officer; Society of Educational Officers

s.e.o.o. *sauf erreur ou omission* (French: errors or omissions excepted)

SEP [USA] simplified employee pension

Sep. September; Septuagint

sep. [botany] sepal; separable; separate; separated; separation

SEPA Scottish Environment Protection Agency

SEPM Society of Economic Palaeontologists and Mineralogists

sepn separation

SEPON Stock Exchange Pool Nominees Limited

Sept. *September* (German: September); September; Septuagint

sept. *septem* (Latin: seven); *septembre* (French: September)

seq. sequel; sequence; *sequens* (Latin: the following (one)); *sequente* (Latin: and in what follows); *sequitur* (Latin: it follows)

seq. luce [medicine] *sequenti luce* (Latin: on the following day) (in prescriptions)

seqq. *sequentia* (Latin: the following (ones)); *sequentibus* (Latin: in the following (places))

Ser [astronomy] Serpens

ser. serial; series; sermon; servant; service

SERA Socialist Environment and Resources Association

Serb. Serbia; Serbian

SERC Science and Engineering Research Council (formerly SRC)

Serg. Sergeant

Sergt Sergeant

Serj. Serjeant

Serjt Serjeant

SERL Services Electronics Research Laboratory

SERLANT [US navy] Service Forces, Atlantic

SERPAC [US navy] Service Forces, Pacific

Serps State Earnings-Related Pension Scheme

SERT Society of Electronic and Radio Technicians

serv. servant; service

SES Scientific Exploration Society; [USA] socioeconomic status; Stock Exchange of Singapore

SESCO secure submarine communications

SESDAQ Stock Exchange of Singapore Dealing and Automated Quotation System

SESI Stock Exchange of Singapore Index

SESO Senior Equipment Staff Officer

sess. session

SET Securities Exchange of Thailand; selective employment tax (former tax)

SETI [astronomy] search for extraterrestrial intelligence

S-et-L Saône-et-Loire (French department)

S-et-M Seine-et-Marne (French department)

S-et-O Seine-et-Oise (French department)

Sets Stock Exchange electronic trading system

sett. *settembre* (Italian: September)

sev. sever; several; severe

sevl several

SEW safety-equipment worker

sew. sewage; sewer; sewerage

Sex [astronomy] Sextans

sex. sextet; sexual

Sexag. Sexagesima

sext. sextant

SF [vehicle registration] Edinburgh; San Francisco; science fiction; Senior Fellow; [military] Sherwood Foresters; shipping federation; [telecommunications] signal frequency; [finance] sinking fund; Sinn Féin; Society of Friends; special facilities; special forces; [electrical engineering] standard frequency

Sf [currency] Suriname guilder (from alternative name florin)

sf. [music] *sforzando* (Italian: strengthening, strongly accented)

s.f. [baseball] sacrifice fly; [commerce] *sans frais* (French: no expenses); science fiction; [telecommunications] signal frequency; [finance] sinking fund; *sub finem* (Latin: towards the end)

SFA Scottish Football Association; Securities and Futures Authority; Small Farmers' Association; sulphated fatty alcohol (in detergent); [slang] sweet Fanny Adams (i.e. nothing); [slang] sweet fuck all (i.e. nothing)

SFAC Statement of Financial Accounting Concepts

SFAS Statement of Financial Accounting Standards

SFB *Sender Freies Berlin* (German: Broadcasting Station of Free Berlin)

SFBMS Small Farm Business Management Scheme

SFC specific fuel consumption (of jet engine)

Sfc [USA] Sergeant first class

SFD [obstetrics] small for dates (of baby)

SFEP Society of Freelance Editors and Proofreaders

SFEU Scottish Further Education Unit

SFF [computing] small form factor

sfgd safeguard

SFHEA Scottish Further and Higher Education Association

SFI *Société financière internationale* (French: International Finance Corporation)

SFInstE Senior Fellow, Institute of Energy

SFL Scottish Football League; [aeronautics] sequenced flashing lights (on runway)

sfm surface feet per minute

SFO Senior Flag Officer; Serious Fraud Office; Superannuation Funds Office

SFOF spaceflight operations facility (in NASA)

SFOR Sustaining (or Stabilization) Force (NATO-led peacekeeping force in Bosnia, replacement for IFOR)

sfp [music] *sforzato-piano* (Italian: strongly accented (then) soft)

SFR [finance] sinking fund rate of return

SFr [currency] Swiss franc

SFSR Socialist Federation of Soviet Republics

SFT supercritical fluid technology

SFTCD Senior Fellow of Trinity College, Dublin

SFU signals flying unit; suitable for upgrade (on airline ticket)

sfz. [music] *sforzando* (Italian: strengthening, strongly accented)

SG [vehicle registration] Edinburgh; *Sa Grâce* (French: Her/His Grace); *Sa Grandeur* (French: Her/His Highness); Scots Guards; Seaman Gunner; Secretary-General; *selon grandeur* (French: according to size) (on menus etc.); [US education] senior grade; [astronomy] Seyfert galaxy; ship and goods; Showmen's Guild of Great Britain; Society of Genealogists; Solicitor-General; spin-glass (type of crystal); [UK postcode] Stevenage; Surgeon-General

Sg [chemical element] seaborgium

Sg. Surgeon

sg. [grammar] singular

.sg Singapore (in Internet address)

s.g. specific gravity; steel girder

SGA Scottish Games Association; [obstetrics] small for gestational age; Society of Graphic Art

SGB *Schweizerischer Gewerkschaftsbund* (German: Swiss Federation of Trade Unions)

SGBI Schoolmistresses' and Governesses' Benevolent Institution

SgC Surgeon Captain

SgCr Surgeon Commander

SGD [Freemasonry] Senior Grand Deacon

sgd signed

sgdg *sans garantie du gouvernement* (French: without government guarantee) (of patent)

Sge [astronomy] Sagitta

SGF Scottish Grocers' Federation

SGHWR [nuclear technology] steam-generating heavy-water reactor

sgl. single

S Glam. South Glamorgan

SgLCr Surgeon Lieutenant-Commander

sgle single

SGM Sea Gallantry Medal

SGML [computing] standard generalized markup language

SGO Squadron Gunnery Officer

SGOT [medicine] serum glutamic oxaloacetic transaminase

SGP [international vehicle registration] Singapore

SGPT [medicine] serum glutamic pyruvic transaminase

Sgr [astronomy] Sagittarius

SgRA Surgeon Rear-Admiral

SGRAM [computing] synchronous graphics random-access memory

SGT Society of Glass Technology

Sgt Sergeant

Sgt-Maj Sergeant-Major
SGTS Scottish Gaelic Texts Society
SGU Scottish Gliding Union; Scottish Golf Union
SgVA Surgeon Vice-Admiral
SGW [Freemasonry] Senior Grand Warden
SH [vehicle registration] Edinburgh; [fishing port] Scarborough; Schleswig-Holstein; school house; scrum half (in rugby); sexual harassment; [meteorology] showers; [numismatics] small head; southern hemisphere
Sh. [military] Shipwright
s/h shorthand
sh. shall; [stock exchange] share; sheep; [bookbinding] sheet; shilling; shower (in property or accommodation advertisement)
s.h. [baseball] sacrifice hit; second-hand; shit-house; slant height; slope height
SHA Scottish Hockey Association; Secondary Heads Association; [astronomy, navigation] sidereal hour angle; special health authority; [mathematics] spherical harmonic analysis
SHAC Shelter Housing Aid Centre
SHACT Scottish Housing Associations Charitable Trust
SHAEF Supreme Headquarters Allied Expeditionary Forces (in World War II)
Shak. (William) Shakespeare (English writer)
Shakes. (William) Shakespeare (English writer)
SH&MA Scottish Horse and Motormen's Association
SHAPE Supreme Headquarters Allied Powers Europe (of NATO)
SHC [physics] specific heat capacity
SHCJ Society of the Holy Child Jesus
shd should
SHE safety, health and ergonomics
S/HE [shipping] Sundays and holidays excepted
Shef. Sheffield
SHEFC Scottish Higher Education Funding Council
Sheff. Sheffield
Shet. Shetland Islands
Shetl. Shetland Islands
SHEX [shipping] Sundays and holidays excepted
SHF [radio] superhigh frequency
Sh.F shareholders' funds
SHGF Scottish Hang-Gliding Federation
SHHD Scottish Home and Health Department
shipmt shipment
shipt shipment
s/hist. service history (in car advertisement)
SHM [physics] simple harmonic motion; Society of Housing Managers
SHMIS Society of Headmasters and Headmistresses of Independent Schools
SHMO senior hospital medical officer
SHO senior house officer
SHORAN short-range navigation
SHP [chemical engineering] selective hydrogenation process; [horticulture] single-flowered hardy perennial (rose); [horticulture] single-flowered hybrid perpetual (rose)
shp shaft horsepower
shpg shipping
shpt shipment
SHQ station headquarters; supreme headquarters
shr. share(s)
shrap. shrapnel
SHRG Scottish Homosexual Rights Group
Shrops Shropshire
SHS Shire Horse Society; Social History Society of the United Kingdom; *Societatis Historicae Socius* (Latin: Fellow of the Historical Society)
SHT [horticulture] single-flowered hybrid tea (rose)
sht [bookbinding] sheet
shtg. shortage
SHU Scottish Hockey Union
s.h.v. *sub hac voce* (Latin: under this word) (in reference book); *sub hoc verbo* (Latin: under this word) (in reference book)
SHW safety, health, and welfare
shwr shower (in property or accommodation advertisement)
SI Sandwich Islands (former name of Hawaii); seriously ill; Shetland Islands; Smithsonian Institution (Washington, DC); Socialist International; [USA] Society of Illustrators; South Island (New Zealand); Staff Inspector; (Order of the) Star of India; Staten Island (New York); statutory instrument (of government); styrene–isoprene (polymer); *Système*

International (*d'Unités*) (French: International System (of Units), as in **SI unit**)
Si [chemical element] silicon
.si Slovenia (in Internet address)
s.i. sum insured
SIA Securities Industry Association; Society of Investment Analysts; Spinal Injuries Association
SIAC [USA] Securities Industry Automation Corporation
SIAD Society of Industrial Artists and Designers (former name of CSD)
SIAM [USA] Society of Industrial and Applied Mathematics
SIAS Statement on Internal Auditing Standards
SIB Savings and Investment Bank; Securities and Investments Board; [medicine] self-injurious behaviour; Shipbuilding Industry Board; Special Investigation Branch (of police)
Sib. Siberia; Siberian
SIBH Society for the Interpretation of Britain's Heritage
SIBOR [finance] Singapore Inter-Bank Offered Rate
SIC [USA] Scientific Information Center; Standard Industrial Classification
Sic. Sicilian; Sicily
sic. [pharmacology] *siccus* (Latin: dry)
SICAV *société d'investissement à capital variable* (French: unit trust)
SICOT *Société internationale de chirurgie orthopédique et de traumatologie* (French: International Society of Orthopaedic Surgery and Traumatology)
SID Society for International Development; *Spiritus in Deo* (Latin: her/his spirit is with God); [radio] sudden ionospheric disturbance
SIDA Swedish International Development Authority; [medicine] *syndrome immunodéficitaire acquis* (French: acquired immune deficiency syndrome, Aids)
SIDF system independent data format
SIDS [medicine] sudden infant death syndrome (= cot death)
SIEC Scottish Industrial Estates Corporation
SIESO Society of Industrial and Emergency Service Officers
SIF selective identification feature; [engineering] stress-intensity factor
SIFS special instructors' flying school
SIG [numismatics] signature of engraver present; special interest group
Sig. *Signor* (Italian: Mr); *Signore* (Italian: Sir)
sig. signal; signature; *signetur* (Latin: let it be written, let it be labelled); significant; signification; signifies
SIGAC Scottish Industrial Groups Advisory Council
SIGBI Soroptimist International of Great Britain and Ireland
sig. fig. [mathematics] significant figures
sigill. *sigillum* (Latin: seal)
SIGINT signals intelligence (gathering network)
SIGMA Science in General Management
Sigmn Signalman
sign. signature
signif. significant; signifier
sig. n. pro. [medicine] *signa nomine proprio* (Latin: label with the proper name) (in prescriptions)
Sig. O Signal Officer
SIH Society for Italic Handwriting
SIL [electronics] single in-line; *Société internationale de la lèpre* (French: International Leprosy Association)
Sil. Silesia; Silesian
SIM self-inflicted mutilation; *Société internationale de musicologie* (French: International Musicological Society); survey information on microfilm
sim. similar; similarly; simile
SIMA Scientific Instrument Manufacturers' Association of Great Britain; Steel Industry Management Association; [psychology] system for identifying motivated abilities
SIMC *Société internationale pour la musique contemporaine* (French: International Society for Contemporary Music)
Simca *Société industrielle de mécanique et carrosserie automobiles* (French car manufacturer)
SIMD [computing] single instruction, multiple data
SIME Security Intelligence Middle East
SIMEX Singapore International Monetary Exchange
SIMG *Societas Internationalis Medicinae Gen-*

eralis (Latin: International Society of General Medicine)
SIMM [computing, electronics] single in-line memory module
SIMPL Scientific, Industrial and Medical Photographic Laboratories
SIN [accounting] stores issue note
sin [mathematics] sine
sin. sinecure; *sinistra* (Italian: left)
sinbad [informal] single income, no boyfriend, absolutely desperate
Sing. Singapore; Singaporean
sing. [grammar] singular; [medicine] *singulorum* (Latin: of each) (in prescriptions)
Sinh. Sinhalese
sinh [mathematics] hyperbolic sine
SINS ship's inertial navigation system
SIO senior intelligence officer; [computing] serial input/output
SIOP [USA] single integrated operations plan (for nuclear war)
SIP [computing] single in-line package; [USA] supplemental income plan
SIPC [USA] Securities Investor Protection Corporation
SIPO [computing] serial in, parallel out
SIPRC Society of Independent Public Relations Consultants
SIPRI Stockholm International Peace Research Institute
SIPS side impact protection system (in car bodywork)
SIR [taxation] small income relief
Sir [computing] serial infrared
SIRA Scientific Instrument Research Association
SIRS [medicine] systemic inflammatory response syndrome
SIRTF Space Infrared Telescope Facility
SIS Satellite Information Services; Secret Intelligence Service (= MI6); [New Zealand] Security Intelligence Service
sis [short form] sister
sis. sister
SISD Scottish Information Service for the Disabled; [computing] single instruction, single data
SISO [computing] serial in, serial out; [electronics] single input, single output
SISS submarine integrated sonar system
SISTER Special Institutions for Scientific and Technological Education and Research
SIT Society of Industrial Technology; Society of Instrument Technology; [engineering] spontaneous ignition temperature; [currency] tolar (used in Slovenia)
sit. sitting room (in property advertisement); situated; situation
s.i.t. stopping in transit; storing in transit
SITA *Société internationale de télécommunications aéronautiques* (French: International Society of Aeronautical Telecommunications); Students' International Travel Association
SITC Standard International Trade Classification
sitcom [short form] situation comedy
SITC(R) Standard International Trade Classification (Revised)
SITPRO Simpler Trade Procedures Board (formerly Simplification of International Trade Procedures)
sits vac. situations vacant
sitt. sitting room (in property advertisement)
sit. vac. situation(s) vacant
SIUNA Seafarers International Union of North America
SI unit *Système international* unit
SIV [microbiology] simian immunodeficiency virus
SIW self-inflicted wound
SIWA Scottish Inland Waterways Association
SJ [vehicle registration] Glasgow; Society of Jesus (= Jesuits); supersonic jet
s.j. [law] sub judice
SJA St John Ambulance
SJAA St John Ambulance Association
SJAB St John Ambulance Brigade
SJC standing joint committee; [USA] Supreme Judicial Court
SJCRE Scottish Joint Committee on Religious Education
SJD Doctor of Juridical (or Juristic) Science (from Latin *Scientiae Juridicae Doctor*)
SJF Scottish Judo Federation
SK [vehicle registration] Inverness; Saskatchewan; Sealed Knot (historical reenactment society); [international vehicle registration] Slovakia; [UK postcode] Stockport
Sk [currency] Slovakian koruna
sk sack; sick

sk. sketch
.sk Slovakia (in Internet address)
SKAMP station keeping and mobile platform (unmanned boat)
SKC Scottish Kennel Club
SKFA Scottish Keep Fit Association
Skm Stockholm
s.k.p.o. [knitting] slip one, knit one, pass slipped stitch over
Skr Skipper; [currency] Swedish krona
Skr. Sanskrit
Skt Sanskrit
SKU [commerce] stock-keeping unit
SL [vehicle registration] Dundee; [insurance] salvage loss; Scout leader; sea level; Second Lieutenant; security list; Sergeant-at-Law; [building] short lengths; Sierra Leone; [UK postcode] Slough; Solicitor-at-Law; source language; southern league; south latitude; [commerce] specification limits; Squadron Leader; supplementary list
Sl. Slovak; Slovakian
sl. sleet; slightly; slip
.sl Sierra Leone (in Internet address)
s.l. [insurance] salvage loss; *secundum legem* (Latin: according to law); seditious libel; [bibliography] *sine loco* (Latin: without place (of publication)); support line
SLA School Libraries Association; Scottish Library Association; special landscape area (in conservation); [USA] Special Libraries Association; Symbionese Liberation Army
SLAC Stanford Linear Accelerator Center
SLADE Society of Lithographic Artists, Designers, Engravers and Process Workers
SLAET Society of Licensed Aircraft Engineers and Technologists
Slam standoff land-attack missile
s.l.a.n. [bibliography] *sine loco, anno vel nomine* (Latin: without place, year or name (of publisher))
Slar [military] side-looking airborne radar
SLAS Society for Latin American Studies
SLASH Scottish Local Authorities Special Housing Group
S Lat. south latitude
Slav. Slavic; Slavonian; Slavonic
SLBM submarine-launched ballistic missile
SLC Scottish Land Court; Scottish Law Commission; Scottish Leaving Certificate; Statute Law Committee; Surgeon Lieutenant-Commander
SLCM sea-launched cruise missile; ship-launched cruise missile; submarine-launched cruise missile
SLD self-locking device; Social and Liberal Democrats (former name of Liberal Democrats)
sld sailed; sealed; sold; solid
S Ldr Squadron Leader
SLE [medicine] systemic lupus erythematosus
s.l. et a. [bibliography] *sine loco et anno* (Latin: without place and year (of publication))
S level [education] Special level (formerly Scholarship level)
SLF Scottish Landowners' Federation
s.l.f. [telecommunications] straight-line frequency
SLFP Sri Lanka Freedom Party
SLGA Scottish Ladies' Golfing Association
SLIC [USA] (Federal) Savings and Loan Insurance Corporation
SLIM South London Industrial Mission
SLIP [computing] serial line Internet protocol
Slipar [military] short light pulse alerting receiver (in aircraft)
SLLA Scottish Ladies' Lacrosse Association
SLLW solid low-level (radioactive) waste
SLM ship-launched missile
SLMA [USA] Student Loan Marketing Association
SLMC Scottish Ladies' Mountaineering Club
s.l.n.d. [bibliography] *sine loco nec data* (Latin: without date or place (of publication))
SLO senior liaison officer; [international vehicle registration] Slovenia
SLOA Steam Locomotive Operators' Association
SLOC [computing] source lines of code
SLP Scottish Labour Party; [USA] Socialist Labor Party
slp slip
s.l.p. *sine legitime prole* (Latin: without lawful issue)
SLR satellite laser ranging; self-loading rifle; single-lens reflex (camera)

SLRS Sexual Law Reform Society
SL Rs [currency] Sri Lankan rupee
SLS sodium lauryl sulphate (detergent); Stephenson Locomotive Society
SLSC surf life-saving club
SLSI [electronics] super large-scale integration
SLTA Scottish Lawn Tennis Association; Scottish Licensed Trade Association
Slud [military slang] salivate, lachrymate, urinate, defecate (effects of chemical weapons)
SLV Society of Licensed Victuallers; space launch vehicle; standard launch vehicle
SLW solid low-level (radioactive) waste
sly slowly; southerly
SM [vehicle registration] Carlisle; Master of Science (from Latin *Scientiae Magister*); sadomasochism; sadomasochist; sales manager; *Sa Majesté* (French: Her/His Majesty); *sanctae memoriae* (Latin: of holy memory); *Seine Majestät* (German: Her/His Majesty); senior magistrate; Sergeant-Major; [USA] service mark (registered proprietary name); [astronautics] service module; shipment memorandum; [fishing port] Shoreham; [music] short metre; silver medal; silver medallist; Sisters of Mercy; Society of Miniaturists; Sons of Malta; Staff Major; stage manager; [astronomy] standard model; [USA] state militia; station master; stipendiary magistrate; strategic missile; *Sua Maestà* (Italian: Her/His Majesty); (officer qualified for) Submarine Duties; *Su Magestad* (Spanish: Her/His Majesty); Surgeon Major; [UK postcode] Sutton (Surrey); [medicine] systolic murmur
Sm [chemical element] samarium
s/m sadomasochism; sadomasochist
sm. small
.sm San Marino (in Internet address)
SMA [medicine] spinal muscular atrophy; [USA] Surplus Marketing Administration
SMAC Standing Medical Advisory Committee (of NHS)
SMATV satellite (or small) master antenna television
SMAW shielded metal-arc welding
SMB Bachelor of Sacred Music; *Sa Majesté Britannique* (French: Her/His Britannic Majesty)
SMBA Scottish Marine Biological Association
SMBF Scottish Musicians' Benevolent Fund
SMBG [medicine] self-monitoring of blood glucose (in diabetes)
SMC *Sa Majesté Catholique* (French: Her/His Catholic Majesty); School Meals Campaign; Scottish Mountaineering Club; Scottish Museums Council; [astronomy] Small Magellanic Cloud; [aeronautics] standard mean chord
sm. caps [printing] small capitals
SMC(Disp) Dispensing Certificate of the Worshipful Company of Spectacle Makers
SMD Doctor of Sacred Music; [medicine] senile macular degeneration; [music] short metre double; submarine mine depot; [electronics] surface-mounted device (on printed circuit board)
SMDS [computing] switched multi-megabit data service
SME *Sancta Mater Ecclesia* (Latin: Holy Mother Church); seismic-margin earthquake; [international vehicle registration] Suriname
SMERSH *Smert Shpionam* (Russian: death to spies) (section of KGB)
SMEs small and medium enterprises
SMEX [astronomy] Small Explorer
SMG Scottish Media Group; submachine gun
SMGC Scottish Marriage Guidance Council
SMH [fishing port] St Margaret's Hope (Orkney)
SMHD Higher Diploma in Ophthalmic Optics of the Worshipful Company of Spectacle Makers
SMHI Swedish Meteorological and Hydrological Institute
SMHO Sovereign Military Hospitaller Order (in Malta)
SMI *Sa Majesté Impériale* (French: Her/His Imperial Majesty); Swiss Market Index
SMIA Sheet Metal Industries Association
SMIEEE [USA] Senior Member of the Institute of Electrical and Electronics Engineers
SMIRE [USA] Senior Member of the Institute of Radio Engineers

Smith. Inst. Smithsonian Institution (Washington, DC)
SMJ Sisters of Mary and Joseph
smk. smoke
SML Science Museum Library
sml small; small, medium, large
sml. simulate; simulation; simulator
SMLE short magazine Lee-Enfield (rifle)
SMM Master of Sacred Music; *Sancta Mater Maria* (Latin: Holy Mother Mary)
SMMB Scottish Milk Marketing Board
SMMT Society of Motor Manufacturers and Traders Limited
SMO senior medical officer; Sovereign Military Order
SMON [medicine] subacute myelo-opticoneuropathy
smorz. [music] *smorzando* (Italian: becoming slower and softer)
SMP Society of Mural Painters; statutory maternity pay; [computing] symmetric multiprocessing
s.m.p. *sine mascula prole* (Latin: without male issue)
SMPS Society of Master Printers of Scotland; switched-mode power supply
SMPTE [USA] Society of Motion Picture and Television Engineers
SMR *Sa Majesté Royale* (French: Her/His Royal Majesty); standardized mortality ratio; standard Malaysian rubber; [medicine] standard metabolic rate; standard mortality rate
SMRC Scottish Motor Racing Club
SMRE Safety in Mines Research Establishment
SMRTB Ship and Marine Requirements Technology Board
SMS secondary modern school; Shipwrecked Mariners' Society; synchronous meteorological satellite
SMSA [USA] Standard Metropolitan Statistical Area
SMSO Senior Maintenance Staff Officer
SMT ship's mean time; [computing] surface mount technology
SMTA Scottish Motor Trade Association
SMTF Scottish Milk Trade Federation
SMTO senior mechanical transport officer
SMTP [computing] simple mail transfer protocol
SMTWTFS Sunday, Monday, Tuesday, Wednesday, Thursday, Friday, Saturday
SMV submentovertical (in radiology)
SMW standard metal window
SMWIA [USA] Sheet Metal Workers' International Association
SMWS Scottish Malt Whisky Society
SN [vehicle registration] Dundee; [fishing port] North Shields; [USA] Secretary of the Navy; [international vehicle registration] Senegal; Sergeant Navigator; shipping note; [meteorology] snow; [astronomy] supernova; [UK postcode] Swindon
S/N shipping note; [electronics] signal-to-noise (as in **S/N ratio**)
Sn [chemical element] tin (from Latin *stannum*)
s/n serial number; series number; service number
sn. senior; snow
.sn Senegal (in Internet address)
s.n. *secundum naturam* (Latin: according to nature, naturally); serial number; series number; service number; *sine nomine* (Latin: without name); *sub nomine* (Latin: under the (specified) name)
SNA Scottish Netball Association; [computing] systems network architecture
snafu [slang] situation normal, all fouled (or fucked) up
SNAME [USA] Society of Naval Architects and Marine Engineers
SNAP Shelter Neighbourhood Action Project; systems for nuclear auxiliary power
SNB [stock exchange] sellers no buyers
SNBTS Scottish National Blood Transfusion Service
SNCB *Société nationale des chemins de fer belges* (French: Belgian National Railways)
SNCF *Société nationale des chemins de fer français* (French: French National Railways)
SND Sisters of Notre Dame
Snd Sound (in place-names)
SNECMA *Société nationale d'étude et de construction de moteurs d'aviation* (French: national aeroengine research and construction company)
SNF solids, nonfat (in nutrition); spent nuclear fuel; [USA] strategic nuclear forces
SNFA Standing Naval Force, Atlantic
SNFU Scottish National Farmers' Union

SNG substitute natural gas; synthetic natural gas
Sng. Singapore
SNH Scottish National Heritage
SNIF [finance] short-term note issuance facility
SNIG sustainable noninflationary growth
SNIPEF Scottish and Northern Ireland Plumbing Employers' Federation
SNL Sandia National Laboratories (Albuquerque); standard nomenclature list
SNLA Scottish National Liberation Army
SNLR services no longer required
SNLV strategic nuclear launch vehicle
SNM [USA] Society of Nuclear Medicine; Somali National Movement
SNMP [computing] simple network management protocol
SNO Scottish National Orchestra (former name of RSO); senior naval officer; senior navigation officer; senior nursing officer
SNOBOL string oriented symbolic language (computer programming language)
SNP Scottish National Party
SNPA Scottish National Newspaper Proprietors' Association
SNR [electronics] signal-to-noise ratio; Society for Nautical Research; [astronomy] supernova remnant
Snr Senior
Sñr *Señor* (Spanish: Mr)
snr senior
Snra *Senhora* (Portuguese: Mrs)
Sñra *Señora* (Spanish: Mrs)
Sñrta *Señorita* (Spanish: Miss)
SNSC Scottish National Ski Council
SNSS School Natural Science Society
SNTPC Scottish National Town Planning Council
SNTS Society for New Testament Studies
SNU [astronomy] solar neutrino unit; Spiritualists' National Union
Snug Scottish Network Users' Group
SO [vehicle registration] Aberdeen; scientific officer; Scottish Office; section officer; senior officer; shale oil (residue); Signal Officer; [fishing port] Sligo; [computing] small outline; [international vehicle registration] Somalia; sorting office; [UK postcode] Southampton; [meteorology] southern oscillation; special order; Staff Officer; standing order; Stationery Office; statistical office; suboffice; supply officer; symphony orchestra
S/O section officer; seller's option; shipowner
So. *Sonntag* (German: Sunday); south; southern
so. sonata; south; southern
.so Somalia (in Internet address)
s.o. seller's option; shipping order; *siehe oben* (German: see above); strike out; substance of (weight of paper)
SOA Scottish Orienteering Association; state of the art
SoA Society of Authors
SOAD Staff Officer, Air Defence
SOAP [medicine] subjective, objective, analysis, plan (in patients' records)
SOAS School of Oriental and African Studies (University of London)
SOB [USA] Senate office building; [medicine] shortness of breath; [informal] silly old bastard; [informal] son of a bitch; state office building
s.o.b. [informal] son of a bitch
SOBHD Scottish Official Board of Highland Dancing
SOC Scottish Ornithologists' Club; [informal] slightly off colour
Soc. Socialist; [commerce] *società* (Italian: company); Society; Socrates (ancient Greek philosopher)
soc. social; socialist; society; sociology
SocCE(France) *Société des ingénieurs civils de France* (French: Society of Civil Engineers of France)
Soc. Dem. Social Democrat
sociol. sociological; sociologist; sociology
SOCO scene-of-crime officer
SOCONY Standard Oil Corporation of New York
SOCS Society of County Secretaries
soc. sci. social science; social scientist
Socy Society
sod. sodium
SODAC Society of Dyers and Colourists
SODEPAX Committee on Society, Development and Peace (from Latin *pax*)
SODS ship's operatic and dramatic society (in Royal Navy)
SOE Special Operations Executive (in World War II); state-owned enterprise

SOED Scottish Office Education Department; *Shorter Oxford English Dictionary*
SOEID Scottish Office Education and Industry Department
SOES [US finance] Small Order Execution System (of NASDAQ)
SOF share of freehold (in property advertisement); [chemistry] soluble organic fraction; [cinema] sound on a film
SOFAA Society of Fine Art Auctioneers
sofar sound fixing and ranging
SOFCS self-organizing flight-control system
SOFFEX Swiss Options and Financial Futures Exchange
SOFIA Stratospheric Observatory for Infrared Astronomy
S of S Secretary of State; [Bible] Song of Solomon; [Bible] Song of Songs
S of Sol. [Bible] Song of Solomon
S of T Sons of Temperance
S of TT School of Technical Training
SOGAT Society of Graphical and Allied Trades (became part of GPMU)
SOH sense of humour (in personal advertisement)
SOHC single overhead cam(shaft)
SOHIO Standard Oil of Ohio
SOHO Solar Heliospheric Observatory
SoHo small office/home office (furniture); [USA] South of Houston
Sohyo *Nihon Rodo Kumiai So Hygikai* (Japanese: General Council of Japanese Trade Unions)
SO(I) Staff Officer (Intelligence)
SOIC [electronics] small outline integrated circuit
SO-in-C Signal Officer-in-Chief
SOL [US slang] strictly (or shit) out of luck
Sol. Solicitor; [Bible] Song of Solomon
sol. solicitor; soluble; solution
s.o.l. [insurance] shipowner's liability
Solace Society of Local Authority Chief Executives
Sol-Gen Solicitor-General
soln solution
solr solicitor
solv. solvent
soly solubility
SOM Society of Occupational Medicine
Som. Somerset
SOMA Society of Mental Awareness
SOME Senior Ordnance Mechanical Engineer
SOMPA [USA] System of Multicultural Pluralistic Assessment (intelligence testing)
Som.Sh. [currency] Somali shilling
sonar sound navigation and ranging
SONET [computing] synchronous optical network
SO(O) Staff Officer (Operations)
SOP significant other person; sleeping-out pass; standard operating procedure; [computing] sum of products
sop. [music] soprano
Soph. Sophocles (ancient Greek writer)
soph. sophomore
SOR sale or return; Society of Radiographers
SORD submerged-object recovery device
SORG Stratospheric Ozone Review Group
SORP [accounting] Statement of Recommended Practice
SOS save our souls (international distress signal, letters chosen for ease and clarity of transmission in Morse code); Secretary of State; senior officers' school; services of supply
s.o.s. [medicine] *si opus sit* (Latin: if necessary) (in prescriptions)
SOSc Society of Ordained Scientists
SoSh [currency] Somali shilling
sost. [music] *sostenuto* (Italian: sustained)
SOT stay-on tab
Soton Southampton
SOTS Society for Old Testament Study
Sou. south; Southampton; southern
sou. south; southern
SOV [linguistics] subject-object-verb
Sov. Soviet
sov. sovereign
s.o.v. shut-off valve
Sov. Un. Soviet Union
Soweto Southwestern Townships (South Africa)
SP [vehicle registration] Dundee; [civil aircraft marking] Poland; *Saint-Père* (French: Holy Father); [UK postcode] Salisbury; *Sanctissimus Pater* (Latin: Most Holy Father); Self-Propelled (Antitank Regiment); service pistol; [military] service police; shore patrol; Sisters of Providence; Socialist Party; [building] soil pipe; spark(ing) plug; Staff Paymaster;

standard play (on video recorder); starting price (hence slang meaning 'latest information'); stirrup pump; [banking] stop payment; stop press; stretcher party; submarine patrol; *Summus Pontifex* (Latin: Supreme Pontiff, the pope); supply point; [finance] supra protest

Sp. Spain; Spaniard; Spanish

sp. space; special; specie; [biology] species; specific; specimen; speed; spelling; spirit; sport; *sposa* (Italian: wife)

s.p. self-propelled; [music] *senza pedale* (Italian: without pedal); *sine prole* (Latin: without issue); [electrical engineering] single phase; [advertising] special position; starting point; [banking] stop payment

SPA Saudi Press Agency; Scottish Pipers' Association; Scottish Pistol Association; Scottish Publishers' Association; [USA] Society for Personnel Administration; special protection area (for conservation of wild birds)

SpA [commerce] *società per azioni* (Italian: public limited company, plc)

SPAA Scottish Passenger Agents' Association

SPAB Society for the Protection of Ancient Buildings

SPAC Standing Pharmaceutical Advisory Committee (of NHS)

spac. spacious (in property advertisement)

Sp. Am. Spanish American

Span. Spaniard; Spanish

SPANA Society for the Protection of Animals in North Africa

SPANDAR space and range radar (in NASA)

SPAR member of US Coast Guard women's reserve (in World War II, from Latin motto *Semper paratus* = always ready); superprecision-approach radar

Sp. Ar. Spanish Arabic

SPARC [computing] scalable processor architecture

SPARKS Sport Aiding Medical Research for Kids

SPAS *Societatis Philosophicae Americanae Socius* (Latin: Fellow of the American Philosophical Society)

SPATC South Pacific Air Transport Council

SPBA Scottish Pipe Band Association

SPBP Society for the Preservation of Birds of Prey

SPBW Society for the Preservation of Beers from the Wood

SPC Secretariat of the Pacific Community; Society for the Prevention of Crime; Southern Pacific Commission (former name of the Pacific Community); [commerce] statistical process control; [telecommunications] stored program control

SPCA [USA] Society for the Prevention of Cruelty to Animals

SPCK Society for Promoting Christian Knowledge

SPD Salisbury Plain District; [astronomy] south polar distance; *Sozialdemokratische Partei Deutschlands* (German: Social Democratic Party of Germany)

spd speed (in car advertisement)

s.p.d. [finance] subject to permission to deal

SPDA single-premium deferred annuity

SPDL [computing] standard page description language

SPE Society for Pure English; [USA] Society of Petroleum Engineers; [electronics] solid-phase epitaxy

SPEC [Canada] Society for Pollution and Environmental Control; South Pacific Bureau for Economic Cooperation

spec [short form] specification; [short form] speculation (as in **on spec**)

spec. special; specialist; specially; specific; specifically; specification; specimen; spectrum

special. specialized

specif. specific; specifically; specification

SPECmark Systems Performance Evaluation Cooperative's benchmark

specs [short form] specifications; [short form] spectacles

SPECT [medicine] single photon emission compute(rize)d tomography

SPECTRE Special Executive for Counter-Intelligence, Revenge and Extortion (in James Bond stories by Ian Fleming)

Sp.Ed. [USA] Specialist in Education

SPES South Place Ethical Society

SPET [medicine] single photon emission tomography

SPF South Pacific forum; sun protection factor (in sunscreen)
SPF/DB [aeronautics] super-plastic forming/diffusion bonding (manufacturing method)
SPG Society for the Propagation of the Gospel (in Foreign Parts) (became part of USPG); Special Patrol Group
s.p.g. self-propelled gun
SPGA Scottish Professional Golfers' Association
SPGB Socialist Party of Great Britain
sp. gr. specific gravity
sp. ht specific heat
SPI [finance] selected period investment; [USA] Society of the Plastics Industry
SPIRE [navigation] spatial inertial reference equipment
spirit. [music] *spiritoso* (Italian: with spirit); spiritualism; spiritualistic
SPIW special-purposes individual weapon
SPKC Small Pig Keepers' Council
s.p.l. *sine prole legitima* (Latin: without legitimate issue)
SPLA Sudan People's Liberation Army
SPM scanning proton microscope; [music] short particular metre
s.p.m. *sine prole mascula* (Latin: without male issue)
SPMO senior principal medical officer
SPMU Society of Professional Musicians in Ulster
SPN stop press news
SPNC Society for the Promotion of Nature Conservation
SPNM Society for the Promotion of New Music
SPNR Society for the Promotion of Nature Reserves
SPO senior press officer
SPÖ *Sozialistische Partei Österreichs* (German: Austrian Socialist Party)
SPOA Scottish Prison Officers' Association
SPOD Sexual Problems of the Disabled
SPOE Society of Post Office Engineers
Spool simultaneous peripheral operation on-line
s/pool swimming pool (in property advertisement)
Spore Society for the Preservation of the Rainforest Environment
SPOT single property ownership trust
SPP [medicine] sub-pubic prostatectomy
spp. [biology] species (plural)
SPQR *Senatus Populusque Romanus* (Latin: the Senate and People of Rome); small profits and quick returns
SPR Society for Psychical Research; strategic petroleum reserve
Spr [military] Sapper
spr. spring; sprinkle; sprinkler; sprung
SPRC Society for the Prevention and Relief of Cancer
SPREd Society of Picture Researchers and Editors
SPRI Scott Polar Research Institute (Cambridge)
SPRINT solid-propellant rocket-intercept missile
SPRL Society for the Promotion of Religion and Learning
sprl [commerce] *société de personnes à responsabilité limitée* (French: limited company, Ltd)
SPS Scottish Painters' Society; [physics] Super Proton Synchrotron (at CERN); syndiotactic polystyrene (plastic)
s.p.s. *sine prole supersite* (Latin: without surviving issue)
SPSL Society for the Protection of Science and Learning
SPSO senior principal scientific officer
SPSP St Peter and St Paul
spt seaport; sport; support
sptg sporting
SPTL Society of Public Teachers of Law
SPUC Society for the Protection of the Unborn Child
SPURV self-propelled underwater research vehicle
SPVD Society for the Prevention of Venereal Disease
sp. vol. specific volume
SQ sick quarters; [meteorology] squall; [building] squint quoin; stereophonic-quadraphonic; survival quotient
Sq. Squadron; Square (in road name)
sq. sequence; *sequens* (Latin: the following (one)); squadron; square
SQA Scottish Qualifications Agency; [computing] software quality assurance
sq cm square centimetre
sqd squad
Sqdn Squadron
sqdn squadron
Sqdn Ldr Squadron Leader

sq ft square feet; square foot
sq in square inch
sq km square kilometre
SQL [computing] standard query language; [computing] structured query language
sq m square metre
sq mi square mile
sq mm square millimetre
SQMS Staff Quartermaster-Sergeant
Sqn Squadron
sqn squadron
Sqn Ldr Squadron Leader
SqnQMS Squadron Quartermaster-Sergeant
SqnSM Squadron Sergeant-Major
SqO Squadron Officer
sqq. *sequentia* (Latin: the following (ones))
squid [electronics] superconducting quantum interference device
sq yd square yard
SR [vehicle registration] Dundee; [currency] Saudi riyal; Saunders Roe (aircraft); [USA] Senate resolution; senior registrar; service rifle; [computing] set-reset; Socialist Revolutionary (Party) (in former USSR); Society of Radiographers; sodium ricinoleate (in toothpaste); [USA] Sons of the Revolution; [railways] Southern Region; [physics] special relativity; [military] Special Reserve; [taxation] standard rate; [psychology] stimulus–response; [fishing port] Stranraer; [UK postcode] Sunderland; *Sveriges Radio* (Swedish broadcasting corporation); [physics] synchrotron radiation; synthetic rubber
S/R sale or return
Sr *Senhor* (Portuguese: Mr, Sir); Senior; *Señor* (Spanish: Mr, Sir); *Signor* (Italian: Mr, Sir); Sir; Sister (title of nun); [chemical element] strontium
sr senior; steradian (unit of solid angle)
s/r sunroof (in car advertisement)
.sr Suriname (in Internet address)
s.r. self-raising; shipping receipt; short rate
SRA Squash Rackets Association
Sra *Senhora* (Portuguese: Mrs); *Señora* (Spanish: Mrs)
SRAC [finance] short-run average cost
SRAM short-range attack missile
SRAM [computing] static random-access memory
SR&CC [insurance] strikes, riot and civil commotion
SRAP Scottish Rent Assessment Panel
SRB solid rocket booster; [computing] source route bridge; [microbiology] sulphate-reducing bacteria
SRBC [medicine] sheep red blood cell(s)
SRBM short-range ballistic missile
SRBP synthetic resin-bonded paper
SRC sample return container; Science Research Council (former name of SERC); [commerce] *sociedad regular colectiva* (Spanish: partnership); solvent-refined coal; [chemistry] standard reference compound; [engineering] steam Rankine cycle; Students' Representative Council; Swiss Red Cross
SRCC [insurance] strikes, riot and civil commotion
SRCh State Registered Chiropodist
SRCN State Registered Children's Nurse (former name of RSCN)
SRD service rum diluted
SRDE Signals Research and Development Establishment
SRE *Sancta Romana Ecclesia* (Latin: Holy Roman Church)
S Rept [USA] Senate report
S Res. [USA] Senate resolution
SRG standard reformed gas; Strategic Research Group (market research company)
SRHE Society for Research into Higher Education
SRI *Sacrum Romanum Imperium* (Latin: Holy Roman Empire)
SRIS Science Reference Information Service
Srl. [commerce] *società a responsabilità limitata* (Italian: limited company, Ltd)
SRls [currency] Saudi riyal
SRM short-range missile; speed of relative movement
SRN State Registered Nurse (former name of RGN)
SRNA Shipbuilders and Repairers National Association
sRNA [biochemistry] soluble ribonucleic acid
SRO Scottish Record Office; [finance] self-regulatory organization; [microbiology]

sex-ratio organism; [USA] single room occupancy; sold right out; standing room only; Statutory Rules and Orders; Supplementary Reserve of Officers

s/roof sunroof (in car advertisement)

SRP Society of Recorder Players; State Registered Physiotherapist; suggested retail price; supply refuelling point

SRPA Squash Rackets Professional Association

SRPS Scottish Railway Preservation Society

SRR Society for Research in Rehabilitation

SRS Scottish Record Society; *Societatis Regiae Sodalis* (Latin: Fellow of the Royal Society)

SRs [currency] Seychelles rupee

SRSA Scientific Research Society of America

SRSS [mathematics] square-root sum of squares

Srta *Senhorita* (Portuguese: Miss); *Señorita* (Spanish: Miss)

SRU Scottish Rugby Union

SRWS Scottish Rights of Way Society

SRY Sherwood Rangers Yeomanry

SS [vehicle registration] Aberdeen; *Sacra Scriptura* (Latin: Holy Scripture); Saints; *Santa Sede* (Italian: Holy See); *Sa Sainteté* (French: His Holiness); *Schutzstaffel* (German: protection squad) (Nazi organization); secondary school; Secretary of State; secret service; security service; short sleeves; [computing] single-sided (disk); social security; [chemistry] sodium sulphate; [UK postcode] Southend-on-Sea; Staff Surgeon; stainless steel; standard size; steamship; [fishing port] St Ives; *Strada Statale* (Italian: National Highway); Straits Settlements; Sunday school; surface-to-surface (missile)

S/S same size (of illustrations); silk screen (printing); steamship

SS. Saints; *sanctissimus* (Latin: most holy)

ss. sections; [medicine] *semis* (Latin: half) (in prescriptions); subsection

s.s. screw steamer; *sensu stricto* (Latin: in the strict sense); [music] *senza sordini* (Italian: without mutes); simplified spelling; steamship; *supra scriptum* (Latin: written above)

SSA Scottish Schoolmasters' Association; [computing] serial storage architecture; [USA] Social Security Administration; Society of Scottish Artists; standard spending assessment (in local government)

SSAC Scottish Sub-Aqua Club; Social Security Advisory Committee

SSADM [computing] structured systems analysis and design method

SSAE stamped self-addressed envelope

SSAFA Soldiers', Sailors' and Airmen's Families Association

SSAIB Security Systems and Alarms Inspection Board

SSAP Statement of Standard Accounting Practice

SSB Bachelor of Sacred Scripture (from Latin *Sacrae Scripturae Baccalaureus*); [telecommunications] single-sideband (transmission); [USA] Social Security Board

SSBN [US navy] strategic submarine, ballistic nuclear

SSC Scottish Ski Club; Scottish Sports Council; Sculptors' Society of Canada; [India] Secondary School Certificate; Short Service Commission; [USA] small-saver certificate; *Societas Sanctae Crucis* (Latin: Society of the Holy Cross); [Scotland] Solicitor before the Supreme Court; Species Survival Commission; [physics] Superconducting Super Collider

SScD Doctor of Social Science

SSD Doctor of Sacred Scripture (from Latin *Sacrae Scripturae Doctor*); Social Services Department

SS.D *Sanctissimus Dominus* (Latin: Most Holy Lord, the pope)

ssDNA [biochemistry] single-stranded deoxyribonucleic acid

SSE Society of St Edmund; south-southeast

SSEB South of Scotland Electricity Board

SSEC Secondary School Examinations Council

SSEES School of Slavonic and East European Studies (University of London)

SSEG Scottish Solar Energy Group

SSF single-seater fighter (aircraft); Society of St Francis

SSFA Scottish Schools' Football Association; Scottish Steel Founders' Association

SSgt Staff Sergeant
SSHA Scottish Special Housing Association
SSHC Society to Support Home Confinement
SSI Scottish Symphony Orchestra; site of scientific interest; [electronics] small-scale integration; Social Services Inspectorate; Society of Scribes and Illuminators; [USA] supplemental security income
SSJE Society of St John the Evangelist
SSL Licentiate in Sacred Scripture (from Latin *Sacrae Scripturae Licentiatus*)
SSLH Society for the Study of Labour History
SSM Saturday, Sunday, Monday; [telecommunications] single-sideband modulation; Society of the Sacred Mission; [commerce] soft systems methodology; Staff Sergeant-Major; surface-to-surface missile
SSMA Stainless Steel Manufacturers' Association
SSMH Scottish Society for the Mentally Handicapped
SSN severely subnormal; [USA] Social Security number; Standard Serial Number
SSO senior scientific officer; senior supply officer; Staff Signal Officer; Station Staff Officer
SSP Scottish Socialist Party; statutory sick pay
ssp. [biology] subspecies
SSPCA Scottish Society for the Prevention of Cruelty to Animals
SSPE [medicine] subacute sclerosing panencephalitis
SS.PP. *Sancti Patres* (Latin: Holy Fathers)
sspp. [biology] subspecies (plural)
SSPWB Scottish Society for the Protection of Wild Birds
SSQ [military] station sick quarters
SSR secondary surveillance radar; Small Ships Register; Soviet Socialist Republic
SSRA Scottish Squash Rackets Association
SSRC Social Science Research Council (former name of ESRC)
SSRI [pharmacology] selective serotonin reuptake inhibitor (used to treat depression); [USA] Social Science Research Institute
SSS Secretary of State for Scotland; [USA] Selective Service System (for military mobilization); [medicine] sick sinus syndrome; Simplified Spelling Society; single-screw ship; [fishing port] South Shields; standard scratch score (in golf)
SSSA Scottish Salmon Smokers' Association; Scottish Schools' Swimming Association
SSSI site of special scientific interest
SSSR *Soyuz Sovietskikh Sotsialisticheskikh Respublik* (Russian: Union of Soviet Socialist Republics, USSR)
SSStJ Serving Sister, Order of St John of Jerusalem
SSSU Scottish Speed Skating Union
SST Scottish Scenic Trust; [telecommunications] single-sideband transmission; Society of Surveying Technicians; supersonic transport
SSTA Scottish Secondary Teachers' Association
SSTC sold subject to contract (in property advertisement)
SSU Sunday School Union
s/susp. sports suspension (in car advertisement)
SSV [microbiology] simian sarcoma virus
SSW Secretary of State for War; south-southwest; special security wing (of prison)
SSWA Scottish Society of Women Artists
ST [vehicle registration] Inverness; sanitary towel; septic tank; shipping ticket; (Hubble) Space Telescope; speech therapist; spring tide; Standard Time; [fishing port] Stockton; [UK postcode] Stoke-on-Trent; [civil aircraft marking] Sudan; Summer Time; *Sunday Times*; [building] surface trench; surtax
St Saint; stokes (unit of viscosity); Strait; Street
St [meteorology] stratus
St. Statute; Strait; Street
st seat; strait; street
st. stanza; state; statement; statute; stem; [printing] stet (instruction to restore or retain deleted text); [knitting] stitch; stone (unit of weight); strait; street; strophe (division of verse); [cricket] stumped (by)
s.t. select time; short ton; static thrust; steam trawler

STA Sail Training Association; [USA] Science and Technology Agency; Scottish Typographical Association; Society of Typographic Arts; Swimming Teachers' Association
Sta *Santa* (Italian, Portuguese or Spanish: Saint (female))
sta. station; stationary
StAAA St Andrew's Ambulance Association
stab. stability; stabilization; stabilized; stabilizer; stable
stacc. [music] *staccato* (Italian: detached)
Staffs Staffordshire
STAGS Sterling Transferable Accruing Government Securities
stalag *Stammlager* (German: base camp) (World War II prisoner-of-war camp)
STANAG Standard NATO Agreement
stand. standard
St And. St Andrews (Scotland)
STARCAT Space Telescope Archive and Catalogue
START Strategic Arms Reduction Talks
stat. static; statics; [medicine] *statim* (Latin: immediately) (in prescriptions); stationary; statistic(s); statistical; statuary; statue; statute
STATE [military] simplified tactical approach and terminal equipment
Stat. Hall Stationers' Hall (London)
stats [short form] statistics
STAUK Seed Trade Association of the United Kingdom
STB Bachelor of Sacred Theology (from Latin *Sacrae Theologiae Baccalaureus*); Scottish Tourist Board
stbd starboard
stbt steamboat
STC Samuel Taylor Coleridge (British poet); satellite test centre; Senior Training Corps; Short-Title Catalogue; Standard Telephones and Cables Limited; state total cost; [India] State Trading Corporation; subject to contract (in property advertisement)
STD Doctor of Sacred Theology (from Latin *Sacrae Theologiae Doctor*); salinity-temperature-depth (sensor system); [medicine] sexually transmitted disease; Society of Typographic Designers; [computing] state transition diagram; [New Zealand] subscriber toll dialling; subscriber trunk dialling
Std. *Stunde* (German: hour)
std standard; started
STE Society of Telecom Executives
Ste *Sainte* (French: Saint (female))
Sté [commerce] *société* (French: company, Co.)
STEL short-term exposure level (of radiation); short-term exposure limit (of radiation)
STEM scanning transmission electron microscope (or microscopy)
Sten Shepherd and Turpin (inventors of Sten gun)
sten. stenographer; stenographic(al); stenography
steno. stenographer; stenographic(al); stenography
stenog. stenographer; stenographic(al); stenography
STEP Solar/Terrestrial Energy Programme; Special Temporary Employment Programme
ster. stereophonic; stereotype; sterling
stereo [short form] stereophonic
stereo. stereotype
St. Ex. Stock Exchange
stg seating; sterling
StGB *Strafgesetzbuch* (German: Penal Code)
stge storage
STGWU Scottish Transport and General Workers' Union
STH [biochemistry] somatotrophic hormone
STh Scholar in Theology
Sth South
sthn southern
STI Straits Times Index (of Singapore Stock Exchange)
STIM scanning transmission ion microscope
STINGS [aeronautics] stellar inertial guidance system
stip. stipend; stipendiary; stipulation
Stir. Stirling(shire)
s.t.i.r. surplus to immediate requirements
stk stock
STL Licentiate in Sacred Theology (from Latin *Sacrae Theologiae Licentiatus*); *Sacrae Theologiae Lector* (Latin: Reader in Sacred Theology); Standard Telecom-

munications Laboratories; [telecommunications] studio-to-transmitter link
stlg sterling
STLO Scientific Technical Liaison Office; Scientific Technical Liaison Officer
STLV [microbiology] simian T-lymphotropic virus
STM Master of Sacred Theology (from Latin *Sacrae Theologiae Magister*); scanning tunnelling microscope (or microscopy); scientific, technical and medical (as in **STM publishing**); [psychology] short-term memory; [computing] synchronous transfer module
STMS [finance] short-term monetary support (in EMS)
stmt statement
stn stain; station
STO sea transport officer; senior technical officer; standing order
Sto *Santo* (Portuguese: Saint)
STOL [aeronautics] short take-off and landing
STOLVCD [aeronautics] short take-off and landing, vertical climb and descent
S'ton Southampton
STOP Students Tired of Pollution; suction termination of pregnancy
STOPP Society of Teachers Opposed to Physical Punishment
S to S ship to shore; station to station
STP [informal] hallucinogenic drug related to mescaline (from its energizing effect, facetiously compared to that of the oil substitute STP); Professor of Sacred Theology (from Latin *Sacrae Theologiae Professor*); [trademark] scientifically treated petroleum (oil substitute); sewage treatment plant; [computing] shielded twisted pair; standard temperature and pressure
s.t.p. standard temperature and pressure
STPMA Scottish Theatrical Proprietors' and Managers' Association
Str. Strait; *Strasse* (German: Street); Street
str seater; steamer
str. straight; strait; street; strength; [music] string(s); [music] stringed; stringer (in journalism); [rowing] stroke (oar); strong; structural; structure
s.t.r. surplus to requirements
STRAC [USA] strategic air command; strategic army corps
STRAD signal transmitting, receiving and distribution
Strad [short form] Stradivarius (violin)
stratig. stratigraphy
strd stranded
strep. streptococcal; streptococcus
STRG Scottish Tory Reform Group
STRICOM [USA] Strike Command
string. [music] *stringendo* (Italian: compressing, with increasing speed)
STROBE satellite tracking of balloons and emergencies
STS Scottish Tartan Society; Scottish Text Society; [astronautics] space transportation system
Sts Saints
STSF Scottish Target Shooting Federation
STSO Senior Technical Staff Officer
st. st. [knitting] stocking stitch
STTA Scottish Table Tennis Association
STUC Scottish Trades Union Congress
stud. student
Stuka *Sturzkampfflugzeug* (German: dive bomber)
STV Scottish Television; single transferable vote; standard test vehicle; [USA] subscription television
stvdr. stevedore
stwy stairway
SU [civil aircraft marking] Egypt; [vehicle registration] Glasgow; Scripture Union; [fishing port] Southampton; Soviet Union; [physics] strontium unit
Su. Sudan; Sudanese; Sunday
s.u. set up; *siehe unten* (German: see below)
SUA [USA] State Universities Association
SUB [USA] supplemental unemployment benefits
sub [short form] sub-edit; [short form] submarine; [short form] subscription
sub. subaltern; [music] *subito* (Italian: immediately, suddenly); subject; [grammar] subjunctive; submarine; subordinate; subordinated; subscription; subsidiary; subsidy; subsistence; [grammar] substantive; substitute; suburb; suburban; subvention; subway
SUBAW Scottish Union of Bakers and Allied Workers
subd. subdivide; subdivision
sub-ed. sub-edit; sub-editor

subj. subject; subjective; subjectively; [grammar] subjunctive
SUBLANT [US navy] Submarine Forces, Atlantic
Sub-Lieut. Sub-Lieutenant
Sub-Lt Sub-Lieutenant
subord. [grammar] subordinate; [grammar] subordinating
SUBPAC [US navy] Submarine Forces, Pacific
SUBROC submarine rocket
subs [short form] subscription
subs. subsidence; subsidiary; subsistence
subsc. subscription
subsec. subsection
subseq. subsequent; subsequently
subsp. [biology] subspecies
subspp. [biology] subspecies (plural)
subsq. subsequent; subsequently
subst. [grammar] substantive; substantively; substitute; substitution
substand. substandard
suc. succeed; success; successor; suction
succ. succeed; succeeding; success; successive; successor
SUD [international vehicle registration] Sudan
SUDS [medicine] sudden unexplained death syndrome
suf. [grammar] suffix
Suff. Suffolk; Suffragan
suff. sufficient; [grammar] suffix
suffoc. suffocation
Suffr. Suffragan
sug. suggest; suggestion
SUIT Scottish and Universal Investment Trust
suiv. *suivant* (French: following)
Sult. Sultan
SUM surface-to-underwater missile
sum. [medicine] *sumat* (Latin: let her/him take it) (in prescriptions); [medicine] *sumendum* (Latin: let it be taken) (in prescriptions); summary; summer
sums. summons
Sun. Sunday
Sund. Sunday
SUNFED Special United Nations Fund for Economic Development
SUNS sonic underwater navigation system
SUNY State University of New York
sup. superficial; superfine; superior; superlative; [grammar] supine; supplement; supplementary; supply; support; supporter; *supra* (Latin: above); supreme
sup. ben. supplementary benefit
Sup. Ct Superior Court; Supreme Court
Supdt Superintendent
super. superficial; superfine; superior; supernumerary
superl. superlative
SUPLO Scottish Union of Power Loom Overlookers
supp. supplement; supplementary
suppl. supplement; supplementary
Supp. Res. Supplementary Reserve (of officers)
supr superior; supervisor
supr. superior; supreme
Supt Superintendent
supvr supervisor
SUR [commerce] set-up reduction
Sur. Surrey
sur. surface; surplus
SURF spent unreprocessed fuel
surg. surgeon; surgery; surgical
Surg. Cdr Surgeon Commander
Surg. Comdr Surgeon Commander
Surg. Gen. Surgeon General
Surg. Lt-Cdr Surgeon Lieutenant-Commander
Surg. Maj. Surgeon Major
Surr. Surrey
surr. surrender; surrogate
surro. surrogate
SURV standard underwater research vessel
surv. survey; surveying; surveyor; survive; surviving; survivor
Surv-Gen Surveyor-General
SUS Scottish Union of Students; Students' Union Society
Sus. [Bible] Susanna (book of Apocrypha); Sussex
sus [short form] suspicious
SUSI Sydney University Stellar Interferometer
susp. suspend; suspension
Suss. Sussex
Sustrans Sustainable Transport
SUT Society for Underwater Technology
Suth. Sutherland
SUV [USA] sport-utility vehicle
SV safety valve; *Sancta Virgo* (Latin: Holy Virgin); *Sanctitas Vestra* (Latin: Your Holi-

ness); [microbiology] simian virus; stroke volume (of engine)
Sv sievert (unit of radiation dose equivalent)
s/v [insurance] surrender value
.sv El Salvador (in Internet address)
s.v. sailing vessel; side valve; *sub verbo* (Latin: under the word) (in reference book); *sub voce* (Latin: under the word) (in reference book); [insurance] surrender value
SVA Scottish Volleyball Association
SVC [medicine] superior vena cava; [computing] supervisor call
svc. service
svce service
SVD [veterinary science] swine vesicular disease
svg saving
SVGA [computing] super video graphics array
svgs savings
SVO Scottish Variety Orchestra; [linguistics] subject-verb-object; superintending veterinary officer
SVP saturated vapour pressure
s.v.p. *s'il vous plaît* (French: (if you) please)
SVQ Scottish Vocational Qualification
s.v.r. [medicine] *spiritus vini rectificatus* (Latin: rectified spirit of wine) (in prescriptions)
SVS still-camera video system
SVTP sound velocity, temperature, pressure
s.vv. *sub verbis* (Latin: under the words) (in reference book)
s.v.v. *sit venia verbo* (Latin: pardon the expression)
svy survey
SW [vehicle registration] Carlisle; [vehicle registration] Glasgow; senior warden; shipper's weight; shock wave; [radio] short wave; small women's (clothing size); South Wales; southwest; southwestern; [UK postcode] southwest London; standard weight
S/W [computing] software
Sw. Sweden; Swedish; Swiss
s/w salt water; sea water; seaworthy
sw. switch
s.w. salt water; sea water
Swab. Swabia; Swabian
SWACS space warning and control system
SWALK sealed with a loving kiss (on envelope of love letter)
SWANU South West Africa National Union
SWANUF South West Africa National Union Front
SWAP Scottish Women Against Pornography
SWAPO South West Africa People's Organization
SWAS Submillimetre Wave Astronomy Satellite
SWAT [USA] Special Weapons and Tactics (police unit)
SWB [military] South Wales Borderers
s.w.b. short wheelbase (in car advertisement)
swbd switchboard
SWCI [computing] software configuration item
swd [bookbinding] sewed
SWE [USA] Society of Women Engineers
SWEB South Wales Electricity Board; Southwest Electricity Board
Swed. Sweden; Swedish
SWET Society of West End Theatre(s)
SWF single white female (in accommodation advertisement)
SwF [currency] Swiss franc
SWFA Scottish Women's Football Association
SWG Song Writers' Guild of Great Britain; standard wire gauge
SWH solar water heating
SWHA Scottish Women's Hockey Association
SWIE South Wales Institute of Engineers
SWIFT Society for Worldwide Interbank Financial Transactions
Swing [finance] Sterling Warrant into Gilt-edged Stock
Swit. Switzerland
Switz. Switzerland
SWL safe working load
SWLA Society of Wildlife Artists
SWM single white male (in accommodation advertisement)
SWMF South Wales Miners' Federation
SWO Station Warrant Officer
SWOA Scottish Woodland Owners' Association

SWOPS single-well oil-production system
SWOT [marketing] strengths, weaknesses, opportunities and threats (of new product)
SWP safe working pressure; Socialist Workers' Party
SWPA South-West Pacific Area
SWPF single white professional female (in accommodation advertisement)
SWPM single white professional male (in accommodation advertisement)
SWR [telecommunications] standing-wave ratio
SWRB Sadler's Wells Royal Ballet (former name of Royal Ballet)
SWRI Scottish Women's Rural Institute
SWS static water supply
SWSWU Sheffield Wool Shear Workers' Union
SWT Scottish Wildlife Trust
Swtz. Switzerland
SWWJ Society of Women Writers and Journalists
SX [vehicle registration] Edinburgh; [civil aircraft marking] Greece; soft X-rays; [shipping] Sundays excepted
Sx Sussex
SXR soft X-radiation; soft X-rays
SXT sextant
SY [international vehicle registration] Seychelles; [UK postcode] Shrewsbury; steam yacht; [fishing port] Stornoway
Sy supply; Surrey
Sy. Seychelles; Syria
.sy Syria (in Internet address)
SYB *Statesman's Yearbook*
S Yd Scotland Yard
Syd. Sydney
SYHA Scottish Youth Hostels Association
syl. syllable; syllabus
Sylk [computing] symbolic link
syll. syllable; syllabus
sym. symbol; symbolic; symmetrical; symmetry; symphonic; symphony; symptom
symp. symposium
symph. symphony
syn. synchronize; synod; synonym; synonymous; synonymy; synthetic
sync [short form] synchronization (as in **out of sync**)
sync. synchronization; synchronize; synchronized; synchronous
Syncom synchronous communications satellite
synd. syndicate; syndicated
synon. synonymous
synop. synopsis
synth. [music] synthesizer; synthetic
Sy PO Supply Petty Officer
SYR [international vehicle registration] Syria
Syr. Syria; Syriac; Syrian
syr. [pharmacology] syrup
sys. system
syst. system; systematic
SZ [vehicle registration] Down
sz. size
.sz Swaziland (in Internet address)

T

T [physics] surface tension; tablespoon(ful); [music] *tace* (Italian: be silent); tanker; target; [chemistry] tautomeric effect; [horticulture] tea (rose); teacher; telegraph; telegraphic; telephone; temperature; [music] tempo; temporary; [music] tenor; tera- (indicates 10^{12}, as in **Tm** = terametre); Territorial; Territory; tesla (unit of magnetic flux density); Testament; [international vehicle registration] Thailand; thermometer; [advertising] third of a page (area of type); Thursday; [immunology] thymus (as in **T-cell**); time; torpedo; [photography] total light transmission (as in **T-number**); trainer (aircraft); [fishing port] Tralee; transaction(s); translation; transport; transportation; [obstetrics] transverse (presentation); Treasury; Trinity; [chemistry] tritium; [shipping] tropical (load line); true; Tuesday; Turkish; [knitting] twist
T [physics] kinetic energy; [physics] period;

[physics] thermodynamic temperature; [engineering, physics] torque
t [astronomy] hour angle; [music] te (in tonic sol-fa); thickness; [meteorology] thunder; tonne; [physics] top (quark flavour)
t Celsius temperature; [chemistry] tertiary (isomer); [chemistry] transport number
t. table; tabulated; [sports] tackle; taken (from); [commerce] tare; teaspoon(ful); teeth; temperature; [music] tempo; *tempore* (Latin: in the time of); [music] tenor; [grammar] tense; terminal; territorial; territory; thunder; time; *tome* (French: volume (of book)); ton; tonne; *tonneau* (French: ton); town; township; transit; [grammar] transitive; troy (weight); tun; turn
T2 [civil aircraft marking] Tuvalu
T3 [civil aircraft marking] Kiribati
T7 [civil aircraft marking] San Marino
5T [civil aircraft marking] Mauritania
7T [civil aircraft marking] Algeria
TA [vehicle registration] Exeter; [taxation] table of allowances; [UK postcode] Taunton; [USA] teaching assistant; telegraphic address; temporary admission; [computing] terminal adapter; Territorial Army; [physics] thermal analysis; tithe annuity; training adviser; Training Agency (formerly TSA); [psychology] transactional analysis; [USA] transit authority; travel(ling) allowance; Tricycle Association
T/A technical assistant; temporary assistant
Ta [chemical element] tantalum
ta. tableau; tablet
t.a. target area; time and attendance; true altitude
TAA Territorial Army Association; test of academic aptitude; Trans-Australia Airlines; Transportation Association of America
TA&VRA Territorial Auxiliary and Volunteer Reserve Association
TAB tabulator (key) (on typewriter); Technical Assistance Board (of UN); Total Abstinence Brotherhood; [Australia, New Zealand] Totalizator Agency Board; [medicine] typhoid, paratyphoid A, paratyphoid B (vaccine)
tab. table; tableau; tablet; tabulate; tabulation; tabulator
TABA Timber Agents' and Brokers' Association of the United Kingdom
TABMAC The All British Martial Arts Council
TAC [US air force] Tactical Air Command; Technical Assistance Committee (of UN); Television Advisory Committee; The Athletics Congress; Theatres Advisory Council; Tobacco Advisory Committee; Trades Advisory Council
Tac. (Publius Cornelius) Tacitus (Roman historian)
TACAN tactical air navigation
tach. tachometer
tacho [short form] tachograph
TACL Training for Action-Centred Leadership
TACMAR tactical multifunction array radar
TACS tactical air-control system
TACV tracked air-cushion vehicle; *Transportes Aéreos de Cabo Verde* (Portuguese: Cape Verde airline company)
Tads [military] target acquisition and designation sight
TAF Tactical Air Force
TAFE technical and further education
tafu [slang] things are fouled (or fucked) up
tafubar [slang] things are fouled (or fucked) up beyond all recognition
TAG [USA] The Adjutant-General; Towpaths Action Group
Tag. Tagalog (language)
T/Agt [USA] transfer agent
TAH [medicine] total abdominal hysterectomy
TAI *temps atomique international* (French: International Atomic Time, IAT)
Tai. Taiwan
TAL [insurance] traffic and accident loss
Tal. Talmud
tal. *talis* (Latin: such)
Talisman [stock exchange] Transfer Accounting Lodgement for Investors and Stock Management
tal. qual. *talis qualis* (Latin: average quality)
TAM tactical air missile; Television Audience Measurement
Tam. Tamil (language)

Tamba Twins and Multiple Births Association
tan [mathematics] tangent
TANCA Technical Assistance to Non-Commonwealth Countries
T&A [US slang] tits and ass; [medicine] tonsillectomy and adenoidectomy; [medicine] tonsils and adenoids
T&AFA Territorial and Auxiliary Forces Association
T&AVR Territorial and Army Volunteer Reserve
t&b top and bottom
T&CPA Town and Country Planning Association
T&E test and evaluation; [informal] tired and emotional (i.e. drunk); travel and entertainment; trial and error
T&G Transport and General Workers' Union
t&g tongue(d) and groove(d) (in woodworking)
t&o taken and offered (in betting)
t&p [insurance] theft and pilferage
T&RA Tennis and Rackets Association
T&S transport and supply
t&s toilet and shower (in property or accommodation advertisement)
T&SG Television and Screenwriters' Guild
T&T taxed and tested (in car advertisement); Trinidad and Tobago
Tang. Tangier
tanh [mathematics] hyperbolic tangent
TANS terminal-area navigation system; Territorial Army Nursing Service (became part of QARANC)
TANU Tanganyika African National Union
TAO Technical Assistance Operations (of UN)
TAOC [USA] Tactical Air Operations Center
TAP [USA] Technical Assistance Program; *Transportes Aéreos Portugueses* (Portuguese airline company)
Tapi [trademark] telephony application programming interface
Tapline Trans-Arabian Pipeline Company
TAPPI [USA] Technical Association of the Pulp and Paper Industry
TAPS Trans-Alaska Pipeline System
TAR terrain-avoidance radar; Territorial Army Regulations; [accounting] throughput accounting ratio; thrust-augmented rocket
tar. tariff; tarpaulin
TARA Technical Assistant, Royal Artillery; Territorial Army Rifle Association
TARAN test and replace as necessary
TARDIS time and relative dimensions in space (Doctor Who's time machine used in BBC science fiction series)
tarfu [slang] things are really fouled (or fucked) up
TARO Territorial Army Reserve of Officers
TARS Technical Assistance Recruitment Service; The Arthur Ransome Society
TAS torpedo antisubmarine (course); [aeronautics] true air speed
Tas. Tasmania; Tasmanian
TASI [telecommunications] time-assignment speech interpolation
TASM tactical air-to-surface missile
Tasm. Tasmania; Tasmanian
TASMO tactical air support of maritime operations
TASR terminal area surveillance radar
TASS Technical, Administrative and Supervisory Section (of AEU); Transport Aircraft Servicing Specialist (in RAF)
Tass *Telegrafnoye Agentstvo Sovetskovo Soyuza* (Russian: Telegraph Agency of the Soviet Union)
TAT [psychology] thematic apperception test; [medicine] tired all the time; transatlantic telephone (cable)
TATSA transportation aircraft test and support activity
Tau [astronomy] Taurus
TAUN Technical Assistance of the United Nations
TAURUS [stock exchange] Transfer and Automated Registration of Uncertified Stock
taut. tautology
t.-à-v. *tout-à-vous* (French: yours ever) (at end of letter)
tav. tavern
TAVR Territorial and Army Volunteer Reserve
TAVRA Territorial Auxiliary and Volunteer Reserve Association
t.a.w. twice a week
tax. taxation
taxn taxation
TB [vehicle registration] Liverpool; [com-

puting] terabyte; torpedo boat; torpedo bomber; training battalion; training board; Treasury bill; [book-keeping] trial balance; [medicine] tubercle bacillus; [medicine] tuberculosis

Tb [computing] terabyte; [chemical element] terbium (formerly Tr)

t.b. [printing] take back; temporary buoy; [baseball] total bases; [book-keeping] trial balance; true bearing

TBA tyres, batteries and accessories

t.b.a. [commerce] to be advised; to be agreed; to be announced

tb&s top, bottom and sides

TBCEP tri-beta-chloroethyl phosphate (flame retardant)

t.b.c.f. to be called for

TBD torpedo-boat destroyer

t.b.d. to be decided; to be determined

TBF Teachers' Benevolent Fund

TBI [engineering] throttle-body injection; [medicine] total body irradiation

T-bill Treasury bill

TBL through bill of lading

t.b.l. [knitting] through back of loop

TBM tactical ballistic missile; [surveying] temporary benchmark; [medicine] tuberculous meningitis; tunnel-boring machine

TBO [aeronautics] time between overhauls; [theatre] total blackout

T-bond Treasury bond

TBS talk between ships (radio apparatus); [computing] tape backup system; tight building syndrome; training battle simulation

tbs. tablespoon(ful)

tbsp. tablespoon(ful)

TBSV [microbiology] tomato bushy stunt virus

TBT tributyl tin (antifouling agent in marine paint)

TC [vehicle registration] Bristol; Tank Corps; [USA] Tariff Commission; [law] Tax Cases; technical college; temporary clerk; Temporary Constable; tennis club; touring club; town clerk; town council; town councillor; training centre; training college; training corps; [military] Transport Command; traveller's cheque; [music] *tre corde* (Italian: three strings) (instruction to release soft pedal of piano); Trinity College; (Order of the) Trinity Cross (in Trinidad and Tobago); [meteorology] tropical cyclone; Trusteeship Council (of UN); tungsten carbide; [civil aircraft marking] Turkey; twin carburettors

Tc [chemical element] technetium

tc. [music] tierce (organ stop)

t.c. temperature control; terracotta; till cancelled; time check; [navigation] true course

TCA trichloroacetic acid (herbicide); [pharmacology] tricyclic antidepressant

TCB [US slang] take care of business; Thames Conservancy Board; [medicine] tumour cell burden

TCBM transcontinental ballistic missile

TCC [telecommunications] time compression coding; Transport and Communications Commission (of UN); Trinity College, Cambridge; [USA] Troop Carrier Command

TCCB Test and County Cricket Board

TCD Trinity College, Dublin

TCDD tetrachlorodibenzodioxin (environmental pollutant)

TCE trichloroeth(yl)ene (solvent)

TCF Temporary Chaplain to the Forces; time-correction factor; *Touring Club de France* (French: French Touring Club)

tcf [USA] trillion cubic feet (used to measure natural gas)

TCFB Transcontinental Freight Bureau

TCGF [immunology] T-cell growth factor

TCH [international vehicle registration] Chad (from French *Tchad*)

tchg teaching

tchr teacher

TCI *Touring Club Italiano* (Italian: Italian Touring Club)

TCJCC Trades Council Joint Consultative Committee

TCL Trinity College (of Music) London

T-CLL [medicine] T-cell chronic lymphatic leukaemia

TCM Trinity College of Music (London)

TCMA Telephone Cable Makers' Association

TCO test control office; *Tjänstemännens Centralorganisation* (Swedish: Central Organization of Salaried Employees) (Swedish trade union); Trinity College, Oxford

TCP [computing] transmission control

protocol; [trademark] trichlorophenylmethyliodisalicyl (antiseptic)
TCPA Town and Country Planning Association (or Act)
TCP/IP [computing] transmission control protocol/Internet protocol
TCR [immunology] T-cell receptor; [physics] temperature coefficient of resistance
TCRE [medicine] transcervical resection of the endometrium
TCS target cost system; [USA] traffic control station
tctl tactical
TCU [USA] Transportation, Communications, International Union
TD [UK postcode] Galashiels; [vehicle registration] Manchester; [military] Tactical Division; tank destroyer; [medicine] tard(at)ive dyskinesia; Teaching Diploma; [Ireland] *Teachta Dála* (Gaelic: Member of the Dáil); technical development; technical drawing; Territorial (Efficiency) Decoration (in Territorial Army); Tilbury Docks; torpedo depot; [sports] touchdown; [USA] traffic director; [USA] Treasury Department; trust deed; [currency] Tunisian dinar
td. touchdown
.td Chad (in Internet address)
t.d. technical data; [medicine] *ter in die* (Latin: three times a day) (in prescriptions); test data; time delay; tractor-drawn
TDA tax-deferred annuity; Timber Development Association
TDB *temps dynamique barycentrique* (French: barycentric dynamical time); total disability benefit
TDC Temporary Detective Constable; through-deck cruiser
t.d.c. [engineering] top dead centre
TDD telecommunications device for the deaf; Tubercular Diseases Diploma
TDDL [telecommunications] time-division data link
TDE total digestible energy
TDG Timeshare Developers Group; twist drill gauge
TDH tall, dark and handsome (in personal advertisement)
TDK *Tokyo Denkikagaku Kogyu KK* (Japanese electronics company)
TDL tunable diode laser
TDM telemetric data monitor; [telecommunications] time-division multiplexing
TDMA [telecommunications] time-division multiple access
TDN total digestible nutrients
T-DNA [genetics] transferred deoxyribonucleic acid
TDP technical development plan
TDR [computing] time domain reflectometer; [finance] Treasury deposit receipt
t.d.r. *touts droits réservés* (French: all rights reserved)
TDRSS tracking and data-relay satellite system
TDS [computing] tabular data stream
t.d.s. [medicine] *ter (in) die sumendus* (Latin: to be taken three times a day) (in prescriptions)
TDT [astronomy] terrestrial dynamical time
TE [vehicle registration] Manchester; telecommunications engineering; [biochemistry] trace element; trade expenses; [telecommunications] transverse electric
Te [chemical element] tellurium
t/e time-expired; twin-engined
t.e. thermal efficiency; tinted edge (of paper); trailing edge; trial and error; turbine engine
TEA Terminal Education Age
TEAC Technical Educational Advisory Council
TEACH Teacher Education Admissions Clearing House
Tear The Evangelical Alliance Relief (Fund)
TEC Training and Enterprise Council
tec [short form] detective
tech [short form] technical college
tech. technical; technically; technician; technique; technological; technology
Tech(CEI) Technician (Council of Engineering Institutions)
techn technician
techn. technical; technique
technol. technological; technologically; technologist; technology
Tedco Thames Estuary Development Company
TEDIS Trade Electronic Data Interchange System

TEE Telecommunications Engineering Establishment; Torpedo Experimental Establishment; total energy expenditure; [railways] Trans-Europe Express
TEF Textile Employers' Federation; toxicity equivalence factor
TEFL teaching (of) English as a foreign language
t.e.g. [bookbinding] top edges gilt
Teh. Tehran
TEL tetraethyl lead (petrol additive); [astronautics] transporter-erector-launcher
Tel [astronomy] Telescopium
tel. telegram; telegraph; telegraphic; telephone
telecom. telecommunication(s)
teleg. telegram; telegraph; telegraphic; telegraphy
teleph. telephone; telephony
telex teleprinter exchange
telly [short form] television
TELNET [computing] teletype network
tel. no. telephone number
TELO Tamil Eelam Liberation Organization
TEM Territorial Efficiency Medal; transmission electron microscope (or microscopy); [telecommunications] transverse electromagnetic
TEMA Telecommunications Engineering and Manufacturing Association
temp [short form] temporary (worker)
temp. temperance; temperate; temperature; [music] tempo; temporal; temporary; *tempore* (Latin: in the time of)
Templar tactical expert mission planner (military computer)
temp. prim. [music] *tempo primo* (Italian: at the original speed)
tempy temporary
ten. tenant; tenement; [music] tenor; [music] *tenuto* (Italian: held, sustained)
tency tenancy
Tenn. Tennessee
TENS [medicine] transcutaneous electrical nerve stimulation
tepid [informal] tastes expensive, pension inadequate, dammit
TEPP tetraethyl pyrophosphate (pesticide)
Ter. Terence (Roman writer); Terrace (in road name); Territorial; Territory
ter. terrace; territorial; territory
terat. teratology
TERCOM [aeronautics] terrain contour matching (or mapping)
term. terminal; terminate; termination; terminology
Terr. Terrace (in road name); Territorial; Territory
terr. terrace; territorial; territory
terrd terraced (in property advertisement)
tert. tertiary
TES thermal-energy storage; *Times Educational Supplement*
Tesco T. E. Stockwell and J. Cohen (supermarket chain)
TESL teaching (of) English as a second language
TESOL teaching of English to speakers of other languages
TESSA Tax-Exempt Special Savings Account (replaced by ISA)
test. testament; testator; testatrix; testimonial; testimony
TET Teacher of Electrotherapy
T-et-G Tarn-et-Garonne (French department)
TETOC technical education and training for overseas countries
tet. tox. tetanus toxin
TEU [shipping] twenty-foot equivalent unit
Teut. Teuton; Teutonic
TeV teraelectronvolt
TEWT [military] tactical exercise without troops
Tex. Texan; Texas
text. textile(s); textual
text. rec. *textus receptus* (Latin: the received text)
TF [civil aircraft marking] Iceland; [vehicle registration] Reading; task force; [UK postcode] Telford; Territorial Force; [electronics] thin film; [biochemistry] transcription factor; [shipping] tropical freshwater (load line)
t.f. tabulating form; tax-free; training film; *travaux forcés* (French: hard labour)
TFA Tenant Farmers' Association; [biochemistry] total fatty acids
TFAP Tropical Forestry Action Plan
tfc traffic
TFD [electronics] thin-film detector
TFECG Training and Further Education Consultative Group

TFEL [computing] thin-film electroluminescent display
TFOF Taxi Fleet Operators' Federation
TFR Territorial Force Reserve; total fertility rate
tfr transfer
TFS [medicine] testicular feminization syndrome
TFSC Turkish Federated State of Cyprus
TFSK Turkish Federated State of Kibris (Turkish name for Cyprus)
TFSR Tools for Self Reliance
TFT [electronics] thin-film transistor
TFTA Traditional Farm-Fresh Turkey Association
TFTR [nuclear technology] Tokamak Fusion Test Reactor
TFU telecommunications flying unit
TFW [military] tactical fighter wing
TFX tactical fighter experimental (aircraft)
TG [vehicle registration] Cardiff; [civil aircraft marking] Guatemala; Tate Gallery; temporary gentleman; [informal] thank God; [USA] Theater Guild; [international vehicle registration] Togo; Townswomen's Guild; training group; transformational-generative (grammar); transformational grammar; Translators' Guild
tg [mathematics] tangent
.tg Togo (in Internet address)
t.g. tail gear; [biology] type genus
TGA [chemistry] thermal gravimetric analysis
TGAT [education] Task Group on Assessment and Testing
T-gate [computing] ternary selector gate
TGB *très grande bibliothèque* (French: very large library) (popular name for French national library)
t.g.b. tongued, grooved and beaded (in woodworking)
TGE [medicine] transmissible gastroenteritis
TGF [medicine] transforming growth factor
TGI [marketing] Target Group Index
TGIA Toy and Giftware Importers' Association
TGIF [informal] thank God it's Friday
TGM torpedo gunner's mate
TGMV [microbiology] tomato golden mosaic virus
T-group training group
TGT [aeronautics] turbine gas temperature
tgt target
TGV *train à grande vitesse* (French: high-speed train)
TGWU Transport and General Workers' Union
TH [vehicle registration] Swansea; *Technische Hochschule* (German: technical college, technical university); [fishing port] Teignmouth; Territory of Hawaii; [numismatics] toothed border; town hall (on map); Toynbee Hall; Transport House; Trinity House
Th [chemical element] thorium
Th. Theatre; Theology; Thursday
th. thermal
.th Thailand (in Internet address)
Thai. Thailand
thanat. thanatology
ThB Bachelor of Theology (from Latin *Theologiae Baccalaureus*)
THC tetrahydrocannabinol (active component of cannabis); [New Zealand] Tourist Hotel Corporation
THD total harmonic distortion (in recording)
ThD Doctor of Theology (from Latin *Theologiae Doctor*)
THE Technical Help to Exporters (division of British Standards Institution)
theat. theatre; theatrical
THELEP Therapy of Leprosy
Theoc. Theocritus (ancient Greek poet)
theol. theologian; theological; theology
Theoph. Theophrastus (ancient Greek philosopher)
theor. theorem; theoretical; theory
theoret. theoretical
theos. theosophical; theosophist; theosophy
therap. therapeutic; therapeutics
therapeut. therapeutic; therapeutics
therm. thermometer; thermometry; thermostatic
thermochem. thermochemical; thermochemistry
thermodyn. thermodynamic; thermodynamics
thermom. thermometer; thermometry
THES *Times Higher Education Supplement*
thes. thesis
thesp. thespian

Thess. [Bible] Thessalonians; Thessaly
THF Trusthouse Forte plc
THI temperature–humidity index
t.h.i. time handed in
thk thick
ThL Licentiate in Theology
ThM Master of Theology (from Latin *Theologiae Magister*)
tho' though
thor. thoracic; thorax
thoro. thoroughfare
Thos. Thomas
thou. thousand
thp thrust horsepower
THR [medicine] total hip replacement
thr their
thr. through; thrust
throt. throttle
ThSchol Scholar in Theology
THT Terrence Higgins Trust
Thu. Thursday
Thuc. Thucydides (ancient Greek historian)
Thur. Thursday
Thurs. Thursday
THWM Trinity (House) high-water mark
THz terahertz
TI [civil aircraft marking] Costa Rica; technical inspection; technical institute; temperature indication; temperature indicator; Texas Instruments; thermal imaging; tourist information
T/I target identification; target indicator
Ti [chemical element] titanium
Ti. Tiberius (Roman emperor); Tibet
TIA Tax Institute of America; Telecommunications Industry Association; [medicine] transient ischaemic attack (minor stroke)
TIB tourist information bureau
Tib. Tibet; Tibetan
TIBC [medicine] total iron-binding capacity
TIBOR [finance] Tokyo Inter-Bank Offered Rate
TIC [law] taken into consideration; Timber Industries Confederation; total inorganic carbon; tourist information centre
TICCIH The International Committee for the Conservation of the Industrial Heritage
t.i.d. [medicine] *ter in die* (Latin: three times a day) (in prescriptions)
TIE Theatre in Education
tier. [music] tierce (organ stop)
TIF [computing] tagged image format; telephone influence factor; telephone interference factor; Theatre Investment Fund; [biochemistry] transcription initiation factor; *Transports internationaux par chemin de fer* (French: International Rail Transport)
TIFF [computing] tagged image file format
TIG tungsten inert gas (in welding)
TIGR Treasury Investment Growth Receipts (type of bond, pronounced 'tiger')
TIH Their Imperial Highnesses
TIIAL The International Institute of Applied Linguistics
TIL [medicine] tumour-infiltrating lymphocyte
TILS Technical Information and Library Service
TIM transient intermodulation distortion (in recording)
Tim. [Bible] Timothy
t.i.m. time is money
timp. [music] timpani
timps [short form] timpani
TIMS The Institute of Management Sciences
TIN [USA] taxpayer identification number
TINA [informal] there is no alternative (phrase originally associated with Margaret Thatcher)
tinct. tincture
TIO technical information officer
TIP [computing] terminal interface processor
Tip. Tipperary
Tipp. Tipperary
TIR [optics] total internal reflection; *Transport international routier* (French: International Road Transport)
TIRC Tobacco Industry Research Committee
TIROS television and infrared observation satellite
TIS technical information service
tis. tissue
Tit. [Bible] Titus
tit. title; titular

TIU Telecommunications International Union
TJ [civil aircraft marking] Cameroon; [vehicle registration] Liverpool; [international vehicle registration] Tajikistan; talk jockey; terajoule; [athletics] triple jump
.tj Tajikistan (in Internet address)
TJR [currency] Tajik rouble
TK [vehicle registration] Exeter
Tk [currency] taka (used in Bangladesh)
tk tank; truck
tkg taking
tkgs takings
TKO [boxing] technical knockout
tkr tanker
tks thanks
tkt ticket
TL [civil aircraft marking] Central African Republic; [vehicle registration] Lincoln; target language; [physics] thermoluminescence; [physics] thermoluminescent (as in **TL-dating**); Torpedo Lieutenant; [insurance] total loss; [US informal] trade-last (exchange of compliments); transmission line; [currency] Turkish lira
T/L [banking] time loan; [insurance] total loss
Tl [chemical element] thallium
tl [meteorology] thunder and lightning
t.l. test link; [engineering] thrust link; time length; title list; total load; [insurance] total loss; trade list
TLA three-letter abbreviation (or acronym); Toy Libraries Association
TLB [computing] translation look-aside buffer
t.l.b. temporary lighted buoy
TLC tender loving care; [chemistry] thin-layer chromatography; [medicine] total lung capacity; [Australia] Trades and Labour Council
tld tooled
TLEH true love and everlasting happiness (in personal advertisement)
TLF transferable loan facility
TLG Theatrical Ladies' Guild
TLMI The Leprosy Mission International
TLO technical liaison officer
t.l.o. [insurance] total loss only
TLP [astronomy] transient lunar phenomenon
TLR Times Law Reports; [photography] twin-lens reflex
tlr tailor; trailer
TLRS Tramway and Light Railway Society
TLS *Times Literary Supplement*; typed letter, signed
tltr translator
TLU [computing] table look-up
TLV [electronics] threshold-limit value
TLWM Trinity (House) low-water mark
TM [vehicle registration] Luton; tactical missile; technical manual; technical memorandum; test manual; Their Majesties; [telecommunications] tone modulation; trademark; trained man; training manual; transcendental meditation; [telecommunications] transverse magnetic; trench mortar; tropical medicine; [computing] Turing machine; [international vehicle registration] Turkmenistan
Tm [chemical element] thulium
.tm Turkmenistan (in Internet address)
t.m. temperature meter; true mean
TMA Theatrical Management Association; Trans-Mediterranean Airways (Lebanese airline company)
TMB travelling medical board
TMBA Twins and Multiple Births Association
tmbr timber
TMC [USA] Tanglewood Music Center; The Movie Channel
TMD [military] theatre missile defence
TMI [USA] Three Mile Island
TMJ [medicine] temporomandibular joint
tmkpr timekeeper
TML [chemistry] tetramethyl lead; [shipping] three-mile limit
TMMG Teacher of Massage and Medical Gymnastics
TMO telegraph(ic) money order
TMP thermomechanical pump
TMPDF Trade Marks, Patterns and Designs Federation
tmpry temporary
tmr timer
TMS Tramway Museum Society
TMT turbine motor train
TMV [microbiology] tobacco mosaic virus; true mean value
TN [civil aircraft marking] (Republic of)

Congo; [vehicle registration] Newcastle upon Tyne; [US postcode] Tennessee; [UK postcode] Tonbridge; tradename; [fishing port] Troon; true north; [international vehicle registration] Tunisia
tn ton; tonne; town; train; transportation
.tn Tunisia (in Internet address)
t.n. technical note; telephone number
TNA Tamil National Army
TNC Theatres National Committee; total numerical control; transnational corporation
TNF [military] theatre nuclear forces; [medicine] tumour necrosis factor
TNG [USA] The Newspaper Guild
tng training; turning
TNIP [South Africa] Transkei National Independence Party
TNM tactical nuclear missile; [medicine] tumour, node, metastasis
T-note [finance] Treasury note
TNP *Théâtre national populaire* (French: National Popular Theatre)
TNPG The Nuclear Power Group
tnpk. turnpike
TNT trinitrotoluene (explosive)
TNTC too numerous to count
TNW tactical nuclear warfare; [military] theatre nuclear weapon
TO [vehicle registration] Nottingham; [commerce] table of organization; tax officer; technical officer; telegraphic order; telegraph office; telephone office; telephone order; Torpedo Officer; trained operator; transport officer; [fishing port] Truro; turn over (page)
T/O turnover
To. Togo
.to Tonga (in Internet address)
t.o. take-off; [printing] take over; turnover
TOB temporary office building
ToB [cycling] Tour of Britain
Tob. [Bible] Tobit (book of Apocrypha)
tob. tobacco; tobacconist
TobRV [microbiology] tobacco ringspot virus
TOC total organic carbon
Toc H Talbot House (original headquarters of society, from former telegraphic code for TH)
TOD time of delivery; trade and operations division
TOE [physics] theory of everything
t.o.e. ton oil equivalent
TOEFL test(ing) of English as a foreign language
TOET test of elementary training
TOF [physics] time of flight
TOFC trailer on flat car (freight container)
TOFPET [medicine] time-of-flight positron-emission tomography
tog. together
togr together
Tok. Tokyo
TOL Tower of London
TOM *territoire d'outre mer* (French: overseas territory); total organic matter
tom. tomato; *tomus* (Latin: volume (of book))
tomat. tomato
TOMCAT theatre of operations missile continuous-wave antitank weapon
TOMS Total Ozone Mapping Spectrometer
TON total organic nitrogen
tonn. tonnage
TOO time of origin; [commerce] to order only
TOP [computing] technical office protocol; temporarily out of print; termination of pregnancy
TOPIC [stock exchange] Teletext Output Price Information Computer
topog. topographer; topographical; topography
topol. topological; topology
TOPS Theatre Organ Preservation Society; Training Opportunities Scheme
TOR Tertiary Order Regular of St Francis
Tor. Toronto
t.o.r. time of receipt; time of reception
torn. tornado
torp. torpedo
t.o.s. temporarily out of service; temporarily out of stock; terms of service
TOSD Tertiary Order of St Dominic
TOSF Tertiary Order of St Francis
Toshiba *Tokyo Shibaura Denki KK* (Japanese electrical corporation)
tot. total; totally
t.o.t. time on target; time over target
TOTC time-on-target computation (military computer)
tote [short form] totalizator
TOTP *Top of the Pops* (BBC television programme)

tour. tourism; tourist
tourn. tournament
TOW tube-launched optically tracked wire-guided (antitank missile); tug-of-war
tox. toxicological; toxicology
toxicol. toxicological; toxicologist; toxicology
TP [vehicle registration] Portsmouth; target practice; taxpayer; teaching practice; technical paper; technical publication; teleprinter; [computing] teleprocessing; [music] *tempo primo* (Italian: at the original speed); *tempore Paschale* (Latin: at Easter); test panel; [insurance] third party; town planner; town planning; [computing] transaction processing; Transvaal Province; treaty port; trig point; true position; turning point
tp township; troop
t.p. *timbre-poste* (French: postage stamp); title page; to pay; toilet paper; [commerce] *tout payé* (French: all (expenses) paid)
TPA [medicine] tissue plasminogen activator
TPC [USA] The Peace Corps; [Australia] Trade Practices Commission; Transaction Processing Council
tpd tons per day
tph tons per hour
TPI tax and price index; [computing] terminal phase initiation; [Australia] totally and permanently incapacitated; Town Planning Institute; transpolyisoprene (synthetic rubber); Tropical Products Institute
tpi [engineering] teeth per inch; [engineering, textiles] threads per inch; [shipping] tons per inch (immersion); [computing] tracks per inch; [engineering] turns per inch
tpk. turnpike
TPLF Tigrean People's Liberation Front
TPM third-party maintenance; [commerce] total productive management
tpm tons per minute
TPN [medicine] total parenteral nutrition
TPO travelling post office; Tree Preservation Order
TPR [medicine] temperature, pulse, respiration
Tpr Trooper
tpr teleprinter
TPS Tax Payers' Society; Thomas Paine Society; toughened polystyrene
tpt transport; trumpet
tptr trumpeter
TQ [banking] tel quel (exchange rate); [computing] text quality; [UK postcode] Torquay; [commerce] total quality
TQM [commerce] total quality management
TR [civil aircraft marking] Gabon; [vehicle registration] Portsmouth; target rifle; tariff reform; Telephone Rentals plc; *tempore reginae* (Latin: in the time of the queen); *tempore regis* (Latin: in the time of the king); Territorial Reserve; test run; Theodore Roosevelt (US president); tons registered; tracking radar; transmit–receive; [UK postcode] Truro; trust receipt; [international vehicle registration] Turkey
T/R transmitter–receiver
Tr [chemical element] terbium (former symbol, replaced by Tb); [geology] Triassic
tr. [medicine] *tinctura* (Latin: tincture); trace; track; tragedy; train; trainee; transaction(s); transfer; [grammar] transitive; translate; translated; translation; translator; transport; transportation; [printing] transpose; transposition; treasurer; [music] treble; [music] trill; troop; truck; trumpet; trumpeter; trust; trustee
.tr Turkey (in Internet address)
TRA [USA] Thoroughbred Racing Association
TrA [astronomy] Triangulum Australe
trac. tracer; tractor
TRACALS [aeronautics] traffic control and landing system
TRACE task reporting and current evaluation; [aeronautics] test equipment for rapid automatic checkout evaluation
trad [short form] traditional
trad. tradition; traditional; *traducteur* (French: translator); *traduction* (French: translation); *traduttore* (Italian: translator); *traduzione* (Italian: translation)
TRADA Timber Research and Development Association
trag. tragedian; tragedy; tragic
TRAM [medicine] transverse rectus abdom-

inus myocutaneus (breast reconstruction)
TRAMPS temperature regulator and missile power supply
trannie [short form] transistor (radio)
Trans. Transvaal
trans. transaction(s); transfer; transferred; transit; [grammar] transitive; transitory; translate; translated; translation; translator; transparent; transport; transportation; [printing] transpose; transposition; transverse
transcr. transcribed; transcription
transf. transfer; transference; transferred
transl. translate; translated; translation; translator
translit. transliterate; transliterated; transliteration
transp. transport; transportation; [printing] transpose
trany transparency
trav. travel; traveller; travels
Trb. Tribune
trbn. trombone
TRC Thames Rowing Club; Tobacco Research Council
tr. co. trust company
tr. coll. training college
Trd Trinidad
TRDA Timber Research and Development Association
Treas. Treasury
treas. treasurer; treasury
trem transport emergency (card) (carried by chemical tankers)
trem. [music] *tremolando* (Italian: trembling); [music] tremulant (organ device)
TRF [biochemistry] thyrotrophin-releasing factor; tuned radio frequency
trf tariff
trf. transfer
TRG Tory Reform Group
trg touring; training
trg. [music] triangle
trge [music] triangle
TRH Their Royal Highnesses; [biochemistry] thyrotrophin-releasing hormone
TRI Television Reporters International; [USA] Textile Research Institute; Thrombosis Research Institute
Tri [astronomy] Triangulum
trib. tribal; tribunal; tributary; tribute
TRIC Television and Radio Industries Club; [medicine] trachoma inclusion conjunctivitis
trid. [medicine] *triduum* (Latin: three days) (in prescriptions)
trig [short form] triangulation (as in **trig point**)
trig. trigger; trigonometric(al); trigonometry
TRIGA [engineering] training, research and isotope-production reactors – General Atomic
trigon. trigonometric(al); trigonometry
trike [short form] tricycle
trim. trimester
Trin. Trinidad; Trinidadian; Trinity
Trip. Tripos (final examination at Cambridge University)
tripl. triplicate
trit. triturate
TRJ turboramjet (engine)
TRLFSW tactical range landing-force support weapon
trlr trawler
TRM trademark
trml terminal
t.r.n. technical research note
tRNA [biochemistry] transfer ribonucleic acid
TRNC Turkish Republic of Northern Cyprus
trng touring; training
TRO [law] temporary restraining order
TROBI Tree Register of the British Isles
trom. trombone
tromb. trombone
trombst trombonist
Tron [computing] the real-time operating system nucleus
trop. tropic; tropical
Trop. Can. Tropic of Cancer
Trop. Cap. Tropic of Capricorn
trop. med. tropical medicine
trp troop
TRRL Transport and Road Research Laboratory
TRS [computing] term rewriting system; Torry Research Station (Scotland)
trs. transfer; [printing] transpose; trustees
TRSB time reference scanning beam
trsd transferred; transposed
trsp. transport
TRSR taxi and runway surveillance radar

TRSSGM tactical range surface-to-surface guided missile
TRSSM tactical range surface-to-surface missile
trt turret
Truron. *Truronensis* (Latin: (Bishop) of Truro)
try. truly
TS [UK postcode] Cleveland; [vehicle registration] Dundee; [music] *tasto solo* (Italian: one key alone); Television Society; Theosophical Society; Tolkien Society; tool steel; [slang] tough shit; [medicine] Tourette's syndrome; training ship; [chemistry] transition state; transsexual; Treasury Solicitor; [medicine] tuberous sclerosis; tub-sized (paper); [civil aircraft marking] Tunisia; typescript
T/S transshipment
t.s. temperature switch; tensile strength; test summary; till sale; turbine ship; twin screw; type specification
TSA The Securities Association Limited; [statistics] time-series analysis; total surface area; Training Services Agency (former name of TA); Training Support Agency; [medicine] tumour-specific antigen
TSAPI telephony services application programming interface
TSB Trustee Savings Bank
TSBA Trustee Savings Banks Association
TSD Tertiary of St Dominic
TSDS two-speed destroyer sweeper
TSE Tokyo Stock Exchange; Toronto Stock Exchange; [medicine] transmissible spongiform encephalopathy
TSF two-seater fighter
TSFA The Securities and Futures Authority
tsfr transfer
TSgt Technical Sergeant
TSH Their Serene Highnesses; [biochemistry] thyroid-stimulating hormone
Tsh [currency] Tanzanian shilling
TSH-RF [biochemistry] thyroid-stimulating-hormone-releasing factor
TSH-RH [biochemistry] thyroid-stimulating-hormone-releasing hormone
tsi tons per square inch
TSO The Stationery Office (replacement for HMSO); town sub-office; trading standards officer
TSP textured soya protein; [computing] travelling salesman problem
tsp. teaspoon(ful)
TSR tactical strike reconnaissance; terminate but stay resident (computer program); torpedo-spotter reconnaissance; Trans-Siberian Railway
TSRB Top Salaries Review Body
TSS time-sharing system; [medicine] toxic shock syndrome; turbine steamship; twin-screw steamship; typescripts
TSSA Transport Salaried Staffs Association
tstr tester
t.s.u. this side up
TSV [microbiology] tobacco streak virus
t.s.v.p. *tournez s'il vous plaît* (French: please turn over, PTO)
TSW Television South West
TT [civil aircraft marking] Chad; [vehicle registration] Exeter; [fishing port] Tarbert; technical training; teetotal; teetotaller; [banking] telegraphic transfer; [geology] Tertiary; tetanus toxoid; [cycling] time trial; torpedo tube; Tourist Trophy (motorcycle race); transit time; [international vehicle registration] Trinidad and Tobago; Trust Territories; tuberculin-tested (milk)
.tt Trinidad and Tobago (in Internet address)
TTA Teacher Training Agency; Travel Trade Association
TTAW Table Tennis Association of Wales
TTB tetragonal tungsten bronze
TTBT Threshold Test Ban Treaty
TTC teachers' training course; technical training centre; [military] Technical Training Command; [medicine] transcutaneous transhepatic cholangiography
TTF Timber Trade Federation
TTFN [informal] ta-ta for now
TTL [photography] through the lens; to take leave; [electronics] transistor-transistor logic; tribal trust land (in Zimbabwe)
TTM [commerce] time to market
Tto Toronto
TTRA Tourist Trophy Riders' Association
TTS teletypesetter; teletypesetting; [acoustics] temporary threshold shift; [computing] text-to-speech

TTT [cycling] team time trial; [banking] telegraphic transfer; Tyne Tees Television Limited
TTTA Timber Trade Training Association
TTY [USA] teletypewriter
TU [vehicle registration] Chester; [civil aircraft marking] Côte d'Ivoire (Ivory Coast); thermal unit; toxic unit; trade union; [telecommunications] traffic unit; training unit; [telecommunications, acoustics] transmission unit; Tupolev (former Soviet aircraft, as in **TU-144**)
Tu. Tudor; Tuesday
TUA Telecommunications Users' Association
TUAC Trade Union Advisory Committee
tub. [cycling] tubular (tyre)
TUBCS Trade Union Badge Collectors' Society
TUBE The Union of Bookmakers' Employees
tuberc. tubercular; tuberculosis
TUC Trades Union Congress
Tuc [astronomy] Tucana
TUCC Transport Users' Consultative Committee (or Council)
TUCGC Trades Union Congress General Council
Tue. Tuesday
Tues. Tuesday
TUG Telephone Users' Group
TUI Trade Unions International of Public and Allied Employees
TUIAFPW Trade Unions International of Agricultural, Forestry and Plantation Workers
TUIREG Trade Unions International Research and Education Group
TUIWC Trade Unions International of Workers in Commerce
TUIWE Trade Unions International of Workers in Energy
TULF Tamil United Liberation Front
TULRA Trade Union and Labour Relations Act
TUM Trades Union Movement
TUPE Transfer of Undertakings (Protection of Employment) Regulations
TUR [medicine] transurethral resection
TURB [meteorology] turbulence
turb. turbine
Turk. Turkey; Turkish
TURP [medicine] transurethral resection of the prostate
turps [short form] turpentine
TV [vehicle registration] Nottingham; television; [finance] terminal value; [informal] transvestite
.tv Tuvalu (in Internet address)
t.v. terminal velocity; test vehicle
TVA *taxe à la valeur ajoutée* (French: value-added tax, VAT); Tennessee Valley Authority
TVE Television Trust for the Environment
TVEI Technical and Vocational Educational Initiative
Tvl Transvaal
tvl travel
TVO tractor vaporizing oil
TVP textured vegetable protein (meat substitute)
TVR television rating; [physics] temperature variation of resistance; Trevor (Wilkinson) (founder of sports car company)
TVRO television receive only (type of aerial)
TW [vehicle registration] Chelmsford; [telecommunications] travelling wave (as in **TW antenna**); [UK postcode] Twickenham
.tw Taiwan (in Internet address)
t.w. tail wind
TW3 *That Was The Week That Was* (former television comedy series)
TWA Thames Water Authority; time-weighted average; Trans-World Airlines
TWh terawatt hour
TWI The Welding Institute
TWIF Tug of War International Federation
TWIMC to whom it may concern
TWN teleprinter weather network
TWO this week only
TWOC taking without owner's consent (theft of car)
twp township
TWR Trans World Radio
TWT transonic wind tunnel; [electronics] travelling-wave tube
TWU Tobacco Workers' Union; Transport Workers' Union of America
TWX [USA] teletypewriter exchange service
twy twenty

TX [vehicle registration] Cardiff; [US postcode] Texas
Tx transmission (in broadcasting)
tx tax; taxation; thanks
TY [civil aircraft marking] Benin; [vehicle registration] Newcastle upon Tyne
Ty Territory
ty truly (in correspondence)
TYC Thames Yacht Club
TYMV [microbiology] turnip yellow mosaic virus
t.y.o. [horseracing] two-year-old
typ. typical; typically; typing; typist; typographer; typographic(al); typography
typh. typhoon
typo [short form] typographical error
typo. typographer; typographic(al); typography
typog. typographer; typographic(al); typography
typw. typewriter; typewriting; typewritten
Tyr. Tyrone
Tyrol. Tyrolean; Tyrolese
TYVM thank you very much
TZ [vehicle registration] Belfast; [civil aircraft marking] Mali
.tz Tanzania (in Internet address)

U

U rate of heat loss; Union; Unionist; Unit; United; [cinema] universal (film classification); University; unsatisfactory; upper; [informal] upper class (as in **U and non-U**); [chemical element] uranium; urinal; Utah; you (phonetic spelling, as in **while U wait**)
U [physics] potential difference
u [meteorology] ugly threatening sky; [chemistry] unified atomic mass unit; [physics] up (quark flavour)
u [physics] instantaneous potential difference
u. uncle; *und* (German: and); unit; unsatisfactory; *unter* (German: under, among); upper; utility
U3A University of the Third Age
5U [civil aircraft marking] Niger
9U [civil aircraft marking] Burundi
UA [vehicle registration] Leeds; [international vehicle registration] Ukraine; Ulster Association; United Artists Corporation; University of Alabama
U/a [insurance] underwriting account
.ua Ukraine (in Internet address)
u.a. unauthorized absence; under age; *unter anderem* (German: among other things); *usque ad* (Latin: as far as)
UAA United Arab Airlines
UAB Unemployment Assistance Board; Universities Appointments Board; University of Alabama in Birmingham
UABS Union of American Biological Societies
UAC Ulster Automobile Club
UADW Universal Alliance of Diamond Workers
UAE United Arab Emirates
UAI *Union des associations internationales* (French: Union of International Associations)
UAL United Airlines
UAM underwater-to-air missile
u&o use and occupancy
UAOD United Ancient Order of Druids
UAOS Ulster Agricultural Organization Society
UAP United Australia Party
UAPT *Union africaine des postes et télécommunications* (French: African Postal and Telecommunications Union)
UAR United Arab Republic (former official name of Egypt)
UARS upper-atmosphere research satellite
UART [computing, electronics] universal asynchronous receiver/transmitter
UAS University Air Squadron
u.a.s. upper airspace
UAU Universities Athletic Union
UAV unmanned air vehicle
UAW [USA] United Automobile Workers (United International Union of Automobile, Aerospace and Agricultural Implement Workers of America)

u.A.w.g. *um Antwort wird gebeten* (German: an answer is requested)
UB [vehicle registration] Leeds; United Brethren; [UK postcode] Uxbridge
UB40 registration card for unemployment benefit
UBA [medicine] ultrasonic bone analysis
UBC University of British Columbia (Vancouver)
UBF Union of British Fascists
UBI Understanding British Industry
U-boat German submarine (from German *Unterseeboot*)
UBR [taxation] Uniform Business Rate; University Boat Race
UBS United Bible Societies
UBV [astronomy] ultraviolet, blue, visual
UC [vehicle registration] central London; [music] *una corda* (Italian: one string) (instruction to use soft pedal of piano); under construction; undercover; University College; upcast shaft (in civil engineering); [theatre] up centre (of stage); Upper Canada; urban council; *urbe condita* (Latin: the city being built); [obstetrics] uterine contraction
Uc [cinema] universal, particularly suitable for children (film classification)
u/c [commerce] undercharge
u.c. [printing] upper case
UCA United Chemists' Association
UCAE Universities' Council for Adult Education
UCAR Union of Central African Republics
UCAS Universities and Colleges Admissions Service
UCATT Union of Construction, Allied Trades and Technicians
u.c.b. unless caused by
UCBSA United Cricket Board of South Africa
UCC Union Carbide Corporation; Universal Copyright Convention; University Computing Company
UCCA Universities' Central Council on Admissions (became part of UCAS)
UCCD United Christian Council for Democracy
UCD University College, Dublin; upper critical depth (in oceanography)
UCET Universities Council for Education of Teachers
UCG underground coal gasification
UCH University College Hospital (London)
UCHD usual childhood diseases
UCI *Union cycliste internationale* (French: International Cycling Union); United Cinemas International; University of California, Irvine
UCITS [finance] Undertakings for Collective Investment in Transferable Securities
UCJG *Alliance universelle des unions chrétiennes de jeunes gens* (French: World Alliance of Young Men's Christian Associations)
UCL University College London; upper control limit
u.c.l. [engineering] upper cylinder lubricant
UCLA University of California at Los Angeles
UCM University Christian Movement
UCMJ [USA] uniform code of military justice
UCMSM University College and Middlesex School of Medicine
UCNS Universities' Council for Non-academic Staff
UCNW University College of North Wales
UCR [psychology] unconditioned reflex; [psychology] unconditioned response; [computing] under-colour removal; [USA] Uniform Crime Report
UCS [psychology] unconditioned stimulus; Union of Concerned Scientists; [computing] universal multiple-octet coded character set; University College School (London); Upper Clyde Shipbuilders
UCSB University of California, Santa Barbara
UCSD University of California, San Diego
UCSW University College of South Wales
UCTA United Commercial Travellers' Association
UCV [USA] United Confederate Veterans
UCW Union of Communication Workers; University College of Wales
UCWRE Underwater Countermeasures and Weapons Research Establishment
UD [vehicle registration] Oxford; United Dairies
U/D [USA] under deed

u.d. unfair dismissal; [medicine] *ut dictum* (Latin: as directed) (in prescriptions)
UDA Ulster Defence Association
UDAG [USA] Urban Development Action Grant
UDC [USA] United Daughters of the Confederacy; universal decimal classification; Urban Development Corporation; urban district council
u.d.c. upper dead centre
UDCA Urban District Councils' Association
UDE Underwater Development Establishment
UDEAC *Union douanière et économique de l'Afrique centrale* (French: Central African Customs and Economic Union)
UDEAO *Union douanière des états d'Afrique d'Ouest* (French: Customs Union of West African States)
UDF Ulster Defence Force; [South Africa] Union Defence Force; Union of Democratic Forces (in Bulgaria); *Union pour la Démocratie Française* (French: French Democratic Union) (political party); [South Africa] United Democratic Front
u.d.f. *und die folgende* (German: and the following)
u. dgl. *und dergleichen* (German: and the like)
UDHR Universal Declaration of Human Rights
UDI unilateral declaration of independence
UDM Union of Democratic Mineworkers
UDN [veterinary science] ulcerative dermal necrosis (disease of fish)
UDP United Democratic Party
UDR Ulster Defence Regiment; *Union des démocrates pour la république* (French: Union of Democrats for the Republic) (former name of RPR)
UDSR *Union démocratique et socialiste de la résistance* (French: Democratic and Socialist Union of the Resistance)
UDT United Dominions Trust
UDUP Ulster Democratic Unionist Party
UE [vehicle registration] Dudley; university entrance (examination)
UEA Universal Esperanto Association; University of East Anglia
UED University Education Diploma
UEF *Union européenne des fédéralistes* (French: European Union of Federalists); *Union européenne féminine* (French: European Union of Women)
u.e.f. universal extra fine (screw)
UEFA Union of European Football Associations
UEI Union of Educational Institutions
UEIC United East India Company
UEL United Empire Loyalists
UEMOA *Union économique et monétaire ouest-africaine* (French: West African Economic and Monetary Union)
UEO *Union de l'Europe occidentale* (French: Western European Union, WEU); unit education(al) officer
UEP *Union européenne de paiements* (French: European Payments Union); [genetics] unit evolutionary period
UEPS *Union européenne de la presse sportive* (French: European Sports Press Union)
UER *Union européenne de radiodiffusion* (French: European Broadcasting Union, EBU); university entrance requirements; unsatisfactory equipment report
UETA [USA] universal engineer tractor, armoured
UETRT [USA] universal engineer tractor, rubber-tyred
UF [vehicle registration] Brighton; United Free (Church of Scotland); [India] United Front; urea–formaldehyde (as in **UF resin**); utilization factor (of electric light)
u/f unfurnished (in accommodation advertisement)
UFA *Universum Film-Aktiengesellschaft* (European media company); [biochemistry] unsaturated fatty acid
UFAW Universities Federation for Animal Welfare
UFC United Free Church (of Scotland); Universities Funding Council
UFCW [USA] United Food and Commercial Workers International Union
UFF Ulster Freedom Fighters
uff. *ufficiale* (Italian: official)
UFFI urea–formaldehyde foam insulation
UFO unidentified flying object
u.f.p. unemployed full pay
UFT [physics] unified field theory; [USA] United Federation of Teachers
UFTAA Universal Federation of Travel Agents' Association

UFTU Union of Free Trades Union (in Romania)
UFU Ulster Farmers' Union
UFW United Farm Workers of America
UG [vehicle registration] Leeds
Ug. Uganda; Ugandan
u/g underground
.ug Uganda (in Internet address)
Ugan. Uganda; Ugandan
UGC underground gasification of coal; University Grants Committee
UGLE [Freemasonry] United Grand Lodge of England
UGT *Unión General de Trabajadores* (Spanish: General Union of Workers)
UGWA United Garment Workers of America
UH [vehicle registration] Cardiff
UHA [South Africa] Union House of Assembly
UHB [informal] urban haute bourgeoisie
UHCC Upper House of the Convocation of Canterbury
UHCY Upper House of the Convocation of York
UHF [radio] ultrahigh frequency
UHT ultra-heat-treated (as in **UHT milk**); ultrahigh temperature
UHV ultrahigh vacuum; ultrahigh voltage
UI [vehicle registration] Londonderry; [USA] unemployment insurance; [computing] user interface
u/i under instruction
u.i. *ut infra* (Latin: as below)
UIA Union of International Associations
UIAA *Union internationale des associations d'alpinisme* (French: International Union of Mountaineering Associations)
UIC *Union internationale des chemins de fer* (French: International Union of Railways)
UICC *Union internationale contre le cancer* (French: International Union against Cancer)
UICN *Union internationale pour la conservation de la nature et ses resources* (French: International Union for Conservation of Nature and Natural Resources)
UICPA *Union internationale de chimie pure et appliquée* (French: International Union of Pure and Applied Chemistry, IUPAC)
UIE *Union internationale des étudiants* (French: International Union of Students)
UIEO Union of International Engineering Organizations
UIHPS *Union internationale d'histoire et de philosophie des sciences* (French: International Union of the History and Philosophy of Science)
UIJS *Union internationale de la jeunesse socialiste* (French: International Union of Socialist Youth)
UIL *Unione Italiana del Lavoro* (Italian: Italian Federation of Trade Unions); United Irish League
UIMS [computing] user-interface management system
UIP *Union internationale de patinage* (French: International Skating Union); *Union interparlementaire* (French: Inter-Parliamentary Union)
UIPC *Union internationale de la presse catholique* (French: International Catholic Press Union)
UIPM *Union internationale de pentathlon moderne* (French: International Modern Pentathlon Union)
UIPPA *Union internationale de physique pure et appliquée* (French: International Union of Pure and Applied Physics, IUPAP)
UIS *Union internationale de secours* (French: International Relief Union)
UISB *Union internationale des sciences biologiques* (French: International Union of Biological Sciences)
UISM *Union internationale des syndicats des mineurs* (French: Miners' Trade Unions International)
UISPP *Union internationale des sciences préhistoriques et prohistoriques* (French: International Union of Prehistoric and Prohistoric Sciences)
UIT *Union internationale des télécommunications* (French: International Telecommunications Union, ITU); unit investment trust
UITF [accounting] Urgent Issues Task Force
UITP *Union internationale des transports publics* (French: International Union of Public Transport)
UIU Upholsterers' International Union of North America

UJ [vehicle registration] Shrewsbury; Union Jack; [engineering] universal joint
UJC Union Jack Club (London)
UJD Doctor of Canon and Civil Law (from Latin *Utriusque Juris Doctor*)
UK [vehicle registration] Birmingham; United Kingdom; [civil aircraft marking] Uzbekistan
.uk United Kingdom (in Internet address)
UKA Ulster King of Arms; United Kingdom Alliance
UK(A) [athletics] United Kingdom Allcomers
UKAC United Kingdom Automation Council
UKADGE United Kingdom Air Defence Ground Environment
UKAEA United Kingdom Atomic Energy Authority
UKAPE United Kingdom Association of Professional Engineers
UKBG United Kingdom Bartenders' Guild
UKCC United Kingdom Central Council for Nursing, Midwifery and Health Visiting (replacement for GNC)
UKCIS United Kingdom Chemical Information Service
UKCOSA United Kingdom Council for Overseas Students' Affairs
UKCSBS United Kingdom Civil Service Benefit Society
UKCTA United Kingdom Commercial Travellers' Association
UKDA United Kingdom Dairy Association
UKFBPW United Kingdom Federation of Business and Professional Women
UKgal United Kingdom gallon
UKIAS United Kingdom Immigrants' Advisory Service
UKIRT United Kingdom Infrared Telescope (Mauna Kea, Hawaii)
UKISC United Kingdom Industrial Space Committee
UKLF United Kingdom Land Forces
UKMF(L) United Kingdom Military Forces (Land)
UKMIS United Kingdom Mission
UK(N) [athletics] United Kingdom National
UKOOA United Kingdom Offshore Operators Association
UKOP United Kingdom Oil Pipelines
UKPA United Kingdom Pilots' Association
UKPIA United Kingdom Petroleum Industry Association Limited
Ukr. Ukraine; Ukrainian
UKSATA United Kingdom South Africa Trade Association
UKSLS United Kingdom Services Liaison Staff
UKSMA United Kingdom Sugar Merchant Association Limited
UKST United Kingdom Schmidt Telescope (Siding Spring, Australia)
UKW *Ultrakurzwelle* (German: ultrashort wave)
UL [vehicle registration] central London; [fishing port] Ullapool; [USA] Underwriters' Laboratories (on electrical appliance labels); university library; [biochemistry] unsaturated lipid; [theatre] up left (of stage); [computing] upload (on Internet); [medicine] upper limb
u.l. upper left; upper limit
ULA [computing] uncommitted logic array
ULC [theatre] up left centre (of stage)
ULCC ultralarge crude carrier (oil tanker); University of London Computer Centre
ULCI Union of Lancashire and Cheshire Institutes
ULF [radio] ultralow frequency; upper limiting frequency
ULICS University of London Institute of Computer Science
ULM ultrasonic light modulator; universal logic module
ULMS underwater long-range missile system
ULP University of London Press
ULS [finance] unsecured loan stock
ULSEB University of London School Examinations Board
ULT United Lodge of Theosophists
ult. ultimate; ultimately; *ultimo* (Latin: in the last (month), of the last (month)) (used in formal correspondence)
ulto *ultimo* (Latin: in the last (month), of the last (month)) (used in formal correspondence)
ult. praes. [medicine] *ultimum praescriptum* (Latin: last prescribed)
ULTRA Unrelated Live Transplant Regulatory Authority
ULV ultralow volume

UM [vehicle registration] Leeds; [currency] ouguiya (used in Mauritania); unaccompanied minor (on aircraft); University of Minnesota
u/m undermentioned
um. unmarried
UMA *Union du Maghreb Arabe* (French: Arab Maghreb Union) (customs union)
UMa [astronomy] Ursa Major
UMB *Union mondiale de billard* (French: World Billiards Union); [computing] upper memory block
umbl. umbilical
UMC University of Missouri, Columbia
UMCP University of Maryland, College Park
UMDS United Medical and Dental Schools
UMEJ *Union mondiale des étudiants juifs* (French: World Union of Jewish Students)
UMF Umbrella Makers' Federation
UMFC United Methodist Free Churches
UMi [astronomy] Ursa Minor
UMIST University of Manchester Institute of Science and Technology
UMNO United Malaysia National Organization
ump. umpire
UMT universal military training
UMTS universal military training service (or system)
UMW United Mine Workers (of America)
UMWA United Mine Workers of America
UN [vehicle registration] Exeter; [civil aircraft marking] Kazakhstan; United Nations
un. unified; union; united; unsatisfactory
UNA United Nations Association
UNAA United Nations Association of Australia
unab. unabridged
UNACC United Nations Administrative Committee and Coordination
unacc. unaccompanied
unaccomp. unaccompanied
UNACOM universal army communication system
unan. unanimous
UNARCO United Nations Narcotics Commission
unasgd unassigned
unatt. unattached
unattrib. unattributed
UNAUS United Nations Association of the United States
unauth. unauthorized
unauthd unauthorized
UNB universal navigation beacon; University of New Brunswick
unb. unbound
unbd unbound
UNBRO United Nations Border Relief Operation
UNC [numismatics] uncirculated; *Union National Camerounaise* (French: Cameroon National Union); United Nations Command; University of North Carolina
unc. uncertain; uncle
UNCAST United Nations Confederation on the Applications of Science and Technology
UNCC United Nations Cartographic Commission
UNCCP United Nations Conciliation Commission for Palestine
UNCDF United Nations Capital Development Fund
UNCED United Nations Conference on Environment and Development
UNCID Uniform Rules of Conduct for Interchange of Trade Data by Teletransmission
UNCIO United Nations Conference on International Organization
uncir. uncirculated
uncirc. uncirculated
UNCITRAL United Nations Commission on International Trade Law
unclas. unclassified
unclass. unclassified
UNCLE United Network Command for Law and Enforcement (in 1960s television series *The Man from UNCLE*)
UNCLOS United Nations Conference on the Law of the Sea
uncond. unconditional
uncor. uncorrected
UNCSTD United Nations Conference on Science and Technology for Development
UNCTAD United Nations Conference on Trade and Development
UND University of North Dakota
UNDC United Nations Disarmament Commission

UNDCP United Nations Drug Control Programme
undergrad [short form] undergraduate
UNDOF United Nations Disengagement Observer Force (peacekeeping force in Syria)
UNDP United Nations Development Programme
UNDRO United Nations Disaster Relief Organization
undsgd undersigned
undtkr undertaker
UNE underground nuclear explosion
UNEC United Nations Education Conference
UNECA United Nations Economic Commission for Asia
UNEDA United Nations Economic Development Administration
UNEF United Nations Emergency Force
UNEP United Nations Environment Programme
UNESCO United Nations Educational, Scientific and Cultural Organization
UNETAS United Nations Emergency Technical Aid Service
unexpl. unexplained; unexploded; unexplored
UNFAO United Nations Food and Agriculture Organization
UNFB United Nations Film Board
UNFC United Nations Food Conference
UNFICYP United Nations (Peacekeeping) Force in Cyprus
UNFPA United Nations Fund for Population Activities
unfurn. unfurnished (in accommodation advertisement)
ung. [medicine] *unguentum* (Latin: ointment)
UNGA United Nations General Assembly
UNHCR United Nations High Commissioner for Refugees
UNHQ United Nations Headquarters
UNI *Ente Nazionale Italiano di Unificazione* (Italian: Italian Standards Association); United News of India
uni [short form] university
UNIC United Nations Information Centre
UNICA *Union internationale du cinéma d'amateurs* (French: International Union of Amateur Cinema)
UNICE *Union des industries de la communauté européenne* (French: Union of Industries of the European Community)
UNICEF United Nations Children's Fund (formerly United Nations International Children's Emergency Fund)
UNICOM universal integrated communication system
UNIDO United Nations Industrial Development Organization
UNIDROIT *Institut international pour l'unification du droit privé* (French: International Institute for the Unification of Private Law)
unif. uniform
UNIFIL United Nations Interim Force in Lebanon
UNIKOM United Nations Iraq–Kuwait Observation Mission (peacekeeping force)
UNIMA *Union internationale des marionettes* (French: International Union of Puppeteers)
UNIO United Nations Information Organization
UNIP United National Independence Party (in Zambia)
UNIPEDE *Union internationale des producteurs et distributeurs d'énergie électrique* (French: International Union of Producers and Distributors of Electrical Energy)
UNIS United Nations International School
unis. [music] unison
UNISCAT United Nations Expert Committee on the Application of Science and Technology
UNISIST Universal System for Information in Science and Technology
Unit. Unitarian; Unitarianism
UNITA *União Nacional para a Independência Total de Angola* (Portuguese: National Union for the Total Independence of Angola)
UNITAR United Nations Institute for Training and Research
Univ. Universalist; University
univ. universal; universally; university
UNIVAC universal automatic computer
UNIX [trademark] type of computer operating system (originally Unics, short for Uniplexed Information and Computing System)

UNJSPF United Nations Joint Staff Pension Fund
unkn. unknown
UNLC United Nations Liaison Committee
UNM University of New Mexico
unm. unmarried
UNMC United Nations Mediterranean Commission
UNMIBH United Nations Mission in Bosnia-Herzegovina (peacekeeping force)
unmod. unmodernized (in property advertisement)
UNMOGIP United Nations Military Observer Group in India and Pakistan (peacekeeping force)
UNO United Nations Organization
UNOG United Nations Office at Geneva
UNOMA United Nations Observer Mission in Angola (peacekeeping force)
UNOMIG United Nations Observer Mission in Georgia (peacekeeping force)
UNOMIL United Nations Observer Mission in Liberia (peacekeeping force)
unop. unopened; unopposed
UNOSOM United Nations Operation in Somalia
UNOV United Nations Office at Vienna
UNP United National Party (in Sri Lanka)
unp. unpaged; unpaid
UNPA United Nations Postal Administration
UNPC United Nations Palestine Commission
unpd unpaged; unpaid
UNPREDEP United Nations Preventive Deployment Force (peacekeeping force in FYROM)
UNPROFOR United Nations Protection Force (in former Yugoslavia)
unpub. unpublished
unpubd unpublished
UNREF United Nations Refugee Emergency Fund
UNRISD United Nations Research Institute for Social Development
UNRRA United Nations Relief and Rehabilitation Administration
UNRWA United Nations Relief and Works Agency (for Palestine Refugees in the Near East)
unsat. unsatisfactory; unsaturated
UNSC United Nations Security Council; United Nations Social Commission
UNSCC United Nations Standards Coordinating Committee
UNSCCUR United Nations Scientific Conference on the Conservation and Utilization of Resources
UNSCOM United Nations Special Commission
UNSF United Nations Special Fund for Economic Development
UNSG United Nations Secretary-General
UNSR United Nations Space Registry
UNSSM United Nations Special Services Medal
unst. unstable
UNSW University of New South Wales
UNTAA United Nations Technical Assistance Administration
UNTAB United Nations Technical Assistance Board
UNTAC United Nations Transitional Authority in Cambodia
UNTAG United Nations Transition Assistance Group (in Namibia)
UNTAM United Nations Technical Assistance Mission
UNTC United Nations Trusteeship Council
UNTSO United Nations Truce Supervision Organization (peacekeeping force)
UNTT United Nations Trust Territory
UNU United Nations University
UNV United Nations Volunteers
UNWCC United Nations War Crimes Commission
UO [vehicle registration] Exeter
u.ö. *und öfters* (German: and often)
u.o.c. ultimate operating capability
UOD ultimate oxygen demand (in water conservation)
U of A University of Alaska
U of NC University of North Carolina
U of S University of Saskatchewan
U of T University of Toronto
UOM Union of Myanmar
UP [vehicle registration] Newcastle upon Tyne; Ulster Parliament; Union Pacific; United Party; United Presbyterian; United Press (news agency); United Provinces (former name of Uttar Pradesh); University of Paris; University of Pennsylvania; University of Pittsburgh; Uni-

versity Press; unsaturated polyester; [USA] Upper Peninsula; Uttar Pradesh
up. upper
u.p. underproof (of alcohol)
UPA *Union postale arabe* (French: Arab Postal Union); United Productions of America (company producing animated films)
UPC Uganda People's Congress; *Union des Populations Camerounaises* (French: Union of the Populations of Cameroon); United Presbyterian Church; Universal Postal Convention; universal product code (bar code)
UPD united port district; Urban Planning Directorate
upd unpaid
UPF untreated polyurethane foam
UPGC University and Polytechnic Grants Committee
UPGWA United Plant Guard Workers of America
uphd uphold
uphol. upholsterer; upholstery
UPI United Press International
UPIGO *Union professionelle internationale des gynécologues et obstétriciens* (French: International Union of Professional Gynaecologists and Obstetricians)
UPIU [USA] United Paperworkers International Union
UPNI Unionist Party of Northern Ireland
UPOA Ulster Public Officers' Association
UPOW Union of Post Office Workers (became part of UCW)
UPP United Peasant Party (in Poland)
UPPP [medicine] uvulopalatopharyngoplasty
UPR [insurance] unearned premiums reserve; Union Pacific Railroad
UPS uninterruptible power supply; [trademark] United Parcel Service; United Publishers' Services
UPU Universal Postal Union (formerly GPU)
UPUP Ulster Popular Unionist Party
uPVC unplasticized polyvinyl chloride
UPW Union of Post Office Workers (became part of UCW)
UR [vehicle registration] Luton; [civil aircraft marking] Ukraine; [psychology] unconditioned reflex; [psychology] unconditioned response; uniform regulations; [theatre] up right (of stage); urban renewal
Ur. Urdu; Uruguay; Uruguayan
ur. [medicine] urine
URA Urban Regeneration Agency; [USA] Urban Renewal Administration
Uran. Uranus
urb. urban
URBM ultimate-range ballistic missile
URC United Reformed Church; [theatre] up right centre (of stage)
Urd. Urdu
URF *Union des services routiers des chemins de fer européens* (French: Union of European Railways Road Services); uterine relaxing factor
urg. urgent; urgently
URI [medicine] upper respiratory infection
URL [computing] Uniform Resource Locator (address of Internet location); Unilever Research Laboratory
urol. urologic(al); urology
URSI *Union radio scientifique internationale* (French: International Scientific Radio Union)
URT upper respiratory tract
URTI [medicine] upper respiratory tract infection
URTU United Road Transport Union
Uru. Uruguay; Uruguayan
Urupabol Uruguay, Paraguay and Bolivia (commission for international cooperation)
URW United Rubber, Cork, Linoleum and Plastic Workers of America
US [vehicle registration] Glasgow; *ufficio stampa* (Italian: press office); [medicine] ultrasonic scanning; [medicine] ultrasound scanning; [USA] Uncle Sam; [psychology] unconditioned stimulus; undersecretary; [USA] United Service; United States (of America); United States highway (as in **US66**); unsaleable
u/s unserviceable; useless
.us United States of America (in Internet address)
u.s. *ubi supra* (Latin: where (mentioned) above); *ut supra* (Latin: as above)
USA United States Army; United States of America; [international vehicle registration] United States of America; United Synagogue of America

USA/ABF United States of America Amateur Boxing Federation
USAC United States Air Corps; United States Auto Club
USAEC United States Atomic Energy Commission
USAF United States Air Force
USAFA United States Air Force Academy
USAFC United States Army Forces Command
USAFE United States Air Forces in Europe
USAFI United States Armed Forces Institute
USAFR United States Air Force Reserve
USAID United States Agency for International Development
USAMC United States Army Materiel Command
USAMedS United States Army Medical Service
USAR United States Army Reserve
USASA United States Army Security Agency
USASigC United States Army Signal Corps
USASMC United States Army Supply and Maintenance Command
USAT United States Army Transport
USATDC United States Army Training and Doctrine Command
USATEC United States Army Test and Evaluation Command
USAWC United States Army Weapons Command
USB [computing] universal serial bus
USBC United States Bureau of the Census
USBM United States Bureau of Mines
USC Ulster Special Constabulary; United Services Club; United Somali Congress; United States Code; United States Congress; United States of Colombia; University of South Carolina; University of Southern California
USCA United States Code Annotated
USCC United States Circuit Court
USCCA United States Circuit Court of Appeals
USCG United States Coast Guard
USCGA United States Coast Guard Academy
USCGC United States Coast Guard Cutter
USCGR United States Coast Guard Reserve
USCGS United States Coast and Geodetic Survey
USCL United Society for Christian Literature
USCRC United States Citizens Radio Council
USCSC United States Civil Service Commission
USD US dollars
USDA United States Department of Agriculture
USDAW Union of Shop, Distributive and Allied Workers
USDOE United States Department of Energy
USEA United States Energy Association
U/sec. Undersecretary
USECC United States Employees' Compensation Commission
USES United States Employment Service
USF United States Forces
usf. *und so fort* (German: and so on, etc.)
USFL United States Football League
USG United States Government; United States Standard Gauge
USGA United States Golf Association
USgal United States gallon
USGPO United States Government Printing Office
USGS United States Geological Survey
Ush [currency] Uganda shilling
USHA United States Housing Authority
USI United Schools International; United Service Institution; United States Industries
USIA United States Information Agency
USIS United States Information Service
USITC United States International Trade Commission
USL United States Legation; United States Lines
USLTA United States Lawn Tennis Association
USM ultrasonic machining; underwater-to-surface missile; United States Mail; United States Marines; United States Mint; [stock exchange] unlisted securities market
USMA United States Military Academy
USMC United States Marine Corps; United States Maritime Commission
USMH United States Marine Hospital
USMS United States Maritime Service
USN United States Navy

USNA United States National Army; United States Naval Academy
USNC United States National Committee
USNG United States National Guard
USNI United States Naval Institute
USNO United States Naval Observatory
USNR United States Naval Reserve
USNRC United States Nuclear Regulatory Commission
USNS United States Navy Ship
USO [USA] United Service Organization
US of A [informal] United States of America
USP unbleached sulphite pulp (for papermaking); [advertising] unique selling proposition (distinctive feature of product); United States Patent; United States Pharmacopeia
USPat. United States Patent
USPC Ulster Society for the Preservation of the Countryside
USPCA Ulster Society for the Prevention of Cruelty to Animals
USPG United Society for the Propagation of the Gospel
USPHS United States Public Health Service
USPO United States Post Office
USPS United States Postal Service
USR United States Reserves; Universities' Statistical Record
USRA [USA] Universities Space Research Association
USRC United States Reserve Corps
USS [medicine] ultrasound scanning; Undersecretary of State; *Union Syndicale Suisse* (French: Swiss Federation of Trade Unions); United States Senate; United States Service; United States Ship; United States Steamer; United States Steamship; Universities Superannuation Scheme
USSAF United States Strategic Air Force
USSB United States Shipping Board
USSC United States Supreme Court
USSCt United States Supreme Court
USSR Union of Soviet Socialist Republics
USSS United States Steamship
UST undersea technology
USTA United States Tennis Association; United States Trademark Association
USTC United States Tariff Commission
USTS United States Travel Service
usu. usual; usually
USV United States Volunteers
USVA United States Volleyball Association
USVB United States Veterans' Bureau
USVI United States Virgin Islands
USW [radio] ultrashort wave; ultrasonic waves; underwater sea warfare
usw. *und so weiter* (German: and so forth, etc.)
USWA United Steelworkers of America
USWB United States Weather Bureau
USWI United States West Indies; urban solid-waste incinerator
UT [vehicle registration] Leicester; ultrasonic testing; ultrasonic transducer; [India] Union Territory; unit trust; Universal Time (= GMT); University of Texas (at Austin); [medicine] urinary tract; [US postcode] Utah
U/T under trust
Ut. Utah
ut. untrained; utility
u.t. universal trainer; user test
UTA Ulster Transport Authority; *Union de Transports Aériens* (French airline company); Unit Trust Association
UTC Universal Time Coordinated; University Training Corps
Utd United
UTDA Ulster Tourist Development Association
ut dict. [medicine] *ut dictum* (Latin: as directed) (in prescriptions)
utend. [medicine] *utendus* (Latin: to be used)
UTI [medicine] urinary-tract infection
util. utility room (in property advertisement)
ut inf. *ut infra* (Latin: as below)
UTK University of Tennessee, Knoxsville
UTP [computing] unshielded twisted pair
UTS ultimate tensile strength
ut sup. *ut supra* (Latin: as above)
UTU Ulster Teachers' Union; [USA] United Transportation Union
UTW Union of Textile Workers
UTWA United Textile Workers of America
UU [vehicle registration] central London; Ulster Unionist
u.U *unter Umständen* (German: circumstances permitting)

UUA [USA] Unitarian Universalist Association
UUCP [computing] UNIX-to-UNIX copy
UUM underwater-to-underwater missile
UUP Ulster Unionist Party
UUUC United Ulster Unionist Coalition; United Ulster Unionist Council
UUUP United Ulster Unionist Party
u.u.V *unter üblichem Vorbehalt* (German: errors and omissions excepted)
UV [vehicle registration] central London; ultraviolet
UVA ultraviolet radiation of wavelength 320–380 nanometres
UVAS ultraviolet astronomical satellite
uvaser ultraviolet amplification by stimulated emission of radiation
UVB ultraviolet radiation of wavelength 280–320 nanometres
UVF Ulster Volunteer Force
UVL ultraviolet light
UVR ultraviolet radiation
UW [vehicle registration] central London; underwater; University of Washington; unladen weight
U/W [law] under will; underwriter
u/w underwater; unladen weight
UWA University of Western Australia
UWC Ulster Workers' Council
UWCE Underwater Weapons and Countermeasures Establishment
UWI University of the West Indies
UWIST University of Wales Institute of Science and Technology
UWT Union of Women Teachers (became part of NAS/UWT)
UWUA Utility Workers Union of America
UWUSA United Workers' Union of South Africa
UX [vehicle registration] Shrewsbury
ux. *uxor* (Latin: wife)
UXB unexploded bomb
UY Universal Youth; [vehicle registration] Worcester
.uy Uruguay (in Internet address)
UZ [vehicle registration] Belfast; University of Zürich
Uz. Uzbek; Uzbekistan
.uz Uzbekistan (in Internet address)

V

V [Roman numeral] five; Valiant (aircraft) (as in **V bomber**); [chemical element] vanadium; [immunology] variable region (of immunoglobulin chain); [international vehicle registration] Vatican City State; [currency] vatu (used in Vanuatu); Venerable; *Vergeltungswaffe* (German: reprisal weapon, as in **V-1**, **V-2**); version; Very (in titles); very; vespers; *Via* (Italian: Street); Vicar; Vice (in titles); Victor (aircraft) (as in **V bomber**); victory (as in **V-sign**); Viscount; Viscountess; volt; [music] *volti* (Italian: turn over); voltmeter; Volunteer(s); Vulcan (aircraft) (as in **V bomber**)
V electric potential; [physics] luminous efficiency; [physics] potential difference; [physics] potential energy; volume (capacity)
v [Roman numeral] five; variable absorption (in spectroscopy); [meteorology] (abnormally good) visibility; [physics] (instantaneous) voltage
v [physics] instantaneous potential difference; [chemistry] specific volume; [physics] velocity; *versus* (Latin: against); [chemistry] vibrational quantum number
v. vacuum; vagrant; vale; valley; valve; vein; *vel* (Latin: or); ventilator; ventral; [grammar] verb; verbal; verse; version; [printing] verso (left-hand page); versus; vertical; very; via; vicar; vicarage; *vice* (Latin: in place of); victory; *vide* (Latin: see); village; violin; virus; visibility; [medicine] vision; [grammar] vocative; [music] *voce* (Italian: voice); [music] voice; volcano; volume; *von* (German: of) (in names); *votre* (French: your); vowel
V-1 *Vergeltungswaffe 1* (German: reprisal weapon 1) (World War II flying bomb)

V¹ [music] *violino primo* (Italian: first violin)
V2 [civil aircraft marking] Antigua
V-2 *Vergeltungswaffe 2* (German: reprisal weapon 2) (World War II ballistic missile)
V² [music] *violino secondo* (Italian: second violin)
V3 [civil aircraft marking] Belize
V5 [civil aircraft marking] Namibia
V6 car engine with six cylinders arranged in V-shape
V8 [civil aircraft marking] Brunei; car engine with eight cylinders arranged in V-shape
5V [civil aircraft marking] Togo
6V [civil aircraft marking] Senegal
9V [civil aircraft marking] Singapore
VA [vehicle registration] Peterborough; value-added; [commerce] value analysis; [medicine] ventricular arrhythmia; [USA] Veterans' Administration; Vicar Apostolic; Vice-Admiral; (Order of) Victoria and Albert; [US postcode] Virginia; [medicine] visual acuity; Voice of America; Volunteer Artillery; Volunteers of America; *Vostra Altezza* (Italian: Your Highness); *Votre Altesse* (French: Your Highness); *Vuestra Alteza* (Spanish: Your Highness)
V/A voucher attached
Va Virginia (US state)
va [music] viola
.va Vatican City State (in Internet address)
v.a. [commerce] value analysis; [grammar] verb active; [grammar] verbal adjective
VAB [astronautics] vehicle assembly building (of NASA)
VABF Variety Artists' Benevolent Fund
VABM [surveying] vertical angle benchmark
VAC vector analogue computer
vac [short form] vacation
vac. vacancy; vacant; vacation; vacuum
vacc. vaccination; vaccine
VAD Voluntary Aid Detachment
VADAS [medicine] voice-activated domestic appliance system
V-Adm Vice-Admiral
VAF Variety Artists' Federation
VAFC [computing] VESA advanced feature connector
vag. vagabond; vagina; vaginal; vagrancy; vagrant
VAH [USA] Veterans' Administration Hospital
val. valley; valuable; valuation; value; valued
valid. validate; validation
valn valuation
Valpo Valparaiso
vamp. vampire
VAN [computing] value-added network
van [short form] advantage (in tennis); [short form] vanguard
van. vanilla
Vanc. Vancouver
V&A Victoria and Albert Museum
V&L vodka and lime
V&M Virgin and Martyr
V&T vodka and tonic
V&V [computing] verification and validation
VANS [computing] value-added network service
VAPI [aeronautics] visual approach path indicator
vapor. vaporization
VAR [computing] value-added reseller; visual aural range; Volunteer Air Reserve; *Votre Altesse Royale* (French: Your Royal Highness)
var. variable; variant; variation; [botany] variety; variometer; various
VARIG *Viação Aérea Rio Grandense* (Portuguese: Brazilian airline company)
var. lect. *varia lectio* (Latin: variant reading)
varn. varnish
VAS [medicine] ventricular-atrial shunt
vas. vasectomy
VASARI [computing] Visual Art System for Archiving and Retrieval of Images
vasc. vascular
Vascar visual average speed computer and recorder
VASI [aeronautics] visual approach slope indicator
VASP *Viação Aérea São Paulo* (Portuguese: Brazilian airline company)
VAT value-added tax
Vat. Vatican
VATE versatile automatic test equipment
Vat. Lib. Vatican Library

vaud. vaudeville
v. aux. [grammar] auxiliary verb
VAV variable air volume (in air-conditioning system)
VAWT vertical-axis wind turbine
VAX [trademark, computing] virtual address extension (range of computers)
VB [vehicle registration] Maidstone; [chemistry] valence bond; volunteer battalion
vb [grammar] verb
vb. verbal
v.b. vehicle borne; vertical bomb
VBI [medicine] vertebrobasilar insufficiency
vbl verbal
V bomber Valiant bomber; Victor bomber; Vulcan bomber
VBR [computing] variable bit rate
VBRA Vehicle Builders and Repairers Association Limited
VC [vehicle registration] Coventry; [engineering] vapour compression; Vatican City; [cycling] velo club; [finance] venture capital; [USA] Veterinary Corps; Vice-Chairman; Vice-Chamberlain; Vice-Chancellor; Vice-Consul; Vickers Commercial (aircraft) (as in **VC10**); Victoria Cross; Viet Cong; [chemistry] vinyl chloride; [physiology] vital capacity
vc. (violon)cello
.vc St Vincent and the Grenadines (in Internet address)
v.c. valuation clause; vehicular communication; visual communication
VCA [chemistry] vinyl carbonate; [medicine] viral capsid antigen; [USA] Volunteer Civic Association
VCAS Vice-Chief of Air Staff
VCC Veteran Car Club of Great Britain; Vice-Chancellors' Committee
VCCS [electronics] voltage-controlled current source
VCDS Vice-Chief of the Defence Staff
VCE variable-cycle engine
Vce Venice
VCG vertical centre of gravity; Vice-Consul-General
VCGS Vice-Chief of the General Staff
VCH *Victoria County History* (reference book)
v.Chr. *vor Christus* (German: before Christ, BC)
VCI volatile corrosion inhibitor
vcl. (violon)cello; vehicle
VCM vinyl chloride monomer (plastic)
vcm vacuum
VCNS Vice-Chief of Naval Staff
vcnty vicinity
VCO [India] Viceroy's Commissioned Officer; voltage-controlled oscillator; voluntary county organizer (in Women's Institute)
VCPI [computing] virtual control program interface
VCR video cassette recorder; visual control room (at airfield)
Vcr Vancouver
vcs voices
VCT venture capital trust
V Cz Vera Cruz (Mexico)
VD [medicine] vascular dementia; venereal disease; Victorian Decoration; Volunteer Decoration
vd void
v.d. vapour density; various dates
V-Day Victory Day
VDC Volunteer Defence Corps
Vdc volts direct current
VDF [computing] voice data fax
VDH [medicine] valvular disease of the heart
VDI [computing] virtual device interface
VDJ video disc jockey
VDM *Verbi Dei Minister* (Latin: Minister of the Word of God); [computing] Vienna Development Method (notation)
VDQS *vin délimité de qualité supérieure* (French: superior-quality wine)
VDR variable-diameter rotor; video-disc recording
VDRL Venereal Disease Research Laboratory (test)
VDS variable-depth sonar
VDT [computing] visual display terminal; [computing] visual display unit
VDW [chemistry] van der Waals (as in **VDW force**)
VE [vehicle registration] Peterborough; [medicine] vaginal examination; [chemistry] valence electron; valve engineering; Victory in Europe (as in **VE Day**); vocational education; *Vostra Eccellenza* (Italian: Your Excellency); *Votre Éminence* (French: Your Eminence); *Vuestra Excelencia* (Spanish: Your Excellency)

ve. *veuve* (French: widow)
.ve Venezuela (in Internet address)
VEB *Volkseigener Betrieb* (German: People's Concern) (state-owned company in former East Germany)
vec. vector
ved. *vedova* (Italian: widow)
VE Day Victory in Europe Day (8 May 1945)
veg [short form] vegetable(s)
veg. vegetable; vegetarian; vegetation
veh. vehicle; vehicular
Vel [astronomy] Vela
vel. vellum; velocity; velvet
Ven. Venerable; Venetian; Venezuela; Venezuelan; Venice
ven. *vendredi* (French: Friday); veneer; *venerdì* (Italian: Friday); venereal; venery; venison; venom; venomous; ventral; ventricle
Venet. Venetian
Venez. Venezuela; Venezuelan
vent. ventilate; ventilation; ventriloquist
Ver. [commerce] *Verein* (German: association, company)
ver. verification; verify; vermilion; verse; version
VERA versatile reactor assembly; vision electronic recording apparatus
verb. *verbessert* (German: improved, revised)
verb. et lit. [law] *verbatim et literatim* (Latin: word for word and letter for letter)
verb. sap. *verbum sapienti* (*sat est*) (Latin: a word (is enough) to the wise)
verb. sat *verbum sapienti sat est* (Latin: a word is enough to the wise)
Verf. *Verfasser* (German: author)
Verl. *Verlag* (German: publisher)
verm. vermiculite; vermilion
vern. vernacular
vers [mathematics] versed sine; [mathematics] versine
vers. version
vert. vertebra; vertebral; vertical; vertigo
VES Voluntary Euthanasia Society
ves. [medicine] *vesica* (Latin: bladder); [medicine] *vesicula* (Latin: blister); [medicine] *vespere* (Latin: in the evening) (in prescriptions); vessel; vestry
VESA Video Electronics Standards Association
vesp. [medicine] *vespere* (Latin: in the evening) (in prescriptions)
VESPER Voluntary Enterprises and Services and Part-time Employment for the Retired
vet [US short form] veteran; [short form] veterinary surgeon
vet. veteran; veterinarian; veterinary
Vet. Admin. [USA] Veterans' Administration
veter. veteran; veterinarian; veterinary
VetMB Bachelor of Veterinary Medicine
vet. sci. veterinary science
vet. surg. veterinary surgeon; veterinary surgery
VF [vehicle registration] Norwich; [medicine] ventricular fibrillation; [Roman Catholic Church] Vicar Forane; video frequency; [telecommunications] voice frequency
v.f. very fair; very fine
VFA [Australia] Victorian Football Association; [chemistry] volatile fatty acid
Vfat [computing] virtual file allocation table
VFD [computing] vacuum fluorescent display; verified free distribution; [USA] volunteer fire department
VFL [Australia] Victorian Football League
VFM value for money; variable-frequency oscillator
VFOAR [US air force] Vandenberg Field Office of Aerospace Research
VFR [aeronautics] visual flight rules
VFT [Australia] very fast train
VFU [computing] vertical format unit
VFW [USA] Veterans of Foreign Wars
vfy verify
VG [vehicle registration] Norwich; *vaisseau de guerre* (French: warship); very good; Vicar-General; [Freemasonry] Vice Grand; *Votre Grâce* (French: Your Grace); *Votre Grandeur* (French: Your Highness)
Vg. [ecclesiastical] Virgin
.vg Virgin Islands (British) (in Internet address)
v.g. *verbi gratia* (Latin: for example); *verbigracia* (Spanish: for example); very good
VGA [computing] video graphics adapter; [computing] video graphics array
v.g.c. very good condition (in advertisement)
VGH very good health

VGL very good-looking (in personal advertisement)
vgl. *vergleiche* (German: compare)
VGPI [aeronautics] visual glide path indicator (in World War II)
VGSOH very good sense of humour (in personal advertisement)
VH [civil aircraft marking] Australia; [vehicle registration] Huddersfield; *Votre Hautesse* (French: Your Highness)
v.h. vertical height; very high
v.h.b. very heavy bombardment
VHC very highly commended
VHD [computing] very high density; video high density (system)
VHE very high energy
VHF very high fidelity (in sound recording); [radio] very high frequency
VHLW vitrified high-level (radioactive) waste
VHN [engineering] Vickers hardness number
VHO very high output
VHP [India] Vishwa Hindu Parishad (militant group)
VHS [trademark] Video Home System
VHT very high temperature
VHV very high vacuum
VI Vancouver Island; [cartography] vertical interval; Virgin Islands; virgo intacta; viscosity index; volume indicator
.vi Virgin Islands (US) (in Internet address)
v.i. [grammar] verb intransitive; *vide infra* (Latin: see below)
VIA [computing] versatile interface adapter; Visually Impaired Association
viad. viaduct
VIASA *Venezolana Internacional de Aviácion, Sociedad Anónima* (Spanish: Venezuelan International Airways Limited)
VIB vertical integration building
vib. [music] vibraphone; vibrate; vibration
VIC Victoria Institute of Colleges
Vic. Vicar; Victoria; Victorian
vic. vicar; vicarage; vicinity; victory
Vict. Victorian
VID [computing] virtual image display
vid. *vide* (Latin: see); [law] *vidua* (Latin: widow)
Vien. Vienna; Viennese
vier. *viernes* (Spanish: Friday)
VIF variable import fee
vig. vignette
vign. vignette
vil. village
vill. village
v. imp. [grammar] verb impersonal
v. imper. [grammar] verb imperative
VIN [USA] vehicle identification number
vin. vinegar
vind. vindicate; vindication
vini. viniculture
VIO Veterinary Investigation Officer
VIP [medicine] vasoactive intestinal peptide; very important person
VIR *Victoria Imperatrix Regina* (Latin: Victoria Empress and Queen)
Vir [astronomy] Virgo
Vir. Virgil (Roman poet)
vir. *viridis* (Latin: green)
Virg. Virgil (Roman poet); Virginia (USA)
v. irr. [grammar] verb irregular
Vis. Viscount; Viscountess
vis. viscosity; visibility; visible; visiting; visual
Visc. Viscount; Viscountess
visc. viscosity
Visct Viscount; Viscountess
VISS VHS index search system
VISTA Volunteers in Service to America
vit. vital; vitamin; vitreous
VITA Volunteers for International Technical Assistance
viti. viticulture
vitr. *vitreum* (Latin: glass)
vit. stat. vital statistics
viv. [music] *vivace* (Italian: lively, animated)
vivi. vivisection
vix. *vixit* (Latin: (he/she) lived)
viz *videlicet* (Latin: namely)
VJ [vehicle registration] Gloucester; [Australia] Vaucluse Junior (yacht); Victory over Japan (as in **VJ Day**); video jockey
v.J *vorigen Jahres* (German: last year)
VJ Day Victory over Japan Day (15 August 1945)
VK [vehicle registration] Newcastle upon Tyne
v.k. vertical keel
VL [vehicle registration] Lincoln; Vulgar Latin
vl. violin
v.l. *varia lectio* (Latin: variant reading)

VLA [astronomy] Very Large Array (of radio telescopes in New Mexico)
vla [music] viola
Vlad. Vladivostok
VLB vertical-lift bridge; [computing] VESA local bus
VLBA [astronomy] very long baseline array
VLBC [shipping] very large bulk carrier
VLBI [astronomy] very long baseline interferometry
VL-Bus [computing] VESA local bus
VLBW [medicine] very low birth weight
VLCC [shipping] very large crude carrier
VLCD very low calorie diet
VLDB [computing] very large database
VLDL [biochemistry] very low-density lipoprotein
VLE [chemistry] vapour–liquid equilibrium
vle [music] violone (double-bass viol)
VLF [radio] very low frequency
VLFMF very low-frequency magnetic field
VLIW [computing] very long instruction word
VLLW very low-level (radioactive) waste
vln violin
VLR very long range (aircraft); Victoria Law Reports
VLS [physics] vapour–liquid–solid
VLSI [electronics] very large-scale integration
VLT very large telescope
vltg. voltage
vlv. valve; valvular
VM [vehicle registration] Manchester; [physics] velocity modulation; Victory Medal; Viet Minh; Virgin Mary; [computing] virtual machine; [computing] virtual memory; [chemistry] volatile matter; *Votre Majesté* (French: Your Majesty)
v.M *vorigen Monats* (German: of last month)
VMC [computing] VESA medium channel; [aeronautics] visual meteorological conditions
VMCCA Veteran Motor Car Club of America
VM/CMS [trademark, computing] virtual machine, conversational monitor system
VMD Doctor of Veterinary Medicine (from Latin *Veterinariae Medicinae Doctor*)
VME [trademark, computing] Versa Module Eurocard (bus)
VMH Victoria Medal of Honour (Royal Horticultural Society award)
VMO [astronomy] very massive object
VMS vertical marketing system; [computing] virtual machine system; Voluntary Medical Services
v.m.t. very many thanks
VN [vehicle registration] Middlesbrough; Vietnam; [international vehicle registration] Vietnam; Vietnamese
vn violin
.vn Vietnam (in Internet address)
Vna Vienna
VNM [Canada] Victoria National Museum
VNTR [genetics] variable number tandem repeat
VO [vehicle registration] Nottingham; valuation officer; verbal order; very old (brandy etc.); veterinary officer; (Royal) Victorian Order; voice-over
vo. [printing] verso (left-hand page)
VOA Voice of America; Volunteers of America
VOC Vehicle Observer Corps; volatile organic chemical; volatile organic compound
voc. vocal; vocalist; vocation; vocational; [grammar] vocative
vocab. vocabulary
VOCAL Voluntary Organizations Communication and Language
vocat. [grammar] vocative
voc. ed. vocational education
voctl vocational
VOD velocity of detonation
VODAT voice-operated device for automatic transmission
VOH Vehicle on Hire (certificate)
Vol [astronomy] Volans
Vol. volume (of book); Volunteer
vol. volatile; volcanic; volcano; volume; voluntary; volunteer
volc. volcanic; volcano
Vols volumes
vols volumes
volum. volumetric
voly voluntary
VONA vehicle of the new age (rapid shuttle)

VOP very oldest procurable (brandy etc.)
VOR [navigation] very-high-frequency omnidirectional radio range
vorm. *vormals* (German: formerly); *vormittags* (German: in the morning, a.m.)
Vors. *Vorsitzender* (German: chairman)
vou. voucher
vox pop [short form] *vox populi* (Latin: voice of the people)
VP [vehicle registration] Birmingham; [civil aircraft marking] British Colonies and Protectorates; [physics, chemistry] vapour phase; [building] vent pipe; [grammar] verb phrase; Vice-President; Vice-Principal; victory points; *vita patris* (Latin: during the life of her/his father)
v.p. [photography] vanishing point; vapour pressure; variable pitch; [grammar] verb passive
VPC *vente par correspondence* (French: mail order)
vpd vehicles per day
vph vehicles per hour
v.ph. vertical photography
VPL visible panty line
vpm vehicles per mile
VPO Vienna Philharmonic Orchestra
Vpo Valparaiso
VPop [computing] virtual point of presence
VPP [India] value payable post; [veterinary science] virus pneumonia of pigs; Volunteer Political Party
VPRGS Vice-President of the Royal Geographical Society
VPRP Vice-President of the Royal Society of Portrait Painters
VPRS Vice-President of the Royal Society
vps vibrations per second
VPZS Vice-President of the Zoological Society
VQ [civil aircraft marking] British Colonies and Protectorates
VQMG Vice-Quartermaster-General
VR [civil aircraft marking] British Colonies and Protectorates; [vehicle registration] Manchester; variant reading; [physics] velocity ratio; [medicine] ventricular reflux; Vicar Rural; *Victoria Regina* (Latin: Queen Victoria); [computing] virtual reality; voltage regulator; Volunteer Reserve; vulcanized rubber
v.r. variant reading; *vedi retro* (Italian: please turn over, PTO); [grammar] verb reflexive
VRA [USA] Vocational Rehabilitation Administration
VRAM [computing] video random-access memory
VRB [meteorology] variable
VRC Vehicle Research Corporation; Volunteer Rifle Corps
VRD Royal Naval Volunteer Reserve Officers' Decoration
v. refl. [grammar] verb reflexive
V Rev. Very Reverend
VRG [biochemistry] vaccinia rabies glycoprotein
vrg [meteorology] veering
VRI *Victoria Regina et Imperatrix* (Latin: Victoria Queen and Empress); [medicine] viral respiratory infection; [aeronautics] visual rule instrument (landing)
VRM [USA] variable-rate mortgage
VRN [finance] variable-rate note
VRO vehicle registration office
Vry Viceroy
VS [vehicle registration] Luton; [Freemasonry] Venerable Sage; veterinary surgeon; *vieux style* (French: Old Style) (in dates); [chemistry] volatile solid; [music] *volti subito* (Italian: turn over quickly); *Vostra Santità* (Italian: Your Holiness); *Votre Sainteté* (French: Your Holiness)
vs. versus
v.s. variable speed; *vide supra* (Latin: see above); [music] *volti subito* (Italian: turn over quickly)
VSAM [computing] virtual storage access method
VSB [telecommunications] vestigial sideband
vsby visibility
VSC Volunteer Staff Corps
VSCC Vintage Sports Car Club
VSD vendor's shipping document; [medicine] ventricular septal defect
VSI [navigation] vertical speed indicator
VSL Venture Scout leader
VSM [telecommunications] vestigial sideband modulation
vsn vision
VSO [linguistics] verb-subject-object (as in **VSO language**); [computing] very small outline; very superior old (brandy

etc.); Vienna State Opera; Voluntary Service Overseas
VSOP very special old pale (brandy etc.); very superior old pale (brandy etc.)
VSQ very special quality
VSR very short range; very special reserve (wine)
VSS [medicine] vital signs stable
vst violinist
VSTOL [aeronautics] vertical and short take-off and landing
VSUK Vegetarian Society of the United Kingdom Limited
VSV [medicine] vesicular stomatitis virus
VSW vitrified stoneware
VSWR [telecommunications] voltage standing-wave ratio
VT [civil aircraft marking] India; [vehicle registration] Stoke-on-Trent; variable time; [currency] vatu (used in Vanuatu); [medicine] ventricular tachycardia; [US postcode] Vermont
Vt Vermont
v.t. vacuum technology; variable transmission; [grammar] verb transitive
VTC Volunteer Training Corps; voting trust certificate
VTE [psychology] vicarious trial and error
Vte *Vicomte* (French: Viscount)
Vtesse *Vicomtesse* (French: Viscountess)
VTFL [computing] variable-to-fixed length (code)
vtg voting
VTL [computing] variable threshold logic
VTMoV [microbiology] velvet tobacco mottle virus
VTO [aeronautics] vertical take-off
VTOHL [aeronautics] vertical take-off, horizontal landing
VTOL [aeronautics] vertical take-off and landing
VTOVL [aeronautics] vertical take-off, vertical landing
VTR videotape recorder; videotape recording
VTVL [computing] variable-to-variable length (code)
VU [vehicle registration] Manchester; [medicine] varicose ulcer; [acoustics] volume unit
.vu Vanuatu (in Internet address)
Vul [astronomy] Vulpecula
Vul. Vulgate
Vulg. Vulgate
vulg. vulgar; vulgarly
VV [vehicle registration] Northampton
vv. verbs; verses; [music] (first and second) violins; [music] voices; volumes
v.v. vice versa; viva voce
VVD *Volkspartij voor Vrijheid en Democratie* (Dutch: People's Party for Freedom and Democracy)
vve *veuve* (French: widow)
vv.ll. *variae lectiones* (Latin: variant readings)
VV.MM. *Vos Majestés* (French: Your Majesties)
VVO very very old (brandy etc.)
VW [vehicle registration] Chelmsford; [computing] van Wijngaarden (grammar); Very Worshipful; *Volkswagen* (German vehicle manufacturer)
VWH Vale of the White Horse
VX [vehicle registration] Chelmsford
vx vertex
VY [vehicle registration] Leeds
vy very
v.y. [bibliography] various years
VYAH very young at heart (in personal advertisement)
VZ [vehicle registration] Tyrone
VZIG [immunology] varicella zoster hyperimmune globulin

W

W [genetics] sex chromosome of birds and insects; [chemical element] tungsten (from former name wolfram); Wales; Warden; [fishing port] Waterford; watt; Wednesday; Welsh; Wesleyan; west; western; [UK postcode] west London; white; wide; widow; widowed; widower; width; [shipping] winter (load line);

women; women's (clothing size); [currency] won (used in Korea)
W [engineering] load; [physics] weight; [physics] work
w [meteorology] dew
w [chemistry] mass fraction
w. waist; wall; war; warm; waste; water; weather; week; weight; wet; white; [cricket] wicket; [cricket] wide; width; wife; win; wind; wire; with; woman; won; wooden; word; work; wrong
5W [civil aircraft marking] Samoa
6W [civil aircraft marking] Senegal
WA [vehicle registration] Sheffield; [UK postcode] Warrington; [US postcode] Washington; [USA] Welfare Administration; West Africa; West African; Western Australia; Westminster Abbey; [fishing port] Whitehaven; [netball] wing attack; [insurance] with average; [US banking] withholding agent; Woodworkers of America
w.a. with answers
WAA Women's Auxiliary Association
WAAA Women's Amateur Athletic Association
WAAAF Women's Auxiliary Australian Air Force
WAAC Women's Army Auxiliary Corps
WAAE World Association for Adult Education
WAAF Women's Auxiliary Air Force; Women's Auxiliary Australian Air Force
WAAS Women's Auxiliary Army Service; World Academy of Art and Science
WAC [USA] Women's Army Corps (in World War II); World Aeronautical Chart
WACB World Association for Christian Broadcasting
WACC [accounting] weighted average cost of capital; World Association for Christian Communications
WACCC Worldwide Air Cargo Commodity Classification
WACSM [USA] Women's Army Corps Service Medal
WADEX word and author index
WADF [USA] Western Air Defense
WADS wide-area data service
w.a.e. when actually employed
WAF West African Forces; [USA] Women in the Air Force
w.a.f. with all faults
WAFC West African Fisheries Commission
W Afr. West Africa; West African
WAFS [USA] Women's Auxiliary Ferrying Squadron; Women's Auxiliary Fire Service
WAG [international vehicle registration] (West Africa) Gambia; Writers' Action Group; Writers' and Artists' Guild
WAGBI Wildfowl Association of Great Britain and Ireland
WAGGGS World Association of Girl Guides and Girl Scouts
WAIF World Adoption International Fund
WAIS [psychology] Wechsler Adult Intelligence Scale; [computing] wide-area information service
WAL [international vehicle registration] (West Africa) Sierra Leone
Wal. Walloon
WAM wife and mother; work analysis and measurement; [USA] wrap-around mortgage
WAN [computing] wide-area network
w&i weighing and inspection
W&L [USA] Washington and Lee University
W&M William and Mary (joint sovereigns of England)
W&S whisky and soda
w&t wear and tear
WANS Women's Australian National Service
WAOS Welsh Agricultural Organization Society
WAP work assignment plan; work assignment procedure
WAPC Women's Auxiliary Police Corps
WAPOR World Association for Public Opinion Research
WAR West Africa Regiment
War. Warsaw; Warwick(shire)
war. warrant
WARC [USA] Western Air Rescue Center; World Administrative Radio Conference; World Alliance of Reformed Churches
WARI [Australia] Waite Agricultural Research Institute
Warks Warwickshire
warn. warning
warr. warranty

warrty warranty
WASA Welsh Amateur Swimming Association
Wash. Washington
WASP [USA] White Anglo-Saxon Protestant; [USA] Women Airforce Service Pilots
WAST Western Australia Standard Time
WAT [aeronautics] weight, altitude, temperature; [psychology] word association test
Wat. Waterford
WATA World Association of Travel Agencies
WATFOR [computing] University of Waterloo Fortran
WATS [USA] Wide Area Telephone Service
W Aus. Western Australia
W Aust. Western Australia
WAV [computing] waveform
WAVES [US navy] Women Accepted for Volunteer Emergency Service
WAWF World Association of World Federalists
WAY World Assembly of Youth
WAYC Welsh Association of Youth Clubs
WB [vehicle registration] Sheffield; warehouse book; Warner Brothers (film studio); water board; [telecommunications] waveband; [commerce] waybill; weather bureau; [psychology] Wechsler–Bellevue (Intelligence Scale); [insurance] weekly benefits; World Bank
W/B warehouse book; [telecommunications] waveband; [commerce] waybill
Wb weber (unit of magnetic flux)
w.b. wage board; waste ballast; water ballast; [commerce] waybill; wheel base; [knitting] wool back
WBA West Bromwich Albion (football club); whole-body activity; World Boxing Association
WBAFC [USA] Weather Bureau Area Forecast Center
WBAN [USA] Weather Bureau, Air Force and Navy
WBC [medicine] white blood cell; [medicine] white blood (cell) count; World Boxing Council
WBF World Bridge Federation
WBGT [meteorology] wet-bulb globe temperature; [meteorology] wet-bulb globe thermometer
WBI [medicine] whole-body irradiation
w.b.i. will be issued
WbN west by north
WBR [medicine] whole-body radiation
WBS [medicine] whole-body scan; [physics] wide-band spectrometer; [physics] wide-band spectrum
WbS west by south
w.b.s. [engineering] walking-beam suspension; [insurance] without benefit of salvage
WBT [meteorology] wet-bulb temperature
WC [vehicle registration] Chelmsford; walking club; war cabinet; war council; water closet (= toilet); Wesleyan chapel; [UK postcode] west central London; [military] Western Command; working capital; [computing] world coordinates
W/C Wing Commander
w.c. watch committee; water closet (= toilet); water cock; wheelchair; without charge
WCA Wholesale Confectioners' Alliance; Wildlife and Countryside Act; Women's Christian Association
w.c.a. worst-case analysis
WCAT Welsh College of Advanced Technology
WCC War Crimes Commission; World Council of Churches
W/Cdr Wing Commander
WCEU World Christian Endeavour Union
WCF World Congress of Faiths
WCL World Confederation of Labour
WCP World Climate Programme; World Council of Peace
WCRA [USA] Weather Control Research Association; Women's Cycle Racing Association
WCT World Championship Tennis
WCTU [USA, Canada] Women's Christian Temperance Union
WCWB World Council for the Welfare of the Blind
WD [international vehicle registration] (Windward Islands) Dominica; [vehicle registration] Dudley; War Department; [UK postcode] Watford; [fishing port] Wexford; [astronomy] white dwarf; [netball] wing defence; Works Department

wd ward; warranted; weed; wood; word; would; wound
W/D wind direction; [banking] withdrawal
w/d warranted; well developed
2WD two-wheel drive
4WD four-wheel drive
WDA Welsh Development Agency; Women's Diocesan Association; [taxation] writing-down allowance
WDC War Damage Commission; [USA] War Damage Corporation; Woman Detective Constable; World Data Centre
w.d.f. wood door and frame
wdg winding
WDM [telecommunications] wavelength division multiplex
Wdr Wardmaster
WDS Woman Detective Sergeant
wd sc. wood screw
WDSPR [meteorology] widespread
WDV [taxation] written-down value
WE [vehicle registration] Sheffield; War Establishment
w/e weekend; week ending
WEA (Royal) West of England Academy; Workers' Educational Association
wea. weapon; weather
WE&FA Welsh Engineers' and Founders' Association
WEARCON weather observation and forecasting control system
WEC wave energy converter; wind energy converter; World Energy Conference
WECOM [USA] Weapons Command
Wed. Wednesday
WEDA Wholesale Engineering Distributors' Association
Wednes. Wednesday
Weds. Wednesday
w.e.f. with effect from
WEFC World European Fisheries Conference
WEFT [aeronautics] wings, engine, fuselage, tail
Wel. Welsh
weld. welding
Well. Wellington (New Zealand)
WEN Women's Environmental Network
w/end weekend
WES Women's Engineering Society; World Economic Survey
Wes. Wesleyan
WES/PNEU Worldwide Education Service of Parents' National Educational Union
west. western
Westm. Westmeath; Westminster; Westmorland
WET Western European Time
WETUC Workers' Educational Trade Union Committee
WEU Western European Union (replacement for BTO)
Wex. Wexford
Wexf. Wexford
WF [vehicle registration] Sheffield; [UK postcode] Wakefield; [physics] wave function; [USA] Wells Fargo and Company; white female
w.f. [sports] wing forward; [knitting] wool forward; [printing] wrong font
WFA White Fish Authority; Women's Football Association; World Friendship Association
WFB World Fellowship of Buddhists
WFC World Food Council (of UN)
WFD World Federation of the Deaf
w.fd [knitting] wool forward
WFDY World Federation of Democratic Youth
WFEO World Federation of Engineering Organizations
WFF [logic] well-formed formula; World Friendship Federation
WFGA Women's Farm and Garden Association
WFL Women's Freedom League
Wfl Worshipful
WFMH World Federation for Mental Health
WFMW World Federation of Methodist Women
WFN World Federation of Neurology
WFP World Food Programme (of UN)
WFPA World Federation for the Protection of Animals
WFSW World Federation of Scientific Workers
WFTC Working Families Tax Credit
WFTU World Federation of Trade Unions (replacement for IFTU)
WFUNA World Federation of United Nations Associations
WG [international vehicle registration] (Windward Islands) Grenada; [vehicle registration] Sheffield; water gauge;

weight guaranteed; Welsh Guards; West Germanic (language group); [informal] W(illiam) G(ilbert) Grace (British cricketer); wire gauge; working group
wg weighing; wing
w.g. water gauge; weight guaranteed; wire gauge
WGA Writers' Guild of America
WGC Welwyn Garden City; World Gold Council; [Freemasonry] Worthy Grand Chaplain
Wg/Cdr Wing Commander
WGer West Germanic (language group)
WGG [Freemasonry] Worthy Grand Guardian; [Freemasonry] Worthy Grand Guide
WGGB Writers' Guild of Great Britain
WGI world geophysical interval
w. gl. wired glass
W Glam. West Glamorgan
WGM [Freemasonry] Worthy Grand Master
WGmc West Germanic (language group)
WGPMS warehouse gross performance measurement system
WGS [Freemasonry] Worthy Grand Sentinel
WGU Welsh Golfing Union
WH [vehicle registration] Manchester; water heater; [fishing port] Weymouth; [cycling] wheelers; [USA] White House; [banking] withholding
Wh watt hour
w/h [banking] withholding
wh. wharf; which; whispered; white
w.h. [sports] wing half
WHA World Health Assembly (of WHO); World Hockey Association
W'hampton Wolverhampton
w.h.b. wash-hand basin
whd warhead
WhF Whitworth Fellow
whf wharf
whfg. wharfage
whfr wharfinger
Whi. Whitehall (London)
whis. whistle
whmstr weighmaster
WHO [USA] White House Office; World Health Organization
WHOA! [USA] Wild Horse Organized Assistance
WHOI [USA] Woods Hole Oceanographic Institution
whp water horsepower
whr whether
WHRA World Health Research Centre
whs. warehouse
WhSch Whitworth Scholar
whse warehouse
whsle wholesale
whsmn warehouseman
whsng warehousing
WHT William Herschel Telescope (La Palma)
WHTSO Welsh Health Technical Services Organization
w.h.y. what have you
WI West Indian; West Indies; Windward Islands; [fishing port] Wisbech; [US postcode] Wisconsin; Women's Institute; wrought iron
w.i. [finance] when issued
WIA wounded in action
WIBC [USA] Women's International Bowling Congress
WICA Warsaw International Consumer Association
Wick. Wicklow
WID West India Docks (London)
wid. widow; widower
WIDF Women's International Democratic Federation
WIF West Indies Federation
Wig. Wigtownshire
Wigorn. *Wigorniensis* (Latin: (Bishop) of Worcester)
wilco will comply (in radio communications)
WILPF Women's International League for Peace and Freedom
Wilts Wiltshire
WIMP [physics] weakly interacting massive particle; [computing] windows, icons, menus and pointers
WIN [USA] Work Incentive
Winch. Winchester
W Ind. West Indian; West Indies
Wind. I Windward Islands
Wings [finance] warrants in negotiable government securities
Winn. Winnipeg
wint. winter
Winton. *Wintoniensis* (Latin: (Bishop) of Winchester)

WIP waste incineration plant; work in progress
WIPO World Intellectual Property Organization
WIRA Wool Industries Research Association
WIRDS weather information reporting and display system
Wis. Wisconsin
WISC [psychology] Wechsler Intelligence Scale for Children
Wisd. [Bible] Wisdom of Solomon (book of Apocrypha)
Wisd. *Wisden* (*Cricketers' Almanack*)
WISP wide-range imaging spectrometer
wit. witness
WITA Women's International Tennis Association
withdrl withdrawal
witht without
Wits. Witwatersrand
WIZO Women's International Zionist Organization
WJ [vehicle registration] Sheffield
WJC World Jewish Congress
WJEC Welsh Joint Education Committee
WK [vehicle registration] Coventry; [fishing port] Wick
Wk Walk (in road name)
wk weak; week; work; wreck
w.k. warehouse keeper; well known
wkg working
wkly weekly
WKN [meteorology] weakening
wkr walker; worker; wrecker
wks weeks; works
wks. workshop
wkt [cricket] wicket
WL [vehicle registration] Oxford; [international vehicle registration] (Windward Islands) St Lucia; *wagon-lit* (French: sleeping car); waiting list; water line; wavelength; West Lothian; Women's Liberation
W/L wavelength
wl wool
w.l. water line
WLA Women's Land Army
WLAN [computing] wireless local area network
WLB [USA] War Labor Board
Wld World
wld would
wldr welder
WLF Women's Liberal Federation
wl fwd [knitting] wool forward
WLGS Women's Local Government Society
WLHB Women's League of Health and Beauty
WLI workload index
WLM Women's Liberation Movement
Wln Wellington (New Zealand)
W Long. west longitude
W Loth. West Lothian
WLPSA Wild Life Preservation Society of Australia
WLR Weekly Law Reports
WLRI World Life Research Institute
WLS [statistics] weighted least squares
WLTBU Watermen, Lightermen, Tugmen and Bargemen's Union
WLTM would like to meet (in personal advertisement)
WLU World Liberal Union
WLUS World Land Use Survey
wly westerly
wlz waltz
WM [vehicle registration] Liverpool; war memorial; washing machine (in accommodation advertisement); wattmeter; well maintained (in advertisement); white male; wire mesh; [Freemasonry] Worshipful Master
W/M [shipping] weight or measurement
Wm. William
WMA Working Mothers' Association; World Medical Association
WMAA Whitney Museum of American Art
WMC [USA] War Manpower Commission (in World War II); Ways and Means Committee; working men's club; Working Men's College; World Meteorological Centre; World Methodist Council
WMCIU Working Men's Club and Institute Union Limited
WMF [trademark, computing] Windows metafile format
wmk watermark
WMM World Movement of Mothers
WMO World Meteorological Organization
WMP with much pleasure
WMS Wesleyan Missionary Society; World Magnetic Survey

WMTC Women's Mechanized Transport Corps
WN [vehicle registration] Swansea; [UK postcode] Wigan; [fishing port] Wigtown
WNA [shipping] winter North Atlantic (load line)
WNB weekly news bill
WNCCC Women's Nationwide Cancer Control Campaign Limited
w.n.d.p. with no down payment
wndw window
WNE Welsh National Eisteddfod
WNL within normal limits
WNLF Women's National Liberal Federation
WNO Welsh National Opera
WNP Welsh National Party
WNW west-northwest
WO [vehicle registration] Cardiff; walkover; War Office; Warrant Officer; welfare officer; wireless operator; [fishing port] Workington; [commerce] written order
w/o without; [accounting] written off
w.o. walkover; *wie oben* (German: as mentioned above); [commerce] written order
WOA Wharf Owners' Association
w.o.a. without answers
WOAR Women Organized Against Rape
w.o.b. washed overboard
WOC [building] waiting on cement (setting)
w.o.c. without compensation
WOCA world outside centrally planned economic areas
WOCS [building] waiting on cement setting
w.o.e. without equipment
WOF [New Zealand] Warrant of Fitness (for vehicles)
w.o.g. water, oil or gas; with other goods
w.o.l. wharf-owner's liability
WOM wireless operator mechanic
WOMAN World Organization for Mothers of All Nations
w.o.n. [knitting] wool on needle
WOO Warrant Ordnance Officer; World Oceanographic Organization
WoO *Werke ohne Opuszahl* (German: works without opus number) (works by Beethoven not listed in standard catalogue)
woopie [informal] well-off older person
w.o.p. with other property; without personnel
w.o.p.e. without personnel or equipment
WOR without our responsibility
Wor. Worshipful
WORC [USA] Washington Operations Research Council
Worcs Worcestershire
WORM [computing] write once, read many (times)
WOSAC worldwide synchronization of atomic clocks
WOSB War Office Selection Board
wotcha [informal] wonderful old thing, considering her/his age
WOW waiting on weather; War On Want; Women Against the Ordination of Women
WP Warsaw Pact; weather permitting; West Point (US military academy); Western Province (South Africa); White Paper (government report); [USA] wire payment; [law] without prejudice; [vehicle registration] Worcester; word processing; word processor; working paper; working party; working pressure; [Freemasonry] Worthy Patriarch; [Freemasonry] Worthy President
Wp. Worship; Worshipful
w.p. waste paper; waste pipe; weather permitting; [baseball] wild pitch(es); will proceed; [law] without prejudice; word processing; word processor
WPA Water Polo Association; Western Provident Association; [insurance] with particular average; [USA] Work Progress Administration; [USA] Work Projects Administration; World Parliament Association; World Pool–Billiard Association; World Presbyterian Alliance
WPB [USA] War Production Board (in World War II); wastepaper basket
w.p.b. wastepaper basket
WPBL [USA] Women's Professional Basketball League
WPBSA World Professional Billiards and Snooker Association
WPC War Pension(s) Committee; Woman Police Constable; wood–plastic composite; wood–polymer composite; World Petroleum Congress
WPCA [USA] Water Pollution Control Administration

WPCF [USA] Water Pollution Control Federation
WPE white porcelain enamel
WPFC West Pacific Fisheries Commission
Wpfl Worshipful
wpg waterproofing
WPGA Women's Professional Golfers' Association
WPHC Western Pacific High Commission
WPI wholesale price index; World Press Institute
WPL warning-point level
wpm words per minute
WPMSF World Professional Marathon Swimming Federation
wpn weapon
WPPSI [psychology] Wechsler Preschool and Primary Scale of Intelligence
WPRL Water Pollution Research Laboratory
w.p.s. with prior service
WPT Women's Playhouse Trust
WR [vehicle registration] Leeds; wardrobe; ward room; warehouse receipt; war reserve; [medicine] Wassermann reaction; [railways] Western Region; West Riding (former division of Yorkshire); *Wilhelmus Rex* (Latin: King William); [astronomy] Wolf–Rayet (stars); [UK postcode] Worcester
w.r. warehouse receipt; [insurance] war risk; water repellent
WRA [USA] War Relocation Authority; Water Research Association; [horticulture] Wisley Rose Award
WRAAC Women's Royal Australian Army Corps
WRAAF Women's Royal Australian Air Force
WRAC Women's Royal Army Corps
WRAF Women's Royal Air Force
WRAM [computing] Windows random-access memory
WRANS Women's Royal Australian Naval Service
WRAP [USA] weapons readiness analysis program
WRC Water Research Centre; [USA] Welding Research Council
WRE [Australia] Weapons Research Establishment
w. ref. with reference (to)
w. reg. with regard (to)
WRI war risks insurance; Women's Rural Institute
w.r.n. [knitting] wool round needle
WRNG [meteorology] warning
WRNR Women's Royal Naval Reserve
WRNS Women's Royal Naval Service (hence informal name Wrens)
wrnt warrant
WRO Weed Research Organization
w.r.o. [insurance] war risks only
WRP Workers' Revolutionary Party
WRRA [cycling] Women's Road Records Association
wrt wrought (iron)
w.r.t. with respect to
WRU Welsh Rugby Union; Wesleyan Reform Union; who are you?
WRVS Women's Royal Voluntary Service (formerly WVS)
WS [vehicle registration] Bristol; [international vehicle registration] (Western) Samoa; [UK postcode] Walsall; water-soluble; weapon system; West Saxon; wind speed; [Scots law] Writer to the Signet [Scotland]
.ws Samoa (in Internet address)
WSA [USA] War Shipping Administration
W Sam. Western Samoa
WSC World Series Cricket
WSCF World Student Christian Federation
WSF Wake Shield Facility; [chemistry] water-soluble fraction
w/shop workshop
WSI Writers and Scholars International
WSJ *Wall Street Journal*
WSL Warren Spring Laboratory (Stevenage, Hertfordshire)
WSM Women's Suffrage Movement
WSP water supply point
WSPU Women's Social and Political Union
WSSA Welsh Secondary Schools Association
WSTN World Service Television News
WSTV World Service Television
WSU Wichita State University
WSW west-southwest
WT [vehicle registration] Leeds; Warrant Telegraphist (in Royal Navy); war transport; watertight; weekly takings; [fishing port] Westport; wireless telegraphy; wireless telephony; withholding tax

W/T wireless telegraphy; wireless telephony
wt warrant; watertight; weight; without
WTA winner takes all; Women's Tennis Association; World Transport Agency
WTAA World Trade Alliance Association
WTAU Women's Total Abstinence Union
WTB Welsh Tourist Board
Wtb. *Wörterbuch* (German: dictionary)
WTC Wheat Trade Convention
WTD watertight door
wtd wanted; warranted; watered
Wtf. Waterford
WTG wind turbine generator
WTH whole-tree harvesting
wthr weather
WTIS World Trade Information Service
WTMH watertight manhole
WTN Worldwide Television News
WTO Warsaw Treaty Organization; World Tourism Organization; World Trade Organization (replacement for GATT)
WTP willingness to pay; willing to pay (in advertisement)
wtr water; winter; writer
WTRC Wool Textile Research Council
WTS Women's Transport Service
WTT World Team Tennis
WTTA Wholesale Tobacco Trade Association of Great Britain and Northern Ireland
WTTC World Travel and Tourism Council
WTUC World Trade Union Conference
WTUL Women's Trade Union League
WU [vehicle registration] Leeds; Western Union
WUCT World Union of Catholic Teachers
WUF World Underwater Federation
WUJS World Union of Jewish Students
WUPJ World Union for Progressive Judaism
WUS World University Service
WUSL Women's United Service League
WV [vehicle registration] Brighton; [international vehicle registration] (Windward Islands) St Vincent; water valve; [US postcode] West Virginia; [UK postcode] Wolverhampton
w/v water valve; [chemistry] weight in volume (of solution)
WVA World Veterinary Association
W Va West Virginia
WVD *Wereldverbond van Diamant Bewerkers* (Dutch: Universal Alliance of Diamond Workers)
wvd waived
WVF World Veterans' Federation
WVS Women's Voluntary Service (former name of WRVS)
WVT water vapour transfer; water vapour transmission
WVU West Virginia University
WW [vehicle registration] Leeds; wall-to-wall (in property advertisement); walnut wood (trim) (in car advertisement); warehouse warrant; warrant writer; whitewall (tyre); *Who's Who*; World War; worldwide
W/W wall-to-wall (in property advertisement); warehouse warrant
w/w weight for weight
WW1 World War One
WW2 World War Two
WWDC World War Debt Commission
WWDSHEX [shipping] weather working days, Sundays and holidays excluded
Wwe *Witwe* (German: widow)
WWF Worldwide Fund for Nature (formerly World Wildlife Fund); World Wrestling Federation
WWI World War One
WWII World War Two
WWMCCS World Wide Military Command and Control System
WWO Wing Warrant Officer
WWSSN worldwide standard seismograph network
WWSU World Water Ski Union
WWW *Who Was Who*; World Weather Watch (of WMO); [computing] World Wide Web
WWY (Queen's Own) Warwickshire and Worcestershire Yeomanry
WX [vehicle registration] Leeds; women's extra (large) (clothing size)
WY [vehicle registration] Leeds; [fishing port] Whitby; [US postcode] Wyoming
Wy Way (in road name)
Wy. (John) Wycliffe (English religious reformer); Wyoming
Wycl. (John) Wycliffe (English religious reformer)
Wyo. Wyoming
WYR West Yorkshire Regiment

wysiwyg [computing] what you see is what you get
WZ [vehicle registration] Belfast; *Weltzeit* (German: universal time)
Wz. *Warenzeichen* (German: trademark)
WZO World Zionist Organization

X

X Christ (transcription of Greek letter chi); Cross (as in **Charing X**); error; exchange; experiment; experimental; explosive; extension; extra; extraordinary; [cinema] for over-18s only (former film classification); [chemistry] halogen; kiss (on letter, card, etc.); location on map; [genetics] sex chromosome; [Roman numeral] ten; unknown person or thing; X-ray; xylonite (plastic)
X [physics] exposure dose
x cross (as in **x-section**); [commerce] ex (= from); [finance] ex (= without); extra; [meteorology] hoar-frost; [Roman numeral] ten; trans- (as in **xformer**)
x [mathematics] algebraic variable; [mathematics] (horizontal) coordinate (as in ***x*-axis**)
3X [civil aircraft marking] Guinea
4X [civil aircraft marking] Israel
5X [civil aircraft marking] Uganda
XA [civil aircraft marking] Mexico
xa [finance] ex all (i.e. without any benefits)
XB [civil aircraft marking] Mexico
xb [finance] ex bonus
Xber December
XBT expendable bathythermograph
xbt exhibit
XC [USA, Canada] cross-country (as in **XC skiing**); [civil aircraft marking] Mexico
xc [finance] ex capitalization; [finance] ex coupon (i.e. without interest on coupon)
x.c.l. [insurance] excess current liabilities
xcp [finance] ex coupon (i.e. without interest on coupon)
xcpt except
XCT [medicine] X-ray compute(rize)d tomography
XD [physics] X-ray diffraction
xd [finance] ex dividend
x'd crossed; executed
xdiv [finance] ex dividend
XDR extended dynamic range (of cassettes)
Xdr crusader
Xe [chemical element] xenon
Xen. Xenophon (ancient Greek historian)
xf extra fine
xfer transfer
xfmr transformer
xg crossing
XGA [computing] extended graphics array
XG Midi extended general musical instrument digital interface
xhst exhaust
xhy extra heavy
XI [vehicle registration] Belfast; [medicine] X-ray imaging
xi [finance] ex interest
xin [finance] ex interest
XL extra large (clothing size)
xlnt excellent
x.l.w.b. extra-long wheelbase
XM experimental missile
Xmas Christmas
xmit transmit
XML [computing] extensible markup language (used on Internet)
XMS [computing] extended memory specification
xmsn transmission
xmtr transmitter
Xn Christian
xn [finance] ex new (i.e. without right to new shares)
x/nt excellent
Xnty Christianity
XO cognac of superior quality; executive officer
XP Christ (transcription of Greek letters chi and rho); Christianity; express paid; [medicine] xeroderma pigmentosum
x.p. express paid
xpl. explosive

xplt exploit
xpn expansion
xq cross-question
XR X-ray(s)
Xr examiner
xr [finance] ex rights
X-ray electromagnetic radiation of very short wavelength (from originally unknown nature of this radiation)
XRD [physics] X-ray diffraction
Xrds crossroads
XRE X-ray emission
x-ref. cross-refer; cross-reference
XRF X-ray fluorescence
XRM [medicine] X-ray mammography
XRMA X-ray microprobe analysis
XRT [medicine] X-ray therapy
XRT [medicine] X-ray tomography
xrts [finance] ex rights
XS cross-section; excess
xs expenses
XT [civil aircraft marking] Burkina Faso; extended technology
Xt Christ
xtal crystal
XTE [astronomy] X-ray Timing Explorer
X-tgd [building] cross-tongued
Xth tenth
Xtian Christian
xtra extra
xtry extraordinary
Xty Christianity
XU [civil aircraft marking] Cambodia
XUI [computing] X user interface
XUV [astronomy] extreme ultraviolet
xw [finance] ex warrants
x/wb extra-long wheelbase
XX double-strength beer
XXX triple-strength beer
XY [civil aircraft marking] Myanmar (formerly Burma)
xyl. xylophone
XZ [vehicle registration] Armagh; [civil aircraft marking] Myanmar (formerly Burma)

Y

Y [genetics] sex chromosome; [currency] yen (used in Japan); Yeomanry; [fishing port] Youghal; [chemical element] yttrium; [currency] yuan (used in China); Yugoslavia
Y [physics] hypercharge
y [meteorology] dry air
y [mathematics] algebraic variable; altitude; [mathematics] (vertical) coordinate (as in ***y*-axis**); [aeronautics] lateral axis
y. yacht; yard; year; yellow; young; youngest
Y2K Year 2000
5Y [civil aircraft marking] Alaska
6Y [civil aircraft marking] Jamaica
9Y [civil aircraft marking] Trinidad and Tobago
YA [civil aircraft marking] Afghanistan; [vehicle registration] Taunton; [insurance] York–Antwerp (Rules); [USA] young adult
YABA Young American Bowling Alliance
YAC [genetics] yeast artificial chromosome(s)
YACC [computing] yet another compiler-compiler
YAG [electronics] yttrium–aluminium garnet
YAH young at heart (in personal advertisement)
YAL Young Australia League
Y&LR York and Lancaster Regiment
YAR [international vehicle registration] Yemen (Arab Republic); [insurance] York–Antwerp Rules
Y-ARD Yarrow-Admiralty Research Department
YAS Yorkshire Agricultural Society
YAVIS [US informal] young, attractive, verbal, intelligent and successful
YB [vehicle registration] Taunton; yearbook
Yb [chemical element] ytterbium
y.b. [knitting] yarn back
YC [vehicle registration] Taunton; yacht club; [USA] Yale College; Young Conservative; youth club
YCA Youth Camping Association

YC&UO Young Conservative and Unionist Organization
YCL [USA] Young Communist League
YCNAC Young Conservative National Advisory Committee
YCS (International) Young Catholic Students
yct yacht
YCW [informal] you can't win; (International) Young Christian Workers
YD [vehicle registration] Taunton
yd yard (unit of length)
y'day yesterday
ydg yarding
yds yards (unit of length)
YE [vehicle registration] central London; [civil aircraft marking] Yemen; Your Excellency
.ye Yemen (in Internet address)
YEA [USA] Yale Engineering Association
yearb. yearbook
YEB Yorkshire Electricity Board
yel. yellow
Yel. NP [USA] Yellowstone National Park
Yem. Yemen; Yemeni
YEO Youth Employment Officer
yeo. yeoman; yeomanry
YER [finance] yearly effective rate (of interest)
YES Youth Employment Service; Youth Enterprise Scheme
yesty yesterday
YF [vehicle registration] central London
y.f. [knitting] yarn forward
YFC Young Farmers' Club; Youth for Christ
YFCU Young Farmers' Club of Ulster
YFG [electronics] yttrium–ferrite garnet
YG [vehicle registration] Leeds
YH [vehicle registration] central London; [fishing port] Yarmouth; [numismatics] young head (of Queen Victoria); youth hostel
YHA Youth Hostels Association
YHANI Youth Hostels Association of Northern Ireland
YHVH Hebrew name for God (the Tetragrammaton)
YHWH Hebrew name for God (the Tetragrammaton)
YI [civil aircraft marking] Iraq
Yi. Yiddish
Yid. Yiddish
YIG [electronics] yttrium–iron garnet
YIP [USA] Youth International Party
Yippie [US informal] member of Youth International Party
YJ [vehicle registration] Brighton; [civil aircraft marking] Vanuatu
YK [vehicle registration] central London; [civil aircraft marking] Syria
YL [vehicle registration] central London; [civil aircraft marking] Latvia; yield limit
YLI Yorkshire Light Infantry
YM [vehicle registration] central London
YMBA Yacht and Motor Boats Association
YMCA Young Men's Christian Association
YMCath.A [USA] Young Men's Catholic Association
YMCU Young Men's Christian Union
YMFS Young Men's Friendly Society
YMHA Young Men's Hebrew Association
YMV [microbiology] yellow mosaic virus
YN [vehicle registration] central London; [civil aircraft marking] Nicaragua
YNP [USA] Yellowstone National Park
YO [vehicle registration] central London; [UK postcode] York
y.o. [knitting] yarn over; year(s) old
y.o.b. year of birth
YOC Young Ornithologists' Club (of RSPB)
y.o.d. year of death
y.o.m. year of marriage
YOP Youth Opportunities Programme (former government scheme)
Yorks Yorkshire
YP [vehicle registration] central London; yield point (in mechanics); young people; young person; young prisoner
y.p. year's purchase
YPA Young Pioneers of America
YPFB *Yacimientos Petroliferos Fiscales Bolivianos* (Spanish: Bolivian state petroleum organization)
YPSCE [USA] Young People's Society of Christian Endeavour
YPSL [USA] Young People's Socialist League
YPTES Young People's Trust for Endangered Species
YR [vehicle registration] central London; [civil aircraft marking] Romania
yr year; younger; your
YRA Yacht Racing Association

yrbk yearbook
YRls [currency] Yemeni riyal
yrly yearly
Yrs Yours
yrs years
YS [civil aircraft marking] El Salvador; [vehicle registration] Glasgow; yield strength (in mechanics); Young Socialists
Ys. Yugoslavia; Yugoslavian
YSA Young Socialist Alliance
YSAG [electronics] yttrium–scandium–aluminium garnet
YSO [astronomy] young stellar object
yst youngest
YT [vehicle registration] central London; Yukon Territory
yt yacht
YTD [accounting] year to date
YTS Youth Training Scheme
YTV Yorkshire Television
YTYTK you're too young to know
YU [vehicle registration] central London; [USA] Yale University; [civil aircraft marking] Yugoslavia; [international vehicle registration] Yugoslavia
.yu Yugoslavia (in Internet address)
Yugo. Yugoslavia; Yugoslavian
Yuk. Yukon
YUP Yale University Press
yuppie [informal] young upwardly-mobile professional; [informal] young urban professional
YV [vehicle registration] central London; [civil aircraft marking] Venezuela; [international vehicle registration] Venezuela
YVF Young Volunteer Force
YVFF Young Volunteer Force Foundation
YW [vehicle registration] central London
YWCA Young Women's Christian Association
YWCTU Young Women's Christian Temperance Union
YWF Young World Federalists
YWHA Young Women's Hebrew Association
YWS Young Wales Society; Young Workers' Scheme
YX [vehicle registration] central London
YY [vehicle registration] central London
YZ [vehicle registration] Londonderry

Z

Z [genetics] sex chromosome of birds and insects; [international vehicle registration] Zambia; *Zeit* (German: time); zero (as in **Z-hour**); [civil aircraft marking] Zimbabwe; Zion; Zionist; *Zoll* (German: customs); zone
Z [physics] proton number
z [meteorology] haze
z [mathematics] algebraic variable; [chemistry] charge number; [mathematics] coordinate (as in **z-axis**)
z. zenith; zero; zone
ZA [civil aircraft marking] Albania; [international vehicle registration] South Africa (from Afrikaans *Zuid Afrika*)
za. *zirca* (German: approximately)
.za South Africa (in Internet address)
Zag. Zagreb
Zam. Zambia
ZAMS [astronomy] zero-age main sequence
Zan. Zanzibar
ZANU Zimbabwe African National Union
ZANU(PF) Zimbabwe African National Union (Patriotic Front)
Zanz. Zanzibar
ZAP [military] zero anti-aircraft potential
ZAPU Zimbabwe African People's Union
ZB Zen Buddhism; Zen Buddhist
z.B *zum Beispiel* (German: for example, e.g.)
ZBB [US finance] zero-base(d) budgeting
ZC Zionist Congress
ZCCT Zoo Check Charitable Trust
ZD [electronics] Zener diode; [astronomy] zenith distance; zero defect(s)
Z-DNA [biochemistry] zigzagged deoxyribonucleic acid
ZE [UK postcode] Lerwick
ZEBRA [nuclear technology] zero-energy breeder-reactor assembly
Zech. [Bible] Zechariah

ZEEP [nuclear technology] zero-energy experimental pile
ZEG zero economic growth
zen. zenith
ZENITH [nuclear technology] zero-energy nitrogen-heated thermal reactor
Zeph. [Bible] Zephaniah
zepp. zeppelin
ZETA [nuclear technology] zero-energy thermonuclear apparatus (or assembly)
ZETR [nuclear technology] zero-energy thermal reactor
ZF zero frequency; [military] zone of fire
ZFGBI Zionist Federation of Great Britain and Ireland
ZG zero gravity; zoological gardens
z-g zero gravity
ZH zero hour
z.H *zu Händen* (German: for the attention of, f.a.o., care of, c/o)
ZHR [astronomy] zenithal hourly rate
ZI [military] zone of interior
Ziana Zimbabwe Inter-Africa News Agency
ZIF [electronics] zero insertion force
ZIFT [medicine] zygote intrafallopian transfer (infertility treatment)
ZIL [computing] zigzag in-line
zip [computing] zigzag in-line package; [USA] zone improvement plan (as in **zip code**, US postcode)
ZK [civil aircraft marking] New Zealand
ZL [civil aircraft marking] New Zealand
Zl [currency] zloty (used in Poland)
ZM [civil aircraft marking] New Zealand
.zm Zambia (in Internet address)
ZN [civil aircraft marking] New Zealand
Zn [chemical element] zinc
ZO Zionist Organization
ZOA Zionist Organization of America
zod. zodiac
zoo [short form] zoological garden
zool. zoological; zoologist; zoology
ZP [civil aircraft marking] Paraguay
ZPG zero population growth
Zr [chemical element] zirconium
.zr Democratic Republic of Congo (formerly Zaïre) (in Internet address)
ZS [civil aircraft marking] South Africa; Zoological Society
Zs. *Zeitschrift* (German: periodical, journal)
ZSI Zoological Society of Ireland
ZSL Zoological Society of London
ZST zone standard time
ZT [civil aircraft marking] South Africa; zone time
z.T *zum Teil* (German: partly)
Ztg *Zeitung* (German: newspaper)
ZU [civil aircraft marking] South Africa
Zulu. Zululand
ZUM Zimbabwe Unity Movement
Zür Zürich
ZV zoomed video
ZW [international vehicle registration] Zimbabwe
zw. *zwischen* (German: between, among)
.zw Zimbabwe (in Internet address)
ZZ [vehicle registration] vehicle temporarily imported by foreign visitor
Zz. [medicine] *zingiber* (Latin: ginger)
z.Z *zur Zeit* (German: at present)
zz zigzag

READ MORE IN PENGUIN

In every corner of the world, on every subject under the sun, Penguin represents quality and variety – the very best in publishing today.

For complete information about books available from Penguin – including Puffins, Penguin Classics and Arkana – and how to order them, write to us at the appropriate address below. Please note that for copyright reasons the selection of books varies from country to country.

In the United Kingdom: Please write to *Dept. EP, Penguin Books Ltd, Bath Road, Harmondsworth, West Drayton, Middlesex UB7 0DA*

In the United States: Please write to *Consumer Services, Penguin Putnam Inc., 405 Murray Hill Parkway, East Rutherford, New Jersey 07073-2136.* VISA and MasterCard holders call 1-800-631-8571 to order Penguin titles

In Canada: Please write to *Penguin Books Canada Ltd, 10 Alcorn Avenue, Suite 300, Toronto, Ontario M4V 3B2*

In Australia: Please write to *Penguin Books Australia Ltd, 487 Maroondah Highway, Ringwood, Victoria 3134*

In New Zealand: Please write to *Penguin Books (NZ) Ltd, Private Bag 102902, North Shore Mail Centre, Auckland 10*

In India: Please write to *Penguin Books India Pvt Ltd, 11 Community Centre, Panchsheel Park, New Delhi 110017*

In the Netherlands: Please write to *Penguin Books Netherlands bv, Postbus 3507, NL-1001 AH Amsterdam*

In Germany: Please write to *Penguin Books Deutschland GmbH, Metzlerstrasse 26, 60594 Frankfurt am Main*

In Spain: Please write to *Penguin Books S. A., Bravo Murillo 19, 1°B, 28015 Madrid*

In Italy: Please write to *Penguin Italia s.r.l., Via Vittorio Emanuele 45/a, 20094 Corsico, Milano*

In France: Please write to *Penguin France, 12, Rue Prosper Ferradou, 31700 Blagnac*

In Japan: Please write to *Penguin Books Japan Ltd, Iidabashi KM-Bldg, 2-23-9 Koraku, Bunkyo-Ku, Tokyo 112-0004*

In South Africa: Please write to *Penguin Books South Africa (Pty) Ltd, P.O. Box 751093, Gardenview, 2047 Johannesburg*

READ MORE IN PENGUIN

LITERARY CRITICISM

The Penguin History of Literature

Published in ten volumes, *The Penguin History of Literature* is a superb critical survey of the English and American literature covering fourteen centuries, from the Anglo-Saxons to the present, and written by some of the most distinguished academics in their fields.

New Bearings in English Poetry F. R. Leavis

'*New Bearings in English Poetry* was the first intelligent account of the work of Eliot, Pound and Gerard Manley Hopkins to appear in English and it significantly altered critical awareness . . . Leavis gave to literary criticism a thoroughness and respectability that has never since been equalled' Peter Ackroyd, *Spectator*. 'The most influential literary critic of modern times' *Financial Times*

The Uses of Literacy Richard Hoggart

Mass literacy has opened new worlds to new readers. How far has it also been exploited to debase standards and behaviour? 'A vivid inside view of working-class culture and one of the most influential books of the post-war era' *Observer*

Epistemology of the Closet Eve Kosofsky Sedgwick

Through her brilliant interpretation of the readings of Henry James, Melville, Nietzsche, Proust and Oscar Wilde, Eve Kosofsky Sedgwick shows how questions of sexual definition are at the heart of every form of representation in this century. 'A signal event in the history of late-twentieth-century gay studies' Wayne Koestenbaum

Dangerous Pilgrimages Malcolm Bradbury

'This capacious book tracks Henry James from New England to Rye; Evelyn Waugh to a Hollywood as grotesque as he expected; Gertrude Stein to Spain to be mistaken for a bishop; Oscar Wilde to a rickety stage in Leadsville, Colorado . . . The textbook on the the transatlantic theme' *Guardian*

READ MORE IN PENGUIN

LITERARY CRITICISM

The Practice of Writing David Lodge

This lively collection examines the work of authors ranging from the two Amises to Nabokov and Pinter; the links between private lives and published works; and the different techniques required in novels, stage plays and screenplays. 'These essays, so easy in manner, so well-built and informative, offer a fine blend of creative writing and criticism' *Sunday Times*

A Lover's Discourse Roland Barthes

'May be the most detailed, painstaking anatomy of desire we are ever likely to see or need again ... The book is an ecstatic celebration of love and language ... readers interested in either or both ... will enjoy savouring its rich and dark delights' *Washington Post*

The New Pelican Guide to English Literature Edited by Boris Ford

The indispensable critical guide to English and American literature in nine volumes, erudite yet accessible. From the ages of Chaucer and Shakespeare, via Georgian satirists and Victorian social critics, to the leading writers of the twentieth century, all literary life is here.

The Structure of Complex Words William Empson

'Twentieth-century England's greatest critic after T. S. Eliot, but whereas Eliot was the high priest, Empson was the *enfant terrible* ... *The Structure of Complex Words* is one of the linguistic masterpieces of the epoch, finding in the feel and tone of our speech whole sedimented social histories' *Guardian*

Vamps and Tramps Camille Paglia

'Paglia is a genuinely unconventional thinker ... Taken as a whole, the book gives an exceptionally interesting perspective on the last thirty years of intellectual life in America, and is, in its wacky way, a celebration of passion and the pursuit of truth' *Sunday Telegraph*

READ MORE IN PENGUIN

REFERENCE

The Penguin Dictionary of the Third Reich
James Taylor and Warren Shaw

This dictionary provides a full background to the rise of Nazism and the role of Germany in the Second World War. Among the areas covered are the major figures from Nazi politics, arts and industry, the German Resistance, the politics of race and the Nuremberg trials.

The Penguin Biographical Dictionary of Women

This stimulating, informative and entirely new Penguin dictionary of women from all over the world, through the ages, contains over 1,600 clear and concise biographies on major figures from politicians, saints and scientists to poets, film stars and writers.

Roget's Thesaurus of English Words and Phrases
Edited by Betty Kirkpatrick

This new edition of Roget's classic work, now brought up to date for the nineties, will increase anyone's command of the English language. Fully cross-referenced, it includes synonyms of every kind (formal or colloquial, idiomatic and figurative) for almost 900 headings. It is a must for writers and utterly fascinating for any English speaker.

The Penguin Dictionary of International Relations
Graham Evans and Jeffrey Newnham

International relations have undergone a revolution since the end of the Cold War. This new world disorder is fully reflected in this new Penguin dictionary, which is extensively cross-referenced with a select bibliography to aid further study.

The Penguin Guide to Synonyms and Related Words
S. I. Hayakawa

'More helpful than a thesaurus, more humane than a dictionary, the *Guide to Synonyms and Related Words* maps linguistic boundaries with precision, sensitivity to nuance and, on occasion, dry wit' *The Times Literary Supplement*